Derivatives Applications in Asset Management

Frank J. Fabozzi · Marielle de Jong
Editors

Derivatives Applications in Asset Management

From Theory to Practice

palgrave
macmillan

Editors
Frank J. Fabozzi
Carey Business School
Johns Hopkins University
Baltimore, MD, USA

Marielle de Jong
Grenoble Ecole de Management
Paris, France

ISBN 978-3-031-86353-0 ISBN 978-3-031-86354-7 (eBook)
https://doi.org/10.1007/978-3-031-86354-7

This Palgrave Macmillan imprint is published by the registered company Springer Nature Switzerland AG
The registered company address is: Gewerbestrasse 11, 6330 Cham, Switzerland

Preface

Derivatives have become indispensable tools in modern asset management, offering the flexibility and precision needed to navigate increasingly complex financial markets. Their ability to enhance portfolio returns, manage risk exposures, and maintain liquidity makes them a cornerstone of effective portfolio management. However, while derivatives hold immense potential, their complexity often leads to misunderstandings and misuse. Many practitioners find themselves overwhelmed by the technicalities of pricing models or the operational challenges of implementation, which can limit their ability to harness the full power of these instruments.

The need for a practical, application-oriented resource on derivatives has never been greater. Traditional texts on derivatives often emphasize theoretical pricing models, such as the Black-Scholes equation, providing a solid foundation for understanding the mechanics of these instruments. However, they frequently do not consider the real-world complexities that asset managers face when using derivatives in live portfolios. Issues such as managing margin requirements, rolling contracts, navigating transaction costs, and adapting strategies to volatile markets are often overlooked in favor of abstract models and idealized scenarios.

This book seeks to bridge the gap between theory and practice by focusing on the practical applications of derivatives in asset management. Rather than relying on simplified or contrived examples, the book draws from real-world case studies and the lived experiences of practitioners. It demonstrates how derivatives are used to solve tangible problems in portfolio management, offering insights into the challenges and nuances of implementing these strategies effectively. By doing so, the book provides the tools asset managers need to navigate the unpredictable, dynamic world of asset management, where derivatives are not merely theoretical constructs but essential components of a robust and flexible investment strategy.

Bridging the Gap Between Theory and Practice

The study of derivatives has traditionally centered on theoretical models, such as the Black-Scholes framework and binomial trees, which provide a mathematical foundation for understanding the pricing and valuation of these instruments. While these models are invaluable for grasping the mechanics of derivatives, their dominance in academic instruction often comes at the expense of addressing the practical realities of using derivatives in asset management. The result is a persistent gap between the abstract concepts taught in classrooms and the operational challenges practitioners face in the real world.

This book aims to bridge that gap by shifting the focus from pricing theory to practical applications. While pricing models remain an essential part of understanding derivatives, the actual value of these instruments lies in their ability to address concrete challenges in portfolio management. Derivatives are tools for managing risk, optimizing portfolio exposures, achieving strategic investment objectives, and potentially enhancing returns—not merely theoretical constructs.

While theoretical pricing models such as Black-Scholes have long been central to derivatives education, their dominance in academic instruction often overshadows the practical applications needed in real-world asset management. This imbalance is particularly evident considering the high pricing efficiency of derivatives markets, where market-generated prices quickly reflect all available information. As a result, the manual calculation of pricing models has become less relevant in professional contexts, where practitioners rely on automated systems for real-time analytics.

This book challenges the traditional emphasis on pricing derivations by demonstrating how derivatives can effectively manage risk, adjust portfolio exposures, and optimize returns. Shifting the focus to operational challenges, such as margin management, rolling contracts, and mitigating basis risk, equips professionals with the tools and insights required to navigate the complexities of modern derivatives use. The goal is to ensure that practitioners are well-versed in the mechanics of derivatives and adept at implementing strategies that align with the realities of contemporary financial markets.

In professional settings, derivatives are far removed from the neat, controlled scenarios often presented in textbook examples. Practitioners face a range of complexities, including managing margin requirements, navigating transaction costs, and mitigating basis risk when rolling futures or options contracts. Additionally, derivatives strategies must adapt to market realities such as liquidity constraints, volatility spikes, and geopolitical events that can disrupt the best investment strategies. These operational and strategic challenges are rarely captured in theoretical treatments but are at the heart of this book's approach.

This book bridges the divide between theory and practice by incorporating realistic case studies and practitioner insights. It provides a conceptual understanding of derivatives while also demonstrating how to apply them effectively in asset management, where success depends on navigating unpredictability and adapting to changing conditions. This practical focus equips students and professionals to tackle real-world finance complexities with confidence and competence.

While this book focuses on the practical applications of derivatives in asset management, ignoring the widespread public perception of these instruments is impossible. The media often emphasizes the dramatic and negative stories associated with derivatives, such as their role in financial crises, large-scale losses, and corporate failures. Events like the 2007-2008 global financial crisis, the collapse of Lehman Brothers, or high-profile derivative missteps involving institutions like Barings Bank dominate public discourse, reinforcing the view of derivatives as risky and overly complex financial tools.

However, these narratives overlook how derivatives are used responsibly and effectively to manage risk and enhance financial stability. These success stories rarely make headlines, as they lack the drama and immediacy of financial collapses. Yet, they underscore the indispensable role derivatives play in supporting the global economy.

This book provides a balanced perspective by addressing both the challenges and the successes of derivatives. It aims to educate students and practitioners on employing derivatives responsibly and effectively, ensuring their potential is harnessed for constructive purposes. This approach bridges the gap between theory and practice and counters the often one-sided portrayal of derivatives, demonstrating their critical importance in modern asset management.

The Unique Approach of This Book

This book distinguishes by prioritizing the practical realities of derivatives in asset management. While many existing texts offer a theoretical foundation for understanding derivatives, their reliance on simplified examples and abstract models often fails to capture the complexities that practitioners encounter in real-world scenarios. This book takes a different approach, emphasizing how derivatives are applied to solve problems faced by portfolio managers and risk professionals.

Central to this approach are detailed case studies and walkthrough illustrations that bring the nuances of derivative strategies to life. These examples are not contrived or overly simplistic; they are drawn from real-world applications where asset managers must navigate unpredictable market conditions, liquidity constraints, and operational challenges. Through these cases, readers are guided step by step through designing, implementing, and adjusting derivative strategies, gaining insight into the decision-making frameworks and practical trade-offs that shape successful outcomes.

By providing these illustrations, the book seeks to educate readers about the practical mechanics of derivatives and shift the narrative toward a more balanced understanding of their role in asset management. These stories highlight the transformative potential of derivatives when used with due diligence and strategic intent, offering a counterpoint to the predominantly negative portrayal seen in mainstream media.

What makes this book particularly valuable is the integration of practitioner insights. The contributors are experienced professionals with years of expertise in using derivatives to enhance portfolio returns, manage risks, and optimize exposures. Their collective experience provides a depth and authenticity that theoretical models alone cannot offer. By sharing their experiences, these practitioners help illuminate the practical realities of derivatives, including their challenges.

By combining realistic examples, practitioner insights, and a focus on operational challenges, this book offers a fresh and efficient perspective on derivatives in asset management. It empowers readers to move beyond theoretical understanding, equipping them to use derivatives confidently and effectively in their professional roles. In doing so, the book bridges the gap between academic instruction and the demands of the real world, making it an indispensable resource for aspiring and experienced asset managers.

Case Studies

A case study is an in-depth exploration of a specific situation, event, individual, organization, or phenomenon. It aims to examine cause-and-effect relationships, evaluate strategies, or extract insights that can be applied broadly. A case study typically begins with a clear definition of the issue or scenario being investigated and provides background information to establish the relevant context, such as market dynamics, institutional frameworks, or historical trends. The methodology used to examine the situation is then outlined, often incorporating models, frameworks, or analytical tools. This is followed by the presentation of data and analysis, which could include empirical evidence, simulations, or real-world examples that substantiate the findings. Insights and implications are then discussed, emphasizing practical applications, risks, trade-offs, or broader lessons learned. The case study concludes with a summary of its findings and their relevance to similar contexts or decision-making processes.

A detailed illustration using real-world data can also qualify as a case study if it focuses on a specific situation or application, rather than presenting a general analysis or broad discussion. It should follow a structured format with a clear problem statement, methodology, analysis, and conclusion, offering practical insights or lessons that are applicable to similar contexts. The use of actual data enhances its real-world relevance and demonstrates the practical implications of decisions or strategies. For example, an analysis that uses real-world data to explore how a portfolio manager implemented a hedging strategy during a market downturn and breaks down the methodology, outcomes, and lessons learned would be a case study. However, a purely descriptive analysis without a clear focus or actionable takeaways would not meet the threshold. In this book, the case studies fall into this second category, providing readers with focused, real-world examples that illustrate practical applications and insights in the contexts being explored.

The Educational Value of Practical Applications

The value of this book lies in its ability to integrate theory with practice, a critical need in derivatives education that has often been overlooked. While theoretical pricing models such as Black-Scholes and binomial trees provide the conceptual underpinnings of derivatives, they do not prepare professionals for the real-world complexities of using these instruments in asset management. The focus of this book shifts toward practical applications, ensuring that readers not only understand derivatives conceptually but also gain the tools and skills necessary to navigate the implementation challenges.

The inherent pricing efficiency of derivatives markets also justifies emphasizing real-world applications over theoretical pricing. Decades of empirical research have demonstrated that market prices for derivatives are reliable benchmarks, quickly incorporating all available information. This efficiency reduces the need for extensive manual pricing exercises and shifts the focus to interpreting these prices and using them strategically.

Practical applications enhance the relevance of education, equipping readers with skills directly transferable to professional settings. For instance, case studies in this book simulate real-world scenarios, such as navigating a market downturn with protective puts, using futures contracts to adjust duration in a fixed income portfolio, or managing currency risks in a globally diversified fund. These examples are designed to reflect the complexities of live portfolio management, allowing readers to develop a deeper understanding of how derivatives function as tools for risk control and performance enhancement.

This practical approach ensures that readers are well-versed in the mechanics of derivatives and capable of applying them in a dynamic and often unpredictable financial landscape. By bridging the gap between academic instruction and real-world application, this book serves as both a learning resource for students and a practical guide for professionals, ensuring that the next generation of asset managers is fully equipped to harness the potential of derivatives in portfolio management.

Target Audience

This book is tailored to meet the needs of a diverse audience, encompassing both aspiring and experienced professionals in asset management, finance, and related fields. Its practical focus makes it an essential resource for portfolio managers, risk managers, and traders who actively use derivatives to manage exposures, enhance returns, and optimize portfolio performance. At the same time, its structured approach and clear explanations make it an invaluable guide for students of finance and economics seeking to deepen their understanding of derivatives beyond theoretical models.

For portfolio managers, the book provides actionable insights into integrating derivatives into asset management strategies. It addresses real-world challenges such as managing margin requirements, mitigating basis risk, and rolling contracts effectively and equips professionals with tools to refine their decision-making in dynamic market environments. The emphasis on case studies and practitioner insights ensures that the content resonates with those who actively navigate the complexities of financial markets, offering lessons that can be immediately applied to professional practice.

Risk managers and financial analysts will find the book particularly useful for exploring operational and strategic considerations in derivatives use. From designing hedging strategies to balancing risk and return in a portfolio context, the book comprehensively examines how derivatives can manage volatility, protect downside risks, and achieve specific investment objectives. It also delves into regulatory considerations and liquidity management, which are critical to effective derivatives strategies in institutional settings.

Students of finance, economics, and business will benefit from the book's ability to bridge the gap between academic instruction and professional application. While traditional derivatives textbooks often focus on pricing models and theoretical frameworks, this book places greater emphasis on how these instruments function in practice. By presenting realistic scenarios and addressing practical challenges, it provides a foundation that prepares students for the realities of the financial industry, equipping them with the skills needed to succeed in portfolio management, trading, and risk control.

The book's utility extends beyond individual professionals and students, making it a valuable resource for educators and trainers. Professors of finance and business can incorporate its case studies and practical examples into their curricula, enriching classroom discussions with content that reflects the complexities of modern financial markets. Similarly, training programs within financial institutions can use the book to equip employees with the technical knowledge and operational expertise required for derivatives management.

By addressing the needs of such a broad audience, this book positions itself as a versatile resource that bridges the gap between theory and practice. Whether for seasoned practitioners looking to refine their strategies, students seeking to transition from academic studies to professional roles, or educators striving to modernize their instruction, this book offers insights and guidance that are both relevant and actionable in today's financial landscape.

Structure of the Book

The book has four parts, each serving a distinct purpose. Part I, "Derivatives Fundamentals for Asset Managers," provides a comprehensive foundation for understanding and applying derivatives in asset management, the different types of derivatives, and an overview of their use in asset management. After an introduction to the book, the following four chapters review the various types of derivatives categorized by asset class: equity, bond-related, foreign exchange, and volatility derivatives. These chapters offer an overview of their characteristics and applications.

Building on this foundation, Part I then transitions into decision-making frameworks for asset managers. These include strategies for managing volatility, rebalancing multi-asset portfolios, designing option income strategies, and addressing advanced themes such as the use of derivatives for liquidity management, performance attribution when derivatives are used, and extracting market views from derivative prices. By progressing from fundamental concepts to more advanced topics, Part I equips readers with the theoretical knowledge and practical tools for effective derivative usage in asset management.

Parts II–IV shift focus to real-world applications through an extensive collection of 22 case studies. These case studies are organized into thematic sections that address specific challenges and objectives in asset management. Part II illustrates strategies for managing risk and ensuring capital protection, showcasing how derivatives can mitigate various financial risks. Part III examines leverage and exposure management, demonstrating how derivatives can optimize market exposure, hedge systematic risks, and enhance portfolio flexibility. Finally, the book concludes with strategies for income enhancement, presenting innovative approaches for generating returns using derivatives, such as harvesting volatility risk premiums and replicating bond returns with credit default swaps covered in Part IV.

This structure ensures a logical flow, guiding the reader from foundational concepts in derivatives to their sophisticated applications in real-world scenarios. By blending theoretical insights with practical case studies, the book provides a comprehensive and actionable guide for asset managers seeking to leverage derivatives effectively.

Baltimore, MD, USA — Frank J. Fabozzi
Paris, France — Marielle de Jong

Acknowledgments

We would like to express our deepest gratitude to all the contributors whose expertise and insights have been instrumental in shaping this book. Each chapter and case reflects the dedication, intellectual rigor, and thoughtful perspectives of the authors, and we are profoundly grateful for their commitment to this endeavor.

We also extend our heartfelt thanks to the organizations that supported their work. Without the resources, encouragement, and collaborative environments provided by these institutions, the contributions to this book would not have been possible. The organizations represented by our contributors have played a crucial role in advancing the research and ideas presented in this volume.

We would also like to extend our gratitude to the organizations that employ our contributors and have provided them with the support, resources, and intellectual environments that enabled their valuable contributions to this book. These organizations have been instrumental in fostering the research, ideas, and perspectives shared in this volume, and we deeply appreciate their role in making this collaborative effort possible.

Disclaimer

This book brings together contributions from professionals working at leading financial institutions around the world. While their expertise and insights reflect years of experience in the derivatives and asset management industry, it is important to note that the views expressed in this book are solely those of the individual contributors. These perspectives do not necessarily represent the official views, policies, or positions of the organizations they are affiliated with.

Additionally, the content in this book is intended for informational and educational purposes only. It should not be construed as financial, investment, or legal advice. Readers are encouraged to consult with their own professional advisors for guidance tailored to their specific circumstances. This disclaimer ensures transparency and reinforces the independence of the contributors' analyses and opinions.

Contents

Notes on Contributors

The contributors to this book are all highly experienced practitioners in the field of derivatives, bringing a wealth of expertise and practical knowledge to the topics covered. The group includes professionals who are currently active in the industry as well as individuals who have transitioned from practice to academia, enriching their perspectives with both real-world and theoretical insights. Collectively, these contributors represent a truly global perspective, hailing from the United States, the United Kingdom, Germany, Finland, France, the Netherlands, Canada, Singapore, and Abu Dhabi. This diversity ensures that the book reflects a wide range of market practices, regulatory environments, and innovative approaches from across the world.

The contributors share their experiences in their own words with a generosity and a spontaneity that bring the study cases to life. The explanations they give to the decisions taken in the particular market circumstances they lived through are valuable. Those stories tend to be passed on between asset managers from older to younger generations, however are not often heard away from the asset management desks, which is a loss, as they are of interest for a much larger audience.

Below is the list of contributors detailing their current positions and professional experience. This listing will give readers a deeper understanding of the credentials and expertise of the individuals behind the chapters and case studies they prepared for this book.

Arik Ben Dor, Ph.D., is a managing director at Barclays and a member of the Quantitative Portfolio Strategy Group. He has co-authored four books on quantitative investing, published over 30 articles in practitioner journals, and serves on the editorial boards of The Journal of Portfolio Management and The Journal of Fixed Income. Recognized in Institutional Investor's Fixed Income Research Survey, he ranked second in the US and Europe for Quantitative Analysis in 2023. Arik holds a US patent for synthetic hedge fund replication. He previously worked at Lehman Brothers and Morgan Stanley.

Vineer Bhansali, Ph.D., is the founder and chief investment officer of LongTail Alpha, a firm specializing in risk mitigation strategies for institutional investors. Prior to LongTail Alpha, he was a managing director and portfolio manager at PIMCO as Head of Analytics and Founder and Head of PIMCO's Quantitative Portfolios Team. He started PIMCO's Tail Risk Hedging Business and PIMCO's first hedge fund. Prior to PIMCO, he was a trader at Salomon Brothers CSFB and Citibank, where he started the Hybrid Options desk. He has received the *Financial Analysts Journal's* Graham and Dodd Scroll Award and *TIME* magazine's college achievement award.

John Burrello, CFA, CAIA, is a senior portfolio manager at Invesco, focusing on derivatives-based multi-asset and equity investment strategies, including options-based income, hedging strategies, and global macro. Prior to joining Invesco, from 2004 to 2012, he was a partner at Continental Advisors, a Chicago-based equity long/short hedge fund, where he focused on derivative strategies, equity research, and portfolio construction.

William Cazalet, CAIA, CMA, was most recently a global investment strategist at Newton Investment Management. Previously, he oversaw multi-factor equity and fixed income at Mellon and active equity at Mellon Capital. Prior to Mellon Capital, he worked at Commonfund and AXA Investment Managers and was a derivatives trader at Morgan Stanley. He started his career at Royal Dutch Shell.

Eddie Cheng, CFA, is the head of International Portfolio Management for the Multi-Asset team at Allspring Global Investments. He joined Allspring from its predecessor firm, Wells Fargo Asset Management. Prior to that, Eddie was a senior portfolio manager at Schroders, focusing on quantitative strategies. Earlier, he served as a research analyst at the Institute of Information Science, Academia Sinica. Eddie is a regular guest lecturer at Warwick Business School.

Dimitri Curtil is the global head of multi-asset solutions at Newton Investment Management. He leads the portfolio managers and researchers responsible for, and the research underpinning, the firm's systematic multi-asset strategies. Dimitri's areas of research include absolute return and total return strategies, risk parity, alternative risk premia and tail-risk hedging solutions. Previously, Dimitri was the CIO and head of multi-asset strategies, and the head of asset allocation research at Mellon Investments Corporation and Mellon Capital (BNY group companies).

Johan Duyvesteyn, Ph.D., CFA, is a portfolio manager in the Quant Fixed Income team of Robeco. His areas of expertise include quantitative credit strategies, credit beta market timing, government bond market timing, country sustainability, and emerging-market debt. He has published in both academic and practitioner-oriented journals. Johan started his career in the industry in 1999 at Robeco.

Redouane Elkamhi, Ph.D., is a professor of Finance at the Rotman School of Management, University of Toronto. His research has been published in top finance journals, presented at major conferences, and recognized with numerous awards and honors (e.g., ICPM, PCAM, GARP, and the Development Bank of Japan). In addition to his academic career, he advises major Canadian pension funds and hedge funds, specializing in asset allocation, total fund management, and private assets. Elkamhi is also a nine-time recipient of the MBA Teaching Excellence Award.

Frank J. Fabozzi, Ph.D., CFA, CPA, is a professor of practice at Carey Business School at Johns Hopkins University, editor of *The Journal of Portfolio Management and co-editor of The Journal of Financial Data Science.* From 1988 to 2023, he served on the board of directors of the BlackRock fixed income complex, where he chaired the performance committee and oversaw the monitoring of fund managers' use of derivatives. He received the CFA Institute Research Foundation's James R. Vertin Award and the C. Stewart Sheppard Award in 2007 and was inducted into the Fixed Income Society's Hall of Fame.

Bruce J. Feibel, CFA, serves as the global head of Strategy for State Street's Alpha Platform, a comprehensive front-to-back investment technology solution for institutional investors. Previously, he was the head of Performance & Risk Analytics at BNY Mellon Asset Management, following his tenure at Eagle Investment Systems, where he developed performance and attribution software products.

Mr. Feibel is the author of Investment Performance Measurement and co-author of Complying with the Global Investment Standards, both published by Wiley. He serves on the advisory board of The Journal of Performance Measurement. In recognition of his contributions to the field, he has been inducted into the journal's Performance & Risk Measurement Hall of Fame.

Jingling Guan, Ph.D., is a director in the Quantitative Portfolio Strategy Group at Barclays based in New York. She focuses on cross-asset-class research and has worked on using credit signals in equity investments, systematic credit strategies, and the empirical analysis of credit portfolio risk. Her research has been used by the largest institutional investors globally. The co-author of a book on measuring ESG effects in systematic investing, she has published multiple articles in leading industry journals. Previously, Jingling was an assistant professor at Georgia State University.

Robert Harlow, CFA, CAIA, is the associate head of Global Multi-Asset Research at T. Rowe Price and a member of both the Investments Derivatives Committee and Investment Advisory Committee of the Global Allocation Fund. He is a vice president of T. Rowe Price Group, Inc., and T. Rowe Price Associates, Inc. He also manages several equity derivative mandates on behalf of broader multi-asset portfolios.

Scott Hixon, CFA, is a senior portfolio manager and head of Research for Invesco's Global Asset Allocation team, which invests in worldwide stock, bond, and commodity markets. Scott oversees and helps steer the team's research initiatives in model and strategy development and portfolio construction. He has been responsible for Invesco's tactical allocation strategies since joining the firm in 1994.

Patrick Houweling, Ph.D., is the head of the Quant Fixed Income team of Robeco and lead portfolio manager of its quantitative credit strategies. He joined Robeco in 2003. Patrick has published in academic and practitioner-oriented journals on such topics as factor investing, risk management, liquidity, and credit derivatives. He is a recipient of the Graham and Dodd Scroll Award of Excellence for 2017 awarded by the *Financial Analysts Journal*. Patrick is a guest lecturer at several universities. Prior to joining Robeco, he was a researcher in the Risk Management department at Rabobank International where he started his career in 1998.

Marielle de Jong, Ph.D., is an associate professor of Finance at Grenoble Ecole de Management, Paris, France, where she also serves as the academic director of the DBA program. She is the editor-in-chief of the Journal of Asset Management. From 2011 to 2020, she led the fixed income quantitative research team at Amundi, and before that, she served as the vice president of Financial Engineering at Sinopia Asset Management from 1997 to 2010. Marielle is a recipient of the prestigious Bernstein Fabozzi/Jacobs Levy Award for publishing an outstanding article in the Journal of Portfolio Management.

Mounia Khamlich Fischer is the head of Real Asset Management at Assurances du Crédit Mutuel, a French insurance company based in Paris. She has notably worked as a fund manager for Edmond de Rothschild Group deploying Absolute Return Strategies (involving arbitrage on derivative instruments), and managing capital guaranteed funds (structured products and actively managed funds). Mounia also held various positions as the head of Financial Risk Management overseeing insurance portfolios, traditional funds, and hedge funds.

Adam Kobor, Ph.D., CFA, is a managing director of Investments at New York University. He is responsible for strategic asset allocation, private credit, and fixed income investments. Prior to joining NYU, Mr. Kobor was a director at the Rock Creek Group, focusing on asset allocation and emerging markets equity investments. Earlier, he was a senior manager at Apple Inc., responsible for risk and analytics of Apple's investment portfolio. Prior to Joining Apple, Mr. Kobor worked for the World Bank, where he managed mortgage-backed securities portfolios, and advised central bank clients.

Gueorgui S. Konstantinov, Ph.D., CAIA, FDP, is a senior portfolio manager with more than 18 years of experience. He has managed global bond portfolios and currencies for institutional investors and pension funds. He is an editorial board member of *The Journal of Portfolio Management*, *The Journal of Alternative Investments*, and *The Journal of Financial Data Science.*

Pravesh Kumar is a quantitative researcher within the Multi-Asset (Investment Solutions Group) Research team at State Street Global Advisors. Pravesh played a key role in developing the portfolio construction suite, which is used by multiple teams across the firm to carry out strategic and tactical asset allocation processes and facilitate target date fund activities. He is researching to enhance the tactical alpha models for multiple asset classes and target volatility models. Before joining ISG in 2019, Pravesh had a brief stint in Marketing Analytics as a Data Scientist.

Jacky S. H. Lee is the senior managing director and head of the Total Portfolio Group at the Healthcare of Ontario Pension Plan (HOOPP) in Canada.

He also serves on the Editorial Advisory Boards of The Journal of Portfolio Management and The Journal of Financial Data Science. Previously, he was the managing director of Total Fund Management at the Ontario Teachers' Pension Plan (OTPP). Jacky publishes research in academic journals on asset allocation and risk management. He has received research awards from the Kroner Center for Financial Research and the International Centre for Pension Management.

Wai Lee, Ph.D., is the co-head of Systematic Research and senior portfolio manager at Allspring Global Investments. He joined Allspring from its predecessor, Wells Fargo Asset Management. Previously, he worked at Neuberger Berman as the head of quantitative investments and a senior portfolio manager, Credit Suisse Asset Management as the head of the quantitative engineering group, and J.P. Morgan Investment Management, where he oversaw quantitative research and risk management for the global balanced group. Wai has authored several articles and a book on asset allocation. He serves on the editorial board of *The Journal of Portfolio Management* and *The Journal of Systematic Investing*.

Han Liang, CFA, is a research analyst on the Global Asset Allocation team at Invesco, specializing in creating, maintaining, and enhancing systematic investment strategies using quantitative methods across multiple asset classes. He joined Invesco through the acquisition of OppenheimerFunds, where he developed and managed multi-alternative strategies involving financial derivatives. Before his time at Oppenheimer, Han served as a senior quantitative analyst at The Options Clearing Corporation and as a quantitative analyst at Bank of America Merrill Lynch. Before that, he held quantitative trading positions at Infinium Capital Management and G.H. Financials, focusing on market making and arbitrage.

Lodewijk van der Linden is a portfolio manager in the Quant Fixed Income team of Robeco. His areas of expertise include quantitative government bond selection strategies, credit beta market timing, government bond market timing, and defensive strategies. He joined Robeco in August 2018. In the period 2015-2018 Lodewijk worked at Aegon Asset Management where he was a risk associate and a team manager for Client Reporting. Lodewijk started his career at PwC as an actuarial consultant in 2013.

Joseph Niehaus, CFA, is a senior vice president with the CUFS | Credit Union Financial Services Group at Jefferies, where he leverages the Jefferies investment banking platform for the evolving financial needs of credit unions.

Joseph is also a doctoral candidate with the Grenoble Ecole de Management with a research focus on financial cooperative economics and the relationship between social factors and the value of credit union membership. He is a past president of the CFA Society Sacramento.

Alexander Rudin, Ph.D., heads quantitative research efforts across Multi-Asset (Investment Solutions Group) and Fixed Income Cash and Currency (FICC) business lines for State Street Global Advisors. Within ISG, he drives a quantitative research agenda supporting tactical and strategic asset allocation processes, portfolio construction analytics, target volatility models, and the target date fund franchise. Within FICC, Alex oversees quantitative research for enhanced indexing, systematic credit, ETF management, and top-down active fixed income processes. Alex collaborates with ISG and FICC teams to deliver innovative ideas, products, and thought leadership to clients and has published articles in finance and theoretical physics journals.

Vincenzo Russo, Ph.D., is the head of Group Life and Health Risk Capital Modeling at Generali Group. From 2006 to 2014, he served as a risk manager at the Intesa Sanpaolo Bank Group. Prior to that, he worked as an Insurance and Financial Sales Agent for leading Italian insurance companies. He has authored scientific publications on quantitative models for financial and insurance risk modeling. Vincenzo is a member of the editorial advisory board of *The Journal of Portfolio Management*.

Marco Salerno, Ph.D., is an assistant advisor at the Abu Dhabi Investment Authority, focusing on portfolio strategy and strategic asset allocation. Previously, he was a principal at the Healthcare of Ontario Pension Plan (HOOPP). His research spans asset pricing, portfolio allocation, and topics such as stable equities, factor investing, and portfolio construction. Marco's work has earned awards from the Kroner Center for Financial Research and the International Centre for Pension Management.

Kris Shen is a Ph.D. candidate in Finance at Fisher College of Business at the Ohio State University in Columbus, Ohio, United States. He is a former equity trader at Seven Points Capital in New York City, specializing in market making, dark pool trading, and high-frequency trading. He is also a former retail-loan trading analyst at Goldman Sachs. Kris' primary research fields are asset pricing, climate finance, and labor finance.

Christopher Small is the director of Trading at Windham Capital Management, LLC. He has worked at Windham since 2015 and in the investment management industry since 2004. Chris manages the implementation of Windham's investment solutions across domestic and foreign equities, fixed income, commodities, and currencies, and has experience in a wide variety of investment vehicles including ETFs, futures, forwards, and swaps. Prior to Windham, Chris was a senior trader and manager at Windhaven Investment Management.

Anil Sood leads the AI Governance practice at EY US in New York, with over 18 years of experience in technology and capital markets. He was previously an executive director in Model Risk Governance at JPMorgan Chase, a software engineer at Microsoft, and a desk strategist at Deutsche Bank. Anil has also worked as a high-frequency trader and has several years of experience in options trading.

James Stavena is the head of portfolio management for Newton Investment Management's multi-asset solutions team and oversees the portfolio management team responsible for its global multi-asset strategies. Since joining in 1998, James has been the lead portfolio manager for the Dynamic US Equity strategy. He is a key contributor to the development, refinement, and risk management of the team's multi-asset strategies and signals, focusing on using derivatives in quantitative investment strategies. Previously, he was a portfolio manager and senior portfolio manager at Mellon Investments Corporation and Mellon Capital (BNY group companies).

Shubham Upadhyay is a quantitative researcher within the Multi-Asset ("Investment Solutions Group") Research team of SSGA. He is presently researching to enhance the Tactical Asset Allocation Model for commodities. Furthermore, he has been involved in the development and expansion of ISG's Exposure Management suite of products (Hedge Fund replication). Before joining ISG in 2022, Shubham conducted academic research in the Indian School of Business's Finance department and had a brief stint in investment banking and management consulting.

Kari Vatanen, CFA, FRM, is the head of asset allocation and alternative investments at Elo Mutual Pension Insurance Company in Finland. Previously, he worked as a chief investment officer at Veritas Pension Insurance, as a head of cross-asset derivatives and as a chief risk officer at Varma Mutual Pension Insurance Company. Mr. Vatanen is a member of the Editorial Advisory Board of *the Journal of Portfolio Management*, and he has written articles on asset allocation, risk management, and alternative risk premia investing.

Suprita Vohra, Ph.D., is an active financial professional specializing in foreign exchange and interest rate derivatives. Over the past two decades, she has held several senior roles across global banks, providing solutions to investors and risk managers. Suprita has contributed articles focusing on using FX derivatives in active currency management. She frequently presents at key industry events like the FX-Markets and Asia Risk Congress.

Andrew Weisman is a co-founder of MRP, an economics consultancy. He previously served as CIS of Windham Capital and as CIO for: Janus Capital's alternatives group, Merrill Lynch's hedge fund group, and Nikko Securities International. He is a recipient of the Bernstein Fabozzi /Jacobs Levy Award from the Journal of Portfolio Management and the Roger F Murray Prize (First Place) from the Institute for Quantitative Research in Finance. He is a board member of the International Association for Quantitative Finance, The Institute for Quantitative Research in Finance, and the Editorial Advisory Board of *The Journal of Portfolio Management*.

Shaojun Zhang, Ph.D., is an assistant professor of Finance at the Ohio State University in Columbus, Ohio, United States. She is a former portfolio manager at the Vanguard Corporation and China Investment Corporation, managing US, international, and global active factor ETFs and mutual funds. She is an advisory editorial board member of *The Journal of Portfolio Management*. Shaojun's primary research fields are asset pricing, sustainable investing, and international finance. She has published extensively in leading academic and practitioner journals. Her work has been extensively featured in various media, including Harvard Law School Forum, ProMarket at Chicago Booth, IBKRCampus.

List of Exhibits

Part I

Derivatives Fundamentals for Asset Managers

1

Introduction

Frank J. Fabozzi and Marielle de Jong

Derivative instruments are essential tools in modern asset management, offering flexibility and precision in implementing a diverse range of investment strategies. From mitigating risks to enhancing income and adjusting exposures, derivatives enable portfolio managers to address the subtleties of today's dynamic financial markets. This chapter provides an overview of how these instruments are employed to achieve various objectives, including effective risk management, asset allocation optimization, and income generation while aligning investment strategies with regulatory and operational considerations.

The chapter begins by examining the foundational concepts of derivatives, distinguishing between risk-sharing and insurance-type contracts. Through detailed discussions on instruments such as futures, options, and swaps, it highlights how these tools are tailored to specific portfolio goals. In addition to their practical benefits, derivatives provide a window into commonly shared market views, sentiments, and expectations. Portfolio managers can extract insights that inform strategic decisions by analyzing derivative pricing and implied market views. This ability to bridge quantitative analysis with

F. J. Fabozzi (✉)
Carey Business School, Johns Hopkins University, Baltimore, MD, USA
e-mail: ffabozz1@jhu.edu

M. de Jong
Grenoble Ecole de Management, Paris, France

F. J. Fabozzi and M. de Jong (eds.), *Derivatives Applications in Asset Management*,
https://doi.org/10.1007/978-3-031-86354-7_1

tactical execution highlights derivatives' dual role in asset-price evaluation and optimizing portfolio performance.

At the end of this chapter, we briefly describe the 22 cases included in this book.

General Classification of Derivatives

Derivatives are financial instruments whose value is based on the performance of an underlying asset, commodity, index, or reference rate. This underlying component, often referred to simply as the "underlying," is the foundation from which the derivative derives its value.

The primary economic purpose of a derivative is to serve as an efficient tool for managing and mitigating risk.

Derivatives are broadly categorized into two types: risk-sharing arrangements and insurance arrangements. Risk-sharing derivatives are named as such because both parties to the agreement mutually protect each other while foregoing the opportunity to benefit from favorable market movements. Insurance-type derivatives are financial instruments that protect one party from specific risks by transferring the potential downside to another party compensated in exchange by a premium or fee. Unlike risk-sharing derivatives, where both parties share risks and potential benefits, insurance-type derivatives provide asymmetrical protection: one party hedges against unfavorable outcomes while the counterparty assumes the associated risk.

Types of Risk-Sharing Derivative Contracts

A futures contract is a standardized agreement that obligates one party to buy and the other party to sell an underlying asset at a designated future date and a predetermined price. These contracts are traded on organized exchanges. The buyers of a futures contract are said to be "long the futures contract," meaning they benefit if the price of the underlying asset increases but incur losses if the price decreases. Conversely, the seller is "short the futures contract" and gains when the price of the underlying decreases while losing when it increases. In a futures contract, the clearinghouse associated with the exchange acts as the counterparty to both parties in the transaction, effectively eliminating counterparty risk.

A forward contract is a customized agreement between two parties to buy or sell an underlying asset at a specified future date and price. Unlike futures contracts, forward contracts are not standardized and are traded over-the-counter (OTC). Because the agreement is traded OTC, it is a private transaction between two parties without the involvement of a clearinghouse. To mitigate counterparty risk, parties often rely on several arrangements: collateral agreements, netting arrangements, and credit support annexes (an addendum to the International Swaps and Derivatives Association (ISDA) Master Agreement, which governs the overall relationship between the two parties in derivatives transactions).

Swaps are financial contracts in which two parties agree to exchange cash flows over a specified period. These instruments can serve different purposes, and their classification as either risk-sharing or insurance depends on their structure and objectives. In risk-sharing swaps, both parties mutually exchange exposures to manage their financial risks more effectively. These swaps are designed to help both parties achieve specific objectives without transferring all the risk to one side. An example is a generic interest rate swap where one party agrees to pay a fixed interest rate while receiving a floating rate from the other party. This allows the fixed-rate payer to hedge against rising interest rates while the floating-rate payer hedges against falling rates. Both parties share the benefits and risks of the swap based on changes in interest rates. Consequently, risk-sharing swaps involve a mutual exchange of risks, where both parties retain some level of exposure and benefit from favorable market movements.

In contrast, insurance-type swaps, such as credit default swaps (CDS), are designed to transfer risk entirely from one party to another. In a CDS, the buyer of the swap pays a regular premium to the seller in exchange for protection against the risk of a credit event (e.g., a default) affecting a specific reference entity, such as a corporation. If a credit event occurs, the seller compensates the buyer for their loss, insuring them against the default.

The key distinction lies in the risk transfer. In risk-sharing swaps, both parties actively manage and share financial risks, benefiting from favorable outcomes while accepting some exposure. In insurance-type swaps like CDS, the risk is fully transferred to the seller, who assumes responsibility for the defined risk in exchange for a fee. This asymmetry makes insurance-type swaps more akin to traditional insurance contracts, where one party seeks protection while the other provides it for a premium.

Insurance-Type Derivatives

Insurance-type derivatives include options, CDSs, caps, and floors. We have already described why a CDS is an insurance-type derivative.

Options

An option is a contract that gives the buyer the right, but not the obligation, to buy or sell an asset from the writer (or seller) at a specified price within a specified period or on a specific date. In exchange for granting this right, the writer receives a payment from the buyer known as the option price or option premium. The specified price at which the asset can be bought or sold is the exercise price or strike price. The date the option expires and becomes void is called the expiration date. The maximum amount that an option buyer can lose is the option price. The maximum profit that the option writer can realize is the option price. The option buyer has substantial upside return potential, while the option writer has substantial downside risk. Options may be traded on an organized exchange or in the OTC market.

When an option gives the buyer the right to purchase the underlying instrument from the writer (seller), it is called a call option or simply a call. Conversely, when the option grants the buyer the right to sell the underlying instrument to the writer, it is referred to as a put option or put. Options are also classified based on when the buyer can exercise the option, a characteristic known as the option's exercise style. The two most common exercise styles are American, which allows exercise at any time before expiration, and European, which permits exercise only at expiration. Other exercise styles, such as Bermudan options, which can be exercised on specific dates, and Asian options, which depend on the average price of the underlying asset over a specified period, also exist.

Understanding the classification of options as in-the-money (ITM), at-the-money (ATM), or out-of-the-money (OTM) is essential for evaluating their potential profitability and developing effective trading and hedging strategies. These classifications reflect the relationship between the option's strike price and the underlying asset's market price. An option is said to be ITM, and when exercising, it would result in a positive payoff for the holder. Options are classified as **ATM** when the underlying asset's market price is equal to, or very close to, the strike price. In this case, exercising the option would neither generate a profit nor result in a loss, as the price at which the option allows the holder to buy or sell matches the market price. An option is considered **OTM**, but exercising it would not result in a payoff for the holder.

Caps and Floors

In the financial market, agreements exist where one party, in exchange for a fee (referred to as a premium), agrees to compensate the other if a specified reference deviates from a predetermined level. The buyer is the party paying the premium and receiving compensation if the reference deviates. The party accepting the premium and committing to making the payment in the event of such a deviation is the seller.

An agreement is a cap when the seller agrees to compensate the buyer if the designated reference exceeds a predetermined level. Conversely, it is called a floor when the seller agrees to compensate the buyer if the designated reference falls below a predetermined level. Such arrangements are also embedded in certain fixed-income securities, such as inflation-linked bonds, which often include a deflation floor, which activates when the inflation rate drops below zero.

The designated reference could be a specific interest rate, the rate of return on a domestic or foreign stock market index such as the S&P 500 or the DAX (the German stock market index), or an exchange rate, such as the exchange rate between the U.S. dollar and the Japanese yen. The predetermined level is referred to as the strike.

Derivatives Fundamentals for Asset Managers

The 11 chapters in Part I describe the fundamentals about derivatives that asset managers should know. Chapters 2 to 5 describe the different types of derivatives based on the underlying.

Chapter 6 focuses on advanced derivative strategies to illustrate their application in managing risk and generating absolute returns. These strategies demonstrate derivatives' strategic flexibility, enabling portfolio managers to address specific objectives such as risk control and return optimization. This chapter is illustrative and vital for understanding how derivatives may enhance quantitative portfolio management.

Chapter 7 covers how derivatives, particularly futures, can address the subtleties of managing multi-asset portfolios with both public and private investments. It discusses the challenges of maintaining strategic asset allocation amid private investments' illiquidity and long-term nature. The chapter provides practical examples of using futures to offset allocation drifts, ensuring portfolios remain balanced without requiring direct asset liquidation. This discussion is essential for institutional investors who face the dual challenges of managing private assets and achieving timely portfolio rebalancing in dynamic markets.

Chapter 8 focuses on the design of derivatives income strategies, drawing attention to factors determining the instruments' choice and their application. The ultimate investment goal in the market context in which it is pursued gives guidance as to whether risk-sharing- or insurance-type derivatives are preferred. More concretely, is the priority given to the price-locking facility of futures contracts, to the tailored cash exchanges inherent to swaps, or the non-binding aspect of options? Furthermore, implementation considerations are addressed in this chapter, depending on practical issues such as portfolio size or mandatory constraints.

Chapters 8, 9, and 10 examine advanced themes in applying derivatives for asset management, covering topics such as liquidity management, performance evaluation, and the extraction of market views. These chapters provide essential frameworks and practical insights into how derivatives can enhance portfolio construction, facilitate strategic decision-making, and align with investment objectives. By addressing the unique characteristics of derivatives and their multifaceted roles, the last three chapters in Part I provide asset managers with the tools to navigate the complexities of modern financial markets.

How stock index futures can be used to manage liquidity efficiently within portfolios is explained in Chapter 9. It examines scenarios where portfolio managers face liquidity challenges, particularly during market stress or when managing allocations involving illiquid asset classes. Stock index futures provide a practical solution for maintaining market exposure while preserving liquidity. The chapter provides examples of using futures to hedge equity exposures, meet redemption demands, and navigate liquidity constraints in multi-asset portfolios. The discussion highlights key considerations, such as transaction costs, basis risk, and margin requirements, which influence the effective use of futures. The chapter demonstrates how stock index futures can bridge liquidity management and maintain portfolio objectives by providing theoretical insights and real-world applications.

Performance attribution analysis evaluates and breaks down the sources of a portfolio's returns to determine how different investment decisions contributed to its overall performance. This analysis helps portfolio managers and clients understand the effectiveness of various strategies. Chapter 10 describes the intricacies complexities and methodologies involved in performance attribution when derivatives are included in a portfolio. It highlights the unique challenges posed by derivatives, such as leverage, non-linear payoffs, and their role in modifying exposures rather than directly generating returns. The chapter emphasizes the need to adapt traditional attribution models by incorporating notional values and effective return calculations to account for derivatives' amplified impacts on portfolio performance. It also provides detailed discussions on specific derivative types—futures, options, and swaps—outlining tailored approaches to their performance attribution.

Chapter 11 examines how derivative pricing can derive actionable market insights. By analyzing prices of instruments like options, futures, and swaps, portfolio managers can uncover market expectations regarding volatility, risk, and economic trends. The chapter introduces techniques such as extracting risk-neutral densities (RNDs) from option prices and deriving implied forward rates from interest rate derivatives, demonstrating their application in forecasting and scenario analysis. The chapter also addresses the limitations of these techniques, stemming from data sparsity and market inefficiencies, while providing methodologies for refining predictions through tools like kernel density estimation. Asset managers can enhance decision-making and align their investments with anticipated market dynamics by integrating these derivative-based insights into portfolio strategies.

Applications to Asset Management

Parts II, III, and IV provide the case studies. The applications are categorized into three primary areas: managing risk and capital protection, leverage and exposure management, and strategies for income enhancement. These three areas provide a comprehensive framework for applying derivatives in asset management, addressing various objectives from protecting capital to boosting returns. With this application classification, we briefly introduce the cases in this book.

Part II: Managing Risk and Capital Protection

Managing risk and capital protection focuses on safeguarding investments against adverse market movements. This includes strategies such as hedging, which mitigate specific risks like interest rate fluctuations, currency volatility, or equity market declines. The goal is to reduce potential losses while preserving the overall value of a portfolio, ensuring stability even during periods of heightened market uncertainty. These techniques are especially valuable for managing tail risks or protecting critical capital assets.

The nine cases in Part II provide applications for managing risk and capital protection. Collectively, they illustrate diverse methods of managing financial risks and protecting capital across different asset classes and institutional contexts.

Chapter 12 explores risk management in equity portfolios by examining hedging strategies with stock index futures and put options. It discusses the practicalities of implementing these two approaches to reduce the directional beta exposure to the S&P 500 index, emphasizing the tradeoffs between futures-based and options-based hedging. Using a hypothetical portfolio, the case compares outcomes during the COVID-19 market sell-off, illustrating the effectiveness of each strategy under extreme conditions. The options approach demonstrated higher gains due to unexpectedly high realized market volatility. Still, it also highlighted the accounted-for higher upfront costs and the potential impact of the volatility risk premium.

Chapter 13 addresses tail risk hedging using options, focusing on how portfolio managers can proactively protect against rare but severe market events. The case demonstrates how portfolio managers can cushion portfolios against extreme downside risks while preserving exposure to the market upside by structuring and implementing options-based hedging strategies. A hypothetical scenario examines the practicalities of using OTM put options for hedging an equity portfolio, providing insight into their costs and performance under adverse conditions.

Chapter 14 focuses on bond portfolio hedging with U.S. Treasury futures, highlighting interest rate risk management. A hypothetical bond portfolio demonstrates how portfolio managers use futures to adjust the portfolio's duration and mitigate exposure to adverse yield curve shifts. By examining hedging strategies with 2-year, 5-year, and 10-year Treasury futures, the case illustrates the benefits of using a tailored basket of futures contracts to optimize the portfolio's key-rate duration profile, effectively neutralizing the impact of rate changes while preserving positive carry.

Chapter 15 discusses a real-world application of interest rate swaps in consumer mortgage portfolio hedging, as implemented by a credit union. Facing a liability-sensitive balance sheet, the credit union uses pay-fixed swaps to reduce asset duration and align it with liability duration, thereby stabilizing equity during interest rate fluctuations. The case details the operational and accounting benefits of using the "last-of-layer" method under updated accounting standards, showcasing how derivatives can be strategically employed for balance sheet stability in community financial institutions.

Chapter 16 examines how life insurance companies hedge interest rate risk using swaps as part of their asset-liability management processes. It focuses on mitigating the duration mismatch between long-term liabilities and shorter-term assets by incorporating interest rate derivatives into the asset portfolio. The illustration demonstrates how a receiver swap can be used to increase asset duration, reducing the duration gap and stabilizing profits against interest rate fluctuations. The case emphasizes the importance of effective duration as a metric and the role of optimization in aligning asset and liability sensitivities to market changes.

Chapter 17 examines strategies for managing systematic risk in high-yield credit portfolios. It highlights the limitations of traditional approaches, such as shorting high-yield ETFs, due to high costs, illiquidity, and basis risk between cash and synthetic markets during stress periods. Instead, it demonstrates the effectiveness of equity index derivatives in hedging high-yield portfolios, particularly a combination of equity futures and put options. The study underscores that equity futures and options offer effective hedging reliability, particularly during volatile market conditions when effective hedging is most important. Cross-asset instruments offer effective hedging ability due to the strong linkage between high-yield bonds and synthetic equity markets. It recommends refining hedging strategies with additional economic indicators to enhance accuracy and flexibility.

Chapter 18 describes how mortgage originators hedge the gain-on-sale income from their mortgage pipeline using to-be-announced (TBA) securities. The timeline from rate lock to funding, which often ranges from 15 to 60 days, exposes originators to interest rate risk. To mitigate this, they enter TBA contracts corresponding to the characteristics of the mortgages they are originating. The case explores the mechanics of the TBA market, which is a critical component of the secondary mortgage market, allowing originators to manage risk efficiently and maintain profitability. A practical illustration demonstrates how originators use TBA contracts to hedge pipeline risk, balance liquidity needs, and navigate market volatility, ensuring stability during periods of fluctuating rates.

Chapter 19 examines the use of foreign exchange (FX) options as a versatile tool for managing currency risks in globally diversified portfolios. It begins by outlining the challenges faced by portfolio managers operating in multi-currency environments, such as mitigating FX volatility and balancing risk with cost-effectiveness. The study emphasizes the flexibility of FX options, such as ATM options, average rate (Asian) options, and contingent options, which allow portfolio managers to tailor hedging strategies to specific objectives while accounting for market nuances like delta, volatility, and moneyness. Through several case studies, this case illustrates practical applications of FX options in diverse scenarios. The study compares hedging tools, including FX forwards and ATM FX options, highlighting their respective impacts on portfolio returns. It also describes average rate options, which are particularly effective in hedging sustained currency weakness while offering cost efficiency. The study concludes that FX options offer critical advantages for navigating the complexities of global investments.

Chapter 20 explores the strategic use of FX forward contracts to manage currency risks in globally diversified institutional portfolios. The study provides theoretical and practical insights into managing FX exposure, showcasing scenarios where forward contracts stabilize returns effectively. The study begins with a simple illustration of a U.S.-based portfolio manager hedging 50% of a portfolio's euro exposure. Entering an FX forward contract, the portfolio manager locks in an exchange rate to mitigate potential losses from euro depreciation. This hedging mechanism demonstrates how portfolio managers can reduce currency risks, ensuring portfolio performance aligns with investment objectives. A real-world illustration analyzing an international equity portfolio exposed to various currencies is provided. The analysis reveals the impact of equity index value changes and FX rate fluctuations on portfolio performance. The effectiveness of FX hedging strategies is highlighted through detailed performance analysis. When currencies are hedged using FX forwards, portfolio losses due to FX rate fluctuations are significantly reduced. The study also examines basis risk, which arises from mismatches between the hedging instrument and the underlying exposure and interaction effects between equity and FX movements.

Part III: Leverage and Exposure Management

Leverage and exposure management, the central theme in Part III, involves optimizing a portfolio's risk-return profile by adjusting market exposures and employing leverage. This consists in using derivatives to gain or reduce exposure to specific asset classes, sectors, or markets without requiring large capital outlays. For example, derivatives can be used to rebalance portfolios efficiently, manage systematic risks, or implement tactical asset allocation strategies.

Chapter 21 focuses on how equity swaps are utilized in portfolio management to achieve strategic objectives, manage risk, and enhance operational efficiency. Equity swaps are derivative contracts allowing two parties to exchange cash flows, typically one tied to an equity index or stock basket and the other to a fixed or floating interest rate. This setup offers a cost-effective and flexible means for portfolio managers to gain equity exposure, rebalance portfolios, hedge risk, and access restricted markets without directly owning the underlying securities. Multiple applications of equity swaps, including speculation, where portfolio managers can bet on stock movements without purchasing the assets, and hedging, which protects against potential losses by procuring the economic effects of selling an equity position without physically divesting it. Additionally, equity swaps facilitate asset allocation adjustments, allowing portfolio managers to achieve desired exposure levels efficiently. They also enable leverage, offering amplified market exposure with less initial capital and providing access to markets that may be restricted due to regulations or high entry costs. Equity swaps can also tailor tax efficiency and operational risk management, reducing transaction costs and simplifying the management of diverse portfolios.

How portfolio managers use derivatives to address the challenges posed by cash drags in investment portfolios is demonstrated in Chapter 22. Cash drags occur when uninvested cash within a portfolio generates lower returns than the portfolio's benchmark, particularly during low or negative interest rates. This performance gap can erode a portfolio's competitiveness. Cash equitization offers a solution by using derivatives to align cash positions with the intended market exposure, maintaining investment objectives, and mitigating the negative impact of holding cash. The case focuses on a global equity-enhanced income fund benchmarked against the MSCI All-Country World Index (ACWI). The fund uses cash equitization to manage daily cash inflows and outflows. By employing liquid derivatives, such as S&P E-mini futures contracts, the portfolio management team replicates the fund's exposure to global equity markets while awaiting cash deployment into long-term investments. This approach minimizes opportunity costs, enhances operational efficiency, and reduces trading complexities. For example, the fund uses nearby futures contracts due to their high liquidity and low transaction costs, ensuring cost-effective execution and well-managed market exposure.

Chapter 23 focuses on strategies for managing and profiting from event-driven market risks, such as earnings announcements, elections, or macroeconomic policy decisions. These events often trigger sharp changes in market volatility, which traditional risk models, like the Black–Scholes model, struggle to capture due to their constant volatility assumption. The case introduces a technique for extracting forward implied volatility, which uses options with overlapping maturities to isolate expected volatility changes during event-specific periods, offering a precise tool for analyzing market reactions to these discrete events. A practical example involves Amazon's stock (AMZN) leading up to an earnings announcement. The study examines two trading strategies: the first consists of buying a straddle (a combination of call and put options) that expires after the announcement. In contrast, the second combines this position with selling a straddle expiring before the announcement. These strategies aim to capitalize on anticipated volatility increases during the earnings period. By analyzing implied volatility before and after the event, the study demonstrates how forward implied volatility provides insights into market expectations, enabling traders to focus on event-specific risks. The case highlights challenges in trading around event risk, such as managing option sensitivities ("Greeks") and market volatility mispricing.

Chapter 24 describes the challenges of managing interest rate exposure within high-yield bond portfolios. It identifies the complexities of traditional hedging techniques and the unique dynamics of high-yield bonds, particularly the interaction between interest rate changes and credit spreads. The case explores the theoretical underpinnings of hedging strategies, practical applications, and the often counterintuitive outcomes of conventional duration-based approaches. The case begins with explaining hedging objectives, such as minimizing portfolio variance through an optimal hedge ratio. For high-yield bonds, duration—a measure of sensitivity to interest rates—is traditionally used to calculate this ratio. However, the case demonstrates that high-yield bonds often behave differently due to the inverse relationship between interest rate changes and credit spreads. This phenomenon, driven by market responses to economic conditions, results in an empirical duration for high-yield bonds that is much lower—and sometimes even negative—than the analytical duration. Using the Bloomberg U.S. Corporate High-Yield Bond Index as a case study, the analysis illustrates how hedging with Treasury futures based on duration often leads to increased portfolio volatility, contrary to the intended purpose.

The strategic use of futures contracts in tactical asset allocation is demonstrated in Chapter 25. The case presents practical applications of futures through a balanced portfolio based on a 60/40 allocation model, showing how futures streamline asset allocation shifts. For instance, a portfolio manager can adjust equity and bond exposures by trading futures contracts rather than directly buying or selling individual securities. The illustration details scenarios such as increasing equity exposure or reducing bond allocations by incorporating futures, enabling portfolio managers to align tactical decisions with market expectations dynamically. Through detailed illustrations, the case underscores the precision of futures contracts in achieving desired allocations while minimizing leverage and transaction complexity. Finally, the study highlights the tax advantages of futures for tactical investment horizons under the 60/40 tax rule, which treats 60% of gains as long-term and 40% as short-term. This favorable tax treatment, combined with the liquidity and cost benefits of futures, positions them as an optimal tool for short-term tactical adjustments in taxable and tax-exempt portfolios. By examining the practical mechanics and strategic advantages of futures, the case establishes their critical role in modern portfolio management, enabling managers to achieve flexible, cost-effective, and tax-efficient allocation adjustments.

The use of derivatives in constructing tactical asset allocation TAA overlays for multi-asset portfolios is demonstrated in Chapter 26. It illustrates how derivatives enable portfolio managers to achieve additional returns while managing risks. Using instruments like equity index futures, government bond futures, and options, portfolio managers can implement TAA overlays to diversify and generate uncorrelated returns, known as "portable alpha," without disrupting the core portfolio. The case also explains the mechanics of using derivatives, emphasizing basis risk, initial margin requirements, and duration mismatches to achieve efficient exposure to various asset classes. The study highlights the strategic role of options for downside protection and upside capture, showcasing their effectiveness during market volatility, such as the COVID-19 pandemic. By integrating call options into a TAA overlay, portfolio managers benefited from the convex payoff profile, allowing dynamic risk-level adjustments. Options mitigate losses during sharp drawdowns and facilitate participation in market recoveries. The use of options is presented as a more flexible tool than linear instruments like futures, providing portfolio managers with a robust means to navigate uncertain market conditions. The case underscores the advantages of derivatives in multi-asset portfolio construction through detailed calculations and illustrations.

The final chapter in this section, Chapter 27, demonstrates how institutional investors use derivatives to manage FX risk in globally diversified portfolios. The case examines the implementation of centralized currency hedging overlays, which streamline FX risk management by using derivatives such as forwards, swaps, futures, and options to neutralize or reduce currency exposure. Currency hedging overlays separate FX risk management from the broader asset allocation process, enabling consistent, efficient, and transparent management of currency exposures across portfolios. The case emphasizes the importance of defining optimal hedging ratios and balancing risk reduction with hedging costs, including transaction fees, margin requirements, and opportunity costs. Factors such as currency volatility, correlations with portfolio assets, and interest rate differentials influence the choice of hedging instruments and the extent of hedging. By centralizing these decisions, institutions can enhance operational efficiency, reduce portfolio volatility, and better align currency management with investment objectives. The case also considers the decision between managing currency overlays internally or outsourcing to external specialists. Internal management offers greater control and customization but requires significant resources and expertise, while external managers provide specialized knowledge, cost efficiencies, and advanced monitoring tools. A hybrid approach, combining internal oversight with outsourced execution, can balance control and efficiency. Through detailed analysis, the case demonstrates how portfolio managers can design and implement effective currency hedging strategies that align with their operational capabilities, investment goals, and market conditions.

Part IV: Income Enhancement Strategies

Strategies for income enhancement, the subject of Part IV, seek to generate additional returns by leveraging specific market opportunities. These strategies often involve using derivatives to monetize volatility, implementing covered call strategies, or replicating income streams through instruments like credit default swaps or options. Focusing on yield optimization enables portfolio managers to enhance their portfolios' income potential while effectively managing associated risks.

Chapter 28 addresses the challenges associated with path dependency in option income strategies, such as covered call and cash-secured put strategies. Path dependency is inherent in these strategies, as the outcomes depend on the underlying asset's final price and the sequence and timing of price movements. This case focuses on understanding and mitigating these challenges to achieve consistent portfolio performance and sustainable income generation. The case uses the CBOE S&P 500 BuyWrite Monthly Index (BXM) as a benchmark to illustrate how single-path strategies can underperform in certain market conditions. The BXM generates income by systematically writing ATM call options tied to fixed expiration dates, but its rigid structure makes it vulnerable to adverse market timing. During rapid market rallies, the capped upside of ATM options limits participation in growth, and in declining markets, the premiums collected can fail to significantly offset losses. Historical data reveals that single-path strategies like BXM frequently experience inconsistent results, highlighting the need for diversification to reduce reliance on specific market outcomes. To address these issues, the case emphasizes the importance of laddering—a strategy that diversifies option expirations and strike levels across different timeframes. By staggering option trades, laddering smooths income streams and reduces the impact of timing-related risks associated with single-path strategies. Additionally, the case explores the importance of balancing yield and total return.

The volatility risk premium (VRP) refers to the consistent difference between the implied volatility in option prices and the realized volatility of the underlying asset arising from market participants' demand for protection against uncertainty. This premium, driven by institutional hedging activity and behavioral biases, offers a systematic opportunity for generating absolute returns. Chapter 29 explains how asset managers can harvest the VRP through strategies that sell options to monetize this discrepancy while managing associated risks. More specifically, it provides an in-depth analysis of a one-month ATM straddle strategy on the S&P 500 Index, where both call and put options are sold to collect premiums, paired with daily delta hedging using futures to minimize directional risk. This strategy is highlighted for its ability to capture the VRP systematically while mitigating the potential for large losses during sharp market moves. The discussion further explores alternative approaches, such as safer structures like iron condors, which add additional out-of-the-money hedges to limit downside risks. The case emphasizes the importance of disciplined risk management in executing VRP-based strategies, addressing challenges such as volatility spikes and market dislocations. Refinements, including more frequent hedging and diversification across strike prices and expiration dates, are suggested to improve performance and reduce exposure to sudden market shocks.

Chapter 30 describes a strategy to enhance the performance of covered call strategies by integrating stock index options. Using Nvidia, a high-growth stock with high implied volatility, as the central example, the case demonstrates how portfolio managers can generate additional income while mitigating risks associated with short call positions. The analysis introduces the fundamental mechanics of covered calls, where a portfolio manager sells OTM call options on held shares to collect premiums, generating income as long as the stock price remains below the strike price. The case contrasts single-stock options, like Nvidia's, with index options, emphasizing differences in implied volatility dynamics. The case underlines a real-world example that illustrates the strategy, demonstrating the importance of position sizing to balance cash flow and delta alignment. By maintaining a proportional relationship between Nvidia and S&P 500 option positions based on beta and price correlation, the portfolio manager effectively hedges against potential losses while optimizing risk-adjusted returns. The case concludes by discussing the importance of evaluating correlation, implied volatility, and option premiums when designing adaptive covered call strategies. This case offers a robust framework for managing high-growth equities while enhancing income generation and risk management through innovative hedging techniques.

The practical application of covered calls and cash-secured puts to generate consistent income while managing risk is presented in Chapter 31. These strategies allow portfolio managers to earn premium income by selling options on underlying assets, providing flexibility to target specific income levels while participating in market movements. The case analyzes three approaches to income targeting—adjusting strike prices, modifying portfolio weights, and combining covered calls with cash-secured puts—and evaluates their performance based on metrics like premium income, risk-adjusted returns, and downside risk. The case highlights the similarities and differences between covered calls and cash-secured puts. Both strategies share the same payoff profile when implemented with identical strike prices and expirations. However, combining the two strategies provides diversification and the ability to balance market participation and income generation. For instance, adjusting call strikes higher allows more equity-like returns, while lowering put strikes adds defensive characteristics. This flexibility enables investors to customize their strategies to meet income objectives while managing downside risk. The case also emphasizes the importance of volatility skew in optimizing option-based income strategies. Skew dynamics, where OTM puts often carry higher premiums than OTM calls, create opportunities to enhance yields and defensiveness by incorporating puts. A comparison of three illustrative strategies demonstrates that combining OTM puts and calls with variable strikes results in lower beta, reduced volatility, and more stable risk-adjusted returns compared to strategies that rely solely on calls.

CDS indices, such as CDX and iTraxx, can be an efficient alternative to physical corporate bond portfolios. These indices enable portfolio managers to replicate corporate bond market exposure, benefiting from enhanced liquidity, lower transaction costs, and operational flexibility. By combining CDS indices with government bonds, managers can achieve similar risk-return profiles to traditional corporate bond indices while mitigating the challenges of investing in physical bonds, particularly in illiquid or distressed market conditions. Chapter 32 details the mechanics of CDS index replication, highlighting how CDS indices allow portfolio managers to gain credit risk exposure while government bonds provide interest rate exposure. Compared to physical bonds, CDS indices offer higher liquidity and lower trading costs, making them an efficient tool for managing large portfolios. Additionally, the historical performance of CDS index-based portfolios shows lower volatility and default rates than traditional corporate bond portfolios, particularly during crises such as the 2007–2008 Global Financial Crisis and the COVID-19 market turmoil. CDS indices exhibit large relative risk (tracking error) for portfolio managers who benchmark against physical bond indices. However, patient managers focusing on long-term results may benefit from comparable returns with reduced volatility and fewer defaults. Moreover, the case demonstrates that dynamic beta allocation strategies using CDS indices can enhance portfolio returns. By employing a trend-following strategy based on past performance, managers can adjust credit exposure to capitalize on favorable market conditions while reducing risk during downturns.

The final case in the book, Chapter 33, demonstrates how CDS can be integrated into fixed-income strategies to improve portfolio performance and mitigate risks associated with issuer defaults. The analysis is based on a hypothetical buy-and-hold bond portfolio of 30 corporate bonds structured to generate regular cash flows over a multi-year horizon. The case highlights the potential of CDS overlays to transform passive investment strategies by introducing active risk management elements, protecting against credit events while maintaining yield objectives. The portfolio used in the case comprises a mix of investment-grade and lower-rated bonds, exposing it to varying levels of credit risk. Using Monte Carlo simulations, the study evaluates the impact of defaults on the portfolio, employing metrics such as Value at Risk and Conditional Value at Risk to assess tail risks. Without a CDS overlay, the portfolio faces significant downside risks. A partial CDS overlay strategy is used to address this. The overlay reduces the portfolio's downside risk without impacting its yield-to-maturity, demonstrating its effectiveness in mitigating extreme losses while preserving returns. The case underscores the importance of evaluating the cost–benefit tradeoffs of CDS integration, considering both nominal and present-value metrics. This analysis provides practical insights into using CDS for navigating credit risks and enhancing portfolio stability in volatile market environments.

Summary

This chapter describes the basic derivative products and then introduces derivatives' applications in modern asset management, highlighting their essential role in addressing complex portfolio objectives. Derivatives offer portfolio managers unparalleled flexibility and efficiency, enabling portfolio managers to enhance asset allocation strategies, manage risks, and generate income. The chapter establishes a foundational understanding of their design and purpose by categorizing derivatives into risk-sharing and insurance-based instruments. It further introduces practical applications such as futures for tactical asset allocation, options for income generation, and swaps for managing interest rate and credit risks, demonstrating their value in aligning portfolios with strategic goals.

The chapter describes the versatility of derivatives in managing specific risks, from hedging against tail risks during market downturns to addressing currency exposure in global portfolios. Instruments like put options, Treasury futures, and credit default swaps are introduced and detailed as critical tools for mitigating market, interest rate, and credit risks. Moreover, for globally diversified portfolios, FX forwards and options are presented as indispensable for preserving returns amidst currency volatility. These applications illustrate how derivatives equip managers with the tools to navigate increasingly dynamic and interconnected financial markets.

In addition to risk management, the chapter emphasizes the strategic use of derivatives in multi-asset portfolios. Derivatives allow managers to implement tactical overlays, portable alpha strategies, and sector-specific exposures, offering a seamless balance of short-term opportunities with long-term allocation objectives. By providing a robust framework for integrating derivatives into portfolio management, this chapter sets the stage for the detailed case studies and advanced applications in the book, offering a practical guide for asset managers seeking to leverage derivatives effectively.

2

Equity Derivatives

Frank J. Fabozzi

Exchange-traded equity derivatives, including options and futures, are integral to modern financial markets, providing tools for controlling risks, enhancing returns, and achieving precise market exposures. Investors widely use these instruments to manage portfolio risks, speculate on market movements, and implement tactical adjustments efficiently. While this chapter focuses on the structural and operational aspects of equity options and futures, it does not delve into their pricing mechanics nor equity volatility derivatives covered in Chapter 5 and equity swaps covered in Chapter 21. Additionally, the applications of equity derivatives are not described in this chapter, as these are explored through practical examples in the cases presented throughout the book.

This chapter also includes a detailed discussion on managing maintenance margins and rolling contracts, which, while covered in the context of equity derivatives, are equally applicable to other financial derivatives. Effective management of these aspects is essential to ensure consistent exposure to the underlying assets and to avoid risks such as forced liquidation due to unmet margin requirements. By focusing on these foundational elements, this chapter aims to provide operational insights necessary to utilize equity derivatives effectively while mitigating associated risks.

F. J. Fabozzi (✉)
Johns Hopkins University's Carey School of Business, Baltimore, MD, USA
e-mail: ffabozz1@jhu.edu

F. J. Fabozzi and M. de Jong (eds.), *Derivatives Applications in Asset Management*,
https://doi.org/10.1007/978-3-031-86354-7_2

Types of Exchange-Traded Equity Options and Futures

Exchange-traded equity derivatives are financial instruments whose value is derived from individual stocks or stock indices. These derivatives primarily include stock options, stock index options, single-stock futures, and stock index futures, each offering unique features and uses. This section focuses on the structure and mechanics of these instruments, providing foundational knowledge essential for understanding their applications.

Stock options grant the holder the right, but not the obligation, to buy or sell a specific stock at a predetermined price, called the strike price, within a certain time period. In the United States, exchange-traded stock options typically represent 100 shares of the underlying stock per contract. Options are standardized based on characteristics such as expiration cycles, strike prices, and settlement methods. American-style options, the standard in U.S. markets, can be exercised anytime before expiration, offering the holder flexibility. Variants of standard options include Long-Term Equity Anticipation Securities (LEAPS), which extend expiration periods to up to three years, and weekly options, which provide shorter durations for tactical trading strategies. In contrast, European-style options stipulate a single exercise date.

Stock index options are derivatives based on the value of a stock index, such as the S&P 500 or Nasdaq-100. These options allow investors to gain or hedge exposure to an entire index without holding individual stocks. Because they track an index, settlement is typically cash-based rather than involving the delivery of securities. The dollar value of the underlying index is calculated by multiplying the index level by a predefined contract multiplier. Index options have been modified over time to accommodate a broader range of market participants, with e-mini and micro e-mini contracts providing lower notional values and making them accessible to retail investors.

Equity futures obligate the holder to buy or sell a specific amount of an equity or equity index at a predetermined price on a future date. These contracts are exchange-traded and require initial and maintenance margins. The less commonly used single-stock futures focus on individual stocks, while index futures provide exposure to equity indices.

Pricing Efficiency in Equity Derivatives Markets

The pricing efficiency of equity derivatives markets is a critical factor that underpins their practical application in asset management. Pricing efficiency refers to the degree to which the prices of derivatives accurately and promptly reflect all available information about the underlying assets. When markets are efficient, arbitrage opportunities are minimized, and derivative prices provide reliable benchmarks for managing financial risk and implementing strategies.

Pricing efficiency has profound implications for the strategic use of derivatives. In efficient markets, derivatives can be employed confidently for dynamic portfolio rebalancing, volatility arbitrage, and tail-risk protection. The reliability of market-generated prices ensures that these strategies are executed effectively, minimizing the need for extensive manual intervention.

Over the past half-century, empirical studies have supported the consistent pricing efficiency of stock options and stock index options.[1] Mispricing was found to be rare, and it was quickly wiped out when it occurred. Moreover, empirical evidence suggests that markets have become more efficient over time, driven by increased competition, advanced trading algorithms, and greater regulatory oversight. Finally, it is essential to acknowledge that the pricing efficiency of derivatives markets has stood the test of time. The empirical studies establishing efficiency were conducted decades ago, but no evidence suggests that markets have become less efficient. On the contrary, technological advancements and improvements in market infrastructure have likely enhanced their efficiency.

Liquidity, transparency, and robust regulatory oversight contribute to pricing efficiency in equity derivatives markets. Highly liquid markets facilitate quick price adjustments and minimize transaction costs, while transparent information flows ensure that prices accurately reflect underlying risks and opportunities. Regulatory frameworks, such as those enforced by the Commodity Futures Trading Commission (CFTC) and the European Securities and Markets Authority (ESMA), play a vital role in maintaining fair and efficient markets by preventing manipulation and ensuring investor protection.

Pricing efficiency also has significant implications for strategy implementation. For instance, efficient markets enable precise targeted risk control using

[1] Early studies on the pricing efficiency of stock options are provided by Chiras and Manaster (1978), Galai (1980), Phillips and Smith (1980), and Blomeyer and Klemkosky (1983). For stock index options, empirical evidence supporting pricing efficiency is provided by Evnine and Rudd (1985) and Chance (1987).

metrics such as the "Greeks," allowing portfolio managers to adjust their positions dynamically in response to market changes. Cost-effective hedging strategies, such as using options and futures, rely on pricing that closely aligns with theoretical models, which presume prices to be information efficient. Furthermore, efficient pricing supports the use of equity derivatives for dynamic portfolio rebalancing, tail-risk protection, and volatility arbitrage, all of which are critical for modern risk management.

While equity derivatives markets are generally efficient, occasional inefficiencies allow well-positioned market participants to exploit mispricings. Deviations from expected volatility patterns or temporary pricing anomalies can create strategic advantages for sophisticated investors. However, these opportunities are fleeting, underscoring the importance of rapid response and advanced analytical tools in exploiting such inefficiencies.

A Closer Look at Exchange-Traded Equity Derivatives

This section delves into the characteristics and applications of exchange-traded equity derivatives, focusing on their structure, mechanics, and practical utility. By examining the nuances of these derivatives, a deeper understanding of their use in investment strategies is gained.

Options on Individual Stocks

A defining characteristic of stock options is their standardized contract size, which typically represents 100 shares of the underlying stock in most markets. This standardization ensures uniformity across contracts and facilitates liquidity in the options market. The strike price determines the price at which the option can be exercised and is set at regular intervals based on the stock's trading price. Expiration dates are another critical component, with stock options offering a range of maturities from weekly options, which expire in a few days, to long-term options like Long-Term Equity Anticipation Securities (LEAPS) extending up to three years. This flexibility allows investors to select options that align with their investment horizons and strategic objectives.

Options on individual stocks in the United States are primarily American style, which means they can be exercised at any time before expiration. Unlike cash-settled derivatives discussed later, stock options are generally physically settled, meaning that the actual shares of the stock are transferred if the option is exercised. This feature closely ties the derivative to the underlying asset, enhancing its utility for managing direct equity exposure.

Stock options are priced based on a combination of extrinsic value and intrinsic value. The latter reflects the difference between the stock price and the strike price, representing the immediate exercise value of the option. Extrinsic value, on the other hand, accounts for factors such as time to expiration, implied volatility, and prevailing interest rates. For example, a call option with a strike price below the stock's current price will have a positive intrinsic value, while one with a higher strike price will derive its value entirely from intrinsic factors. Based on the relationship between the stock price and the strike price, each type of option can be categorized as in-the-money (ITM), at-the-money (ATM), or out-of-the-money (OTM). This classification influences the pricing and likelihood of exercise.

Broad-Based Stock Index Options

Stock index options offer portfolio managers exposure to the performance of an entire stock market index, sector, or investment characteristics rather than individual stocks. For broad-based stock index options, the underlying asset is a stock index such as the S&P 500, Nasdaq-100, or Russell 2000, typically cash-settled. This means that upon expiration, the settlement involves a cash payment based on the difference between the index level and the strike price rather than the physical delivery of the index's component stocks.

A critical aspect of any stock index options is the **contract multiple**, which determines the dollar value of the index underlying the contract. The dollar value of the underlying index is calculated as:

$$\text{Dollar Value of Index} = \text{Index Level} \times \text{Contract Multiple}$$

For example, if the S&P 500 is trading at 4,000, the dollar value of the underlying index would be 4,000 times the contract multiple. For the S&P500 index option, the contract multiple is \$100. The contract value would be \$400,000 (4,000 × \$100).

To cater to smaller investors and provide more flexibility, exchanges introduced e-mini and micro e-mini stock index options. These contracts have reduced contract multiples, such as \$50 for e-mini S&P 500 and \$5 for micro e-mini options. This scaling down allows investors with smaller capital bases to participate in index derivatives markets while tailoring their exposure to desired levels.

Broad-Based Stock Index Futures

Stock index futures are standardized contracts that obligate the buyer to purchase or the seller to deliver the cash value of a stock index at a specified future date. As with index options, stock index futures have a contract multiple. For example, the S&P 500 Index futures contract has a standard contract multiple of $250. If the index level is 4,000, the contract represents a notional value of $1,000,000 (4,000 × $250). The e-mini S&P 500 futures contract, designed for smaller investors, has a contract multiple of $50, reducing the notional value for the same index level to $200,000. Micro-e-mini contracts lower the entry barrier, with a contract multiple of $5, allowing retail investors to manage smaller exposures effectively.

Single-Stock Futures

Single-stock futures are standardized financial contracts that obligate the buyer to purchase, or the seller to deliver, a specific number of shares of an individual stock at a predetermined price on a future date. Single-stock futures are typically standardized, ensuring uniformity and facilitating trading. Each contract is based on a specific stock, typically a large-cap or liquid stock with significant trading volume, and generally represents 100 shares of the underlying stock per contract, mirroring the lot size of standard stock options. Contracts are available with multiple expiration dates, typically spaced at quarterly intervals, aligning with the expiration cycles of other equity derivatives. Most single-stock futures are physically settled, meaning the actual shares of the underlying stock are delivered upon contract expiration. Some exchanges may offer cash-settled variants.

Stock Index Options and Futures in U.S. Sectors

Stock index options and futures tied to U.S. sector indices play a crucial role in facilitating targeted exposure to specific segments of the economy. These instruments allow portfolio managers to control exposure or rebalance portfolios based on the performance of industry sectors such as technology, healthcare, financials, energy, and more. Sector-specific derivatives provide flexibility for investors looking to isolate and manage risks unique to particular economic areas, making them valuable tools for active portfolio management.

Exhibit 2.1 shows the S&P 500 sectors for the stock index futures and options. The European-style exercise characteristic ensures that options can only be exercised at expiration, aligning with their role in managing broad sectoral risks rather than frequent trading.

The settlement involves a cash payment based on the difference between the index's level at expiration and the option's strike price. For example, a portfolio manager holding a portfolio concentrated in technology stocks may purchase put options on the S&P 500 Technology Sector Index to protect against potential sector-wide declines. Conversely, traders anticipating outperformance in the healthcare sector might buy call options on the corresponding index to leverage their investment thesis.

The flexibility of sector index options also supports more complex strategies, such as pairs trading. This involves taking opposing positions on two sectors, allowing investors to exploit relative performance differences. Spread strategies, such as calendar spreads, further enhance the ability to target specific outcomes based on market views or economic conditions.

Sector-specific derivatives offer distinct advantages, making them valuable tools for portfolio managers. One key benefit is their ability to provide targeted exposure to specific industries without requiring the purchase of individual stocks. This makes it easier for portfolio managers to gain or adjust exposure to sectors like technology, healthcare, or financials cost-effectively and streamlined. Additionally, these derivatives facilitate efficient portfolio diversification by allowing investors to access underrepresented or emerging sectors.

Another advantage of sector-specific derivatives is their capital efficiency. By utilizing futures or options, investors can achieve significant exposure with only a fraction of the capital required for outright stock purchases. This leverage amplifies potential returns and allows for more strategic capital allocation. Furthermore, these instruments often exhibit high liquidity in well-traded sectors, which ensures ease of execution and narrow bid-ask spreads, minimizing transaction costs for investors.

Sector-specific derivatives, as do derivatives in general, also provide insights into market expectations. For example, the pricing of sector-based options reflects implied volatility and market sentiment about the underlying sector, offering valuable information for decision-making. This forward-looking data can guide investors in adjusting strategies or anticipating market shifts. The flexibility of these instruments supports a variety of strategies, including risk management and sector rotation, allowing investors to navigate dynamic market conditions effectively.

Instrument	Underlying Index	Contract Multiplier	Exercise Style	Application
E-mini S&P 500 Technology Futures	S&P 500 Technology Sector Index	$50	N/A	Provides leveraged exposure to the technology sector of the S&P 500.
E-mini S&P 500 Healthcare Futures	S&P 500 Healthcare Sector Index	$50	N/A	Targets exposure to the healthcare sector of the S&P 500.
E-mini S&P 500 Energy Futures	S&P 500 Energy Sector Index	$50	N/A	Provides exposure to the energy sector for hedging or speculative trades.
E-mini S&P 500 Financials Futures	S&P 500 Financials Sector Index	$50	N/A	Focuses on financial sector stocks in the S&P 500 for dynamic allocation.
E-mini S&P 500 Utilities Futures	S&P 500 Utilities Sector Index	$50	N/A	Enables exposure to the defensive utilities sector in the S&P 500.
E-mini S&P 500 Industrials Futures	S&P 500 Industrials Sector Index	$50	N/A	Tracks industrial sector performance for tactical portfolio adjustments.
S&P 500 Technology Index Options	S&P 500 Technology Sector Index	$100	European	Allows hedging or speculation on the technology sector's performance.
S&P 500 Healthcare Index Options	S&P 500 Healthcare Sector Index	$100	European	Provides tools for managing risks in the healthcare sector.
S&P 500 Energy Index Options	S&P 500 Energy Sector Index	$100	European	Targets exposure to the energy sector, particularly for oil and gas stocks.
S&P 500 Financials Index Options	S&P 500 Financials Sector Index	$100	European	Facilitates risk management in the financial services sector.
S&P 500 Utilities Index Options	S&P 500 Utilities Sector Index	$100	European	Enables exposure to the defensive utilities sector.
S&P 500 Industrials Index Options	S&P 500 Industrials Sector Index	$100	European	Tracks industrial sector risk or opportunities for tactical strategies.

Exhibit 2.1 Key features of the S&P 500 E-Mini stock index futures and options

Despite their numerous benefits, sector-specific derivatives come with challenges that portfolio managers must carefully manage. Liquidity can vary significantly between sectors, with popular sectors like technology or financials typically exhibiting high trading volumes, while smaller or less prominent sectors may suffer from lower liquidity. This can result in wider bid-ask spreads, higher transaction costs, and potential difficulties in executing large trades efficiently.

Correlation risks also pose a challenge when using sector-specific derivatives. While these instruments are designed to provide exposure to specific industries, sectors often maintain a degree of correlation with broader market movements. For example, a downturn in the overall market may affect all sectors somewhat, reducing the precision of hedging strategies or diluting the effectiveness of sector-specific bets.

Complexity in analyzing sector-specific drivers adds another layer of difficulty. Unique factors, such as regulatory changes, commodity price fluctuations, or technological advancements, influence each sector. For instance, the healthcare sector may be affected by policy reforms, while the energy sector's performance is closely tied to global oil prices. Understanding these dynamics requires specialized knowledge and careful analysis to ensure that investment strategies align with the specific risks and opportunities of the sector.

Finally, the leverage inherent in sector-specific derivatives magnifies both potential gains and losses, requiring disciplined risk management. Poorly timed or unhedged positions can result in significant financial exposure, particularly in volatile or rapidly changing markets.

Stock Index Futures and Options Based on Investment Factors

Stock index futures and options based on investment factors, such as value and growth, represent a specialized subset of equity derivatives designed to provide exposure to specific investment styles or risk premia. These contracts are linked to indices that track the performance of stocks grouped by characteristics, allowing investors to target factor exposures directly rather than indirectly through broader market indices. They have become increasingly important as factor-based investing has grown in popularity among institutional and retail investors.

Exhibit 2.2 provides a summary of the key features of stock index futures and options based on investment factors.

Instrument	Underlying Index	Contract Multiple	Exercise Style	Application
E-mini S&P 500 Growth Futures	S&P 500 Growth Index	$50	N/A	Provides leveraged exposure to growth stocks in the S&P 500.
E-mini S&P 500 Value Futures	S&P 500 Value Index	$50	N/A	Targets exposure to value stocks in the S&P 500.
Russell 1000 Growth Futures	Russell 1000 Growth Index	$100	N/A	Tracks large-cap growth stocks in the Russell 1000 for hedging or speculation.
Russell 1000 Value Futures	Russell 1000 Value Index	$100	N/A	Provides exposure to large-cap value stocks in the Russell 1000.
E-mini Russell 2000 Growth Futures	Russell 2000 Growth Index	$50	N/A	Targets small-cap growth stocks for tactical allocation or hedging.
E-mini Russell 2000 Value Futures	Russell 2000 Value Index	$50	N/A	Enables exposure to small-cap value stocks for portfolio adjustments.
S&P 500 Growth Index Options	S&P 500 Growth Index	$100	European	Hedging or speculating on the growth segment of the S&P 500.
S&P 500 Value Index Options	S&P 500 Value Index	$100	European	Efficient tools for managing exposure to value stocks in the S&P 500.
Russell 1000 Growth Index Options	Russell 1000 Growth Index	$100	European	Strategic allocation to large-cap growth stocks in the Russell 1000.
Russell 1000 Value Index Options	Russell 1000 Value Index	$100	European	Provides access to the value factor within the Russell 1000.
MSCI USA Growth Index Options	MSCI USA Growth Index	$100	European	Direct exposure to U.S. growth stocks based on MSCI's methodology.
MSCI USA Value Index Options	MSCI USA Value Index	$100	European	Allows investors to manage U.S. value stock exposure using MSCI indices.

Exhibit 2.2 Key features of the stock index futures and options based on investment factors

Value and growth are among the most prominent factors in equity investing. Value indices typically include companies with low price-to-earnings (P/E), price-to-book (P/B), or price-to-sales (P/S) ratios, reflecting the market's perception that these stocks are undervalued relative to their fundamentals. Growth indices, on the other hand, focus on companies with strong earnings or revenue growth potential, often characterized by high P/E ratios and reinvestment of earnings into expansion rather than dividends. Futures and options on these indices allow investors to gain or hedge exposure to these specific investment styles efficiently.

Futures on factor-based indices operate similarly to traditional stock index futures but are tied to value or growth indices, such as the S&P 500 Value Index or S&P 500 Growth Index. These contracts provide leveraged exposure to the performance of the underlying factor indices, with settlement based on the index level at expiration. They are cash-settled and standardized, ensuring ease of trading and minimizing counterparty risk. The notional value of these contracts is determined by the index level multiplied by the contract-specific multiplier, typically $50 for e-mini contracts. Institutional investors widely use these futures to adjust portfolio factor exposures dynamically or implement long-short strategies between value and growth.

Options on factor indices, such as those based on growth or value benchmarks, offer similar functionality but with greater flexibility. By allowing the holder to buy or sell the index at a predetermined strike price, these options facilitate strategies for risk control or potential income enhancement based on relative factor performance. For example, portfolio managers who have a view on value stocks outperforming outperform growth stocks might buy call options on a value index while selling call options on a growth index. These options are typically cash-settled and European-style, aligning with the needs of institutional investors focusing on strategic portfolio adjustments rather than physical delivery of underlying securities.

The appeal of factor-based derivatives lies in their precision and efficiency. Instead of constructing a portfolio of individual stocks to achieve factor exposure, portfolio managers can use a single derivative contract, significantly reducing transaction costs and complexity. Moreover, these instruments are precious for traders seeking to execute pairs trades, such as long value and short growth, where traders seek to capitalize on the relative performance of these factors.

Despite their advantages, factor-based futures and options are not without challenges. Liquidity can be an issue for less popular factor indices, and pricing dynamics may be influenced by changes in market sentiment or macroeconomic conditions that affect factor performance. Additionally, the methodology used to construct factor indices varies across providers, introducing potential discrepancies in performance and risk profiles.

Non-U.S. Stock Index Futures and Options

Non-U.S. stock index futures and options are critical for portfolio managers and traders seeking exposure to international equity markets. These derivatives enable them to control risks, diversify portfolios, or take a view on the performance of foreign stock indices without directly investing in the underlying securities. The global nature of these instruments provides a flexible and cost-effective way to access international markets, whether in Europe, Asia, or emerging economies.

Exhibit 2.3 outlines key non-U.S. stock index futures and options, highlighting the underlying indices, contract multipliers, and exchanges where they are traded. For example, the Euro STOXX 50 Futures, traded on Eurex, is a widely used contract for gaining exposure to blue-chip European stocks. Similarly, the Nikkei 225 Futures, offered by the Osaka Exchange, provides access to Japan's leading publicly traded companies. These instruments are vital in managing regional market exposures and implementing strategies tailored to specific economic regions.

The structure and mechanics of these derivatives are like those of their U.S. counterparts, with standardized contract terms, initial and maintenance margin requirements, and cash-settlement mechanisms for many options. However, differences in regulatory environments, market conventions, and trading hours add unique considerations for investors operating in non-U.S. markets. For instance, the DAX Futures contract on Eurex features a contract multiplier of €25, making it suitable for managing exposures to Germany's leading stock market index.

Non-U.S. stock index futures and options also provide opportunities for hedging and speculation in emerging markets. Instruments like the MSCI Emerging Markets Index Futures, traded on the CME, allow investors to gain exposure to a diversified basket of emerging market equities. Similarly, the FTSE China A50 Index Futures on SGX targets China's largest A-share companies, facilitating precise regional strategies.

Exhibit 2.3 illustrates that these instruments cover a wide range of geographies, including Europe, Asia, Australia, and emerging markets. They are integral to global portfolio management, offering diversification and flexibility while allowing for dynamic adjustments to market views or economic conditions.

Margin Requirements for Equity Derivatives

Margin requirements are critical to trading equity derivatives. They ensure participants meet their financial obligations and mitigate counterparty risk. The requirements vary by the type of derivative, the nature of the position, such as buying or selling options or futures, and whether the trades are standard or customized.

Buyers must pay the total premium upfront for stock options, representing the maximum potential loss. Because the risk is capped, option buyers have no additional margin requirements. In contrast, sellers of stock options face substantial risk, particularly with uncovered positions. To address this, exchanges impose initial margin requirements based on a percentage of the stock's market value plus a portion of the premium received. Sellers must also maintain a lower maintenance margin to cover potential losses. Covered options, where the seller owns the underlying stock or has offsetting positions, reduce margin requirements due to the decreased risk.

Country/Region	Instrument	Underlying Index	Multiplier	Exchange	Application
Europe	Euro STOXX 50 Futures	Euro STOXX 50 Index	€ 10	Eurex	Hedging or gaining exposure to blue-chip European stocks.
	Euro STOXX 50 Index Options	Euro STOXX 50 Index	€ 10	Eurex	Managing risk in the European equity market or capitalizing on volatility.
	FTSE 100 Index Futures	FTSE 100 Index	€ 10	ICE Futures Europe	Exposure to the UK's largest publicly traded companies.
	DAX Futures	DAX Index	€ 25	Eurex	Managing risk or speculating on Germany's leading stock market index.
Asia	Nikkei 225 Futures	Nikkei 225 Index	¥1,000	Osaka Exchange (OSE)	Exposure to Japan's largest publicly traded companies.
	Hang Seng Index Futures	Hang Seng Index	HK$50	Hong Kong Futures Exchange (HKFE)	Managing risk or speculating on Hong Kong's equity market.
	Nifty 50 Index Futures	Nifty 50 Index	₹50	NSE India	Exposure to India's largest companies in a diverse set of industries.
Australia	SPI 200 Futures	S&P/ASX 200 Index	A$25	ASX	Managing risk or gaining exposure to Australia's top 200 publicly traded companies.
Emerging Markets	MSCI Emerging Markets Index Futures	MSCI Emerging Markets Index	$50	CME	Exposure to a diversified basket of emerging market equities.
	FTSE stChina A50 Index Futures	FTSE China A50 Index	$1	SGX (Singapore)	Targeted exposure to China's largest A-share companies.

Exhibit 2.3 Non-U.S. stock indexes

Stock index options have similar margin structures but are tailored to the broader exposures of these instruments. As with stock options, buyers of index options pay the premium upfront with no further margin requirements. Sellers, however, are subject to initial and maintenance margin rules that consider the notional value of the underlying index, adjusted for factors like delta and market volatility. Index options' risk and margin requirements are typically higher than those for stock options, reflecting the broader market exposure and higher notional values involved.

Equity futures require both an initial margin and a maintenance margin. The initial margin is a percentage of the contract's notional value, which varies by the exchange but typically ranges from 5 to 15%. For instance, an E-mini S&P 500 futures contract with a notional value of $200,000 might require an initial margin of $10,000. The maintenance margin is slightly lower and ensures that positions are adequately funded as market conditions fluctuate. Futures are marked to the market daily, with gains or losses settled at the end of each trading session, necessitating active monitoring of margin balances to avoid position liquidation.

Managing margin requirements effectively ensures financial stability and avoids adverse outcomes. Sufficient cash reserves or liquid collateral must be maintained to meet margin calls, especially during volatile market conditions. Large price swings can lead to sudden increases in margin requirements, placing traders at risk of forced liquidation if they cannot fulfill the additional demands. Forced liquidations often result in positions being closed at unfavorable prices, exacerbating financial losses.

Monitoring volatility is another essential component of managing margins. Exchanges frequently adjust margin requirements in response to market turbulence, which can catch traders off guard if they are unprepared. Adherence to regulatory standards is also critical to maintaining compliance and avoiding penalties or restrictions. Traders must carefully plan their strategies to anticipate margin needs, using offsetting positions or dynamic portfolio adjustments to optimize their capital efficiency.

Effective collateral management is equally important, as high-quality assets such as cash or government securities are commonly used to meet margin requirements. Ensuring that these assets remain liquid and readily available minimizes the risk of sudden shortfalls. Strategic planning, combined with a proactive approach to monitoring market conditions, helps traders and portfolio managers navigate the complexities of margin management, reduce risks, and enhance the utility of equity derivatives in achieving their financial objectives.

Margin requirements are a technical necessity and a cornerstone of risk management in equity derivatives trading. By understanding their nuances and actively managing them, market participants can safeguard their positions, maintain financial stability, and optimize their use of derivative instruments.

The collapse of Archegos, a family office managing billions of dollars, is a stark reminder of the dangers of excessive leverage and poor risk management. Archegos used highly leveraged total return swaps to gain exposure to individual stocks, amplifying its positions through borrowed money.

When the value of some underlying stocks dropped, Archegos faced margin calls from multiple banks. Unable to provide additional collateral, the firm defaulted, triggering a fire sale of its assets. Major institutions like Credit Suisse and Nomura incurred massive losses, with billions wiped out in the aftermath. This case underscores the importance of maintaining sufficient liquidity buffers, monitoring leverage levels, and adhering to sound margin management practices to mitigate financial risks in derivatives trading.

Best Practices for Managing Liquidity

There are best practices for managing these liquidity requirements. Holding a sufficient liquidity buffer is one of the most effective ways to prepare for unexpected margin calls. This involves setting aside a portion of capital in highly liquid assets such as cash, U.S. Treasury bills, or money market instruments. The buffer size should be based on historical margin call requirements, expected market volatility, and the size of open positions. Maintaining a buffer ensures that liquidity is readily available without selling long-term or illiquid investments.

Monitoring trading positions and market conditions is essential to anticipate potential margin calls. By keeping track of factors, such as leverage levels, price movements, and market volatility, traders can estimate when margin requirements might increase. Tools like real-time margin calculators, scenario analysis, and stress testing can help assess the impact of adverse market moves on liquidity requirements.

Diversifying the types of collateral used for margin requirements can enhance flexibility. In addition to cash, many brokers and clearinghouses accept high-quality securities, such as government bonds, as collateral. Diversification reduces the need to liquidate specific assets under stress and ensures access to multiple sources of liquidity.

Some brokers allow margin offsets when positions are hedged or partially netted. For instance, holding long and short positions in related instruments may reduce the overall margin requirement. Structuring portfolios to take advantage of these offsets minimizes the capital in margin accounts, freeing liquidity for other purposes.

Leverage, the key characteristic of derivatives, amplifies the potential for profits and increases the risk of large-margin calls during adverse market movements. Maintaining prudent leverage levels is a best practice to ensure that liquidity needs remain manageable.

Establishing credit lines or access to liquidity facilities before they are needed can provide an additional safety net for margin calls. Banks or prime brokers often offer secured credit facilities against high-quality collateral. These arrangements ensure funds can be drawn quickly during market stress without selling assets at unfavorable prices.

Automated systems monitoring margin balances and requirements can help traders respond quickly to changes. Many trading platforms offer alerts when margin balances fall below a predefined threshold, enabling proactive account funding before a margin call is issued. Automation reduces the likelihood of missing critical warnings during volatile market conditions.

Regular stress tests and scenario analyses allow traders to evaluate extreme market movements' impact on margin requirements and liquidity needs. For example, simulating a 10% drop in the underlying asset price can help determine whether liquidity reserves are sufficient. Incorporating these tests into risk management processes ensures preparedness for unforeseen events.

Margin requirements should be considered within broader portfolios and enterprise risk management. Setting firm-wide liquidity thresholds, aligning trading strategies with risk appetite, and integrating margin requirements into daily operations provide a comprehensive approach to mitigating liquidity risks.

Finally, regularly communicating with brokers or clearinghouses can help traders stay informed about changes in margin requirements, especially during periods of heightened volatility. Understanding the timing, calculation methods, and settlement processes for margin calls can prevent surprises and allow smoother liquidity management.

Rolling Strategies with Equity Derivatives

Rolling is a critical operational strategy in equity derivatives and derivatives generally that ensures continuous exposure to the underlying asset or strategy. Because derivatives contracts have fixed expiration dates, portfolio managers and traders must either close their positions or transition them to new contracts with later expirations to maintain uninterrupted market participation. This process, known as rolling, plays a vital role in managing derivative-based strategies effectively while addressing risks associated with liquidity, transaction costs, and market conditions.

The Mechanics of Rolling

Rolling involves two steps: closing an existing position in a contract nearing expiration and simultaneously opening a new position in a later-dated contract. For instance, a portfolio manager with an S&P 500 futures contract expiring in June would sell that contract and purchase a September contract to extend exposure seamlessly. Similarly, a portfolio manager employing a call option strategy would sell the expiring call option and buy another with the same strike price but a later expiration.

This process ensures that investors maintain their desired exposure to the underlying asset or strategy without interruption. Rolling is particularly important for institutional investors managing long-term strategies, such as equity market hedging or systematic risk management, where gaps in exposure could significantly impact performance.

The Importance of Rolling

Equity derivatives strategies often rely on the continuous application of contracts to achieve their objectives. For instance, a portfolio manager using index futures to hedge equity market risk must roll these contracts regularly to preserve the hedge. Without rolling, the contract's expiration could expose the portfolio to market fluctuations, undermining the intended strategy.

Rolling also addresses liquidity concerns. As derivative contracts approach expiration, trading activity shifts to later-dated agreements, reducing the liquidity of the expiring contracts. By rolling positions, investors ensure they participate in the most liquid contracts, minimizing the impact of transaction costs and maintaining market efficiency.

Challenges of Rolling: Roll Yield and Basis Risk

Rolling derivatives contracts introduce several challenges that can significantly impact portfolio performance. Two key challenges are roll yield and basis risk, which arise when transitioning from an expiring contract to a new one. These issues are particularly critical as they can affect a portfolio's overall cost, return, and risk profile. Here, we explain these two challenges in detail, starting with roll yield.

Roll Yield

Roll yield is the return generated or lost when transitioning a position from a near-expiring derivative contract to a later-dated one. This occurs because of price differences between contracts with varying expiration dates, influenced by the forward curve's shape (contango or backwardation). Roll yield is particularly relevant in equity derivatives, such as futures, where maintaining a continuous position requires rolling contracts forward.

For instance, consider a portfolio manager holding a long position in an equity index futures contract, such as an E-mini S&P 500 futures contract set to expire in March. To maintain exposure to the S&P 500 index, the investor must close the March contract before its expiration and open a new position in the June contract. If the price of the March contract is 4,000 and the June contract is 4,020, the portfolio manager incurs a cost of 20 points during the roll. Since the contract multiplier is $50 per point, this results in a $1,000 cost per contract. This situation illustrates a negative roll yield because the later-dated contract is more expensive than the expiring one.

The concept of roll yield depends significantly on the structure of the futures market. When the market is in contango, the prices of later-dated contracts are higher than those of near-term contracts. As shown in the example above, this scenario often leads to negative roll yield and is typical in stable or bullish equity markets. Conversely, later-dated contracts are priced lower than near-term contracts in backwardation, resulting in a positive roll yield. While less common in equity derivatives, backwardation can occur in bearish markets or under specific conditions, such as anticipated dividend adjustments.

Roll yield is critical for strategies requiring continuous exposure to an underlying asset. A negative roll yield introduces an ongoing cost, reducing overall returns. Conversely, a positive roll yield can enhance performance, contributing to profits. This factor is particularly significant for institutional investors, such as exchange-traded funds and mutual funds that use equity index futures to replicate benchmark performance. Roll yield management becomes essential to minimize tracking errors and optimize costs.

Understanding roll yield and its implications enables portfolio managers and traders to adapt their strategies to market conditions effectively. It ensures that costs or returns from rolling contracts align with broader investment goals, mitigating the potential erosion of performance over time. This is a crucial component of managing derivative portfolios.

Basis Risk

Basis risk presents a significant challenge in rolling strategies for equity derivatives, as it arises from discrepancies between the pricing of expiring and newly initiated contracts. These pricing differences occur naturally due to the structure of derivatives markets and the influence of various external factors, making it difficult to perfectly align the exposure of rolled positions with the original strategy. When basis risk is present, the effectiveness of a derivative strategy can be compromised, leading to unintended consequences that may affect performance.

Rolling an equity derivative position involves closing an expiring contract and simultaneously entering a new contract with a later expiration date. However, the prices of these contracts are often not identical because they are influenced by factors such as interest rates, expected dividends, and market volatility. For instance, in futures markets, the price of an expiring contract typically converges to the spot price of the underlying asset. In contrast, the price of the new contract reflects market expectations for future conditions. This divergence creates a "basis," which introduces risk as the rolled position may no longer provide the exact exposure intended by the original strategy.

Several market dynamics influence basis risk. Market expectations, such as anticipated changes in interest rates or dividends, often shift between the periods represented by the expiring and new contracts, leading to pricing discrepancies. Volatility is another critical factor, as it can amplify differences between contract prices, particularly during market uncertainty or heightened economic risk. Additionally, liquidity plays a significant role; the expiring contract may experience declining trading activity as its expiration approaches, while the newly introduced contract may have wider bid-ask spreads, further contributing to basis risk. Structural market events, such as regulatory changes or macroeconomic developments, can also impact the relationship between expiring and new contracts, complicating the rolling process.

The implications of basis risk for rolling strategies are far-reaching. One primary concern is the potential for mismatched exposures. A discrepancy between the intended and actual exposures of the rolled position can undermine the effectiveness of hedging or speculative strategies. For example, a portfolio manager rolling S&P 500 futures contracts to hedge against market risk might find that the new position offers less precise coverage due to basis risk. In addition to mismatched exposures, basis risk can increase transaction costs. Pricing differences between contracts, particularly in periods of low liquidity or high volatility, can result in higher costs, reducing the overall profitability of the strategy. Basis risk can also introduce tracking errors for portfolios replicating an index using derivatives. For instance, an ETF using futures to track the S&P 500 may experience performance deviations if the basis risk during the roll period is significant. Moreover, unexpected basis risk can lead to short-term performance volatility, disrupting investment objectives and potentially increasing the portfolio's risk profile.

Effectively managing basis risk requires a proactive approach to planning and execution. Timing the roll is critical, as poor timing can exacerbate pricing discrepancies and increase costs. Rolling during periods of high liquidity, such as near official roll dates designated by exchanges, can help reduce the impact of basis risk. Monitoring market conditions, including volatility levels and shifts in interest rates or dividend expectations, provides valuable insights that can guide the timing and execution of rolling strategies. Diversifying the execution of rolls over multiple trading days is another effective approach. By spreading the process across several sessions, traders can reduce the risk of executing the entire roll under unfavorable market conditions.

Analytical tools and data-driven approaches also play an essential role in managing basis risk. Historical data and real-time market information can be used to model and predict basis risk, allowing for more informed decision-making during the rolling process. Additionally, selecting contracts with deep liquidity and tighter spreads minimizes potential adverse price movements during execution. When integrated into a comprehensive rolling strategy, these practices can significantly mitigate the challenges basis risk poses.

Basis risk is an inherent challenge in rolling equity derivative positions, driven by the natural discrepancies between expiring and new contracts. These discrepancies can undermine strategy effectiveness, increase costs, and introduce tracking errors. However, with careful planning, market analysis, and advanced tools, traders and portfolio managers can navigate basis risk effectively, preserving the integrity of their derivative strategies. Addressing this challenge is essential for maintaining consistent and reliable outcomes in rolling equity derivative positions.

Applications of Rolling Strategies

Rolling is integral to implementing and maintaining various equity derivative strategies. In hedging strategies, such as using index futures to offset market risks, rolling ensures the hedge remains active as contracts expire. Similarly, rolling supports long-term speculative positions, such as betting on directional market movements using options or futures.

Dynamic portfolio management often involves rolling strategies to adjust exposures or rebalance positions. For instance, an investor implementing a volatility-based strategy may roll options contracts to maintain consistent exposure to market volatility while avoiding the risks of holding expiring contracts.

Strategic Considerations in Rolling

Investors must consider several factors to optimize rolling strategies, including market conditions, transaction costs, and timing. Choosing the optimal timing for rolling positions can minimize costs and reduce exposure to adverse price movements. Additionally, managing roll yields effectively can enhance the strategy's cost efficiency, ensuring it aligns with broader investment objectives.

Rolling strategies are a cornerstone of equity derivatives management, enabling investors to maintain consistent exposure, manage risks, and adapt to changing market conditions. While the process introduces specific challenges, careful planning and execution can ensure that rolling strategies remain effective and aligned with the derivative strategy's goals. The seamless transition of contracts through rolling underscores the versatility and importance of equity derivatives in modern financial markets.

Summary

This chapter describes the structure and mechanics of exchange-traded equity derivatives: stock options, stock index options, stock futures, and stock index futures. It highlights how these instruments enable portfolio managers to manage risk, implement risk-control strategies, and achieve portfolio diversification. A detailed discussion on margin requirements underscores the importance of maintaining adequate collateral to mitigate counterparty risk and avoid forced liquidations. The chapter also emphasizes the pricing efficiency of exchange-traded equity derivatives markets, particularly stock options and stock index options, where market forces and technological advancements have minimized inefficiencies, reducing the need for manual pricing models in education and practice.

The chapter further examines operational challenges associated with derivatives usage, such as managing roll yield and basis risk when rolling over contracts. These challenges, alongside practical considerations like market volatility and liquidity, are critical for practitioners aiming to optimize returns and manage portfolio exposures effectively.

3

Bond-Related Derivatives

Frank J. Fabozzi, Marielle de Jong, and Mounia Khamlich Fischer

Bond-related derivatives come in many formats, ranging from futures, forwards, swaps to options. They allow portfolio managers to adjust interest rate exposure, protect against unexpected credit events, and enhance portfolio performance. Derivatives contracts can be tailored to help achieve specific financial goals, for example, managing exposure to short-term interest rate movements with futures contracts or offsetting credit risks through credit default swaps. The versatility of bond derivatives allows them to be used as both risk management tools and as speculative instruments to capitalize on anticipated market trends.

In this chapter, we describe the primary categories of bond-related derivatives in the following order: interest rate futures, interest rate forwards, swaps, in particular interest rate, inflation- and credit default swaps, and options. As to the latter category, we cover options on bonds, futures, and swaps. Each section delves into these instruments' unique characteristics, mechanics, and applications within bond portfolio management. By understanding these tools investors gain insights into constructing and managing a bond portfolio

F. J. Fabozzi
Johns Hopkins University's Carey School of Business, Baltimore, MD, USA

M. de Jong (✉)
Grenoble Ecole de Management, Paris, France
e-mail: marielle.de-jong@grenoble-em.com

M. Khamlich Fischer
Assurances du Crédit Mutuel, Paris, France

F. J. Fabozzi and M. de Jong (eds.), *Derivatives Applications in Asset Management*,
https://doi.org/10.1007/978-3-031-86354-7_3

that balances risk, return, and flexibility in a constantly evolving financial landscape.

This chapter outlines the core structural components of bond-related derivatives, emphasizing their basic framework rather than their practical application, contract variations (such as puts, calls, and day-count conventions), or the risks and strategic considerations involved in their use. Other chapters cover these latter aspects in detail, so they are intentionally not addressed here.

Interest-Rate Futures

Interest rate futures are standardized contracts traded on regulated exchanges. They are vital instruments in managing bond portfolios' sensitivity to interest rate fluctuations. Portfolio managers frequently use interest rate futures to adjust portfolio duration, hedge against rate movements, and, in some cases, enhance yield. These contracts offer flexibility, liquidity, and implementation efficiency, making them a preferred choice for institutional investors.

Interest rate futures contracts based on securities with a maturity greater than one year are typically called "bond futures" or "interest rate bond futures." These contracts differ from short-term interest rate futures in that their underlying instruments are medium- to long-term debt securities, such as U.S. Treasury notes and bonds.

Short-interest rate futures are tied to short-term benchmarks like the Secured Overnight Financing Rate (SOFR), the Federal Funds rate, or Euribor. They focus on interest rate movements over short time horizons up to one year. In contrast, bond futures encompass a wider range of maturities, starting from two years (e.g., 2-year U.S. Treasury note futures) and extending up to 30 years or beyond (including 30-year Treasury bond futures and ultra-long Treasury bond futures).

This classification helps distinguish futures linked to short-term interest rates from those based on securities with longer maturities. It provides market participants with transparency to align their strategies with specific segments of the yield curve, addressing different durations and interest rate exposures.

Short Interest Rate Futures

Various futures contracts are available within this subcategory, enabling practitioners to take positions regarding rates representing the lending rates between banks, either with collateral (e.g., SOFR, Euribor) or without collateral (e.g., federal fund rate, €STR). These listed contracts are available on various maturities, albeit trading volumes are sufficient and prices meaningful only for the shortest maturities.

Euribor Futures

The buyer of a Euribor future enters into a forward transaction by buying a theoretical bond that yields the Euribor rate. Euribor Futures are listed products, the precise characteristics of which are defined by the exchange platform, the Eurex. These characteristics include the contract value per index point, which stands at €2,500, and the maturity.

Exhibit 3.1 details a 3-month Euribor futures contract bought on November 29, 2024, and maturing on December 15, 2025. On the purchase day, it had an effective annual yield of 1.8%, as reflected by the quotation price; that is, a price of 98.2 translates into a yield of 100–98.2 = 1.8. The value of one contract is €245,000€ in the example (= €2,500 × 98.2).

The buyer's profit and loss (P&L) at maturity will depend on the spot rate at maturity, registering a loss if yields are lower than 1.8% and a gain if higher. In case the price will be 97.0 on December 15, 2025, meaning a yield of 3%, the loss will be €3,000 (= €2,500 × (97.0–98.2)), whereas with a price at 99.0 the gain will be €2,000 (=€2,500 × (99.0–98.2)). The loss or gain will be settled in cash, as Euribor futures are always cash settled.

Underlying	3M Euribor	
Future maturity date	December 2025	
Value of 1 point	€2,500	
Price	98.2	[effective yield at 100% − 98.2% = 1.8%]
Value of 1 contract	€245,500	[= €2,500 × 98.2]
Scenario 1		
Price on 12/15/25	97.0	[effective yield at 3%]
Cash settlement	-€3,000	[= €2,500 × (97.0 − 98.2)]
Scenario 2		
Price on 12/15/25	99.0	[effective yield at 1%]
Cash settlement	€2,000	[= €2,500 × (99.0 − 98.2)]

Exhibit 3.1 Three-Month (3 M) Euribor future in different scenarios

SOFR Futures

Following the shift away from LIBOR in 2023, SOFR (Secured Overnight Financing Rate) futures have emerged as the preferred benchmark for short-term interest rates in the US. These futures track the daily interest rates for overnight repurchase agreements, providing a lower-risk alternative to the preceding Eurodollar futures. Bond managers are increasingly using SOFR futures to hedge US short-term rate exposures, which are gaining traction as the market adapts to the transition away from LIBOR.

SOFR futures work similarly to Euribor futures, having two underlying indexes available, the one-month and the three-month. The specific parameters of the two contract types differ: the value of 1 point is $4,167 for the former and $2,500 for the latter. Users should be particularly cautious about contract sizes to avoid hedging mistakes.

For example, a fund manager, who must pay 30-day interests on a notional of $10,000,000 in March 2025 at the 1-month SOFR rate, wants to hedge against a rate hike concerning the prevailing level at 4.55% as of December 2024. In case of a 1% hike, the payment will become 5.55% × 30/360 × $10,000,000 = $46,250, which is $8,333 more than the status quo. To avoid the extra burden, the manager can sell two 1-month SOFR futures contracts (= 8333/4167 ≈ 2).

Euro-STR Futures

As of 2022, the Euro Short-Term Rate (€STR) futures, based on the overnight lending rate between banks in the Eurozone, have replaced the EONIA futures, which stood for Euro Overnight Index Average. They are traded on the Eurex and on the Intercontinental Exchange® (ICE). These futures are widely used in the Eurozone for managing short-term interest rate risk and are crucial for hedging against movements in euro-denominated interest rates.

Federal Fund Futures

The 30-day federal fund futures are quoted on the Chicago Board of Trade (CBOT). The underlying rate is the arithmetic average of the daily effective Federal Fund rates over a month. Fed fund rate targets are set by the Federal Open Market Committee (FOMC), meaning that the Federal Funds Futures fluctuations can be directly influenced by the U.S. Federal Reserve's monetary policy.

Canadian CORRA Futures

The Canadian Overnight Repo Rate Average (CORRA) is the rate of overnight repo transitions in Canada. In 2023, CORRA futures replaced the BAX futures, which were based on the three-month Canadian Bankers' Acceptance rate, reflecting the short-term lending rates among Canadian banks. These futures offer a hedge for short-term Canadian interest rate risk.

Bond Futures

Long Treasury bond futures are based on long-term Treasury bonds, typically with maturities from two years up to 30 years. These contracts are widely used to manage the duration of portfolios focused on long-term bonds.

US Treasury Note Futures

U.S. Treasury Note futures contracts are standardized and actively traded on exchanges such as the Chicago Mercantile Exchange (CME), making them highly liquid and widely used by market participants. These contracts are categorized by the maturity of the underlying Treasury security and play a critical role in managing interest rate risk across various time horizons. They are the 2-year Treasury note futures, which are based on 2-year U.S. Treasury notes, the 5-year Treasury note futures, the 10-year Treasury note futures, and the 30-year Treasury bond futures. Together, these Treasury futures provide a flexible suite of instruments for managing interest rate risk along the yield curve, catering to various hedging and speculative strategies. Each contract type serves a distinct purpose, allowing market participants to tailor their risk management approach to specific maturity segments and economic outlooks.

Exhibit 3.2 gives an example of a 10-year U.S. Treasury Note Future. The underlying is a hypothetical 10-year Treasury bond with a 6% coupon paid semi-annually. A notable feature of these futures is their quotation system, whereby prices are quoted as a percentage of the face value in increments of 1/32 of 1%. For instance, a quote price of 111–07 + translates into 111 plus 7.5/32 (or 111.23438% of the face value), meaning the contract represents a transaction at $111,234.38 for a $100,000 par value bond. The yield-to-maturity, or simply the yield, corresponding to a price of $111,234.38, is the

Underlying	10Y US 6%	
Future maturity date	March 2025	
Contract Size	$100,000	
Value of 1 point	$1,000	
Price	111-07+	[=111 + 7.5/32=111.2438] [effective yield at 4.587%]
Value of 1 contract	$111,234.38	[111.2438 × $1,000]
Spot rate on 12/01/24	4.22%	[corresponding price 114.36]
Scenario 1		
Spot rate on 12/15/25	3%	[corresponding price 125]
Cash settlement	$13,766	[= $1,000 × (125 - (111+7.5/32))]
Scenario 2		
Spot rate on 12/15/25	5%	[corresponding price 107.7]
Cash settlement	-$3,514	[= $1,000 × (107.7 - (111+7.5/32))]

Exhibit 3.2 Ten-Year U.S. (10Y US) treasury note future in different scenarios

(discount) rate that sets the sum of discounted cash flows equal to this price. The reader can verify that this rate is 4.587%, see Exhibit 3.2.

In Treasury futures contracts and bond futures generally, the short position, or the party obligated to deliver, is granted significant flexibility in how and when they fulfill their delivery obligation. These options (choices) are designed to allow the seller to minimize their costs and optimize the delivery strategy, which can impact the futures contract's pricing and valuation. The delivery options include the ability to choose the specific bond from a list of eligible securities (the "cheapest-to-deliver" or CTD option), the timing within the delivery month, and the "wild card" option, which permits delivery after the daily settlement price has been determined.

These options give the short position leverage to select the bond and timing that best aligns with market conditions and their cost structure. For the long position, however, this flexibility introduces uncertainty about the exact security and timing of delivery, adding complexity to hedging and valuation strategies. The delivery options available to the short are crucial to understanding the dynamics of Treasury futures, as they directly influence contract pricing and provide strategic opportunities in Treasury futures trading.

Most portfolio managers close out their futures positions before maturity to avoid taking delivery of the underlying bonds. Hedging positions are often "rolled" a few days before the maturity date to maintain exposure without triggering delivery obligations. For specialists seeking to optimize their hedging strategies, a thorough understanding of the delivery mechanisms can provide valuable insights and opportunities to seize.

Cheapest-to-Deliver Option: This is one of the most strategic delivery options granted to the short position (the seller) in a Treasury futures contract. It allows the seller to select from a list of eligible Treasury bonds or notes specified by the exchange and choose the security that minimizes their cost of fulfilling the delivery obligation. The CTD option is valuable because Treasury securities differ in terms of coupon rates, maturities, and market prices, which can affect the relative cost for the seller.

To determine the CTD for a given Treasury futures contract, the seller assesses each eligible bond to determine the "cheapest" one to deliver. The determination is based on calculating the implied repo rate for each bond, which reflects the return the seller could theoretically earn by buying the bond in the market, holding it, and then delivering it at the futures settlement price. The bond with the highest implied repo rate—indicating the highest relative profitability or the lowest cost—is selected as the CTD.

Each eligible bond has an associated conversion factor, which standardizes the invoice price of the futures contract to reflect differences in coupon rates and maturities. The exchange assigns these factors to align the bond prices with the notional price of a standardized 6% coupon bond. This means the settlement price of the futures contract is adjusted by the conversion factor of the chosen bond, thereby affecting the final delivery price. The invoice price for the CTD bond is calculated as follows:

$$\begin{aligned}\text{Invoice Price} &= \text{Contract Size} \times \text{Futures Settlement Price}\\ &\quad \times \text{Conversion Factor} + \text{Accrued Interest}\end{aligned}$$

Market conditions, such as shifts in interest rates, can influence which bond becomes the CTD over the life of the futures contract. As interest rates change, the relative cost and attractiveness of delivering different bonds also shift, meaning that the CTD bond can vary until the delivery date. The seller monitors these changes to ensure they optimize delivery based on the latest market conditions.

The CTD option affects future prices, as the contract price tends to align more closely with the price of the CTD bond than any other deliverable bond. This also introduces complexity for the long position (the buyer), as the identity of the CTD bond—and, consequently, the precise value of the futures position—can fluctuate. As a result, hedging and valuation require close monitoring of the CTD dynamics to maintain effectiveness.

Timing Option: This option grants the short position (the seller) the flexibility to determine the precise timing of delivery within the designated delivery month. This flexibility allows the seller to choose any day within the month to deliver the underlying bond, optimizing for advantageous market conditions and potentially reducing costs. This timing option is beneficial because it enables the short position to observe interest rate movements throughout the month and strategically decide when to fulfill their obligation. If interest rates fluctuate, the short can select a delivery date that maximizes their financial advantage or minimizes any potential loss.

For example, if interest rates decline during the delivery month, the seller may delay delivery to benefit from any favorable changes in bond values. Conversely, if rates increase, the short may opt to deliver earlier to avoid the cost implications of further rate increases. This timing flexibility is an essential part of the broader delivery options package, which also includes the quality and wildcard options, adding layers of strategic consideration for the short position and introducing uncertainty for the long position regarding the exact timing and nature of the delivery.

Wild Card Option: This option allows the seller to wait until after the futures market has closed for the day to decide whether to deliver the Treasury bond at that day's settlement price, even if the after-hours cash market prices have shifted. Here is how it works.

Treasury futures have a daily settlement price determined when the futures market closes, typically at 3:00 PM CT. However, the cash market for Treasury securities continues to trade after this official settlement time, and bond prices may fluctuate during these after-hours trades. The wild card option allows the short to observe these after-hours price movements and decide whether to initiate delivery that day at the official settlement price.

Suppose the cash price of the deliverable bond falls below the day's futures settlement price after hours. In that case, the seller can opt to deliver, effectively locking in a higher price than the current cash market value. Conversely, if the cash market price rises, the seller may wait, retaining the option to deliver on a later day within the delivery month. This flexibility is particularly valuable in volatile markets, where after-hours price movements can create profitable opportunities for the short.

For the buyer (long position), the wild card option introduces uncertainty, as they cannot be sure which day the delivery will occur or the exact market conditions. This variability makes hedging and valuation more complex for the long position, as they need to account for the possibility that the short will exercise the wild card option when it is most favorable to them.

Non-U.S. Bond Futures

Euro-Bund, Euro-Bobl, and Euro-Schatz Futures: The most-traded bond futures in the Eurozone are those defined on the German government debt, which is regarded the safest credit-risk freest debt in the region. Three contracts, traded on the Eurex, are the most popular: the Bund futures, based on long-term German bonds with maturities of 8.5 to 10.5 years, the Bobl futures, based on medium-term German bonds with maturities of 4.5 to 5.5 years, and the Schatz futures based on short-term German bonds with maturities of 1.75 to 2.25 years. A fourth type, the Buxl futures, is becoming increasingly popular, covering long-term German bonds up to 30 years. These futures are essential for European portfolio managers to manage interest rate risk along the yield curve and are highly liquid.

Exhibit 3.3 gives an example of a 10-year Bund future. The future's underlying is a theoretical 10-year German government bond paying a 6% coupon annually. The futures prices are defined on this bond. At maturity, the seller will deliver a real bond with characteristics close to this theoretical bond. Each futures contract is valued according to the specifications set by the Eurex. The Bund future size is 100 000€, so the value of one index point is 1 000€.

The value of one contract is equal to the quote price times the contract size, which is thus in the example 136.3% × €100,000 = €136,300. If the quote price shifts to 137.3, the value of the contract shifts to €137,300 (i.e., €1,000€ × 137.3). Exhibit 3.3 illustrates two scenarios where the evolution of the yield and associated futures prices enable the holder to register a gain or a loss respectively on the future contract.

Gilt Futures: Traded on the London International Financial Futures and Options Exchange (LIFFE), gilt futures are based on U.K. government bonds, commonly referred to as gilts. The contracts allow hedging against fluctuations in British interest rates and include both long and short gilt

Underlying	Bund 10y 6%	
Future maturity	March 2025	
Contract Size	€100,000	
Value of 1 point	€1,000	
Price	136.3	[effective yield 1.96%]
Value of 1 contract	€136,300	
Settlement	Physical	
Spot rate on purchase day 11/29/24	2,10%	[corresponding price 134.85]
Scenario 1		
Spot rate on 12/15/25	125.6	[effective yield 3%]
Loss	-€10,700	[= €1,000 x (125.6 - 136.3)]
Scenario 2		
Spot rate on 12/15/25	147.4	[effective yield 1%]
Gain	€11,050	[= €1,000 x (147.4 - 136.3)]

Exhibit 3.3 Ten-Year Bund future in different scenarios

contracts, covering different maturity ranges (10 years and 2 years), though liquidity can be low on the short end.

Japanese Government Bond (JGB) Futures: Traded on the Tokyo Stock Exchange (TSE), JGB futures are based on Japanese government bonds with maturities of 10 or 20 years. Mini JGB Futures, available on the Singapore Exchange (SGX), offer smaller contract sizes—one-tenth the size of standard JGB Futures—providing greater flexibility for portfolio managers and traders. However, these smaller contracts typically have lower liquidity compared to their standard counterparts.

Australian Government Bond Futures: The Australian Securities Exchange (ASX) offers bond futures based on Australian government bonds, particularly the 3-year and 10-year bond futures. These contracts allow investors to hedge against movements in Australian interest rates and are important for managing rate exposure in Australian dollars.

Italian Government Bond (BTP) Futures: BTP futures are based on Italian government bonds, with maturities of around 3 and 10 years. They provide a way to hedge against interest rate movements specific to Italian debt, which can be more volatile than core Eurozone countries due to varying credit conditions.

French Euro OAT Futures: French Euro OAT Futures are derivatives contracts based on French government bonds, known as **Obligations Assimilables du Trésor (OATs).** OATs are medium- to long-term debt instruments issued by the French Treasury, typically with maturities ranging from five to fifty years. These bonds are widely used as a benchmark for euro-denominated sovereign debt. French Euro OAT Futures are primarily traded on platforms such as Eurex, and they are designed to provide investors and portfolio managers with a tool to hedge or speculate on interest rate movements in the Eurozone, specifically relating to French government debt.

Forward Rate Agreements

A forward rate agreement (FRA) is an over-the-counter (OTC) contract where two parties agree on an interest rate to be paid on a notional principal amount at a future date. FRAs are often used to lock in rates on short-term borrowing or lending positions. For example, a portfolio manager anticipating rate increases might use an FRA to secure today's rate for funds needed in the future, thus hedging against potential rate hikes. Using FRA instead of futures enables fund managers to tailor their hedging more precisely, taking into account the effective cash flows of their portfolio. Yet, these products are less liquid than futures (closing a position before maturity may have a cost), and bilateral contracts are to be placed with the counterparty before initiating any trade. As the value fluctuation of the products may entail a credit risk on the counterparty, it is generally covered with bilateral frequent margin calls.

The mechanics of an FRA involve a customized OTC between two parties to secure an interest rate on a notional principal amount for a specified future period. While the notional amount itself is never exchanged, the cash settlement of the FRA is based on the difference between the agreed-upon forward rate and the actual market interest rate, known as the reference rate, at the start of the agreed future period.

The process begins with two parties agreeing on the terms of the FRA. These terms include the notional principal amount, the start and end dates of the contract period, the fixed forward interest rate, and the reference rate that will determine the actual market interest rate. For instance, the contract might specify a notional amount of $20 million with a forward rate of 5% per annum for a future period beginning three months from now and lasting for three months.

At the start of the contract period, the reference rate is observed and compared to the forward rate agreed upon in the FRA. If the reference rate is higher than the forward rate, the seller of the FRA compensates the buyer, as the buyer has effectively locked in a lower borrowing rate. Conversely, if the reference rate is lower than the forward rate, the buyer compensates the seller, as the seller benefits from locking in a higher lending rate. The settlement amount is discounted to its present value at the time of settlement, reflecting the difference in interest rates over the contract period.

FRAs are commonly described using a shorthand notation, such as "3 × 6," which provides a concise way to specify the timing of the contract period. The first number, "3," represents the time in months from the current date to the start of the contract period, while the second number, "6," represents the time in months from the current date to the end of the contract period. In this example, the FRA covers a three-month period beginning three months from today and ending six months from today. This notation is widely used in financial markets for its simplicity and clarity, allowing market participants to identify the timing of the agreement without extensive explanation quickly. For instance, a "1 × 4" FRA would denote a contract that begins one-month from now and lasts for three months, ending four months from today. Similarly, a "6 × 12" FRA indicates a contract starting in six months and lasting for six months, ending one year from the current date.

Swaps

Swaps are financial derivatives that involve an agreement between two parties to exchange cash flows or financial obligations based on a predetermined set of terms. Portfolio managers widely use these instruments to manage risks. Swaps are highly versatile and can be tailored to address a variety of financial exposures, making them a cornerstone of modern financial risk management.

There are several types of swaps commonly used in financial markets. **Interest rate swaps** allow parties to exchange fixed and floating interest rate payments, enabling them to manage interest rate exposure. **Inflation swaps** provide a mechanism to hedge against changes in inflation by exchanging fixed (nominal) payments for inflation-linked payments. **Credit default swaps** transfer the credit risk of a reference entity between two parties, offering a tool to protect against or speculate on default risk. Other widely used swaps include **currency swaps**, which involve the exchange of principal and interest payments in different currencies, and **equity swaps**, which allow parties to exchange returns on equity instruments for fixed or floating payments.

There are non-standardized swap instruments and, since 2009, standardized instruments. For the former the swap rate is the (market) rate that equates the net present value of the fixed cash flows to that of the floating cash flows at the inception of the swap contract. This rate is influenced by a multiple of factors under which the current interest rates, the expectations of future rate changes, and the credit quality of the parties involved. The swap rate essentially represents the equilibrium point, where neither party has a financial advantage based on projected rates. At inception, the swap is thus liable to trade at par (around zero net value), however, during the swap's life its value may divert from zero considerably as market conditions evolve. In case the swap trades, the difference is settled via an upfront payment.

In the aftermath of the global financial crisis standardized instruments appeared, notably for swapping credit default risk, with predefined swap rates. For those instruments there is always a non-zero upfront payment even at inception, which can be either positive or negative. These payments can become sizeable to the extent that, intentionally or not, they can play a determining role in the cash management or in the capital-reinvestment policies that are in place for the portfolio to which the swaps are added.

In this section, we focus exclusively on interest rate swaps, inflation swaps, and credit default swaps. These swaps play a critical role in managing interest rate-, inflation-, and credit risk, and their versatility has made them indispensable for managers of financial institutions and asset managers. While currency and equity swaps are important in their own right, they fall outside the scope of this chapter.

Interest Rate Swaps

An interest rate swap is an exchange of cash flows between two parties over a certain period, often involving a fixed and floating leg. In a so-called fixed-for-floating swap, the fixed leg consists of periodic payments based on a fixed interest rate. In contrast, the floating leg is based on a variable rate that resets periodically depending on the prevailing market conditions. Payments are usually netted, meaning that only the difference between the fixed and floating cash flows are exchanged. This minimizes transaction costs and simplifies the cash flow management for both parties.

Interest rate swaps are among the most widely used financial derivatives, offering flexibility to manage interest rate exposure across various scenarios. While the fundamental structure of an interest rate swap involves the exchange of fixed and floating interest rate payments, these instruments can be tailored to meet diverse investment objectives, eventually resulting in several distinct types of swaps. Each type addresses specific market conditions, hedging needs, or speculative opportunities.

Fixed-for-Floating Interest Rate Swap

The most common type is the ***plain vanilla interest rate swap***, where one party pays a fixed rate and receives a floating rate while the other party does the opposite. This swap type allows portfolio managers to lock in a fixed rate or take advantage of fluctuating short-term rates. This straightforward structure is the foundation for managing interest rate risk in debt portfolios and optimizing financing costs.

Exhibit 3.4 provides an example of an interest rate swap denominated in euro, whereby the receiver gets an annual coupon payment of 2.2% times the €10 M notional, and the payer pays a quarterly interest based on the prevailing 3-month Euribor. This swap may be of interest to a fund manager invested in a leveraged loan portfolio yielding 3-month Euribor plus 400bps, for instance. Negotiating this swap will give this manager more visibility on the portfolio's yield over the next 10 years.

Start date	12/10/2024		
Maturity date	02/12/2034		
Notional amount	€10 million		
Leg 1 : Receive fixed rate		**Leg 2 : Pay floating rate**	
Coupon	2.20%	**Index**	3-month Euribor
Pay frequency	annual	**Pay frequency**	quarterly
		Reset frequency	quarterly

Exhibit 3.4 Fixed for floating rate swap

Basis Swap

Beyond the plain vanilla swap, ***basis swaps*** involve the exchange of two floating rates, often tied to different benchmarks such as SOFR and Euribor. These swaps are useful for entities managing exposure to multiple floating rate benchmarks or mismatches in cash flows.

In a basis swap, both parties exchange floating rate payments based on different benchmarks, such as SOFR against Euribor or two different tenors of SOFR. This structure can adjust exposure to different segments of the interest rate market or hedge against benchmark risk. The example in Exhibit 3.5 illustrates a 10-year basis swap exchanging two floating rates, the euro short-term rate (€STR) against three-month Euribor. Note that to make the swap value equal to zero, the receiver will get a floating rate plus a fixed spread. This swap can be used by a fund manager whose portfolio is benchmarked to the euro short-term rate, while a part of the portfolio is offering a yield indexed to three-month (3 M) Euribor.

Start date	10/12/2024		
Maturity date	12/02/2034		
Notional amount	€10,000,000		
Leg 1 : Receive floating rate		**Leg 2 :Pay floating rate**	
Index	€STR	**Index**	3M Euribor
Pay frequency	Quarterly	**Pay frequency**	Quarterly
Reset frequency	Quarterly	**Reset frequency**	Quarterly
Spread	13bp		

Exhibit 3.5 Basis swap

Constant Maturity Swaps

A ***Constant Maturity Swap*** **(CMS)** is a type of interest rate swap where one party pays a rate indexed to an invariant benchmark while the other party pays a floating rate that is periodically reset to a long-term interest rate or swap rate with a specified constant maturity. Unlike plain vanilla interest rate swaps, where the floating leg is tied to a short-term benchmark, the floating leg of a CMS is linked to a fixed longer-term interest rate, such as the 5-year or 10-year swap rate. Exhibit 3.6 provides an example. The purpose of a CMS is to manage exposure to changes in the slope or shape of the yield curve rather than focusing solely on the level of short-term interest rates.

Other variations include **amortizing swaps**, where the notional principal decreases over time to match the declining balance of an underlying loan or liability, and ***forward-starting swaps***, which begin on a future date and are used to hedge against anticipated changes in interest rates.

Inflation Swaps

Though inflation swaps made their entry onto the capital markets a while ago in the early 2000s, they still seem to receive relatively little attention today in the finance literature and in pedagogical textbooks. Yet the instrument is an effective tool for fund managers, in particular for those seeking to take position with respect to inflation risk. An inflation swap may provide protection against purchase power loss of invested capital stemming from the price erosion incurred over the investment period, or conversely, it can help gain exposure to the inflation rate as part of an active investment strategy.

Inflation swaps work similarly to regular interest rate swaps in that they exchange a fixed cash flow for a floating one. In this swap one party pays a fixed (nominal) rate on a notional principal amount while the other party pays a floating rate linked to an inflation index, typically the Consumer Price

Start date	10/12/2024
Maturity date	12/02/2030
Notional amount	€10,000,000

Leg 1 : Receive – rate of invariant index		**Leg 2 : Pay- ten-year swap rate (fixed maturity)**	
Index	6M Euribor	**Index**	10-year Swap rate
Pay frequency	Quarterly	**Pay frequency**	Quarterly
Reset frequency	Quarterly	**Reset frequency**	Quarterly

Exhibit 3.6 Constant maturity swap

Index (CPI). To be precise, since these price indices are not instantly available but are published with a delay by the public accounting authorities, the floating rate payments are indexed on a lagged inflation rate, of three to six months.

There are two types of inflation swaps, namely the zero coupon- and the year-on-year inflation swap. The zero coupon, also called the breakeven swap, does not involve intermediate payments during the swap's tenor period and is thus essentially a forward rate contract; it is a forward contract on the future inflation rate. At the maturity date, the protection buyer pays a compounded fixed-rate payment on the notional amount, while the protection seller pays back the notional payment adjusted for the inflation incurred over the holding period up to maturity. In case of a year-on-year swap, there is one netting-out exchange of cash flows per year based on the same principles.

Inflation swaps are critical tools for managing inflation risk. They provide flexibility and efficiency for institutions with inflation-sensitive assets or liabilities and help investors gain targeted exposure to inflation trends. As inflation becomes a key economic factor, inflation swaps play an increasingly important role in risk management and financial planning.

Credit Default Swaps

Credit default swaps (CDS) are a type of credit derivative that allows investors to manage the risk of default on specific bonds or credit instruments. These swaps are agreements in which the buyer of protection makes periodic payments to the seller. In return, the seller agrees to compensate the buyer if a defined credit event—such as a default or a restructuring—occurs on the referenced entity's debt. CDS have become indispensable tools for bond portfolio managers, providing a way to hedge against credit risk, enhance yield, and manage exposure to credit spreads without directly buying or selling the bonds in question.

Basics of Credit Default Swaps

In a CDS contract, the two main parties are the protection buyer and the protection seller. The protection buyer seeks to hedge credit risk by paying the seller a periodic premium, referred to as the CDS spread. The protection seller is the party assuming the credit risk, who receives the premium in exchange for bearing the obligation to cover losses if a credit event occurs.

The underlying asset in a CDS can be a single bond or loan (single-name CDS) or a basket of credits (CDS index). Suppose a credit event, such as bankruptcy or failure to pay, occurs. In that case, the CDS contract triggers, and the protection seller compensates the buyer by paying an agreed amount, either as a cash settlement or by taking delivery of the defaulted bond.

CDS contracts are commonly traded OTC, providing customization options for the notional amount, maturity, and credit events covered. Standardized CDS contracts, governed by the International Swaps and Derivatives Association (ISDA), ensure consistency in definitions and terms, streamlining their use across markets.

The reference entity is the issuer whose credit risk is being hedged. The reference obligation is the specific debt instrument or group of instruments the CDS is tied to. This clarity allows both parties to understand the precise asset whose credit quality is at stake.

A credit event triggers the CDS payment. Credit events include bankruptcy, failure to pay, and restructuring. These events are standardized by the ISDA, in an effort to ensure that the parties involved share a common understanding of what constitutes a triggering event. The exact definitions and conditions the ISDA upholds are continuously challenged by market participants, at times voraciously so, leading in certain cases to reforms. The wipeout in 2023 of the subordinated AT1 bonds issued by Credit Suisse, which were not covered by the bank's CDS protection, and similarly for Silicon Valley Bank bonds in the same year, have reignited the ongoing debate.

Credit Spread Quotation Mechanics in CDS

In a CDS, the credit spread (or CDS spread) represents the cost of insuring against the default of a reference entity such as a corporation or government. The spread is quoted as an annualized percentage of the notional amount of the swap and is paid quarterly in arrears. This spread reflects the perceived risk of default: the higher the credit risk, the wider the spread. In particular, a CDS on an investment-grade company has a spread of 100 basis points (1%), whereas a CDS on a high-yield (riskier) entity has a spread of 500 basis points (5%).

This market standard has been introduced by the International Swaps and Derivatives Association (ISDA) in the aftermath of Lehman Brothers' default in 2009 and is referred to as the "Big Bang" reform. The standardized spreads of 1% and 5% help streamline the trading of CDS contracts, reducing the need to negotiate unique terms for each contract. When the actual credit risk justifies a spread different from the standardized rate, an upfront payment is made to adjust the total cost of protection. This upfront amount represents the present value difference between the agreed-upon spread and the standardized rate.

For example, consider a CDS on an investment-grade corporation with a notional amount of $10 million. Let's assume the current market spread for the corporation's CDS is 2% (200 basis points) annually, indicating the market's perception of its credit risk. Since the corporation is investment-grade, the standardized spread for the CDS contract would be 1% (100 basis points). Using the standardized spread, the quarterly payment would be calculated as follows:

$$\text{Quarterly Payment} = \text{Notional Amount} \times \text{Standardized Spread} \times \left(\text{Days in Quarter}/360\right)$$

For simplicity, assuming 90 days in the quarter:

$$\text{QuarterlyPayment} = \$10,000,000 \times 0.01 \times 90/360 = \$25,000$$

So, under the standardized spread, the protection buyer would pay $25,000 at the end of each quarter.

The actual market spread (2%) is higher than the standardized spread (1%), so the protection buyer must make an upfront payment to account for this difference. This upfront payment is the present value of the 1% difference over the contract's term, discounted by a rate agreed upon by both parties.

For example, let's assume the contract term is five years, and the discount rate is 3%. The upfront payment would be calculated as follows:

$$\text{UpfrontPayment} = \text{NotionalAmount} \times \left(\text{MarketSpread} - \text{StandardizedSpread}\right) \times \text{PresentValueFactor}$$

Here, with a present value factor based on a 3% discount over 5 years (approximately 4.58):

$$\text{UpfrontPayment} = \$10,000,000 \times (0.02 - 0.01) \times 4.58 = \$458,000$$

Thus, the protection buyer would make a one-time upfront payment of $458,000 in addition to the quarterly payments based on the standardized 1% spread.

Now, let's consider a high-yield entity with a market spread of 4% (400 basis points) on a notional amount of $10 million. The standardized high-yield spread is 5% (500 basis points), and the **quarterly running premium is 5%.**

$$\text{QuarterlyPayment} = \$10,000,000 \times 0.05 \times 90/360 = \$125,000$$

Since the market spread (4%) is lower than the standardized 5% for high-yield entities, the protection seller would pay the buyer upfront to compensate for the excess 1% being paid in the quarterly premiums. The present value calculation would similarly use the difference and the discount rate.

Interest Rate Options

Interest rate options are derivatives that give the holder the right, but not the obligation, to buy (call option) or sell (put option) an interest rate-sensitive instrument—such as a bond, an interest rate futures or a swap—at a specified price before or at expiration. These options provide bond portfolio managers with flexible tools for hedging against interest rate volatility, adjusting portfolio exposure, and enhancing yields. Unlike futures, which obligate the holder to fulfill the contract terms, options allow more nuanced positioning to protect against downside risks while retaining upside potential.

As is the case for equity options, there are various types depending on the execution rights. There are American options, which can be exercised any time before expiration, and European options, which can only be exercised at maturity. Most hedging strategies combine the use of various options in an effort to reduce the hedging costs.

Options on Physical Bonds

Options on bonds give the holder the right to buy or sell a specific bond at a predetermined price before or when the option expires. For several reasons, options on futures discussed next are preferred over options on physical bonds. First, options on futures eliminate the need for payments related to accrued interest, simplifying transactions. Secondly, futures options reduce the risk of delivery squeezes, as they typically have an ample deliverable supply, unlike certain physical bonds that may face short supply at the time of delivery. Third, futures prices are generally more readily available than current bond prices, which aids in accurately pricing options. Lastly, options on physical bonds are mainly OTC products, which makes them less liquid.

Options on Bond Futures

An option on a futures contract, also known as a *futures option*, provides the buyer with the right, but not the obligation, to enter into a futures contract at a specified price, that is, the exercise or strike price. A **call option on futures** grants the buyer the right to buy the underlying futures contract at the exercise price while the **put option on futures** grants the buyer the right to sell the underlying futures contract at the exercise price. Upon exercising the option, the buyer acquires a position in the futures contract at the exercise price, and this position is immediately marked to the market at the current futures price. The buyer's profit or loss on exercising the option is determined by the difference between the exercise price and the current futures price.

For example, suppose a portfolio manager buys a call option on a futures contract with an exercise price of 80. If the current futures price rises to 90, and the portfolio manager decides to exercise the option, the mechanics work as follows. Upon exercising the call option, the investor acquires a long position in the futures contract at the exercise price of 80. Simultaneously, the option writer (seller) takes the corresponding short futures position at the same price of 80. Since the prevailing futures price is now 90, the portfolio manager's long position is immediately marked to market, meaning it is evaluated at the current futures price of 90 rather than the exercise price of 80. The portfolio therefore realizes a gain based on the difference between the current futures price (90) and the exercise price (80), which is a profit of 10. This gain represents the economic benefit of having exercised the option. After exercising the option, the portfolio has the choice to either sell the futures contract at the current futures price (90), locking in the gain of 10 immediately, or maintain the long position in the futures contract, exposing the investment to further price movements and the standard profit/loss dynamics of a futures contract.

If the same portfolio manager had purchased a put option with an exercise price of 80, and the futures price dropped to 75, the portfolio manager faces the following. The buyer of the put takes in effect a short position in the futures contract at the exercise price of 80, while the option writer takes the corresponding long position. With the current futures price at 75, the short futures position held by the portfolio manager is marked to market at this prevailing price. The portfolio profits by the difference between the exercise price (80) and the current futures price (75), for a gain of 5. After exercising, the portfolio manager can either buy a futures contract at the current market price (75), the portfolio locks in the gain of 5, or the portfolio manager may choose to keep the short futures position, continuing to profit if the futures price declines further, but also exposing themselves to potential losses if futures prices subsequently increase.

Many future options are listed on various stock exchanges. The maturities of the options are generally quite short term. It is difficult to find options over two years, as liquidity fades on this type of maturity and the quoted price may not seem relevant. Portfolio managers would usually use listed options to hedge on a rolling basis a variable interest rate exposure. If the portfolio manager has a clear long-term view on its hedging purpose, he or she would rather resort to OTC options, for a long-term hedging.

In summary, exercising options on futures converts the option into a futures contract position at the strike price, which is then marked to market at the current futures price. The profit or loss from exercising is immediately realized based on the difference between the exercise price and the prevailing futures price, providing a clear and structured mechanism for managing market expectations through options on futures.

Options on Short-Term Interest Futures

Options on short-term interest futures are listed products available on various exchanges. The principle is similar to that of bond futures described in the previous section. Like all listed options, the most liquid products are those with the shortest maturity and a strike close to the spot price.

Exhibit 3.7 provides an example. At the end of November 2024, a portfolio manager plans to receive a 3-month Euribor future expiring in March 2025 on a €2 million contract and aims for the yield to approximate the current spot rate of around 2%. To achieve this, the manager purchases two call options, as shown below. If yields were to drop to 0%, for instance, the manager would exercise the options to secure the intended cash flow.

Options on Swaps

Swaptions are options on a swap, granting the buyer the right, but not the obligation, to enter into a swap under specific conditions. These are over-the-counter (OTC) products, customized to meet the unique requirements of the holders. There are several types of swaptions: a call swaption (known as a “receiver swaption”), which gives buyers the right to enter into a swap

Underlying	3M Euribor March25	
Option maturity date	03/17/2025	
Strike price	98	[effective yield 100-98=2%]
Notional amount	€1,000,000	
Value of 1 point	€2,500 €	[= €1,000,000 / 100 / 4]
Option price per 1 point	0.06500	
Option price for 1 contract	162.50	
Spot rate on 11/29/24	97.83	[effective yield 100-97.83=2.17%]
Scenario 1		
Spot rate on 03/17/25	100	[effective yield 0%]
Cash settlement	€5,000	[= €2,500 x (100 - 98)]
Scenario 2		
Spot rate on 03/17/25	95	[effective yield 100-95=5%]
Cash settlement	-€7,500	[= €2,500 x (95 - 98)]

Exhibit 3.7 Call option on 3-Month (3 M) Euribor future

where they receive the fixed leg and pay the floating leg, and a put swaption (known as a "payer swaption"), which gives buyers the right to enter into a swap where they pay the fixed leg and receive the floating leg. Additionally, there are more exotic variations of swaptions designed for specific market scenarios.

Exhibit 3.8 illustrates an example of a European receiver swaption with a strike rate of 2.23% and an expiry in one year as of December 1, 2024. At maturity, the buyer has the right to enter into the swap, receiving a fixed leg at an annual rate of 2.23% and paying a floating rate based on the 6-month (6 M) Euribor. This instrument can be useful for servicing predefined liability payments. A pension fund may want to buy the receiver swaption displayed in the Exhibit for instance, who prepares to pay fixed annuities over a ten-year period starting next year.

Interest Rate Caps and Floors

Caps and floors are OTC options that a portfolio manager can use to establish boundaries on interest rates, providing protection within a specified range. A cap sets an upper limit on interest rates, effectively limiting the cost of borrowing for a portfolio with floating rate debt. Conversely, a floor sets a minimum rate, providing a hedge against declines in income from floating rate assets. Caps and floors are often structured as a series of options, called caplets and floorlets, offering flexibility in managing rate sensitivity. The cap and floor options are particularly helpful in managing portfolios with floating rate bonds, as instruments to control income volatility.

Option	
Style	European
Option maturity	11/27/2025
Notional amount	€10 million

Underlying swap	
Start date	12/01/2026
Maturity date	12/01/2036

Leg 1 : Receive fixed rate		Leg 2 : Pay floating rate	
Coupon	2.20%	**Index**	6M Euribor
Pay frequency	Annual	**Pay frequency**	Quarterly
		Reset frequency	Quarterly

Exhibit 3.8 Receiver swaption

By definition, as OTC products are not standardized, their characteristics can be negotiated on a bilateral basis. The underlying can be a fixed interest rate at a particular maturity, or a floating rate, as illustrated in the following example displayed in Exhibit 3.9. The instrument allows the buyer to cap the annual interest rate payment obligation in force due to the underlying 10-year fixed-for floating swap at a strike of 2.175%, corresponding to the prevailing 10-year rate, any time in the coming two years (American call convention). In case of an interest rate hike, for example an upward shift of 2% (200bps), the buyer will receive compensation via a cash flow payment. This compensation will be €20,000, i.e., 2% times the nominal value.

Purchasing bond-related options for a hedging strategy can be quite costly. To reduce these expenses, asset managers often employ various cost-saving techniques. One common approach is to use an option call or put spread, such as buying a call with a 2% strike and partially financing it by selling a call with a 3% strike, which provides partial hedging at a lower cost. Another

Contract Underlying	10Y Swap Rate		
Start date	12/05/2024		
Option maturity date	12/05/2026		
Strike (Cap)	2.175%		
Notional amount	€1,000,000		
Option price	€6,816		
Spot today 12/05/24	2.175%		
Scenario: upward +200bps			
1. Fixing rate on 12/05/25	4.1750%	cash flow received 12/05/25	€20,000
2. Fixing rate on 12/05/26	4.1750%	cash flow received 12/05/26	€20,000

Exhibit 3.9 Cap option on 10-year interest rate swap

method is to purchase out-of-the-money options, which are less expensive than at-the-money options. Alternatively, an asset manager might buy a call and offset the cost by selling a put with a lower strike price. These strategies help balance hedging effectiveness with cost efficiency. A number of case studies in this book elaborate on those possibilities.

Summary

This chapter provides an overview of bond-related derivatives, focusing on their structures and mechanics, and gives a brief explanation of their use in bond portfolio management. These instruments, which include futures, forwards, swaps, and options, are essential tools for portfolio managers to adjust interest rate exposure, hedge against credit risks, and enhance overall portfolio performance.

Interest rate futures are a key category of standardized contracts that help manage sensitivity to fluctuations in interest rates. The chapter explains short-interest rate futures alongside longer-maturity bond futures like U.S. Treasury and Euro-Bund futures. These contracts are widely used to hedge portfolio duration or protect against interest rate risks.

Forward rate agreements (FRAs) are another focus. These customizable OTC contracts allow parties to lock in interest rates for future periods. While FRAs are particularly useful for managing short-term interest rate risk, they come with additional counterparty and liquidity risks compared to exchange-traded futures.

Swaps, including interest rate, inflation, and credit default swaps (CDS), are discussed in detail. Interest rate swaps allow parties to exchange fixed and floating interest payments, while inflation swaps are used to hedge inflation risk. CDS are highlighted for their role in hedging credit risk and their standardization under ISDA regulations, which ensure consistency across markets.

Options on fixed-income instruments, including bonds, futures, and swaps, are also covered. These instruments provide significant flexibility in managing interest rate volatility and developing hedging strategies. Swaptions, or options on swaps, and caps and floors, which establish interest rate boundaries for floating rate exposures, are among the examples discussed.

4

Foreign Exchange Derivatives

Frank J. Fabozzi, Gueorgui S. Konstantinov, and Suprita Vohra

Foreign exchange (FX) derivatives are financial instruments based on exchange rates between two or more currencies. The FX derivatives market is primarily divided into two segments. The over-the-counter (OTC) market includes instruments such as currency forwards, swaps, and options, which are customized to meet the specific needs of participants. These OTC contracts are negotiated directly between parties, usually through financial institutions, and are neither standardized nor traded on formal exchanges. In contrast, the exchange-traded segment consists of standardized futures and options on major currency pairs available on regulated exchanges like the Chicago Mercantile Exchange (CME), offering transparency, liquidity, and reduced counterparty risk.

FX derivatives play a critical role in managing currency risk, providing tools for risk control, enhancing liquidity, and addressing cross-border financial exposures. These instruments, including forwards, futures, options, and

F. J. Fabozzi
Johns Hopkins University's Carey School of Business, Baltimore, MD, USA

G. S. Konstantinov (✉)
Senior Portfolio Manager of Fixed Income & Currencies, Frankfurt am Main, Germany
e-mail: georgi.konstantinoff@gmail.com

S. Vohra
Financial Professional Specializing in Foreign Exchange and Interest Rate Derivatives , Barclays, Singapore

F. J. Fabozzi and M. de Jong (eds.), *Derivatives Applications in Asset Management*,
https://doi.org/10.1007/978-3-031-86354-7_4

swaps, serve distinct purposes depending on the portfolio manager's investment objectives.

This chapter provides an overview of the foundational elements of these FX derivative products. It is important to note that the chapter focuses on the structural characteristics of FX derivatives rather than their applications, specific contract forms (such as puts, calls, swaps, and futures), associated risks, or considerations in their use. Those topics are explored comprehensively in other chapters and are not repeated here.

Currency Forward Contracts

Currency forward contracts are private agreements between two parties to exchange a specified amount of one currency for another at a fixed rate on a predetermined future date. Unlike spot transactions, where the currency exchange happens immediately, forward contracts allow the parties to secure an exchange rate in advance, setting the rate today for a transaction that will take place later. This structure makes forwards one of the most widely used tools in foreign exchange for managing exposure to currency risk.

A defining feature of currency forward contracts is their customization level. Since forwards are traded OTC, there is no standardization in contract size, duration, or settlement terms, allowing the two parties to shape the contract to their specific needs. This flexibility is especially beneficial for corporations with predictable foreign currency cash flows or anticipated expenses in different currencies, as they can arrange forward contracts to match their unique payment schedules. The ability to tailor the exact amount, date, and currency pair also means that companies with future obligations in foreign currencies can manage these transactions in a controlled way, reducing the unpredictability of future costs or revenue streams.

The mechanism of currency forward contracts is largely influenced by the interest rate differential between the two currencies in the contract. The forward rate is calculated based on the current spot rate and adjusted to account for this differential, which represents the opportunity cost of holding one currency over the other for the duration of the contract. When the acquired currency has a higher interest rate than the base currency, the forward rate generally reflects a discount, compensating for the higher return associated with holding that currency. On the other hand, if the base currency has a higher interest rate, the forward rate usually includes a premium, acknowledging the lower opportunity cost associated with holding that currency. This method of adjusting forward rates ensures that both parties consider the financial implications of carrying one currency relative to the other over time.

A currency forward contract can be settled in two ways on maturity: physical delivery or cash settlement. For example, a one-month forward contract for a customer to buy EUR 100 million against USD 105 million at a forward rate of 1.05 USD/EUR. After one month, the customer can send USD 105 million to the bank and receive EUR 100 million. Alternatively, the customer can settle the transaction in cash in USD or EUR. If the USD/EUR exchange rate at the time of settlement is 1.10 USD/EUR, then the customer will receive USD 5 million, calculated as 100 million × (1.10–1.05). This offers market participants flexibility to manage their currency risks without necessarily having to gross settle large cash flows.

Many currencies, especially in emerging markets, are not fully convertible outside the country. Such currencies often develop two kinds of markets, a local market and an offshore market. Depending on the regulations, the offshore FX market may exclusively trade as USD-cash settled or other hard currencies, since the local currency is not deliverable outside the country. Such markets are known as non-deliverable markets and are popular venues for global corporations and funds to hedge emerging market FX risks in their portfolio. For such non-deliverable markets, the market usually follows a fixing page[1] as the standard FX rate against which the cash-settlement USD amount is calculated. Indian rupee (INR), Indonesian rupiah (IDR), Egyptian pound (EGP), and Brazilian real (BRL) are some examples that have a local FX market and an offshore FX non-deliverable market.

Currency Futures Contracts

Currency futures contracts are standardized agreements to exchange a specific amount of one currency for another at a predetermined rate on a set future date. Unlike currency forwards, which are customized and traded over the counter, currency futures are traded on regulated exchanges. This distinction makes futures more accessible to a broader range of investors, providing them with transparency, standardized contract terms, and reduced counterparty risk. These qualities make currency futures an essential tool for managing

[1] A fixing page refers to a platform, page, or source (often provided by financial data providers like Reuters or Bloomberg) that publishes official benchmark exchange rates at a specific, pre-determined time. The fixing page provides benchmark exchange rates, considered the "official" rates at a specific time of the day.

foreign exchange exposure, particularly in markets where liquidity and ease of access are key considerations.

The exchange predates the terms in a typical currency futures contract, including the contract size, maturity dates, and settlement procedures. By removing the need for customization, exchanges like the CME ensure that currency futures are highly liquid and readily tradable. Each contract has a fixed notional value representing a standard quantity of the underlying currency, allowing participants to make precise adjustments to their currency exposure without engaging in complex negotiations. The standardization extends to settlement dates, with maturities usually set at regular intervals, such as quarterly, allowing traders and investors to align their positions with specific timeframes.

Currency futures are marked to market daily, meaning gains or losses are settled at the end of each trading day based on that day's closing price. This daily settlement process minimizes the risk of large, unmanageable losses by requiring each party to maintain margin—a form of collateral—on deposit with the exchange. If the value of a futures position moves unfavorably, the trader must deposit an additional margin to maintain the position.

Currency futures, therefore, serve as a critical instrument for managing and gaining exposure to foreign exchange rates. Their standardized, exchange-traded nature gives market participants transparency, liquidity, and reduced counterparty risk, qualities that make them a mainstay in global FX markets. For both hedging and speculation, currency futures offer a structured approach to managing currency exposure in an efficient and accessible manner.

Currency Options Currency options are financial contracts that give the holder the right, but not the obligation, to exchange a specific amount of one currency for another at a predetermined rate, known as the strike price, on or before a specified expiration date. Currency options are available in both over-the-counter (OTC) and exchange-traded formats. OTC options offer customization, allowing parties to tailor the contract size, strike price, expiration date, and exotic features to meet specific hedging or speculative needs. However, OTC options involve counterparty risk, as they are private agreements without the guarantees provided by a clearinghouse. Exchange-traded options, on the other hand, are standardized and traded on platforms like the CME. These options offer greater liquidity, transparency, and security through daily settlement processes, making them accessible to a broad range of investors who seek more standardized currency option contracts without the complexities of customization.

Currency options are also classified based on their "moneyness," determining their intrinsic value at a given point. Moneyness is commonly categorized as in-the-money (ITM), at-the-money (ATM), or out-of-the-money (OTM), depending on the relationship between the option's strike price and the current spot exchange rate. Delta, a measure of an option's sensitivity to changes in the underlying exchange rate, provides a critical metric for assessing the likelihood of an option expiring ITM. For example, ATM options generally have a delta of approximately 0.50, meaning a 50% probability of expiring in the money.

Currency options can be exercised in **European style, American style,** or **Bermudian style,** depending on the contract terms. European-style options allow the holder to exercise the option only on the expiration date, providing a single opportunity for execution. In contrast, American-style options offer greater flexibility, enabling exercise at any time up to and including the expiration date. Bermudian options combine features of both, allowing exercise only on specific, predetermined dates, often aligned with business days, referred to as "BuAdd" (Business Add).[2] This structure balances flexibility and control, making Bermudian options particularly useful in structured products and customized hedging strategies.

Notably, the option contracts have different prices. For example, the EUR/USD currency pair is the most traded, but the option price depends on the usual determinants like volatility, time decay, and interest rates. Despite being the most liquid currency pair, options on EUR/USD are expensive instruments to apply for hedging, and their choice depends on the effectiveness of the manager in predicting currency movements and, most importantly, their range. For example, the put option premium of, say, 1.6% might be an expensive hedge instrument on an ongoing basis. Put differently, FX option contracts on several currency pairs might be a serious performance drag. In this respect, FX forwards are the most effective and less expensive instrument, which can be combined in multiple strikes and structures.

Currency Swaps

Currency swaps are a type of FX derivative contract in which two parties agree to exchange equivalent amounts of two different currencies and commit to a series of periodic interest payments over a specified term. At the end of this term, they swap back the principal amounts at a predetermined rate, unlike

[2] The "BuAdd" or "Business Add" defines these allowable exercise dates and aligns them with business days, avoiding holidays or weekends where markets may be closed.

other FX derivatives, which primarily hedge against changes in exchange rates or interest rates; currency swaps are often used to manage both currency and interest rate risk simultaneously, particularly for long-term obligations in foreign currencies.

The structure of a currency swap typically involves an initial exchange of principal amounts, where each party provides the agreed-upon amount of one currency to the other at the prevailing exchange rate. The parties exchange interest payments on the principal amounts they received throughout the swap. These interest payments can be structured in various ways, depending on the counterparties' needs. A common arrangement is the fixed-for-floating rate swap, where one party pays a fixed interest rate in one currency while the other pays a floating rate based on a benchmark rate in the other currency. Other arrangements may involve both parties paying fixed rates or floating rates. At the swap's conclusion, the principal amounts are exchanged back at the same rate agreed upon at the start, which mitigates the exchange rate risk associated with the principal.

Currency swaps are almost exclusively traded OTC rather than on exchanges, making them highly customizable. This OTC nature allows the contract terms, including notional amounts, interest rate structures, and maturity dates, to be tailored to meet each party's unique requirements. However, because they are private contracts, currency swaps carry counterparty risk, which can be a significant consideration for long-term agreements. To mitigate this risk, swaps are often collateralized, and participants may choose to work with highly creditworthy institutions to ensure greater security.

Here are two examples of how a global portfolio manager could use currency swaps.

Suppose an asset manager oversees a bond portfolio that includes US dollar-denominated and euro-denominated debt securities. The portfolio manager seeks to hedge the currency risk associated with the euro-denominated bonds, ensuring that the portfolio's returns are not adversely affected by USD/EUR exchange rate fluctuations. The portfolio manager enters into a currency swap with a financial institution, exchanging a notional amount of euros for US dollars at the current spot rate. Under the terms of the swap, the portfolio manager agrees to pay the counterparty a fixed interest rate in euros. In contrast, the counterparty pays a floating interest rate in dollars based on some US reference rate. At the swap's maturity, the principal amounts are exchanged at the original spot rate, ensuring the portfolio manager is fully hedged against currency fluctuations during the investment horizon. This structure allows the portfolio manager to focus on credit risk and yield opportunities in the bond portfolio without being impacted by exchange rate volatility.

In our second example, suppose an asset manager of a global balanced fund wants to enhance yield by investing in high-yield corporate bonds from an emerging market, such as India but does not wish to take on the currency risk of holding Indian rupee-denominated assets. To achieve this, the manager enters a currency swap to synthetically transform the exposure from rupees to US dollars. In this swap, the portfolio manager exchanges rupee-denominated coupon payments for US dollar payments based on a fixed interest rate. The principal amounts in rupees and US dollars are exchanged at the start of the swap and will be exchanged at the same rate upon maturity. By doing so, the portfolio manager gains access to the higher yields of Indian corporate bonds while mitigating currency risks associated with the rupee. This approach ensures the portfolio benefits from geographic diversification and higher returns without exposing it to excessive currency volatility.

Exotic FX Derivatives

Exotic FX derivatives are specialized financial contracts beyond the standard structures of forwards, futures, options, and swaps. These derivatives are designed to meet the complex and unique needs of corporations, financial institutions, and investors seeking customized exposure to currency movements or hedge-specific, often intricate, currency risks. Exotic FX derivatives can vary significantly in structure and payoff, with many featuring additional conditions or tailored elements that respond to specific market scenarios. Despite their flexibility and precision, exotic FX derivatives involve higher levels of complexity and are generally less liquid than standard FX derivatives. The lack of standardization, combined with the bespoke nature of these contracts, means that exotic derivatives are typically traded OTC, where they can be customized but carry additional counterparty risks. Additionally, the conditionality in exotic options, such as the barrier triggers in knock-in or knock-out options, requires portfolio managers to deeply understand market dynamics and monitor their positions as market conditions change carefully.

Range Forward FX Derivatives

Range Forward FX derivatives combine features of both call and put options. They are customized instruments that enable portfolio managers to establish a predefined range of exchange rates within which currency transactions will occur. These derivatives are useful in asset management for hedging portfolio exposures to foreign currencies while retaining the potential to benefit from favorable FX movements within a set range. Range forwards balance cost efficiency and tailored risk management, making them appealing to asset managers with global investment portfolios.

The mechanics of a range forward involve defining two strike rates: the lower strike, linked to the put option, and the upper strike, linked to the call option. These strike rates form the range within which currency transactions are executed. If the spot rate at maturity lies within the range, the portfolio manager transacts at the prevailing market rate. However, specific obligations are triggered if the spot rate breaches either the upper or lower strike. If the spot rate rises above the upper strike, the counterparty exercises the call option, obligating the manager to transact at the upper strike rate. Conversely, if the spot rate falls below the lower strike, the portfolio manager exercises the put option, ensuring a minimum exchange rate for the transaction. The cost-neutral nature of the range forward eliminates the need for an upfront premium, as the cost of purchasing the put is offset by selling the call.

A range forward is composed of several key structural components. The lower strike establishes a floor, protecting against currency depreciation, while the upper strike sets a ceiling, capping potential gains from favorable currency movements. The notional amount specifies the size of the exposure being hedged, and the maturity date determines when the contract settles. These instruments are beneficial for managing currency risk in global portfolios where exposure to foreign currencies can affect returns.

For example, consider the portfolio manager of a global equity fund. The fund is denominated in US dollars but has significant exposure to European equities priced in euros. The portfolio manager is concerned about potential euro depreciation against the dollar over the next six months but does not want to forgo all possible benefits of favorable euro movements. First, it is crucial to understand the currency pairs. The EUR/USD expresses the price of one euro in US dollars. The currency pair EUR/USD of 1.15 expresses the US dollar price of one euro. The convention is that the first currency in the pair (EUR in our example) denotes the "foreign" currency, and the second term refers to the reference or base currency. In this respect, the second currency in a currency pair is associated with the currency in which the portfolio is denominated. In other words, the EUR is the long position, and the USD is the short position in this currency pair.

Within this framework, the portfolio manager might be concerned about EUR/USD moving to levels lower than 1.05. In other words, a move from

EUR/USD of 1.10 to 1.02 is a euro depreciation for a US dollar-based portfolio manager and US dollar appreciation for a European-based portfolio manager whose portfolio is denominated in euros. Suppose the euro depreciates to 1.02 EUR/USD at maturity. In that case, the portfolio manager exercises the put option, securing the minimum rate of 1.05 EUR/USD to convert euro-denominated gains back into dollars. Alternatively, if the euro appreciates to 1.18 EUR/USD, the counterparty exercises the call option, and the portfolio manager transacts at the capped rate of 1.15 EUR/USD. The portfolio manager transacts at the prevailing market rate if the exchange rate remains within the range (e.g., 1.10 EUR/USD).

Range forwards offer several advantages for asset management. They provide a cost-efficient method of managing currency risk, as they involve no upfront premium while allowing participation in favorable exchange rate movements within the range. However, the upper strike limits the upside potential, and the manager must fulfill obligations if the exchange rate moves outside the predefined range. Despite these limitations, range forwards provide a tailored and effective solution for currency risk management in global investment portfolios, ensuring a balance between stability and opportunity.

Barrier Option FX Derivatives

Barrier option FX derivatives are unique instruments whose existence or activation depends on the underlying exchange rate reaching or surpassing a specified price level, known as the "barrier." These derivatives, often called knock-in or knock-out options, are particularly valuable in asset management for managing currency exposures in global portfolios. Barrier options provide asset managers with cost-efficient solutions by tailoring risk management strategies to specific market conditions, reducing costs compared to standard options.

The mechanics of barrier options depend on whether they are structured as knock-in or knock-out options. A knock-in option becomes active only when the underlying exchange rate reaches or breaches the barrier level during the option's life. Until the barrier is breached, the option has no value. In contrast, a knock-out option is invalidated or ceases to exist once the exchange rate touches the barrier level, providing the holder with cost savings in scenarios where the hedged event becomes unlikely. Barrier levels are usually set above (for call options) or below (for put options) the current exchange rate, depending on the hedging or speculative objective.

Barrier options have several structural components. The strike price determines the rate at which the option can be exercised if it becomes active, while the barrier level determines whether it is activated or deactivated. These instruments are often cheaper than standard options due to the conditionality of their activation or existence, making them particularly attractive for cost-conscious foreign exchange risk management. The notional amount and maturity date define the volume and timeline of the hedge, aligning the option's parameters with the asset manager's portfolio needs.

For example, a portfolio manager oversees a global fixed-income fund denominated in US dollars, with a significant allocation to Japanese government bonds priced in yen (JPY). The USD value of the yen bond portfolio declines if the yen weakens, and the portfolio manager is keen to hedge against that. One way to do so is to buy a USD call/JPY put option, which requires paying an option premium. Let a 1-year USD call/JPY put option with a strike price of 150 JPY/USD cost 2.50% USD at an exchange rate of 150, determined as a combination of interest rate differential and time value of the option.

To circumvent this cost, the fund manager could use the barrier option and purchase a 1-year USD call/JPY put with the same strike price of 150 and a knock-out (KO) barrier at 170. This alternative lowers the cost by 60%, reducing it to 1.0% USD. However, this cost saving comes with a tradeoff, namely that the hedge is capped. The fund manager is protected against JPY weakening as long as the exchange rate does not exceed 170. If 170 is reached or surpassed, the option is knocked out and becomes invalid. Therefore, if the fund manager anticipates that JPY may weaken but not beyond 170, the barrier option offers a cost-effective and appealing solution. On the other hand, if there is a possibility that JPY could weaken significantly beyond 170, the vanilla option, despite its higher cost, provides a more comprehensive protection.

In practice, fund managers actively assess various structures to identify the most suitable options based on their market outlook, cost considerations, and investment horizons. Currency options are not only used for hedging currency risk but also for enhancing portfolio returns. This can be illustrated by a scenario where a portfolio manager leverages option premiums to boost returns. For instance, the manager might sell deep out-of-the-money USD/JPY options—such as options with a strike price of 190—based on the expectation that the yen will weaken but not more than the level of 170 against the US dollar. By selling these options, the manager collects the option premium, adding to portfolio returns if the currency remains within expected levels.

However, if the yen appreciates against the US dollar, it could result in a negative payoff for the manager.

Writing currency puts and calls is a common strategy among currency managers but requires stringent risk management to handle the inherent option risks. These strategies, often classified as volatility strategies in FX management, depend on the market environment, as well as the relationship between implied and realized FX volatility. Such strategies are generally more suitable for liquid currencies, where markets are deep and efficient, rather than for emerging market (EM) currencies, which typically involve higher risks and lower liquidity.

Barrier options can be used by portfolio managers who seek to manage currency risks under specific market scenarios. Compared to standard options, their cost efficiency makes them an attractive choice for hedging exposures in portfolios where extreme currency movements are deemed unlikely. Knock-in options, for instance, suit managers who want a hedge only if the underlying exchange rate moves into a predefined range, ensuring that the cost is incurred only when the hedge is necessary. Conversely, knock-out options benefit managers who wish to limit the cost of hedging when specific adverse currency movements are highly improbable.

These derivatives can also enhance returns for global portfolios. By incorporating conditionality into the hedge, barrier options enable asset managers to allocate capital more efficiently, directing resources toward strategies with higher expected returns. For instance, a manager may use barrier options to hedge a portion of the portfolio exposed to emerging market currencies, reducing overall hedging costs while maintaining protection against moderate currency risks.

Currency Basket Option FX Derivatives

Currency basket options FX derivatives derive their value from a weighted average of multiple currencies, known as a "currency basket," relative to a base currency. Depending on the hedging or speculative objectives, they can be structured as calls or puts. These options allow portfolio managers to manage currency risks associated with a group of currencies within a single contract, making them particularly efficient for global asset management strategies. Unlike standard options based on a single currency pair, currency basket options provide diversified exposure to multiple exchange rates, reducing the need for separate hedging arrangements.

The mechanics of currency basket options involve specifying the base currency, the constituent currencies in the basket, their weights, and the strike price. The weighted average exchange rate of the basket currencies relative to the base currency is calculated based on the predefined weights, which are typically proportional to the portfolio's exposures to those currencies. The option's payoff depends on the movement of this weighted average exchange rate relative to the strike price. For instance, consider a global equity portfolio denominated in US dollars with significant exposures to the euro (EUR), Japanese yen (JPY), and Swiss franc (CHF). A currency basket option could be structured with weights reflecting the proportion of the portfolio's exposure to each currency, such as 55% EUR, 30% JPY, and 15% CHF. The option would provide a payoff based on the movement of these currencies' weighted average exchange rate relative to the US dollar.

However, liquidity in exotic currencies remains a significant challenge. Despite the FX market being the most liquid globally, as noted by the Bank for International Settlements, exotic currency markets are prone to heightened risks and lack sufficient liquidity during periods of financial market stress. This can make managing exposures in these currencies more complex, particularly during market turmoil.

The structure of currency basket options allows for considerable customization, enabling managers to align the instrument with their portfolio's specific exposures. The weights of the constituent currencies can be adjusted to reflect the portfolio's risk profile or expected market movements. The strike price and maturity can also be tailored to the manager's hedging horizon and risk tolerance. Currency basket options also offer cost efficiencies compared to managing individual options for each currency pair. They reduce transaction costs and simplify risk management by consolidating multiple hedges into a single instrument. However, they also present challenges, such as the potential for over- or under-hedging if the basket's composition does not perfectly align with the portfolio's exposures.

Dual-Currency Options

Dual currency options give the holder a choice of two payout currencies at maturity, depending on predetermined conditions. These options are particularly valuable for asset managers seeking to hedge or speculate on the relative movements of two currencies without committing to a single currency payout. Dual currency options are structured to offer flexibility and cost efficiency, making them an effective tool for managing multi-currency exposures in global investment portfolios.

The mechanics of dual currency options involve specifying the two currencies, the strike price, and the notional amount. At maturity, the payout is determined by comparing the relative performance of the two currencies against the strike price or a predefined reference level. The option's holder has the right to receive the payout in the more favorable currency, as determined by the contract terms. This feature allows the holder to benefit from favorable currency movements while limiting downside risks.

For example, consider an asset manager overseeing an equity fund that invests in Asian emerging market countries. Two countries it is invested in are India and China, creating exposure to the Indian rupee and the Chinese yuan. To hedge potential currency risks, the asset manager could purchase a dual currency option with the rupee and yuan as the underlying currencies. If, at maturity, the rupee appreciates significantly relative to the yuan, the asset manager receives the payout in rupees. Conversely, if the yuan appreciates relative to the rupee, the payout is settled in yuans. This flexibility allows the asset manager to optimize returns while mitigating adverse currency movements.

Dual currency options can be structured as either calls or puts, depending on the hedging or speculative objectives. A dual currency call option allows the holder to choose which currency to receive if the exchange rate moves favorably, while a dual currency put option provides the right to deliver the less favorable currency. These options are typically used in scenarios where the portfolio manager expects significant volatility in the relative exchange rates of the two currencies but is uncertain about the direction of movement.

The structure of dual currency options includes several customizable components. The strike price defines the threshold at which the relative value of the two currencies is compared, and the notional amount determines the size of the exposure being hedged. The maturity date specifies the contract's expiration, aligning with the portfolio manager's risk horizon. The payout mechanism can also be adjusted to reflect the manager's specific needs, such as targeting a particular currency allocation within the portfolio.

Cross-Rate Derivatives

Cross-rate derivatives are designed to manage exchange rate risks directly between two foreign currencies, bypassing the portfolio manager's domestic currency. These derivatives are particularly valuable for global portfolios in asset management, including investments denominated in multiple foreign currencies. Their relevance lies in mitigating currency mismatches within portfolios, preserving returns, and enabling efficient currency risk management in diversified investment strategies.

Asset managers often employ cross-rate forwards to lock in exchange rates between two foreign currencies for a specified future date. These contracts are essential when managing expected cash flows or portfolio rebalancing involving two non-domestic currencies. For example, a European asset manager investing in Japanese equities might use a EUR/JPY forward contract to hedge the currency risk between euros and yen, ensuring the portfolio's value is protected against adverse exchange rate movements. Consider for example that the EUR/JPY is trading at a level of say, 150. The movement of the EUR/JPY to the level of say 170 represents a yen weakness and euro strength. In other words, the yen will depreciate against the euro and the portfolio will suffer losses. Movements to levels of say, 120 represents a yen strength and euro weakness. The economic rationale of the derivative is that the portfolio manager enters a long forward at the strike of 150 which should provide protection of the portfolio against yen weakness. The pricing of the forward considers the interest rate differential between the euro and the yen. Suppose that the portfolio has exposure in both US dollar-denominated and Japanese yen-denominated bonds. The portfolio manager might use cross-rate derivatives. Extending the previous example, the portfolio manager might use a forward contract on the USD/JPY currency pair to hedge the potential depreciation of the JPY to a level of say 170 and thus mitigate the negative impact of the JPY-depreciation against the USD-denominated bonds. The cross-rate forward assures that the portfolio exposure is hedged without implementing hedge instruments involving the base currency of the portfolio which is EUR in this case.

Cross-rate options provide additional flexibility by granting the right, but not the obligation, to exchange one foreign currency for another at a specified rate. This flexibility benefits asset managers seeking to hedge or speculate on currency movements without committing to a fixed rate. For example, a USD fund manager investing in both Australian and British markets could use a GBP/AUD option to hedge cross-currency risk while retaining upside potential from favorable exchange rate fluctuations.

Cross-rate swaps, meanwhile, are essential tools for long-term currency risk management in asset management. These instruments involve the exchange of cash flows in two foreign currencies, allowing asset managers to more structurally align their portfolio's income and liabilities. For instance, a USD asset manager with euro-denominated liabilities and yen-denominated income streams from European and Japanese bond investments might use a EUR/JPY swap to internally balance off cash flows and reduce currency exposure within the portfolio.

The valuation and pricing of cross-rate derivatives are critical for asset management applications. These instruments are often valued based on the spot exchange rates and interest rate differentials between the two currencies involved. For instance, arbitrage relationships such as covered interest parity ensure that the pricing of cross-rate forwards is consistent with the underlying market conditions. An asset manager could use these pricing dynamics to identify cost-effective hedging opportunities and improve the portfolio's overall risk-adjusted return.

Cross-rate derivatives are particularly useful in asset management strategies that involve global diversification. By hedging direct exposures between foreign currencies, these instruments allow asset managers to focus on generating alpha from investment decisions rather than being hindered by unmanaged currency risks. For example, in a global multi-asset portfolio, cross-rate forwards or swaps could be used to optimize the portfolio's currency exposures without over-relying on domestic currency hedges, thereby enhancing overall performance.

Contracting Over-The-Counter FX Derivatives

The process by which a portfolio manager or trader contracts with a third party, typically a bank or financial institution, to create an OTC FX derivative is structured and collaborative. It involves negotiating the terms of the derivative, formalizing the agreement, adhering to collateral and margin requirements, and addressing termination provisions. Due to the customizable nature of OTC FX derivatives, this process is highly tailored to the specific needs of the portfolio manager, enabling effective currency risk management or speculative opportunities.

The process begins with the portfolio manager identifying the need for an OTC FX derivative. This need often arises to hedge currency exposure in a global portfolio, optimize returns, or execute a specific trading strategy. The portfolio manager then engages a counterparty, such as an investment bank, to initiate negotiations. During this stage, the parties discuss the specific parameters of the derivative, including the underlying currency pair, the notional amount reflecting the volume of currency exposure, the tenor or maturity date of the contract, and the type of derivative to be created (i.e., forward, swap, or option). Pricing terms, such as the strike price, premium (if applicable), and settlement terms, are also determined, ensuring that the derivative aligns with the portfolio manager's objectives. This negotiation stage is crucial in tailoring the contract to meet the unique requirements of the portfolio.

Once the negotiation is complete, the contract terms are formalized in a legal agreement, typically governed by an International Swaps and Derivatives Association (ISDA) Master Agreement. The Master Agreement is bilaterally negotiated between each customer and the bank. The ISDA template is the industry standard for definitions, documentation, and the legal framework for these Master Agreements. This document outlines the rights and responsibilities of each party, ensuring clarity and legal uniformity. The agreement specifies the settlement terms, including whether the derivative will be physically settled through the exchange of currencies or cash-settled based on the exchange rate differential. The valuation methodology for the derivative is detailed, defining how its value will be calculated under varying market conditions. The contract also includes provisions for collateral and margin requirements and termination clauses that define the conditions under which the agreement can be terminated prematurely. There is a small minority of currency forwards that are traded without a Master Agreement, where bespoke conditions exist. Such transactions are documented on short-form confirmations or long-form confirmations as needed.

Following the 2007–2008 global financial crisis, there was a strong push to mitigate counterparty risks associated with bilateral transactions. This resulted in a reform program spearheaded by the Basel Committee on Banking Supervision (BCBS), which introduced margining requirements. These requirements have since become a standard practice in the FX OTC derivatives market, aiming to reduce counterparty credit risk by mandating the posting of both initial and variation margin as collateral.

Margin requirements are crucial in managing credit risk in OTC FX derivatives. As with other derivatives, two types of margin are typically involved: the initial margin, which is collateral posted at the start of the contract to cover potential future exposures, and the variation margin, which is periodically adjusted based on market movements to reflect the current value of the derivative. The specific terms of margin requirements are laid out in a Credit Support Annex (CSA), a supplementary document to the ISDA agreement. The CSA outlines the minimum exposure thresholds at which margin must be posted, the types of assets acceptable as collateral, and the discounts, or haircuts, applied to these assets to account for market risk. These measures ensure that potential losses are mitigated, reducing the risk of default by either party.

The above-mentioned ISDA/CSA form an important part of any derivative pricing. Any OTC derivative would likely have four pricing components.

The first is the market prevailing FX rate which is the closest equivalent to the traded level in the interbank market. Second component would be a collateral adjustment, to account for variations in the CSA arrangements with the customer. A CSA arrangement can have variations in currency, thresholds, and frequency of collateral posting, all of which impact the pricing. Third component is the counterparty risk, calculated as CVA (credit valuation adjustment). Simply put, this is driven by the relative credit-worthiness of the customer, as well as tenor and cashflow frequencies of the underlying derivative. The fourth component is the capital impact of the derivative on the bank's balance sheet and the return that the bank is required to generate on the capital consumption. In summary, any FX Forward, Swap, or Option would have a contracted FX Rate with a customer which would include not only the market FX forward rate, but also the above-mentioned associated components. Any market practitioner, as a result, needs to be well-versed in these components and factors impacting them, to manage FX risks in their portfolio efficiently.

Termination provisions are a key aspect of the contract, addressing situations where the agreement needs to be ended before its scheduled maturity. Termination can occur by mutual agreement between the parties, often to unwind a hedge or adjust to new market conditions. It may also occur due to a default or breach of contract, such as a failure to post the required margin or deliver payments. In some cases, external market events, such as force majeure or significant disruptions, may also trigger early termination. When a contract is terminated, the agreement specifies the procedure for calculating settlement amounts, typically based on the mark-to-market value of the derivative at the time of termination. The ISDA Master Agreement provides standardized methods for resolving disputes and calculating termination payments, ensuring a fair and efficient process.

FX derivative transactions are increasingly conducted electronically, particularly for the most liquid currencies and product types, such as spot, forwards, swaps, and vanilla options. Electronic platforms allow market participants to access pricing from multiple banks in a single venue, promoting better pricing and execution efficiency. Many of the largest "aggregator platforms" are now non-bank entities, such as CME and Bloomberg, which provide comprehensive services, including price discovery, liquidity access, and pre-and post-transaction analytics. Additionally, non-bank financial institutions have become significant intermediaries in the FX market, complementing and, in some cases, competing directly with large banks across various areas of the market.

Many large portfolio managers actively employ **algorithmic trading**[3] to execute sizable FX transactions with the goal of minimizing costs, reducing market impact, and maximizing execution efficiency. The use of algorithms has grown significantly in recent years, offering a variety of strategies, from straightforward approaches like volume-weighted average price (VWAP) to more advanced, highly customized solutions. However, for more exotic derivatives or tailored solutions, the market remains predominantly reliant on **voice execution**,[4] where prices are bilaterally negotiated between the transacting parties.

Summary

Foreign exchange (FX) derivatives offer diverse instruments for managing currency exposure, controlling FX risk, and taking advantage of currency movements in a globalized market. This chapter has explored various FX derivative products, from foundational tools like forwards, futures, options, and swaps to more complex instruments like exotic and cross-rate derivatives. Each of these products serves distinct purposes, providing flexibility and targeted solutions for corporations, financial institutions, investors, and even speculators seeking exposure to currency fluctuations or protection from currency risk.

Currency forwards are often chosen for their simplicity and customization. They provide a direct means to lock in exchange rates for future transactions tailored to specific needs regarding notional amounts, maturity, and currency pairs. Exotic FX derivatives, including range forwards, barrier options, and currency baskets, are designed to meet specific hedging or investment objectives that standard products may not cover. These tailored instruments allow firms to address unique or complex exposures with precision, albeit with added complexity and lower liquidity. Cross-rate derivatives, similarly, serve an essential role for participants with indirect currency exposures by providing a way to manage relationships between foreign currencies without involving the domestic currency. Cross-rate forwards, futures, and

---

[3] Algorithmic trading, also known as algo trading or automated trading, involves using computer programs or algorithms to execute trades automatically based on predefined parameters such as price, volume, timing, or other market data.

[4] Voice execution refers to the process of conducting trades or transactions through direct communication between two parties, typically via phone calls or other verbal communication channels, rather than through electronic or automated trading platforms. It involves manual, real-time negotiation of prices and terms between the buyer and seller (or their representatives), making it more personalized and flexible. This method is commonly used for less liquid or more complex financial products, such as exotic FX derivatives.

options enable companies and investors to strategically handle multi-currency portfolios, balance indirect risks, and pursue speculative opportunities in global FX markets.

Market participants must consider practical factors such as liquidity, cost, and counterparty risk when selecting and utilizing these FX derivatives. Liquidity, especially for exotic or cross-rate derivatives, can vary greatly, impacting the ease of entering or exiting positions. Costs, including premiums, margin requirements, and collateral obligations, should be assessed based on the level of protection or exposure the derivative offers. Counterparty risk, while mitigated in exchange-traded products, remains a consideration for OTC contracts, where careful selection of counterparties and use of collateral agreements are common practices.

5

Volatility Derivatives

Kari Vatanen

Exchange-traded volatility derivatives are financial instruments whose value is derived from the volatility of an underlying asset or market index. They are standardized contracts and publicly traded on regulated exchanges, which makes them transparent, liquid, and accessible to a broad range of investors, from institutional traders to retail participants.

Volatility derivatives enable investors to hedge or speculate on future volatility without taking a position on the actual price movements of the underlying asset from which the volatility is derived. Institutional investors commonly use volatility derivatives to hedge against large market drawdowns since volatility tends to rise when equity markets decline. Traders and hedge funds also use these instruments to speculate on future changes in market volatility, whether they expect an increase or decrease in volatility.

Exchange-traded volatility derivatives are standardized contracts, meaning that the expiration dates, contract sizes, and strike prices are fixed in advance. Standardization provides transparency and liquidity by making contracts more accessible for trade and comparison across different markets. Data on prices, volumes, and open interest for exchange-traded volatility derivatives are publicly available in real-time, and the presence of market makers contributes to narrower bid-ask spreads, which reduces trading costs. Most exchange-traded volatility derivatives are cash-settled, meaning there is no

K. Vatanen (✉)
Elo Mutual Pension Insurance Company, Espoo, Finland
e-mail: kari.vatanen@elo.fi

F. J. Fabozzi and M. de Jong (eds.), *Derivatives Applications in Asset Management*,
https://doi.org/10.1007/978-3-031-86354-7_5

physical delivery of an asset at expiration. Instead, contracts are settled in cash based on the final value of the underlying index.

In addition to their applications for hedging and speculation, these instruments enable investors to employ advanced trading strategies that capitalize on unique features of the volatility term structure. The VIX carry strategy, for example, systematically sells short-dated VIX futures to benefit from the roll yield, albeit with significant risks during volatility spikes. Complementing this, the curve carry strategy combines short positions in short-dated futures with long positions in longer-dated futures to reduce risk and balance returns. These strategies demonstrate how volatility derivatives can be used not only for risk management but also for generating returns in sophisticated investment frameworks.

Overview of Exchange-Traded Volatility Derivatives

The most common volatility indices used as underlying assets for volatility derivatives are the Chicago Board Options Exchange (CBOE) Volatility Index (VIX) and the Euro Stoxx 50 Volatility Index (VSTOXX). In addition, volatility derivatives are tied to other stock indices, individual stocks, and Treasury bond volatility. Volatility indices are not themselves investable, but they represent the implied volatility estimated from options prices, reflecting the market's assessment of future volatility. They serve as indicators of the market's expectations regarding price fluctuations in the underlying assets.

The CBOE Volatility Index or VIX Index, introduced in 1993, is the world's most widely followed measure of investor sentiment and expected equity market risk. The VIX is often called the *market's fear gauge* as it spikes during market uncertainty, stress, or economic turbulence and falls when markets are calm and stable. The VIX Index is calculated based on the prices of S&P 500 Index options, and it represents the market's expectation of future volatility over the next 30 days. The VIX uses both call and put options on the S&P 500 Index, and it considers a wide range of strike prices to capture a comprehensive measure of the implied volatility of the options expiring over the next 30 days. Since the VIX index is based on the implied volatilities of options, it includes a *volatility risk premium*, i.e., the values of the VIX index tend to be higher than the realized historical volatility.

Similarly, the Euro Stoxx 50 Volatility Index (VSTOXX) is designed to reflect investor sentiment and overall economic uncertainty by measuring the 30-day implied volatility of the Eurozone equity market. The VSTOXX is based on options prices for the Euro Stoxx 50 index, which includes 50 of the largest blue-chip stocks from 11 Eurozone countries. It reacts essentially to European political and economic developments and to decisions of the European Central Bank, though global events can also affect it.

The VIX index possesses a few stylized characteristics. First, it is mean reverting around a long-term average. While the VIX typically spikes during market turmoil, it tends to fall back as conditions normalize. Exhibit 5.1 shows the evolution of the VIX Index from 1990 to October 2024.

Second, the distribution of VIX index levels is positively skewed. The VIX may remain moderately below its long-term average for extended periods but can rise to multiples of its average or median levels. Additionally, it is lower-bounded, as volatility cannot reach negative values. Exhibit 5.2 illustrates the distribution of the VIX index levels. The median VIX index level is 17.6. A VIX level below 15 indicates a stable and calm market where significant price swings are not expected in the near future. The VIX level over 20 signals rising market uncertainty, and levels above 30 generally occur during extreme market downturns, crises, or sharp corrections.

Third, the VIX has an inverse relationship with equity markets. It tends to rise when stock prices fall, and then decline when stock markets start to recover. The correlation between the VIX and the S&P 500 Index is remarkably negative (−0.75), which is why volatility derivatives are used to hedge against large equity market drawdowns. Exhibit 5.3 shows the negative correlation between weekly changes in VIX index levels and S&P 500 index returns.

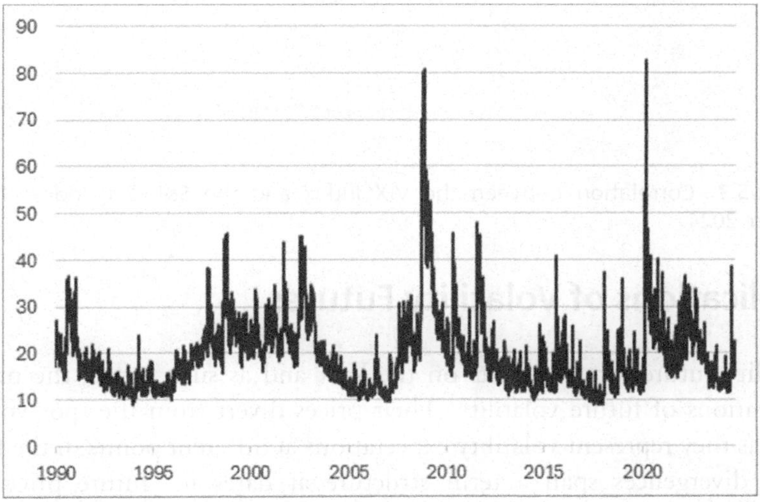

Exhibit 5.1 VIX index: 1990 to October 2024

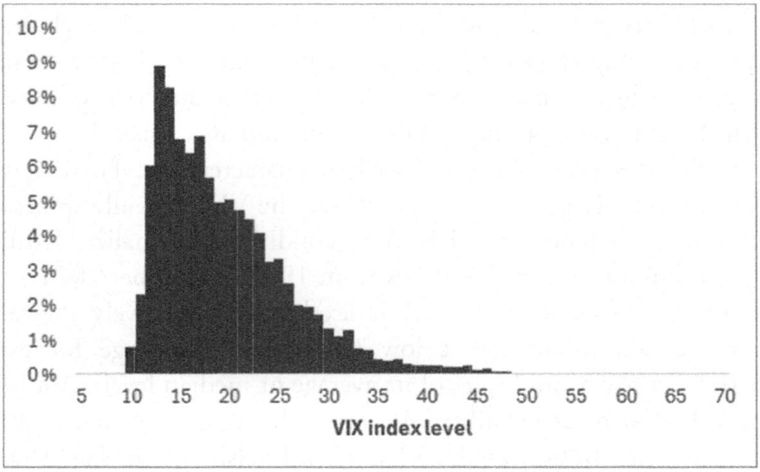

Exhibit 5.2 The distribution of the VIX index levels: 1990 to October 2024

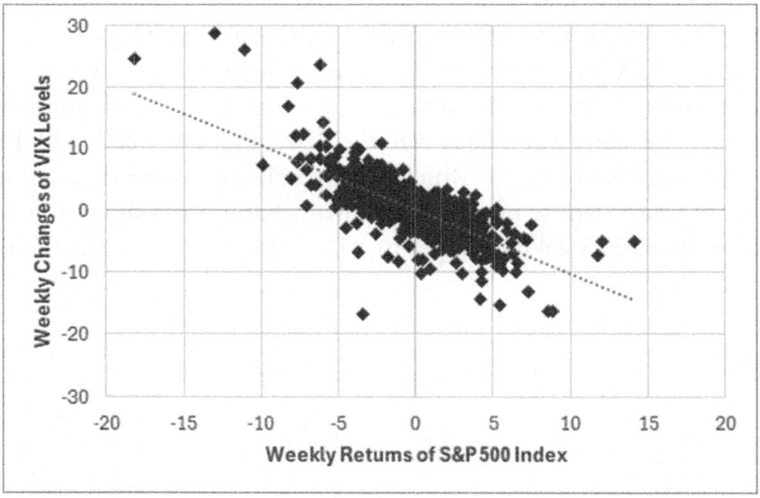

Exhibit 5.3 Correlation between the VIX Index and the S&P 500 Index: 1990 to October 2024

Applications of Volatility Futures

Volatility futures are contracts on the VIX and as such reflect the market's expectations of future volatility. Their prices divert from the spot volatility index as they represent volatility expectations at different points in the future. These divergences span a term structure at dates for future prices with varying expiration.

Investors use volatility futures to hedge against market risk or speculate on future changes in market volatility. Volatility futures typically hedge an equity portfolio against specific event risks, such as elections, the publication of economic reports, or geopolitical developments that could trigger market volatility spikes. Speculators can use volatility futures both to express their views on changes in market volatility and to take advantage of the volatility term structure, profiting from the pricing dynamics of different expiration dates across various futures contracts.

VIX futures were launched in March 2004 for trading on the CBOE Futures Exchange. They are traded electronically with a $1,000 multiplier and are regulated by the US Commodity Futures Trading Commission. The underlying value of one VIX futures contract is the multiplier of $1,000 times the future price. For example, if the price of the nearest maturing VIX future is 18.5, the value of one futures contract is $18,500.

The expiration and cash settlement for VIX futures usually occur on Wednesday mornings in the United States. The final settlement date for a monthly contract is on the Wednesday that falls 30 days before the third Friday of the following calendar month, which is when the underlying S&P 500 options, from which the VIX index is derived, will expire. The settlement of VIX futures contracts results in the delivery of a cash settlement amount on the business day immediately following the final settlement date. The cash settlement amount on the final settlement date is the final mark-to-market amount based on the final settlement value of the VIX futures, based on the final settlement value of VIX futures multiplied by $1,000.

VIX futures are listed across multiple expiration months, up to 9 months from the spot date. In addition, the exchange may list up to six near-term weekly expirations for trading. Futures contracts with different expiration dates have different prices, and together, they span a price curve known as the futures term structure of the volatility index. When the futures term structure is ascending, it is said to be *in contango*, meaning that futures contracts with longer time until expiration have higher prices than those with shorter time to expiration. Conversely, when the futures term structure is descending, it is referred to as *backwardation*, where longer-term futures have lower prices than short-term futures.

Exhibit 5.4 illustrates the term structure of the VIX futures at two separate points in time. Over the long term, the term structure has been in contango approximately 80% of the time. Backwardation generally occurs when the VIX index rises significantly above its long-term average.

During significant spikes in the VIX index (as in the case of backwardation in Exhibit 5.4), holding near-term VIX futures produces gains, but these were

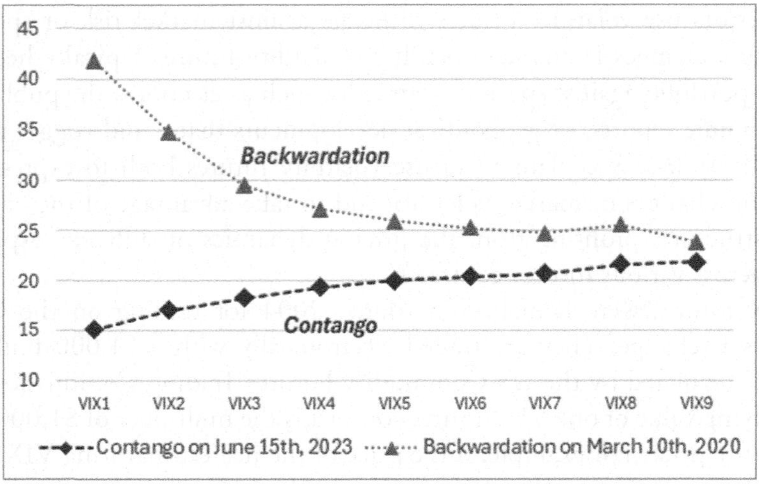

Exhibit 5.4 Term structure of the VIX futures

smaller than the moves in the VIX index itself. Longer-dated VIX futures saw even smaller increases. The sensitivity, called the volatility beta, of VIX futures prices relative to the changes of the VIX index is always below one and decreases as the maturity of the futures contracts increases. It means that the prices of futures move less than the VIX index and the movement diminishes as the maturity lengthens. This is because volatility tends to be mean reverting, and futures reflect volatility expectations for the 30 days following their expiration date rather than for the next 30 days.

The VIX futures term structure is usually in contango, which means that the prices of shorter-term futures contracts are generally lower than those of longer-term ones. As futures contracts approach expiration, their prices tend to decline over time. This implies that VIX futures have a negative roll yield or carry cost, and the returns on VIX futures are likely to be negative if the VIX index remains unchanged.

Exhibit 5.5 shows the performance of rolling futures indices for VIX futures expiring in the nearest, second nearest, and third nearest months. These indices replicate hypothetical VIX futures portfolios that reflect VIX expectations one, two, and three months out by rolling futures continuously from one contract to the following one. The index values increase when volatility rises, but the rolling cost is significant across all indices. The average annual rolling cost for the first-month VIX futures contracts has been approximately −50% compared to the notional value of the futures, while for the second- and third-month contracts, it has been around −30% and −20%, respectively.

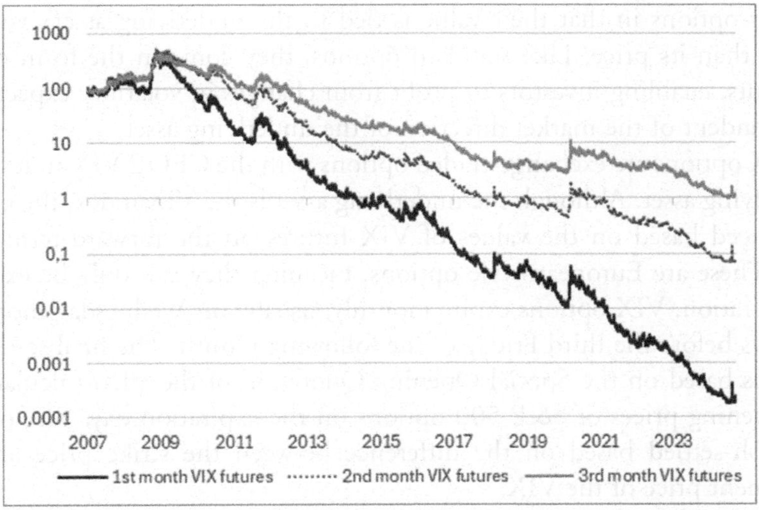

Exhibit 5.5 Rolling futures indices for the VIX futures expiring next, 2nd, and 3rd month in a logarithmic scale

Due to the substantial rolling costs, investors and portfolio managers typically use VIX futures as temporary tactical hedges against potential equity market drawdowns. Long VIX futures positions are taken ahead of specific events, such as elections, Central Bank meetings, or geopolitical developments, to hedge against the risk of significant equity market drops, which often cause spikes in volatility. Investors can reduce the negative rolling cost of VIX futures hedges by moving to longer-dated contracts along the term structure. However, the effectiveness of these hedges decreases as futures further along the curve respond less to changes in volatility.

Speculators and traders aim to profit from increases in volatility and its eventual reversion to the mean. Therefore, they take long and short positions in VIX futures based on their market expectations. The strategy of systematically selling VIX futures to benefit from the high rolling costs within the VIX futures term structure is even more common.

Applications of Volatility Options

Volatility options are financial derivatives that give investors the right to speculate on or hedge against changes in the volatility of an underlying asset without being obligated to do so. These options are ideal for those who expect a significant price movement for an asset but are uncertain whether the movement will be upward or downward. Volatility options differ from regular options in that their value is tied to the underlying asset's volatility rather than its price. Like standard options, they come in the form of calls and puts, enabling investors to profit from changes in volatility expectations independent of the market direction of the underlying asset.

VIX options are exchange-traded options with the CBOE VIX Index as the underlying asset. Although the underlying asset is the VIX index, the options are priced based on the values of VIX futures on the forward-term structure. These are European-style options, meaning they can only be exercised at expiration. VIX options expire monthly, usually on Wednesday mornings, 30 days before the third Friday of the following month. The final settlement value is based on the Special Opening Quotation of the VIX, calculated on the opening prices of S&P 500 options on the expiration day. VIX options are cash-settled based on the difference between the strike price and the settlement price of the VIX.

VIX options were launched in February 2006 with a $100 multiplier. They are regulated by the US SEC and traded electronically on an open outcry trading floor at CBOE. The value of one VIX option contract is the multiplier $100 × the option price, and the notional value of the option contract is the multiplier $100 × the strike VIX Index level. VIX options have historically ranked among the most actively traded options in the U.S. markets, often holding the second-highest traded option after S&P 500 Index options.

VSTOXX options are similar to VIX options, but the underlying asset is the VSTOXX future instead of the VSTOXX index. VSTOXX options are American-style, meaning that an option can be exercised up to the end of the Post-Trading Full Period on any exchange day during the option's lifetime. These options involve physical delivery at settlement, but since the underlying future expires on the same day, it is settled in cash. VSTOXX options are traded on the Eurex Exchange and are quoted in euros with a €100 multiplier. They tend to have lower liquidity compared to VIX options, as the Eurozone volatility market is smaller in scale than the U.S. market.

Volatility options are generally used to hedge an investment portfolio against spikes in market volatility, to speculate on changes in future volatility before and after specific events, or to benefit from the negative roll yield of the volatility term structure. VIX options are often used as a macroeconomic hedge against rising uncertainty in financial markets. Since the VIX index typically rises when stock prices fall, investors can buy VIX call options to protect their portfolios. If equity markets drop sharply, causing increased volatility, the value of VIX call options rises, offsetting some of the losses in their equity holdings. VIX options are an efficient hedge against rare but extreme tail-risk events like the 2008 financial crisis or the COVID-19 market crash in March 2020. A sharp rise in volatility can make VIX options highly profitable, providing protection when traditional assets fall.

The main disadvantage of VIX options is their high cost of carry. VIX options are priced based on the term structure of VIX futures. Since the VIX futures term structure is typically in contango, the underlying price tends to decline over time, reducing the moneyness of call options. For example, suppose an investor buys an at-the-money call option with four months until expiration. In that case, it will gradually become more out-of-the-money as time passes, assuming the VIX index remains unchanged. Additionally, the implied volatility of the VIX index, which is used to price VIX options, is relatively high, leading to significant time decay. These two factors combined make VIX options an expensive hedging tool over the long term.

Exhibit 5.6 shows the term structure of VIX futures in contango, starting from the VIX Index spot price and extending to the ninth-month future contract. If an investor enters into an at-the-money call option with a strike price of 22 and a four-month expiration, the strike price will remain far from the underlying futures prices as they approach the VIX spot price. Meanwhile, an out-of-the-money put option with a strike price of 18 becomes in-the-money over time as the futures prices decline toward the VIX spot price.

Instead of relying on expensive hedging or speculating on expected changes in volatility, an investor could benefit from the negative roll yield of the VIX

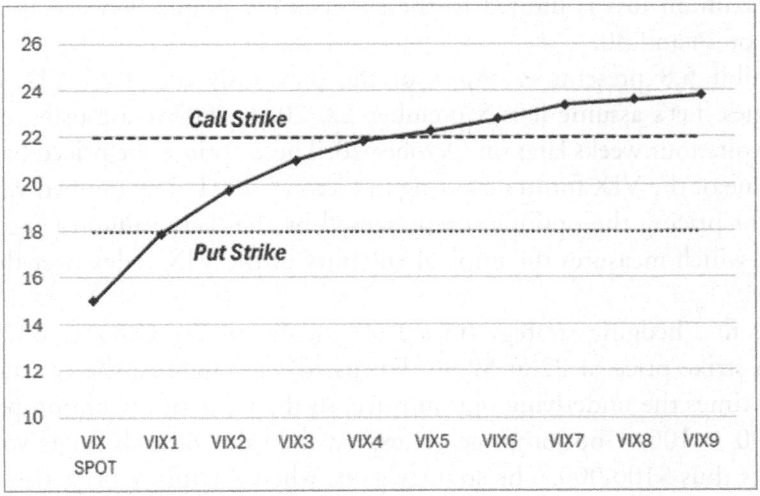

Exhibit 5.6 The normal term structure of the VIX futures with option strike levels at 18 and 22

term structure. A risk-averse strategy would be to systematically buy out-of-the-money put options each month, expecting them to expire in-the-money. An example of this is shown in Exhibit 5.6, where an out-of-the-money put option with a strike price of 18 and a four-month expiration turns in-the-money before expiry.

A more risk-tolerant approach is to systematically sell at-the-money call options, collect the premium, and anticipate that the options will expire worthless. This strategy benefits from both the negative roll yield of the VIX term structure and the *volatility-of-volatility risk premium* embedded in VIX options. The volatility-of-volatility risk premium refers to the implied volatility of options whose underlying asset is volatility. While the return from this strategy can be high, it is also exposed to significant and deep drawdowns if the VIX index suddenly spikes to high levels. A more risk-conscious strategy is to sell out-of-the-money call spreads each month. This allows the investor to collect the premium and expect the call spread to expire worthless most of the time but with limited and predictable risk in the event of a sudden VIX spike.

Exhibit 5.7 illustrates the term structure of VIX futures and the range of a call spread with strike prices of 24 and 30. In this example, an investor sells a call option with a strike price of 24 and hedges the upside risk by buying a call option with a strike price of 30. The investor collects a positive premium since the sold option with the lower strike price is more expensive than the bought option with the higher strike price. If the VIX index rises, the maximum loss is limited to the six volatility points between the strike prices of 24 and 30.

Exhibit 5.8 presents examples of the previously described VIX option strategies. Let's assume it is September 22, 2021, and we are using options that expire four weeks later on October 20. These options are priced based on the value of the VIX futures expiring in October 2021. The implied volatility used for pricing the options is represented by the daily values of the VVIX Index, which measures the implied volatility of the VIX Index over the next 30 days.

The first hedging strategy buys 1,000 at-the-money October 2021 calls with a strike price of 22 at $2.90. For listed VIX options, the contract size is 100 times the underlying option price, so the value of the option position is 1,000 × 100 × option price. At expiry, the value of each single volatility point is thus $100,000. The strategy gains when the future price rises above the strike price, but it quickly starts to lose value as the future price declines. In this example, the option expires worthless when the settlement price is below the strike price.

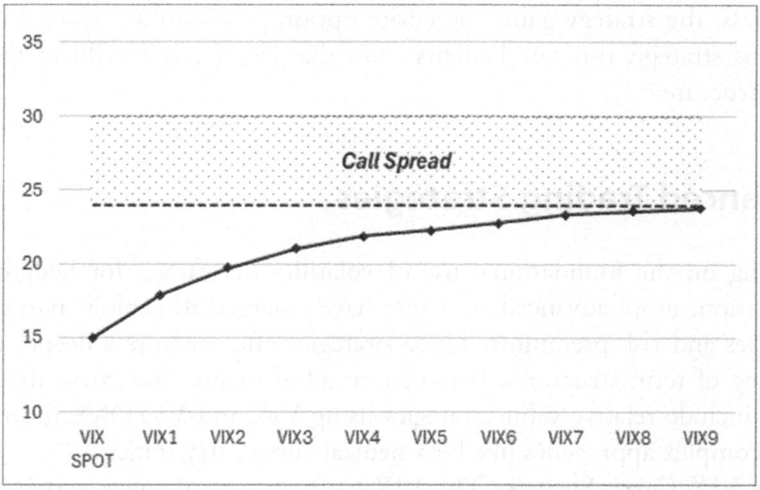

Exhibit 5.7 The term structure of the VIX futures and the range of a call spread with option strike prices of 24 and 30

Date	VIX Oct 21 Future	VIX Oct21 Call 22	1000 bought 22 Calls	VIX Oct 21 Put 18	1000 bought 18 Puts	VIX Oct21 Call 24	VIX Oct21 Call 30	Call Spread 24/30	1000 sold 24/30 CS
9/22/2021	22,10	2,90	290 000	1,04	104 000	2,13	0,78	1,35	-135 000
9/29/2021	22,99	3,08	308 000	0,63	63 000	2,19	0,71	1,48	-148 000
10/6/2021	21,22	1,50	150 000	0,55	55 000	0,87	0,13	0,74	-74 000
10/13/2021	19,15	0,30	30 000	0,63	63 000	0,09	0,00	0,09	-9 000
10/20/2021	15,35	0,00	0	2,65	265 000	0,00	0,00	0,00	0
Profit/loss			-290 000		161 000				135 000

Exhibit 5.8 Examples of VIX option strategies

The second strategy buys 1,000 out-of-the-money October 2021 puts with a strike price of 18 at \$1.04. Again, the value of the option position is 1,000 × 100 × the option price, and the value of each single volatility point is \$100,000 at expiry. The options strategy loses its time value if the future remains unchanged but gains when the future price falls below the strike price. In this example, the put option expires deep in the money with the settlement value of \$2.65. The profit of the strategy is 1,000 × 100 × (\$2.65 – \$1.04) = \$161,000. The strategy benefits from the negative roll yield of the VIX term structure.

The third strategy sells 1,000 out-of-the-money call spreads to collect the option premium. The call spread consists of buying 24 calls and selling 30 calls, creating a range of six volatility points from a strike price of 24 to a strike price of 30. The value of the 1,000 sold call spreads is -1,000 × 100 × the call spread price, which is the difference between the prices of the 24 calls and 30 calls. The strategy collects an option premium of \$135,000 by selling 1000 call spreads at \$1.35. Since the out-of-the-money options expire worthless, the strategy gains the entire option premium at expiry. Like the previous strategy, this one benefits from the negative roll yield of the VIX term structure.

Advanced Trading Strategies

Building on the foundational use of volatility derivatives for hedging and speculation, more advanced strategies have emerged to exploit market inefficiencies and risk premiums. These strategies often require a deeper understanding of term structures, beta-neutral adjustments, and curve dynamics. These include relative value strategies using VIX and VSTOXX futures and more complex approaches like beta-neutral curve carry trades.

The VIX Carry Strategy The VIX carry strategy involves systematically selling VIX futures to harvest the carry embedded in the term structure. This requires selling the nearest first-month futures contracts and rolling them into the subsequent contracts before expiration. The front end of the term structure typically offers the highest carry due to the curve's steepness in contango markets. Capitalizing on this roll-down effect provides a systematic approach to capturing consistent returns.

While this strategy can generate substantial returns in calm markets, it carries significant risks during periods of heightened volatility. The value of short-dated VIX futures can triple or even quadruple during market stress, such as financial crises or sudden geopolitical shocks. Investors must, therefore, be prepared to endure potential drawdowns of three to four times the notional amount of the futures contracts. Despite these risks, the mean-reverting nature of volatility often facilitates a rapid recovery, making the strategy appealing to those with a long-term investment horizon.

Numerical Analysis of the VIX Carry Strategy

Exhibit 5.9 depicts its historical performance to help assess the VIX carry strategy's practical implications. The first six columns of the exhibit display the weekly prices of VIX futures expiring between August and December 2021. Settlement prices at expiration are marked with the symbol *). The VIX Aug21 future is the front-month contract at the beginning of the sample period, and after its expiration, the VIX Sep21 contract becomes the new front-month contract.

An example of the VIX carry strategy is presented in the seventh column of Exhibit 5.9:

Initial Trade: Selling 100 contracts of the first-month Aug21 VIX futures contracts on July 28th at $20.11.

Roll Mechanism: As the contracts approach expiration, they are repurchased back a day before expiry on August 17th at $17.58, and a new position is opened in the subsequent Sep21 contract at $20.17. Similarly, the Sep21 contracts are bought back at $19.72 a day before expiry on September 14th, and Oct21 contracts are sold at $21.56. The Oct21 contracts expire at $15.35 on October 20th.

Profit Calculation: The roll generates a gain of 1,000 × ($20.11 – $17.58) = $2530 per contract for the expiring Aug21 position as the future was sold at $20.11 and repurchased back at $17.58. Similarly, a gain for the expiring Sep21 position is 1,000 × ($20.17 – $19.72) = $450 per contract. The Oct21 has generated a gain of 1,000 × ($21.56 – $15.35) = $6210 per contact at the expiry as the contract was sold at $21.56 and it expires at $15.35 The total profit of the VIX carry strategy is the sum of the gains of consecutive contracts: $2530 + $450 + $6210 = $9190 per contract at the expiry.

Key findings from the analysis are:

Average Annual Return: The strategy delivers an average annual gross return of approximately 50% in stable market conditions, driven by the predictable roll yield.

Drawdowns: Extreme volatility events, such as those in March 2020, resulted in losses of up to $2 million for a notional position of $500,000, reflecting the importance of robust risk management.

Recovery: Following such drawdowns, the mean-reversion of volatility enabled the strategy to recover losses within 6–12 months, showcasing its resilience when applied with disciplined execution.

Exhibit 5.9 provides a detailed breakdown of the strategy's profitability, and Exhibit 5.10 shows the strategy's performance across varying market regimes, including its cumulative returns and periods of drawdown.

The VIX carry strategy exemplifies how investors can leverage the term structure of volatility futures to extract returns. However, its success depends on disciplined execution, a thorough understanding of volatility dynamics, and robust risk management practices. By pairing this strategy with well-considered hedging mechanisms or incorporating it into a diversified portfolio, investors can further mitigate risks while optimizing returns. This strategy also serves as a foundation for more sophisticated approaches, such as the curve carry strategy, which integrates additional hedging elements to balance risk and return effectively.

The curve carry strategy builds on the principles of the VIX carry strategy, adding a hedging component to reduce risk while retaining exposure to the term structure's roll yield. By combining short positions in short-dated futures with long positions in longer-dated futures, this strategy aims to balance risk and reward more effectively. It is particularly useful in mitigating the severe drawdowns that can occur during volatility spikes.

Mechanism of the Curve Carry Strategy

The curve carry strategy involves selling short-dated futures contracts with the highest carry and buying longer-dated futures contracts that are less sensitive to short-term volatility shocks. This structure enables the investor to profit from the roll yield of the short-dated contracts while using the long-dated contracts as a hedge.

A dollar-neutral curve carry strategy ensures that the vega notional values of the sold and purchased futures are identical. For example, if $1 million in short-dated futures contracts is sold, $1 million in long-dated futures contracts is purchased. This balances the dollar-denominated impact of price changes on both the short and long positions, minimizing directional risk while maintaining exposure to the term structure dynamics.

Beta-Neutral Adjustment

In practice, futures contracts with different maturities have varying sensitivities to changes in the VIX index, often measured by beta. To achieve a truly market-neutral position, a beta-neutral curve carry strategy adjusts the number of longer-dated contracts purchased relative to the beta of the short-dated contracts.

For instance, if the beta of the third-month futures contract relative to the first-month futures contract is 0.67, then approximately 1.5 third-month contracts are required to neutralize the market risk of one sold first-month contract with a beta of 1. This adjustment ensures that the hedge is calibrated to the differential sensitivities of the futures contracts, providing more robust protection against volatility spikes.

Numerical Illustration

Exhibit 5.9 provides a detailed analysis of the curve carry strategy's performance.

The delta-neutral carry strategy, shown in the tenth column in Exhibit 5.9, sells 100 front-month futures contracts and hedges the risk by buying 100 third-month contracts. On July 28th, the strategy sells 100 Aug21 contracts and buys 100 Oct21 futures contracts, so the net position in VIX futures contracts is zero. The long hedging leg is rolled over a day before the short front-month Aug21 contract expires, executed by selling 100 Oct21 contracts at $21.68 and buying 100 Nov21 contracts at $22.31. A similar roll is executed a day before the short Sep21 contract expires by selling the Nov21 contracts and buying Dec21 contracts. The cumulative profit/loss of the delta-neutral carry strategy is the sum of the profit/loss from the 100 sold first-month contracts and the 100 bought third-month contracts, as presented in the seventh and eighth columns.

The performance of the beta-neutral carry strategy is shown in the eleventh column of Exhibit 5.9. This strategy is identical to the delta-neutral carry strategy, except that the long hedging leg buys 150 third-month futures contracts instead of 100. The cumulative profit/loss of the beta-neutral carry strategy is the sum of the profit/loss from the 100 sold first-month contracts and the 150 bought third-month contracts, as presented in the seventh and ninth columns. The beta-neutral carry strategy provides better protection against changes in the VIX index, but the larger number of hedging contracts reduces the strategy's return.

The example shows two things. First, with respect to price dynamics, selling 100 short-dated futures contracts at $20.11 and buying 100 longer-dated futures contracts at $22.63 creates an initial spread of $2.52 per contract. Over the life of the trade, the short-dated contracts decline to $17.58 by the rolling date, generating a gain of $2530 per contract, while the longer-dated contracts decline to $21.68, resulting in a loss of $950 per contract. The spread between the contracts widens to $4.10, resulting in a net profit of $1580 per contract.

Second, with respect to risk mitigation, during volatility spikes, the long position in longer-dated futures offsets losses in the short position, significantly reducing overall drawdowns. For example, in March 2020, when short-dated futures spiked by 400%, the long-dated contracts rose by 200%, mitigating the net loss by half. In the beta-neutral version, the loss mitigation was even 75%.

	VIX Aug21 Future	VIX Sep21 Future	VIX Oct21 Future	VIX Nov21 Future	VIX Dec21 Future	100 Sold 1st Future Contracts	100 Bought 3rd Future Contracts	150 Bought 3rd Future Contracts	Delta Neutral Carry	Beta Neutral Carry
7/28/2021	20.11	21.80	22.63	22.93	23.01	0	0	0	0	0
8/4/2021	19.85	21.76	22.79	23.20	23.30	25,950	16,650	24,975	42,600	50,925
8/11/2021	17.44	19.73	21.22	21.93	22.36	266,460	-141,230	-211,845	125,230	54,615
8/17/2021	17.58	20.17	21.68	22.31	22.62	253,020	-94,380	-141,570	158,640	111,450
8/18/2021	18.58*)	21.71	22.93	23.34	23.43	99,410	8,010	12,015	107,420	111,425
8/25/2021		19.23	21.29	22.20	22.50	346,710	-105,790	-158,685	240,920	188,025
9/1/2021		18.08	20.45	21.51	21.97	461,940	-174,990	-262,485	286,950	199,455
9/8/2021		18.77	20.93	22.19	22.61	393,410	-106,130	-159,195	287,280	234,215
9/14/2021		19.72	21.56	22.67	23.31	298,490	-58,550	-87,825	239,940	210,665
9/15/2021		19.79*)	20.84	22.30	23.04	370,750	-84,830	-127,245	285,920	243,505
9/22/2021			22.10	23.13	23.54	244,600	-35,290	-52,935	209,310	191,665
9/29/2021			22.99	23.78	24.01	155,420	12,120	18,180	167,540	173,600
10/6/2021			21.22	22.66	23.27	332,830	-62,470	-93,705	270,360	239,125
10/13/2021			19.15	21.11	22.13	539,480	-176,480	-264,720	363,000	274,760
10/20/2021			15.35*)	19.32	21.05	919,540	-284,050	-426,075	635,490	493,465

* Settlement prices. Calculations made by the author.

Exhibit 5.9 Examples of VIX Carry strategies

Advantages and Limitations

The curve carry strategy provides several advantages. First, the long-dated futures act as a hedge, reducing exposure to extreme volatility spikes. Second, the strategy's risk-adjusted returns are typically higher due to the reduced volatility of outcomes (i.e., higher Sharpe ratio). Third, by incorporating different parts of the term structure, the strategy diversifies sources of return.

However, the hedge diminishes the overall roll yield compared to an unhedged VIX carry strategy. Achieving a beta-neutral position requires accurate estimates of beta and frequent rebalancing. Finally, longer-dated futures may be less liquid, leading to higher transaction costs.

Exhibit 5.10 presents the simulated performance of the VIX carry strategies, both with and without hedging via longer-dated futures. The number of sold futures contracts is assumed equivalent across all strategies and remains constant over time. The unhedged, short-dated VIX carry strategy delivers the highest returns over time but exhibits the greatest risk and largest drawdowns. Adding a hedging component by purchasing third-month contracts (dollar-neutral curve carry strategy) reduces drawdowns but diminishes long-term returns. The beta-neutral strategy has the lowest drawdown risk, but the carry can remain negative for extended periods. However, hedging improves the strategies' Sharpe ratio, as the risk reduction outpaces the decline in long-term carry returns.

There is yet another way to hedge the VIX carry strategy, namely by using European VSTOXX futures. VSTOXX futures are, in many ways, very similar to VIX futures, except that they are based on the European VSTOXX volatility index. They are traded on the Eurex Exchange and quoted in euros with a €100 multiplier, meaning that the underlying value

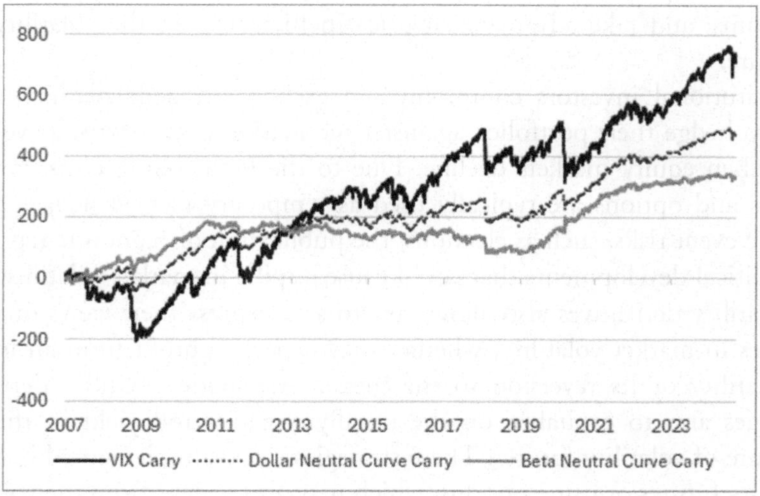

Exhibit 5.10 Simulated performance of the VIX carry strategies with a constant number of futures contracts

of one VSTOXX futures contract is calculated as €100 multiplied by the futures price. Although VSTOXX futures reflect the volatility expectations of the European equity market, they are highly correlated with US-based VIX futures, particularly during global market selloffs.

The VIX and VSTOXX futures can be used together to construct hedged relative value carry trades. Carry can be harvested with a short leg on the term structure with the steeper contango, and the long hedging leg can be set to the flatter volatility curve. Another way to construct a relative value strategy between VIX and VSTOXX futures is to measure the divergence of the two futures curves from their long-term average and expect them to revert to their average level over time, and as such seize a pricing equilibrium opportunity across markets. However, a trader should remember that the VIX futures are quoted in USD with a multiplier of $1,000 and the VSTOXX futures in euros with a multiplier of €100.

Summary

Exchange-traded volatility derivatives provide investors and traders with a flexible and effective way to hedge against market risks or speculate on changes in market volatility. Whether through futures or options, these derivatives enable investors to manage portfolio risk, capture volatility risk premiums, and take advantage of price inefficiencies in the volatility term structure.

Institutional investors commonly use exchange-traded volatility derivatives to hedge their portfolios against large market drawdowns, as volatility rises when equity markets decline. Due to the high rolling costs, volatility futures and options are typically used as temporary tactical hedges against specific event risks, such as elections, the publication of economic reports, or geopolitical developments that could cause a spike in market volatility.

Volatility derivatives also allow investors to express their views on future changes in market volatility, whether they expect to profit from an increase in volatility or its reversion to the mean. Systematic volatility derivatives strategies aim to capitalize on the usually negative roll yield in the term structure of volatility futures. These strategies can be implemented by selling volatility futures or using options, which may also benefit from the volatility-of-volatility risk premium.

Advanced strategies, such as the VIX and curve carry strategies, offer more sophisticated methods for seizing performance opportunities. The VIX carry strategy exploits the high roll yield at the front end of the term structure but carries significant drawdown risks during volatility spikes. The curve carry strategy mitigates these risks by incorporating longer-dated futures as a hedge, providing a more balanced risk-return profile. These approaches underscore the potential of volatility derivatives as risk management tools and return-generating instruments in a diversified portfolio.

Using these derivatives requires a thorough understanding of volatility dynamics, term structures, and the associated risks. With disciplined execution and proper risk management, they can provide valuable opportunities for both institutional and retail investors.

6

Managing Volatility and Capturing Returns Through Derivatives

Alexander Rudin, Pravesh Kumar, and Shubham Upadhyay

In asset management, derivatives play a crucial role beyond traditional hedging applications. Their versatility, high liquidity, and cash efficiency make them powerful tools for active management, where they can be employed for precise exposure control and targeted return enhancement. This chapter provides two advanced uses of derivatives in quantitative portfolio management, illustrating how they can support both exposure management and absolute return strategies.

Specifically, we examine two primary applications of derivatives outside of hedging. The first application, exposure management, uses a Target Volatility Strategy (TVS) to maintain consistent risk levels by dynamically adjusting exposure to risky assets based on observed market volatility. TVS is widely utilized across investment products—from variable annuities to risk-parity portfolios—where managing volatility at a target level is essential. In our example, equity futures are used to create notional leverage within this strategy, allowing managers to efficiently achieve their desired risk exposure without tying up large amounts of capital.

The second application is an absolute return strategy based on commodity carry, which leverages the differences in futures contract prices along the commodity term structure to capture returns. By holding futures contracts in markets exhibiting favorable carry conditions (e.g., backwardation), managers can potentially capture positive returns independently from the general

A. Rudin (✉) · P. Kumar · S. Upadhyay
State Street Global Advisors, Boston, MA, USA
e-mail: Alexander_Rudin@ssga.com

F. J. Fabozzi and M. de Jong (eds.), *Derivatives Applications in Asset Management*,
https://doi.org/10.1007/978-3-031-86354-7_6

market direction. This section provides an in-depth look at constructing a long/short commodity portfolio, using carry signals derived from futures prices to dynamically allocate positions based on market conditions.

Together, these two applications showcase how derivatives extend the capabilities of active managers. They offer the opportunity for precise positioning, efficient capital deployment, and enhanced return potential across different asset classes. Each application in this chapter demonstrates the strategic flexibility that derivatives provide, highlighting their role in modern quantitative portfolio management.

In the following sections, we will describe each strategy in detail, discussing the theoretical foundations, practical implementation choices, and empirical results that underscore the advantages of using derivatives in portfolio construction. By contrasting a derivatives-free approach with a derivatives-overlay version in our TVS example, we illustrate the incremental benefits derivatives can bring to a strategy. Similarly, we detail the data, signals, and construction methods essential to building a robust carry strategy in commodities, underscoring the value derivatives add to absolute return pursuits. Through these applications, the chapter emphasizes the strategic role of derivatives in enhancing both risk-adjusted returns and absolute return potential.

Target Volatility Strategy

Target Volatility Strategy (TVS) refers to an investment approach that involves scaling position sizes of risky assets in an inverse proportion to their observed volatility. The approach is utilized in many insurance and asset management pockets. One example is variable annuities, whereby equity returns are passed to investors after conforming to a target volatility level. Another example is a risk-parity product category, popular among wealth managers. The risk budget is allocated across many asset classes and then controlled at a target level within each class, often by utilizing a version of the TVS. The alternative investment industry is also among adopters. For example, managed futures managers often size market positions inversely proportionally to their estimated volatility.

Theoretical Foundations

The classical volatility management approach to equity investing involves taking positions X_t in the amount that is inversely proportional to the estimated market volatility:

$$X_t = \frac{\sigma_{\text{target}}}{\sigma_t}, \tag{6.1}$$

where

σ_{target} is "target" volatility
σ_t is observed (estimated) volatility at time t.

Since target volatility is a manager-provided constant while market volatility tends to be persistent over time, such an approach creates a return stream that is much more stable than a passive buy-and-hold equity investing strategy (see Exhibit 6.1). In the absence of constraints on the position size X_t, the Eq. (6.1) creates a return stream with a volatility close to the target σ_{target}, hence the strategy name.

In the last decade, academic researchers have followed practitioners and paid considerable attention to target volatility strategies. It wasn't the property of such strategies to deliver outcomes with well-controlled risk characteristics that interested academics—that aspect was trivial. It was TVS's apparent ability to deliver that outcome with a visible improvement in risk-adjusted returns (see Exhibit 6.2). The improvement is very robust to the choice of the volatility estimation model and survives inclusion of realistic transaction costs and other practical constraints.

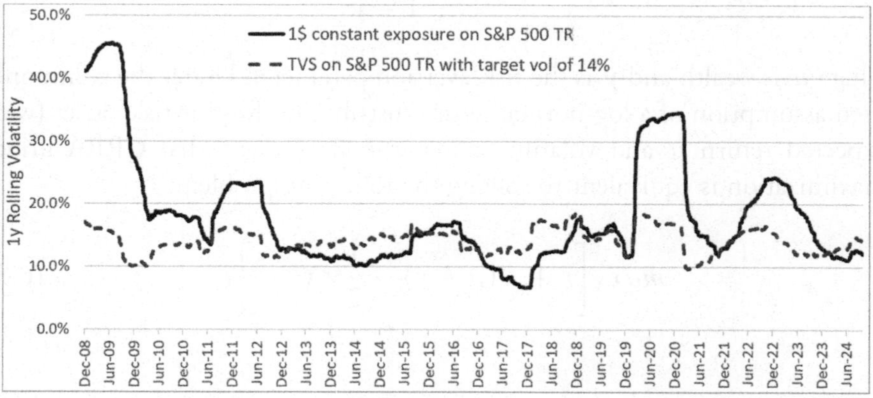

Exhibit 6.1 Rolling daily volatility of the S&P 500 TR vs that of TVS on S&P 500 TR that targets 14% annualized volatility

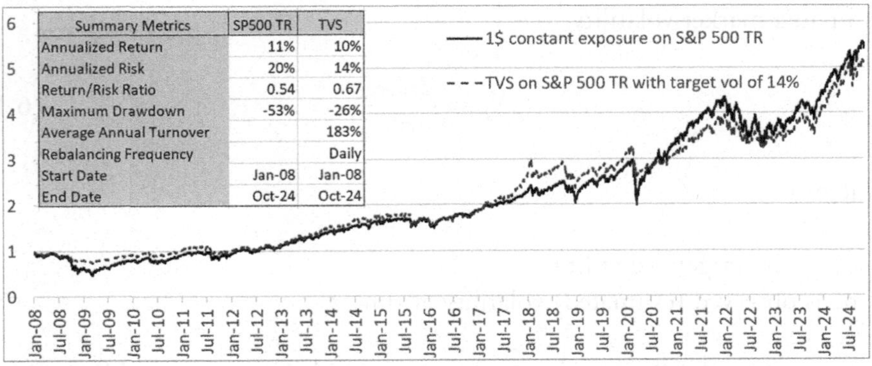

Exhibit 6.2 Cumulative performance of a TVS approach applied to S&P 500 TR; target volatility is 14%

What stands behind this improvement in the risk-adjusted returns? To answer that, we need an appropriate framework.[1] It starts with a question: If we could invest in a risky asset, what would be the right position size for that asset as a function of time?

We could consider this question through the lens of wealth management. We could construct a utility function for an investor that balances benefits (wealth increases) with risks (uncertainty of those increases) and find an optimum. The Constant Relative Risk Aversion (CRRA) utility function is commonly used for such problems, which has the following form:

$$\mathrm{U(W)} = \frac{W^{1-\gamma} - 1}{1-\gamma}, \tag{6.2}$$

where w is wealth and γ is the risk-aversion parameter. Under the commonly used assumption of a log-normal return distribution for our risky asset (with expected return μ and volatility σ), it can be shown[2] that CRRA utility maximization is equivalent to solving the following problem:

$$max_X\left[r + X(\mu - r) - \frac{1}{2}\gamma X^2\sigma^2\right]T, \tag{6.3}$$

[1] For some helpful background, see for example, Campbell R. Harvey, Edward Hoyle, Russell Korgaonkar, Sandy Rattray, Matthew Sargaison, and Otto Van Hemert, "The Impact of Volatility Targeting," *Journal of Portfolio Management*, 45(1), 2018, 14–33, and Alan Moreira and Tyler Muir, "Volatility Managed Portfolios", NBER working paper 22208 (2017).

[2] See, for example, Jamil Baz and Helen Guo, "An Asset Allocation Primer: Connecting Markowitz, Kelly, and Risk Parity," PIMCO Quantitative Research, 2017.

where r is the risk-free rate, and T is the time horizon (we removed subscript t for brevity).

Our problem boils down to mean-variance optimization for the position size X, which can be easily solved. Optimal positioning is proportional to the expected return of our risky asset divided by the square of its expected volatility:

$$X_t = \frac{\mu_t - r}{\gamma \sigma_t^2} = \frac{S_t}{\gamma \sigma_t} \tag{6.4}$$

where $S_t = \frac{\mu_t - r}{\sigma_t}$ is the expected Sharpe ratio of the risky asset. This well-known solution is often called a "Merton's fraction."

Comparing Eqs. (6.4) and (6.1), we see that TVS is theoretically optimal (matches Merton's fraction) if the Sharpe ratio of our risky asset does not change over time.

This is an important observation. We see target volatility implementation as a more appropriate implementation of the Merton fraction's inspired position sizing than other target risk varieties, such as Muir-Moreira's target variance approach.[3] The existence of risk premia—investors demanding higher returns for experiencing higher risks—is foundational to finance.[4] The target variance strategy of Muir and Moreira implies that expected returns do not change (or change slowly) even when risks change materially. The target volatility strategy, however, implies that the ratio of expected returns to risks does not change (or changes slowly). The latter assumption is consistent with the existence of risk premia in the markets and the principles behind the foundational Capital Asset Pricing Model.

Equations (6.1) and (6.4) together give a practical interpretation of the target volatility choice. Target volatility is simply a ratio of the expected (constant) Sharpe ratio of the risky assets and the investor's risk-aversion coefficient.

Implementation Options

Say we would like to implement a target volatility strategy on a major equity market such as the S&P 500. We could choose to use derivatives from the very beginning, but we find it instructive to first illustrate the benefits

[3] See Moreira, Alan and Tyler Muir. 2017. "Volatility Managed Portfolios," NBER working paper 22208.

[4] See, for example, Aswath Damodaran, "Equity Risk Premiums (ERP): Determinants, Estimation, and Implications—The 2024 Edition," https://papers.ssrn.com/sol3/papers.cfm?abstract_id=4751941.

and—more importantly, given the focus of this chapter—limitations of a derivatives-free version of the TVS.

How would we implement a TVS without derivatives? First, we need to choose our investment universe. We would use an S&P 500 index return stream as a "risky asset" and a 1–3 month Treasury bill index return (LD12TRUU Index in Bloomberg) stream as a proxy for risk-free cash. Both could be easily implemented through existing exchange-traded funds (ETFs) or index funds.

Suppose we have $1 of capital. The target volatility approach suggests allocating this capital to a blend of equities and cash, using X_t from Eq. (6.1) as a guide. When market volatility is above target, the recommended position size X_t is below $1 and can be implemented unimpeded, with the rest of our $1 capital going to our cash instrument.

When, however, market volatility subsides below target and recommended position size X_t is above 1, we are facing a challenge. The unavailability of leverage or derivatives effectively caps equity exposure at $1: we cannot implement our target volatility model fully and symmetrically. As our empirical tests will later show, such a lack of ability to over-allocate to a risky asset in low-volatility environment is a severe handicap. Risk-adjusted returns of the Derivatives-Free Target Volatility Strategy (DF TVS) do show some improvement over a simple buy and hold, constant-exposure equity investment strategy, but this advantage erodes for higher levels of the target volatility σ_{target}. As the Results section of this chapter demonstrates, DF TVS is unable to outperform pure equity investments on the absolute return basis over the time period studied.

Let us now imagine that we have S&P 500 futures added to our investment universe. Then when X_t rises above 1, we can use S&P 500 futures to leverage equity exposure and create a much more complete, symmetrical implementation of the TVS. We will name such modification a TVS with a Derivatives Overlay (DO TVS) when describing empirical studies and as a differentiator to the DF TVS.

In the end, we will place the results of both approaches onto an efficient frontier, allowing fair comparisons between the two.

The Data

A TVS requires very little data to implement—only equity and cash returns are needed. However, details matter: Different equity market proxies may have similar volatility but are not the same.

Equity ETFs and index funds generally reflect the most complete picture of equity returns,[5] including dividend income alongside equity price appreciation. We will use S&P 500 TR index returns (SPXT Index in Bloomberg) as a source for those return figures. We use 1–3-month Treasury bill total returns as a proxy for our cash instruments. For S&P 500 Futures, we use generic SP500 futures stitched at expiration from Bloomberg (Exhibit 6.3).[6]

Date	Index			Daily Returns		
	S&P 500 TR	1-3m Tbill Index	S&P 500 Futures	S&P 500 TR	1-3m Tbill Index	S&P 500 Futures
10/1/2024	12490.87	225.98	5759.75			
10/2/2024	12493.35	226.02	5760.25	0.02%	0.02%	0.01%
10/3/2024	12472.39	226.05	5749.50	-0.17%	0.01%	-0.19%
10/4/2024	12586.91	226.12	5800.00	0.92%	0.03%	0.88%
10/7/2024	12466.41	226.15	5744.75	-0.96%	0.01%	-0.95%
10/8/2024	12587.25	226.18	5800.50	0.97%	0.01%	0.97%
10/9/2024	12677.16	226.21	5841.25	0.71%	0.01%	0.70%
10/10/2024	12652.84	226.23	5829.00	-0.19%	0.01%	-0.21%
10/11/2024	12729.52	226.35	5859.75	0.61%	0.05%	0.53%
10/14/2024	12827.63	226.35	5908.25	0.77%	0.00%	0.83%
10/15/2024	12731.10	226.38	5862.75	-0.75%	0.01%	-0.77%
10/16/2024	12790.84	226.41	5887.00	0.47%	0.01%	0.41%
10/17/2024	12788.78	226.44	5887.00	-0.02%	0.01%	0.00%
10/18/2024	12840.30	226.52	5906.00	0.40%	0.04%	0.32%
10/21/2024	12817.39	226.55	5896.25	-0.18%	0.01%	-0.17%
10/22/2024	12811.36	226.58	5892.50	-0.05%	0.01%	-0.06%
10/23/2024	12693.82	226.61	5837.75	-0.92%	0.01%	-0.93%
10/24/2024	12721.05	226.64	5849.00	0.21%	0.01%	0.19%
10/25/2024	12717.34	226.73	5846.00	-0.03%	0.04%	-0.05%
10/28/2024	12751.22	226.76	5861.50	0.27%	0.01%	0.27%
10/29/2024	12771.80	226.79	5871.00	0.16%	0.01%	0.16%
10/30/2024	12729.73	226.82	5852.00	-0.33%	0.01%	-0.32%
10/31/2024	12493.74	226.85	5738.50	-1.85%	0.01%	-1.94%

Exhibit 6.3 A snapshot of data for October 2024

[5] For simplicity, we ignore fees charged by managers of those funds.

[6] We will ignore complexities related to the fact that technically "buy and hold" is impossible when futures contracts are involved. Futures contracts have specific expiration (every month or quarter) and if an investor wishes to maintain a particular exposure, periodic rolling to the next contract is required. There is a lot of flexibility in how an investor can execute this process. An investor can roll all at once a certain number of days prior to expiration… or roll gradually over some period. Possibilities are endless but principally trivial. Data providers such as Bloomberg long ago created functionality to generate "stitched" time series of futures contracts under user-defined rules, which is very helpful for modeling purposes. An investor can set up a preferred method in Bloomberg; we chose one for our empirical studies to roll and stitch contracts immediately after the last trade date.

The Signal

As Eq. (6.1) implies, implementing a Target Volatility Strategy starts with picking a method for volatility estimation. Studies have shown[7] that essentially all reasonable volatility estimation methods lead to very similar outcomes for this particular strategy, so for our study, we will pick a straightforward volatility estimation methodology that is equivalent to the exponentially weighted variance:

$$\sigma_t^2 = \lambda\sigma_{t-1}^2 + (1-\lambda)r_t^2. \tag{6.5}$$

where

λ is the decay factor ($0 < \lambda < 1$),
r_t is the daily return, and
σ_t is the volatility at time t.

We use λ of 0.98 for the remainder of this sub-section; it corresponds to a medium-term volatility smoothing (2–3 months half-life).

Also, to be realistic in our strategy development, we would introduce transaction costs of 5bps, a minimal trade size of 2.5%, and an implementation delay of 1 day into our TVS simulation.

Exhibit 6.4 illustrates our volatility and signal calculation. For example, to evaluate volatility figure as of October 2, 2024, we do the following:

- We first get the daily volatility (we denote it V) as of Oct 1, 2024. It is $V = 0.1405/\text{sqrt}(252) = 0.00885$
- Then we calculate variance for October 2, 2024, using Eq. (6.9) as Variance $= 0.98 \times V^2 + (1 - 0.98) \times r^2$, where r is the realized return for October 2. Substituting $V = 0.0085$ and $r = 0.0002$, we get Variance $= 0.0000767$
- Finally, we calculate volatility on October 2 and annualize it as $V = \text{sqrt(Variance)} \times \text{sqrt}(250) = 13.9\%$

Each day, the theoretical position is estimated as the ratio of target volatility to realized volatility as per Eq. (6.1). Since we have an implementation delay of one day, we lag our positions by 1. We also apply a minimum trade size constraint of 2.5%.

---

[7] See, for example, Harvey et al., "The Impact of Volatility Targeting" or Robert Benson, Timothy Furbush, and Christopher Goolgasian, "Targeting Volatility: A Tail Risk Solution When Investors Behave Badly," *Journal of Index Investing*, 4(4), 2014, 4, 88–101.

Date	Daily Returns	EWM Vol (annualized)	Theoretical Position	Theoretical Position Lagged
10/1/2024	-0.93%	14.05%	99.7%	99.8%
10/2/2024	0.02%	13.90%	100.7%	99.7%
10/3/2024	-0.17%	13.77%	101.7%	100.7%
10/4/2024	0.92%	13.79%	101.6%	101.7%
10/7/2024	-0.96%	13.82%	101.3%	101.6%
10/8/2024	0.97%	13.85%	101.1%	101.3%
10/9/2024	0.71%	13.80%	101.4%	101.1%
10/10/2024	-0.19%	13.67%	102.4%	101.4%
10/11/2024	0.61%	13.60%	102.9%	102.4%
10/14/2024	0.77%	13.57%	103.1%	102.9%
10/15/2024	-0.75%	13.54%	103.4%	103.1%
10/16/2024	0.47%	13.45%	104.1%	103.4%
10/17/2024	-0.02%	13.31%	105.2%	104.1%
10/18/2024	0.40%	13.21%	106.0%	105.2%
10/21/2024	-0.18%	13.08%	107.0%	106.0%
10/22/2024	-0.05%	12.95%	108.1%	107.0%
10/23/2024	-0.92%	12.99%	107.8%	108.1%
10/24/2024	0.21%	12.87%	108.8%	107.8%
10/25/2024	-0.03%	12.74%	109.9%	108.8%
10/28/2024	0.27%	12.62%	110.9%	109.9%
10/29/2024	0.16%	12.50%	112.0%	110.9%
10/30/2024	-0.33%	12.40%	112.9%	112.0%
10/31/2024	-1.85%	12.97%	107.9%	112.9%

Exhibit 6.4 Signal calculation

Results

Here, we present the results of applying a target volatility strategy—with and without derivatives overlay—to the S&P 500 equity market. We will always compare those results with a natural benchmark corresponding to a constant-exposure blend of equities and cash.

The three panels of Exhibit 6.5 present results for both the DF TVS and DO TVS versions of the strategy. A few observations come to mind. First, the results are generally supportive of TVS. Risk-adjusted returns achieved through both versions of the target volatility approach are superior[8] to a constant-exposure equity/cash blend over a broad range of volatilities. Second, the efficient frontier for the derivatives-free, constrained version of

[8] Exhibit 5 covers 16 years. Results over shorter periods show some level of variability but are still supportive of the TVS approach, with perhaps the exception of 2020–2021 period. The latter was characterized by an extreme level of government support for risk assets making most dynamic management decisions detrimental to portfolio outcomes.

the strategy (DF TVS) saturates at higher levels of risk. This is a direct result of a lack of leverage access. Constrained target volatility strategy struggled to compete with pure equity investments, especially in the post-COVID period of rallying equity markets, even if it outperformed pure equities on adjusted and risk-adjusted basis. Finally, adding derivatives overlay cures this problem. The efficient frontier for DO TVS shows the added value of the approach and its ability to outperform pure equities not only on the risk-adjusted but also on the absolute return basis.

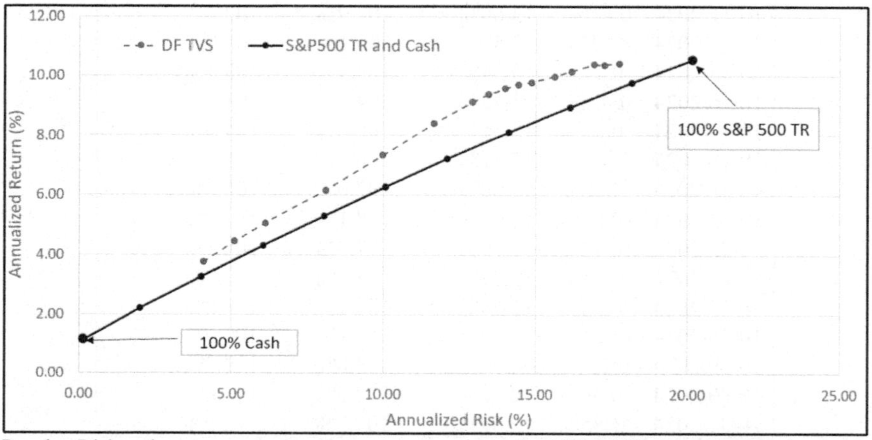

Panel a: Risk and return comparison between a constant mix of S&P 500 and cash on one end and TVS applied to the same market. Derivatives are disallowed. January 2008 to October 2024.

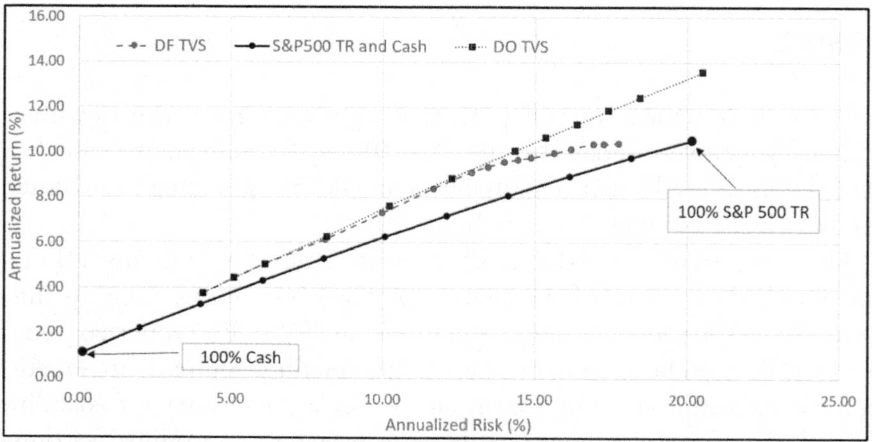

Panel b. The same as panel a, but with the addition of a TVS strategy with derivatives overlay. January 2008 to October 2024.

Exhibit 6.5 Outcomes of the TVS, with (DO) and without (DF) derivatives overlay

DF TVS				DO TVS		
Target Volatility (%)	Annualized Return	Annualized Risk	Return/Risk Ratio	Annualized Return	Annualized Risk	Return/Risk Ratio
4	3.76	4.09	0.92	3.76	4.09	0.92
5	4.45	5.11	0.87	4.45	5.11	0.87
6	5.07	6.12	0.83	5.07	6.12	0.83
8	6.16	8.11	0.76	6.29	8.16	0.77
10	7.33	9.98	0.73	7.64	10.21	0.75
12	8.40	11.66	0.72	8.87	12.27	0.72
14	9.13	12.92	0.71	10.07	14.33	0.70
15	9.37	13.45	0.70	10.67	15.36	0.69
16	9.57	13.99	0.68	11.28	16.38	0.69
17	9.70	14.43	0.67	11.89	17.41	0.68
18	9.78	14.85	0.66	12.46	18.45	0.68
20	9.98	15.64	0.64	13.59	20.51	0.66

Panel c. Data corresponding to panels a and b

Exhibit 6.5 (continued)

Concluding Remarks

We revisited a well-known target volatility approach, re-established its theoretical foundations and empirically observed advantages. Sizing risky assets inversely proportional to their observed volatility not only helps produce a relatively stable return stream in terms of their rolling volatility but also delivers theoretically justified improvements in terms of risk-adjusted returns.

While it is possible to implement a version of TVS without using derivatives, such implementation is suboptimal for medium to high target volatility levels. Lack of access to notional leverage limits the strategy's ability to over-invest in equity markets during low-volatility periods, which tends to be most rewarding. Adding a derivative overlay cures this handicap and improves absolute and risk-adjusted returns.

A Commodity Carry Strategy for Absolute Return

We will use a commodity carry as an example of an absolute return strategy. Commodity carry is the annualized return an investor would experience when holding a commodity futures contract while the spot price remains unchanged. We will illustrate how to calculate it based on future prices. Such return varies materially over time and reflects many factors, from storage costs to supply/demand imbalances.

When the commodities price term structure is upward sloping (called "contango"), carry returns are negative. Conversely, when the term structure is downward sloping (called "backwardation"), carry returns are positive.

"Carry" strategies are generally designed to capture this income, so they tend to go long contracts that happen to be in deep backwardation (positive carry income) at the expense of contracts that are in deep contango (negative carry). Investors building such a strategy need to articulate three key aspects of it:

1. How do they get the right data for signal generation and backtesting of the strategy?
2. How do they construct the carry signal?
3. How do they construct the portfolio itself?

Let's tackle these items one by one.

The Data

As we mentioned before, futures contracts have specific expiration (every month or quarter), and if an investor wishes to maintain exposure to a specific commodity, periodically rolling to the next contract is required. There is a lot of flexibility in how an investor can execute this process. We chose to roll and stitch contracts immediately after the last trade date.

Now that we have decided the structure of the data, an investor must choose specific contracts for the strategy. For this example, we selected 10 commodities that together form 67% of the broad Bloomberg Commodities Index. They include (1) corn, (2) WTI crude oil, (3) Brent crude, (4) gold, (5) copper, (6) aluminum, (7) natural gas, (8) soybeans, (9) silver, and (10) sugar. We needed to download "stitched" data for the next and second-next futures contract for each of those commodities to run our carry strategy.

The Signal

Carry can be defined in several ways. We generate a carry signal as an annualized ratio of prices of the next contract and the second-next contract for the given day. For example, for oil,

$$\text{Carry} = \left(\frac{\text{CL1}}{\text{CL2}}\right)^{12/\text{GAP}} - 1 \tag{6.6}$$

GAP is the difference (in months) in maturity between these two contracts, which usually amounts to one, two, or three months. For CL1 and CL2, the gap is equal to 1.

Exhibit 6.6 shows a short history of first and second oil futures contracts from November 2023. On 11/30/2023 our carry signal would be

$$\text{Carry} = \left(\frac{75.96}{75.05}\right)^{\frac{12}{1}} - 1 = -1.41$$

By design, the values of such signals will differ before and after each futures contract roll. These differences do not reflect some deep economic meaning, and it is advisable to smooth the signal. Since the contracts are mostly rolled

	First-nearby contract	Second-nearby contract
	CL1 Comdty	CL2 Comdty
11/1/2023	80.44	80.10
11/2/2023	82.46	82.16
11/3/2023	80.51	80.23
11/6/2023	80.82	80.60
11/7/2023	77.37	77.21
11/8/2023	75.33	75.31
11/9/2023	75.74	75.75
11/10/2023	77.17	77.15
11/13/2023	78.26	78.19
11/14/2023	78.26	78.17
11/15/2023	76.66	76.79
11/16/2023	72.90	73.09
11/17/2023	75.89	76.04
11/20/2023	77.60	77.83
11/21/2023	77.77	77.92
11/22/2023	77.10	77.25
11/23/2023	77.10	77.25
11/24/2023	75.54	75.77
11/27/2023	74.86	75.09
11/28/2023	76.41	76.59
11/29/2023	77.86	77.99
11/30/2023	75.96	76.05

Exhibit 6.6 Data to support the carry signal calculation

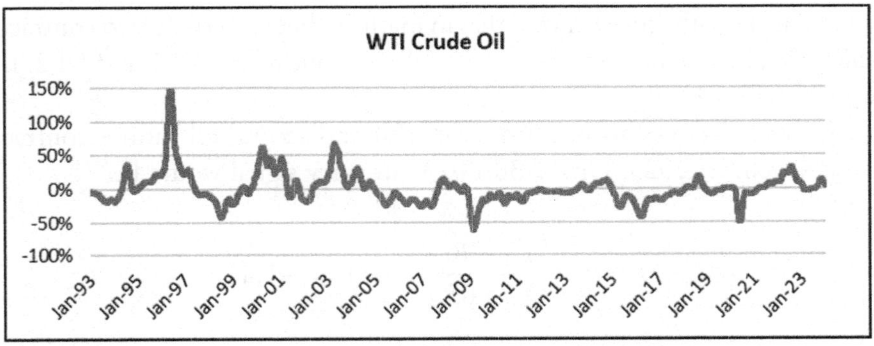

Exhibit 6.7 Historical values of smooth carry for WTI crude oil (1993–2023)

monthly or quarterly, we used the 63 trading days (three-month equivalence) rolling value of Carry as a signal. We refer to it as "Smooth Carry." Exhibit 6.7 shows the history of Smooth Carry for the CL contract.

Portfolio Construction

In constructing a portfolio, we select an approach that is simple but comes with two important characteristics: (1) the portfolio is long/short and approximately dollar neutral, at least over the long term, and (2) the position sizing is risk-aware (lower position sizes for higher volatility assets). The process itself was straightforward:

- Each day, all commodities were ranked based on the Smoothed Carry strength (10th highest rank, 1st lowest rank). Commodities with low ranks (from 1 to 5) were allocated to the "short portfolio," while commodities with high ranks (from 6 to 10) were allocated to the "long portfolio."
- Dollar sizing within such long and short portfolios was chosen to be inversely proportional to 252-day rolling volatility of commodity contracts themselves (we chose ones that are next to expiration, like CL1).

We show this process schematically in Exhibit 6.8.

Let's now walk through the main calculations. We already illustrated how to calculate the Smooth Carry signal for a given commodity. Smooth Carry is always a numerical value and is easy to rank, so the ranking step is trivial. Our volatility calculation methodology involves taking a contract's daily time series (say, CL1) and calculating its standard deviation over a 252-trading day period (1-year equivalence). Final portfolio weights are calculated according to formulas given in Exhibit 6.8, and aim to have a long/short portfolio

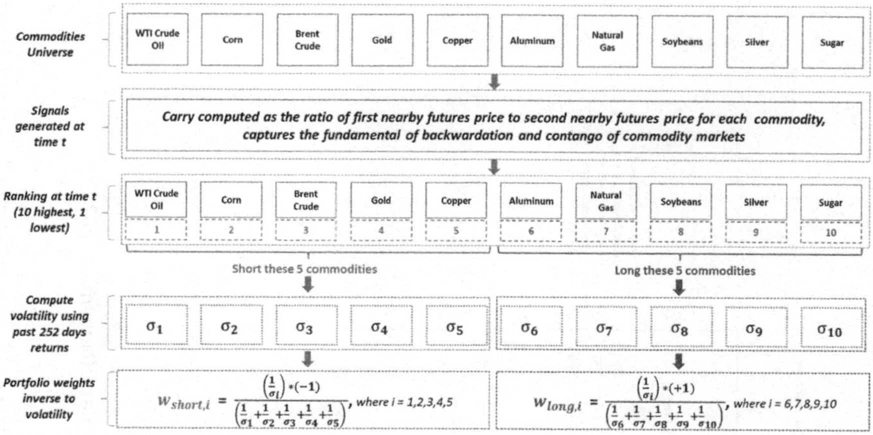

Exhibit 6.8 Portfolio construction process for the active commodity futures carry strategy

that is dollar-neutral overall, allocating capital inversely proportional to the calculated volatility values.

Exhibit 6.9 contains values for Smooth Carry, Rankings, Volatility, and Final Weights for a small subset of data (November 2023) so that an interested reader can verify.

Results

The hypothetical performance of such a strategy (portfolio rebalanced at the end of each month) is shown in Exhibit 6.10. We calculated active returns of the long-short commodities strategy using prices of next contracts as our assets. Notably, our calculation corresponds to unfunded, *excess* returns associated with the strategy. Funding commodity futures requires little cash (exchange margin requirements are usually a tiny fraction of notional exposure), which is one of the key benefits of using derivatives for risk-taking. If we funded the strategy entirely, we would earn cash income in addition to the active futures strategy returns.

As can be seen, our approach succeeded, at least in our illustration, in creating an active commodities strategy with positive returns over a variety of market environments and a reasonable level of turnover. Such a strategy also has low correlation to core asset classes such as equities, bonds, or even long-only commodities themselves and hence may play a role as a diversifier in a broad institutional portfolio.

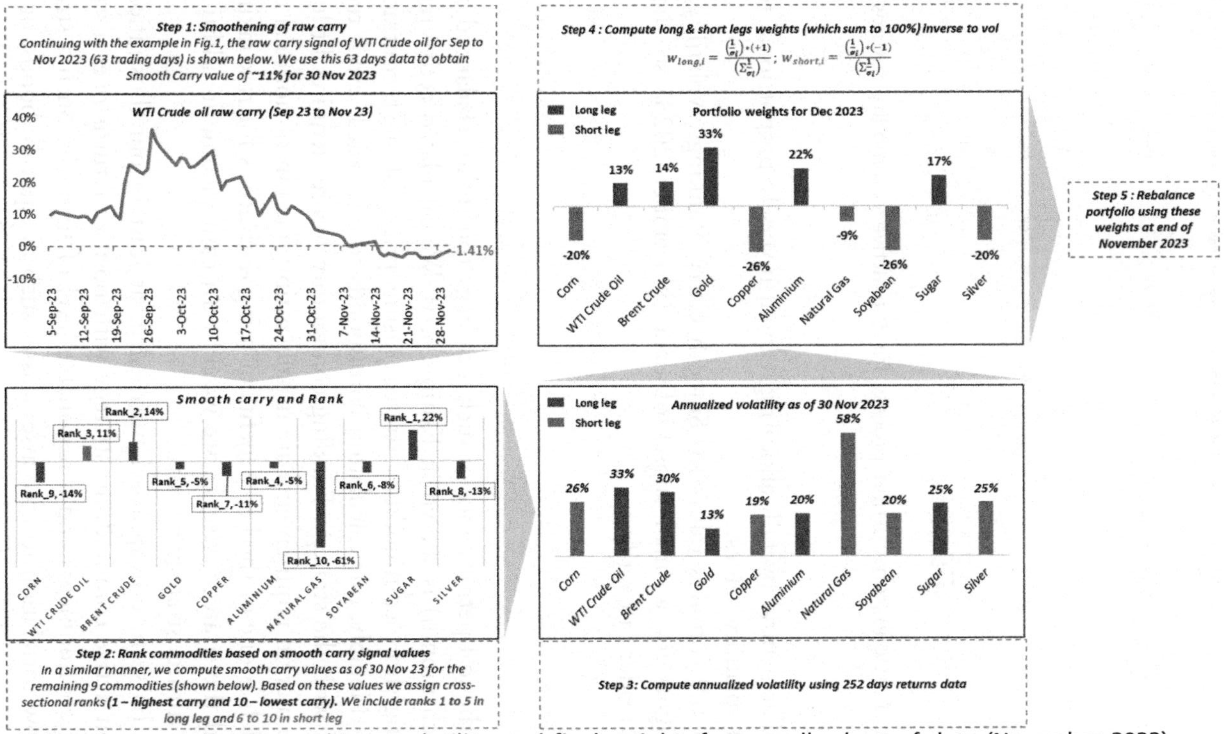

Exhibit 6.9 Values for smooth carry, rankings, volatility, and final weights for a small subset of data (November 2023)

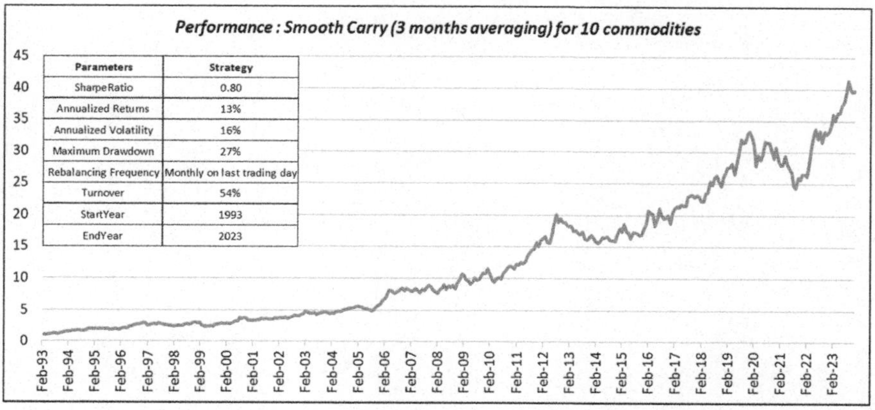

Exhibit 6.10 Active commodities carry strategy hypothetical performance

Summary

This chapter presents advanced applications of derivatives in quantitative portfolio management, focusing on two specific strategies beyond traditional hedging. The first strategy, a Target Volatility Strategy (TVS), aims to manage portfolio risk by dynamically adjusting exposure based on observed market volatility. This approach is used widely in investment products that require consistent risk levels, such as risk-parity portfolios and variable annuities. We demonstrate both a derivatives-free version of TVS, which faces limitations due to lack of leverage, and an enhanced version with a derivatives overlay that uses equity futures to provide notional leverage. This addition enables more precise risk targeting, even in low-volatility environments, and improves risk-adjusted returns.

The second strategy is a commodity carry strategy designed to capture absolute returns by exploiting the term structure of commodity futures. By taking long positions in commodities with favorable carry conditions (typically backwardation markets) and short positions in contango markets, the strategy seeks to generate positive returns independent of market direction. The steps for constructing this strategy, including data selection, signal generation, and risk-aware portfolio construction based on volatility-adjusted position sizes, are provided.

In both applications, derivatives allow for strategic flexibility, efficient capital deployment, and enhanced return potential. Practical illustrations highlight derivatives' value to portfolio management by enabling precise positioning and adaptation to changing market conditions.

7

Using Derivatives When Rebalancing a Multi-Asset Portfolio with Private Investments

Redouane Elkamhi, Jacky S. H. Lee, and Marco Salerno

For multi-asset managers, such as pension funds, professional family offices, and other large institutional investors, managing a diverse portfolio that includes both public and private assets presents unique challenges. The goal is often to achieve a balanced, diversified portfolio that aligns with the institution's long-term investment objectives. However, maintaining this balance can be difficult when private assets, such as private equity, real estate, or infrastructure, are involved in the portfolio, which has become the norm for most institutional investors.

Private market investing differs significantly from public market investing in several key aspects, each contributing to the complexity of portfolio management. Private assets are inherently illiquid. Unlike public equities, which can be bought and sold on exchanges relatively easily, private assets often require long-term commitments, sometimes extending over several

R. Elkamhi
Rotman School of Management, University of Toronto, Toronto, ON, Canada

J. S. H. Lee (✉)
Total Portfolio Group at Healthcare of Ontario Pension Plan (HOOPP), Toronto, ON, Canada
e-mail: jlee5@hoopp.com

M. Salerno
Abu Dhabi Investment Authority, Abu Dhabi, UAE

F. J. Fabozzi and M. de Jong (eds.), *Derivatives Applications in Asset Management*,
https://doi.org/10.1007/978-3-031-86354-7_7

years or even decades. This illiquidity arises from the nature of the assets themselves—private equity investments involve taking significant stakes in companies that are not publicly traded, real estate investments require acquiring and managing physical properties, and infrastructure investments often involve large-scale projects with substantial capital requirements and long-term payback periods.

The process of transacting in private markets is also considerably more complex than in public markets. Acquiring or divesting a private equity stake, for example, involves extensive due diligence, lengthy negotiations, and legal issues, all of which contribute to longer transaction times and higher costs. Similarly, real estate and infrastructure transactions require also the negotiation of terms, which often involves regulatory approvals and compliance with local laws, adding further delays. These factors make it difficult for portfolio managers to quickly adjust private market holdings in response to changing market conditions or shifts in the strategic asset allocation.

Private market investments are thus associated with higher transaction costs and longer investment horizons than their public market counterparts. A private equity investment might involve significant upfront, management, and performance fees, all of which reduce the net returns to investors. Additionally, the returns on private equity investments are generally realized over a longer time horizon, as the value of the investment depends on the successful growth and eventual exit of the portfolio companies, either through a sale, merger, or public offering. Real estate and infrastructure investments, too, require time to mature, as the income generated from these assets often accrues slowly over many years, and the capital appreciation realizes only upon sale.

When investing in private funds, such as those focused on private equity, private credit, real estate, or infrastructure, the timing of capital deployment and returns adds another layer of complexity. These funds often take months or even years to fully deploy the committed capital, as they wait for suitable investment opportunities. Once invested, the timing of distributions to investors is uncertain and typically occurs years into the future, depending on the success and exit strategies of the underlying investments. This unpredictability in both the deployment and distribution phases makes it difficult for portfolio managers to precisely control the allocation of private funds within a multi-asset portfolio. Consequently, this can lead to unintentional over- or under-weighting of private assets relative to the portfolio's strategic asset allocation, i.e., the desired portfolio weights.

Given their illiquid nature and different risk/return profile compared to public assets, private investments can appreciate at a rate that differs significantly from public assets, causing deviations from the portfolio's target allocation. For instance, during a period of strong economic growth, private equity investments might outperform public equities due to their leveraged nature and the operational improvements made by private equity managers. This can result in an overweight position in private equity, increasing the portfolio's overall risk profile and necessitating rebalancing to bring the asset allocation back in line with strategic targets.

Rebalancing within a portfolio is a critical activity that ensures that the portfolio remains aligned with its strategic asset allocation (i.e., the desired long-term weights of the investor). However, rebalancing private assets is particularly difficult due to their illiquidity and the long-term nature of these investments. Even when private equity investments are made through funds, investors have limited control over when capital is deployed or returned. The timing of capital calls and distributions is at the discretion of the fund managers, who decide when to invest in new opportunities and when to exit existing investments. This lack of control can make it challenging for investors to promptly rebalance their private equity holdings, potentially leading to prolonged periods of overweight or underweight positions relative to the target allocation.

In addition to the challenges posed by private market investments, public market investments can complicate the portfolio management as well, particularly when active strategies are employed. In the public markets, fund managers might engage in security selection within asset classes like equities or credit, making investment decisions based on detailed research and analysis. These active strategies often lead to more concentrated portfolios, where managers take larger positions in a smaller number of securities they believe will outperform. However, this concentration can increase the portfolio's volatility, especially if the chosen securities experience significant price fluctuations. Furthermore, active managers might choose to hold positions for extended periods, either due to a long-term buy-and-hold strategy or to avoid market impact when exiting large positions. This can result in deviations from the target allocation, particularly if the market moves against the concentrated positions, necessitating portfolio adjustments in order to maintain the intended balance.

Given these challenges, derivatives, specifically futures contracts, offer a powerful tool for managing the overall portfolio's asset allocation. Futures contracts allow for quick adjustments in the portfolio's exposures to various asset classes without needing to trade the underlying securities directly. This flexibility is particularly valuable when managing private assets, for which direct transactions are cumbersome and slow. For example, suppose a private equity allocation becomes overweight due to a strong performance. In that case, the portfolio manager can sell equity-index futures to reduce the portfolio's overall equity exposure without having to sell the private equity holdings directly. Similarly, suppose a public equity manager's active strategy leads to an underweight in a particular asset class. In that case, futures can be used to temporarily increase the exposure until the manager can realign the portfolio through direct trades. It is important to note that using futures contracts can lead to basis risk if there is a mismatch between the underlying equity exposure of the futures contracts and the intended equity exposures they are meant to hedge.

Hence, by using futures, portfolio managers can offset overweights or underweights that arise due to market movements or due to the inherent characteristics of certain asset classes, ensuring that the portfolio remains aligned with its strategic asset allocation. This approach provides a dynamic and efficient means to manage public and private asset exposures, allowing for timely rebalancing that would otherwise be difficult or impossible to achieve through direct transactions alone.

In this application, we will illustrate how futures contracts can be utilized to manage the equity exposure within a multi-asset portfolio. While the principles discussed broadly apply across various asset classes, we will focus on managing the exposure from private equity holdings and from actively managed public equities. The example demonstrates how derivatives can be effectively employed to maintain the desired asset allocation, ensuring that the portfolio remains aligned with its strategic objectives despite the challenges stemming from the different asset classes.

Investment Example

This example is based on a multi-asset fund with $100 million USD in capital. The fund is overseen by a Chief Investment Officer (CIO) who is responsible for managing the overall asset allocation. The fund also involves specialized portfolio managers: one manages the private equity portfolios, and another actively manages the public equity portfolio. The role of these managers is to select securities within their respective asset classes, while the CIO focuses on maintaining the strategic asset allocation across the entire portfolio.

Let's consider the initial target asset allocation for the fund:

- U.S. Private Equity 20%
- Public U.S. Active Equities 10%
- Europe Private Equity 30%
- U.S. Treasuries 40%

Over time, the allocations shift, and at a certain moment (before a rebalancing) the portfolio's composition is as follows:

- U.S. Private Equity 25%
- Public U.S. Active Equities 9%
- Europe Private Equity 32%
- U.S. Treasuries 34%

This deviation from the target allocation has resulted in an overweight position in Europe Private Equity and U.S. Private Equity and an underweight position in Public U.S. Active Equities. To bring the equity exposure back in line with the target allocation, the CIO decides to use futures contracts to rebalance the portfolio:

Overall U.S. Equity (public and private): The total U.S. equity exposure must be reduced by 4% to align with the target. This reduction comprises:

- U.S. Private Equity 5% reduction ($5 million USD)
- Public U.S. Active Equities 1% increase ($1 million USD)

Overall Europe Equity: The total European equity exposure must be reduced by 2% of the portfolio:

- Europe Private Equity 2% reduction ($2 million USD)

Since U.S. private equity is overweight by 5% (more than the 1% underweight in U.S. public equities), the CIO decides to sell futures contracts on the S&P 500 E-mini index to reduce U.S. equity exposure. Similarly, the CIO sells futures on the Euro Stoxx 50 index to reduce European equity exposure.[1] The relevant details are:

[1] Note that selling equity futures reduces the portfolio's total equity exposure (including both public and private equity). However, this action could increase tracking error relative to the benchmark, depending on the benchmark's composition.

- ***S&P 500 E-mini Futures***:
  - Index value: 5500
  - Contract size: $50 per index point
- ***Euro Stoxx 50 Index Futures***:
  - Index value: 5000
  - Contract size: €10 per index point
  - FX rate: 1 EUR = 1.1 USD

Calculating the Notional Value of Futures to Trade

1. ***For U.S. Equity (S&P 500 E-mini Futures)***:
   - Total notional amount to adjust: USD 4 million
   - Notional value per contract = 5500 (index value) × $50 = USD $275,000
   - Number of contracts to sell = $4,000,000 ÷ $275,000 ≈ 14.55 contracts (rounded up to 15)
2. ***For Europe Equity (Euro Stoxx 50 Futures)***:
   - Notional amount to reduce: $2 million USD
   - Notional value per contract = 5000 (index value) × €10 = €50,000
   - Convert to USD: €50,000 × 1.1 (FX rate) = $55,000 USD
   - Number of contracts to sell = $2,000,000 ÷ $55,000 ≈ 36.36 contracts (rounded up to 37)

The CIO would sell 15 S&P 500 E-mini futures and 37 contracts Euro Stoxx 50 futures contracts.

Revised Portfolio Allocation

Exhibit 7.1 illustrates the portfolio's target allocation, the allocation before rebalancing and after rebalancing.

Exhibit 7.1 shows that U.S. Private Equity component is 25%, with the Public U.S. Active Equities slightly underweight at 9%. The CIO reduces the overall U.S. equity exposure by using S&P 500 E-mini futures to achieve the target of 30%. The European Private Equity component is slightly overweight at 32%, offset by a −2% position in Euro Stoxx 50 futures, bringing the total European equity allocation back to the target 30%. The U.S. Treasuries allocation is increased to 40% from 34%.

Asset Class	Target Allocation	Allocation *before rebalancing*	Allocation *after rebalancing*
U.S. Equity	**30%**	**34%**	**30%**
- U.S. Private Equity	20%	25%	25%
- Public U.S. Active Equities	10%	9%	9%
- U.S. Equity (via S&P 500 Futures)	0%	0%	-4%
Europe Equity	**30%**	**32%**	**30%**
- Europe Private Equity	30%	32%	32%
- Europe Equity (via Euro Stoxx 50 Futures)	0%	0%	-2%
U.S. Treasuries	**40%**	34%	**40%**
Total Portfolio	**100%**	**100%**	**100%**
Effective Equity Exposure	*60%*	*66%*	*60%*

Exhibit 7.1 Target vs. Actual Allocation

Risk Analysis

The example above demonstrates how futures manage equity exposure within a portfolio and reduce deviations from strategic asset allocation weights. In this section, we analyze how these actions impact the portfolio's overall risk profile. We begin by outlining the assumptions used in our analysis and calculating the portfolio volatility under different allocation scenarios. Lastly, we examine the risk contributions of each asset class and grouped asset classes.

Portfolio Volatility Calculation

The portfolio volatility measures the overall risk, considering the asset classes' individual volatilities and their correlations. The formula below aggregates the asset volatilities adjusted by their correlations and weights, to produce the overall portfolio volatility (σ_p), as follows:

$$\sigma_p = \sqrt{\sum_{i=1}^{n}\sum_{j=1}^{n} w_i w_j \sigma_i \sigma_j \rho_{ij}}$$

where:

- w_i and w_j are the portfolio weights of asset classes i and j
- σ_i and σ_j are the volatilities of asset classes i and j
- ρ_{ij} is the correlation between asset classes i and j
- n is the number of asset classes.

Risk Contribution Calculation

Risk contribution, denoted *RC*, measures how much each asset class contributes to the portfolio's total risk (volatility). The risk contribution for each asset class *i* is calculated using the following formula:

$$RC_i = w_i \cdot MRC_i$$

where:

- w_i is the portfolio weight of asset class i
- MRC_i is the marginal risk contribution of asset class i, which represents the sensitivity of the portfolio's volatility to changes in the weight of asset class i. It is calculated as:

$$\text{MRC}_i = \frac{\partial \sigma_p}{\partial w_i} = \frac{\sum_{j=1}^{n} w_j \sigma_j \rho_{ij}}{\sigma_p}$$

The total portfolio risk is the sum of the individual risk contributions:

$$\sigma_p = \sum_{i=1}^{n} RC_i$$

These calculations help to understand the impact of each asset class on the overall portfolio risk and how rebalancing can influence the distribution of risk within the portfolio.

Assumptions for the Investment Example

Exhibits 7.2 and 7.3 summarize the volatility and correlation assumptions, respectively, used in the risk analysis.

Asset Class	Volatility (%)
U.S. Private Equity	20%
Public U.S. Active Equities	18%
U.S. Equity (via S&P 500 Futures)	15%
Europe Private Equity	22%
Europe Equity (via Euro Stoxx 50 Futures)	18%
U.S. Treasuries	7%

Exhibit 7.2 Volatility assumptions

Asset Class	U.S. Private Equity	Public U.S. Active Equities	U.S. Equity (via S&P 500 Futures)	Europe Private Equity	Europe Equity (via Euro Stoxx 50 Futures)	U.S. Treasuries
U.S. Private Equity	100%	70%	80%	80%	75%	0%
Public U.S. Active Equities	70%	100%	90%	65%	85%	5%
U.S. Equity (via S&P 500 Futures)	80%	90%	100%	75%	95%	10%
Europe Private Equity	80%	65%	75%	100%	80%	0%
Europe Equity (via Euro Stoxx 50 Futures)	75%	85%	95%	80%	100%	5%
U.S. Treasuries	0%	5%	10%	0%	5%	100%

Exhibit 7.3 Correlation assumptions

Risk Results

Using the assumptions above, the portfolio volatility of the target allocation, the allocation before rebalancing, and after rebalancing are:

Allocation	Portfolio Volatility (%)
Target	11.79%
Before rebalancing	12.87%
After rebalancing	12.16%

Exhibit 7.4 shows the risk contributions from each asset class for the three allocations.

Asset Class	Target Allocation	Allocation before rebalancing	Allocation after rebalancing
U.S. Private Equity	3.58%	4.57%	4.53%
Public U.S. Active Equities	1.38%	1.24%	1.20%
U.S. Equity (via S&P 500 Futures)	0.00%	0.00%	-0.50%
Europe Private Equity	6.14%	6.61%	6.58%
Europe Equity (via Euro Stoxx 50 Futures)	0.00%	0.00%	-0.30%
U.S. Treasuries	0.69%	0.45%	0.65%

Exhibit 7.4 Risk contribution per asset class

To give a broader perspective, the risk contributions have also been grouped into the three main buckets: overall U.S. Equity, overall European Equity, and U.S. Treasuries, shown in Exhibit 7.5.

Asset Class	Target Allocation	Allocation before rebalancing	Allocation after rebalancing
Overall U.S. Equity	4.96%	5.81%	5.23%
Overall Europe Equity	6.14%	6.61%	6.28%
U.S. Treasuries	0.69%	0.45%	0.65%

Exhibit 7.5 Risk contribution grouped by asset class and region

Margin Requirements Calculation

The fund must post margin as collateral when trading futures contracts to cover potential losses on these derivative positions. The margin requirements serve as a financial safeguard to ensure that the fund can meet its obligations during adverse market movements. It is important to note that the margin requirements discussed here are representative examples, and actual margin requirements can vary depending on the broker and market conditions. Additionally, these figures represent maintenance margins, which must be maintained throughout the duration of the futures contracts. If the fund were to initiate these futures positions for the first time, the initial margin required would likely be higher than the maintenance margin.

Based on the example after rebalancing, where the fund decides to sell futures contracts, the margin requirements are calculated as indicated below. Note that the number of contracts is rounded up to the nearest whole number:

- ***S&P 500 E-mini Futures***:
  - Number of contracts: 15 (rounded up from 14.55)
  - Maintenance margin per contract: $15,000
  - Total maintenance margin required: 15 × 15,000 = $225,000
- ***Euro Stoxx 50 Futures***:
  - Number of contracts: 37 (rounded up from 36.36)
  - Maintenance margin per contract: €4,000
  - Total maintenance margin required: 37 × 4,000 = €148,000

Therefore, the fund needs to post a total maintenance margin of $225,000 for the S&P 500 E-mini futures and €148,000 for the Euro Stoxx 50 futures. We report the maintenance margins to simplify our discussion. If the fund were to initiate these futures trades, it would likely be required to post a higher initial margin, which provides an additional buffer against potential losses when entering the positions. This margin is critical to managing the risk associated with trading derivatives, ensuring the fund has sufficient collateral to cover potential adverse market movements.

Discussion

Futures contracts offer several strategic advantages as a rebalancing tool for multi-asset portfolios and require careful consideration of various factors. This discussion explores the key aspects of the portfolio's exposure, risk profile, and margin requirements before and after rebalancing, providing a comprehensive understanding of how futures contribute to effective portfolio management.

Exposure Before and After Rebalancing

Before rebalancing, the portfolio had drifted from its target allocations due to the performance of different asset classes. In the example, the U.S. Private Equity allocation increased to 25%, and the European Private Equity allocation increased to 32%, exceeding their respective target allocations. This overweight in private equity indicates an increased concentration in higher-risk, less liquid assets, exposing the portfolio to heightened volatility and illiquidity issues, which could lead to adverse events, particularly during market downturns.

In contrast, the allocation to Public U.S. Active Equities decreased slightly to 9%, below the target allocation of 10%. This underweight in publicly traded equities meant that the portfolio had less exposure to more liquid and potentially lower-risk assets, reducing its ability to adjust to market changes quickly.

The rebalancing process involved selling futures contracts on the S&P 500 and Euro Stoxx 50 indices to reduce the overall equity exposure and bring the portfolio back in line with its target allocations. After rebalancing, the effective U.S. Equity exposure (comprising U.S. Private Equity, Public U.S. Active Equities, and U.S. Equity via S&P 500 Futures) was adjusted to precisely 30%, restoring the balance in the portfolio. Similarly, the European Equity exposure (including European Private Equity and European Equity via Euro Stoxx 50 Futures) was brought back to its target of 30%. This adjustment ensured that the portfolio's exposure to different asset classes aligned with the strategic asset allocation, reducing the risk of unintended concentration in any area.

Risk Profile Before and After Rebalancing

The portfolio's risk profile changed significantly due to the drift in allocations. Before rebalancing, the portfolio's volatility increased to 12.87%, up from the target volatility of 11.79%. This increase was primarily driven by the overweight positions in U.S. and European private Equity, which are inherently more volatile than other asset classes like U.S. Treasuries. The elevated risk highlighted the potential for greater fluctuations in the portfolio's value, which could be detrimental in periods of market stress.

After rebalancing, the portfolio's volatility was reduced to 12.16%. While this is still slightly above the target volatility, it represents a significant reduction from the pre-rebalance level. The use of futures allowed the CIO to quickly adjust the portfolio's risk profile without liquidating the underlying assets, demonstrating the effectiveness of derivatives in managing short-term deviations from strategic asset allocations. This approach helps mitigate the excess risk associated with the overweight in private equity and ensures that the portfolio's overall risk is more evenly distributed across the various asset classes.

The risk contribution analysis further supports this outcome. Before rebalancing, the risk contributions from U.S. and European equities were disproportionately high, reflecting the overweight in these asset classes. After rebalancing, the risk contributions were more balanced and closer to the original targets, with U.S. Treasuries regaining a more appropriate share of the portfolio's risk. This rebalancing of risk contributions underscores the importance of using futures to maintain a diversified risk profile, which is crucial for achieving long-term investment objectives.

Margin Requirements

The use of futures contracts to rebalance portfolios also introduces considerations related to margin requirements. In the example, the portfolio manager decided to sell 15 S&P 500 E-mini futures contracts and 37 Euro Stoxx 50 futures contracts, and the fund was required to post margin as collateral. The total maintenance margin required was $225,000 for the S&P 500 futures and €148,000 for the Euro Stoxx 50 futures. This margin is a safeguard to cover potential losses on these derivative positions.

While the margin requirements are relatively small compared to the overall size of the portfolio, they nonetheless require careful management. The fund must maintain sufficient liquidity to meet these margin calls, particularly during periods of market volatility when futures prices can fluctuate significantly. Furthermore, these margin requirements represent an additional layer of complexity in portfolio management, as they necessitate maintaining a cash buffer or liquid assets that can be readily converted to cash if needed.

It is also important to note that the figures provided represent maintenance margins only, which must be maintained throughout the duration of the futures contracts. If the fund were to initiate these futures positions for the first time, the initial margin required would likely be higher, providing an additional buffer against potential losses when entering the positions. The CIO must consider these factors when using futures as a rebalancing tool, ensuring that the fund has adequate resources to meet margin requirements without disrupting the broader investment strategy.

Advanced Topic: Refining the Use of Derivatives

In the example provided above, we assumed that the S&P 500 futures were used as a one-to-one substitute for private equity, thus implying a market beta of 1. This approach simplifies the rebalancing process by treating the public and private equity exposures as having identical sensitivities to market movements. However, in practice, more sophisticated portfolio managers can refine the use of derivatives to more accurately reflect the unique characteristics of different asset classes and the nuances of their sensitivities to market factors.

One way to refine the approach is by adjusting the beta used for rebalancing. For instance, if the portfolio manager believes the private equity portfolio has a higher sensitivity to market movements than the public indices embed, they might use a beta greater than 1 when selecting futures contracts. This adjustment acknowledges that private equity could have a higher expected volatility or market correlation than public equities and using a higher beta in the rebalancing process can better align the portfolio's risk profile with its intended exposure.

To illustrate this, let's revise our example with a refined approach. Suppose the CIO determines that the U.S. Private Equity portfolio has a beta of 1.5 relative to the S&P 500. For every 1 unit of U.S. Private Equity, 1.5 units of S&P 500 futures are needed to balance the exposure. The same adjustment is applied to European Private Equity with respect to the Euro Stoxx 50 futures.

Given this adjustment, the CIO's task is now to rebalance the portfolio using these adjusted beta values.

Adjusted Example with Beta Refinement

The target allocation remains the same:

- U.S. Private Equity 20%
- Public U.S. Active Equities 10%
- Europe Private Equity 30%
- U.S. Treasuries 40%

The portfolio composition before rebalancing is as follows:

- U.S. Private Equity 25%
- Public U.S. Active Equities 9%
- Europe Private Equity 32%
- U.S. Treasuries 34%

The CIO must now account for the higher beta when using futures contracts to bring the equity exposure back in line with the target allocation.

- ***Overall U.S. Equity (public and private)***: The total U.S. equity exposure needs to be reduced by 4%. However, with the beta adjustment, 5% of the U.S. Private Equity translates to 7.5% in S&P 500 futures. Additionally, 1% needs to be added back for Public U.S. Active Equities, resulting in a net adjustment of −6.5% in S&P 500 futures.
- ***Overall European Equity***: The total European equity exposure needs to be reduced by 2%. With the beta adjustment, 2% of Europe Private Equity translates to 3% in Euro Stoxx 50 futures.

With these adjustments, the CIO decides to sell futures contracts on the S&P 500 E-mini index and the Euro Stoxx 50 index.

Exhibit 7.6 illustrates the portfolio's target allocation, the allocation before rebalancing, and the allocation after rebalancing with the beta adjustment.

In Exhibit 7.6, the U.S. Private Equity component still represents 25% of the portfolio. However, 7.5% of the portfolio's value is offset by S&P 500 futures rather than the initial 5% to account for the higher beta. Since the Public U.S. Active Equities requires a 1% increase, the overall S&P 500 futures position is −6.5%.

The European Private Equity component is slightly overweight at 32%, offset by a −3% position in Euro Stoxx 50 futures after adjusting for the beta of 1.5 rather than the initial 2% reduction.

Asset Class	Target Allocation (%)	Allocation Before rebalancing (%)	Allocation after rebalancing (%)
U.S. Equity	**30%**	**34%**	**27.5%**
- U.S. Private Equity	20%	25%	25%
- Public U.S. Active Equities	10%	9%	9%
- U.S. Equity (via S&P 500 Futures)	0%	0%	-6.5%
Europe Equity	**30%**	**32%**	**29%**
- Europe Private Equity	30%	32%	32%
- Europe Equity (via Euro Stoxx 50 Futures)	0%	0%	-3%
U.S. Treasuries	**40%**	34%	**40%**
Total Portfolio	**100%**	**100%**	**96.5%**
Effective Equity Exposure	***60%***	***66%***	***56.5%***

Exhibit 7.6 Target vs. actual allocations with beta refinement

Another refinement involves characteristics matching, where the derivatives used for rebalancing are selected based on specific attributes such as region, sector, or market capitalization—provided that suitable futures contracts are available. For example, if a private equity portfolio consists of 50% large private equity funds and 50% venture capital investments, the manager might choose to use S&P 500 futures for the large private equity funds while employing Russell 2000 or Nasdaq futures contracts to hedge the venture capital exposure. This tailored approach allows for a more precise management of the portfolio's exposures and risks, potentially leading to better alignment with the portfolio's strategic objectives.

This concept can also extend to other asset classes like infrastructure and real estate. For instance, if a real estate portfolio is viewed as a combination of equity and fixed-income characteristics, a more refined approach might involve rebalancing with a mix of S&P 500 futures and U.S. Treasury futures. This strategy reflects the hybrid nature of real estate investments, capturing both the growth potential typically associated with equities and the income stability of bonds.

While these refinements can lead to more effective risk management and exposure control, they also introduce additional complexity. For example, when the market beta is not 1, the notional value of the futures contracts used for rebalancing may not sum to 100% of the portfolio's value. This can make the portfolio's overall exposure less straightforward to interpret and manage.

Despite the complexity, many sophisticated funds employ these advanced techniques because they allow for more precise control over the portfolio's risk and exposure profiles. Such funds often incorporate strategic asset allocation with a factor-based approach, emphasizing managing the portfolio's exposure to underlying risk factors rather than simply adhering to traditional asset class boundaries. In this context, derivatives become a powerful tool for fine-tuning the portfolio's factor exposures, helping to achieve a more nuanced and effective risk management strategy within a multi-asset portfolio.

Summary

Applying futures contracts in rebalancing a multi-asset portfolio offers a dynamic and effective means to maintain target allocations and manage risks associated with public and private assets. By utilizing futures, portfolio managers can swiftly address deviations from strategic allocations without directly trading in less liquid underlying assets, particularly in private equity and actively managed public equities. This approach not only restores balance in the portfolio but also allows for a more controlled risk profile, as demonstrated by the reduced volatility after rebalancing.

However, while futures provide significant flexibility and efficiency, they also introduce additional considerations, such as managing margin requirements and understanding the potential for basis risk. These factors must be carefully managed to ensure that the use of derivatives aligns with the institution's overall investment philosophy and risk management framework. Moreover, ongoing monitoring and prudent risk management are essential to successfully integrating futures into a portfolio's broader asset allocation strategy.

In summary, futures contracts are valuable in the multi-asset manager's toolkit. They enable the precise and timely rebalancing of portfolios in response to market movements and asset performance. When used thoughtfully, they help maintain the desired balance between asset classes, ultimately contributing to achieving the portfolio's long-term investment objectives.

8

Option Income Strategies Design

John Burrello and Frank J. Fabozzi

Income enhancement derivatives strategies have become integral to modern portfolio management because they can achieve various investment objectives, from income generation to risk management. These strategies are no longer confined to hedge funds or institutional portfolios; technological advancements and the growing accessibility of financial markets have made them an essential tool for a broader range of portfolio managers. With instruments such as options, futures, and swaps, portfolio managers can craft highly customized approaches for enhancing returns through income-generating techniques.

Derivatives have gained prominence for their ability to adapt to various market environments. Strategies such as covered calls, cash-secured puts, and protective puts are commonly employed to generate consistent cash flow, mitigate risk, or capitalize on volatility. Futures and swaps, on the other hand, provide mechanisms to lock in prices or exchange cash flows based on the performance of underlying assets. The flexibility inherent in these instruments makes them indispensable for addressing diverse portfolio management challenges.

J. Burrello (✉)
Invesco Global Strategies, Atlanta, GA, USA
e-mail: John.Burrello@invesco.com

F. J. Fabozzi
Carey Business School, Johns Hopkins University, Baltimore, MD, USA

F. J. Fabozzi and M. de Jong (eds.), *Derivatives Applications in Asset Management*,
https://doi.org/10.1007/978-3-031-86354-7_8

Designing effective strategies begins with clearly understanding the objectives they seek to achieve. Whether the goal is to generate additional income, protect against downside risks, or exploit pricing inefficiencies, the foundational principles of a derivative strategy design remain the same. A structured approach is essential, incorporating elements such as (1) defining investment goals, (2) understanding market views, (3) selecting the appropriate instruments, and (4) evaluating risk-reward trade-offs. These considerations ensure that the chosen strategy aligns with the broader portfolio objectives and remains adaptable to changing market conditions.

The importance of thoughtful design cannot be overstated. Poorly constructed strategies may fail to deliver the intended outcomes or expose portfolios to unnecessary risks. For instance, targeting yields that exceed the portfolio's total return potential can lead to capital erosion over time, while misaligned derivative positions can result in inconsistent performance. By focusing on the core principles of alignment, balance, and flexibility, portfolio managers can craft strategies that achieve immediate goals and sustain long-term portfolio growth.

This chapter lays the foundation for understanding the key principles of option income strategy design. It discusses how these strategies are critical in portfolio management and outlines the essential considerations for developing practical approaches. Cases later in this book will delve deeper into specific techniques and applications, with references to practical cases such as "Managing Path Dependency" and "Targeting Options-Based Income with Puts and Calls," offering actionable insights for portfolio managers. Through this exploration, the chapter aims to provide a comprehensive framework for integrating option income strategies into a disciplined and sustainable investment process.

The Role of Derivative and Option Income Strategies

Option income strategies are central in modern portfolio management, offering versatility and adaptability to address various investment objectives. These strategies enable portfolio managers to generate consistent income, manage risk, and maintain exposure to market opportunities, all while tailoring approaches to specific goals. Unlike traditional asset allocation methods, derivatives provide customization and precision that allow for highly targeted solutions, making them indispensable in stable and volatile market environments.

At their core, derivative strategies revolve around two primary functions: income generation and risk mitigation. Income-focused strategies, such as covered calls and cash-secured puts, provide a predictable stream of cash flows that can supplement traditional sources like dividends or bond coupons. These strategies are particularly valuable in low-interest-rate environments, where generating meaningful income from traditional cash instruments can be challenging. In contrast, risk-focused strategies like protective puts offer downside protection by limiting potential losses on underlying assets, making them ideal for preserving capital during periods of heightened market uncertainty.

The adaptability of derivative instruments enhances their appeal in portfolio construction. For example, options allow portfolio managers to take advantage of specific market conditions by capitalizing on volatility or expressing directional views. Futures contracts provide a mechanism to lock in prices or hedge against unfavorable price movements, while swaps enable the exchange of cash flows to manage interest rate or currency risks. This flexibility allows portfolio managers to address short-term tactical needs and long-term strategic objectives.

A key advantage of derivative strategies lies in their ability to shape risk-return profiles to align with clients' unique needs. For instance, a portfolio manager seeking additional income for a client in a moderately bullish market may implement a covered call strategy, which generates premiums while maintaining exposure to potential stock price appreciation. Similarly, a cash-secured put can provide an attractive entry point for acquiring stocks at lower prices while also collecting premiums. These strategies are effective in generating income and contribute to portfolio stability by offsetting some of the risks associated with market volatility.

However, the effective use of derivatives requires thoughtful design and disciplined execution. The alignment between the underlying portfolio and the derivative positions is crucial to achieving consistent outcomes. Misaligned exposures, such as index options with a concentrated or actively managed equity portfolio, can lead to performance discrepancies and unanticipated risks. Furthermore, derivative strategies must be carefully tailored to the market environment, considering factors such as volatility, interest rates, and liquidity conditions, which can significantly influence their effectiveness.

Understanding the role of derivative income strategies goes beyond their immediate benefits. They serve as tools that enhance portfolio performance and offer resilience in the face of market challenges. By combining flexibility, precision, and adaptability, these strategies enable portfolio managers to navigate complex financial markets while meeting the diverse needs of their clients. The principles and considerations introduced in this chapter set the stage for a deeper exploration of the critical design elements and practical applications covered later in this chapter.

Designing Effective Option Income Strategies

The design of option income strategies is a deliberate and structured process that ensures alignment with investment objectives and adaptability to dynamic market conditions. Success in this endeavor hinges on a comprehensive understanding of the instruments involved, clearly articulating the strategy's purpose and disciplined execution. Each step in the design process builds upon the others, creating a cohesive framework for achieving specific investment goals.

The first step in crafting an effective strategy is defining the overarching objectives. For income-focused strategies, the aim may be to supplement portfolio returns through consistent cash flow, often achieved via covered calls or cash-secured puts. In contrast, risk-focused strategies like protective puts prioritize capital preservation by providing downside protection. Speculative objectives, on the other hand, may involve leveraging derivatives to capitalize on anticipated price movements or volatility spikes. The clarity of the objectives shapes every subsequent decision, from the selection of instruments to the choice of risk management tools.

Market outlook plays a crucial role in determining the structure of a derivative strategy. A bullish perspective, for example, might lead to the selection of strategies that capitalize on upward price movements, such as writing covered calls or using cash-secured puts to acquire assets at favorable prices. Conversely, a bearish view may prompt the use of protective puts to shield against losses or short futures contracts to benefit from declining prices. A neutral market view, where little price movement is anticipated, often leads to strategies such as calendar spreads,[1] which profit from time decay and stable markets. For some portfolio managers, the focus may shift from price direction to volatility, leading to straddles or strangles[2] to capture profits from significant market swings, irrespective of direction.

---

[1] A calendar spread is an options strategy that involves buying and selling options on the same underlying asset at the same strike price but with different expiration dates.

[2] A straddle involves buying or selling both a call option and a put option on the same underlying asset, with the same strike price and expiration date. A strangle involves buying or selling both a call option and a put option on the same underlying asset but with different strike prices and the same expiration date.

The choice of derivative instrument further refines the strategy's design. Options, with their inherent flexibility, are often favored for income and risk management due to their customizable strike prices and expiration dates. Futures contracts, by contrast, are more suited for price locking or speculation due to their standardized terms and obligation-based structure. Swaps, such as interest rate or commodity swaps, are particularly valuable for managing cash flows tied to fluctuating financial metrics. Selecting the right instrument requires careful consideration of the strategy's objectives and the market environment in which it will operate.

A critical element in strategy design is determining the appropriate strike prices and expiration dates for options. Strike price selection reflects the investor's market outlook and risk tolerance. A covered call written at-the-money generates the highest premium but limits upside potential, while an out-of-the-money call sacrifices some income for greater participation in price appreciation. Similarly, expiration dates influence the balance between cost and flexibility. Longer expirations provide more time for market moves to materialize but come at a higher premium, whereas shorter expirations lower costs but may require more frequent adjustments.

Risk management is integral to designing derivative strategies. It begins with evaluating the risk-reward profile of the proposed approach, considering potential losses, expected returns, and the position's sensitivity to market variables such as price, time, and volatility. Metrics such as the Greeks—delta, gamma, theta, vega, and a range of others measuring higher-order sensitivities—are essential for assessing the behavior of options under different scenarios. For futures and swaps, understanding margin requirements and the potential for margin calls ensures the strategy remains viable during adverse market conditions. Regularly monitoring positions is critical, allowing for timely adjustments in response to changing market dynamics.

Finally, implementation and ongoing management ensure the strategy's continued alignment with its investment objectives. Executing trades through reliable platforms, setting appropriate position sizes, and adhering to pre-established stop-loss or profit-taking levels are key to maintaining discipline. Over time, the strategy may need to be adjusted by rolling expiring contracts forward, increasing or reducing exposure, or shifting focus in response to evolving market conditions. Such adaptability is essential for maintaining effectiveness and relevance in dynamic markets.

Designing option income strategies is a multifaceted process that combines technical expertise with practical insights. Each decision, from defining investment objectives to managing positions, contributes to the strategy's ability to meet the portfolio manager's goals for a client while navigating the complexities of financial markets. The principles outlined in this chapter provide a structured framework for creating robust strategies, paving the way for more detailed discussions of specific techniques and case applications later in this book.

Key Principles for Strategy Design

The design of option income strategies requires adherence to foundational principles that ensure alignment with investment objectives, sustainability of income generation, and effective risk management. These principles serve as a guide for structuring strategies that are both robust and adaptable to changing market conditions. Outlined below are three critical considerations: (1) aligning equity and derivative portfolios, (2) managing path dependency, and (3) balancing growth with yield.

Aligning Equity and Derivative Portfolios

A well-aligned equity and derivative portfolio is essential for achieving consistent performance. Misaligned exposures, such as writing index options against a portfolio of actively managed stocks, can lead to unpredictable outcomes and undermine the strategy's effectiveness. For example, if the underlying equity portfolio focuses on dividend-paying or low-volatility stocks, pairing it with broad-based index options may result in mismatched risk-return profiles. Proper alignment involves selecting derivatives that closely correspond to the composition and objectives of the equity portfolio. This synchronization minimizes tracking errors, enhances predictability, and ensures the strategy complements the broader portfolio framework.

Path Dependency

Path dependence is a key characteristic of option income strategies. It refers to how the outcomes of these strategies are influenced not only by the final price of the underlying asset but also by the sequence and magnitude of its price movements over time. Unlike traditional buy-and-hold strategies, where the ending value determines the outcome, option income strategies are impacted by fluctuations in the underlying asset's price throughout the option's life and the timing of trades, such as rolling or closing positions before expiration.

In practical terms, path dependence arises because the value of an option is not solely determined at expiration but fluctuates during its life based on factors like implied volatility, time decay, and changes in the underlying asset's price. For example, in a covered call strategy, if the underlying asset experiences a significant price spike early in the option's life, the call may limit further upside potential until the path ends when the trade is closed. Conversely, a sudden price drop might reduce the risk mitigation potential until the trade is closed and additional premium is earned from selling future options, negatively affecting the strategy's overall defensive properties.

This path-dependent nature means that option income strategies require active management and decision-making during the life of the options. Portfolio managers must consider when to roll options, adjust strike prices, or close positions early to optimize outcomes, as these decisions depend heavily on how the underlying asset's price has moved and how it is expected to move in the future. Thus, understanding and managing path dependence is essential for effectively executing option income strategies and achieving desired results.

For example, strategies such as the CBOE S&P 500 BuyWrite Index, which involves selling monthly at-the-money call options, are heavily influenced by market environments on expiration dates. This dependency on a single path increases the strategy's vulnerability to unexpected outcomes. Diversification through laddering can mitigate these risks. Laddering involves staggering option expirations and strike prices across multiple time horizons, enabling the portfolio to capture a broader range of market scenarios. Reducing reliance on specific outcomes smooths income generation and improves the strategy's resilience to market fluctuations.

Balancing Growth with Yield

Another cornerstone of strategy design is achieving a sustainable balance between income generation and long-term portfolio growth. While high yields may appear attractive, they often come at the expense of capital appreciation or downside protection. For example, selling at-the-money covered calls across the entire portfolio can cap upside potential, limiting participation in bullish markets. Similarly, setting overly aggressive yield targets that exceed the portfolio's expected total return can lead to capital erosion over time. Effective strategies balance yield expectations with realistic growth potential, ensuring that the portfolio's overall performance supports income distributions. Adjusting strike prices and allocations based on market conditions allows for flexibility while maintaining this balance.

Integrating these principles into strategy design ensures that derivative and option income strategies align with investment goals and market realities. Alignment between equity and derivative portfolios provides consistency, managing path dependency reduces vulnerabilities to specific outcomes, and balancing growth with yield sustains long-term portfolio health. These considerations form the foundation of a disciplined approach to designing strategies that generate income, manage risk, and support portfolio resilience. The principles outlined here will be further explored in practical applications and case studies in the subsequent sections of this chapter.

Evaluating Option Income Strategies

Evaluating the effectiveness of option income strategies is critical, as well as ensuring alignment with investment objectives and adapting to changing market conditions. This evaluation involves assessing the strategy's consistency in delivering results, capacity to manage inherent risks, and resilience against common pitfalls. A thorough and disciplined approach to evaluation enhances the strategy's reliability and mitigates potential drawbacks that can undermine its success.

Consistency in income generation is one of the primary metrics for evaluating an option income strategy. Reliable performance across various market conditions is essential, particularly for investors who depend on these strategies as a significant source of cash flow. Strategies that yield strong returns during high volatility but falter during calmer markets may fail to meet long-term expectations. For example, a covered call strategy that generates substantial premiums in a volatile market but limits upside participation in a strong bullish trend could lead to dissatisfaction over time. A well-designed strategy should demonstrate a balance, ensuring that income is generated predictably without compromising the broader portfolio's objectives. This requires the careful selection of strike prices, expiration dates, and the proportion of the portfolio allocated to derivative positions.

Risk management is an equally important consideration in the evaluation process. Options, futures, and swaps are inherently complex instruments with unique risk profiles. For options-based strategies, understanding the Greeks—such as delta (price sensitivity), theta (time decay), and vega (volatility sensitivity)—is crucial for gauging how positions will respond to changes in market conditions. These metrics provide valuable insights into the behavior of the strategy and help portfolio managers make informed adjustments. For futures and swaps, risk management involves monitoring margin requirements, understanding potential margin calls, and assessing the liquidity of the underlying assets. A comprehensive evaluation of the strategy's risk-reward profile ensures it remains robust even in adverse market environments.

Another key aspect of evaluating derivative and option income strategies is identifying and avoiding common pitfalls. One of the most significant risks is the temptation to chase unsustainable yields. While higher yields may appear attractive in the short term, they often come with increased risks, such as reduced upside participation or potential capital erosion. For instance, targeting annual yields that exceed the portfolio's total return potential can deplete the principal over time, jeopardizing the strategy's long-term sustainability. Misalignment between the equity and derivative components of the portfolio is another common issue. If the derivative strategy does not correspond closely to the underlying portfolio's structure and goals, performance can become inconsistent and unpredictable, introducing unnecessary risks.

Resilience to market dynamics is also an important factor in evaluating the effectiveness of these strategies. Markets are inherently volatile, and strategies that lack flexibility may underperform during periods of significant change. For example, strategies designed for stable markets may struggle during heightened volatility, while those built for volatile conditions may fail to capitalize on calm market environments. The ability to adjust positions dynamically, such as rolling options to later expiration dates or altering strike prices in response to market shifts, enhances the strategy's adaptability and ensures its relevance across various scenarios.

Practical Considerations for Strategy Implementation

Successfully implementing option income strategies may require a systematic approach that bridges theoretical design with real-world execution. Translating strategy design into actionable trades involves careful consideration of market conditions, precise execution, and ongoing management to ensure the strategy remains aligned with its objectives. Implementation is not merely the final step in strategy design—it is a continuous process of monitoring, adjusting, and refining the strategy to adapt to evolving market dynamics.

One of the first practical considerations is ensuring that the trading platform and tools used for execution are well-suited to the strategy. Derivative strategies often involve complex calculations, sensitive timing, and precise order placement, necessitating platforms with advanced pricing, analytics, and real-time monitoring capabilities. For example, platforms that provide insights into options Greeks, volatility metrics, and implied pricing are invaluable for executing and managing options-based strategies. Futures and swaps, on the other hand, may require platforms capable of handling margin calculations, reporting requirements, and liquidity assessments.

Executing the strategy involves determining the appropriate trade size, selecting the instruments, and setting up the initial positions. For example, when implementing a covered call strategy, the portfolio manager must decide which underlying assets to target, which strike prices to select, and how far out to set expiration dates. Similarly, implementing a protective put strategy involves buying put options on selected assets to hedge against downside risk. Precision during this stage is crucial because deviations from the designed parameters can affect the strategy's risk-return profile. Once the trades are placed, careful attention must be paid to transaction costs, slippage, and execution quality, which can erode the strategy's performance if not managed effectively.

Monitoring market conditions and portfolio positions is a cornerstone of effective strategy implementation. Market dynamics such as changes in volatility, interest rates, or the underlying asset's price can significantly impact derivative positions. For options, shifts in implied volatility or time decay (theta) may require adjustments to ensure the strategy remains aligned with its goals. For futures and swaps, movements in underlying asset prices or changes in margin requirements necessitate vigilance to avoid margin calls or unfavorable shifts in cash flows. Regular monitoring ensures that portfolio managers can make timely adjustments, such as rolling options to a later expiration date, closing positions to lock in profits, or rebalancing derivative allocations to reflect market shifts.

Adaptability is also critical during implementation. Market conditions often deviate from expectations, requiring flexibility to modify the strategy. For instance, if an investor holding a covered call strategy anticipates a significant upward move in the underlying stock, they may roll the call option to a higher strike price to capture additional upside. Conversely, suppose a protective put strategy becomes less relevant due to underlying price and/or volatility changes. In that case, the portfolio manager may close or adjust the position to reduce costs. The ability to adapt dynamically while staying true to the overarching strategy objectives ensures that the strategy remains effective under varying conditions.

Closing or adjusting positions is another practical consideration. As derivative contracts approach expiration, decisions must be made on whether to close the position, roll it forward, or allow it to expire. Rolling involves extending the exposure by replacing expiring contracts with new ones with later expiration dates, maintaining the strategy's objectives while adapting to changing market conditions. Closing positions, whether to lock in profits or limit losses, is equally important for preserving portfolio value. Predefined exit strategies, such as profit-taking thresholds or stop-loss levels, help maintain discipline and ensure decisions are guided by the original strategy design rather than emotional reactions to market movements.

Effective implementation also requires a long-term perspective. Strategies should be evaluated over multiple market cycles to assess their robustness and adaptability. This involves documenting key performance metrics, analyzing the impact of adjustments, and learning from deviations between expected and actual outcomes. A disciplined approach to implementation, paired with continuous evaluation, provides the insights necessary for refining future strategies.

The practical considerations of implementing derivative and option income strategies emphasize the importance of precision, adaptability, and ongoing management. By bridging the gap between design and execution, portfolio managers can ensure their strategies deliver their intended objectives while navigating the complexities of financial markets. These implementation principles provide a foundation for real-world application of the concepts discussed throughout this chapter and prepare the groundwork for the following in-depth case studies.

Summary

The design and implementation of derivative and option income strategies demand a disciplined approach that integrates theoretical principles with practical execution. These strategies are vital tools for modern portfolio management because they can generate consistent income, manage risk, and enhance portfolio adaptability. However, their success depends on a comprehensive understanding of the instruments involved, careful alignment with portfolio objectives, and continuous adaptability to dynamic market conditions.

Throughout this chapter, we have explored the foundational principles that underpin effective strategy design, including aligning derivative positions with equity portfolios, managing path dependency through diversification, and balancing growth with sustainable yield generation. These principles provide a framework for structuring robust strategies that can withstand market fluctuations and deliver consistent results. Additionally, strategy evaluation has been emphasized as a critical process to ensure reliability, effective risk management, and avoiding common pitfalls such as chasing unsustainable yields or failing to align portfolio components.

Practical considerations in strategy implementation underscore the importance of precision in execution, ongoing monitoring, and adaptability. The ability to make timely adjustments, roll positions, and respond to market changes ensures that strategies remain relevant and practical in various conditions. The integration of tools such as options Greeks monitoring, margin analysis, and volatility metrics enables portfolio managers to manage risks effectively and optimize the performance of derivative positions.

This chapter serves as a conceptual foundation and a practical guide to designing and implementing derivative and option income strategies. The insights provided here pave the way for deeper exploration of specific techniques and real-world applications in the cases presented later in this book.

Successful application of these strategies requires technical expertise, a commitment to disciplined execution, and ongoing learning. By adhering to the principles outlined in this chapter and applying the practical insights discussed, portfolio managers can create derivative and option income strategies that achieve their objectives while navigating the complexities of today's financial markets. The cases and applications presented in the subsequent sections will further illustrate these concepts, offering actionable guidance for portfolio managers seeking to enhance their practice.

9

Liquidity Management with Stock-Index Futures

Kris Shen and Shaojun Zhang

Active funds in the United States managed assets exceeding $13 trillion in 2023, playing an important role in the financial markets. Institutional and retail investors frequently use these funds to enact their trading views, and these rebalancing actions generate strong flows in active funds. Managing such large asset movements requires active fund managers to be proficient in liquidity management within an ever-changing market environment.

While this chapter provides an overview of liquidity management for active mutual fund managers, the primary focus will be on how derivatives, particularly stock-index futures contracts, are deployed as a key tool for efficient liquidity management. By using these derivatives, fund managers can strategically manage exposures and address liquidity needs without large-scale asset liquidation.

Basics of Liquidity Management

Liquidity management refers to managers' strategic control of funds' cash holdings, liquid assets, and illiquid assets to ensure sufficient liquidity to cover both expected and unexpected liquidity needs. The expected liquidity needs

K. Shen · S. Zhang (✉)
Fisher College of Business, The Ohio State University, Columbus, OH, USA
e-mail: zhang.7805@osu.edu

F. J. Fabozzi and M. de Jong (eds.), *Derivatives Applications in Asset Management*,
https://doi.org/10.1007/978-3-031-86354-7_9

typically include regular investor redemptions and scheduled portfolio rebalances. Most mutual funds trade once daily, with the execution price based on the next available net asset value (NAV) after the close of the market. Hence, most active mutual funds face daily redemption pressures and need sufficient liquidity to manage these regular cash outflows. Furthermore, fund managers periodically rebalance their portfolios for many reasons, such as the impending expiration of current assets that necessitate rollovers.

Liquidity management is important for several reasons. First, active funds must be able to meet investor redemption requests promptly. For example, mutual fund investors expect to redeem their shares at the NAV without significant delays. If a fund lacks sufficient liquidity, it may struggle to fulfill these redemptions, potentially forcing the fund manager to sell assets quickly at unfavorable prices. This can lead to a "fire sale" situation, where assets are sold at a steep discount, negatively impacting investors' returns.

Second, liquidity management allows fund managers to adhere to their investment strategy without being forced to make decisions based on cash flow needs rather than market opportunities. If a fund is compelled to sell its positions to meet redemptions, it may incur losses and deviate from its intended asset allocation and strategy. Maintaining adequate liquidity helps fund managers continue pursuing their strategy and target returns without undue disruption.

Third, funds that effectively manage their liquidity can be better positioned to capitalize on market opportunities. In times of market volatility or undervalued assets, having liquid assets on hand allows fund managers to make timely investments. Conversely, funds that are fully invested or have poor liquidity may miss out on these opportunities, limiting their potential for generating alpha (excess returns over a benchmark). For example, the COVID-19 Crisis in 2020 triggered substantial financial market turbulence, characterized by elevated equity market volatility and diminished market liquidity. During this liquidity crisis, substantial and abnormal outflows from active funds were primarily driven by a sharp increase in redemption demands. Moreover, significant mispricing also arises during such market episodes, and only well-capitalized managers can exploit the trading opportunities.

Fourth, liquidity management can reduce the transaction costs that the fund incurs. Illiquid assets can result in higher transaction costs when buying or selling, eroding fund performance. Effective liquidity management helps minimize these costs by ensuring that transactions can be executed under normal market conditions rather than during periods of forced liquidation.

This cost management is particularly important in volatile markets, where bid-ask spreads can widen, and the cost of liquidity can increase significantly.

Ultimately, effective liquidity management helps maintain investor confidence, which is crucial for the reputation and success of an active fund. Funds that cannot meet redemption requests or are forced to sell assets under pressure can suffer reputational damage, leading to further redemptions and a negative feedback loop. On the other hand, funds with a track record of good liquidity management are more likely to retain and attract investors, which can reduce liquidity shocks that the fund must deal with.

It is worth noting that liquidity management can be more important for active funds than for passive funds. Managers of passive funds aim to mimic benchmark performances. In contrast, active fund managers frequently adjust their portfolios and engage in active trading in order to seize market opportunities. Therefore, liquidity management is crucial to ensure that all transactions are conducted effectively and without excessively large transactions that could impede the funds' overall performance and lead to prompt fund outflows by concerned investors. In addition, effective liquidity management will reduce the risk of tracking error, i.e., the difference between the fund's actual performance and its benchmark, which can result from delayed or suboptimal trades.

Tools and Techniques for Liquidity Management

Active mutual fund managers must be experts in utilizing different tools and techniques for effective liquidity management. Their ability to navigate various tools under different circumstances is crucial for supporting daily operations and ensuring the fund's capability to meet market opportunities and investor demands. The typical liquidity management tools used by active managers are cash buffers and liquid assets (Exhibit 9.1). We discuss each of the tools below.

Among the tools available, derivatives play a central role in liquidity management by enabling managers to manage risk exposures and meet liquidity demands with minimal transaction costs. This chapter first provides an overview of the tools available to active managers and then focuses on how stock-index futures can be effectively utilized for these purposes.

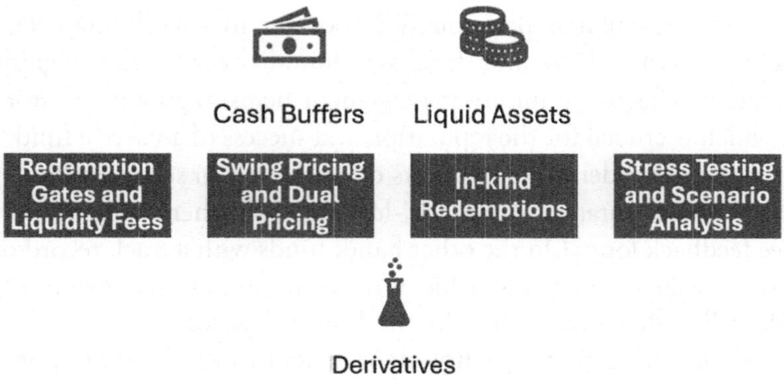

Exhibit 9.1 Liquidity management tools

Cash Buffers

Active mutual funds usually hold a proportion of their portfolio in cash or cash equivalents to meet daily redemption requests. Sufficient cash buffers enable managers to cover daily transactions and unexpected withdrawals without fire-selling other assets. In some cases, the active mutual funds can hold more than 5% cash in the portfolio. For example, according to Morningstar, one of the largest value funds, a $97.9 billion American Mutual A Fund (AMRMX), held 5.2% in cash and cash equivalents as of May 13, 2024.

Liquid Assets

Active mutual funds invest in various liquid assets to gain earnings and maintain financial flexibility for immediate liquidity needs. These liquid assets include bonds and other debt securities issued by the U.S. government and by federal agencies, instrumentalities, and highly liquid stocks. Holding stocks also contributes to the fund's liquidity pool with earnings from dividends or interest payments. For example, Morningstar reports that one of Vanguard's active mutual funds, namely the Vanguard Advice Select Global Value Fund (VAGVX), held 55.83% in U.S. equity and 43.29% in non-U.S. equity as of Jun 30, 2024. Among those equity holdings, most are highly liquid stocks that could be sold easily to meet redemption requests. Their U.S. equity holdings include Adobe Inc., Morgan Stanley, and Delta Air Lines Inc. Their non-U.S. equity holdings include the Chinese Tencent Holdings Ltd, Japanese Sony Group Corp, and Canadian Natural Resources Ltd.

While it is beyond the scope of this chapter, active managers have additional liquidity management tools that they can deploy, in particular under unusual circumstances. The second row in Exhibit 9.1 shows examples of such measures, including redemption gates and liquidity fees, alternative pricing mechanisms, and in-kind redemptions. Such measures need higher-level approval senior to portfolio managers at the fund's inception or in exceptional market conditions.

Redemption Gates and Liquidity Fees

In extreme market conditions, active mutual funds may implement mechanisms like redemption gates or liquidity fees to constrain large-scale withdrawals by investors. Redemption gates allow funds to temporarily suspend (or gate) redemptions when the proportion of weekly liquid assets drops below a predetermined threshold, such as 30%. Concurrently, in scenarios where liquid assets become insufficient, a fund may impose a liquidity fee of up to 2% on all redemptions. These tools and techniques are designed to protect the overall health of the fund by preventing rapid asset depletion so that the fund remains stable during volatile periods.

Swing Pricing and Dual Pricing

Some funds deploy alternative pricing mechanisms, such as swing pricing or dual pricing, to shield existing investors from the costs incurred from large redemption orders. Swing pricing involves adjusting a fund's NAV in accordance with the trading volumes following net fund flows, ensuring that both redemptions and subscriptions occur at the same price. Dual pricing operates similarly to swing pricing, with the key distinction that redemption prices may differ from subscription prices. This approach allows funds to control transaction costs associated with investor entries and exits more effectively.

In-kind Redemptions

In-kind redemptions, primarily reserved for large institutional investors, allow funds to fulfill redemption requests using security baskets that are equivalent in value instead of cash. This method effectively transfers the transaction costs associated with the sale of securities to the redeeming investors. Moreover, funds retain the discretion to select which securities to distribute through in-kind redemptions, providing a strategic advantage in managing portfolio impacts. Funds tend to distribute illiquid securities in-kind to discourage large redemptions. Mutual funds formalize the option for in-kind redemptions by means of filing Form N-18F-1 with the Securities and Exchange Commission (SEC). For instance, Vanguard's policies specify that "Because a trade may be disruptive to a fund's operation or performance, the portfolio manager has the authority to accept, reject, or delay such a purchase; delay the delivery of redemption proceeds for up to seven days; or issue a redemption in kind." This approach allows managers to opt for in-kind redemptions, providing flexibility to manage trades that could impact the fund adversely.

Stress Testing and Scenario Analysis

The success or effectiveness of a fund's liquidity management policy can be assessed via stress testing and scenario analysis. The regulation of liquidity management in active mutual funds dates back to the enactment of the Investment Company Act in 1940 in the United States, which outlines mutual funds' responsibilities and requires that funds return all proceeds to shareholders within seven days of a share redemption request. Over the years, regulatory frameworks have evolved, particularly in response to financial crises that exposed vulnerabilities. For example, the 2007–2008 Global Financial Crisis highlighted the liquidity risks of active mutual funds, especially those invested in markets like mortgage-backed securities involved in defaulted subprime mortgages. In response to these events, regulatory bodies worldwide tightened liquidity requirements to ensure that funds can adequately meet redemption requests even during market downturns. In the United States, the SEC adopted the Rule 22e-4 in 2016, which mandates comprehensive liquidity-risk management programs, and specific reporting and disclosure obligations for mutual funds.

Furthermore, regulators often mandate that active mutual funds conduct regular stress testing and scenario analysis to ensure their resilience during financial turbulence. For instance, following the 2014 reform of money market mutual funds by the SEC, it became a requirement for funds to test their ability to maintain a minimum of 10% in liquid assets on a one-week horizon under several SEC-defined stress scenarios.[1] This reform necessitates that funds evaluate their hypothetical responses to potential crises that could trigger immediate large-scale redemption demands from investors. The scenarios include a prompt increase in short-term interest rates, a downgrade

[1] For more details, see Jeremy Berkowitz, "Money Market Mutual Funds: Stress Testing and New Regulatory Requirements," National Economics Research Associates, July 14, 2015, https://corpgov.law.harvard.edu/2015/07/14/money-market-mutual-funds-stress-testing-new-regulatory-requirements.

or default of specific securities, and a widening of credit spreads relative to the indexes to which the portfolio securities are benchmarked. Such stress testing helps ensure that funds can manage unexpected financial pressures while maintaining necessary liquidity levels.

Derivatives

Finally, we conduct an in-depth examination of the application of derivatives in liquidity management, offering a comprehensive set of case studies across various market conditions. Derivatives, including futures, options, and swaps, play a pivotal role in liquidity management for active mutual funds. These sophisticated financial instruments empower fund managers to hedge against diverse risks and efficiently manage exposures without the necessity of holding substantial quantities of the underlying assets. Fund managers can effectively align their assets by strategically adjusting derivative positions within their portfolios to meet short-term liquidity demands, such as unexpected redemption requests. This flexibility is particularly valuable in volatile market conditions, where rapid adjustments may be necessary to maintain the fund's desired risk profile and performance objectives.

An illustrative example of derivatives used for liquidity management is the $20 billion JPMorgan Hedged Equity Fund (JHQAX) as of August 16, 2024. According to the fund's Summary Prospectus, it implements a Put/Spread Collar strategy utilizing index options. This options-based approach allows the fund to potentially generate income and provide downside protection, enhancing its liquidity profile. Additionally, the fund employs index futures contracts to manage equity exposure from its cash positions strategically. These futures serve a dual purpose, also acting as a hedge for the fund's portfolio when direct options for its overlay strategy are not feasible to write. This multifaceted use of options and futures exemplifies the sophisticated liquidity management techniques available through derivatives, enabling the fund to maintain desired exposure levels while providing the flexibility to meet liquidity needs efficiently. This example of JHQAX underscores how active mutual funds can leverage a combination of derivative instruments to optimize their liquidity management strategies, potentially enhancing risk-adjusted returns and operational efficiency in dynamic market environments.

Challenges in Liquidity Management

Active funds bear higher levels of active and fund-specific risks than passive funds do. As such, the funds are more liable to deviate from the benchmark in terms of performance. This active performance prompts frequent and substantial investor flows, and managing these flows is challenging. In this section, we will discuss several key challenges that impede fund managers' ability to achieve superior results consistently due to liquidity strategies. These challenges include volatile market conditions, transaction costs, issues related to the market structure, irrational investor behavior, and the uncertainty stemming from evolving market regulation. Each of these factors plays an important role in the overall performance of active funds.

Market Conditions

Overall market conditions greatly influence the liquidity management of active mutual funds. Fund managers typically adopt different liquidity strategies following the prevailing market conditions. A recent study finds that, during periods of high market volatility, managers prioritize the use of cash and highly liquid assets to satisfy redemption requests while preserving a certain level of liquidity. Conversely, managers are less likely to use cash buffers in a stable market characterized by adequate market liquidity. When markets are stable, fund managers tend to reduce holdings in liquid assets and increase investments in illiquid assets, adjusting the portfolio composition to optimize returns when the market liquidity risk seems low.

However, it is important to note that different types of funds may adopt different liquidity strategies irrespective of the overall market conditions. Active mutual funds, particularly those that aim to seize liquidity premiums, might retain their holdings in illiquid assets even during market downturns. For instance, Morningstar reports that the Fidelity Real Estate Income Fund (FRIFX), which holds assets totaling $4.8 billion as of July 31, 2024, maintains a significant portion of its portfolio in inherently less liquid investments such as home financing, real estate, and Commercial Mortgage-Backed Securities.

Transaction Costs

High transaction costs, conveyed by bid-ask spreads, or brokerage fees, are obstructive to effective liquidity management for active fund managers.

Active funds, which inherently engage in more frequent trading than their passive counterparts, are particularly susceptible to these costs. Despite a substantial reduction in transaction costs since the 1970s due to technological advancements in trading systems, numerous studies demonstrate that these transaction costs often subsume a considerable portion of the active returns generated by mutual funds.

Effective liquidity management entails strategic planning to mitigate transaction costs. One common approach is through economies of scale, allowing fund managers to transact large volumes of securities in a single operation rather than executing multiple trades for individual securities. This method, however, poses greater challenges for smaller funds due to their limited capacity to trade in bulk. Alternatively, fund managers may employ financial instruments like index futures to replicate market exposure. This strategy avoids the need for frequent transactions of large quantities of underlying securities, thereby reducing transaction costs.

Market Structure

Futures contracts, while essential for hedging and speculation in financial markets, come with several structural characteristics that can impact their effectiveness and usage. One key aspect is that these contracts are standardized and come in predefined lot sizes, which may not always align perfectly with an investor's specific hedging needs. This standardization can lead to over- or under-hedging, potentially introducing basis risk. Additionally, futures contracts are typically issued monthly, which can create timing mismatches for hedgers whose risk exposure doesn't neatly align with these monthly cycles.

Another important consideration is the ex-dividend trading period associated with futures contracts. During this period, the market value of current holdings may not accurately reflect the liquidity needs due to the impending dividend payment. As such, portfolio managers need to adjust their derivative positions cautiously and manage their true liquidity needs.

Furthermore, futures markets often experience variations in liquidity across different contract months, with near-term contracts generally being more liquid than those with longer maturities. This liquidity differential can impact transaction costs and the ease of entering or exiting positions, particularly for larger trades or in less actively traded markets.

Investor Behavior

Liquidity management for active fund managers is further challenged by unpredictable investor behavior, influenced by cognitive biases such as representativeness heuristics, the disposition effect, and mental accounting. Representativeness heuristics describe the tendency of investors to base their expectations of a fund's future performance on its recent past returns, often leading to behavior in which investors chase past performance. The disposition effect refers to the reluctance of investors to sell underperforming funds while quickly selling those performing well. Mental accounting involves investors' differential responses to various resources of fund expenses, such as transaction costs and management fees, often affecting their investment decisions and actions. These behaviors introduce additional complexity and uncertainty to active fund managers' liquidity management tasks.

Regulatory Uncertainty

Regulatory uncertainty poses another challenge to active fund managers, as regulations can change relatively quickly, particularly following major events that cause financial turbulence. These regulatory shifts can either decrease or increase mutual fund managers' costs. For instance, the abovementioned Rule 22e-4 implemented in 2016 substantially increased operating costs for active mutual funds and subjected them to higher public monitoring pressure.

However, regulatory changes can also benefit mutual fund managers and decrease the costs during liquidity crises. For example, during the COVID-19 pandemic, mutual funds, particularly money market funds (MMFs), faced significant redemption pressures. In response, the Federal Reserve established the Money Market Mutual Fund Liquidity Facility (MMLF) in March 2020. This facility was designed to support MMFs by enabling them to sell high-quality assets, such as U.S. Treasuries and agency-backed securities, to meet redemption demands without fire sales, thus helping stabilize the funds during the liquidity crisis.

Case Study

In this section, we present a few cases of liquidity management for active funds. We begin by providing an overview of the instruments. Then, we discuss a few examples, including reinvesting dividend payments, rolling futures contracts, dealing with flows, and finally, the mixed use of options and futures. It is worth noting that although we focus on active funds in this section, the discussions here also apply to passive funds. Managers of passive funds usually adopt the instruments we discuss here to complement the tools specific to passive funds, such as in-kind trades.

Cash flows of active funds can seep through from several sources.

- *Dividends*: When a mutual fund receives dividends from the stocks or other holdings in its portfolio, the dividends cumulate into the mutual fund's cash holdings rather than being immediately paid out to shareholders. Mutual funds can have different dividend distribution strategies, like distributing fully in cash, reinvesting a portion in the fund itself, or giving investors a choice between cash and reinvestment. For example, mutual funds can periodically distribute the accumulated dividends to shareholders on pre-announced ex-dividend dates, monthly, quarterly, or annually. Shareholders effectively receive their portion of the dividends earned.
- *Inflows and Outflows*: Mutual funds experience inflows and outflows of investor capital through subscriptions and redemptions, respectively. When investors purchase shares of a mutual fund, the fund receives cash inflows, which the portfolio manager must invest following the fund's investment strategy. Conversely, when investors redeem their shares, the fund must sell some of its holdings to generate the cash needed to meet these redemptions. This constant ebb and flow of capital can significantly impact the fund's liquidity management. Substantial outflows may force the manager to liquidate holdings at inopportune times or unfavorable prices to raise the necessary cash. Effective liquidity management is crucial for mutual funds to ensure they meet redemption requests while minimizing the impact on the remaining shareholders and adhering to the fund's investment objectives.

Instrument for Liquidity Management

A key instrument of liquidity management is stock-index futures contracts. These contracts are derivative instruments that allow investors to speculate on or hedge against the future value of a specific market index. These contracts derive their value from an underlying index, such as the S&P 500, the Nasdaq 100, or the Dow Jones Industrial Average. The buyer of a stock-index futures contract takes a long position when expecting the index to rise in value. In

Contract	Underlying Index	Contract Size	Exchange
E-Mini S&P 500	S&P 500 Index	$50 times Index	CME
E-Micro S&P 500	S&P 500 Index	$5 times Index	CME
E-Micro Nasdaq 100	Nasdaq 100 Index	$2 times Index	CME
E-Mini Nasdaq 100	Nasdaq 100 Index	$20 times Index	CME
E-Mini Russell 2000 Index	Russell 2000 Index	$50 times Index	CME
E-Mini Dow Jones Industrial	Dow Jones Industrial Average (DJIA) Index	$5 times Index	CBOT
Bloomberg Commodity Index	Bloomberg Commodity Index	$100 times Index	CBOT
E-Mini S&P MidCap 400 Index	S&P MidCap 400 Index	$100 times Index	CME
S&P GSCI - Goldman Sachs Commodity Index	Goldman Sachs Commodity Index	$250 times Index	CME

Exhibit 9.2 Examples of U.S. stock-index futures contracts

contrast, the seller takes a short position when anticipating a decline in the index's value.

The active manager often selects index futures that closely mimic the benchmark index's performance but with sufficient liquidity and low transition costs. Exhibit 9.2 presents the most active index futures in the United States. The E-mini S&P 500 futures contract has a notional value of 50 times the value of the S&P 500 index. For example, if the S&P 500 index is trading at 5,000, the notional value of one contract would be $250,000 (5,000 × $50). As such, the notional value of the contracts can be relatively high for funds with lower assets under management (AUM) to use for liquidity management. In those cases, the funds can also use micro E-mini S&P futures contracts, which have a notional value of 5 times the value of the S&P 500 index, to complement E-mini S&P 500 futures.

Reinvesting Dividends Through Index Futures

Consider an active mutual fund with a benchmark of the Russell 3000 index. The mutual fund's mandate is to maximize its exposure to the quality factor according to proprietary trading signals and outperform the benchmark. The mutual fund uses both the E-mini and micro E-mini S&P futures contracts to help manage its liquidity.

On March 1, 2024, the mutual fund had 2,310,000 shares outstanding, and the market price is $134.68 per share. The portfolio had been recently rebalanced to boost the so-called *quality* exposure according to proprietary signals. The quality signal exposure calculated internally at 0.82, is favorable compared to the average exposure in the preceding three months, 0.78.

At the beginning of the day, the portfolio carried over its outstanding futures positions as follows. The cash, or the U.S. dollar amount, had increased compared to the end of the previous day because the fund had received a dividend payment of $158,922.00. Exhibit 9.3 presents the positions of liquid assets, including cash.

Given the portfolio's positions and the additional cash of $158,922 from the dividend payment, the portfolio manager (PM) can either invest the cash into individual stocks or in stock-index futures contracts. While investing in individual stocks could potentially increase the portfolio's exposure to the quality factor, the PM examines the quality exposure and determines that the quality exposure meets the target exposure because he has recently rebalanced the portfolio.

Therefore, the PM decides to reinvest the cash into index futures contracts. This strategy allows the PM to maintain broad exposure to the S&P 500 index, minimizing potential deviations from the benchmark's performance while reducing transaction costs in managing the fund's liquidity. This approach ensures that the portfolio remains almost fully invested and minimizes potential cash drags. The high liquidity of futures contracts also offers the PM flexibility to adjust the portfolio's exposure efficiently in response to inflows, outflows, or changes in market conditions.

Exhibit 9.4 shows how the PM can proceed:

Description	% of Funds	# of Contracts	Price Per Contract	Notional Value
Micro E-mini S&P500 futures Mar 2024	0.08%	10	$25,558.75	$255,587.50
E-mini futures S&P500 Mar 2024	0.25%	3	$255,587.50	$766,762.50
US Dollar	0.05%			$158,922.00
Subtotal	0.38%			$1,181,272.00

Exhibit 9.3 Liquid/cash positions on March 1, 2024

Description	% of Funds	# of Contracts	Price Per Contract	Notional Value
Micro E-mini S&P500 futures Mar 2024	0.13%	16	$25,558.75	$408,940.00
E-mini futures S&P500 Mar 2024	0.25%	3	$255,587.50	$766,762.50
Cash	<0.01%			$5,569.50
Subtotal	0.38%			$1,181,272.00

Exhibit 9.4 Post-trade liquid/cash positions

- Cash available: $158,922. Since the amount of cash is lower than the price of the E-mini S&P 500 contracts, the PM uses the micro E-mini S&P 500 contracts instead.
- Calculate the number of micro E-mini S&P 500 futures contracts that can be purchased with the available cash:
  Price per micro E-mini S&P contract: $25,558.75
  Number of contracts to buy = $158,922 / $25,558.75 = 6.22 (round down to 6 contracts)

After purchasing six additional micro E-mini S&P 500 futures contracts, the portfolio's new liquid positions would be as shown in Exhibit 9.4.

Rolling Futures Contracts

The contracts have quarterly expiration cycles on the third Friday of March, June, September, and December. Given that all the current futures positions are for the March 2024 contract as today is March 1st, the PM will need to roll these contracts to the next available contract month very soon.

In this case, with the March 2024 E-mini and micro E-mini S&P 500 futures contracts expiring on March 15, the PM should plan to roll these positions in the coming days or weeks. Here are some key considerations:

1. *Next Contract Month*: The PM will likely roll into the June 2024 contract, the next quarterly expiration after March.
2. *Timing*: Many traders aim to roll 1–2 weeks before expiration to avoid illiquidity and potential price distortions very close to expiry.
3. *Roll Spread*: The March and June contracts may have a positive or negative price difference, known as the roll spread or roll yield. The PM should account for this spread.
4. *Execution*: The roll can be executed by selling the March contracts simultaneously and buying an equivalent number of June contracts. Some brokers offer a "roll" order type.
5. *Cash Flow Impact*: Any positive or negative cash flow from the rolled positions must be managed appropriately.

No inflows, outflows, or dividends occurred from March 1 to March 7. However, the price per share of the mutual fund and the S&P 500 index have changed. Exhibit 9.5 presents the updated liquid positions.

Based on the updated positions and prices, if the PM rolls the same number of contracts from the March 2024 expiry to the June 2024 expiry,

Description	% of Funds	# of Contracts	Price Per Contract	Notional Value
Micro E-mini S&P500 futures Mar 2024	0.13%	16	$25,974.00	$415,584.00
E-mini futures S&P500 Mar 2024	0.24%	3	$259,740.00	$779,220.00
Cash	< 0.01%			$5,569.50
Subtotal	0.38%			$1,200,375.50

Exhibit 9.5 Liquid/cash positions on March 7, 2024

Description	% of Funds	# of Contracts	Price Per Contract	Notional Value
Micro E-mini S&P500 futures Jun 2024	0.13%	16	$26,141.25	$418,260.00
E-mini futures S&P500 Jun 2024	0.24%	3	$261,412.50	$784,237.50
Cash	0.00%			($2,124.00)
Subtotal	0.38%			$1,200,373.50

Exhibit 9.6 Hypothetical liquid/cash position after full rolling

there would be a negative cash balance, as shown in Exhibit 9.6. This is because the June 2024 contracts are trading at a higher price than the March 2024 contracts.

Instead, the PM decides to take a balanced approach, rolling most of the existing contracts to the June 2024 expiry while maintaining a positive cash balance. Here are the specific steps:

Step 1: Roll the E-mini futures contracts: The PM rolls all three E-mini futures contracts from March 2024 to June 2024 expiry, maintaining the full exposure for the larger E-mini contract position.

Step 2: Partially roll the micro E-mini futures contracts: The PM rolls 15 out of the 16 micro E-mini contracts from March 2024 to June 2024 expiry. By rolling 15 instead of all 16, the PM can free up some cash to cover the roll cost.

Step 3: Manage the cash balance: The partial roll of the micro E-mini contracts generates enough cash to cover the roll cost. After the roll, the cash balance is $24,017.25, leaving a positive amount. Exhibit 9.7 presents the new portfolio after partial rolling.

Description	% of Funds	# of Contracts	Price Per Contract	Notional Value
Micro E-mini S&P500 futures Jun 2024	0.12%	15	$26,141.25	$392,118.75
E-mini futures S&P500 Jun 2024	0.24%	3	$261,412.50	$784,237.50
Cash	0.01%			$24,017.25
Subtotal	0.38%			$1,200,373.50

Exhibit 9.7 Liquid/cash positions after partial rolling

Dealing with Outflows

The mutual fund experienced an outflow of $909,140.3. The PM needs to raise significant cash while maintaining reasonable S&P 500 exposure. The PM conducts an analysis and executes trades in several steps. With only $24,017.25 in cash, selling futures contracts was necessary. The liquid asset positions are more than enough to cover the outflow, implying that selling some future contracts would be sufficient to meet the redemption needs.

1. The PM first sells all 3 E-mini S&P 500 futures Jun 2024 contracts at $261,412.50 per contract, raising $784,237.50. After the E-mini sales, the remaining cash was $808,254.75 ($24,017.25 + $784,237.50), still short of the $909,140.30 required.
2. The PM then sells 11 of the 15 micro E-mini S&P 500 futures Jun 2024 contracts at $26,141.25 per contract, raising an additional $287,553.75 (11 × $26,141.25).
3. The total cash raised from selling all E-mini and 11 micro E-mini contracts is $1,095,808.50 ($808,254.75 + $287,553.75).
4. After meeting the $909,140.30 redemption, the remaining cash balance was $186,668.20 ($1,095,808.50 − $909,140.30 = $186,668.20).

The updated futures and cash positions are presented in Exhibit 9.8.

In addition, when the fund approaches the pre-announced ex-dividend dates, the fund also needs to liquidate assets to meet the dividend amount. For example, if the fund needs to pay a dividend of $909,140, the PM needs

Description	% of Funds	# of Contracts	Price Per Contract	Notional Value
Micro E-mini S&P500 futures Jun 2024	0.03%	4	$26,141.25	$104,565.00
Cash	0.06%			$186,668.20
Subtotal	0.38%			$291,233.20

Exhibit 9.8 Liquid/cash position after redemption

to trade as if he is facing an outflow of $909,140. As such, the PM would proceed as analyzed in Exhibit 9.8.

Dealing with Inflows

The second column in Exhibit 9.8 shows the portfolio weight (% of the funds) in liquid assets and cash. The portfolio weight invested in liquid assets (index futures and cash) depends on the expectation about flows. If the fund is facing frequent flows, particularly redemptions, the fund manager (PM) may maintain a higher allocation to liquid assets to ensure sufficient liquidity to meet these redemptions without being forced to sell illiquid or strategic holdings at unfavorable prices. Conversely, if the fund is anticipating significant inflows, the PM is less concerned about liquidating individual equity positions and can hold a lower liquidity buffer. Let's examine the actions of the PM.

Consider a period during which the fund has consistently outperformed its benchmark. The fund's inflows have been strong, and the PM is preparing for further expected inflows. Given the strong inflow, the PM is less concerned about incurring high transaction costs when the PM must liquidate individual positions. In sum, the PM decides to deploy all available cash and liquid assets to invest in individual stocks to further boost the quality exposure of the fund and make the most of the signal.

After careful analysis, the PM decides to deploy all available liquid positions and cash into Qualcomm (QCOM, 123.73 per share), which has one of the highest quality scores but is not held by the fund. The PM proceeds as follows:

1. Calculates how many shares to buy: $291,233.20/$123.73 = 2353.78.
2. Round the number of shares down to 2353 shares.
3. The remaining cash equals $291,233.20 − $123.73 × 2352 = $467.70.

Exhibit 9.9 presents the updated positions for the Qualcomm stock and cash.

A Mixed Use of Options and Index Futures

Let's explore a scenario where the fund manager considers a mixed approach combining options and index futures to achieve specific equity exposure and

Description	% of Funds	# Shares	Stock Price	Market Value
Qualcomm (QCOM)	0.09%	2350	123.73	$290,765.50
Description	% of Funds	# of Contracts	Price Per Contract	Notional Value
Cash	0.00%			$467.70

Exhibit 9.9 Liquid/Cash positions after deploying all cash

mitigate risk, particularly when direct option transactions are not feasible for the strategic goals.

To illustrate, let's consider the case of a PM who decides to allocate all available liquid assets to QCOM while implementing a Put/Spread Collar strategy to hedge associated risks. Rather than purchasing all 2350 shares of QCOM as in the previous example, the PM opts to buy only 800 shares, using the remaining cash to establish the hedge. The Put/Spread Collar strategy employed involves several steps:

1. *Buying a Put Option*: The PM purchases a put option with a strike price of $100, which serves to limit potential losses by setting a floor; if QCOM's stock price falls below $100, the fund's maximum losses are fixed.
2. *Selling a Call Option*: To offset the cost of the put, the manager short-sells a call option with a strike price of $148. This action helps finance the put position but caps the portfolio's gains if QCOM's price exceeds $148.
3. *Buying Another Call Option*: Initially, the PM had intended to purchase another call option with a strike price of $172 to extend the potential for gains, should the stock price surge beyond $148. However, we assume that this specific option is unavailable in the market.

Consequently, the PM takes an alternative approach by acquiring a long position in NASDAQ-100 index futures (specifically, the NASDAQ 100 E-Mini) for June 2024. This future has a higher concentration of tech stocks, including Qualcomm, thus aligning with the fund's investment focus. For simplicity, we assume the prices for the $148 strike price call option and the $100 strike price put option are identical at $20 each. The price per NASDAQ 100 E-Mini futures contract is $19,790.75.

Now, the PM can construct the new portfolio. He proceeds as follows:

1. Calculate how much it takes to buy 800 shares of QCOM: $\$123.73 \times 800 = \$98{,}992.00$.
2. Calculate how much it costs to buy the call options and how much it gains to sell the put options: $-800 \times \$20 + 800 \times \$20 = 0$

Description	% of Funds	# Shares	Stock Price	Market Value
Qualcomm (QCOM)	0.03%	800	$123.73	$98,992.00
Description	% of Funds	# of Contracts	Price Per Contract	Notional Value
Call with Strike Price at $148	0.01%	(800)	$20	($16,000)
Put with Strike Price at $100	0.01%	800	$20	$16,000
NASDAQ 100 E-Mini Futures	0.06%	9	$19,790.75	$178,116.75
Cash	0.01%			$14,124.45

Exhibit 9.10 Liquid/cash positions after deploying options and index futures

3. Calculate how many shares of NASDAQ 100 E-Mini Futures contracts can be bought with the remaining money: ($291,233.20 – $98,992.00) / 19,790.75 = 9.714. Round down to 9 shares.
4. The remaining cash will be: $291,233.20 – 9 × $19,790.75 – $98,992.00 = $14,124.45.

Exhibit 9.10 presents the updated positions for the Qualcomm stock, options, index futures, and cash.

This example showcases how index futures can be employed when other derivatives are unavailable to build portfolio exposure and mitigate specific risks. In the scenario described, the fund manager wants to pursue a Put/Spread Collar strategy but cannot fully execute this approach due to the unavailability of specific options. Despite these constraints, fund managers can lever the flexibility of index futures to effectively achieve targeted equity exposure from their cash holdings when the desired options are inaccessible.

In summary, liquidity management is a critical aspect of managing active funds, particularly those designed to beat the performance of a benchmark index, such as the Russell 300 index or S&P 500 index. Index futures contracts, including E-mini and micro E-mini futures, play a pivotal role in effective liquidity management for these funds.

Conclusions

In this chapter, we introduce the basics of liquidity management for active mutual funds, highlighting in what way derivatives can be instrumental Liquidity management is an integral part of day-to-day fund management. Liquidity management needs to adapt to varying market conditions, seek to minimize transaction costs, anticipate and accommodate investor behaviors, and deal with regulatory uncertainty.

There are four key takeaways:

- Liquidity management is crucial for the funds' ability to meet redemption requests and is an indispensable part of risk management.
- Key techniques of liquidity management include maintaining cash buffers to handle daily redemptions, investing in liquid assets for financial flexibility, and using derivatives like futures and options for efficient liquidity risk management. In addition, funds may employ mechanisms like redemption gates or liquidity fees, swing pricing, dual pricing, in-kind redemptions, stress testing, and scenario analysis.
- Despite various tools and techniques, active mutual fund performance varies widely due to several critical challenges in liquidity management. These include volatile market conditions, high transaction costs, issues related to the market structure, unpredictable investor behaviors, and regulatory uncertainties. Seasoned active fund managers need to manage these complex challenges to meet redemption demands and seize market opportunities.
- Stock-index futures are a crucial instrument in the toolkit of active managers for effective liquidity management. These derivatives enable managers to maintain desired market exposures without holding a great amount of the underlying securities. One advantage of index futures is their diversity in terms of product features and price ranges, which enables the construction of a mix of liquidation positions while fulfilling specific redemption needs. For instance, the employment of both E-mini and Micro E-mini S&P 500 futures allows active managers to preserve a certain level of exposure to the S&P 500 while efficiently liquidating assets to meet redemption requests. This flexible use of index futures helps manage the fund's liquidity needs while minimizing the impact on the fund's overall market exposure.

We present a few practical applications in the form of case studies for active fund managers. These implications affect managers' daily liquidity management. Under different scenarios, we show how managers could more effectively manage their liquidity.

- Funds periodically receive dividends, presenting managers with the decision to either retain these dividends in cash or cash equivalents or reinvest them into assets like individual stocks or index future contracts. The choice largely hinges on the fund's strategic needs. If anticipating an increase in redemption requests, conserving dividends as cash is prudent to ensure liquidity. In contrast, if the objective is to adjust portfolio exposure to align with specific risk factors—such as maintaining exposure to quality factors in our case—reinvesting dividends in index futures offers the necessary flexibility to meet this goal efficiently.

- Futures contracts need to be rolled by fund managers regularly to transfer positions from near-expiration contracts to those with later expiration dates. This process requires careful planning regarding timing, selection of appropriate replacement products, and execution to minimize transaction costs and mitigate market impact. Proper execution of rolling futures contracts enables managers to smoothly update old futures positions while maintaining the desired exposure through new contracts, ensuring consistency in the fund's strategic portfolio allocation and risk management framework.
- Managing regular inflows and outflows is a critical responsibility for active mutual fund managers. This case study illustrates strategies for handling both scenarios effectively. On the one hand, when anticipating inflows, fund managers might increase allocations to liquid assets such as index futures. This facilitates swift adjustments in portfolio exposure and liquidity management without incurring significant transaction costs. On the other hand, when anticipating outflows, managers can strategically sell a mix of futures contracts based on their unit prices. This approach ensures they can meet redemption requests while maintaining as much exposure to their desired risk factors as possible.

In summary, liquidity management plays a crucial role in ensuring the smooth operation of a fund, preserving capital, and achieving investment objectives. By effectively managing liquidity with equity index derivatives, fund managers can meet investor needs, maintain investment strategy and enhance their performance, capitalize on market opportunities, manage risks, comply with regulations, reduce transaction costs, and ultimately maintain and improve investors' confidence and the funds' reputation.

10

Performance Attribution Analysis for Derivatives

Bruce J. Feibel and Frank J. Fabozzi

Performance attribution is a critical process that helps investors and portfolio managers understand the sources of returns within a portfolio and relative to a benchmark. Breaking down the performance into different components identifies which decisions contributed to or detracted from overall returns. When derivatives are included in a portfolio, performance attribution becomes more nuanced and complex, as derivatives possess unique characteristics that set them apart from traditional asset classes like bonds and equities.

Performance attribution analysis is a valuable tool for understanding portfolio returns, but the complexity increases significantly when derivatives are included. Unlike traditional asset classes like bonds or equities, derivatives modify exposure rather than generate direct returns. This introduces unique challenges, such as accounting for leverage effects, managing notional versus market values, and recognizing the limitations of standard attribution methods.[1] For instance, derivatives like futures and swaps are leveraged

[1] "Limitations and challenges in attribution analysis." Blog available at https://fastercapital.com/topics/limitations-and-challenges-in-attribution-analysis.html.

B. J. Feibel (✉)
State Street, Boston, MA, USA
e-mail: feibels@yahoo.com

F. J. Fabozzi
Carey Business School, Johns Hopkins University, Baltimore, MD, USA

F. J. Fabozzi and M. de Jong (eds.), *Derivatives Applications in Asset Management*,
https://doi.org/10.1007/978-3-031-86354-7_10

instruments, amplifying both gains and losses, which can distort conventional attribution metrics if not properly adjusted.[2] Additionally, attribution analysis requires careful selection of benchmarks, especially when derivatives create exposures that do not align with conventional benchmarks.[3]

Unlike bonds, which typically generate returns through interest payments and changes in yield curves, or equities, which derive returns from dividends and capital appreciation, derivatives are contracts whose value is based on the performance of an underlying asset. Derivatives often have no initial market value like equities or bonds do, which makes calculating returns and measuring their contributions to portfolio performance more challenging. For instance, futures contracts are leveraged instruments that can alter exposure without requiring significant upfront capital. If improperly adjusted, this can amplify gains and losses and distort traditional attribution metrics.

Another key difference is that derivatives are frequently used to adjust portfolio exposure rather than to generate returns independently. In contrast to equities, where the main objective might be growth, or bonds, where the focus might be on stable income, derivatives are often employed for hedging, risk management, or achieving targeted leverage. These functions mean that derivatives may serve multiple purposes within a portfolio, from minimizing currency risk to altering interest rate exposure or providing synthetic market access. As a result, performance attribution for portfolios containing derivatives must account for gains or losses on individual derivative positions and their intended function and impact on broader portfolio objectives. This necessitates specialized approaches in attribution analysis that extend beyond the conventional frameworks for bonds and equities, ensuring that derivative impacts are accurately measured and contextually understood.

The chapter examines the complexities of performance attribution for portfolios containing derivatives, emphasizing the need for specialized approaches. It begins by discussing the unique role of derivatives in portfolio management, including their use in hedging, leveraging, and managing specific exposures. The chapter then describes methodologies for accurately attributing performance to derivatives, such as adapting the Brinson model, discussed below, and using notional values to account for leveraged exposure. It guides handling futures, options, and swaps, each requiring specific

---

[2] Bruce J. Feibel, "A comprehensive approach to derivatives in performance attribution," *Journal of Derivatives*, *29*(3), 2022, 121–138.

[3] Dan DiBartolomeo, "Performance attribution inclusive of derivatives," Webinar Presentation December 2023, Northfield. Available at https://www.northinfo.com/documents/1103.pdf.

attribution adjustments. The chapter also addresses common challenges—like leverage effects and data limitations—and concludes with best practices to improve accuracy and transparency in derivatives attribution.

While performance attribution for derivatives is essential for understanding portfolio outcomes, it is fraught with challenges. Key obstacles include data quality and availability, and potential model biases, which are often overlooked. Furthermore, derivatives introduce non-linear relationships, complicating the attribution model assumptions. Recognizing these limitations is crucial to approach attribution with a critical lens.[4] Best practices call for using specialized models that account for leveraged exposure and consider underlying price changes and time decay in options.[5]

As attribution models continue to evolve, incorporating these best practices can help enhance the accuracy and relevance of performance insights, especially when derivatives play a significant role. By aligning analytical frameworks with the specific characteristics of derivatives, portfolio managers and analysts can better understand the true drivers of portfolio performance.

Effective attribution analysis, therefore, requires an adaptive approach that reflects the dynamic nature of derivative instruments. This adaptability allows for a comprehensive performance assessment across various market conditions and investment strategies, contributing to a more complete picture of risk and return.

A widely accepted approach for attribution analysis, the Brinson-style attribution model, can be adapted for derivatives by focusing on effective exposures. When derivatives are used, especially leveraged instruments, the standard Brinson decomposition—security selection, asset allocation, and interaction effects—must consider economic exposure rather than just market value. By incorporating notional values, as demonstrated by Feibel[6] and supported by Northfield,[7] analysts gain a more accurate view of derivatives' impact on portfolio outcomes. This is essential, as derivatives like futures contracts alter exposure without significant upfront capital, necessitating adjustments to the basic attribution inputs.

The notional approach also involves using effective return calculations, which consider the leveraged nature of derivatives. For instance, futures and options often have minimal initial values but can significantly impact portfolio performance due to changes in the underlying asset prices. In attribution analysis, adjusting return calculations to reflect the derivative's intended role

---

4 This is highlighted in "Limitations and challenges in attribution analysis."

5 DiBartolomeo, "Performance attribution inclusive of derivatives."

6 Feibel, "A comprehensive approach to derivatives in performance attribution."

7 DiBartolomeo, "Performance attribution inclusive of derivatives."

in the portfolio, whether for hedging, achieving leverage, or accessing specific asset exposures is crucial.

Overview of Derivatives in Performance Attribution

Derivatives play a distinct and versatile role in portfolios, often serving functions beyond straightforward return generation. Unlike traditional assets such as bonds or equities, derivatives can modify portfolio exposure to various risk factors without requiring significant initial investment. This capability allows investors to use derivatives for various purposes, including hedging, leveraging, and managing exposure to specific asset classes or risk factors like currency or interest rates. In performance attribution analysis, it is essential to recognize these unique characteristics to assess the contribution of derivatives accurately.

The primary complexity in attributing performance to derivatives lies in their notional exposures and how they influence the overall portfolio. Derivatives typically have notional values far greater than their market values, meaning that their exposure to the portfolio is disproportionate to their initial capital requirement. For example, a futures contract might have a notional exposure of several times its market value, which significantly magnifies its impact on portfolio performance compared to a similarly valued equity or bond position. Consequently, effective performance attribution for derivatives requires a framework that accounts for this amplified exposure and evaluates returns based on notional value rather than market value alone.

Another critical element in derivative attribution is the calculation of returns and weights, as standard methods used for bonds and equities do not always apply. For derivatives, effective return calculations must consider the leveraged nature of these instruments. Futures, options, and swaps often have minimal initial value but can significantly impact portfolio returns due to changes in underlying asset prices. In attribution analysis, it is important to adjust return calculations to reflect the derivative's intended role in the portfolio, whether it's hedging against downside risk, achieving specific leverage, or accessing certain asset exposures. This requires a shift from conventional market-value-based returns to methods incorporating the derivative's exposure-adjusted performance, providing a clearer view of its contribution to the overall portfolio.

Key Concepts in Derivatives Attribution Analysis

Attributing performance in a portfolio containing derivatives requires adapting traditional metrics to account for the unique nature of these instruments. One of the core concepts in derivatives attribution is *notional exposure*, which reflects the total economic exposure a derivative provides rather than its initial market value. This differs significantly from standard equity or bond investments, where the amount invested typically corresponds to the actual exposure. In derivatives, notional exposure can be multiple times the initial investment, creating a leveraged effect that amplifies gains and losses. For accurate attribution, analysts use notional exposure to scale returns and assess the derivative's impact on overall portfolio performance.

Effective return calculations for derivatives present another critical concept, as standard market-value returns are not always meaningful. Since derivatives often have minimal or no upfront capital requirements, their returns must be assessed differently to reflect their economic impact. Effective returns are calculated by adjusting for the derivative's leverage, where its performance is scaled to its notional value rather than its market value. This approach provides a clearer view of how derivatives influence portfolio outcomes, ensuring that performance attribution captures the full extent of risk and return associated with these positions. Finally, each derivative type's return and weight calculations must be adapted to achieve an accurate performance attribution. For instance, futures contracts require adjustments for daily variation margin, while options demand careful consideration of delta to capture changes in value relative to the underlying asset. Swaps also need specialized treatment in attribution analysis, as their value and returns are based on the movement of interest rates, currencies, or credit spreads. By tailoring return and weight calculations to each derivative type, performance attribution can more precisely capture the contribution of these instruments, aligning the analysis with the derivative's intended role within the portfolio.

Performance Attribution Methodologies Adapted for Derivatives

To accurately capture the performance contribution of derivatives within a portfolio, performance attribution methodologies must be adapted to address the unique characteristics of these instruments. One widely used framework in attribution analysis, Brinson-style attribution,[8] can be modified to incorporate derivative positions by focusing on value-added components such as security selection, asset allocation, and interaction effects.

In the Brinson analysis, value added is broken down into the following three active management effects:

Management effect	Measured by
Security Selection effect	(Portfolio segment return – Benchmark segment return) × Benchmark segment weight
Asset Allocation effect	(Portfolio segment weight – Benchmark segment weight) × (Benchmark segment return – Benchmark total return)
Interaction effect	(Portfolio segment weight – Benchmark segment weight) × (Portfolio segment return – Benchmark segment return)

An example gives illustration. The example portfolio begins with a 30% allocation to cash and a 70% allocation to equity, relative to a benchmark of 40% cash and 60% equity. The Brinson breakdown, given in Exhibit 10.1, illustrates the attribution without derivatives, where the three management effects, i.e., allocation, selection, and interaction effects contribute to a total outperformance of 1.7%. Using market-value-based returns and weights, the performance attribution is calculated traditionally, breaking down the value added into the three effects. This method assumes that portfolio exposure is directly proportional to the invested capital without leverage or synthetic exposure adjustments.

To incorporate derivatives into the analysis, we introduce notional adjustments reflecting the economic exposure of derivative instruments, in this case futures. Derivatives modify portfolio exposures, enabling leverage or precise asset allocation adjustments. This approach reclassifies cash and derivative-related gains into relevant asset classes, capturing the economic impact of the instruments more accurately. Exhibit 10.2 details the recalculated attribution after the exposure adjustments.

	Begin Weights			Returns			Attribution of Value Added			
Segment	**Portfolio**	**Benchmark**	**Difference**	**Portfolio**	**Benchmark**	**Value Added**	**Allocation**	**Selection**	**Interaction**	**Total**
Cash	30.00%	40.00%	-10.00%	7.00%	7.00%	0.00%	0.18%	0.00%	0.00%	0.18%
Equity	70.00%	60.00%	10.00%	12.00%	10.00%	2.00%	0.12%	1.20%	0.20%	1.52%
Total	**100.00%**	**100.00%**		**10.50%**	**8.80%**	**1.70%**	**0.30%**	**1.20%**	**0.20%**	**1.70%**

Exhibit 10.1 Performance Attribution of the example portfolio without Derivatives

[8] Gary P. Brinson, L. Randolph Hood, and Gilbert L. Beebower, "Determinants of Portfolio Performance," *Financial Analysts Journal*, *42* (4), 1986, 39–44.

	Portfolio Return Inputs - Base Currency				Begin Weights	Returns - Base Currency
Asset Class	**Begin Value**	**Income**	**End Value**	**Market Value + Income**	**Portfolio**	**Portfolio**
Cash	$ 100.00	$ 4.00	$ 100.00	$ 104.00		
Notional Cash	$ (90.00)	$ (3.60)	$ (90.00)	$ (93.60)	5.00%	4.00%
Equities	$ 100.00	$ 5.00	$ 120.00	$ 125.00	50.00%	25.00%
Futures	$ -	$ -	$ 20.00	$ 20.00		
Notional Futures	$ 90.00	$ 3.60	$ 90.00	$ 93.60	45.00%	26.22%
	$ 200.00	**$ 9.00**	**$ 240.00**	**$ 249.00**	**100.00%**	**24.50%**

	Portfolio Return Inputs - Base Currency				Begin Weights	Returns - Base Currency
Asset Class	**Begin Value**	**Income**	**End Value**	**Market Value + Income**	**Portfolio**	**Portfolio**
Cash	$ 10.00	$ 0.40	$ 10.00	$ 10.40	5.00%	4.00%
Equities	$ 190.00	$ 8.60	$ 230.00	$ 238.60	95.00%	25.58%
Total	**$ 200.00**	**$ 9.00**	**$ 240.00**	**$ 249.00**	**100.00%**	**24.50%**

Exhibit 10.2 Futures attribution: returns after exposure adjustments

The inclusion of derivatives transforms the calculation by incorporating notional exposures. In the case of futures, the portfolio's effective exposure increases while cash serves as collateral. The performance attribution captures the manager's true exposure intentions by reflecting both the notional value and cash income. Gains and losses from futures contracts and interest from backing cash are reclassified under the equity segment, aligning attribution with the portfolio's economic reality.

The comparison, without and with derivatives, illustrates how derivatives enhance attribution by more accurately reflecting the impact of leverage and synthetic exposures on performance. The recalibration aligns observed returns with the portfolio's economic exposures, revealing the contribution of derivative instruments beyond traditional metrics.

Within a Brinson-style framework, *interaction effects* capture the combined effect on the performance. For example, suppose the portfolio manager overweights an outperforming asset class relative to the portfolio's benchmark and simultaneously selects better-performing securities within the asset class. In that case, there is a positive synergy between the two decisions.

Derivative portfolios often benefit from modifying the basic Brinson analysis, introducing *notional attribution models* that directly incorporate the leveraged exposure of derivatives. Notional models analyze returns relative to notional exposure, providing a more realistic view of performance for instruments like futures and swaps. This method helps to align attribution with the derivative's actual economic impact, as it accounts for the leverage inherent in notional positions. Notional attribution is particularly useful when managing portfolios with significant derivative exposure, as it reveals the true contribution of these instruments to portfolio returns beyond what traditional market-value-based metrics would suggest.[9]

To analyze the impact of the use of derivatives on portfolio performance, we replace the use of market-value-based returns and weights with *notional returns* and *notional exposures* reflecting the underlying economic exposure of the derivative contracts. As illustrated in the example using futures, the leverage inherent in the futures contract increases the portfolio's exposure to the underlying compared to an equivalent dollar investment in a cash market instrument. The leverage has the effect of repositioning cash balances to an economic exposure to the underlying. Exhibit 10.2 shows how, in our example, we modify the calculation of returns and weights, inputs to the basic Brinson analysis, to reflect the use of futures to equitize cash.

The example portfolio aims to maximize returns while maintaining exposure to equity markets, even when significant cash holdings are present. To achieve this, equity index futures are used to equitize cash holdings, ensuring continuous participation in equity market performance while allowing the cash to earn interest. Futures contracts in this context act as instruments that synthetically replicate the economic exposure of direct equity investments. By entering into long equity futures positions, the portfolio substitutes a portion of its cash with exposure to the equity market, effectively reallocating the portfolio's economic exposure.

Exhibit 10.2 illustrates how futures are used to equitize cash and how this impacts the portfolio's performance attribution. The portfolio starts with a 50% allocation to cash and a 50% allocation to equities. A long futures position covering 90% of the cash is introduced. This adjustment shifts the effective equity allocation to 95% while maintaining a small residual 5% cash allocation. The futures contract allows the portfolio to track equity market gains or losses while earning interest on the backing cash. Income and gains from the futures contract are reclassified under the equity segment. As shown in Exhibit 10.2, the adjusted returns reflect the cash income of 4% and interest on backing cash, and they reflect the economic exposure of the futures contract, which adds to the equity segment's returns. By consolidating futures gains and cash income into the equity segment, the analysis aligns with the manager's intended exposure, providing a clearer view of performance attribution.

This adjustment process demonstrates how futures contracts transform the economic exposure of cash holdings, allowing the portfolio to capture

9 Feibel, "A comprehensive approach to derivatives in performance attribution."

equity market performance effectively while optimizing cash utilization. Exhibit 10.2 quantifies this adjustment, showing a 95% effective equity allocation that drives a 24.50% total portfolio return.

This attribution methodology highlights the integral role of derivatives in optimizing portfolio performance and clarifies their economic impact relative to traditional cash and equity allocations.

In the example portfolio, an initial allocation of 50% cash and 50% equities yielded a 25% equity return and 4% cash return, with an additional long equity futures position covering 90% of the cash, repositioning the portfolio to a 95% equity allocation. The futures contract provided daily variation margin adjustments that tracked underlying equity gains and losses while cash backing earned interest. The analysis reclassifies cash income, futures gains, and effective exposure adjustments to better capture performance, attributing these to the equity segment rather than a separate "Futures" asset class. This adjustment process clarifies the manager's exposure intentions by reflecting income from cash backing and effective exposure gains within the equity segment.

Attribution for Specific Types of Derivatives

Each type of derivative instrument—futures, options, and swaps—presents unique challenges in attribution. Futures require adjustments for daily variation margin, capturing gains or losses based on notional values rather than initial capital. Options attribution relies on sensitivity measures like delta to account for price changes in underlying assets, while swaps use effective exposure adjustments to represent the derivative's intended economic role. This method aligns with the Brinson-style attribution by adjusting inputs to reflect the derivative's economic impact within the portfolio accurately.[10] Feibel further underscores the importance of effectively leveraging notional exposure, especially with interest rate or currency swaps, to attribute returns based on actual economic exposure, aligning with portfolio objectives.[11]

Futures and Forwards

Futures and forward contracts allow leveraged exposure to an underlying asset without requiring substantial initial capital. As we have seen, performance attribution for these instruments must account for the impact of daily

[10] DiBartolomeo, "Performance attribution inclusive of derivatives."

[11] Feibel, "A comprehensive approach to derivatives in performance attribution."

variation margin (in the case of futures) or final settlement (for forwards). Futures attribution focuses on how the gains or losses realized through daily margin adjustments contribute to overall portfolio returns. Since futures provide a leveraged exposure, the notional value of each contract is typically used to assess its performance impact, capturing the amplified effect of small price changes in the underlying asset. Forwards, although settled at maturity rather than daily, similarly require consideration of their notional exposure to attribute performance accurately.

Options

Options are more complex due to their asymmetric payoff structure, time decay, and sensitivity to changes in the underlying asset's price, volatility, and time to expiration. Key metrics such as delta, gamma, and theta are essential for understanding how an option's value changes in response to market movements. In attribution analysis, delta captures the option's directional sensitivity to changes in the underlying asset, while gamma measures the rate of change in delta as the asset's price shifts. Theta, or time decay, reflects the option's loss in value as expiration approaches. Incorporating these factors into performance attribution allows analysts to gauge the option's direct returns and the influence of market dynamics on its performance over time.

Let's examine performance attribution when a portfolio manager uses call options to gain exposure to an underlying stock. Our objective is to demonstrate how options contribute to portfolio performance. The examples will underscore the importance of understanding the ex-ante intended use of an option contract, a consideration even more significant than futures and forwards.

Because options strategies often combine multiple options, security, and cash positions, this section demonstrates *strategy-based performance attribution* in addition to traditional approaches.

Options attribution differs from futures and forwards in several keyways:

- *Intrinsic value at inception*: Options have a premium representing their initial market value.
- *Asymmetric performance*: Options respond asymmetrically to the price movements of their underlying assets.
- *Exposure quantification methods*: Multiple valid methods exist to quantify the effective exposure of options to the underlying assets.

Metric	Value
Option Premium	$2.00
Total Contracts	100
Shares per Contract	100
Total Shares	20,000
Initial Stock Price	$10.00
Delta (Start)	0.50
Delta (End)	0.60
Final Stock Price	$11.50

Exhibit 10.3 Inputs for options attribution

We illustrate options attribution using a call purchase strategy, where the portfolio manager seeks exposure to gains in an underlying stock.[12] In this example, the inputs are 100 call contracts on 20,000 shares of an underlying stock purchased at $2.00 per share for a total premium of $20,000. The outcome is that the stock price increases by $1.50 per share, raising the value of the calls to $40,000. During the period, the options' delta changes from 0.5 to 0.6.

Exhibit 10.3 provides the input data, while Exhibits 10.4, 10.5, and 10.6 explore three methods for analyzing the impact of options on portfolio performance.

Each method provides unique insights into how options contribute to returns as summarized below:

Attribution Method	Option Treatment
Direct Method (Partial Exposure)	Treats the option as a distinct portfolio segment, similar to equity or bonds, reflecting its market value
Delta Method (Full Exposure)	Adjusts portfolio weights and returns to reflect the economic exposure of the options to the underlying
Gross Method (Strategy Attribution)	Allocates cash and positions ex-ante to define the strategy's return denominator, useful for quantifying the impact of broader allocation decisions

[12] These examples draw from Feibel, "A comprehensive approach to derivatives in performance attribution." They are based on foundational work by John C. Stannard, "Measuring investment returns of portfolios containing futures and options," *The Journal of Performance Measurement*, 1(1), 1996, 27–33; John C. Stannard, "Measuring investment returns of portfolios containing derivatives: Part II—Performance attribution," *The Journal of Performance Measurement*, 1 (3), 1997, 5–9, and; Stuart Morgan, "Performance attribution of options: Defining single-stock option exposures and understanding the Brinson-Fachler effects," *The Journal of Portfolio Management*, 40 (2), 2014, 103–111.

	Begin	End	Gain/Loss
Cash	$ 200,000.00	$ 200,000.00	$ -
Cash Offset	$ -	$ -	$ -
Change in Offset	$ -	$ -	$ -
Equity	$ 200,000.00	$ 230,000.00	$ 30,000.00
Equity Adjustment			$ -
Options	$ 20,000.00	$ 40,000.00	$ 20,000.00
Options Adjustment	$ -	$ -	$ -
Total	$ 420,000.00	$ 470,000.00	$ 50,000.00
	Weight	**Return**	**Contribution**
Cash	47.62%	0.00%	0.00%
Cash Offset	0.00%	0.00%	0.00%
Equity	47.62%	15.00%	7.14%
Options	**4.76%**	**100.00%**	**4.76%**
Total Portfolio	**100.00%**	**11.90%**	**11.90%**

Exhibit 10.4 Direct Method

Direct Method

The Direct Method treats the option as a standalone portfolio segment. The weight of the option within the portfolio is calculated as the initial option premium as a percentage of the total portfolio value (20,000/420,000 = 4.76%). The return is calculated as the change in option value divided by the initial premium (20,000 / 20,000 = 100%), and the option's contribution to the total portfolio return equals the weight multiplied by return (4.76% × 100% = 4.76%). While intuitive, this approach does not fully capture the option's economic exposure to the underlying stock.

Delta Method

Exhibit 10.5 illustrates the Delta Method of attributing the performance of options. It provides a more nuanced performance analysis by considering the full range of factor exposures rather than only changes in holdings, making it particularly useful for portfolios with complex exposure profiles. The method assesses the impact of various factors on portfolio performance, breaking down returns based on exposures to different asset classes, sectors, or factors, such as duration, credit quality, or specific economic sectors. The Delta Method examines how differences between the portfolio and benchmark exposures to these factors contribute to performance differences, allowing managers to analyze the effects of strategic or tactical allocation choices. Attribution using the Delta Method requires several adjustments to the portfolio accounting to reflect the economic exposure of the options. The Delta Method is also known as the Full Exposure method. We can adjust segment exposures to reflect the economic exposure to option contracts:

1. Increase the equity segment equal to the option's effective exposure.
2. Decrease in the options segment equal to the option premium value.
3. Decrease in the cash segment reflecting the difference between the first two adjustments.
4. Reclassify the income earned on the options cash backing to the equity segment.

The option increases the portfolio risk exposure to the underlying equity positions as measured by the option delta. And because the portfolio is unlevered, meaning the beginning market value of the total portfolio has not changed from $420,000, the option serves to reduce the portfolios cash exposure:

1. *Equity Adjustment*: Option Delta × Option Multiplier x #Contracts × Underlying Stock Price.
2. *Option Adjustment:* (−1 × Options Premium).

	Begin	End	Gain/Loss
Cash	$ 200,000.00	$ 200,000.00	$ -
Cash Offset	$ (30,000.00)	$ (30,000.00)	$ -
Change in Offset	$ -	$ 1,000.00	$ 1,000.00
Equity	$ 200,000.00	$ 230,000.00	$ 30,000.00
Equity Adjustment	$ 50,000.00	$ 69,000.00	$ 19,000.00
Options	$ 20,000.00	$ 40,000.00	$ 20,000.00
Options Adjustment	$ (20,000.00)	$ (40,000.00)	$ (20,000.00)
Total	$ 420,000.00	$ 470,000.00	$ 50,000.00

	Weight	Return	Contribution
Cash	47.62%	0.00%	0.00%
Cash Offset	-7.14%	0.00%	0.00%
Equity	47.62%	15.00%	7.14%
Options	**11.90%**	**40.00%**	**4.76%**
Total Portfolio	**100.00%**	**11.90%**	**11.90%**

Exhibit 10.5 Delta Method

3. *Cash Offset:* (−1 × (Equity Adjustment + Option Adjustment)).

The bottom section of Exhibit 10.5 shows how the method reflects the true economic exposure of the options within the equity segment. This method reduces the apparent return of the options to 40%, as it attributes gains to the underlying stock exposure. The lower options return using the direct method vs. the delta-effective method may not be intuitive. Using the delta-effective method, the denominator of the return calculation equals $50,000, which is the effective exposure to the underlying stock at the beginning of the period. The numerator equals $20,000, equivalent to the gain on this "virtual" underlying stock, $19,000, plus a $1000 increase in the offset. The offset is included in the return because it is, in effect, a transfer of value from cash to the equity segment over the period due to the gains in the stock and option. The Delta method can similarly be extended to reflect the option and portfolio exposure to gamma, vega, theta, and other risk factors.

Gross Method

The Gross Method pre-allocates cash to the strategy. Here, $100,000 is dedicated to the options strategy and subtracted from the cash segment. Exhibit 10.6 illustrates an example of *Strategy Attribution*, or Gross Method,[13] for handling options. Strategy attribution is a handy methodology for many strategies, not just those using derivatives. Here, we note the cash value and positions dedicated to the strategy on an *ex-ante* basis and use this value as the return denominator. The portfolio manager has decided that $100,000 will be devoted to the strategy and the options purchase. $100,000 notional cash is transferred from the equity to the cash segment.

As with the delta-effective method, these adjustments reduce the representation of the portfolio's net cash position from 47.62% to 23.81%, with a corresponding increase in the options segment. This leads to the options strategy being ascribed to a 16.67% return.

The Gross Method allocates cash contributions to the covered call options strategy upfront. Here, we assume that $100,000 was contributed to the portfolio managers' options strategy at the beginning of the period. Again, we assume that the portfolio is not leveraged. Therefore, the strategy value is subtracted from the cash exposure.

[13] Morgan, "Performance attribution of options: Defining Single-stock option exposures and understanding the Brinson-Fachler effects."

	Begin	End	Gain/Loss
Cash	$ 200,000.00	$ 200,000.00	$ -
Cash Offset	$ (100,000.00)	$ (100,000.00)	$ -
Change in Offset	$ -	$ -	$ -
Equity	$ 200,000.00	$ 230,000.00	$ 30,000.00
Equity Adjustment	$ -	$ -	$ -
Options	$ 20,000.00	$ 40,000.00	$ 20,000.00
Options Adjustment	$ 100,000.00	$ 100,000.00	$ -
Total	$ 420,000.00	$ 470,000.00	$ 50,000.00
	Weight	**Return**	**Contribution**
Cash	47.62%	0.00%	0.00%
Cash Offset	-23.81%	0.00%	0.00%
Equity	47.62%	15.00%	7.14%
Options	**28.57%**	**16.67%**	**4.76%**
Total Portfolio	**100.00%**	**11.90%**	**11.90%**

Exhibit 10.6 Gross Method

Summary

Each method offers unique insights into how options contribute to portfolio performance: the Direct Method captures market value, the Delta Method adjusts for economic exposure, and the Gross Method highlights strategic allocations. Managers should choose the method that aligns with their strategy and reporting needs.

Selecting an attribution method depends on strategy goals, reporting needs, and benchmark-relative analysis requirements. Portfolio managers should choose the method most aligned with their reporting objectives, and analysts should consider grouping options with related stocks, industries, or asset classes to understand their contribution to benchmark-relative performance. The portfolio manager must choose the most appropriate method based on the strategy's objectives and reporting requirements. It will sometimes make sense to group options with parent company stocks, industries, and asset classes to analyze their contribution to benchmark-relative performance.

The weights, returns, and contributions calculated in the exhibits are used to determine the management effects using the basic allocation, selection, and interaction effects demonstrated in Exhibit 10.1. Given the range of options for intended usage, analysts need to choose the best combination of direct, delta-effective, and gross methods and level of aggregation.

Swaps

Swaps, such as interest rate swaps, currency swaps, and credit default swaps, require a different approach to attribution because they involve exchanges of cash flows over time rather than a direct investment in an asset. For example, in an interest rate swap, one party pays a fixed rate while receiving a floating rate, or vice versa. Attribution for swaps focuses on the value changes driven by shifts in interest rates, exchange rates, or credit spreads. The notional amount of the swap is critical for determining its impact on portfolio returns, as it represents the principal on which cash flows are calculated. Attribution must account for the derivative's role in either hedging exposure or creating targeted risk exposures.

Swap holdings are adjusted similarly to futures and forwards by calculating effective exposure for each leg, grouping them by portfolio segment, and calculating notional values. Swaps may simplify attribution by often providing separate long and short legs in portfolio accounting. By tailoring attribution analysis to the unique characteristics of each derivative type, portfolio managers can better understand how these instruments contribute to overall performance. Recognizing the distinct behaviors of futures, options, and swaps ensures that performance attribution accurately captures the derivative's intended role within the portfolio, whether for hedging, leveraging, or accessing specific market exposures.

Integrating Derivatives Attribution with Overall Portfolio Analysis

Integrating derivatives attribution into an overall portfolio analysis framework is essential for accurately understanding the full impact of derivatives on performance and aligning this impact with broader portfolio goals. Unlike traditional assets like stocks and bonds, as explained in other chapters, derivatives can serve many roles within a portfolio—they can be used to control risks, provide leverage, or enable exposure to otherwise inaccessible assets. This multifunctionality means that derivatives' contributions to portfolio performance must be analyzed in isolation and with traditional assets to capture their complete influence on risk and return.

To effectively integrate derivatives attribution, assessing how derivatives affect asset class exposures across the portfolio is essential. For instance, a futures position that boosts equity exposure should be included in the portfolio's equity segment, with returns and risks adjusted for the leverage effect. This method involves aligning derivative returns with their respective asset classes (e.g., attributing equity index futures to the equity category), providing a more refined view of performance at the segment level. Another essential step is adjusting for the unique exposures and risk characteristics of derivatives in each asset class. For example, an interest rate swap within the fixed-income category requires adjustments that reflect its unique exposure compared to traditional bonds. By including notional values for swaps or delta adjustments for options, attribution models can capture the true economic impact of derivatives, ensuring their specific contributions are accurately represented in the portfolio's risk and return profile.

Finally, an effective derivatives attribution framework should offer meaningful insights into how these instruments support the portfolio's strategic objectives. Derivatives are often used to maintain target volatility, enhance returns, or provide downside protection, which should be reflected in the attribution analysis. For example, suppose derivatives help maintain volatility within a set range. In that case, attribution results should illustrate their role in stabilizing the portfolio amid market fluctuations, ensuring alignment with its volatility objective.

Integrating derivatives within a broader performance framework requires a clear link between the attribution outcomes and the portfolio's overarching goals, whether risk reduction, diversification, or alpha generation. This means that attribution analysis should go beyond standard returns and exposures and assess how each derivative position fulfills its intended function within the portfolio. For example, options to hedge against downside risk should have their contributions analyzed in terms of performance and how effectively they mitigate losses during market downturns. Similarly, a futures position aimed at gaining sector-specific exposure should show how it aligns with the strategic allocation to that sector.

Moreover, connecting attribution results to strategic goals allows for better decision-making and transparency. By understanding the exact role of derivatives in achieving specific objectives, portfolio managers can make more informed adjustments, fine-tune exposures, and communicate performance outcomes more clearly to stakeholders. This alignment between derivatives attribution and strategic goals ultimately enables a more cohesive portfolio management approach, ensuring that each derivative's contribution supports the portfolio's objectives measurably and transparently.

Challenges and Limitations in Derivatives Attribution

While performance attribution for derivatives offers valuable insights, it is subject to several challenges and limitations that can affect the accuracy and interpretability of results. Understanding these limitations is essential for constructing a reliable attribution framework and managing expectations regarding the precision of attribution analysis in derivative-heavy portfolios.

One significant challenge in derivatives attribution is the *impact of leverage*. Derivatives often allow investors to control large exposures with relatively small capital outlays, resulting in a leveraged effect. This leverage can amplify gains and losses, making it difficult to accurately attribute performance without adjusting for the derivative's notional value. Misinterpreting the effect of leverage can lead to overstated performance contributions and obscure a portfolio's true risk-adjusted returns.

Another critical limitation arises from *currency and interest rate risks* in the context of an investment strategy. Derivatives that expose a portfolio to changes in foreign exchange rates, interest rates, or credit spreads add complexity to the attribution analysis. For example, a currency or an interest rate swap can introduce risk factors that are not directly tied to the underlying assets but significantly impact performance. Accounting for these risks requires specialized attribution models that consider market conditions beyond the typical return metrics for stocks and bonds, especially when these factors fluctuate independently of the primary market exposures in the portfolio.

Finally, *data quality and availability* can pose challenges. Accurate attribution relies on accurate accounting information and precise data for factors such as notional exposures, delta for options, and daily margin adjustments for futures. However, obtaining this data at a granular level is not always possible, particularly for complex or bespoke derivatives that may lack transparent pricing and valuation models. In these cases, attribution results may be estimates rather than precise measurements, limiting the analysis's reliability. Additionally, attribution for derivatives may require more frequent data updates, as derivatives are susceptible to market changes. This need for comprehensive data and frequent recalibration can make derivatives attribution a resource-intensive.

Addressing these challenges requires careful consideration of the data inputs, a robust understanding of leverage effects, and an awareness of external factors such as interest rates and currency fluctuations. By acknowledging these limitations, practitioners can more accurately interpret performance attribution results for derivatives, ensuring a balanced and realistic view of how these instruments contribute to portfolio outcomes.

Conclusion and Best Practices for Derivatives Attribution Analysis

Incorporating derivatives into performance attribution analysis provides valuable insights into how these complex instruments impact portfolio outcomes. However, due to their unique characteristics, derivatives require specialized approaches to measure their contributions accurately. From understanding notional exposures and practical return calculations to adapting Brinson-style and notional attribution models, this chapter has outlined the essential methodologies for evaluating derivatives in a portfolio context. By applying these tailored approaches, practitioners can better understand how derivatives fulfill roles such as hedging, leveraging, and synthetic exposure.

Adopting best practices in derivatives attribution can significantly enhance the reliability of the analysis. First, ensuring data accuracy and availability is crucial, particularly for factors like notional value and delta, which drive the performance of options, futures, and swaps. Ensuring regular updates to data and maintaining a clear record of all relevant metrics helps achieve precise attribution results, as derivatives are susceptible to shifts in underlying market conditions. Practitioners should also prioritize transparency, disclosing the methods and assumptions used in their attribution models. This helps stakeholders interpret results with a clear understanding of any limitations or potential biases.

Attribution analysis for portfolios with derivatives is a powerful tool when applied thoughtfully and rigorously. By recognizing the challenges inherent in measuring the performance of leveraged, non-linear instruments, portfolio managers can better assess the impact of derivatives on overall returns and manage risk more effectively. Adhering to best practices—such as maintaining data quality, selecting the right attribution model, and applying exposure transparency—ensures that derivatives attribution remains a reliable and informative performance analysis technique, helping investors better understand portfolio dynamics.

Summary

This chapter explores the complexities and specialized approaches required to perform performance attribution analysis in portfolios containing derivatives. Recognizing that derivatives differ from traditional assets like bonds and equities, it begins by outlining the unique role of derivatives in portfolio management—primarily as tools for modifying exposures rather than directly generating returns. This distinction introduces challenges, as derivatives bring leverage, non-linear risk profiles, and dynamic exposure adjustments into attribution models.

The chapter reviews the need to adapt standard attribution models, such as the Brinson-style framework, to incorporate notional values and effective exposures that capture derivatives' contributions more accurately. Each derivative type—futures, options, and swaps—requires specific adjustments due to its unique characteristics. Futures, for example, require daily variation margin adjustments, while options need metrics like delta and gamma to assess their sensitivity to underlying asset prices. Swaps demand exposure-based adjustments to reflect their dependency on interest rates, currencies, or credit spreads.

A portfolio manager using derivatives to adjust currency exposures will also want to enhance the basic attribution to reflect the impact of hedging decisions.[14] A portion of the chapter addresses challenges in derivatives attribution, including the effects of leverage, data quality issues, and the need for models that can handle derivatives' non-linear impacts on portfolios. The chapter also presents best practices, such as using notional value-based metrics and maintaining transparency in model assumptions, to improve the accuracy and interpretability of results.

Finally, the chapter emphasizes integrating derivatives attribution with the overall portfolio analysis. Derivatives' multifaceted roles—ranging from hedging to synthetic market exposure—mean their impact must be analyzed with traditional assets to provide a complete view of risk and return. By aligning derivatives' contributions with asset class segments and strategic portfolio objectives, analysts can better understand how derivatives support broader portfolio goals, such as managing volatility, enhancing returns, or controlling risk.

[14] These methods are covered in José Menchero and Ben Davis, "Multi-currency performance attribution," *The Journal of Performance Measurement*, 14(1), 2009, 45–55, and Carl Bacon, *Performance Attribution History and Progress*. Charlottesville, CA: CFA Institute Research Foundation, 2019.

11

Extracting Market Views from Derivative Prices

Andrew Weisman

The financial industry produces many forecasts across a broad range of issues of concern to investors. Notable examples include forecasts of the magnitude and timing of interest rate adjustments effected by Central Banks, forecasts of risk in asset markets typically conceived of in terms of an annualized measure of volatility, and the inherent dependence structure of investible assets expressed in terms of expected correlations between assets or relative to specified benchmarks.

Practitioner forecasts rarely achieve a narrow consensus. Interestingly, it is more often the case that even well-informed, experienced investors vary sharply in their opinions concerning the future, and even the most accomplished investors struggle to forecast markets accurately on a consistent basis.

The difficulty forecasters face is consistent with economic theory, notably the Efficient Markets Hypothesis (EMH), which suggests that the ability to consistently out-think financial markets writ large is nearly impossible, particularly in the case of competitively traded markets. As Niels Bohr, the renowned Danish physicist and Nobel Laureate for his groundbreaking contributions to understanding atomic structure and quantum mechanics, allegedly remarked, prediction is challenging, especially about the future.

Investors can, however, ground their market views and effectively establish market-based "priors" concerning a broad range of issues by extracting such

A. Weisman (✉)
Market Revealed Preference, Boston, MA, USA
e-mail: abweisman1@gmail.com

F. J. Fabozzi and M. de Jong (eds.), *Derivatives Applications in Asset Management*,
https://doi.org/10.1007/978-3-031-86354-7_11

views directly from the derivatives markets. The idea that one can extract such forecasts is grounded in the notion that prices of actively traded assets reflect the collective expectations of market participants. Such expectations are often referred to in the economic literature as "revealed preferences," as they represent investors' aggregate beliefs and preferences as expressed through their trading decisions.[1] The derivatives markets are a particularly rich source of such information. By analyzing the prices of derivatives, it is possible to extract information about market participants' expectations regarding key economic variables, market risk, and asset dependence structure, to name a few.

Below is a discussion that includes three real-world examples of how such views are obtained, including their theoretical frameworks, methods of calculation, and an appendix that provides Python code to develop the forecasts contained in the examples. The three examples presented are (1) forecasting Federal Reserve policy adjustments using federal funds futures prices, (2) forecasting equity market risk using equity option prices, and (3) forecasting currency correlations using currency options prices.

Example 1: Federal Funds Futures and Federal Reserve Policy Adjustments

Background and Theory

The Federal Reserve (the Fed), the Central Bank of the United States, has as one of its primary monetary policy tools, the ability to set short-term interest rates through targeting of the federal funds rate (or simply, the fed funds rate). The fed funds rate is the base interest rate that depository institutions (such as banks and credit unions) lend reserve balances to other depository institutions overnight. This rate is set by the Federal Open Market Committee (FOMC) of the Fed and serves as a key benchmark for short-term interest rates in the U.S. economy.

The setting of this rate is the primary tool used by the Fed to influence economic activity. By adjusting this rate, the Fed can either encourage economic growth (by lowering the rate) or cool down inflationary pressures

[1] The economist Paul Samuelson introduced the concept of revealed preference. His theory was a significant contribution to consumer choice theory, as it provided a way to understand and analyze consumer behavior without relying on the notion of utility, which was more abstract and difficult to measure. See Paul A. Samuelson, "A Note on the Pure Theory of Consumer's Behaviour." *Economica* 5(17), 1938, 61–71.

(by raising the rate). The FOMC sets a target range for the Fed Funds rate, and the actual rate fluctuates within this range based on supply and demand for reserves in the banking system. The Fed uses open market operations, such as buying or selling government securities, to steer the rate toward the target range.

The fed funds rate influences other interest rates in the economy, including rates on mortgages, savings accounts, loans, and other financial products. When the fed funds rate is low, borrowing costs generally decrease, encouraging spending and investment. Conversely, when the rate is high, borrowing costs increase, which can slow economic activity.

Recently, the forecasting of Fed interest rate policy has almost replaced baseball as America's national pastime. Practitioner forecasts tend to be framed in a normative context that simultaneously considers the natural real rate of interest, a desired rate of inflation, and a preferred pace of economic growth. Forecasting rate decisions typically involve gauging the state of the economy, parsing and psychoanalyzing the words of each member of the FOMC, with a "haircut" applied to their place in the Fed's pecking order, while considering any game-theoretic global macro-economic externalities such as the election cycle, to arrive at an estimate of the timing and magnitude of monetary policy decisions. There is subsequently a great deal of leeway to arrive at divergent probability estimates associated with varying outcomes.

Fortunately, the derivatives markets provide a useful means for establishing a more objective policy forecast grounded in the market's aggregate expectation. The fed funds futures market, in combination with a relatively simple mathematical calculation, provides just such a framework.

The fed funds futures market is a financial market where contracts are traded based on the future level of the fed funds rate. Investors, economists, and policymakers closely watch this market because it provides insights into market expectations for future Fed interest rate decisions.

As noted, fed funds futures prices reflect the collective expectations of market participants regarding future Fed interest rate decisions. The price of a fed funds futures contract for a specific month indicates the market's consensus (revealed preference) on the average fed funds rate that will prevail at the maturity of each futures contract month.

Technically, the price of a fed funds futures contract is inversely related to the expected fed funds rate. The contract price is therefore quoted as 100 minus the implied rate. For example, if the futures contract is priced at 94.75, the implied federal funds rate is 5.25% (100 – 94.75 = 5.25%).

Analysts can infer the timing of expected interest rate changes by analyzing the prices of fed funds futures contracts for different months. For example, if the futures prices for a contract month near a FOMC meeting show a significant shift, it suggests that the market anticipates a rate change during that meeting. The magnitude of the expected rate change can also be inferred from the futures prices. A significant change in the implied rate from one month to the next indicates an expectation of a rate move by the Fed. For example, if the implied rate jumps by 0.25% (25 basis points) between consecutive months, the market is pricing in a likely 25-basis-point rate increase.

Historically, the fed funds futures market has been a reasonably accurate predictor of the direction of Fed interest rate changes, particularly in the short term (one to two FOMC meetings ahead). The market's efficiency in aggregating information and the incentives for participants to make accurate predictions contribute to this accuracy.

The fed funds futures market does, however, have limitations. It can be influenced by unexpected economic developments or shifts in Fed policy that the market did not anticipate. Additionally, the further out the prediction (e.g., several months or more), the less reliable the futures market tends to be due to the increasing uncertainty of future economic conditions. Beyond this, certain events, such as major economic reports or geopolitical crises, can cause sudden shifts in futures prices as market participants reassess their expectations. These events can introduce volatility in the fed funds futures market, making predictions more challenging.

In short, the fed funds futures market provides a crucial tool for predicting the timing and magnitude of Fed interest rate decisions. It reflects the collective expectations of market participants and provides a real-time gauge of sentiment regarding future monetary policy. While it is not infallible, the insights derived from this market are valuable for a wide range of economic and financial analyses.

Fed Funds Futures Implied Rate-Cut Probabilities: A Real-World Example

To calculate the implied probability of a rate cut (or any change in the federal funds rate) using fed funds futures, we apply the following simple steps. The data used in this example were collected on August 30, 2024. The analysis provides the probabilities of rate cuts of 25 and 50 basis points (bps) at the upcoming FOMC held on September 17 and 18, 2024. The September 2024 futures contract matures on September 27, 2024, so it has been selected for use in this illustration.

The process begins by obtaining the current fed funds target range. The current target range in our illustration is 5.25% to 5.50%. Therefore, the mid-point, 5.375%, is used as the current target rate. Next, the fed funds futures price relevant to the examined rate-cut timeframe is obtained, 94.80 in our illustration. Given the futures price, the implied rate is obtained:

$$\text{Implied Rate} = 100 - \text{Futures Price} = 5.20$$

Next, the rate cut scenario is defined. In our illustration,

- R_0 = current target rate
- R_1 = rate if the Fed cuts by 25 bps.
- R_2 = rate if the Fed cuts by 50 bps.

The implied probability of the two scenarios. The implied probability for the first scenario is calculated from the observed futures price using the following formula:

$$P_{cut} = \frac{(R_0 - \text{Implied Rate})}{(R_0 - R_1)}$$

By inspection, we see that the resulting probability is a linear approximation derived by comparing what the market has already "priced in" to the change implied by the evaluated target rate.

For Scenario 1:

P_{cut} = the implied probability of a 25-bps rate cut.
R_0 = the current target rate.
R_1 = the target rate after a 25-bps cut.

$$P_{cut} = \frac{(5.375 - 5.20)}{(5.375 - 5.125)} = 70.00\%$$

Similarly, for Scenario 2, the formula is

$$P_{cut} = \frac{(R_0 - \text{Implied Rate})}{(R_0 - R_2)}$$

where

P_{cut} = implied probability of a 50-bps rate cut.
R_0 = current target rate.

R_2 = target rate after a 50-bps cut.

$$P_{cut} = \frac{(5.375 - 5.20)}{(5.25 - 4.875)} = 35.00\%$$

Finally, in degenerate cases where the probabilities exceed 1, we normalize them so they sum to 1 and then calculate the "no change" probability by subtracting the sum of the probabilities from 1. In our illustration

$$P_{25BPScut} = 66.67\%$$

$$P_{50BPScut} = 33.33\%$$

$$P_{Nocut} = 0.00\%$$

Note that the normalized probabilities are calculated by dividing the individual probabilities by the sum of the derived probabilities.

The Python code for this illustration is provided in Code Appendix A. The code contains an automatic data collection feature (using YahooFinance) for populating and obtaining model predictions.

Example 2: Equity Option Prices and the Risk-Neutral Density

Background and Theory

Risk-neutral densities (RNDs) are forward-looking probability distributions that represent the market's collective view of future asset prices, adjusted for risk preferences. An RND is conceptually like a probability density function (PDF) in that they are both mathematical functions that can be used to infer the likelihood of observing specified outcomes associated with random processes. They do, however, have distinct interpretations.

A PDF is a function that describes the relative likelihood that a random variable will take on a given value. In economic analysis, a PDF is often used to determine "real-world" probabilities. An example would be using a time series of daily prices and a maximum-likelihood estimation to parameterize a lognormal density function. The estimated function could then be used to specify the moments (mean and variance) of an asset's returns and ascribe probabilities to various outcomes.

In contrast, an RND is the probability distribution of expected asset prices under the risk-neutral measure. It reflects the market's view of future probabilities, where investors are assumed to care only about expected returns and not the associated risk. It can be derived from an asset's option prices and reflects the probabilities of different outcomes implied by the market, adjusted for risk preferences. This measure of dispersion is made possible because the price of an option is thought of as the expected value of the underlying asset's payoffs under a risk-neutral probability measure (i.e., the payoffs are discounted at the risk-free rate). This risk-neutral measure differs from the real-world probability measure because it adjusts for investors' risk aversion, allowing the focus to be on the pure market consensus about future prices.

Breeden and Litzenberger were pioneers in the development of the concept of the RND from option prices, which represented a significant advancement in financial economics.[2] They introduced a method for extracting the entire distribution of possible future prices of an underlying asset as implied by the market. The key innovation in the work of Breeden and Litzenberger was the insight that taking the second partial derivative of an option's price with respect to its strike price reveals the RND. This density represents the probability distribution of the underlying asset's future price, as implied by the current market prices of options across various strike prices.

Advanced Insights for In-Depth Exploration

This section offers additional details and concepts for those seeking a deeper dive into the theoretical and mathematical foundations. We explore advanced methodologies, providing further insights to enhance your comprehensive understanding of RND.

Consider a European call option, which gives the holder the right (but not the obligation) to buy the underlying asset at a strike price K at maturity T. The price of this call option at time t (denoted as $C(K)$) can be expressed as:

$$C(K) = e^{-r(T-t)} \int_{K}^{\infty} (S_T - K) f(S_T) dS_T$$

where:

S_T = price of the underlying asset at maturity T.

r = risk-free interest rate.

[2] Douglas T. Breeden and Robert H. Litzenberger, "Prices of State-Contingent Claims Implicit in Option Prices." *Journal of Business*, 51(4), 621–651.

$f(S_T)$ = RND function of the underlying asset price at maturity.

The integral represents the expected payoff of the call option under the risk-neutral measure, discounted at the risk-free rate.

To relate the option price to the density, we first take the partial derivative of the call price with respect to the strike price K:

$$\frac{\partial C(K)}{\partial K} = -e^{-r(T-t)} \int_K^\infty f(S_T) dS_T$$

Taking the second partial derivative of the call price with respect to the strike price K gives us the risk-neutral density $f(K)$:

$$\frac{\partial^2 C(K)}{\partial K^2} = e^{-r(T-t)} \cdot f(K)$$

Finally, rearranging this equation, we show that the risk-neutral density $f(K)$ is proportional to the second partial derivative of the call option price with respect to the strike price K.

$$f(K) = e^{rT} \cdot \frac{\partial^2 C(K)}{\partial K^2}$$

The Breeden-Litzenberger method, in its earliest form, does however have some important limitations and requires thoughtful implementation to yield usable results. First, accurately estimating the RND requires a clean and timely dataset of option prices across a range of strike prices. This can be challenging in markets where such data are sparse. Second, the practical extraction of the RND often requires interpolation and smoothing techniques that can introduce biases or inaccuracies. Finally, their method assumes no-arbitrage and the ability to continuously trade options across all strike prices, which might not hold perfectly in real markets.

One final note: although the RND is neutral to risk preferences, it can still fluctuate in response to changes in market conditions, such as shifts in volatility, interest rates, or the underlying asset's price. These factors impact option prices, which in turn influence the derived RND. Since Breeden and Litzenberger's pioneering work, there have been several significant advances in the field of extracting and utilizing RNDs from option prices. These advances have primarily focused on addressing the limitations of the original method, improving accuracy, extending the methodology to more complex financial instruments, and applying the concept to new areas. Some of the key developments include:

- *Smoothing Techniques*: One of the challenges with Breeden and Litzenberger's original approach is the noise introduced when calculating the second derivative of option prices with respect to strike prices. This can lead to unstable and unrealistic RND estimates. Advanced smoothing techniques, such as spline interpolation and kernel smoothing, have been applied to create more stable and accurate estimates of the RND.
- *Nonparametric Methods*: Nonparametric approaches, such as kernel density estimation, allow for a more flexible estimation of RNDs without assuming a specific functional form for the distribution. These methods have gained popularity because they can adapt to the actual shape of the underlying distribution observed in the market.
- *Stochastic Volatility Models*: Breeden and Litzenberger's method assumes constant volatility, which is often unrealistic. Models incorporating stochastic volatility, such as the Heston model, have been developed to address this. These models capture the changing volatility over time and may provide a more accurate representation of the RND.
- *Jump-Diffusion Models*: Another extension is the incorporation of jump processes (e.g., Merton's jump-diffusion model[3]) into the option pricing framework. These models account for sudden, large changes in asset prices, which are common in financial markets and can significantly affect the shape of the RND.
- *Local Volatility Models*: The development of local volatility models, like the Dupire model,[4] has allowed for the extraction of RNDs that change with both time and the level of the underlying asset. These models are particularly useful for capturing the skewness and kurtosis observed in market prices.

Applications of Risk-Neutral Densities

The RND has several important applications in finance, particularly in the areas of derivative pricing, risk management, and market analysis. Some key applications of the RND are:

[3] The Merton Jump-Diffusion model is an extension of the Black-Scholes model that accounts for the possibility of sudden, large movements (jumps) in asset prices and the continuous price movements described by standard diffusion processes. It was initially presented in Robert C. Merton, "Option Pricing When Underlying Stock Returns Are Discontinuous." *Journal of Financial Economics*, 3(1–2), 1976, 125–144.

[4] The Dupire model is a local volatility model used in the pricing and risk management of financial derivatives, particularly options. It extends the Black-Scholes framework by allowing volatility to vary with both the underlying asset price and time rather than being constant. It was initially presented by Bruno Dupire, "Pricing with a Smile." *Risk*, 7(1), 1994, 18–20.

- *Option Pricing*: One of the primary uses of a RND is in pricing options and other derivatives. Since the RND represents the probability distribution of future asset prices under the risk-neutral measure, it allows for calculating an option's expected payoff, which can then be discounted to determine its present value. They can be particularly useful for more complex or exotic derivatives, where payoffs depend on the distribution of future prices in non-linear ways. It allows for precise pricing of instruments like barrier options, Asian options, or lookback options.
- *Value-at-Risk and Conditional Value-at-Risk Estimation*: Value at Risk (VaR) and Conditional Value at Risk (CVaR) are risk management metrics that can be estimated using the RND.By applying the RND to predict the potential future distribution of asset prices, financial institutions can assess the potential for large losses and allocate capital accordingly.
- *Stress Testing*: RND can simulate various market scenarios and stress test portfolios. By altering the input conditions (e.g., volatility, interest rates), risk managers can observe how the RND changes and what impact this has on the value of their portfolios.[5]
- *Implied Volatility Surface Analysis*: The RND can provide insights into the implied volatility surface, which reflects market expectations of future volatility. Analyzing the RND across different strikes and maturities can reveal how market participants view future risks and uncertainties.[6]
- *Market Sentiment Indicators*: The shape of the RND can give clues about market sentiment. For example, a skewed RND might indicate that investors expect significant downside risk or upside potential, reflecting bearish or bullish market sentiment.[7]
- *Pricing Under Different Scenarios*: RND allows for pricing under various hypothetical scenarios. For instance, it can be used to evaluate how an option's value would change under different market conditions, such as shifts in interest rates or volatility.

---

[5] For an illustration of the use of RND for scenario analysis during times of crisis, see William R. Melick and Charles P. Thomas. "Recovering an Asset's Implied PDF From Option Prices: An Application to Crude Oil During the Gulf Crisis." *Journal of Financial and Quantitative Analysis*, 32(1), 1997, 91–115.

[6] For an examination of implied volatility surfaces and their connection to RND, see Bernard Dumas, Jeff Fleming, and Robert E. Whaley. "Implied Volatility Functions: Empirical Tests." *Journal of Finance*, 53(6), 1998, 2059–2106.

[7] D.S. Bates, "The Crash of '87: Was It Expected? The Evidence from Options Markets." *Journal of Finance*, 46(3), 1991, 1009–1044, explains how RND can provide insights into market sentiment before major events.

- *Economic Forecasting*: By studying the evolution of the RND over time, analysts can infer changes in economic expectations, such as the likelihood of recessions, booms, or other economic events.[8]
- *Arbitrage Detection*: RND can help identify arbitrage opportunities by checking the consistency of market prices with theoretical models.
- *Tail Risk Management*: Portfolio managers can use the RND to understand better and manage tail risks, which are the risks of extreme market movements. Managers can adjust their portfolios to minimize potential losses in extreme scenarios by integrating the RND into portfolio optimization models.[9]
- *Hedging Strategies*: The RND can inform the design of hedging strategies, especially for complex portfolios with non-linear exposures. By understanding the distribution of future asset prices, managers can tailor their hedges more effectively.[10]

Extracting the Risk-Neutral Density

In this implementation, the Breeden-Litzenberger method is used, augmented by constraints that accommodate data sparsity and kernel density estimation that assists in smoothing and extrapolating the tails of the derived RND. The result is a simple, relatively robust implementation that provides a forward-looking distribution of returns for the stock market as proxied by the SPY ETF,[11] informed by the aggregate expectations in the SPY options market. In extracting the RND, the following steps are used:

[8] The following article covers nonparametric methods for estimating RND and its use in economic forecasting: Yacine Aït-Sahalia and Andrew W. Lo. "Nonparametric Estimation of State-Price Densities Implicit in Financial Asset Prices." *Journal of Finance*, 53(2), 1998, 499–547.

[9] The following article discusses how RND can be used to manage tail risk by accounting for skewness and kurtosis in option pricing: Gurdip S. Bakshi, Nikunj Kapadia, and Dilip B. Madan. "Stock Return Characteristics, Skew Laws, and the Differential Pricing of Individual Equity Options." *Review of Financial Studies*, 16(1), 2003, 101–143.

[10] The following article discusses the role of pricing kernels related to RND, in designing hedging strategies: Joshua V. Rosenberg and Robert F. Engle. "Empirical Pricing Kernels." *Journal of Financial Economics*, 64(3), 2002, 341–372.

[11] The SPDR® S&P 500® ETF Trust (SPY) is an exchange-traded fund that tracks the performance of the S&P 500® Index, offering broad exposure to 500 of the largest U.S. companies. It was launched in 1993 and is one of the most widely traded ETFs globally.

- *Data Preparation*: The option data is loaded, specifically extracting strike prices and corresponding call option prices.[12] The option-model parameters are input. Time to expiration is set based on the given days to expiration. The risk-free rate is set for discounting purposes.
- *Interpolation of Call Prices*: The implementation provided in the code appendix interpolates the call price function across the strike prices using cubic interpolation. This interpolation ensures a smooth call price function that can be differentiated accurately.
- *Second Partial Derivative Calculation*: The second partial derivative of the call price function with respect to the strike price is then calculated. This second partial derivative is crucial as it relates to the RND under the Breeden-Litzenberger framework, where the RND is proportional to the second partial derivative of the option price function.
- *RND Calculation*: The RND is computed by multiplying the second partial derivative of the call price by the discount factor. To avoid negative densities (non-physical), one sets any negative values to zero and adds a small constant to avoid zero densities.
- Normalization: The area under the curve of the density function is calculated using Simpson's rule,[13] and the density is normalized to ensure it integrates to 1. This step is necessary to interpret the density as a probability distribution.
- *Kernel Density Estimation*: The kernel density estimation (KDE)[14] is applied to the strike prices, weighted by the normalized density, to smooth the distribution, especially to extrapolate the tails beyond the observed strike prices. This helps estimate the tails of the distribution where data is sparse. A Gaussian kernel with a specified bandwidth is used for this smoothing process.
- *Moments Calculation*: The first four moments of the KDE distribution (mean, variance, skewness, and kurtosis) and the standard deviation are calculated. These moments provide insights into the distribution's shape, central tendency, and spread.

---

[12] In this example, call prices on so-called American options (that can be exercised before expiration) are used rather than a European option specified by the Breeden-Litzenberger model. However, the price difference between American and European call options is usually very small, especially when the options are far from expiration or if the underlying asset does not pay dividends.

[13] Simpson's rule is a numerical method for approximating the definite integral of a function. It is particularly useful when the function cannot be integrated analytically or when only discrete data points are available. Simpson's rule works by approximating the integrand with a series of quadratic polynomials.

[14] A kernel is a smooth, symmetric function used to weigh the data points. The kernel function is centered at each data point and spreads its influence over a neighborhood of data points. This creates a smooth curve that represents the density.

- *Plotting*: The final RND, smoothed by the KDE, is plotted against strike prices. The current price and VaR are also marked on the plot for reference. In the code appendix the first four moments, standard deviation and VaR are presented in a text box of the associated figure.

Equity Option Prices and the RND: A Real-World Illustration

In this illustration, data were gathered on 9/4/2024 for a range of call option strike prices on the SPY ETF expiring on 10/18/2024. The prevailing market price was 550.84. The implied forward price (at the money price) was 554.34. The prevailing risk-free rate was 0.0532. The data in the imported Excel file had the format shown in Exhibit 11.1.

To appreciate the RND, it is worth comparing it to the PDF obtained by fitting to historical data. The PDF is determined using a series of daily price changes. The moments of the PDF are determined using an exponentially weighted measure of volatility with a 0.97 decay factor, a generally well-regarded technique employed by several risk engine providers.[15] Panel A of Exhibit 11.2 presents the RND, while panel B presents the PDF.

There are some notable differences between these two densities. First, the backward-looking PDF, shown in panel B of Exhibit 11.2, is symmetric by construction, as it is the result of estimating the parameters of a lognormal distribution and is, therefore, fully defined by its first two moments. Conversely, the forward-looking RND, shown in panel A of Exhibit 11.2, displays a negative skew that is implied by the revealed preferences of market participants as expressed in the options market. Second, the RND portrays a broader expectation of dispersion as represented by the standard deviation (in price terms, 7.06 (RND) versus 1.86 (PDF)) and the VaR (in price terms 9.74 (RND) vs 3.06 (PDF)). Participants in the options market are pricing in much greater downside risk on a forward basis. From a risk management perspective, the additional information provided by the RND is likely to be quite useful. It is an interesting point in history to have performed this comparison since the 9/04/2024 is one day after NVidia[16] dropped 10% in a day, singlehandedly wiping out approximately $280 billion in market capitalization.

---

[15] RiskMetrics, developed by JP Morgan in the 1990s, is a well-known example of this method.

[16] NVIDIA Corporation is a technology company known for designing and manufacturing graphics processing units (GPUs) for gaming, professional visualization, and artificial intelligence (AI) applications, as well as system-on-chip units for the mobile computing and automotive markets.

Strike	CallPrice
539	21.72
540	21.00
541	20.24
542	19.49
543	18.76
544	18.03
545	17.31
546	16.60
547	15.89
548	15.20
549	14.53
550	13.87
551	13.20
552	12.57
553	11.94
554	11.33
555	10.72
556	10.13
557	9.56
558	9.01
559	8.46
560	7.94
561	7.43
562	6.95
563	6.47

Exhibit 11.1 Option Price Data

Example 3: Currency Option Prices and Implied Correlations

Currency implied correlation is a forward-looking measure that reflects the market's expectations about the future relationship between two currency pairs (exchange rates). Unlike a typical Pearson correlation measure based on historical data, implied correlation is derived from the implied volatilities of currency options.

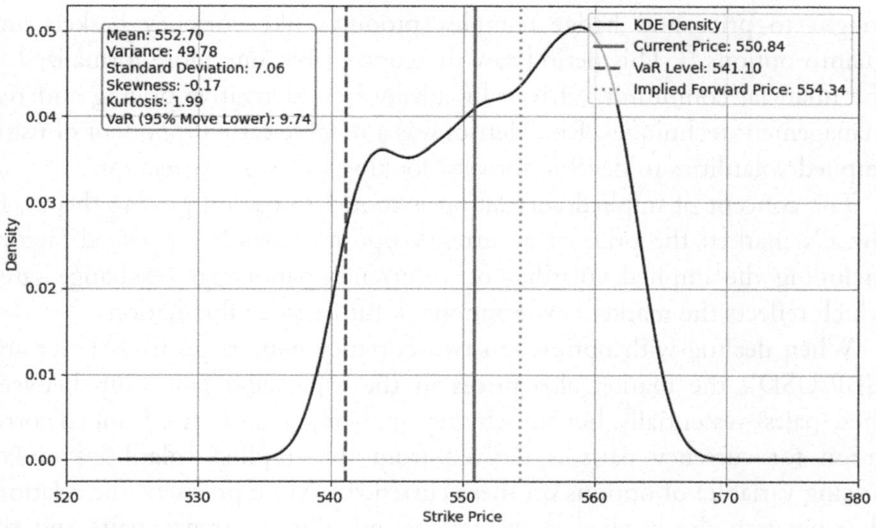

Panel A: Risk Neutral Density

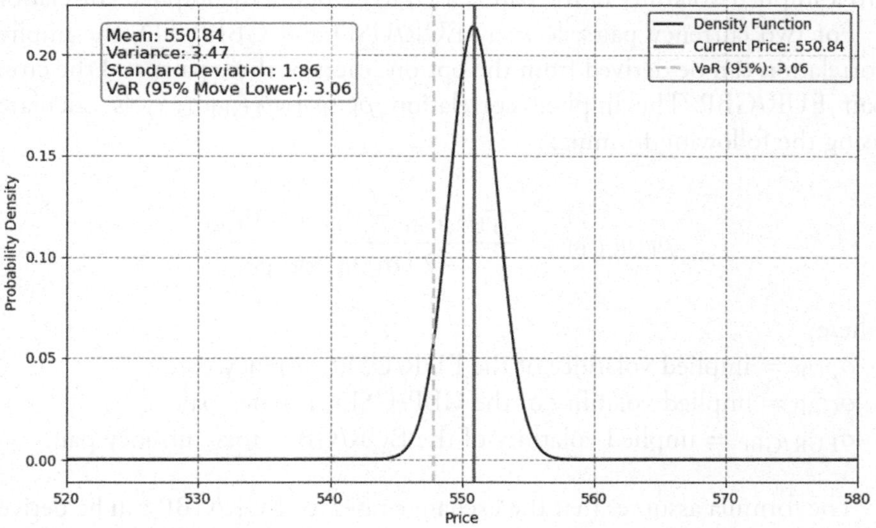

Panel B Probability Density Function

Exhibit 11.2 Risk-Neutral Density versus Probability Density Function

The concept of implied correlation, particularly in the context of the foreign exchange (FX) markets, does not have a single, well-documented originator like some other financial theories. Instead, it evolved over time as part of the broader development of derivative pricing models and the increased sophistication of financial markets. Throughout the 1990s, implied correlation became increasingly important in the FX markets as practitioners sought to price and hedge complex products like currency baskets and quanto options.[17] This period saw the concept become more formalized in the financial community, driven by advances in derivative pricing and risk management techniques. RiskMetrics was a notable early proponent of using implied volatilities to develop forward-looking views on correlation.

The concept of implied correlation is rooted in option pricing theory. In the FX market, the price of a currency option depends on several factors, including the implied volatility of a currency pair (single exchange rate), which reflects the market's expectations of future price fluctuations.

When dealing with options on two currency pairs (e.g., EUR/USD and GBP/USD), the market also prices in the expected relationship between these pairs—essentially, how much they are likely to co-move. Implied correlation for currency pairs is derived from the implied volatilities (a key pricing variable) of options on these currencies. More precisely, the relationship between the implied volatilities of individual currency pairs and the cross-implied-volatility of the pair is used to compute the implied correlation.

For two currency pairs, let's say EUR/USD and GBP/USD, the implied correlation can be derived from the option prices of these pairs and the cross-pair EUR/GBP. The implied correlation $\rho_{\mathrm{EUR/USD,GBP/USD}}$ is calculated using the following formula:

$$\rho_{\mathrm{EUR,GBP}} = \frac{\sigma^2_{\mathrm{EUR/GBP}} - \sigma^2_{\mathrm{EUR}} - \sigma^2_{\mathrm{GBP}}}{-2 \cdot \sigma_{\mathrm{EUR}} \cdot \sigma_{\mathrm{GBP}}}$$

where

σ_{EUR} = implied volatility of the EUR/USD currency pair.
σ_{GBP} = implied volatility of the GBP/USD currency pair.
$\sigma_{\mathrm{EUR/GBP}}$ = implied volatility of the EUR/GBP cross-currency pair.

The formula assumes that the exchange rates for EUR/GBP can be derived as the product of the EUR/USD and GBP/USD rates, which holds true under the assumption of no triangular arbitrage. Note that the formula for implied correlation is related to the Pearson measure of correlation, which is simply the covariance of the two currency pairs divided by the product of their volatilities.

[17] A quanto option is a derivative that allows an investor to gain exposure to the price movements of an underlying asset in one currency while the payoff is denominated in another.

Currency Option Prices and Implied Correlation: A Real-World Example

On 8/16/2024 the data required for this example was collected from Bloomberg. One-month, at the money, implied volatilities for call options on three currency pairs:

$$\sigma_{\text{EUR/USD}} = 0.0532 \quad \sigma_{\text{GBP/USD}} = 0.0612 \quad \sigma_{\text{EUR/GBP}} = 0.043975$$

From the implied volatilities, implied correlation is.

$$\rho_{\text{EUR/USD,GBP/USD}} = \frac{0.001934 - 0.002836 - 0.003745}{-2 \cdot 0.05325 \cdot 0.043975} = 0.7129$$

This calculation revealed an implied correlation of 0.7129. For comparison, the Pearson measure of correlation based on the last 60 days of data (ending on 8/16/2024) provided a similar value of 0.7331. Clearly, investors in the currency markets were not anticipating any undue surprises for the following month, which is potentially useful information. The Python code for this example is provided in the attached Code Appendix.

Appendix A: Fed Funds Rate Decision Probability Model

Includes interactivity & data call.

Andrew B. Weisman

9/24/2024

```
import yfinance as yf
import matplotlib.pyplot as plt
from datetime import datetime


def get_federal_funds_future_price(ticker):
    """
    Retrieves the last price of the Federal Funds future contract from
Yahoo Finance.
    :param ticker: The ticker symbol for the Federal Funds future
contract.
    :return: The last price of the contract.
    """
```

```
    data = yf.Ticker(ticker)
    hist = data.history(period="1d")
    last_price = hist['Close'].iloc[-1]
    return last_price

def calculate_implied_rate(future_price):
    """
    Calculates the implied Federal Funds rate from the future price.
    :param future_price: The price of the Federal Funds future contract.
    :return: The implied Federal Funds rate.
    """
    implied_rate = 100 - future_price
    return implied_rate

def calculate_probability_of_rate_change(implied_rate, current_rate,
potential_rate):
    """
    Calculates the probability of a rate change (hike or cut).
    :param implied_rate: The rate implied by the Federal Funds futures.
    :param current_rate: The current Federal Funds target rate (in basis
points).
    :param potential_rate: The potential new target rate (in basis
points).
    :return: The probability of a rate change.
    """
    if implied_rate > current_rate and potential_rate > current_rate:
        # Probability of a rate hike
        probability_change = (implied_rate - current_rate) / (potential_
rate - current_rate)
    elif implied_rate < current_rate and potential_rate < current_rate:
        # Probability of a rate cut
        probability_change = (current_rate - implied_rate) / (current_
rate - potential_rate)
    else:
        probability_change = 0

    # Ensure the probability is within the valid range [0, 1]
    probability_change = max(0, min(1, probability_change))
    return probability_change

# Query user for inputs
current_target_rate = float(input("Enter the current fed funds target
rate (in basis points, e.g., 537.5 for 5.375%): "))

# Ask user for the date of the FOMC meeting
month = input("Enter the month of the FOMC meeting (format: MM): ")
```

```
day = input("Enter the day of the FOMC meeting (format: DD): ")
year = input("Enter the year of the FOMC meeting (format: YYYY): ")
fomc_meeting_date = f"{month}/{day}/{year}"

# Determine the ticker for the futures contract expiring after the FOMC
meeting
month_to_code = {
  "01": "F", "02": "G", "03": "H", "04": "J", "05": "K", "06": "M",
  "07": "N", "08": "Q", "09": "U", "10": "V", "11": "X", "12": "Z"
}

ticker_month_code = month_to_code[month]
ticker_year_code = year[-2:] # Use the last two digits of the year
ticker = f"ZQ{ticker_month_code}{ticker_year_code}.CBT"

# Ask user whether analyzing cuts or hikes
change_type = input("Are you analyzing potential 'cut' or 'hike'?
").strip().lower()

# Query user for the number of scenarios to analyze
num_scenarios = int(input("Enter the number of scenarios to analyze
(1-8): "))

# Generate the scenarios based on the number of cuts or hikes
scenarios = {}
for i in range(1, num_scenarios + 1):
  rate_change = 25 * i # 25 bps for each scenario increment
  if change_type == "cut":
    potential_rate = current_target_rate - rate_change
    scenarios[f"{rate_change} bps Cut"] = potential_rate
  elif change_type == "hike":
    potential_rate = current_target_rate + rate_change
    scenarios[f"{rate_change} bps Hike"] = potential_rate

# Get the implied rate from the futures contract
implied_rate = (100 - get_federal_funds_future_price(ticker)) * 100

# Calculate probabilities for each scenario
probabilities = {}
total_probability_of_change = 0

for scenario, potential_rate in scenarios.items():
  probabilities[scenario] = calculate_probability_of_rate_
change(implied_rate, current_target_rate, potential_rate)
  total_probability_of_change += probabilities[scenario]
```

```
# Probability of "No Change" is 1 minus the sum of all other
probabilities
probabilities["No Change"] = max(0, 1 - total_probability_of_change)

# Normalize the probabilities only if their sum exceeds 1
total_probability_sum = sum(probabilities.values())

if total_probability_sum > 1:
  for scenario in probabilities:
    probabilities[scenario] /= total_probability_sum

# Print the implied rate
print(f"Implied Rate = {implied_rate:.2f}")

# Print the probabilities (normalized if needed)
for scenario, probability in probabilities.items():
  print(f"Probability of {scenario}: {probability:.2%}")

# Plotting the results
def plot_probabilities(probabilities):
  """
  Creates a bar chart to visualize the probabilities of rate changes.
  :param probabilities: A dictionary with rate change scenarios and
their probabilities.
  """
  scenarios = list(probabilities.keys())
  probs = list(probabilities.values())

  plt.figure(figsize=(8, 6))
  bars = plt.bar(scenarios, probs, color=['#4CAF50', '#FF9800',
'#2196F3'])

  # Add labels to the bars
  for bar in bars:
    yval = bar.get_height()
    plt.text(bar.get_x() + bar.get_width() / 2, yval + 0.01,
f'{yval:.2%}', ha='center', va='bottom')

  # Add the date and time stamp in the upper right-hand corner
  timestamp = datetime.now().strftime("%Y-%m-%d %H:%M:%S")
  plt.text(0.95, 0.95, f"Run on: {timestamp}",
horizontalalignment='right',
         verticalalignment='center', transform=plt.gca().transAxes,
fontsize=10,
        bbox=dict(facecolor='white', alpha=0.5))
```

```
    plt.title("Probability of Federal Funds Rate Change Scenarios")
    plt.ylabel("Probability")
    plt.ylim(0, 1)
    plt.grid(axis='y', linestyle='--', alpha=0.7)
    plt.tight_layout()
    plt.show()

# Call the plot function
plot_probabilities(probabilities)
```

Appendix B: Implied Correlation Between Two Currency Pairs

Sample Case Using One-Month ATM Implied Volatilites:(Data as of close 8/15/24) Andrew B. Weisman

August 16, 2024

```
def calculate_implied_correlation(sigma_eur_usd, sigma_gbp_usd,
sigma_eur_gbp):
    """
    Calculate the implied correlation between EUR/USD and GBP/USD
currency pairs.

    Parameters:
    sigma_eur_usd (float): Implied volatility of EUR/USD currency pair
(annualized).
    sigma_gbp_usd (float): Implied volatility of GBP/USD currency pair
(annualized).
    sigma_eur_gbp (float): Implied volatility of EUR/GBP currency pair
(annualized).

    Returns:
    float: The implied correlation between EUR/USD and GBP/USD.
    """
    # Using the formula to calculate implied correlation
    numerator = sigma_eur_gbp ** 2 - sigma_eur_usd ** 2 - sigma_gbp_usd
** 2
    denominator = -2 * sigma_eur_usd * sigma_gbp_usd

    # Calculate implied correlation
    implied_correlation = numerator / denominator
```

```
  return implied_correlation

# Usage:
if __name__ == "__main__":
  # Example implied volatilities (in decimal form, e.g., 10% = 0.10)
  sigma_eur_usd = 0.0532 # Implied volatility of EUR/USD
  sigma_gbp_usd = 0.0612 # Implied volatility of GBP/USD
  sigma_eur_gbp = 0.043975 # Implied volatility of EUR/GBP

  # Calculate implied correlation
  correlation = calculate_implied_correlation(sigma_eur_usd, sigma_
gbp_usd, sigma_eur_gbp)

  # Output the result
  print(f"The implied correlation between EUR/USD and GBP/USD is:
{correlation:.4f}")
```

Appendix C: Risk-Neutral Density Version 4.0 Andrew B. Weisman 10/4/2024

```
import numpy as np
import pandas as pd
from scipy.interpolate import interp1d
from scipy.integrate import simpson
from numdifftools import Derivative
import matplotlib.pyplot as plt
from sklearn.neighbors import KernelDensity
from datetime import datetime

# Load data from Excel file
file_name = 'CallOptionData2.xlsx'
data = pd.read_excel(file_name)

# Extracting strike prices and call prices from the DataFrame
strikes = data['Strike'].values
call_prices = data['CallPrice'].values

# Current Date
curr_date = datetime(2024, 9, 4)

# Expiration Date
exp_date = datetime(2024, 10, 18)
```

```
# Calculate the number of days between the two dates
days_to_exp = (exp_date - curr_date).days

# Time to expiration in years
T = days_to_exp / 365

# Risk-free rate (you can adjust this as needed)
r = 5.25 / 100

# Interpolating the call price function
call_price_function = interp1d(strikes, call_prices, kind='cubic',
fill_value="extrapolate")

# Using numdifftools to calculate the second derivative of the call
price with respect to strike prices
def second_derivative(strike):
  return Derivative(call_price_function, n=2)(strike)

# Calculating the risk-neutral density
density = np.array([np.exp(r * T) * second_derivative(K) for K in
strikes])

# Ensuring non-negative values by setting negative values to zero
positive_density = np.maximum(density, 0) + 1e-10 # Adding a small
constant to avoid zero densities

# Normalizing the risk-neutral density so that the area under the curve
sums to 1
area_under_curve = simpson(y=positive_density, x=strikes)
normalized_density = positive_density / area_under_curve

# Extend the strike price range for KDE to extrapolate tails better
extended_strike_range = np.linspace(strikes.min() - 20, strikes.max()
+ 20, 500)

# Fit the KDE model with a broader bandwidth to naturally smooth the
tails
kde = KernelDensity(kernel='gaussian', bandwidth=2.0)
kde.fit(strikes[:, None], sample_weight=normalized_density)

# Generate a range of strike prices for the KDE density curve
strike_range_kde = np.linspace(strikes.min() - 20, strikes.max() + ,
500)

# Calculate the KDE log density and exponentiate to get the density
log_density = kde.score_samples(strike_range_kde[:, None])
```

```
density_kde = np.exp(log_density)

# Normalize the KDE density to ensure it integrates to 1
density_kde /= simpson(y=density_kde, x=strike_range_kde)

# Calculate the first three moments of the KDE distribution
mean_kde = simpson(y=strike_range_kde * density_kde, x=strike_range_
kde)
variance_kde = simpson(y=(strike_range_kde - mean_kde) ** 2 * density_
kde, x=strike_range_kde)
std_dev_kde = np.sqrt(variance_kde) # Calculate the standard deviation

# Calculate the third moment (for skewness)
third_moment_kde = simpson(y=(strike_range_kde - mean_kde) ** 3 *
density_kde, x=strike_range_kde)

# Calculate skewness: (third central moment) / (standard deviation^3)
skewness_kde = third_moment_kde / (std_dev_kde ** 3)

# Calculate the fourth moment (for kurtosis)
fourth_moment_kde = simpson(y=(strike_range_kde - mean_kde) ** 4 *
density_kde, x=strike_range_kde)

# Calculate kurtosis: (fourth central moment) / (variance^2)
kurtosis_kde = fourth_moment_kde / (variance_kde ** 2)

# Calculate the current spot price (S_0)
implied_forward_price = 554.34
current_price = implied_forward_price / np.exp(r * T)

# Calculate Value at Risk (VaR)
confidence_level = 0.05 # 95% confidence level
cumulative_density = np.cumsum(density_kde) * (strike_range_kde[1] -
strike_range_kde[0])

# VaR: The strike price corresponding to the (1 - confidence_level)
quantile
var_index = np.where(cumulative_density >= confidence_level)[0][0]
VaR_level = strike_range_kde[var_index]
VaR = current_price - VaR_level # Calculate the size of the move lower

# Plotting the KDE smoothed risk-neutral density with extrapolated
tails
plt.figure(figsize=(10, 6))
plt.plot(strike_range_kde, density_kde, color='black', label='KDE
Density')
```

```
# Adding a vertical line for the current price (solid line)
plt.axvline(x=current_price,      color='gray',      linestyle='-',
linewidth=2, label=f'Current Price: {current_price:.2f}')

# Adding a vertical line for the Value at Risk (VaR) (dashed line)
plt.axvline(x=VaR_level,      color='dimgray',      linestyle='--',
linewidth=2, label=f'VaR Level: {VaR_level:.2f}')

# Adding a vertical line for the implied forward price (dotted line)
plt.axvline(x=implied_forward_price,               color='darkgray',
linestyle=':', linewidth=2, label=f'Implied Forward Price: {implied_
forward_price:.2f}')

# Display the first three moments, standard deviation, VaR, Kurtosis,
and Skewness on the plot
textstr = '\n'.join((
  f'Mean: {mean_kde:.2f}',
  f'Variance: {variance_kde:.2f}',
  f'Standard Deviation: {std_dev_kde:.2f}',
  f'Skewness: {skewness_kde:.2f}', # Adding Skewness
  f'Kurtosis: {kurtosis_kde:.2f}', # Adding Kurtosis
  f'VaR (95% Move Lower): {VaR:.2f}'))

# These are matplotlib.patch.Patch properties
props = dict(boxstyle='round', facecolor='white', edgecolor='black',
alpha=0.5)

# Place the text box on the plot
plt.text(0.05,    0.95,    textstr,    transform=plt.gca().transAxes,
fontsize=10,
     verticalalignment='top', bbox=props)

plt.xlabel('Strike Price')
plt.ylabel('Density')

# Limit the x-axis to the region of interest (between 520 and 580)
plt.xlim(520, 580)

# Update legend to include all lines
plt.legend(loc='upper right') # Set the legend to the upper right
plt.grid(True)
plt.show()
```

Part II

Case Studies: Managing Risk and Capital Protection

12

Risk Management with Stock Index Futures and Put Options

Robert Harlow

Risk management is a cornerstone of portfolio management, enabling fund managers to control risks while aligning portfolio exposures with investment objectives. Within the broad spectrum of risk management strategies, hedging represents a specific and critical subset focused on reducing or eliminating particular risks. In this case study, the focus is on two distinct approaches to hedging excess market exposure in an equity portfolio: stock index futures and put options. These strategies are evaluated in the context of a portfolio manager's need to reduce beta exposure to the S&P 500 index while preserving the underlying portfolio composition.

Using a hypothetical portfolio derived from the top holdings of a T. Rowe Price portfolio as of February 28, 2020, this study demonstrates the mechanics of implementing futures and options-based hedges. Through a step-by-step calculation, it highlights how the manager achieves the desired reduction in effective equity exposure while navigating the implications of market events, specifically the historic sell-off during the onset of the COVID-19 pandemic. By comparing the outcomes of these two approaches, the case study provides valuable insights into the nuances of linear and non-linear hedging strategies, including the trade-offs between simplicity, cost, and risk factor exposure.

This case underscores the importance of aligning hedging strategies with portfolio objectives and explores broader considerations such as transaction

R. Harlow (✉)
Associate Head of Global Multi-Asset Research at T. Rowe Price, Baltimore, USA
e-mail: Robert.Harlow@troweprice.com

F. J. Fabozzi and M. de Jong (eds.), *Derivatives Applications in Asset Management*,
https://doi.org/10.1007/978-3-031-86354-7_12

costs and the volatility risk premium. It is a practical guide for portfolio managers when choosing between futures and options to optimize risk management in varying market conditions.

Illustration

An equity portfolio manager is bullish on all the individual names included in the portfolio shown in Exhibit 12.1,[1] which were determined through bottom-up fundamental research. However, many of the names in the portfolio are high beta, and despite establishing a 5% allocation to cash, the portfolio beta relative to the benchmark, the S&P 500 index, is still higher than 1, at 1.1525. Since the portfolio manager does not have a view on the broader market and being uncomfortable being essentially long 15% versus the benchmark, a decision is made to hedge the excess market exposure. Two approaches are being considered by the portfolio manager for hedging:

Futures approach: Using the existing cash allocation as collateral for the futures position, sell index futures.
Options approach: With a portion of the existing excess cash, buying a 20-delta index put option.

In both cases, the portfolio manager's goal is to reduce exposure to the benchmark without changing the cash market positions. As of February 28, 2020, the S&P 500 index was valued at $2954.22, a March expiry e-mini future contract on the S&P500 was trading at $2951, and a 20-delta put with an expiration identical to the March futures contract was trading at $48.50 and had a strike price of $2660.

---

[1] The hypothetical portfolio used in this mini-case is based on the top 50 names of a T. Rowe Price portfolio as of February 28, 2020, renormalized to have a market value of $150 MN. Additionally, a 5% cash allocation was added to facilitate the illustration. Betas were estimated using historical data between 2016 and February 28, 2020, using historical returns. Futures prices come from Bloomberg and option pricing is from OptionMetrics.

Name	Ticker	Beta	Weight	Market_value ($)
Vmware Inc-Class A	VMW	1.2498	0.4132%	619,871.74
Advanced Micro Devices	AMD	2.0932	0.4219%	632,884.71
Northrop Grumman Corp	NOC	0.6888	0.4244%	636,629.72
Marsh & Mclennan Cos	MMC	0.8124	0.4248%	637,262.16
Fleetcor Technologies Inc	FLT	1.1494	0.4363%	654,479.73
Hilton Worldwide Holdings Inc	HLT	1.0788	0.4761%	714,169.36
Td Ameritrade Holding Corp	AMTD	1.2827	0.4799%	719,794.62
Morgan Stanley	MS	1.4860	0.5116%	767,366.38
Applied Materials Inc	AMAT	1.6340	0.5468%	820,143.18
Lululemon Athletica Inc	LULU	1.0308	0.5777%	866,617.03
Nike Inc -Cl B	NKE	1.0028	0.5840%	875,938.36
Intercontinental Exchange Inc	ICE	0.6993	0.5873%	881,013.40
Hca Healthcare Inc	HCA	0.9182	0.6395%	959,274.51
Costar Group Inc	CSGP	1.0378	0.6602%	990,230.52
S&P Global Inc	SPGI	1.1278	0.7052%	1,057,745.82
Roper Technologies Inc	ROP	1.0107	0.7654%	1,148,066.31
Centene Corp	CNC	1.1444	0.8032%	1,204,819.51
Elevance Health Inc	ELV	0.9379	0.8198%	1,229,760.83
Splunk Inc	SPLK	1.5877	0.9392%	1,408,831.56
Nvidia Corp	NVDA	1.8580	0.9895%	1,484,178.22
Ross Stores Inc	ROST	0.9173	1.0946%	1,641,874.12
Willis Towers Watson Plc	WTW	0.8551	1.0955%	1,643,183.84
Becton Dickinson And Co	BDX	0.8866	1.1209%	1,681,289.97
Thermo Fisher Scientific Inc	TMO	1.1141	1.2231%	1,834,712.23
Workday Inc	WDAY	1.4932	1.2717%	1,907,522.19
Booking Holdings Inc	BKNG	1.1201	1.2810%	1,921,569.00
Danaher Corp	DHR	0.9331	1.3365%	2,004,772.42
Dollar General Corp	DG	0.7246	1.3451%	2,017,631.49
Alphabet Inc Cl A	GOOGL	1.2174	1.4674%	2,201,043.39
Intuitive Surgical Inc	ISRG	1.2110	1.6075%	2,411,221.12
Fiserv Inc	FI	0.9226	1.7371%	2,605,583.68
Stryker Corp	SYK	0.8972	1.8979%	2,846,873.17
Paypal Holdings Inc	PYPL	1.2994	1.9103%	2,865,413.66
Vertex Pharmaceuticals Inc	VRTX	1.3356	1.9832%	2,974,863.08
Boeing Co/The	BA	1.1888	1.9906%	2,985,855.50
Fidelity National Info Serv	FIS	0.9044	2.0030%	3,004,561.13
Cigna Group/The	CI	0.9262	2.0221%	3,033,125.89
UnitedHealth Group Inc	UNH	0.9231	2.0579%	3,086,793.02
Intuit Inc	INTU	1.1724	2.2917%	3,437,607.62
Global Payments Inc	GPN	1.2311	2.3267%	3,490,114.25
Salesforce Inc	CRM	1.3530	2.3625%	3,543,766.71
Netflix Inc	NFLX	1.5280	2.4949%	3,742,282.32
Servicenow Inc	NOW	1.5159	2.6447%	3,966,995.67
Apple Inc	AAPL	1.2968	3.4731%	5,209,703.56
Mastercard Inc - A	MA	1.2873	3.7525%	5,628,709.91
Visa Inc-Class A Shares	V	1.1872	4.3180%	6,476,927.37
Microsoft Corp	MSFT	1.3408	6.1092%	9,163,866.13
Alphabet Inc Cl C	GOOG	1.2213	6.5689%	9,853,284.80
Meta Platforms Inc-Class A	META	1.2136	7.2778%	10,916,684.00
Amazon.Com Inc	AMZN	1.3452	10.7287%	16,093,091.12
Cash USD		0.0000	5.0000%	7,500,000.00
Total		1.1525	100.0000%	150,000,000.00

Exhibit 12.1 Hypothetical Portfolio for Illustration. The hypothetical portfolio used in this mini-case is based on the top 50 names of a T. Rowe Price portfolio as of February 28, 2020, renormalized to have a market value of $150 MN. Additionally, a 5% cash allocation was added to facilitate the illustration. Betas were estimated using historical data between 2016 and February 28, 2020, using historical returns. Futures prices come from Bloomberg and option pricing is from OptionMetrics

Futures-Based Hedging

The general formula for determining the correct number of futures to sell (denoted by $N_{futures}$) is

$$N_{futures} = \frac{\text{Beta target} - \text{Current portfolio beta}}{\text{Futures price} \times \text{Multiplier}} \times \text{Portfolio market value} \quad (12.1)$$

In our illustration, we will use the E-mini futures contracts on the S&P 500. The multiplier for the contact is 50. Therefore, to size the correct number of futures to sell using this contract, the portfolio manager solves Eq. (12.1). For a portfolio market value of $150,000,000 we obtain:

$$N_{futures} = \frac{1.0000 - 1.1525}{\$2951 \times 50} \times \$150{,}000{,}000 = -155 \text{ contracts}$$

The negative sign means that the futures should be shorted. Note that because futures contracts do not have a beta of exactly 1, it is appropriate to use the futures price in the denominator. Additionally, the futures contract requires no initial cash outlay, so the portfolio manager's cash position is unchanged at the time the hedge is added.

Option-Based Hedging

An alternative approach is option-based hedging. This approach involves purchasing 20-delta put options on the S&P 500 index. Delta is a first-order approximation of how much the price of a derivative contract, such as an option, changes, given a move in the underlying asset. Put options provide short exposure to the underlying asset, and a "20-delta put" is a specific put option that is expected to instantaneously gain 20 cents when the underlying falls by $1. These options provide a non-linear hedge, protecting against significant market declines while requiring an upfront cash outlay. The number of put options to purchase (N_{puts}) is determined using the following equation:

$$N_{puts} = \frac{\text{Beta target} - \text{Current portfolio beta}}{\text{Option delta} \times \text{Multiplier} \times \text{Underlying index value}} \times \text{Portfolio market value} \quad (12.2)$$

Options on the S&P 500 used in the illustration have a contract multiplier of 100 and an option delta of -0.20, so the number of put options to buy becomes:

$$N_{puts} = \frac{1.0000 - 1.1525}{-0.20 \times 100 \times 2954.22} \times \$150{,}000{,}000 = 387 \text{ contracts}$$

Note that the cash outlay to purchase these contracts is $1.9 million (387 $48.50 100), which is easily covered by the $7.5 million cash position.

A Note on Derivatives and Their Delta

Delta, often denoted by the Greek symbol Δ, is the expected change in the price of a derivative contract given a corresponding change in the underlying asset. Both futures and options are derivative contracts, and they both have deltas. The fair price of a futures contract, in continuous time, is given by the following equation:

$$F = Se^{(r-d)T}$$

where F is the price of the future, S is the price of the underlying, e is the exponential function, r is the risk free rate, d is the dividend yield of the underlying and T is the time to maturity of the contract. To calculate the delta, or the expected change in the price of the future given a change in the underlying, we would take a derivative of the pricing formula above with respect to S. This results in the expression:

$$\Delta_{\text{future}} = e^{(r-d)T}$$

Note that this provides a way to generalize Eqs. (12.1) and (12.2) in the previous section:

$$N = \frac{\text{Beta target} - \text{Current portfolio beta}}{\Delta \times \text{Multiplier} \times \text{Underlying Index Value}} \tag{12.3}$$

Because the delta of a futures contract multiplied by the underlying index value is equivalent to the futures price, Eq. (12.3) reduces to Eq. (12.1).

In the case of options, the functional form is significantly more complicated. While the derivation is beyond the scope of this chapter, the Black–Scholes model gives the following equation for the price of a put option:

$$P = Ke^{(-rT)}\Phi(-d2) - Se^{(-dT)}\Phi(-d1) \tag{12.4}$$

where Φ is the cumulative distribution function of the normal distribution and we have the following expressions for $d1$ and $d2$:

$$d1 = \frac{ln(S/K) + \left(r - d + \sigma^2/2\right)T}{\sigma\sqrt{T}}$$

$$d2 = d1 - \sigma\sqrt{T}$$

If we take a derivative of (4) with respect to S to find the delta of the put option, we get the following equation for put option delta:

$$\Delta_{put} = e^{(-dT)}(\Phi(d1) - 1)$$

As of February 28, 2020, we have values of 2954.22, 2660, 0.0567, 0.0155, 0.0226, and 0.5720 for S, K, T, r, d, and, respectively. Plugging these values into Eq. (12.4), we get a value of \$48.50 for the price of the put option and a value of -0.20 for the delta, which is consistent with the previous section.

Which Approach is Better?

Now, which approach is better? The answer is, "it depends." Both approaches reduce the effective equity exposure by the same amount at the onset of the trade. However, the futures approach is only exposed to one risk factor (the underlying), and the options approach is exposed to more risk factors (the underlying and the underlying volatility). As it turns out, February 28, 2020, was on the eve of one of the most severe sell-offs in stock market history due to the rapid global spread of the COVID-19 virus. Both these contracts expired on March 20, 2020, when the settlement price on the S&P500 was \$2437.98.

Let's compare the profit and loss (P&L) for each approach:

- *Futures Approach*:

−155 (2437.98 – 2951) 50
= $3,975,905 or a +2.65% contribution to portfolio return

- *Option approach*:

387 [max(2660 – 2437.98, 0) – 48.50] 100
= $6,715,224 or a + 4.48% contribution to portfolio return

The options approach was, with hindsight, more attractive than the futures approach in this example because the realized move in the underlying was large. In other words, the option was underpricing subsequent volatility. However, most of the time, options trade at a premium, a phenomenon known as the "volatility risk premium" (VRP). One way to measure the VRP is to compare option implied volatility to subsequent realized volatility. Historically, this spread is significant and positive, meaning implied volatility is, on average, a few percentage points higher than historical realized volatility, and regular purchasers of index options tend to lose money. Because futures contracts are not exposed to the VRP, they will tend to be less expensive hedging instruments than put options for the same amount of linear exposure reduction. Additionally, transaction costs on futures are far lower than transaction costs on options.

The moral of the story is that when evaluating linear hedges like futures versus non-linear hedges like options (or various combinations of options), portfolio managers should:

- Evaluate apples-to-apples by comparing the net linear exposure of the option positions to the same exposure with futures.
- Use options-based methods when they have a view or preference on risk factors only accessible via options (e.g., volatility).

Summary

This case study explores two approaches to managing excess market exposure in an equity portfolio: hedging with stock index futures and using put options. The portfolio manager, holding a portfolio with a beta of 1.1525 relative to the S&P 500 index, seeks to reduce exposure to align with the benchmark while preserving the underlying equity positions. The study illustrates the mechanics of these strategies, detailing the calculations for sizing futures and options positions. The case further analyzes both methods' profit and loss outcomes during the COVID-19-driven market sell-off in early 2020. The futures approach, exposed only to the underlying index, provided a smaller gain, whereas the options approach, influenced by additional factors like volatility, offered a significantly higher return. This difference underscores the trade-offs between linear and non-linear hedging strategies, emphasizing cost considerations and the volatility risk premium in evaluating their effectiveness.

13

Using Options for Tail Risk Hedging

Vineer Bhansali

Tail risk represents the potential for rare but extreme adverse market events that can significantly impact portfolio performance. While such events occur infrequently, their consequences can be severe, leading to substantial losses and destabilizing an investment strategy. For portfolio managers, managing tail risk is crucial to ensuring resilience and preserving capital during periods of market stress.

Options are powerful instruments for addressing tail risk. By using options-based hedging strategies, portfolio managers can protect against severe downside scenarios while retaining exposure to market upside. This dual benefit makes options an essential component of modern risk management. This case study explores the application of options for tail risk hedging, illustrating how portfolio managers can effectively design, implement, and evaluate hedging programs to mitigate extreme risks.

The case begins by examining the concept of tail risk and the role of options in managing these risks. It then transitions to a detailed case study highlighting the practical application of options for tail risk hedging, including structuring put option strategies, evaluating hedge performance, and balancing cost efficiency with hedge effectiveness. This analysis provides actionable insights for portfolio managers seeking to incorporate tail hedging into their investment strategies.

V. Bhansali (✉)
LongTail Alpha, Newport Beach, USA
e-mail: VBhansali@longtailalpha.com

F. J. Fabozzi and M. de Jong (eds.), *Derivatives Applications in Asset Management*,
https://doi.org/10.1007/978-3-031-86354-7_13

Understanding Tail Risk and Options

Options markets allow portfolio managers to efficiently shape the probability distribution of returns. In exchange for paying a premium to the seller of an option, the buyer of an option can create a contingent payoff for specific market events of interest.

By tail risk, we generally mean rare financial market outcomes but with considerable consequences. Since these events are rare, predicting when and how large such events will occur is usually challenging. However, this does not change the importance of having some securities or strategies in a portfolio that will perform well in such events to provide robustness to the overall portfolio. Tail risk hedging, by definition, is a "just in case" investment strategy as compared to "just in time" investment strategies which rely on responding to an adverse event as it occurs. In other words, using options for tail risk hedging allows a portfolio manager to plan in advance rather than react to the adverse event as it is happening. Options markets are perfectly suited for such risk management applications.

Adverse events can be different for different portfolios.[1] For any adverse event, by committing a small amount of premium to asymmetric options-based strategies helps the underlying portfolio during the period of interest and provides both protection and the ability to take advantage of opportunities via option monetization and redeployment. Such hedging, of course, is not free. For the benefit of getting the protection, the investor usually must pay something (e.g., an option premium, either on a set schedule or by committing capital for protective strategies for a fixed horizon in advance). It is important to realize that once the risk factors of interest are identified, then options on those systematic risk factors can be utilized to reduce the systematic tail risks. Identification and quantification of risk factor exposures is thus the logical first step in designing a tail hedge. For instance, one could use options on the S&P 500 or other market indices if the primary risk factor of interest is aggregate large cap equity beta, or other indices (e.g., options on the Nasdaq 100 index) if the risk is primarily technology sector exposure. Since options are time-decaying assets, the potency of the hedge must be maintained by purchasing new options as old options expire.

[1] For instance, during the 2008–2010 financial crisis, portfolio managers who had overweight credit exposure suffered when credit spreads widened. On the other hand, when inflation suddenly increased in 2021 and 2022, portfolio managers who had been relying on bond markets to diversify their portfolios suffered from sharply rising bond yields. During the COVID-19 pandemic, the sudden decline in equity markets, especially in March 2020, created a significant adverse tail event for equity markets in general.

Illustrating Tail Hedging with a Case Study

This case study illustrates how a portfolio manager can apply options-based hedging strategies to mitigate tail risk and enhance portfolio robustness.

Overview of the Tail Hedging Program

The case study focuses on a portfolio manager overseeing a $100 million equity investment to protect against extreme market downturns while maintaining alignment with long-term strategic goals. This section provides an overview of the hedging program, including the portfolio's characteristics and the key considerations driving the hedging strategy.

When an adverse market event occurs, the options may rise significantly in value. Portfolio managers can choose to do nothing if the view is that the hedge is still needed or monetize it by selling it in the market and redeploying the proceeds into the markets or other investments or just using the cash flows to meet other liabilities. In other words, having options-based hedges during the event in question thus provides endogenous liquidity when such liquidity is valuable for the portfolio. Systematic and discretionary monetization strategies may be used to monetize the increase in the value of the options.

In this illustration, we provide a typical structure of a tail hedging program for hedging equity risk. We consider the problem of a portfolio manager who owns equities and wants to hedge against downside risk. Let's consider a portfolio manager overseeing a $100 million investment in the S&P 500 index via an exchange-traded fund such as the SPDR S&P 500 ETF Trust (SPY) or the iShares Core S&P 500 ETF (IVV).

Assume also that the portfolio manager (1) seeks a strategy that allows the portfolio itself (without the hedge) to absorb the first 20% of potential losses, (2) requires protection against any further decline if the portfolio's value drops below $80 million within a year, and (3) desires a dependable tail hedge mechanism, one that is highly likely to activate and compensate for losses if the S&P 500 index decreases by 20% or more. This scenario assumes that the portfolio manager prefers not to sell or decrease the portfolio's market holdings to mitigate risk. This stance may stem from optimism about a market rebound, fear of missing out on future gains, or concerns about triggering taxable events on unrealized gains, which could present an additional financial burden.

Structuring the Tail Hedge

Considering these objectives, the portfolio manager considers various options-based strategies to structure an effective tail hedge. This section outlines the instruments, strike prices, and maturities selected to meet the desired protection level and explores the key considerations in designing the hedge.

The portfolio manager can consider buying an out-of-the-money put option on the S&P 500 index to implement this hedging strategy. Other alternatives include options on the SPY ETF or the S&P 500 index futures. Suppose the portfolio manager has a relationship with a prime broker or OTC derivative counterparty; a custom OTC option can also be created. The portfolio manager could also explore less reliable but potentially cheaper hedges using instruments in related markets. However, such approaches increase basis risk, and this illustration excludes indirect hedges for simplicity.[2]

Hedge Implementation and Example Calculation

To understand the practicalities of implementing this hedging strategy, we examine an example using a 20% out-of-the-money put option on the S&P 500 index. The following analysis provides a detailed calculation of the option's cost, sensitivities, and potential performance under adverse market conditions.

As a first example of a reliable tail hedge with minimal basis risk, assume that the price of the S&P 500 index is 5150.82 (price as of March 8, 2024). Assume that the portfolio manager wants to hedge the downside risk with a 20% out-of-the-money European-style put option with 90 days to expiration. This short-dated option is usually suitable if the portfolio manager expects a sharp and steep market shock like the one that occurred during the COVID-19 crisis.

Scenario Analysis

To evaluate the effectiveness of this hedging strategy, it is essential to analyze how the options perform under different market scenarios. This section explores the impact of significant market declines and volatility changes on

[2] For a further discussion, see Vineer Bhansali, *Tail Risk Hedging: Creating Robust Portfolios for Volatile Markets*. New York, NY: McGraw-Hill, 2014.

the hedge's value, providing insight into the practical outcomes of using options for tail risk management.

The author has been participating in the options markets for over thirty years and is quite familiar with both simple and complex models that are used by practitioners. Many of these complex models overcome the shortcomings of the Black–Scholes model, which is one of the simplest models in practice, but still sufficiently complex to capture the non-linearities inherent in option pricing and hedging. One of these shortcomings is the assumption of using a constant for the implied volatility in the model. It is common knowledge that volatility is not constant, but is both time varying and level dependent. Despite these shortcomings, the Black–Scholes model is superior to many complex models because of its wide adoption, relatively straightforward implementation, and above all the intuition it captures. Thus, as a practitioner, the author has found that discussing tail hedging with this simple model is a great starting point.

Using the Black–Scholes formula with $5150.82 as the current price, implied volatility of 26.36%, dividend yield of 1.412% for the S&P 500, interest rates of 5.31%, and a strike price of $4120.50 (all data from Bloomberg as of March 8, 2024), the price of this put option is 9.24 S&P 500 points, which, in percentage terms is 0.17% or 17 basis points (9.24/5151.84 = 0.17%). In addition, the delta of the option is –0.033 (–3.3%), the gamma is 0.5581, the vega is 1.87, and the theta is –0.27 (these numbers use the conventions that Bloomberg uses and can be used to compute the change in the value of the option for small changes in the variables that drive the price of the option). The option also has higher-order Greeks, such as the rate of delta change concerning time (called "Charm" or delta decay), which come into play when managing the risks of options over time.

So a portfolio manager can hedge a $100 million portfolio for 0.17% of $100 million (i.e., for a dollar price of $170,000). Since this is a European option, which can only be exercised at expiration, the portfolio manager is paid one-for-one for any decline beyond the 20% strike level if the market falls below the 20% strike level. Since the delta is 3.3%, locally, the exposure is as if the portfolio manager is short $3.3 million, equivalent to the stock market. However, this delta changes rapidly as the market declines or volatility increases, which tends to happen together since market declines increase implied volatility.

Thus, the real potency of the hedge comes from the convexity of the option. For example, if the S&P 500 drops 20% to 4120.66 the value of the hedge will increase by a large multiple of its initial cost. If we assume that the volatility remains unchanged, then because of the change in the level of the

S&P 500 and the put option's gamma, the put option's value will increase to 4.7%, which is a 27-fold increase in value.[3] But the value of options is also very responsive to the level of volatility, which we assumed above to be unchanged. It is difficult to forecast what the level of volatility is going to be for all future paths, but broadly speaking volatility rises sharply when the equity markets fall.[4] If we assume conservatively that for each 10% fall in the market results in a 10-point increase in volatility, then increasing the implied volatility by 20% results in the value of the option increasing to 8.6%, which is a 50-fold increase in its value from its purchase price. Thus, while this selloff in the market results in a loss in the underlying portfolio of 20%, the increase in the option price would cushion a good portion of the losses, thereby providing a tail hedge.

Using a simple Black–Scholes calculator and assumptions for the change in the underlying, the portfolio manager can calculate other scenario payoffs and see if they mitigate the risks as desired or not. For illustration, if we use a 35% decline and 80% volatility level, the new option price would be 30%, a whopping increase of 176 times the initial value of the option. This is how options can hedge "crash" risk, and indeed were able to do so during the COVID-19 pandemic. For other events, such as the gradual but protracted decline in the market in the 2007–2008 Global Financial Crisis, options with longer maturity would be more valuable since they give longer exposure and do not decay as quickly. Portfolio managers can combine options with different strike prices and maturities. For example, suppose a portfolio manager is looking for a hedge that is maintained over time and has a one-year horizon, and resets its strike prices partially as the market changes. The portfolio manager can buy a ladder of options of different maturities (e.g., 3-month, 6-month, 9-month, and 12-month options) each with one quarter of the notional using quarterly options expiration dates and replace expiring options with new 12-month options.

An important thing to remember is that there is a price for the convexity of these options. In the world of option trading, the convexity is known as "gamma", and price is the time decay or "theta". In essence, if the market status quo is maintained (meaning there are no significant changes in market levels or the volatility term structure), the value of the option will decrease over time, along with its effectiveness. So, if one month has elapsed then the

---

[3] During the COVID-19 crisis, the S&P 500 dropped from approximately 3400 to a low of 2200, an almost 35% decline from peak to trough in approximately one month from the middle of February 2020 to the middle of March 2020.

[4] For example, during the one month from February 2020 to March 2020, implied volatility as measured by the CBOE Volatility Index (VIX) rose sharply from 20 to 80, a four-fold increase.

price of the same option will fall to close to half its value (0.09%). Part of this change in value comes from the smaller time left to expiry, and part of the change comes from the implied volatility changing. The "potency" or the delta also decays as time passes (this is the effect of the higher-order Greek "charm" mentioned above). For example, after one month, the delta falls to only −0.02 or −2%, so now the equivalent market short position is only $2 million on this option. This is why to maintain a tail hedge a portfolio manager has to commit new capital periodically to extend the hedge. This is not dissimilar to renewal of an insurance policy where periodic premiums are needed to maintain coverage. Of course, at expiration if the market is not below the strike price, the value of the option is exactly zero, or the insurance/hedge will have expired worthless.

The difference between the implied volatility of at-the-money options and the out-of-the-money options is called the "volatility skew". When this illustration was created, the 20% out-of-the-money put volatility was almost twice the implied volatility for at-the-money options. Thus, another alternative to hedging with puts is to use a put-spread. In a put-spread, the portfolio manager buys a higher strike put option and sells a lower strike put option. For example, the portfolio manager could buy a 5% out-of-the-money put for 0.95% premium (i.e., almost $950,000), and sell a 10% out-of-the-money put for 0.475% (i.e., $475,000) for a difference of approximately 0.475%. Note that the delta of the 5% out-of-the-money put is −21, and the delta of the 10% out-of-the-money put is −10, so the total delta of the put-spread is −11. In other words, to obtain the same delta as the original 20% out-of-the-money put the portfolio manager only has to invest in roughly a third (to obtain the same delta as the original) notional in the put-spread, thus reducing the cost for the put-spread to 0.16% (0.475%/3), which is quite close but not the same as the price of the put.[5] However, the put-spread has a much different payoff profile than the put and can have very different sensitivities ("Greeks"). For instance, if the market falls a large amount within a short period and does not bounce back, the portfolio manager would have been better off buying a put rather than a put-spread. On the other hand, if the market falls only by a moderate amount between the upper and lower strikes of the put-spread then the portfolio manager would do better with a put-spread than with a put. Options traders run scenario shocks to quantify

[5] We should emphasize that the delta of deeply out-of-the-money options can be quite sensitive to the inputs and the model that is used, and especially for tail-hedging applications, many of the assumptions underlying the Black–Scholes model are violated, such as the assumption that the returns are normally distributed. So, care is required in the use of the models for such applications.

the difference between such structures and optimize their decisions to ensure that the desired outcome is achieved at the lowest price.

This illustration highlights several other important aspects of tail risk hedging using options. First, the selection of the instrument and sizing must match the underlying and the objectives must be specified. The objectives can be encapsulated in terms of the underlying (here the S&P 500), the "attachment point" (here the strike of 20%), the expiry (here 3 months), and the budget (here the premium spent of 0.17% per quarter). Since the prices of options vary highly with market conditions, one must solve for these three input variables simultaneously; under certain market conditions, it might not be possible to meet all the objectives. For instance, if one is budgeting only 0.50% per annum, and the desired attachment point is 10% for one year, it might be close to impossible to find a reliable hedge. In such conditions, the portfolio manager might have to compromise by either changing the expiry of the hedge, the strike of the hedges, the mix of hedges (to include indirect hedges, which introduce basis risk) or resorting to timing of the hedges. These all create the possibility of the hedge not performing as originally desired.

Another important aspect of tail hedging arises because the value of options goes up sharply when either markets fall, or volatility rises. As discussed above, the value of a hedge can go up a 100 fold if there is a very sharp fall in the market and a shock to volatility. In such events, a portfolio manager can monetize the options fully or partially and redeploy the monetization proceeds back into the markets. By doing so, the portfolio manager can generate liquidity to purchase assets when they are cheap.[6] Consequently, tail hedging cannot only protect but also result in systematic rebalancing with new liquidity that is very valuable to the portfolio manager. Thus, the cost of the tail hedge must account for the opportunity it provides when such adverse events occur, and whether such opportunity can enhance long-term returns.

While options exist in many markets and there are essentially an infinite variety of combinations of instruments that a portfolio manager can use to hedge exposures, normally it makes sense to stick to liquid markets where hedges can be quickly monetized with low transactions cost. Also counterparty risk should be kept low because financial market distress is correlated with increased stress on counterparties. For this reason, listed options markets, which are traded and cleared on exchanges have become

[6] For instance, during the COVID-19 crisis, any monetization performed in the middle of March 2020 could be redeployed into the equity markets. As the Federal Reserve provided massive amounts of liquidity and purchased assets, the market rallied sharply and resulted in substantial gains.

popular for large institutional hedging programs. For instance, if the underlying equity index is the S&P 500, then using listed options on the S&P 500 index is appropriate to use for tail hedging.

These options markets are quite popular, and options come in many expiration dates and strike prices. The quarterly expiry options are especially popular and liquid which expire on the third Friday of the expiration month. They are "European" style, so they can only be exercised on the expiration date, and trading on these options ceases on the business day before the option expiry. For these options, the multiplier is $100, meaning that the option's price is multiplied by $100 to obtain the total premium per option contract.

Purchasers of options with expiries less than 9 months must pay the full option premium at purchase. For each expiration date, many strike prices are listed, with strike prices spaced out every five S&P 500 points for the near months, and 25 points for far months. These options trade between 8:30 a.m. to 3:15 p.m. central time, and other "extended" and "curb" times. Finally, these options are cash-settled, which means that once the exercise settlement value (SET) is computed using the opening prices in the market for each component of the S&P 500 index, the exercise settlement amount paid to the buyer of the option is the difference between the exercise settlement value and the exercise price of the option, multiplied by $100. The options prices are provided in real-time by many pricing services so portfolio managers can see the value of their hedges and how the total portfolio is doing in aggregate.

Finally, many options markets provide investors with a lot of different types of structures that can be used to reduce the premium cost. However, given the efficiency of the options markets, this cost reduction via creative structuring is rarely free, and investors should ensure that in order to obtain cost reduction, they are not creating scenarios where they might not have a reliable hedge or be obligated to meet capital calls or be exposed to unwanted risks. At the end of the day, the hedge itself should be designed to be cost-effective, reliable, transparent, and add to the robustness of the underlying portfolio it is hedging.

Challenges and Considerations

Implementing tail risk hedging strategies has several practical complexities and potential drawbacks that portfolio managers must navigate carefully. One primary concern is the cost of hedging. Purchasing options, such as out-of-the-money puts, can significantly impact portfolio performance, particularly in calm markets with low volatility where hedges may seem unnecessary. Managers must balance the protection offered by these instruments against their expense, requiring a thoughtful cost–benefit analysis to design a cost-effective hedge.

Liquidity and market conditions also present significant challenges. During periods of extreme market stress, liquidity in derivative markets may dry up, making it challenging to execute hedging strategies or monetize existing positions. Sudden spikes in implied volatility can further complicate the pricing and execution of hedges, increasing costs and operational complexity. Additionally, OTC instruments introduce counterparty and credit risks, as these transactions depend on the financial stability of counterparties. Portfolio managers must mitigate these risks through robust collateral agreements or relying on highly rated counterparties.

Basis risk is another critical consideration, mainly when indirect hedges, such as index futures or ETFs, are used instead of instruments closely aligned with the underlying portfolio. Mismatches between the portfolio and the hedging instrument can lead to inefficiencies, reducing the hedge's effectiveness. Reducing basis risk requires careful alignment of the hedging instrument with the portfolio's specific exposures, though this may not always be feasible in practice.

Operational complexity is an inherent challenge in managing option-based hedges. Portfolio managers must monitor and adjust option sensitivities, such as delta, gamma, and vega, to maintain the hedge's effectiveness over time. This often necessitates frequent rebalancing, particularly in rapidly changing markets, adding to the operational burden. Moreover, managers face strategic and behavioral trade-offs, such as maintaining a commitment to hedging during prolonged market rallies when the need for hedging may seem less apparent. Timing the monetization of hedges during downturns is another critical challenge, as it requires balancing immediate liquidity needs with the possibility of further market declines.

Finally, regulatory and reporting requirements add another layer of complexity. Derivative instruments often come with compliance obligations, requiring portfolio managers to document and report their hedging activities clearly to stakeholders. Transparency in these activities is crucial to maintaining trust and ensuring that the hedging strategy aligns with broader portfolio objectives.

Despite these challenges, a disciplined approach to tail hedging can enhance portfolio resilience if portfolio managers carefully weigh the trade-offs and maintain flexibility to adapt to evolving market conditions. Tail hedging requires technical expertise and a clear strategic vision to balance protection with operational and financial constraints.

Summary

This case study explores options as a strategic tool for tail risk hedging, emphasizing their ability to protect portfolios during extreme market events while maintaining upside potential. Tail risk, defined as rare but severe market downturns, poses significant challenges for portfolio managers seeking to preserve capital and ensure resilience. By employing options-based strategies, such as out-of-the-money put options, portfolio managers can proactively hedge against adverse market conditions, enabling them to mitigate losses and redeploy liquidity effectively during periods of stress.

The case provides a comprehensive framework for designing and implementing tail hedging programs, highlighting key considerations such as cost, instrument selection, and risk factor alignment. A detailed case study demonstrates the practicalities of structuring and evaluating hedges, including scenario analyses to assess performance under various market conditions. The analysis concludes with a discussion of challenges and considerations, such as liquidity constraints, operational complexity, and regulatory requirements, underscoring the importance of disciplined execution and strategic foresight in managing tail risk.

14

Bond Portfolio Hedging with U.S. Treasury Futures

Adam Kobor

This case demonstrates the practical application of U.S. Treasury futures to manage interest rate risk in a bond portfolio. It focuses on how portfolio managers can adjust a portfolio's interest rate sensitivity, or duration, to mitigate potential losses from adverse market movements. Using a hypothetical $133 million bond portfolio, the case illustrates the mechanics of implementing futures-based hedges and evaluates their performance under real-world market conditions.

The portfolio, comprising investment-grade securities with an effective duration of 5.31 years, faces potential risks from changes in the U.S. Treasury yield curve. As of August 31, 2023, the yield curve was inverted due to Federal Reserve rate hikes, with market expectations of a policy shift toward easing. This dynamic creates uncertainty for the portfolio manager, who aims to hedge the portfolio's duration risk fully. The detailed analysis examines various hedging strategies using 2-year, 5-year, and 10-year Treasury futures contracts, providing insights into their effectiveness and trade-offs. Additionally, the case explores a more sophisticated approach involving a basket of futures contracts to match the portfolio's key-rate duration profile, demonstrating how tailored hedging strategies can optimize risk management outcomes.

A. Kobor (✉)
Managing Director of Investments, New York University, New York, USA
e-mail: adam.kobor@nyu.edu

F. J. Fabozzi and M. de Jong (eds.), *Derivatives Applications in Asset Management*,
https://doi.org/10.1007/978-3-031-86354-7_14

ISIN Code	Security Name	Issuer	Sector	Call-able	Maturity	Price	Accrued Interest	Face Value	Market Value	Yield to Worst	Option-Adj. Duration	DV01
US91282CBH34	T 0 ⅜ 01/31/26	U.S. Treasury	Government	No	01/31/2026	90.2420	0.0326%	10,000,000	9,027,460.90	4.70%	2.34	2,113.33
US912828Z781	T 1 ½ 01/31/27	U.S. Treasury	Government	No	01/31/2027	90.7110	0.1304%	10,000,000	9,084,143.50	4.46%	3.24	2,945.99
US91282CDW82	T 1 ¾ 01/31/29	U.S. Treasury	Government	No	01/31/2029	87.9220	0.1522%	10,000,000	8,807,417.40	4.27%	5.02	4,423.09
US912828ZQ64	T 0 ⅝ 05/15/30	U.S. Treasury	Government	No	05/15/2030	79.3120	0.1851%	20,000,000	15,899,424.40	4.20%	6.36	10,104.08
US91282CFV81	T 4 ⅛ 11/15/32	U.S. Treasury	Government	No	11/15/2032	99.9530	1.2218%	20,000,000	20,234,961.40	4.13%	7.45	15,064.93
US3130AFFX04	FHLB 3 ¼ 11/16/28	Fed. Home Loan Bank	Agencies	No	11/16/2028	95.0970	0.9479%	10,000,000	9,604,491.70	4.31%	4.65	4,461.29
US3135G05Q27	FNMA 0 ⅞ 08/05/30	Fannnie Mae	Agencies	No	08/05/2030	79.3530	0.0632%	20,000,000	15,883,238.80	4.36%	6.51	10,336.81
US459058JC89	IBRD 0 ⅞ 05/14/30	IBRD	Supranationals	No	05/14/2030	79.9480	0.2601%	20,000,000	16,041,613.80	4.36%	6.29	10,085.36
US037833BY53	AAPL 3 ¼ 02/23/26	Apple Inc.	Industrials	Yes	02/23/2026	96.1480	0.0722%	10,000,000	9,622,022.20	4.92%	2.25	2,163.03
US172967ME81	C 3.98 03/20/30	Citigroup	Financials	Yes	03/20/2029	92.0350	1.7799%	20,000,000	18,762,988.80	5.67%	4.75	8,903.04
Total Portfolio									**132,967,762.90**	**4.55%**	**5.31**	**70,600.94**

Exhibit 14.1 Bond Portfolio as of August 31, 2023. Data obtained from Bloomberg. The calculations are those of the author

Portfolio Characteristics and Risk Metrics

Exhibit 14.1 shows the details of a simple illustrative bond portfolio worth \$133 million, yielding 4.55%, and comprised of all USD-denominated securities as of August 31, 2023. The portfolio comprises investment-grade securities, including U.S. Treasuries, agencies, supranationals, and corporate and financial sector debt instruments. While diversified bond portfolios typically contain many more securities than the ten securities in this illustrative case, choosing this easy-to-overview portfolio does not impact the hedging considerations and conclusions.

The portfolio's overall effective duration, labeled as the option-adjusted duration in the exhibit, is 5.31 years, and the individual securities' time to maturity and durations fall in the ranges of 2.4–9.2 years and 2.2–7.4 years, respectively. Given the securities' market values, we can also determine the portfolio's DV01, i.e., the dollar sensitivity with respect to 1 basis point yield change:

$$\$132{,}967{,}763.90 \times 5.31 \times 0.0001 = \$70{,}600.94.$$

This means that our \$133 million portfolio would lose about \$71,000, roughly 0.05% of its value.

Market Conditions and Yield Curve Dynamics

Exhibit 14.2 illustrates the U.S. Treasury yield curve as of August 31, 2023. The yield curve at that point is inverted as the Federal Reserve (Fed) had hiked the Fed Fund rate multiple times to fight inflation. At the same time, the market is pricing in a change in the hawkish monetary policy toward an easing policy (i.e., lowering interest rates). Because market expectations are sensitive to inflation and job market reports, the portfolio manager is concerned about the market expecting easing to start too soon. Should these

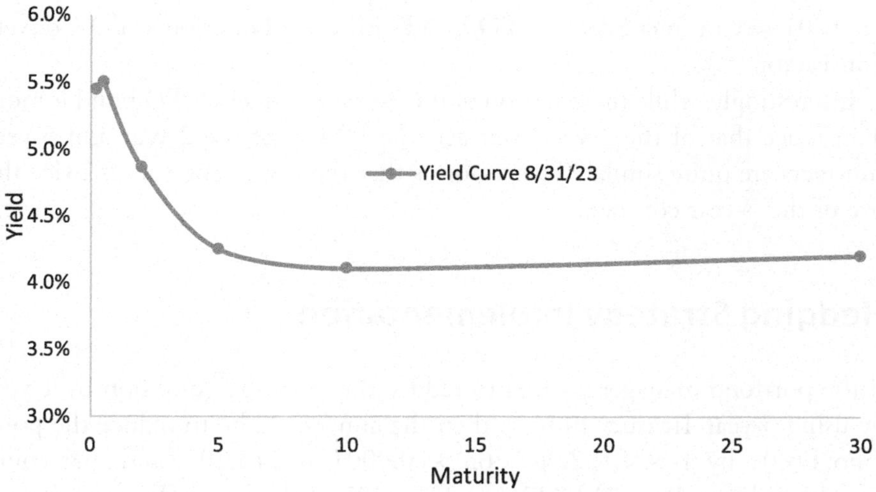

Exhibit 14.2 U.S. Treasury Yield Curve as of August 31, 2023. Data obtained from Bloomberg. The yield curve is constructed by the author

market expectations change, the yield levels would increase, and the yield curve could become less inverted.

Treasury Futures as Hedging Instruments

Given these concerns, the portfolio manager decides to reduce the portfolio duration and wants to initiate a 1-month horizon Treasury futures-based interest rate risk hedge at the end of August, by using the 2023 December Treasury futures contracts, the nearest actively traded month at that time that was practical for a one-month horizon hedge. Exhibit 14.3 shows the key characteristics of 2-year, 5-year, and 10-year Treasury futures contracts as of August 31, 2023.

It is important to note that the DV01 of one futures contract is determined by the cheapest-to-deliver (CTD) bond and is best estimated as.

Ticker	Futures Contract	Underlying	Contract size	Price	1 Contract Value	Cheapest-to-Deliver	CTD Conversion Factor	CTD Bond OAD	DV01 of 1 Contract
TUZ3	US 2YR NOTE (CBT) Dec23	US 2yr 6%	$ 200,000	101.9023	$ 203,805	T 3.5 9/15/25	0.9590	1.89	39.33
FVZ3	US 5YR NOTE (CBT) Dec23	US 5yr 6%	$ 100,000	106.9219	$ 106,922	T 4 2/29/28	0.9272	4.02	43.33
TYZ3	US 10YR NOTE (CBT)Dec23	US 10yr 6%	$ 100,000	111.0313	$ 111,031	T 4.125 8/31/30	0.9003	5.99	66.52

Exhibit 14.3 Treasury Futures Characteristics as of August 31, 2023. Data obtained from Bloomberg. The calculations are those of the authors. CTD = cheapest to deliver; DVO1 = dollar value of 1 basis point

DV01 = Contract Size × CTD Bond's Effective Duration/CTD Conversion Factor.

Interestingly, while the duration of the 5-year contract's CTD bond is more than twice that of the 2-year contract, the DV01s of the 2-year and 5-year contracts are quite similar. The reason is that the 2-year contract is twice the size of the 5-year contract.

Hedging Strategy Implementation

If the portfolio manager wanted to reduce the portfolio's duration by 1 year by using 5-year Treasury futures, then the aim would be to reduce the portfolio DV01 by 1 × $132,967,763 × 0.0001 = $13,297, and that could be achieved by selling $13,297/$43.33 = 307 of the 5-year Treasury futures contracts.

The portfolio manager, however, decides to fully hedge all the Treasury interest rate sensitivity of the portfolio. The portfolio wants to reduce its DV01 of $70,600.94 to zero. The number of contracts to sell, depending on which futures the portfolio manager chooses, would be as follows:

- 2-year contract (TUH4): 70,600.94/39.33 = 1795, or
- 5-year contract (FVH4): 70,600.94/43.33 = 1629, or
- 10-year contract (TYH4): 70,600.94/66.52 = 1061 contracts.

Performance of Hedging Strategies

Exhibit 14.4 shows how the yield curve moved over September, justifying the portfolio manager's initial concerns. While the front end of the curve remained practically unchanged, the curve "bear steepened" as the 2-year, 5-year, and 10-year rates have increased by 18bps, 36bps, and 46bps, respectively. Exhibit 14.5 shows the daily history of the Treasury yields, futures prices, and performance of the futures contracts over September.

Exhibit 14.6 shows the portfolio's value and performance by the end of September 2023, without any derivative hedges. The portfolio's value declined from about $133 million to $130 million, as the portfolio's yield-to-worst increased by 42 basis points to 4.97%. The total monthly profit/loss (P/L) is -1.89%, or ($2,518,736), which includes a coupon payment of $398,000 for the Citibank bond, besides the overall market value change and coupon accruals.

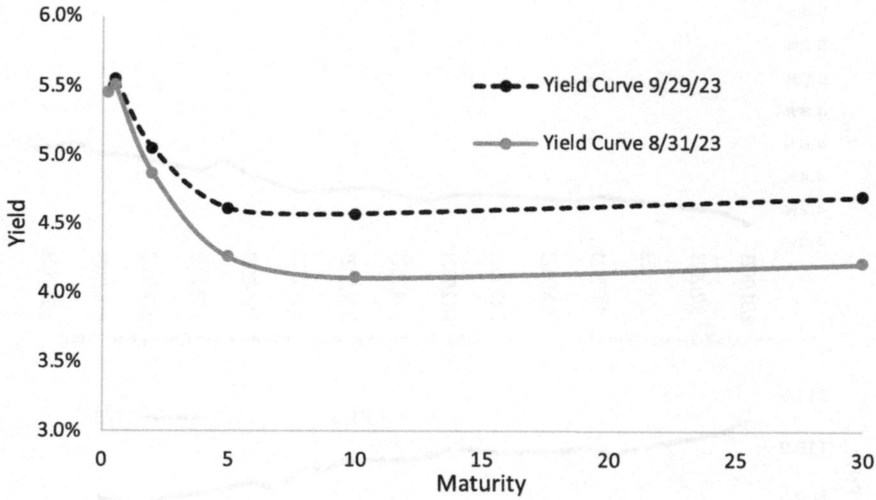

Exhibit 14.4 U.S. Treasury Yield Curve as of August 31, 2023, and September 29, 2023. Data obtained from Bloomberg. The two yield curves are constructed by the author

Exhibit 14.7 compares how the hedges would have performed if the portfolio manager had utilized either the 2-year, 5-year, or 10-year contracts to hedge the portfolio. The column labeled "$ P/L on Bond Portfolio and Futures" displays the sum of the P/L on the short futures contract added to the ($2,518,736) overall negative performance of the bond portfolio. While all three futures transactions DV01 were set equal to the portfolio's DV01, the 2-year contract obviously would have been the poorest choice. This is not surprising since the yield curve did not shift up in a parallel manner, but the front remained unchanged, and longer-dated yields increased by more. The 2-year Treasury yield increased by 18 basis points in September, much less than the 42 basis points yield increase of the portfolio. The 5-year and 10-year Treasury rates' increase of 36 and 46 basis points was closer to the portfolio's overall yield increase. If the par yield curve steepens, the forward rates underlying the Treasury futures price changes increase even more.

Given the portfolio's initial duration of 5.31 years, it is intuitive to expect that the 2-year Treasury futures would not be the most natural choice, as the durations do not match; the 5-year or 10-year contracts would be more natural choices—see their CTD bonds' durations of 4.02 and 5.99 years in Exhibit 14.3.

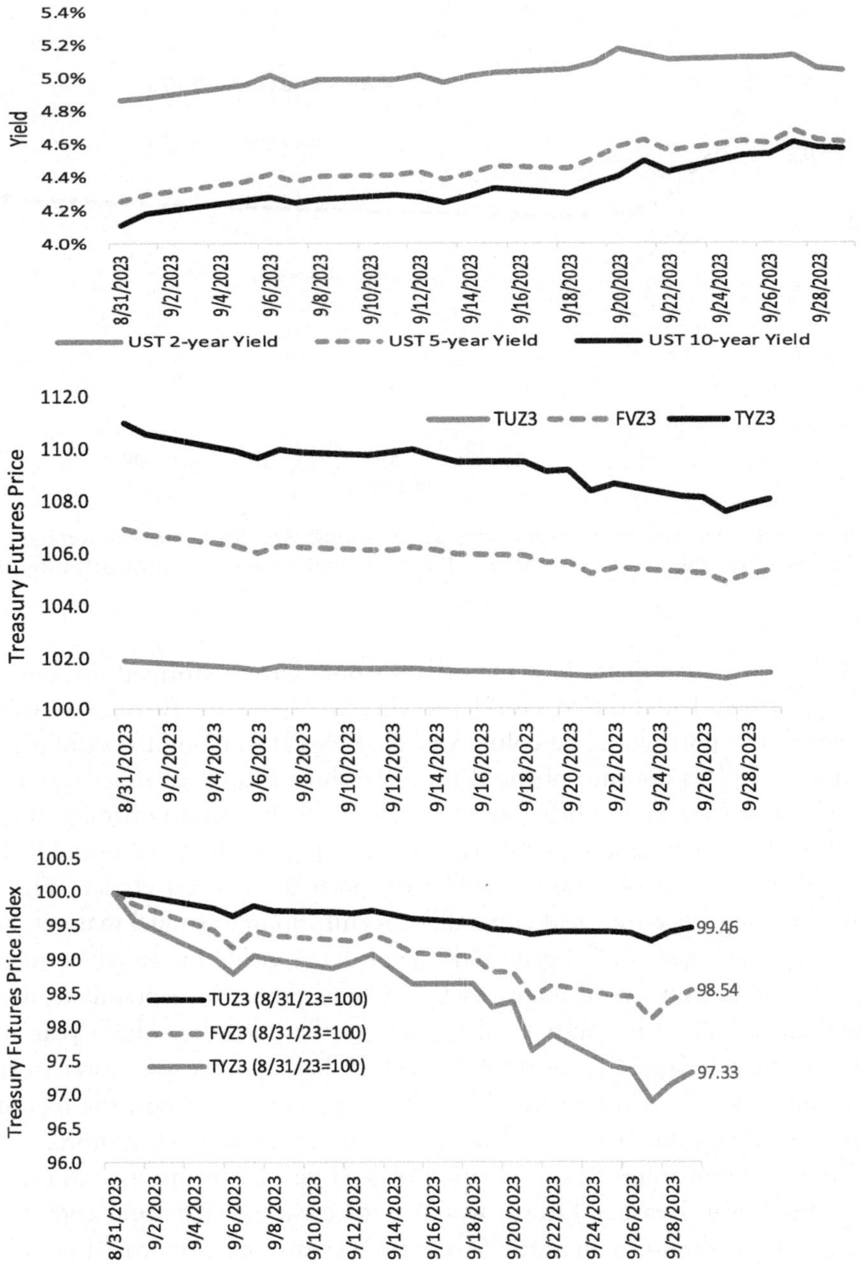

Exhibit 14.5 U.S. Treasury Yields, Treasury Future Prices, and Futures Price Levels from August 31 to September 29, 2023. Data obtained from Bloomberg. The yield curves were constructed by the authors

Security Name	YTW 8/31/23	YTW 9/29/23	Price of 8/31/23	Price of 9/29/23	Accrued Int. 8/31	Accrued Int. 9/29	Face Value	Market Value	Price Return	Accr. Int. Return	Total Return
T 0 ⅜ 01/31/26	4.70%	4.97%	90.2420	90.0080	0.03%	0.06%	10,000,000	9,007,117.90	-0.26%	0.03%	-0.23%
T 1 ½ 01/31/27	4.46%	4.77%	90.7110	90.0390	0.13%	0.25%	10,000,000	9,029,171.70	-0.74%	0.12%	-0.61%
T 1 ¾ 01/31/29	4.27%	4.65%	87.9220	86.4300	0.15%	0.29%	10,000,000	8,672,483.70	-1.70%	0.14%	-1.53%
T 0 ⅝ 05/15/30	4.20%	4.63%	79.3120	77.3910	0.19%	0.24%	20,000,000	15,525,414.60	-2.42%	0.05%	-2.35%
T 4 ⅛ 11/15/32	4.13%	4.61%	99.9530	96.4530	1.22%	1.56%	20,000,000	19,602,216.80	-3.50%	0.34%	-3.13%
FHLB 3 ¼ 11/16/28	4.31%	4.67%	95.0970	93.5760	0.95%	1.22%	10,000,000	9,479,475.00	-1.60%	0.27%	-1.30%
FNMA 0 ⅞ 08/05/30	4.36%	4.81%	79.3530	77.2900	0.06%	0.14%	20,000,000	15,485,222.20	-2.60%	0.07%	-2.51%
IBRD 0 ⅝ 05/14/30	4.36%	4.78%	79.9480	78.0440	0.26%	0.33%	20,000,000	15,675,397.20	-2.38%	0.07%	-2.28%
AAPL 3 ¼ 02/23/26	4.92%	5.26%	96.1480	95.5330	0.07%	0.34%	10,000,000	9,587,605.60	-0.64%	0.27%	-0.36%
C 3.98 03/20/30	5.67%	6.20%	92.0350	89.8130	1.78%	0.12%	20,000,000	17,986,922.20	-2.41%	0.33%	-2.01%
Total Portfolio	**4.55%**	**4.97%**						**130,051,026.90**	**-2.10%**	**0.18%**	**-1.89%**

Exhibit 14.6 Portfolio Performance from August 31 to September 29, 2023

Contract	DV01 of Futures	Traded # Contract	Futures Price 8/31/23	Futures Price 9/29/23	P/L on 1 Contract	P/L on Traded Futures	$ P/L on Bond Portfolio and Futures	% P/L on Bond Portfolio and Futures
US 2YR NOTE (CBT) Dec23	39.33	-1795	101.9023	101.3555	-1,093.75	$ 1,963,281	$ (555,455)	-0.42%
US 5YR NOTE (CBT) Dec23	43.33	-1629	106.9219	105.3594	-1,562.50	$ 2,545,313	$ 26,577	0.02%
US 10YR NOTE (CBT)Dec23	66.52	-1061	111.0313	108.0625	-2,968.75	$ 3,149,844	$ 631,108	0.47%

Exhibit 14.7 Performance of Individual Futures Trades as Hedge. Data obtained from Bloomberg. The calculations are those of the author

Optimizing Hedging with a Basket of Futures

To explore this question of duration matching further, Exhibit 14.8 displays the bond portfolio's key-rate duration profile as of August 31. Based on this information, we can see that the portfolio's overall DV01 $70,601 is mostly concentrated around the 5-year and 10-year key rates, based on Bloomberg's Portfolio Administration tool. Instead of trading with only one of the available futures contracts, the portfolio manager could also determine a basket of 2-year, 5-year, and 10-year contracts to match the portfolio's key-rate DV01 profile best, as shown in Exhibit 14.9. Applying quantitative numerical optimization (such as using a spreadsheet solver) we can determine the optimal number of contracts that minimize the key-rate duration differences between the portfolio and the basket of hedging instruments while ensuring that the DV01 of the hedging basket is matching the DV01 of the portfolio. As a result of the quantitative optimization exercise, by simultaneously shorting 100, 17, and 992 contracts of the 2-year, 5-year, and 10-year Treasury futures, the portfolio's key-rate DV01 profile could be closely matched, resulting in an overall $561,188 ($3,079,924 profit of the hedging basket as shown in Exhibit 14.9 versus the $2,518,736 loss on the underlying bond portfolio as discussed earlier), or + 0.42% P/L net of hedge. While the portfolio manager could successfully eliminate the adverse impact of the yield curve change, it could preserve the positive carry of the portfolio over September.

Security Name	Option-Adj. Duration	OAD Contribution	KRD 6M	KRD 2Y	KRD 5Y	KRD 10Y	KRD 20Y	KRD 30Y
T 0 ⅜ 01/31/26	2.34	0.16	-0.04	1.96	0.42	0.00	0.00	0.00
T 1 ½ 01/31/27	3.24	0.22	-0.03	1.60	1.66	0.00	0.00	0.00
T 1 ¾ 01/31/29	5.02	0.33	-0.02	-0.13	4.67	0.50	0.00	0.00
T 0 ⅝ 05/15/30	6.36	0.76	-0.03	-0.19	4.16	2.42	0.00	0.00
T 4 ⅛ 11/15/32	7.45	1.13	0.00	0.00	1.15	6.29	0.00	0.00
FHLB 3 ¼ 11/16/28	4.65	0.34	-0.01	-0.05	4.47	0.23	0.00	0.00
FNMA 0 ⅞ 08/05/30	6.51	0.78	-0.03	-0.17	3.96	2.75	0.00	0.00
IBRD 0 ⅞ 05/14/30	6.29	0.76	-0.03	-0.17	4.12	2.37	0.00	0.00
AAPL 3 ¼ 02/23/26	2.25	0.16	-0.01	1.89	0.37	0.00	0.00	0.00
C 3.98 03/20/30	4.75	0.67	0.00	-0.01	4.18	0.58	0.00	0.00
Total Portfolio	**5.31**	**5.31**	**-0.01**	**0.30**	**3.03**	**1.99**	**0.00**	**0.00**
Key-Rate DV01	**70,601**		**-159**	**3,989**	**40,289**	**26,461**	**0.00**	**0.00**

Exhibit 14.8 Bond Portfolio Key-Rate Duration Profile as of August 31, 2023. Data obtained from Bloomberg. The calculations are those of the author

Contract	DV01 of Futures	KRD 6M	KRD 2Y	KRD 5Y	KRD 10Y	Traded # Contract	P/L on Traded Futures	$ P/L on Bond Portfolio and Futures	% P/L on Bond Portfolio and Futures
US 2YR NOTE (CBT) Dec23	39.33	-0.01	1.91	0.04	0.00	-100	$ 109,419		
US 5YR NOTE (CBT) Dec23	43.33	0.00	0.59	3.46	0.00	-17	$ 26,229		
US 10YR NOTE (CBT)Dec23	66.52	0.00	0.00	3.59	2.40	-992	$ 2,944,275		
Key-Rate DV01 of Bond Portfolio		**-159**	**3,989**	**40,289**	**26,461**				
Key-Rate DV01 of Futures		**27**	**-3,953**	**-40,252**	**-26,423**				
Performance of Futures Basket							**$ 3,079,924**	**$ 561,187.95**	**0.42%**

Exhibit 14.9 Performance of Basket of Futures Trades as Hedge. Data obtained from Bloomberg. The calculations are those of the author

Summary

This case demonstrates how portfolio managers can use U.S. Treasury futures to manage interest rate risk in bond portfolios. By adjusting the portfolio's interest rate sensitivity or duration, portfolio managers seek to mitigate potential losses resulting from changes in the yield curve. The analysis compares various hedging strategies, including using short positions in 2-year, 5-year, and 10-year Treasury futures and a basket of futures contracts tailored to the portfolio's duration profile.

The results demonstrate that longer-dated futures contracts more closely align with the portfolio's characteristics and provide more effective protection against yield curve movements, particularly when longer-term rates increase more than short-term rates. A basket of futures contracts matched to the portfolio's key-rate duration profile achieves the most precise hedge, effectively neutralizing the impact of rate changes while preserving the portfolio's positive carry. This case highlights the importance of selecting hedging strategies that align with portfolio structure and market conditions to optimize risk management outcomes.

15

Consumer Mortgage Portfolio Hedging with Interest Rate Swaps

Joseph Niehaus

This case study describes how Star One Credit Union, a community-based financial institution headquartered in Sunnyvale, California, effectively mitigated interest rate risk in its mortgage loan portfolio through the use of pay-fixed interest rate swaps. At the end of 2018, facing a liability-sensitive balance sheet, the credit union implemented a hedging strategy to address the duration mismatch between its assets and liabilities, thereby stabilizing the fair value of its equity during periods of interest rate volatility.

By employing the flexibility provided under Accounting Standards Update (ASU) 2017–12, Star One leveraged swaps to designate a portion of its long-term, fixed-rate residential mortgage portfolio as hedged. This approach allowed the credit union to adjust its asset duration while simplifying hedge accounting and maintaining operational efficiency. The case demonstrates how financial institutions can use derivatives not to speculate on interest rate movements but to manage risk and maintain financial stability strategically.

The subsequent sections detail Star One's balance sheet adjustments, the financial outcomes of its hedging program, and the broader lessons this approach offers for community financial institutions navigating similar challenges.

J. Niehaus (✉)
Jefferies | The CUFS Group | Credit Union Financial Services, New York, NY, USA
e-mail: joseph.niehaus@grenoble-em.com

F. J. Fabozzi and M. de Jong (eds.), *Derivatives Applications in Asset Management*,
https://doi.org/10.1007/978-3-031-86354-7_15

Background

To fully understand the role of interest rate swaps in managing Star One Credit Union's balance sheet, it is essential to consider the broader institutional framework and the specific challenges faced by the credit union at the time. The following section examines the organizational context and the key factors influencing its risk management decisions.

Institutional Context

Star One Credit Union, headquartered in Sunnyvale, California, is a community-focused financial institution with a significant residential mortgage portfolio. As of December 31, 2018, the credit union's balance sheet exhibited liability sensitivity, where liabilities had shorter durations than assets. This mismatch meant liabilities would reprice more quickly in response to rising interest rates, with a greater, relative decline in the fair value of assets and a net negative impact to members' equity. Exhibit 15.1 illustrates Star One's interest rate risk profile, highlighting the balance sheet's sensitivity to interest rate movements.

A liability-sensitive balance sheet creates risk in an upward interest rate environment, as the decline in the fair value of liabilities is slower than that of assets. Conversely, in a down-rate scenario, liabilities reprice more slowly, which could support equity valuation. However, the structure of the balance

Assets	**Book Balance**	**Fair Value %**	**Est. Fair Value**	**Est. Effective Duration**
Cash & Cash Equivalents	$ 309,238,359	100%	$ 309,238,359	0.08
Total Investments	$ 4,094,517,870	98%	$ 4,012,627,513	1.88
Net Loans & Leases[1]	$ 3,951,309,826	90%	$ 3,556,178,843	4.71
Other Assets	$ 213,169,040	99%	$ 211,037,350	0.50
Total Assets	$ 8,568,235,095	94%	$ 8,089,082,065	3.02
Liabilities				
Borrowings	$ 684,900,000	95%	$ 650,655,000	2.59
Member Shares (Deposits)[2]	$ 6,837,609,530	91%	$ 6,222,224,672	3.00
Other Liabilities	$ 54,754,216	99%	$ 54,206,674	0.50
Total Liabilities	$ 7,577,263,746	91%	$ 6,927,086,346	2.94
Members' Equity	**$990,971,349**		**$ 1,161,995,718**	**3.49**
Members' Equity Ratio	11.57%		14.36%	

Exhibit 15.1 Star One Credit Union Interest Rate Risk Profile as of December 31, 2018. Data obtained from S&P Capital IQ and Star One Credit Union. The calculations are those of the authors

sheet at year-end 2018 posed greater downside risks in a rising interest rate scenario, with a potential 3.49% decline in equity value for every 100-basis point increase in interest rates.

Regulatory Framework

The implementation of Accounting Standards Update (ASU) 2017–12 provided a robust framework for hedging programs in depository institutions. This update simplified hedge accounting rules, making it easier for institutions like Star One to use interest rate derivatives effectively. Specifically, the "last-of-layer" method enabled the credit union to hedge a portion of its fixed-rate mortgage portfolio without needing to account for prepayments, defaults, or other uncertainties in cash flow timing. This method assumed perfect hedge effectiveness, minimizing the operational and accounting complexities of implementing interest rate swaps.

Interest Rate Risk Profile

Star One's balance sheet included a significant portfolio of fixed-rate mortgages with long durations, particularly loans with terms exceeding 15 years. As of December 31, 2018, the credit union had $3.2 billion in consumer mortgages, $2.4 billion of which were fixed-rate loans with maturities greater than 15 years (see Exhibit 15.2). The balance sheet's overall asset duration was 3.04 years, exceeding the liability duration of 2.94 years. This imbalance resulted in an equity duration of 3.49 years, making the institution particularly vulnerable to interest rate increases.

The risk was compounded by the unpredictable behavior of non-maturing deposit liabilities, such as member shares. These liabilities are highly sensitive to depositor behavior, which can shift dramatically in response to extreme interest rate movements, as demonstrated during the regional banking turmoil of 2023. As a result, treasurers must carefully manage these liabilities to avoid overestimating their durations, which could further destabilize the balance sheet during periods of heightened rate volatility.

Loan Type	Book Balance	Fair Value %	Est. Fair Value	Est. Effective Duration
Unsecured Credit Card Loans & Lines of Credit	$ 48,608,000	97%	$ 47,149,760	0.25
Non-Federally Guaranteed Student Loans	$ 42,982,000	97%	$ 41,692,540	2.00
Other Unsecured Loans and Lines Of Credit	$ 12,208,000	97%	$ 11,841,760	1.00
New Vehicle Loans	$ 149,669,000	97%	$ 145,178,930	1.80
Used Vehicle Loans	$ 129,847,000	95%	$ 123,354,650	1.80
Other Loans and LOC Secured Non-RE	$ 13,408,000	95%	$ 12,737,600	2.00
Loans and LOC Secured 1st Lien 1-4 Family RE	**$ 3,235,753,000**	**89%**	**$ 2,871,092,260**	**5.30**
Loans & LOC Secured Junior 1-4 Family Real Estate	$ 37,874,000	95%	$ 35,980,300	4.00
Other Real Estate Loans and Lines of Credit	$ 285,726,000	95%	$ 271,439,700	3.00
Gross Loans	$ 3,956,075,000	90.0%	$ 3,560,467,500	4.71

Loans and LOC Secured 1st Lien 1-4 Family RE - Detail	
Loans and LOC Secured 1st Lien 1-4 Family RE - Fixed Rate > 15 Years $	*$ 2,352,839,000*
Loans and LOC Secured 1st Lien 1-4 Family RE - Fixed Rate > 15 Years % of Gross Loans	*59%*
Loans and LOC Secured 1st Lien 1-4 Family RE - Fixed Rate > 15 Years % of Total Assets	*27%*

Exhibit 15.2 Star One Credit Union Loan Portfolio Composition as of December 31, 2018. Data obtained from S&P Capital IQ and Star One Credit Union. The calculations are those of the authors

Risk Management Considerations

The treasurer's role is not to predict interest rate movements but to manage the institution's balance sheet to minimize undue risk to equity. Given the sensitivity of Star One's equity to interest rate increases, the treasurer sought to reduce equity duration and improve the balance sheet's resilience. By employing interest rate swaps, the credit union aimed to hedge its exposure to long-duration, fixed-rate mortgage assets and better align asset and liability durations.

Star One's risk management policies also included two key metrics for its derivatives program:

- *Hedge Ratio*: Targeted between 80 and 100%, with a preferred level of 90%, this ratio measured the extent of hedging instruments relative to long-term, fixed-rate mortgage assets.
- *Average Life Ratio*: Targeted between 70 and 90%, with a preferred level of 80%, this ratio ensured the alignment of average durations between hedging instruments and fixed-rate assets.

These metrics underscored Star One's systematic approach to managing interest rate risk and maintaining balance sheet stability.

Analysis of Interest Rate Swaps as A Hedging Strategy

Using interest rate swaps as a hedging strategy represents a pivotal decision in Star One Credit Union's risk management approach. The following analysis explores the practical implementation of this strategy, detailing how the swaps were structured and integrated into the credit union's operations to mitigate balance sheet risk effectively.

Strategic Implementation

To address its balance sheet's liability sensitivity, Star One Credit Union implemented a hedging strategy using $955 million in pay-fixed interest rate swaps. These swaps targeted approximately 40% of the credit union's long-term, fixed-rate residential mortgage portfolio. The swaps converted fixed-rate assets into floating-rate exposure, significantly reducing asset duration and aligning it more closely with the shorter liability durations.

As illustrated in Exhibit 15.3, the duration of the long-term, fixed-rate mortgage portfolio decreased from 6.0 years to 3.67 years, reducing the overall mortgage portfolio duration from 5.3 years to 3.6 years. At the portfolio level, the swaps brought down the total loan portfolio duration from 4.71 years to 3.34 years. Consequently, the weighted average asset duration declined from 3.04 years to 2.42 years. This adjustment reversed the credit union's liability-sensitive position and reduced the equity duration to (0.70) years, significantly improving balance sheet stability.

Accounting Framework

Star One utilized the "last-of-layer" method under ASU 2017–12 to simplify hedge accounting. This method allowed the credit union to hedge a designated portion of its fixed-rate mortgage portfolio without incorporating the risks associated with prepayments, defaults, or other cash flow uncertainties. By assuming perfect hedge effectiveness, Star One avoided mark-to-market impacts on its income statement while recognizing the net coupon spread between the pay-fixed and receive-floating legs of the swaps as an adjustment to loan interest income.

Hedged Mortgage Portfolio and Resulting Est. Effective Durations - January 1, 2019

Loan Type	Book Balance	Fair Value %	Est. Fair Value	Est. Effective Duration
Loans and LOC Secured 1st Lien 1-4 Family RE - Fixed Rate > 15 Years $	$ 2,352,839,000	89%	$ 2,094,026,710	6.00
				Floating Leg
Swapped Mortgage Assets ($ Notional)[5]	**$ 955,000,000**	**89%**	**$ 849,950,000**	***0.25***
	40.6%			
Unhedged Mortgage Assets	$ 1,397,839,000	89%	$ 1,244,076,710	6.00
Adjusted 1st Lien 1-4 Family RE - Fixed Rate > 15 Years Mortgage Portfolio Duration w/Swaps				**3.67**
Remaining Loans and LOC Secured 1st Lien 1-4 Family RE	$ 882,914,000	89%	$ 777,065,550	3.41
Adjusted Loans and LOC Secured 1st Lien 1-4 Family RE Duration				**3.60**

Impact on Total Loan Portfolio - January 1, 2019

Loan Type	Book Balance	Fair Value %	Est. Fair Value	Est. Effective Duration
Unsecured Credit Card Loans & Lines of Credit	$ 48,608,000	97%	$ 47,149,760	0.25
Non-Federally Guaranteed Student Loans	$ 42,982,000	97%	$ 41,692,540	2.00
Other Unsecured Loans and Lines Of Credit	$ 12,208,000	97%	$ 11,841,760	1.00
New Vehicle Loans	$ 149,669,000	97%	$ 145,178,930	1.80
Used Vehicle Loans	$ 129,847,000	95%	$ 123,354,650	1.80
Other Loans and LOC Secured Non-RE	$ 13,408,000	95%	$ 12,737,600	2.00
Loans and LOC Secured 1st Lien 1-4 Family RE	**$ 3,235,753,000**	**89%**	**$ 2,871,092,260**	**3.60**
Loans & LOC Secured Junior 1-4 Family Real Estate	$ 37,874,000	95%	$ 35,980,300	4.00
Other Real Estate Loans and Lines of Credit	$ 285,726,000	95%	$ 271,439,700	3.00
Gross Loans	**$ 3,956,075,000**	**90.0%**	**$ 3,560,467,500**	**3.34**

Impact on Balance Sheet - January 1, 2019

Assets	Book Balance	Fair Value %	Est. Fair Value	Est. Effective Duration
Cash & Cash Equivalents	$ 309,238,359	100%	$ 309,238,359	0.08
Total Investments	$ 4,094,517,870	98%	$ 4,012,627,513	1.88
Net Loans & Leases	**$ 3,951,309,826**	**90%**	**$ 3,556,178,843**	**3.34**
Other Assets	$ 213,169,040	99%	$ 211,037,350	0.50
Total Assets	$ 8,568,235,095	94%	$ 8,089,082,065	2.42
Liabilities				
Borrowings	$ 684,900,000	95%	$ 650,655,000	2.59
Member Shares (Deposits)	$ 6,837,609,530	91%	$ 6,222,224,672	3.00
Other Liabilities	$ 54,754,216	99%	$ 54,206,674	0.50
Total Liabilities	$ 7,577,263,746	91%	$ 6,927,086,346	2.94
Members' Equity	**$ 990,971,349**		**$ 1,161,995,718**	**(0.70)**
Members' Equity Ratio	11.57%		14.36%	

Exhibit 15.3 Star One Credit Union Interest Rate Swap Adjusted Balance Sheet Durations. Data obtained from S&P Capital IQ and Star One Credit Union. The calculations are those of the authors

Impact on Risk Management

Implementing the swaps demonstrated a strategic shift in Star One's risk profile. Exhibit 15.3 highlights how the duration adjustments transformed the balance sheet, reducing sensitivity to interest rate fluctuations. By shortening asset duration, the credit union minimized the impact of rising rates on the fair value of equity. This proactive approach allowed Star One to transition from a liability-sensitive to an asset-sensitive position, enhancing its ability to withstand market volatility.

Alignment with Policy Targets

The hedging program was closely aligned with Star One's internal risk management policies. The hedge ratio, targeted between 80 and 100%, and the average life ratio, targeted between 70 and 90%, were maintained consistently during the implementation of the swaps. By adhering to these metrics, Star One ensured that the hedging strategy addressed the institution's risk tolerance and operational objectives effectively.[1]

Outcomes

Implementing Star One Credit Union's hedging strategy resulted in measurable improvements in its financial stability and risk profile. The strategic use of pay-fixed interest rate swaps reduced the institution's exposure to interest rate volatility and provided substantial benefits to its balance sheet and income statement, as detailed in the following performance metrics and hedge effectiveness analyses.

Performance Metrics

The effectiveness of the swaps is evident in the significant reduction of balance sheet sensitivity to interest rate fluctuations. As illustrated in Exhibit 15.3, the total asset duration declined from 3.04 years to 2.42 years, reversing the liability-sensitive position and shifting to an asset-sensitive profile. The equity duration was reduced from 3.49 years to (0.70) years, minimizing equity volatility and improving resilience to interest rate changes. These adjustments provided a robust buffer against rising interest rates, ensuring that the credit union could sustain the fair value of its equity during volatile market conditions.

Hedge Effectiveness

The pay-fixed swaps proved to be highly effective in offsetting declines in the fair value of the fixed-rate mortgage portfolio. Exhibit 15.4 demonstrates that the fair value of the swaps moved inversely to the U.S. Treasury

---

[1] As of this writing, Star One's hedge ratio target range is 80% to 100%; however, this range has evolved over time and had at one time been 70% to 90%.

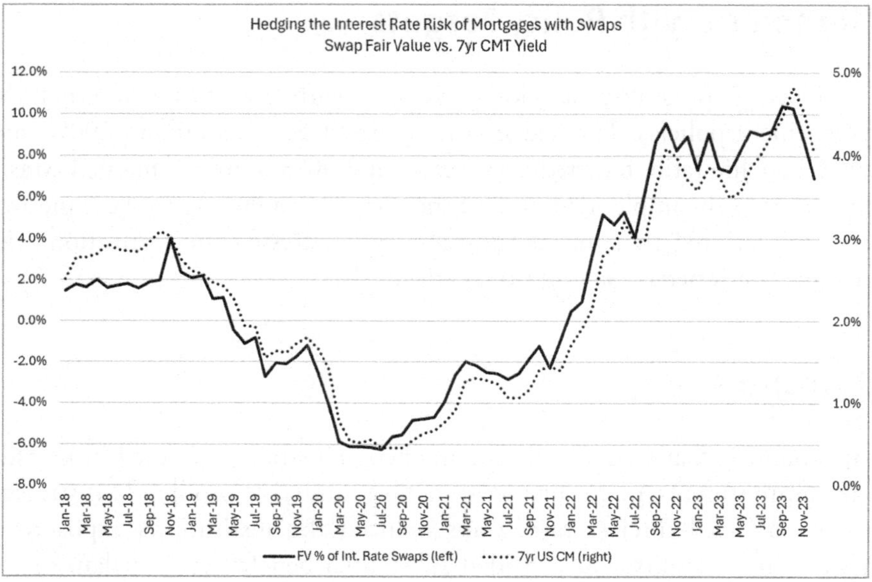

Exhibit 15.4 Fair Value of Interest Rate Swaps vs. 7-Year CMT Yield. Data obtained from S&P Capital IQ, Star One Credit Union, and Bloomberg. The calculations are those of the author

yields of similar duration, highlighting their role as a reliable hedging instrument. Exhibit 15.5 compares the swaps' fair value with the Bloomberg U.S. Mortgage-Backed Security (MBS) Index, showing a strong alignment with the performance of Star One's underlying mortgage portfolio. These analyses confirm the precision and reliability of the hedging program in mitigating interest rate risk.

Financial Impact

The hedging program provided critical income support during a challenging interest rate environment. Exhibit 15.4 tracks Star One's consistent adjustment of hedge ratios and average life ratios between 2018 and 2023, ensuring the program's effectiveness over time. As funding costs rose sharply in 2022 and 2023, the floating leg of the swaps offset these increases, contributing significantly to the credit union's net interest income. Exhibit 15.6 reveals that by the first quarter of 2023, the swaps accounted for approximately 66.7% of Star One's net interest income. Without the swaps, the credit union's net interest income might have turned negative during the latter half of 2023,

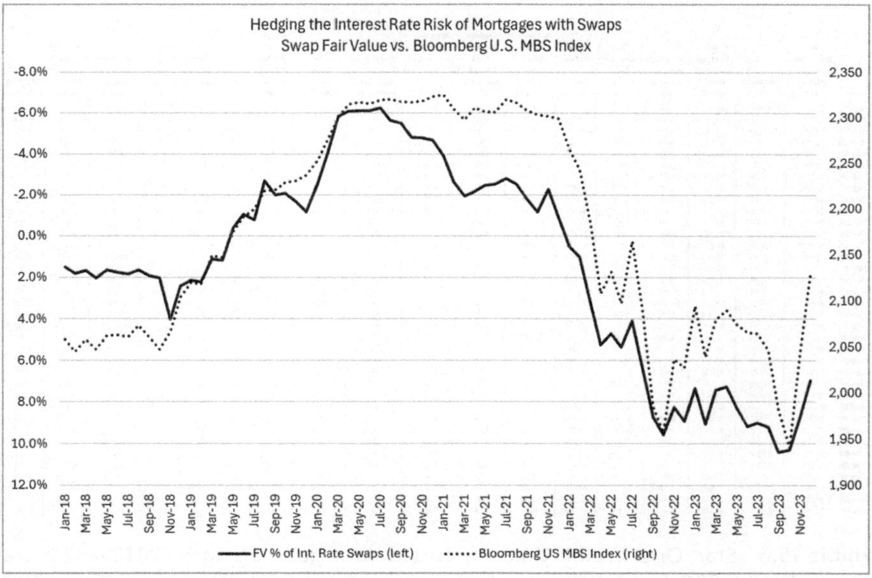

Exhibit 15.5 Fair Value of Interest Rate Swaps vs. Bloomberg U.S. MBS Index. Data obtained from S&P Capital IQ, Star One Credit Union, and Bloomberg. The calculations are those of the authors

underscoring the critical role of the hedging strategy in maintaining financial stability.

Strategic Resilience

The outcomes of Star One's hedging program demonstrate the importance of a disciplined and dynamic approach to risk management. By systematically adjusting its swap positions to align with changes in market conditions and portfolio composition, the credit union mitigated downside risks and enhanced its operational flexibility. The program's success highlights the value of aligning risk management practices with institutional policies to ensure both short-term stability and long-term sustainability.

Exhibit 15.7 demonstrates the significant contribution of the swaps to Star One's net interest income. During the rapid rise in interest rates in 2022 and 2023, the swaps provided critical income support, contributing approximately 66.7% of total net interest income in the first quarter of 2023. Without these swaps, the institution's net interest income would have been severely impacted, potentially turning negative during the latter half of 2023.

										Internal Derivative Policy Targets								
Date	Total Mortgages (Hedge-eligible) (A)	Net Worth (B)	Net Mortgage Assets to be Hedged (A - B)	Borrowings Designated as a Hedge (C)	Total Interest Rate Swap Notional (D)	Total Liability & Derivative Hedges (C + D)	Hedged Loan Portfolio Weighted Average Life (years) (E)	Weighted Average Life of Interest Rate Swaps (F)	Weighted Average Life of Total Hedges ((F*(C+D)+E*B)) / (B+C+D)	Hedge Ratio (C + D) / (A - B) Target Range: 80% to 100%	Average Life Ratio Target Range: 70% to 90%	Hedged Loan Portfolio Weighted Average Coupon	Pay Fixed Interest Rate	Receive Floating Interest Rate	Fair Value of Interest Rate Swaps $ (G)	Fair Value of Interest Rate Swaps % (G / D)	Monthly Average 7yr Constant Maturity Treasury	Bloomberg U.S. MBS Index
Jan-18	$2,689	$985	$1,684	$644	$805	$1,449	7.52	5.19	6.13	86%	82%	3.47%	1.72%	1.61%	$12	1.49%	2.51%	2,058
Feb-18	$2,676	$990	$1,686	$633	$805	$1,438	7.52	5.12	6.10	85%	81%	3.47%	1.72%	1.74%	$14	1.79%	2.78%	2,045
Mar-18	$2,679	$1,000	$1,679	$627	$805	$1,432	7.56	5.03	6.07	85%	80%	3.48%	1.72%	1.87%	$13	1.65%	2.77%	2,058
Apr-18	$2,684	$1,004	$1,680	$624	$805	$1,429	7.56	4.95	6.03	85%	80%	3.49%	1.72%	2.16%	$16	2.02%	2.82%	2,047
May-18	$2,687	$1,009	$1,678	$620	$900	$1,520	7.56	5.06	6.06	91%	80%	3.50%	1.84%	2.31%	$15	1.62%	2.93%	2,062
Jun-18	$2,684	$1,013	$1,671	$620	$900	$1,520	7.59	4.98	6.02	91%	79%	3.51%	1.84%	2.34%	$16	1.73%	2.87%	2,063
Jul-18	$2,676	$1,018	$1,658	$598	$928	$1,526	7.59	4.95	6.01	92%	79%	3.51%	1.87%	2.34%	$17	1.82%	2.85%	2,061
Aug-18	$2,675	$1,022	$1,653	$582	$928	$1,510	7.59	4.87	5.97	91%	79%	3.52%	1.87%	2.33%	$15	1.61%	2.84%	2,073
Sep-18	$2,671	$1,027	$1,644	$570	$928	$1,498	7.59	4.79	5.92	91%	78%	3.52%	1.87%	2.33%	$18	1.90%	2.96%	2,060
Oct-18	$2,669	$1,032	$1,638	$562	$928	$1,490	7.59	4.70	5.88	91%	78%	3.53%	1.87%	2.38%	$19	2.00%	3.09%	2,047
Nov-18	$2,660	$1,034	$1,626	$540	$943	$1,483	7.59	4.66	5.86	91%	77%	3.54%	1.89%	2.50%	$38	4.01%	3.04%	2,066
Dec-18	$2,653	$1,037	$1,616	$535	$943	$1,478	7.58	4.57	5.81	91%	77%	3.55%	1.89%	2.59%	$23	2.39%	2.75%	2,103
Jan-19	$2,647	$1,039	$1,609	$527	$955	$1,482	7.58	4.53	5.79	92%	76%	3.55%	1.90%	2.74%	$20	2.12%	2.61%	2,120
Feb-19	$2,643	$1,040	$1,603	$520	$955	$1,475	7.58	4.45	5.75	92%	76%	3.55%	1.90%	2.74%	$21	2.21%	2.57%	2,118
Mar-19	$2,646	$1,042	$1,603	$499	$955	$1,454	7.50	4.37	5.68	91%	76%	3.56%	1.90%	2.71%	$11	1.11%	2.47%	2,149
Apr-19	$2,650	$1,047	$1,603	$492	$955	$1,447	7.50	4.29	5.64	90%	75%	3.56%	1.90%	2.62%	$11	1.15%	2.43%	2,148
May-19	$2,667	$1,052	$1,615	$480	$967	$1,447	7.50	4.26	5.62	90%	75%	3.56%	1.91%	2.57%	($4)	-0.41%	2.29%	2,175
Jun-19	$2,690	$1,057	$1,633	$480	$967	$1,447	7.42	4.18	5.54	89%	75%	3.56%	1.91%	2.53%	($10)	-1.08%	1.95%	2,191
Jul-19	$2,720	$1,061	$1,659	$470	$997	$1,467	7.42	4.24	5.57	88%	75%	3.55%	1.91%	2.40%	($8)	-0.80%	1.93%	2,200
Aug-19	$2,756	$1,065	$1,691	$470	$997	$1,467	7.42	4.16	5.53	87%	75%	3.55%	1.91%	2.26%	($27)	-2.72%	1.55%	2,219
Sep-19	$2,786	$1,069	$1,716	$470	$997	$1,467	7.39	4.07	5.47	85%	74%	3.54%	1.91%	2.21%	($20)	-2.02%	1.64%	2,221
Oct-19	$2,832	$1,073	$1,759	$450	$1,037	$1,487	7.39	4.22	5.55	85%	75%	3.53%	1.90%	2.06%	($22)	-2.08%	1.62%	2,229
Nov-19	$2,864	$1,077	$1,787	$430	$1,037	$1,467	7.39	4.14	5.51	82%	75%	3.52%	1.90%	1.99%	($18)	-1.69%	1.74%	2,231
Dec-19	$2,913	$1,083	$1,830	$419	$1,037	$1,456	7.26	4.08	5.44	80%	75%	3.52%	1.90%	1.95%	($12)	-1.18%	1.79%	2,237
Jan-20	$2,929	$1,088	$1,841	$419	$1,112	$1,531	7.26	4.32	5.54	83%	76%	3.52%	1.88%	1.86%	($28)	-2.53%	1.67%	2,252
Feb-20	$2,947	$1,094	$1,853	$415	$1,122	$1,537	7.26	4.30	5.53	83%	76%	3.51%	1.87%	1.79%	($46)	-4.06%	1.42%	2,276
Mar-20	$2,965	$1,098	$1,868	$415	$1,127	$1,542	7.23	4.29	5.51	83%	76%	3.49%	1.86%	1.61%	($66)	-5.85%	0.78%	2,300
Apr-20	$3,007	$1,097	$1,910	$415	$1,147	$1,562	7.23	4.29	5.50	82%	76%	3.46%	1.84%	1.28%	($70)	-6.10%	0.55%	2,314
May-20	$3,049	$1,099	$1,951	$425	$1,159	$1,584	7.23	4.27	5.48	81%	76%	3.45%	1.83%	0.89%	($71)	-6.11%	0.53%	2,317
Jun-20	$3,094	$1,100	$1,994	$413	$1,171	$1,584	7.10	4.25	5.42	79%	76%	3.43%	1.82%	0.75%	($72)	-6.12%	0.55%	2,315
Jul-20	$3,101	$1,108	$1,993	$401	$1,199	$1,600	7.10	4.28	5.44	80%	77%	3.41%	1.79%	0.31%	($75)	-6.26%	0.46%	2,319
Aug-20	$3,090	$1,117	$1,973	$394	$1,210	$1,604	7.10	4.25	5.42	81%	76%	3.38%	1.78%	0.27%	($68)	-5.64%	0.46%	2,320
Sep-20	$3,069	$1,125	$1,944	$245	$1,220	$1,465	6.90	4.22	5.38	75%	78%	3.34%	1.77%	0.26%	($67)	-5.52%	0.46%	2,318
Oct-20	$3,063	$1,134	$1,929	$245	$1,237	$1,482	6.90	4.25	5.40	77%	78%	3.27%	1.75%	0.24%	($60)	-4.82%	0.55%	2,317
Nov-20	$3,055	$1,143	$1,911	$245	$1,247	$1,492	6.90	4.21	5.38	78%	78%	3.20%	1.74%	0.23%	($60)	-4.78%	0.63%	2,318
Dec-20	$3,056	$1,152	$1,904	$245	$1,237	$1,482	6.75	4.17	5.30	78%	79%	3.12%	1.73%	0.22%	($58)	-4.68%	0.66%	2,323

Exhibit 15.6 Star One Credit Union Trended Mortgage Hedges, 2018–2023. Data obtained from S&P Capital IQ, Star One Credit Union, and Bloomberg. The calculations are those of the authors

										Internal Derivative Policy Targets								
Date	Total Mortgages (Hedge-eligible) (A)	Net Worth (B)	Net Mortgage Assets to be Hedged (A - B)	Borrowings Designated as a Hedge (C)	Total Interest Rate Swap Notional (D)	Total Liability & Derivative Hedges (C + D)	Hedged Loan Portfolio Weighted Average Life (years) (E)	Weighted Average Life of Interest Rate Swaps (F)	Weighted Average Life of Total Hedges ((F*(C+D)+E*B)) / (B+C+D)	Hedge Ratio (C + D) / (A - B) Target Range: 80% to 100%	Average Life Ratio Target Range: 70% to 90%	Hedged Loan Portfolio Weighted Average Coupon	Pay Fixed Interest Rate	Receive Floating Interest Rate	Fair Value of Interest Rate Swaps $ (G)	Fair Value of Interest Rate Swaps % (G / D)	Monthly Average 7yr Constant Maturity Treasury	Bloomberg U.S. MBS Index
Jan-21	$3,054	$1,163	$1,892	$245	$1,267	$1,512	6.75	4.20	5.31	80%	79%	3.01%	1.72%	0.23%	($50)	-3.94%	0.77%	2,325
Feb-21	$3,059	$1,172	$1,887	$245	$1,255	$1,500	6.75	4.18	5.31	79%	79%	2.94%	1.72%	0.22%	($33)	-2.65%	0.91%	2,310
Mar-21	$3,118	$1,182	$1,936	$245	$1,245	$1,490	6.60	4.13	5.22	77%	79%	2.90%	1.72%	0.22%	($24)	-1.96%	1.27%	2,298
Apr-21	$3,165	$1,188	$1,977	$245	$1,305	$1,550	6.60	4.30	5.30	78%	80%	2.88%	1.69%	0.19%	($28)	-2.17%	1.31%	2,311
May-21	$3,202	$1,195	$2,007	$245	$1,280	$1,525	6.60	4.34	5.33	76%	81%	2.87%	1.68%	0.18%	($32)	-2.49%	1.28%	2,307
Jun-21	$3,227	$1,202	$2,025	$245	$1,280	$1,525	6.56	4.26	5.27	75%	80%	2.85%	1.68%	0.17%	($33)	-2.54%	1.23%	2,306
Jul-21	$3,234	$1,210	$2,024	$245	$1,343	$1,588	6.56	4.38	5.32	78%	81%	2.83%	1.64%	0.13%	($38)	-2.83%	1.07%	2,320
Aug-21	$3,253	$1,217	$2,036	$245	$1,343	$1,588	6.56	4.30	5.28	78%	81%	2.81%	1.64%	0.13%	($34)	-2.54%	1.06%	2,316
Sep-21	$3,278	$1,223	$2,054	$245	$1,323	$1,568	6.51	4.30	5.27	76%	81%	2.80%	1.64%	0.13%	($24)	-1.79%	1.16%	2,308
Oct-21	$3,300	$1,227	$2,073	$229	$1,366	$1,595	6.51	4.41	5.32	77%	82%	2.79%	1.63%	0.13%	($16)	-1.18%	1.40%	2,303
Nov-21	$3,330	$1,230	$2,099	$217	$1,366	$1,583	6.51	4.32	5.28	75%	81%	2.78%	1.63%	0.13%	($31)	-2.28%	1.45%	2,301
Dec-21	$3,344	$1,234	$2,110	$207	$1,349	$1,556	6.49	4.30	5.27	74%	81%	2.78%	1.62%	0.15%	($12)	-0.89%	1.40%	2,299
Jan-22	$3,368	$1,242	$2,125	$199	$1,395	$1,594	6.49	4.36	5.30	75%	82%	2.77%	1.61%	0.21%	$7	0.49%	1.70%	2,265
Feb-22	$3,388	$1,250	$2,138	$184	$1,420	$1,604	6.49	4.24	5.22	75%	80%	2.78%	1.59%	0.28%	$14	0.98%	1.91%	2,243
Mar-22	$2,956	$1,260	$1,696	$184	$1,420	$1,604	6.41	4.15	5.14	95%	80%	2.78%	1.59%	0.39%	$45	3.20%	2.15%	2,185
Apr-22	$2,970	$1,261	$1,709	$174	$1,435	$1,609	6.41	4.28	5.22	94%	81%	2.78%	1.63%	0.83%	$75	5.22%	2.80%	2,108
May-22	$2,972	$1,263	$1,709	$164	$1,435	$1,599	6.41	4.20	5.17	94%	81%	2.79%	1.63%	1.14%	$68	4.71%	2.92%	2,131
Jun-22	$2,973	$1,265	$1,708	$164	$1,435	$1,599	6.41	4.11	5.13	94%	80%	2.80%	1.63%	1.34%	$76	5.33%	3.21%	2,097
Jul-22	$2,975	$1,263	$1,712	$164	$1,500	$1,664	6.41	4.06	5.07	97%	79%	2.81%	1.67%	2.24%	$61	4.08%	2.97%	2,165
Aug-22	$2,964	$1,262	$1,703	$164	$1,455	$1,619	6.41	4.10	5.11	95%	80%	2.82%	1.69%	2.59%	$92	6.33%	2.98%	2,091
Sep-22	$2,959	$1,261	$1,698	$160	$1,435	$1,595	6.70	4.07	5.23	94%	78%	2.83%	1.69%	2.87%	$125	8.71%	3.64%	1,985
Oct-22	$2,950	$1,271	$1,679	$160	$1,410	$1,570	6.70	4.06	5.24	94%	78%	2.83%	1.69%	3.64%	$135	9.55%	4.09%	1,957
Nov-22	$2,938	$1,275	$1,663	$148	$1,385	$1,533	6.70	4.05	5.25	92%	78%	2.84%	1.68%	4.14%	$114	8.26%	3.99%	2,037
Dec-22	$2,932	$1,276	$1,657	$148	$1,370	$1,518	7.03	4.01	5.39	92%	77%	2.85%	1.68%	4.37%	$122	8.92%	3.72%	2,028
Jan-23	$2,923	$1,282	$1,641	$141	$1,415	$1,556	7.03	3.92	5.33	95%	76%	2.86%	1.74%	4.68%	$104	7.34%	3.59%	2,094
Feb-23	$2,915	$1,288	$1,626	$134	$1,397	$1,531	7.03	3.90	5.33	94%	76%	2.87%	1.75%	4.77%	$127	9.07%	3.86%	2,039
Mar-23	$2,909	$1,292	$1,617	$134	$1,377	$1,511	7.38	3.87	5.49	93%	74%	2.88%	1.74%	4.85%	$102	7.43%	3.77%	2,079
Apr-23	$2,901	$1,296	$1,605	$134	$1,322	$1,456	7.38	3.95	5.56	91%	75%	2.89%	1.75%	5.08%	$96	7.26%	3.50%	2,090
May-23	$2,892	$1,298	$1,595	$131	$1,257	$1,388	7.38	4.06	5.66	87%	77%	2.90%	1.74%	5.23%	$104	8.27%	3.58%	2,074
Jun-23	$2,882	$1,300	$1,582	$128	$1,302	$1,430	7.69	3.93	5.72	90%	74%	2.91%	1.83%	5.28%	$120	9.18%	3.85%	2,065
Jul-23	$2,870	$1,301	$1,569	$128	$1,294	$1,422	7.69	3.98	5.75	91%	75%	2.92%	1.87%	5.47%	$117	9.01%	4.03%	2,064
Aug-23	$2,863	$1,300	$1,563	$128	$1,294	$1,422	7.69	3.90	5.71	91%	74%	2.93%	1.87%	5.51%	$119	9.18%	4.26%	2,047
Sep-23	$2,854	$1,300	$1,554	$128	$1,279	$1,407	7.95	3.86	5.82	91%	73%	2.95%	1.88%	5.51%	$133	10.40%	4.46%	1,982
Oct-23	$2,841	$1,294	$1,547	$120	$1,289	$1,409	7.95	3.86	5.82	91%	73%	2.96%	1.94%	5.55%	$133	10.29%	4.82%	1,941
Nov-23	$2,829	$1,289	$1,540	$120	$1,274	$1,394	7.95	3.82	5.80	91%	73%	2.98%	1.94%	5.53%	$112	8.77%	4.53%	2,042
Dec-23	$2,825	$1,285	$1,540	$120	$1,236	$1,356	8.20	3.85	5.97	88%	73%	2.98%	1.96%	5.57%	$86	6.95%	4.04%	2,130

Exhibit 15.6 (continued)

The systematic adjustments to swap positions, guided by Star One's policy targets, enabled the credit union to maintain stability and flexibility during economic uncertainty. By shifting to an asset-sensitive position, Star One reduced its exposure to interest rate volatility while ensuring that its financial position remained robust. The results achieved through this program

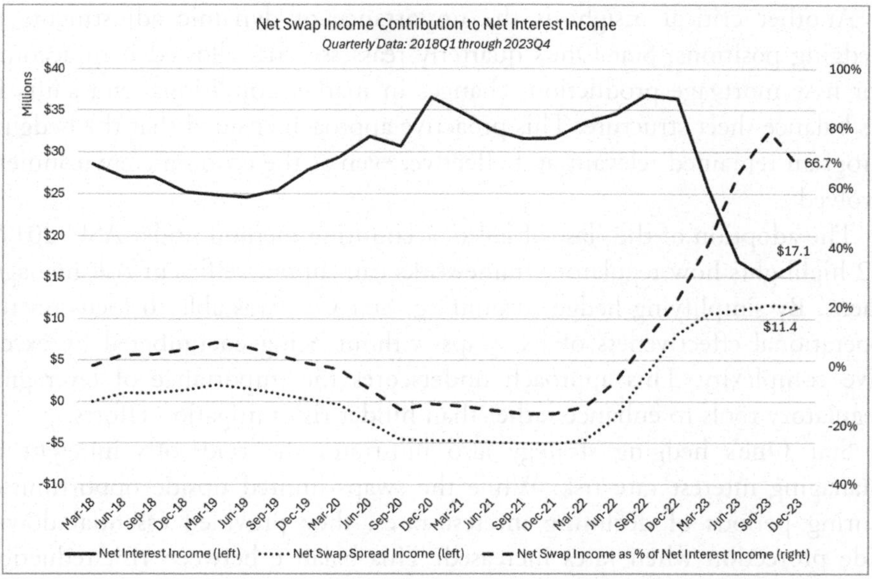

Exhibit 15.7 Net Interest Rate Swap Contribution to Net Interest Income. Data obtained from S&P Capital IQ, Star One Credit Union, and Bloomberg. The calculations are those of the authors

underscore the importance of disciplined and dynamic risk management practices.

Strategic Lessons for Financial Institutions

The experience of Star One Credit Union illustrates the importance of strategic and disciplined risk management in maintaining financial stability, particularly in environments characterized by significant economic volatility. By employing interest rate swaps to hedge duration mismatches, Star One demonstrated how financial institutions can effectively mitigate interest rate risk while preserving their ability to adapt to changing market conditions.

One of the key lessons from this case is the value of aligning risk management strategies with well-defined policies and measurable targets. Star One's adherence to its hedge ratio and average life ratio provided a clear framework for decision-making, ensuring that its hedging activities remained consistent with institutional goals. This disciplined approach not only prevented overhedging or under-hedging but also maintained a balance between reducing risk and preserving flexibility.

Another critical insight is the importance of dynamic adjustments to hedging positions. Star One's quarterly reassessments allowed it to account for new mortgage production, changes in market conditions, and shifts in its balance sheet structure. This proactive approach ensured that the hedging program remained relevant and effective, even as the economic environment evolved.

The adoption of the "last-of-layer" accounting method under ASU 2017–12 highlights how regulatory frameworks can support efficient risk management. By simplifying hedge accounting, Star One was able to focus on the operational effectiveness of its swaps without being encumbered by excessive complexity. This approach underscores the importance of leveraging regulatory tools to enhance rather than hinder risk mitigation efforts.

Star One's hedging strategy also illustrates the trade-offs inherent in managing interest rate risk. While the swaps limited upside opportunities during periods of declining interest rates, they provided essential downside protection when rates increased. This balance between risk reduction and opportunity cost reflects the broader need for financial institutions to prioritize long-term stability over short-term gains.

Finally, this case demonstrates the broader applicability of these strategies to other financial institutions, particularly credit unions and community banks. By integrating systematic risk management practices, institutions can enhance their resilience to economic disruptions, ensuring sustained profitability and stakeholder confidence. The lessons from Star One's experience provide a roadmap for financial institutions seeking to navigate complex market environments while maintaining operational stability and strategic focus.

Summary

Star One Credit Union's implementation of interest rate swaps to hedge its fixed-rate mortgage portfolio underscores the critical role of strategic risk management in ensuring financial stability. By proactively addressing the duration mismatch between assets and liabilities, the credit union successfully reduced its sensitivity to interest rate volatility, safeguarding equity and maintaining operational continuity during periods of economic uncertainty. This shift from a liability-sensitive to an asset-sensitive balance sheet exemplifies how thoughtful hedging strategies can enhance resilience and stability.

The hedging program also provided significant financial benefits, particularly during the challenging rate environment of 2022–2023, when the swaps played a vital role in stabilizing net interest income. This outcome highlights the importance of integrating derivatives into broader risk management frameworks, not for speculation but as tools for preserving institutional health.

A key factor in Star One's success was its disciplined approach to risk management. It aligned hedging activities with clearly defined policies and leveraged regulatory tools such as ASU 2017–12 to streamline implementation. This combination of systematic planning and dynamic execution ensured the program's effectiveness in achieving both short-term and long-term goals.

16

Hedging Interest Rate Risk in Life Insurance Using Interest Rate Derivatives

Vincenzo Russo

As part of their risk management system, life insurance companies must control the risks related to their insurance business. In particular, these companies implement appropriate Asset-Liability Management (ALM) processes to manage the interest-rate risk affecting the assets and liabilities on their balance sheets. In this context, liabilities refer to the provisions that insurance companies make, expressed in terms of expected present values, for the obligations stemming from the insurance policies. Assets typically consist of fixed-income securities that companies hold to fulfill the obligations toward the policyholders. The interest-rate risk lies in the difference in sensitivities between the assets and liabilities to interest-rate movements. On the liability side, obligations tend to be long term, especially those linked to life insurance policies, whereas on the asset side, insurance companies often struggle finding bonds that match these long maturities. Moreover, specific features of life insurance products (e.g., a minimum guaranteed rate, profit-sharing rules, predetermined premium frequencies) can affect the magnitude in which liabilities react to interest-rate movements.

Insurance risk managers widely use duration to measure the sensitivity of assets and liabilities to interest-rate movements. The difference between the duration of an asset and that of a liability is the *duration gap* or *duration*

V. Russo (✉)
Head of Group Life and Health Risk Capital Modeling at Generali Group, Milan, Italy
e-mail: russovincent@gmail.com

F. J. Fabozzi and M. de Jong (eds.), *Derivatives Applications in Asset Management*,
https://doi.org/10.1007/978-3-031-86354-7_16

mismatch. For life insurance companies it is common to have a negative duration gap, which exposes the company to reinvestment risk, as the duration of the assets is shorter than that of the liabilities.

To mitigate this risk, insurance companies can use interest-rate derivatives, such as swaps, to alter the asset sensitivity to interest rates and reduce the duration gap. In case of a negative duration mismatch, the company can enter into a receiver swap to increase the asset duration so that it matches the liability duration. In case of interest-rate fluctuations, the change in the market value of the swap would economically offset any undesired impact of that volatility on the insurance company's balance sheet.

Assumptions, Notation, and Basic Pricing Models

We assume a deterministic risk-free interest-rate environment where $R(t, T_i)$ is the spot annual compounded interest rate prevailing at time $t \geq 0$ and expiring at time T_i, and $P(t, T_i)$ represents the price at time t of a risk-free zero-coupon bond that pays one unit of cash at time T_i. Under this assumption, the following relation holds:

$$P(t, T_i) = \frac{1}{[1 + R(t, T_i)]^{\tau(t, T_i)}} \tag{16.1}$$

where $\tau(t, T_i)$ denotes the time measure between t and T_i computed as a fraction of the year. Given the times $t < T_{i-1} < T_i$ with $i = 1,2, \ldots, n$, the simple compounded forward interest rate fixed at time t, with starting date T_{i-1} and expiring date T_i, denoted by $R(t, T_{i-1}, T_i)$ is

$$R(t, T_{i-1}, T_i) = \left[\frac{P(t, T_{i-1})}{P(t, T_i)} - 1\right] \frac{1}{\tau(T_{i-1}, T_i)} \tag{16.2}$$

We assume deterministic death and surrender[1] rates such that:

- $q_x(T_{i-1}, T_i)$ is the probability that an individual aged x at time T_{i-1} dies within the time T_i[2];
- $l_j(T_{i-1}, T_i)$ is the probability that the contract j is surrendered between T_{i-1} and T_i.

---

[1] Policy cancelations.

[2] Following the actuarial notation, such probability can be denoted by ${}_{T_{i-1}|T_i-T_{i-1}}q_x$

Features of the Asset Portfolio

Let's assume that an asset portfolio is composed of a coupon-bearing bond plus a swap. Denoting by $CBB(t, T_n)$ the spot price at time t of the coupon-bearing bond with maturityT_{n_B}, we have that,

$$CBB\big(t, T_{n_B}\big) = N_B \sum_{i=1}^{n_B} \tau(T_{i-1}, T_i) K_B P(t, T_i) + N_B P\big(t, T_{n_B}\big) \quad (16.3)$$

where N_B is the notional value and K_B is the fixed coupon of the bond.

Denoting by $SWP(t, T_{n_S})$ the spot price at time of a receiver swap with maturity T_{n_S}, we have that,

$$\begin{aligned} SWP\big(t, T_{n_S}\big) = {} & N_S \sum_{i=1}^{n_S} \tau(T_{i-1}, T_i) K_S P(t, T_i) \\ & - N_S \sum_{i=1}^{n_S} \tau(T_{i-1}, T_i) R(t, T_{i-1}, T_i) P(t, T_i) \end{aligned} \quad (16.4)$$

where N_S is the notional value of the swap and K_S is the fixed rate of the fixed leg of the swap.

The total market value of assets (MVA) at time t, denoted by $MVA(t)$, is

$$MVA(t) = CBB\big(t, T_{n_B}\big) + SWP\big(t, T_{n_S}\big) \quad (16.5)$$

Features of the Liability Portfolio

Let's consider a portfolio of N_L life policies with similar features according to which the company pays to the policyholder a capital amount in case of death or surrender events, or in case the insured survives up to the policy maturity without surrendering the contract (i.e., the endowment policy). Let's assume that each life insurance contract starts at time $t = T_0$ and expires at time T_n, and that each policyholder pays to the insurer a single premium Q at the inception of the contract. Under these conditions, the insurer will pay to the policyholder the revaluated capital amount $C(T_n)$ at the maturity T_n of the contract if the insured is still alive at that time and will not have surrendered the contract. Otherwise, the revaluated capital amount $C(T_i)$ is paid in advance by the company at the time $C(T_i)$ in case death occurs before the contract maturity or if the policyholder decides to surrender the policy. Let's assume also that the insurer credits to the policyholder a guaranteed interest rate denoted by g, and that f is the constant fee retained by the insurer. The capital amount $C(T_i)$ is revaluated over time according to the following rule,

$$C(T_i) = C(T_{i-1})(1 + g - f) \tag{16.6}$$

To keep our model tractable, we neglect typical features of endowment policies such as profit-sharing rules, embedded options, or costs charged to the policyholders. For convenience, we assume that all payments related to death and surrender occurring within the period $(T_{i-1}, T_i]$ are postponed to the first discrete time T_i.

To evaluate the fair value of the liability (FVL) related to the portfolio of policies mentioned above, cash flows need to be estimated and projected into the future up to the time when all contracts expire. In this respect, we need to calculate the expected number of insurance contracts in force, denoted by $L(T_i)$, at each date of the projection, given the death and surrender probabilities,

$$L(T_i) = L(T_{i-1})\left[1 - q_x(T_{i-1}, T_i) - l_j(T_{i-1}, T_i)\right] \tag{16.7}$$

Hence, the FVL computed at time for the entire pool of contracts is

$$\begin{aligned} FVL_{x,j}(t) &= N_L \sum_{i=1}^{n_L} p(t, T_i)[C(T_i)L(T_{i-1})q_x(T_{i-1},\ T_i) \\ &\quad + C(T_i)L(T_{i-1})l_j(T_{i-1},\ T_i)] \ + N_L P(t, T_{n_L})C(T_{n_L})L(T_{n_L}). \end{aligned} \tag{16.8}$$

It is worth noting that the difference between MVA and FVL represents the present value of future profits (PVFP) or losses for the insurer on its life insurance activity.

Hedging Strategy

A convenient metric for measuring the sensitivity of assets and liabilities to interest-rate movements is the effective duration. It allows calculating the effective sensitivity to interest rates of any balance sheet item independently from the type of cash flows.[3] Computing the effective duration for assets (EDA) and liabilities (EDL) requires the following quantities:

- market value of assets
- market value of assets in case of a downward parallel shift of the yield curve
- market value of assets in case of an upward parallel shift of the yield curve
- fair value of liabilities
- fair value of liabilities in case of a downward parallel shift of the yield curve
- fair value of liabilities in case of an upward parallel shift of the yield curve

where the shift of the yield curve is denoted by Δ.

The following formulas give the effective duration for assets and liabilities respectively,

$$EDA(t) = \frac{MVA^{-}(t) - MVA^{+}(t)}{2 \times MVA(t) \times \Delta} \tag{16.9}$$

$$EDL(t) = \frac{FVL^{-}(t) - FVL^{+}(t)}{2 \times FVL(t) \times \Delta} \tag{16.10}$$

Hence, the duration gap, denoted by$DGP(t)$, is equal to

$$DGP(t) = EDA(t) - EDL(t)\frac{FVL(t)}{MVA(t)} \tag{16.11}$$

Note that the ratio $\frac{FVL(t)}{MVA(t)}$ in the formula rescales the duration of the liabilities, given that different volumes of assets and liabilities can prevail at time t.

A simple hedging strategy to minimize the duration gap and consequently the interest-rate risk consists of putting in place an optimization procedure to calculate the amount of notional for the swap that minimizes the duration gap:

$$\underset{N_S}{argmin}\left(EDA(t) - EDL(t)\frac{FVL(t)}{MVA(t)}\right) = \underset{N_S}{argmin}(DGP(t)) \tag{16.12}$$

[3] Effective duration allows calculating the sensitivity of a balance sheet item for fixed or floating rates, while the Macaulay Duration or the Modified duration works well only for bonds paying fixed rates.

Practical Example

Let's assume a deterministic and flat risk-free interest rate curve with $R(t, T_i) = r = 3\%$ such that the price of a zero-coupon bond at time $t = 0$ with maturity 10 years ($T_i = 10$) is calculated according to Eq. (16.1) as follows,

$$P(0, 10) = \frac{1}{[1 + 3\%]^{10}} = 0.74 \tag{16.13}$$

As the curve is flat, forward interest rates are also constant at 3% across all periods.

On the asset side, we hold a coupon-bearing bond with $T_{n_B} = 10$, $N_B =$ 10,000 and $K_B = 3\%$, and a swap with $T_{n_S} = 10$, $N_S =$ 1,000 and $K_S =$ 3%. According to the calculations reported respectively in Exhibits 16.1 and 16.2, the value of the CBB at time t is equal to 10,000.00 while the value of the swap is equal to 0.

The price of the swap is equal to 0 because the cash flows of the fixed leg exactly match those of the floating leg, given the flat interest-rate curve, which aligns spot and forward rates. However, the value of the swap will change if interest-rates move.

For example, the value of the swap increases to in case of a parallel shift of the yield curve by -50 bps (i.e., downward scenario) and decreases to in case of parallel shift of the yield curve by + 50 bps (i.e., upward scenario).

On the liability side, we assume deterministic and constant death- and surrender rates of $q_x(T_{i-1}, T_i) = q = 0.1\%$ and $l_j(T_{i-1}, T_i) = l = 5\%$. Following Eq. (16.7), assuming at time $t = T_0 = 0$ an initial number of

Maturity	Zero-coupon Bond Price	Bond Notional	Bond Coupon	Bond Cash Flows	Coupon Bond Price
T_i	$P(t,T_i)$	N_B	K_B	$N_B \times K_B$	$CBB(t,T_n)$
0	1.0000				10,000.00
1	0.9709	10,000.00	3.00%	300.00	
2	0.9426	10,000.00	3.00%	300.00	
3	0.9151	10,000.00	3.00%	300.00	
4	0.8885	10,000.00	3.00%	300.00	
5	0.8626	10,000.00	3.00%	300.00	
6	0.8375	10,000.00	3.00%	300.00	
7	0.8131	10,000.00	3.00%	300.00	
8	0.7894	10,000.00	3.00%	300.00	
9	0.7664	10,000.00	3.00%	300.00	
10	0.7441	10,000.00	3.00%	10,300.00	

Exhibit 16.1 Coupon Bearing Bond Pricing at time $t = 0$

Maturity	Zero-coupon Bond Price	Swap Notional	Swap Fixed Rate	Floating Rate	Fixed Leg Cash Flows	Floating Leg Cash Flows	Swap Price
T_i	$P(t,T_i)$	N_S	K_S	$R(t,T_{i-1},T_i)$	$N_S \times K_S$	$N_S \times R(t,T_{i-1},T_i)$	$SWP(t,T_n)$
0	1.0000						0.00
1	0.9709	1,000.00	3.00%	3.00%	30.00	-30.00	
2	0.9426	1,000.00	3.00%	3.00%	30.00	-30.00	
3	0.9151	1,000.00	3.00%	3.00%	30.00	-30.00	
4	0.8885	1,000.00	3.00%	3.00%	30.00	-30.00	
5	0.8626	1,000.00	3.00%	3.00%	30.00	-30.00	
6	0.8375	1,000.00	3.00%	3.00%	30.00	-30.00	
7	0.8131	1,000.00	3.00%	3.00%	30.00	-30.00	
8	0.7894	1,000.00	3.00%	3.00%	30.00	-30.00	
9	0.7664	1,000.00	3.00%	3.00%	30.00	-30.00	
10	0.7441	1,000.00	3.00%	3.00%	30.00	-30.00	

Exhibit 16.2 Swap Pricing at time $t = 0$

	CBB(t)	SWAP(t)	MVA(t)
Baseline Scenario	10,000.00	0.00	10,000.00
Downward Scenario	10,437.60	43.76	10,481.36
Upward Scenario	9,584.17	-41.58	9,542.59
Effective Duration	**8.5**		**9.4**

Exhibit 16.3 Fair Value of assets evaluated at time $t = 0$

contracts $L(0) = 100$, the number of contracts in force at time $T_1 = 1$ is

$$L(1) = 100 \times [1 - 0.1\% - 5\%] = 94.9 \tag{16.14}$$

Considering a portfolio of life insurance contracts with $T_{n_L} = 20$, $N_L = 100$, $C(0) = 100$, $g = 2{,}5\%$, and $f = 0{,}5\%$, the fair value of the entire portfolio of liabilities (FVL) is equal to 9,405.03 according to the calculations reported in Exhibit 16.4.

Maturity	Zero-coupon Bond Price	Death Rate	Surrender Rate	Number of contracts	Return for policyholder	Capital Insured	Death Cash Flows	Surrender Cash Flows	Maturity Cash Flows	Liability Cash Flows	Fair Value of Liability
T_i	$P(t,T_i)$	$q_x(t,T_{i-1},T_i)$	$l_j(t,T_{i-1},T_i)$	$L(Ti)$	$R(t,T_{i-1},T_i)$	$C(Ti)$	$DCF(T_i)$	$SCF(T_i)$	$MCF(T_i)$	$LCF(T_i)$	$FVL(t)$
0	1.0000			100.00		100.00					9,405.03
1	0.9709	0.10%	5.00%	94.90	2.50%	102.50	10.25	512.50		522.75	
2	0.9426	0.10%	5.00%	90.06	2.50%	105.06	9.97	498.52		508.49	
3	0.9151	0.10%	5.00%	85.47	2.50%	107.69	9.70	484.92		494.62	
4	0.8885	0.10%	5.00%	81.11	2.50%	110.38	9.43	471.70		481.13	
5	0.8626	0.10%	5.00%	76.97	2.50%	113.14	9.18	458.83		468.01	
6	0.8375	0.10%	5.00%	73.05	2.50%	115.97	8.93	446.32		455.24	
7	0.8131	0.10%	5.00%	69.32	2.50%	118.87	8.68	434.14		442.83	
8	0.7894	0.10%	5.00%	65.79	2.50%	121.84	8.45	422.30		430.75	
9	0.7664	0.10%	5.00%	62.43	2.50%	124.89	8.22	410.78		419.00	
10	0.7441	0.10%	5.00%	59.25	2.50%	128.01	7.99	399.58		407.57	
11	0.7224	0.10%	5.00%	56.22	2.50%	131.21	7.77	388.68		396.46	
12	0.7014	0.10%	5.00%	53.36	2.50%	134.49	7.56	378.08		385.64	
13	0.6810	0.10%	5.00%	50.64	2.50%	137.85	7.36	367.77		375.12	
14	0.6611	0.10%	5.00%	48.05	2.50%	141.30	7.15	357.74		364.89	
15	0.6419	0.10%	5.00%	45.60	2.50%	144.83	6.96	347.98		354.94	
16	0.6232	0.10%	5.00%	43.28	2.50%	148.45	6.77	338.49		345.26	
17	0.6050	0.10%	5.00%	41.07	2.50%	152.16	6.59	329.26		335.84	
18	0.5874	0.10%	5.00%	38.98	2.50%	155.97	6.41	320.28		326.68	
19	0.5703	0.10%	5.00%	36.99	2.50%	159.87	6.23	311.54		317.77	
20	0.5537	0.10%	5.00%	35.10	2.50%	163.86	6.06	303.04	5,751.77	6,060.88	

Exhibit 16.4 Fair Value of Liabilities evaluated at time $t = 0$

	MVA(t)	FVL(t)	PVFP(t)	DGP(t)
Baseline Scenario	10,000.00	9,405.03	594.97	
Downward Scenario	10,481.36	10,000.00	481.36	
Upward Scenario	9,542.59	8,858.39	684.19	
Effective Duration	9.4	12.1		-2.0

Exhibit 16.5 Effective duration and duration gap evaluated at time $t = 0$

Under the conditions established above, the present value of future profits for the insurer is,

$$PVFP(t) = MVA(t) - FVL(t) = 10{,}000.00 - 9{,}405.03 = 594.97 \tag{16.15}$$

To implement the hedging strategy, we need to calculate the effective duration for the assets and liabilities, and the duration gap, assuming a shift of the yield curve of $\Delta = 0.5\%$. It allows us to calculate the value of assets and liabilities as a function of the baseline-, the downward- and upward scenario, as reported in Exhibit 16.5.

As shown in the Exhibit, the effective durations for assets and liabilities are equal to 9.4 and 12.1 years respectively, while the duration gap is -2.0 years calculated as follows,

$$DGP(0) = 9.4 - 12.1 \times \frac{9,405.03}{10,000.00} = 9.4 - 12.1 \times 0.9405 = -2.0 \tag{16.16}$$

This is the typical situation that life insurers face, with a negative duration gap, giving rise to reinvestment risk since the duration of the assets is lower than that of the liabilities. The higher (lower) the interest rates, the higher (lower, or even negative) the profits.

To reduce the duration gap and inherently, the interest-rate risk, the insurer can install a hedge that increases the asset sensitivity to interest rates, by increasing the effective duration of the assets, acting on the notional of the receiver swap that is already included in the asset portfolio. When solving the optimization problem according to the Eq. (16.12), the notional of the swap that minimizes the duration gap comes to $N_S = 3{,}376.64$ involving different cash flows and interest-rate sensitivity for the swap as shown in the Exhibit 16.6. Even after the hedging, the value of the swap continues to be equal to in force of the fact that forward rates are assumed equal to the spot rates.

After installing the hedge, the swap's sensitivity to changes in the interest-rate level increases due to the increased notional value, as reported in Exhibit 16.7.

Maturity	Zero-coupon Bond Price	Swap Notional	Swap Fixed Rate	Floating Rate	Fixed Leg Cash Flows	Floating Leg Cash Flows	Swap Price
T_i	$P(t,T_i)$	N_S	K_S	$R(t,T_{i-1},T_i)$	$N_S \times K_S$	$N_S \times R(t,T_{i-1},T_i)$	$SWP(t,T_n)$
0	1.0000						0.00
1	0.9709	3,376.64	3.00%	3.00%	101.30	-101.30	
2	0.9426	3,376.64	3.00%	3.00%	101.30	-101.30	
3	0.9151	3,376.64	3.00%	3.00%	101.30	-101.30	
4	0.8885	3,376.64	3.00%	3.00%	101.30	-101.30	
5	0.8626	3,376.64	3.00%	3.00%	101.30	-101.30	
6	0.8375	3,376.64	3.00%	3.00%	101.30	-101.30	
7	0.8131	3,376.64	3.00%	3.00%	101.30	-101.30	
8	0.7894	3,376.64	3.00%	3.00%	101.30	-101.30	
9	0.7664	3,376.64	3.00%	3.00%	101.30	-101.30	
10	0.7441	3,376.64	3.00%	3.00%	101.30	-101.30	

Exhibit 16.6 Swap Pricing at time $t = 0$ after the hedging

	CBB(t)	SWAP(t)	MVA(t)
Baseline Scenario	10,000.00	0.00	10,000.00
Downward Scenario	10,437.60	147.76	10,585.37
Upward Scenario	9,584.17	-140.41	9,443.76
Effective Duration	**8.5**		**11.4**

Exhibit 16.7 Fair Value of assets evaluated at time $t = 0$ after the hedging

	MVA(t)	FVL(t)	PVFP(t)	DGP(t)
Baseline Scenario	10,000.00	9,405.03	594.97	
Downward Scenario	10,585.37	10,000.00	585.37	
Upward Scenario	9,443.76	8,858.39	585.37	
Effective Duration	**11.4**	**12.1**		**0.0**

Exhibit 16.8 Effective duration and duration gap evaluated at time $t = 0$ after the hedging

Having increased the notional of the receiver swap, the duration of the asset increases from 9.4 to 11.4 and, consequently, the duration gap reduces from to as reported in the Exhibit 16.8.

A comparison between Exhibits 16.5 and 16.8 shows that the hedge reduces the volatility of the company's profits; despite interest-rate level changes of 50 basis points up or down, the profits are stable thanks to the hedge.

Summary

Effective ALM is crucial for life insurance companies to mitigate interest-rate risk and ensure financial stability. By carefully managing the duration gap via a hedge using swaps, these companies can better align their assets and liabilities, thereby protecting their balance sheet from adverse market fluctuations. This proactive approach not only safeguards the company's financial health but also ensures that they can meet their long-term obligations to policyholders.

17

Hedging Systematic Risk in High Yield with Equity Derivatives

Arik Ben Dor and Jingling Guan

How should a high-yield (HY) credit portfolio manager hedge the impact of adverse systematic market changes on the portfolio? The relative illiquidity of the HY market renders scaling down portfolio positions on a tactical basis costly.[1] Another option is "shorting" an ETF, but existing HY ETFs may lack sufficient market depth to be a realistic hedging instrument for institutional-size portfolios and result in high shorting costs.[2]

A different approach involves using index credit default swaps (e.g., CDX, iTraxx). Establishing a position in a standard swap contract is relatively cheap and can be done quickly once the necessary legal documents are in place. We make note that research by the Barclays Quantitative Portfolio Strategy team

[1] Risk can be scaled down by selling positions, switching to cash, or replacing "high beta" names with "low beta" names.

[2] The combined net assets of the two largest HY exchange-traded funds (tickers: HYG and JNK) as of October 2024 were only $22 billion, compared with a market value of $1.3trn for the Bloomberg U.S. HY index.

This chapter is based on Arik Ben Dor and Jingling Guan, "Hedging Systematic Risk in High Yield Portfolios with a Synthetic Overlay: A Comparative Analysis of Equity Instruments vs. Credit Default Swaps," *Journal of Portfolio Management*, *26*(4), 2017, 5–24.

A. Ben Dor (✉) · J. Guan
Quantitative Portfolio Strategy, Barclays Capital, New York, NY, USA
e-mail: arik.bendor@barclays.com

F. J. Fabozzi and M. de Jong (eds.), *Derivatives Applications in Asset Management*,
https://doi.org/10.1007/978-3-031-86354-7_17

highlights the possibility of a large basis risk between the cash and synthetic HY markets, which may play in certain market regimes.[3]

Another choice, what we explore in this chapter, involves equity index derivatives. This idea can be justified by the observation that the reaction of HY bonds to adverse macroeconomic changes, in particular to interest-rate hikes, often resembles that of equities.[4] For example, Exhibit 17.1 shows that since 1999, drawdowns in the U.S. and Euro HY markets (over any six-month period) have followed very closely the dynamics of their respective equity markets in terms of timing and magnitude. This may indicate that equity instruments can offer an effective way to hedge systematic downturns in the HY market despite the difference in asset class dynamics in the underlying constituents.

However, hedging with equity futures could be expensive when applied at periods of positive performance for the hedged portfolio. One way to reduce the hedging costs when using equity futures is to combine them with "writing" out-of-the-money (OTM) short-maturity put options on the underlying equity index. This may improve performance since the option premium is collected consistently (i.e., any time futures are used to hedge). At the same time, the benefit of the futures' hedge would be reduced only in periods when the decline in the futures price is so large (as is also likely the case for the value of the underlying high-yield portfolio) that it trades below the option's strike price. The use of short-maturity OTM put options is motivated by the ample research on the skew in the implied volatility curve reflecting investors' demand for insurance, and the fast decay in the options' value as they approach expiration.

In this chapter, we illustrate the three approaches using a concrete example of a specific month during the great financial crisis when hedging was needed. Moreover, we discuss the effectiveness of hedging in more general settings under different market conditions in the U.S. and Europe. The study covers September 2004 for the U.S. and September 2005 for the Euro market until October 2015.

We first compare the efficacy of equity index derivatives (futures and options) to that of index credit default swaps in hedging the systematic risk of a generic, well-diversified portfolio of HY securities. Since the results would

---

3 Albert Desclée, Anando Maitra, and Simon Polbennikov. "Why CDX.HY and iTraxx.XO have outperformed Barclays High Yield Bond Indices." Barclays Research, January 14, 2016.

4 Unlike investment grade bonds, the "empirical duration" of HY bonds is often close to zero or even negative, similar to the effect interest rates have on the performance of equities. For a more detailed analysis, see Madhur Ambastha, Arik Ben Dor, Lev Dynkin, Jay Hyman, and Vadim Konstantinovksy, "Empirical Duration of Corporate Bonds and Credit Market Segmentation," *Journal of Fixed Income*, 20(1), 2010, pp. 5-27.

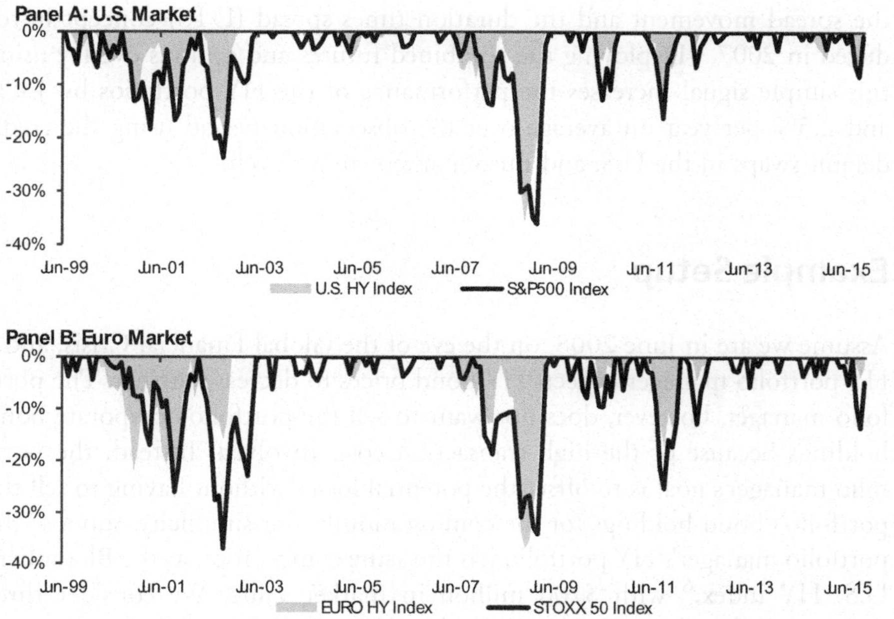

Note: Drawdown is calculated over a rolling 6-month window. Source: Bloomberg, Barclays Research

Exhibit 17.1 Drawdown Dynamics in Bloomberg U.S. and Euro HY indices and Equity Markets. *Note* Drawdown is calculated over a rolling six-month window. *Source* Bloomberg, Barclays Research

reflect not only the properties of the hedging instruments but also additional decisions made by a portfolio manager (e.g., the hedge ratio), we begin with a simple scenario that corresponds to a portfolio manager who employs a passive hedge. In this setup, the manager initially selects only the hedging instrument and the extent to which the portfolio would be hedged (i.e., hedge ratio), which remain unchanged throughout the analysis period. To evaluate the effectiveness of the hedge, we examine the risk reduction based on several measures, including volatility, downside risk, drawdown, and worst monthly loss. Then, we discuss the intuition behind the results.

In the last section, we illustrate active hedging strategies using a simple explicit market-based signal, which delivered a historical hit ratio of over 60%. In this setting, the portfolio manager assesses the risk condition each month and decides whether to hedge. The simple signal we use is based on the spread movement and the duration times spread (DTS) concept introduced in 2007.[5] Deploying the combined futures and options overlay using this simple signal increases the performance of the HY portfolios by 1.4% and 2.5% per year on average over the observation period using the credit default swaps in the U.S. and Euro markets, respectively.

Example Setup

Assume we are in June 2008, on the eve of the Global Financial Crisis, and a HY portfolio manager expects HY bond prices to decrease further. The portfolio manager, however, does not want to sell the portfolio's corporate bond holdings because of the high transaction costs involved. Instead, the portfolio manager's goal is to offset the potential losses without having to sell the portfolio's bond holdings for the coming month. For simplicity, suppose the portfolio manager's HY portfolio has the same composition as the Bloomberg U.S. HY index,[6] with $100 million in market value. We consider three hedging choices for a one-month horizon from June 30 to July 31, 2008:

- *CDX approach*: Buy protection from the on-the-run CDX.NA.HY contract with the same notional as the HY portfolio's market value ($100 million).
- *Futures approach*: Sell short S&P equity futures with three months of maturity at 50% of the portfolio's market value.
- *Futures plus options approach*: Sell short three-month expiry S&P 500 equity futures with 50% of the notional, and write 5% OTM three-month expiry put options with 50% notional to the underlying index.

To understand why we eventually opt for a hedge with equity derivatives that are 50% notional of the underlying index, we will first examine the general risk reduction efficacy of using the CDX index versus using equity futures with different hedge ratios. The optimal hedge ratio should lead to maximum risk reduction.

[5] Arik Ben Dor, Lev Dynkin, Patrick Houweling, Jay Hyman, Erik van. Leeuwen, and Olaf Penninga. "DTS (Duration Times Spread): A New Measure of Spread Exposure in Credit Portfolios," *Journal of Portfolio Management*, 33(2), 2007, 77-100.

[6] In this specific example, we chose to use the Bloomberg U.S. HY index to represent the return profile of a generic HY portfolio. However, since we are looking to hedge *systematic* risk, our results should apply to any well-diversified portfolio of HY securities that exhibit a high correlation with the indices.

Risk Reduction Using Credit Swaps Versus Equity Futures

We also present the analysis in the European market for robustness and comprehensiveness. As credit hedging instruments, we employ the iTraxx.XO in the Euro market, with their performances based on the unfunded returns of the on-the-run contract (i.e., the current contract is rolled to a new series every six months). The European equity hedges (futures and options) are based on the Stoxx 50 Index. The futures' returns are calculated similarly to the swaps, except that the contracts are rolled every quarter. The calculation of the options returns is described in the next section.

To compare credit default swaps and equity futures in terms of their hedging characteristics, we look first at their abilities to reduce portfolio risk at different hedge ratios. The hedge ratio is the notional value of the hedging instrument as a percentage of the portfolio's market value. For simplicity, we keep it constant throughout the entire sample period (starting from September 2004 for U.S./September 2005 for the Euro market and ending in October 2015). Exhibit 17.2 illustrates the change in the indices' risk as the hedge ratio increases from zero to 100% using either the swaps or futures in each market. The results are shown for four different measures of risk that capture progressively more of the tail properties of the return distribution of the hedged indices: total volatility, downside volatility, maximum drawdown, and worst one-month return.

With respect to volatility (Panel A), employing CDX.HY reduces volatility consistently from 2.90%/month for the unhedged index down to 1.93%/month as the hedge ratio attains 76%. Beyond that hedge level, the volatility remains essentially unchanged (fully hedging would result in volatility of 1.96%/month). Using S&P 500 futures instead results in several interesting findings. The volatility of the hedged index declines faster initially while raising the hedge ratio (compared with using CDX.HY), reflecting the futures' higher beta to the index. For hedge ratios above 50%, the volatility stemming from the uncorrelated part of the equity market returns more than offset the hedging benefit, and, as a result, the overall volatility of the hedged index increases. Yet, irrespective of the hedge ratio, the volatility of the hedged index is lower than that of the unhedged index. Hence, even without employing the "optimal" hedge ratio, a portfolio manager using S&P 500 futures would have been able to reduce the portfolio volatility. Moreover, the futures' overlay reduces the HY index risk more effectively than the CDX.HY for any hedge ratio below 58% (as reflected by the line intersection on the chart), and even minimizes volatility to a level only slightly higher

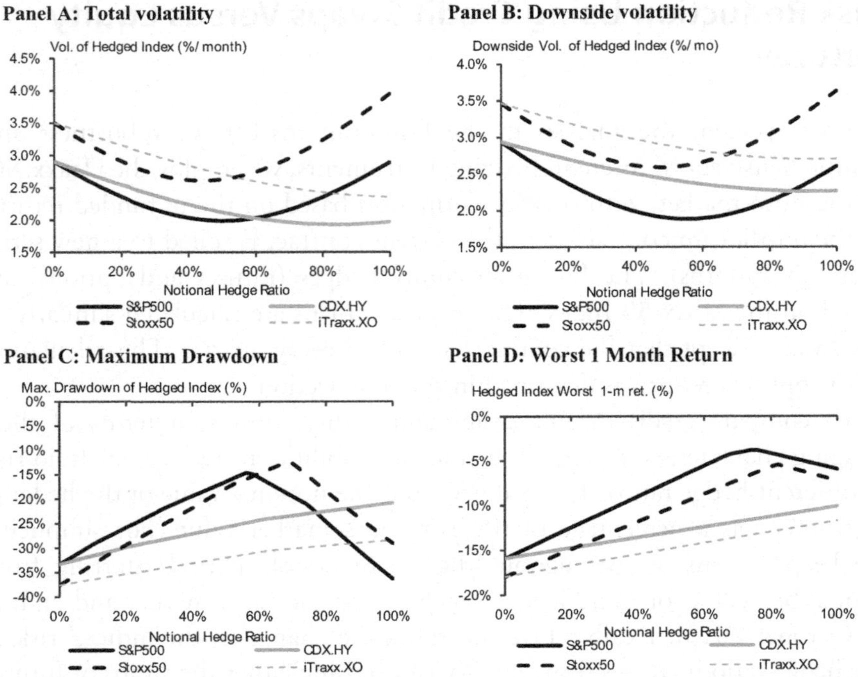

Note: The hedge ratio (the notional value of the hedging instrument as a percentage of the portfolio's market value) remains constant during the analysis period between September 2004 (September 2005 for Euro) and October 2015. Downside volatility is calculated using only months in which the HY Indices earned negative returns. Maximum drawdown represents the largest percentage decline in cumulative returns from peak to the following trough. Source: Bloomberg, Barclays Research. Calculations made by the authors.

Exhibit 17.2 Hedged Indices Performance as a Function of the Hedge Ratio. *Note* The hedge ratio (the notional value of the hedging instrument as a percentage of the portfolio's market value) remains constant during the analysis period between September 2004 (September 2005 for Euro) and October 2015. Downside volatility is calculated using only months in which the HY indices earned negative returns. Maximum drawdown represents the largest percentage decline in cumulative returns from peak to the following trough. *Source* Bloomberg, Barclays Research. Calculations made by the authors

than that reached when using the CDX (1.99%/month versus 1.93%/month, respectively).

Besides total volatility, we examine "downside volatility" (i.e., limit the analysis to months with negative index realizations, Panel B). CDX.HY leads to a maximum reduction of 68 bp/month (with full hedging) while using equity futures lowers downside volatility by as much as 105 bp/month (with a hedge ratio of 56%). The advantage of equity futures over CDX.HY is even more evident in Panels C and D, which examine the changes in maximum drawdown and worst one-month return. With a hedge ratio of 56%, for example, the index hedged with S&P 500 futures experiences a maximum drawdown of 14.6% compared to about 25% if hedged using

CDX.HY. Similarly, the S&P 500 hedge reduces the worst one-month return by 76%, twice the reduction using CDX.HY (36%). For both measures, we continue to see a pattern of persistent reduction in risk when using CDX.HY as opposed to an inverted U-shape (i.e., a minimum) if equity futures are employed. Furthermore, using S&P 500 futures seems to have dominated the CDX.HY hedge irrespective of the hedge ratio over the sample period.

The results for the Euro HY index mimic the U.S. results very closely in terms of both the shape of the hedged index risk-curves (irrespective of the risk measure) using either instrument, and the relative advantage of the futures hedge over the use of iTraxx.XO. It is intriguing that despite the difference in the (absolute) level of risk between the two indices (across all risk measures), the optimal hedge ratios, which minimize the respective risk statistics, are quite similar. The minimum volatility and drawdown for the U.S. Index, for example, are achieved at hedge ratios of 52% and 56%, respectively, while the corresponding figures for the Euro Index were 44 and 68%.

Revisit the Example

Given the results in Exhibit 17.2, we employ an intuitive hedge ratio of 100% for the CDX index and a hedge ratio of 50% that produced the highest average volatility reduction.

Let's first evaluate the performance of the first two choices.

Unhedged Case: By July 31, 2008, the HY index dropped as anticipated and had a loss of 1.33% from June 30, 2008. This translates into a portfolio loss of

$100,000,000 * (−1.33%) = − $1,330,000.

CDX Approach: The CDX price dropped from $93.95 (as of 6/30/2008) to $93.265 (as of 7/31/2008), giving the portfolio manager a payment of

− (93.265 − 93.95)/100 * $100,000,000 = $685,000

The portfolio manager must pay accrued interest, however (from June 30 to July 31, 2008, 31 days) when closing the position: 5% * $100,000,000 * 31/360 = $430,555.56

So, the portfolio manager received a net payment of from the CDX of $685,000 − $430,555.56 = $254,444.44

The net portfolio loss is

− $1,330,000 + $254,444.44 = − $1,075,555.56.

This is a 19% smaller loss than in the unhedged case.

Futures Approach: As of June 30, 2008, the S&P 500 index was valued at $1280, and a September expiry E-mini futures contract on the S&P500

was trading at $1281.10, with a multiplier of 50. We calculate the number of futures contracts needed as follows: $N_{futures}$ = Notional * Hedge Ratio/ (Futures Price * Futures Multiplier) = $100,000,000 * 0.5 / (1281.10 * 50) = 781 contracts.

As of July 31, 2008, the futures contract did not expire and was priced at $1267.10, so by closing the short futures contracts, the portfolio manager makes a profit of

− 781 * ($1267.10 − $1281.10) * 50 = $546,700.

So, the net portfolio loss is

− $1,330,000 + $546,700 = − $783,300.

This is a 41% smaller loss than in the unhedged case.

Consistent with the general results, hedging with either the CDX or equity futures reduces the loss in July 2008. Using equity futures, though at a lower hedge ratio, delivered a higher loss reduction (41%) than CDX (19% loss reduction). The next section will discuss the reasons behind the more efficient risk reduction from equity futures.

Drivers of Difference in Hedging Effectiveness

It is somewhat surprising that the equity futures are more effective in reducing the systematic risk of HY indices, given the almost identical correlation of S&P 500 futures and CDX.HY with the U.S. Index (0.73 and 0.75, respectively). The effect is even more apparent in the Euro market, where the correlation of the Stoxx 50 futures (0.67) is lower than that of the iTraxx.XO (0.74). Indeed, the similar correlation in the U.S. is surprising because the S&P 500 futures represent a different asset class, and there is essentially no overlap between its constituents and those underlying the HY index as opposed to the case of CDX.HY.

The fact that the gap in hedging ability between the futures and credit default swaps increases as our risk measures concentrate more on the left tail of the portfolio return distribution suggests that the relation between the performance of the futures and the HY indices may be asymmetric. Exhibit 17.3 reports the performance of the indices and hedging instruments separately for "good" and "bad" states of the market based on two indicators. The first is based on the monthly performance of the HY market (negative or positive) as represented by the Bloomberg Indices (Panel A). As this indicator is available only ex-post, the second indicator (Panel B) is based on the magnitude of the spread change during the previous month and can, therefore, be observed *ex-ante.*[7]

This indicator may be predictive because of the HY market's relative illiquidity and thus inertia. Illiquidity results in autocorrelation of monthly returns, as new information cannot be incorporated into prices instantaneously. We discuss this in greater detail in the next section.

	High Yield Index	Credit Default Swaps	Equity Futures	High Yield Index	Credit Default Swaps	Equity Futures
Panel A: Index Return (contemporaneous)		Negative			Positive	
	U.S.	CDX.HY	S&P500	U.S.	CDX.HY	S&P500
Avg. Ret (%/mo)	-2.31%	-1.95%	-3.19%	1.86%	1.49%	2.12%
Volatility (%/mo)	2.94%	2.01%	4.05%	1.83%	2.07%	3.19%
Correlation with HY Index	1.00	0.64	0.77	1.00	0.58	0.41
Beta to HY Index	1.00	0.44	1.06	1.00	0.66	0.72
	Euro	iTraxx.XO	Stoxx 50	Euro	iTraxx.XO	Stoxx 50
Avg. Ret (%/mo)	-2.74%	-1.68%	-4.52%	2.06%	1.53%	2.33%
Volatility (%/mo)	3.46%	2.33%	4.85%	2.42%	1.92%	4.06%
Correlation with HY Index	1.00	0.63	0.66	1.00	0.58	0.35
Beta to HY Index	1.00	0.42	0.93	1.00	0.46	0.59
Panel B: Spread Change (ex-ante)		Spread Widening > 1 Std			Other	
	U.S.	CDX.HY	S&P500	U.S.	CDX.HY	S&P500
Avg. Ret (%/mo)	-0.22%	0.25%	-0.19%	0.83%	0.54%	0.73%
Volatility (%/mo)	4.81%	3.70%	6.17%	2.32%	2.30%	3.71%
Correlation with HY Index	1.00	0.81	0.84	1.00	0.72	0.66
Beta to HY Index	1.00	0.63	1.08	1.00	0.71	1.05
	Euro	iTraxx.XO	Stoxx 50	Euro	iTraxx.XO	Stoxx 50
Avg. Ret (%/mo)	-0.78%	0.04%	-0.81%	1.03%	0.74%	0.64%
Volatility (%/mo)	4.81%	3.50%	6.66%	3.06%	2.22%	4.92%
Correlation with HY Index	1.00	0.79	0.84	1.00	0.71	0.58
Beta to HY Index	1.00	0.58	1.17	1.00	0.52	0.93

Note: In Panel A, the sample (in each market) is partitioned based on the index monthly realizations (positive or negative). In Panel B, the sample is partitioned into two states corresponding to the previous month's spreads widening by more than one standard deviation.
Source: Bloomberg, Barclays Research.

Exhibit 17.3 Performance of Indices and Hedging Instruments by Market State. *Note* In Panel A, the sample (in each market) is partitioned based on the index monthly realizations (positive or negative). In Panel B, the sample is partitioned into two states corresponding to the previous month's spreads widening by more than one standard deviation. *Source* Bloomberg, Barclays Research

[7] The spread widening is deemed large if it exceeded the product of spread level at the beginning of the month and 10%. To define a spread change as "large," we do not use an absolute cut-off value but rely on the findings in the following study regarding the relation between spread volatility and spread level: Ben Dor et al, "DTS (Duration Times Spread): A New Measure of Spread Exposure in Credit Portfolios." Specifically, a "negative" market state would correspond to a spread widening larger than one standard deviation (10% * beginning of the month spread) during the previous month. For an illustration of this approach during the global financial crisis, see Madhur Ambastha, Arik Ben Dor, and Lev Dynkin. "DTS (Duration Times Spread) in the Credit Crunch: Did It Live Up to Expectations?" Barclays Research, April 2, 2009.

Panel A reveals that the correlation of equity futures with the indices varies considerably in both HY markets, as one may have expected. In months with negative return realizations, the correlations were 0.77 and 0.66 (U.S. and Euro, respectively), whereas in months with positive performance, they were significantly lower (0.41 and 0.35). Furthermore, because of this asymmetry, the correlations of the indices with the futures in "bad" months were higher than with credit default swaps. Hence, although equity futures and credit default swaps exhibited similar correlations with the HY indices over the entire sample, at times when a portfolio manager would have been most interested in hedging an adverse move in the HY index, equity futures' hedging ability proved superior.

Similar results are also apparent in Panel B when market states were determined ex-ante based on the behavior of spreads in the previous month. S&P 500 futures again exhibited an asymmetry in their correlation with the HY index and had a higher correlation than the CDX.HY in months preceded by large spread widening by historical standards (0.84 versus 0.66, respectively). Moreover, notice that CDX.HY performance in months following significant spread widening was positive (0.25%/month), while the index earned negative returns on average. The same dynamics in the Euro market can be observed concerning the Stoxx 50 futures and iTraxx.XO.

Exhibit 17.4 displays the correlation and beta to the HY indices in the worst months in our sample, in order to highlight the difference in the hedging dynamics of equity futures and credit default swaps. The sample months are sorted in ascending order in terms of monthly index performance, and the correlations and betas are calculated over an increasing number of the worst months (denoted by N) starting with five.

The plots show that in the ten worst performance months—when hedging was most needed, U.S. futures correlated with the HY index at 0.8 or higher, while the correlation between CDX.HY and the HY index was less than 0.3. Furthermore, the betas, which are affected by both correlations and volatilities of the hedging instruments, were stable in these months (suggesting the volatilities of the instruments did not vary much). This last point is crucial since it implies that a manager can have more confidence when sizing the hedge. In the Euro market, the Stoxx 50 beta exhibits more variability than in the U.S., but the patterns are overall similar, boasting a higher correlation with the Euro HY index than the iTraxx.XO.

The dynamics shown in Exhibits 17.3 and 17.4 help explain not only the results in Exhibit 17.2 (i.e., the superior hedging ability of futures over credit default swaps) but also suggest that simple signals such as unusual spread widening may be used to improve the efficacy of an overlay hedging strategy

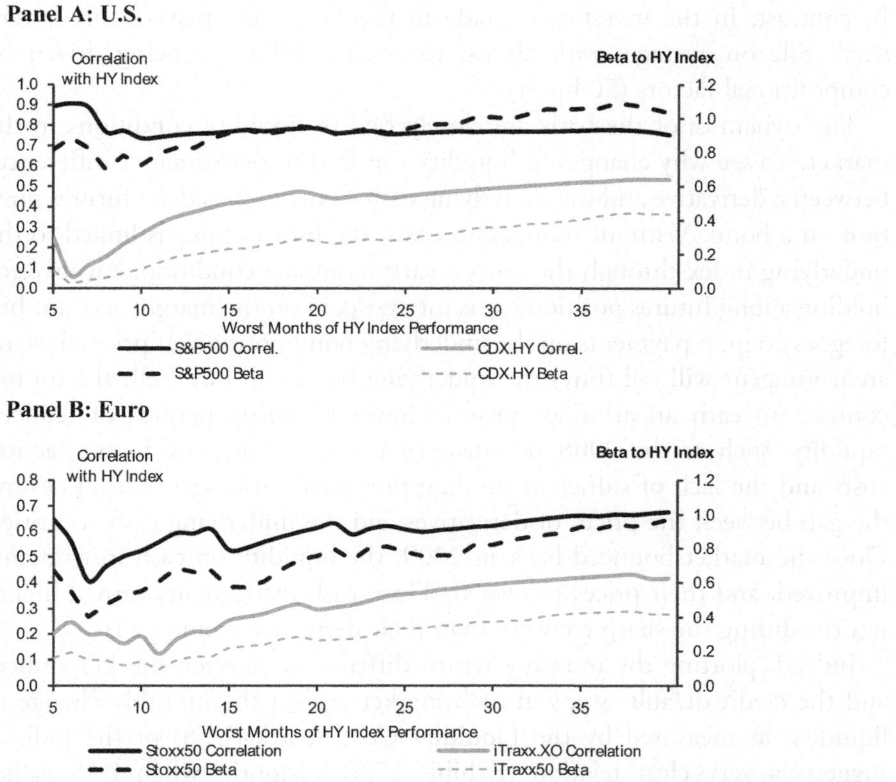

Note: The sample months are sorted by ascending order in terms of monthly index performance. The chart shows the correlations and betas calculated over the N worst months starting with N = 5. Source: Bloomberg, Barclays Research

Exhibit 17.4 Correlation/Beta of Hedging Instruments during Index Worst Months. *Note* The sample months are sorted by ascending order in terms of monthly index performance. The chart shows the correlations and betas calculated over the N worst months starting with N = 5. *Source* Bloomberg, Barclays Research

using equity futures. They do not explain, however, the reason for the relatively poor tracking of the HY indices by the respective credit default swaps contracts (compared with equity futures).

Desclée, Maitra, and Polbennikov analyze the performance difference between the Bloomberg U.S. and Euro HY indices and CDX.HY and iTraxx.XO over the period January 2006 to August 2015.[8] They find that differences in seniority, maturity, quality, sector, and issuer composition account for only a small part (29 bp/yr) of the overall annual tracking error (219 bp/yr). The rest reflects the basis between cash and synthetic markets.

[8] "Why CDX.HY and iTraxx.XO have outperformed Barclays High Yield Bond Indices." Barclays Research, January 14, 2016.

In contrast, in the investment grade market, the basis played only a very small role on average, with almost the entire difference being driven by compositional factors (70 bp/yr).

The dynamics of the basis are closely tied to liquidity conditions in the market. To see why changes in liquidity can lead to performance differences between a derivative and the underlying cash security, consider a futures position on a bond. Without transaction costs, the futures price is linked to the underlying index through the cost-of-carry arbitrage condition. An investor holding a long futures position earns interest paid on the margin account but foregoes coupon payments on the underlying bond position. If prices deviate, an arbitrageur will sell (buy) the underlying bond and buy (sell) the futures contract to earn an arbitrage profit. However, during periods of reduced liquidity, such as the 2008–09 financial crisis, the increase in transaction costs and the lack of sufficient funding prevented arbitrageurs from closing the gap between the prices of derivatives and the underlying cash securities. Once the market bounced back in 2009, the liquidity on cash instruments improved, and their prices recovered. Thus, cash instruments earned higher returns during the sharp recovery than their derivative counterparts.

Indeed, plotting the monthly return differences between the HY indices and the credit default swaps in each market against the monthly change in liquidity, as measured by the Liquidity Cost Scores (LCS) of the indices, suggests a very clear relation (Exhibit 17.5).[9] Months when LCS values increased (i.e., liquidity declined) were generally associated with a larger tracking error between the cash index and the respective CDS contract and vice versa. Hence, although an index credit default swap contract could have been an ideal overlay instrument to hedge against systematic risk in the HY market, it proved ineffective precisely when protection was most needed. These periods of market stress were also generally associated with a decline in liquidity that severed the linkage between cash and synthetic markets due to the reduced ability of arbitrage activity. In equity markets, however, cash and future markets were consistently tightly linked, which resulted in S&P 500 futures being a more effective hedge than index credit default swaps for both U.S. and Euro HY indices.

[9] LCS values represent the cost of an institutional-size round-trip transaction in a bond as a percentage of its market price based on traders' quotes (see Vadim Konstantinovksy, Kwok Yuen Ng, and Bruce Phelps. "Measuring Bond Level Liquidity: Liquidity Cost Scores (LSC)." Barclays Research, July 24, 2015 for more details on LCS).

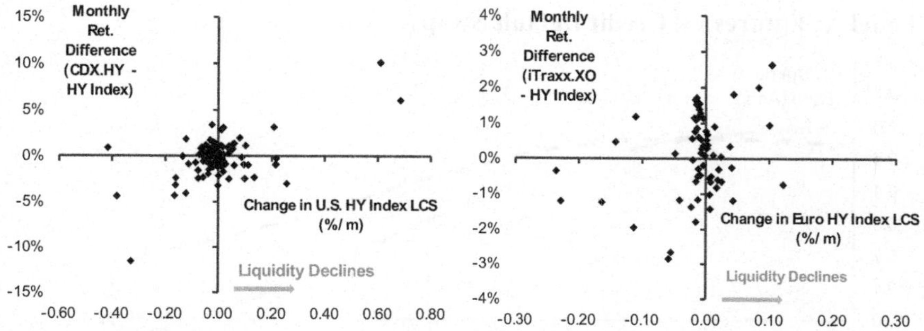

Note: LCS data for U.S. and Euro HY securities start in January 2007 and May 2010, respectively. The changes in index-level LCS are based on aggregating the LCS values of all underlying constituents. Source: Bloomberg, Barclays Research

Exhibit 17.5 Liquidity and Return Differences between CDX/iTraxx and HY indices. *Note* LCS data for U.S. and Euro HY securities start in January 2007 and May 2010, respectively. The changes in index-level LCS are based on aggregating the LCS values of all underlying constituents. *Source* Bloomberg, Barclays Research

Hedging Costs and the Use of Equity Options

The analysis so far focused solely on reducing risk but did not consider costs, which weigh on performance. Incorporating costs is essential not only because hedges generally reduce overall performance but also because it may affect the relative attractiveness of the different instruments.[10]

Panel A of Exhibit 17.6 compares the risk-adjusted performance (i.e., Sharpe Ratios) of the unhedged indices in the two markets with those using the futures and credit default swaps. In the Euro market, Stoxx 50 futures dominated the iTraxx.XO, irrespective of the hedge ratio and resulted in a slight improvement in the Sharpe Ratio of the unhedged index (0.55–0.56 vs. 0.54) for hedge ratios between 4 and 34%. In contrast, S&P 500 futures delivered better Sharpe Ratios than CDX.HY only for hedge ratios below 30%, primarily because Stoxx 50 futures substantially underperformed iTraxx.XO during the sample period (37 and 61 bp/month, respectively), whereas the opposite was the case in the U.S. market. Hence, although S&P 500 futures co-moved more closely with the HY index, as we have previously shown, the degradation in performance more than offset the benefit once the hedge ratio exceeded 30%.

However, irrespective of the hedge ratio, using either CDX.HY, iTraxx.XO or S&P 500 futures resulted in lower Sharpe Ratios than those generated by the unhedged index. Even the unusual performance of the Stoxx 50 futures during the sample (relative to the iTraxx.XO) resulted in a Sharpe Ratio that

[10] The costs associated with deploying a futures' hedge at the "wrong" time may be larger, for example, than those resulting from using credit default swaps.

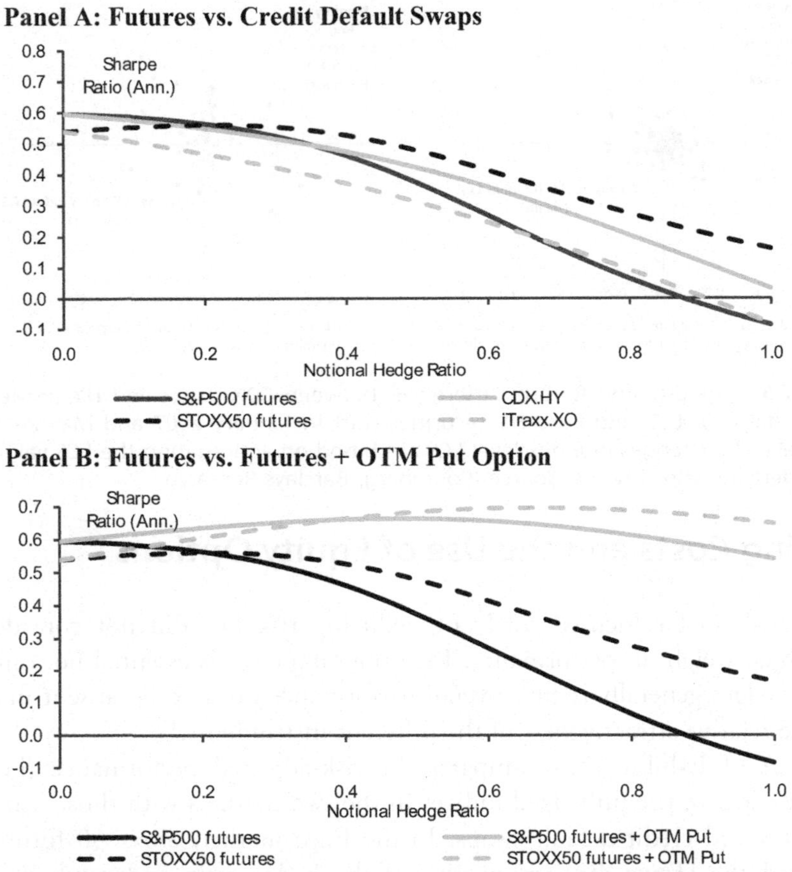

Note: Sharpe Ratios are calculated using returns over 1-month Libor. Source: Bloomberg, Barclays Research

Exhibit 17.6 Sharpe Ratio of Hedged Indices by Instrument and Hedge Ratio. *Note* Sharpe Ratios are calculated using returns over one-month Libor. *Source* Bloomberg, Barclays Research

is essentially the same as that of the unhedged index. These results reflect the fact that a passive hedge might be ineffective either because the underlying portfolio increased in value (i.e., no need to hedge), the correlation between the portfolio and the hedging strategy was negative (i.e., the hedge amplified the magnitude of the loss) or since the scaling of the hedge was inappropriate. Consequently, the risk might decline disproportionally relative to performance.

One possible solution for reducing the hedging costs when using equity futures is to combine them with "writing" an out-of-the-money (OTM) short-maturity put option on the underlying equity index. This may improve performance since the option premium is collected consistently, while the benefit of the futures' hedge would be reduced only in periods when the decline in the futures price was so significant (as was also likely the case for the value of the underlying HY portfolio) that it traded below the strike price of the option. The use of short-maturity OTM put options is motivated by the ample research on the skew in the implied volatility curve reflecting investors' demand for insurance and the fast decay in the options' value as they approach expiration.

To examine this idea, we use S&P 500 and Stoxx 50 put options with strike prices equal to 95% of the then-current spot level of the indices. The options had three months to maturity and were rolled on a monthly basis.[11] We make note that we do not claim that our strike price is optimal. It is possible that using a put option with a different strike price would have resulted in a better trade-off between the income level and the reduction in hedging ability, given the actual return distributions of the equity indices in the sample. Regardless, the 95% strike we use should still illustrate the change in the futures' overlay dynamics.

Exhibit 17.7 plots the put options premiums as a percentage of the underlying index spot value and reveals several interesting patterns. First, as one may expect, the premiums in both markets exhibit similar dynamics, reflecting the generally similar behavior of the underlying markets. Second, the premiums are considerable and amount to an average of 2.67 and 2.11% in the Euro market and the U.S., respectively. The somewhat higher premium in the euro market can be attributed to the difference in the diversification of the underlying index constituents (i.e., the Stoxx50 would be expected to have higher volatility, all else equal). Third, although premium levels varied over time, the adjustment was gradual with long periods of elevated premiums (indicating high levels of implied volatility).

Panel B of Exhibit 17.6 displays the Sharpe Ratios of the U.S. and Euro HY indices hedged with the future/OTM option combination alongside those attained if only futures are used. Two key results applicable to both markets can be observed. First, the future/OTM option combination dominated the futures-only hedge irrespective of the hedge ratio. Second, the performance generated by the option "writing" led to higher Sharpe Ratios than the unhedged index. In the U.S., the Sharpe Ratio increased from 0.6 to 0.66 for hedge ratios between 0.34 and 0.6. Notice that even for somewhat lower or higher hedge ratios, the risk-adjusted performance was higher than that of the unhedged index. Only for hedge ratios beyond 0.85, the

[11] The S&P 500 and Euro Stoxx 50 options are hypothetical contracts priced at the beginning of each month using the contemporaneous implied volatility curve. Their strike prices are set to 95% of the then-current respective index spot level.

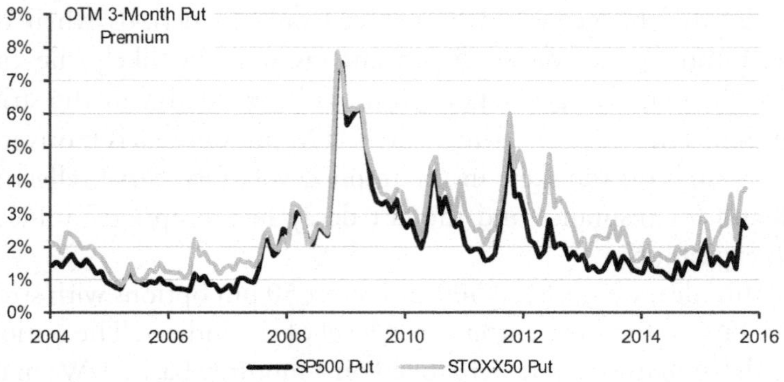

Note: The S&P 500 and Euro Stoxx 50 options are hypothetical contracts priced at the beginning of each month using the contemporaneous implied volatility curve. Their strike prices are set to 95% of the then-current respective index spot level at the beginning of each month. Source: Bloomberg, Barclays Research

Exhibit 17.7 S&P500 and Stoxx50 Put Options Premiums. *Note* The S&P 500 and Euro Stoxx 50 options are hypothetical contracts priced at the beginning of each month using the contemporaneous implied volatility curve. Their strike prices are set to 95% of the then-current respective index spot level at the beginning of each month. *Source* Bloomberg, Barclays Research

resulting Sharpe Ratio was lower than 0.6. In the Euro market, the futures plus OTM option hedge led to consistently higher Sharpe Ratios than the unhedged index.

To better understand the effect of the option inclusion, Exhibit 17.8 breaks down the change in Sharpe Ratio to changes in return and volatility of the hedged indices as a function of the hedge ratio. The charts indicate that the option inclusion led to a substantial reduction in the hedging cost of 5.49% and 4.79% per year in the U.S. and Euro markets, respectively (when the index was fully hedged).[12] In the euro market, the overall performance was higher than that of the unhedged index due to using the OTM option. In contrast, the increase in volatility was quite modest, and for hedge ratios above 0.78 (U.S) and 0.64 (Euro), the inclusion of the option resulted in lower volatility compared with the futures-only case. The difference between the return and volatility dynamics reflects the former's linearity and the latter's non-linear nature. As a result, the benefit of the futures' hedge increases initially. Still, it rapidly declines once the "cost" incurred from either hedging when the HY index rose in value or when the ineffective hedge supersedes the

[12] The annual figures correspond to quarterly values of 1.37 and 1.19% (U.S. and Euro, respectively) compared with the average premium of 2.11 and 2.67% from Exhibit 17.8. The difference reflects the empirical distribution of the underlying futures returns and the fact that the options are not held to expiration but are rolled over monthly.

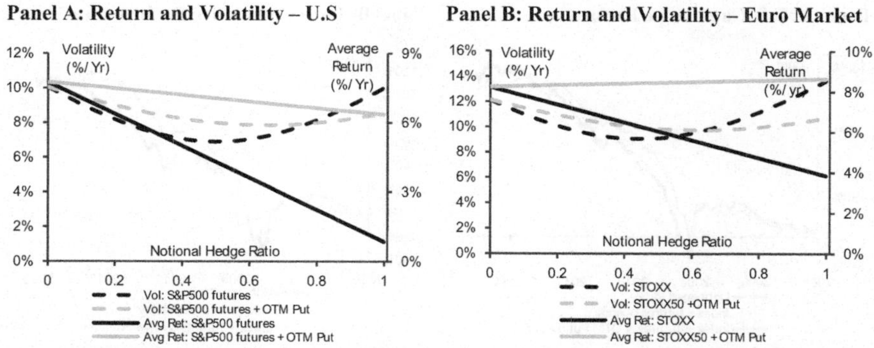

Note: the chart displays the return and volatility of the HY indices when hedged with futures or futures + OTM Put option overlays.
Source: Bloomberg, Barclays Research. Calculations made by the authors.

Exhibit 17.8 Return and volatility of Hedged Indices with OTM Put "Writing". *Note* The chart displays the return and volatility of the HY indices when hedged with futures or futures + OTM Put option overlays. *Source* Bloomberg, Barclays Research. Calculations made by the authors

average benefit. Finally, the minimum volatility with and without the OTM option is similar, although achieved at different hedge ratios.

To see the impact of the futures and futures/OTM option hedges separately on the time-series dynamics of the HY indices, Exhibit 17.9 plots the cumulative performance and drawdown (over trailing six-month intervals), assuming a 50% hedge ratio. The chart includes the unhedged index alongside the results for the index hedged using either of the two equity overlays.

The exhibit (Panels A and B) illustrates the difference in cumulative performance between the futures overlay and the futures + OTM option overlay. Using the latter in the U.S. and Euro markets led to a consistent outperformance over the unhedged index throughout most of the sample period (until early 2013 in the U.S.). In contrast, the index's performance hedged with the futures-only overlay started to deviate from that of the unhedged index in 2009, resulting in a substantial underperformance by the end of the sample. The exhibit also indicates that the same overlay tended to perform similarly across markets with correlations of 0.84 and 0.81 for the active returns (vs. the unhedged index) using the futures only and futures + OTM option hedges.

The advantage of the futures + OTM option overlay can also be seen when looking at the drawdown dynamics of the indices (Panels C and D). Not surprisingly, the exhibits show that with this overlay, the drawdown figures are lower than those of the unhedged index over almost all six-month periods. The results are similar when compared to using the futures overlay except the peak of the financial crisis during the third quarter of 2008 when the futures

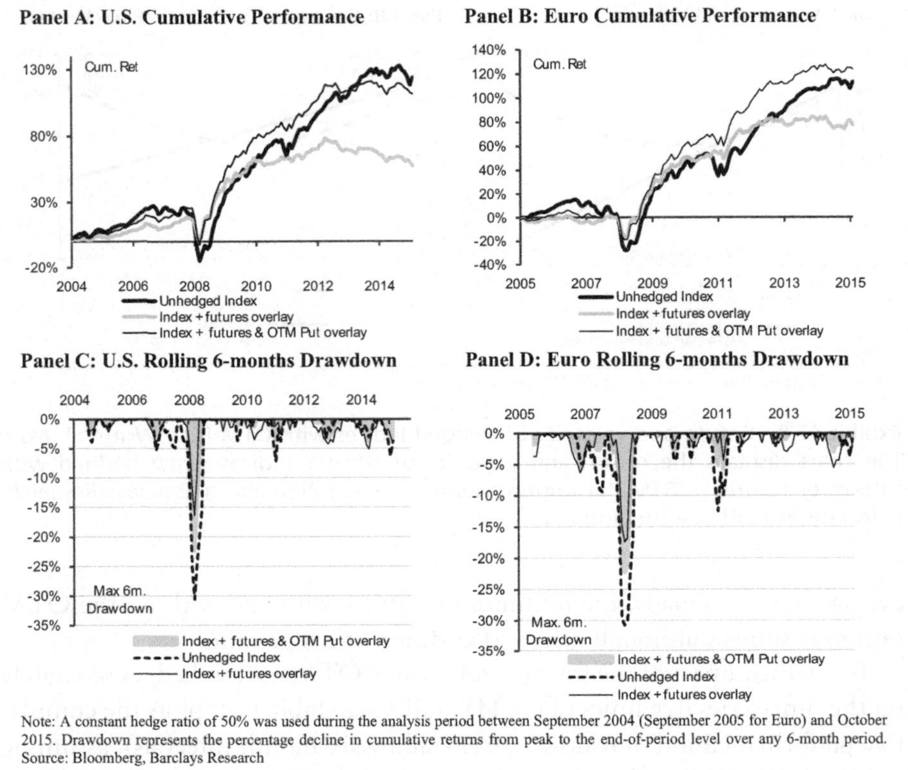

Exhibit 17.9 Cumulative Performance and Drawdown with Equity Overlays. *Note* A constant hedge ratio of 50% was used during the analysis period between September 2004 (September 2005 for Euro) and October 2015. Drawdown represents the percentage decline in cumulative returns from peak to the end-of-period level over any six-month period. *Source* Bloomberg, Barclays Research

overlay resulted in the lowest drawdown in either market as the OTM put options were exercised.

Revisit the Example

Let's go back to the example in the beginning and evaluate the performance of the third choice, the *Futures Plus Options Approach*: A September-expiry put with strike price at $1,225 (closest to the 5% OTM: 95%*1280 = $1,216) was trading at $34.45 on June 30, 2008. The put options have a multiplier of 100. The number of puts to be sold is found as follows: N_{puts} = Notional * Hedge Ratio/(Underlying Index Value * Option Multiplier) = $100,000,000 * 0.5/(1280 * 100) = 391 contracts.

The portfolio manager collected a premium of
$34.45 * 391 * 100 = $1,346,995 on June 30, 2008, from writing the puts.

On July 31, 2008, the same put option was trading at $24.40, so to close the put position, the PM had to pay $24.40 * 391 * 100 = $954,040. The total portfolio loss from selling the futures and writing OTM puts is

Loss on the HY portfolio + payment from futures + premium collected from selling options − payment from closing the option position
= − $1,330,000 + $546,700 + $1,346,995 − 954,040 = − $390,345.

This is a 71% drop from the loss in the unhedged case. Compared to the previous two choices (CDX with 19% loss reduction, equity futures with 41% risk reduction), this choice provided an even bigger risk reduction (71%), benefiting from the premium it collected.

Active Hedging with a Spread Signal

The analysis in the previous section compared the efficacy of different overlays and the extent to which they varied as a function of the hedge ratio. The overlays were deployed passively throughout the analysis period using an unchanged hedge ratio. In practice, it is more likely that an overlay would be deployed on a tactical basis, given the portfolio manager's view of the conditions in the HY market. In this section, we illustrate the idea of active hedging using a simple hedging rule based on the spread widening indicator we introduced in Exhibit 17.3. Despite its simplicity, it results in substantial improvement in the performance of both HY indices.

The relative illiquidity of the HY market results in autocorrelation of monthly returns as new information cannot be incorporated into prices instantaneously. This, in turn, leads to predictable market dynamics anytime large negative adjustments to prices are needed. Investors' behavior may also reinforce the gradual price adjustment. Once the adjustment process has begun, those who anticipate the continued downtrend in the market may sell their holdings, resulting in negative flows, which would tend to increase the down pressure.

Due to high transaction costs, the illiquidity that leads to predictable market patterns also prevents investors from exploiting them directly by trading HY bonds. Nevertheless, a synthetic overlay can be deployed quickly and cheaply based on a quantitative signal and effectively limit the losses of the underlying HY portfolio. Therefore, we assume the overlay is deployed in any month preceded by a spread widening of more than one standard deviation during the previous month.

Exhibit 17.10 reports the signal behavior in up and down (HY) markets in the U.S. and Euro area. The table demonstrates that the spread signal exhibits different success rates in up and down markets. The signal was quite effective in up markets with a success rate of 86% (i.e., 14% of the months with a positive performance for the HY market were preceded by a "large" spread widening). The signal was less successful in down months: identifying only 26% of these periods in the U.S. and 31% in the Euro market. Notice that despite the lower "hit" rates identifying "down" markets, the overall success rates (69% and 70%, respectively) were still much higher than a 50–50% random chance produced by an uninformative signal.

Next, we examine the performance of the different overlays based on the spread widening signal assuming partial (50%) or full (100%) hedging. The results, reported in Exhibit 17.11, offer several interesting insights. First, the futures + OTM options overlay continues to dominate the other overlays when the portfolio is fully hedged in both markets regarding return and Sharpe Ratio. On a standalone basis (i.e., the hedged index returns minus the unhedged index), the overlay generated an information ratio of 0.16 and 0.42 in the U.S. and Euro markets, respectively. Second, while the futures overlay generated equal or slightly higher Sharpe Ratios than the futures + OTM options overlay for partial hedging, overall performance and information ratios were lower because it's costly to implement, as discussed earlier. Lastly, deploying the CDSs overlay led to lower returns than the unhedged index in all cases but still resulted in better Sharpe Ratios (compared with the unhedged indices) due to the reduction in volatilities.

Panels A and B of Exhibit 17.12 plot the cumulative performance of the unhedged index alongside its return when the futures + OTM options overlay (hedge ratio = 100%) is used in both markets (months when the overlay was deployed based on the spread signal are marked in grey). Not surprisingly, the charts indicate that performance started to diverge in early

		U.S.			Euro		
		Ret. <0	Ret. >=0	Overall	Ret. <0	Ret. >=0	Overall
Total		39	95	134	35	87	122
Signal (months)	'Hedge'	10	13	23	11	12	23
	'Don't Hedge'	29	82	111	24	75	99
Prob. Conditional	Correct call	26%	86%	69%	31%	86%	70%
on Ret. Realization	Incorrect call	74%	14%	31%	69%	14%	30%

Source: Bloomberg, Barclays Research

Exhibit 17.10 Relation between Spread Signal and HY Market Behavior. *Source* Bloomberg, Barclays Research

	High Yield Index	Partial Hedging (HR = 0.5) Credit Default Swaps	Partial Hedging (HR = 0.5) Equity Futures	Partial Hedging (HR = 0.5) Equity Futures + OTM Put	Full Hedging (HR = 1) Credit Default Swaps	Full Hedging (HR = 1) Equity Futures	Full Hedging (HR = 1) Equity Futures + OTM Put
U.S.		**CDX.HY**	**SP500**	**SP500**	**CDX.HY**	**SP500**	**SP500**
Avg. Ret (%/mo)	0.65%	0.63%	0.66%	0.68%	0.60%	0.68%	0.72%
Volatility (%/mo)	2.90%	2.58%	2.42%	2.62%	2.45%	2.54%	2.55%
Sharpe Ratio	0.60	0.64	0.74	0.71	0.65	0.73	0.78
Inf. Ratio (Hedged-Unhedged)		-0.10	0.04	0.16	-0.10	0.04	0.16
Euro		**iTraxx.XO**	**Stoxx50**	**Stoxx50**	**iTraxx.XO**	**Stoxx50**	**Stoxx50**
Avg. Ret (%/mo)	0.69%	0.68%	0.76%	0.79%	0.68%	0.84%	0.89%
Volatility (%/mo)	3.50%	3.23%	3.03%	3.18%	3.11%	3.19%	3.07%
Sharpe Ratio	0.54	0.58	0.71	0.71	0.60	0.76	0.85
Inf. Ratio (Hedged-Unhedged)		-0.02	0.19	0.42	-0.02	0.19	0.42

Source: Bloomberg, Barclays Research

Exhibit 17.11 Performance of Active Overlay Strategy with Spread Signal. *Source* Bloomberg, Barclays Research

2007, at the beginning of the financial crisis. The overlay was deployed multiple times between 2007 and 2009, generating an outperformance that increased steadily in the following years. Another observation made clear when looking at both charts is the high degree of similarity between the two markets. The correlation between the returns of the two HY indices was 0.91, while the signals exhibited a correlation of 0.67[13] (i.e., between the "hedge" and "don't hedge" calls).

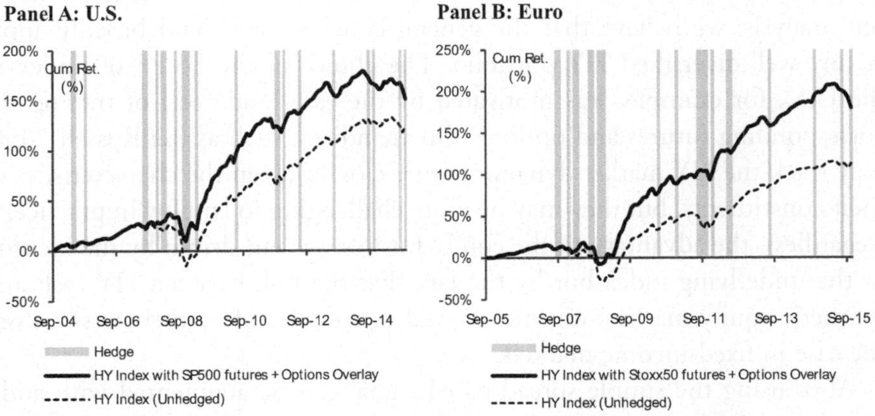

Note: The grey areas represent months where the spread signal made a 'hedge' call. Source: Bloomberg, Barclays Research

Exhibit 17.12 Cumulative Performance with an Active Overlay. *Note* The grey areas represent months where the spread signal made a "hedge" call. *Source* Bloomberg, Barclays Research

[13] The correlation between the signals was calculated by assigning values of 0 and 1 to the decision to hedge or not in each market.

Revisit the Example

On June 30, 2008, the Bloomberg U.S. HY index spread was 7.08%, an increase of 14% from the previous month's end (6.22% May 30). Since the increase is more than 10%, the active hedging rule suggests deploying the hedging for the coming month earlier, which results in loss reduction.

Summary

The chapter offers two key insights to HY portfolio managers who consider hedging systematic downturns in the cash HY market.

Equity futures are good hedges irrespective of the risk measure and hedge ratio used in both U.S. and euro HY markets. Moreover, combining these futures with OTM option "writing" generates income that reduces the hedging costs significantly, with limited effect on risk. As a result, risk-adjusted performance increased and superseded that of the unhedged index even when the overlay is deployed passively. Furthermore, we demonstrate that the predictability of the HY market allows even a simple signal to be the basis for an active hedging strategy that generates consistent outperformance versus the unhedged index.

While the results may be affected to some extent by the specificities of our analysis, we believe that the general conclusions should broadly apply to any well-diversified HY portfolio. The choice of the S&P 500 index in the U.S., for example, was motivated by the ease (and cost) of trading the corresponding futures and options. Other indices, such as the Russell 2000, may track the HY market dynamics more closely, given the characteristics of their constituents, but they may be more challenging to employ in practice.[14] Regardless, the advantage of the equity futures was not driven by the identity of the underlying index but by the fact that the link between HY cash and synthetic equity markets was not severed in episodes of market stress, as was the case in fixed-income markets.

Also, using the simple spread-based signal can be augmented with additional market or economic indicators to generate a more powerful signal with various numeric values. Rather than a binary signal resulting in a hedge being deployed or not, such a signal can be used to vary the hedge ratio over time.

---

[14] The U.S. HY index constituents are more like firms included in the Russell 2000 than in the S&P 500 in terms of size, for example.

Finally, it is important to note that while the magnitude of market dynamics played a significant role in our sample (and affected the results), our findings remain qualitatively similar even if that period was removed from our analysis.

18

Hedging the Mortgage Pipeline with To-Be-Announced (TBA) Securities

Joseph Niehaus

This case demonstrates how the secondary market desk of a mortgage originator, such as a bank or credit union, may choose to hedge the projected gain-on-sale of the mortgages it sells by transacting in to-be-announced (TBA) securities (the derivative).

On a monthly basis, millions of mortgages are originated among thousands of lenders in the United States. The highly competitive primary mortgage market is fully supported and informed by the massive liquidity of the secondary mortgage market. For example, the pricing offered by an originator on any given day for a standard 30-year fixed rate mortgage is most often determined by a target gain-on-sale spread over the purchase price communicated by investors, including Fannie Mae, Freddie Mac, Ginnie Mae (the Agencies), as well as non-agency investors such as large banks. This spread over the purchase price remains relevant for loans that the originator plans to hold on its books since it indicates a degree of liquidity for assets added to the balance sheet. Subsequently, mortgages held on the balance sheet may be hedged to preserve the positive fair value observed at origination[1]; however, that is not the hedging strategy discussed here. The focus is on preserving the

[1] See Joseph Niehaus, "Consumer mortgage portfolio hedging with interest rate swaps," in this book.

J. Niehaus (✉)
Jefferies, The CUFS Group, Credit Union Financial Services, New York, NY, USA
e-mail: joseph.niehaus@grenoble-em.com

F. J. Fabozzi and M. de Jong (eds.), *Derivatives Applications in Asset Management*,
https://doi.org/10.1007/978-3-031-86354-7_18

gain-on-sale targeted at the time of locking a mortgage loan with a consumer by transacting in TBA securities.

The timeline from lock to funding that is typically targeted by mortgage originators may range from 15 to 60 days, depending on whether or not the mortgage is for the purchase of a property or for a refinance transaction, respectively. Once the borrower chooses to lock the loan rate for a given period, e.g., 30 days, the originator is obligated to satisfy that commitment assuming the loan is funded within the initial 30-day window. However, markets may move a considerable amount over a 30-day period, and the originator should not ignore the potential rate volatility as it could have a material adverse impact to profitability if not hedged.

The Secondary Mortgage Market

As of the second quarter of 2024, the United States mortgage market stood at $13.1 trillion, and approximately 65%, or $9.2 trillion, of these mortgages are held in the form of U.S. agency mortgage-backed securities (MBS), according to the Urban Institute.[2] The top three holders of agency MBS are commercial banks, the Federal Reserve, and foreign investors. These large holdings, combined with monthly origination volumes that reach into the hundreds of billions, have spawned a derivatives market by way of TBA contracts with which to hedge and speculate on secondary mortgage market activity.

The majority of trading related to the agency MBS market takes place in the TBA market. TBA securities are forward contracts to buy or sell agency MBS. The market gets its name from the fact that the composition of any MBS is not known until right before settlement. As Berliner and Fabozzi highlight, the liquidity and flexibility provided by the TBA market make it an essential tool for managing interest rate risks and optimizing profitability in mortgage pipeline management.[3] The ability of mortgage originators to trade in the TBA market provides a tremendous amount of flexibility in serving both the borrower and the institution. In the standard mortgage origination process, the originator locks the contract rate with the borrower (the originator is long the loan) and then enters into a contract to sell a TBA

[2] Urban Institute Housing Finance Policy Center, "Housing Finance at a Glance Monthly Chartbook." September 2024, 6–7.

[3] Bill Berliner and Frank J. Fabozzi, "Mortgage originator pipeline management," *Journal of Fixed Income, 34*(3), 2025, 7–25.

with a maturity and coupon directionally consistent with the note rate (originator is short the TBA). Therefore, any fair value gain/loss on the locked loan commitment with the borrower is offset by the TBA contract's fair value gain/loss.

Because of the ability to hedge with TBAs, the borrower gets to lock a rate well ahead of loan closing, and the originator gets to capture a targeted gain-on-sale, even with days or weeks until the loan will be sold to a U.S. agency or other investor. It should be noted that hedging may also be achieved using Treasury futures or mandatory commitments with the agencies, but these methods come with different basis risk considerations. TBAs are often the preferred hedging instrument given the amount of liquidity and the flexibility in managing basis risk due to the similar characteristics of the contract to the underlying loans.

Mortgage Pipeline Milestones

It is important to understand the different stages of the mortgage origination process because the likelihood of loan fallout, i.e., the borrower choosing not to proceed with the loan, is different at each stage. The probability of loan closing increases as the loan moves on from lock to funding. These various probabilities inform the hedge ratio of the mortgage pipeline since the ultimate objective is to hedge the loans that will be funded. Too much unexpected loan fallout will result in excessive hedge costs, thereby reducing overall profitability. Too high of a pull-through ratio (the opposite of fallout) will result in loans closing without being hedged, which also risks an adverse impact to profitability should rates go against the originator.[4]

The steps, or milestones, within the mortgage origination process may be articulated with corresponding estimates of pull-through ratios, i.e., the percentage of loans in each milestone expected to make it to funding. The respective pull-through ratios are calculated by examining data from previously locked loan commitments. Before hedging, originators usually deliver loans to the agencies with commitments of best efforts. The purchase price for these loans offered by the agencies is less than what is offered for mandatory commitments since hedging the lock commitment falls to the agencies under the best efforts commitments. If loans fall out under a best efforts

---

[4] Berliner and Fabozzi emphasize the importance of dynamically adjusting hedge ratios throughout the stages of the pipeline to account for variations in pull-through rates and fallout risks, ensuring that hedging strategies remain effective under fluctuating market conditions. See Berliner and Fabozzi, "Mortgage originator pipeline management.".

commitment, there is no resulting cost to the originator. Under a mandatory commitment, however, loans that are not delivered result in a pair-off fee, which may adversely impact loan profitability.

Illustration of a Mortgage Pipeline Hedge

We show how a mortgage originator decides to hedge the projected gain-on-sale on the mortgages lined up in the pipe by transacting in TBAs, over a period of three consecutive months from June to August 2024. Exhibit 18.1 represents the estimated pull-through rates for the overall pipeline per milestone and per month. For example, mortgages just locked in as of June 2024 have a weighted average estimated probability of 61% to pull through, while mortgages that have reached the milestone of being sent to processing that month have a weighted average 84% pull-through estimate.

Exhibit 18.2 gives a breakdown of the same pipeline in terms of mortgage types, distinguishing between purchase-, rate/term refinance-, and cash-out refinance mortgages. The borrower's behavior and motivations for each type of mortgage transaction are likely different enough to warrant specific pull-through calculations. For example, a homeowner looking to reduce their interest rate does not need to close the transaction by any specified time to obtain a residence, as does the borrower seeking to purchase a home. These analyses are most often completed for each mortgage type and then aggregated, as shown in Exhibit 18.1.

Exhibit 18.3 shows how the mortgage pipeline may be segmented according to loan terms (loan programs) with note rates ranging from

Status	Volume (x 1,000)			Units			Forecasted Pull-Through (Optimal Hedge Ratio)		
	Jun-24	Jul-24	Aug-24	Jun-24	Jul-24	Aug-24	Jun-24	Jul-24	Aug-24
Initial Lock	$3,100	$3,800	$1,800	14	15	7	61%	58%	60%
Sent to Processing	$900	$620	$600	3	2	2	84%	80%	81%
UW* Received	$600	$250	$300	2	1	1	85%	81%	85%
Cond. Approved	$5,000	$3,200	$6,000	21	14	22	87%	82%	85%
Fully Approved	$310	$1,100	$275	1	3	1	97%	93%	95%
Docs Out	$1,700	$700	$2,600	6	2	8	98%	97%	97%
Docs Back	$1,300	$200	$700	4	1	2	99%	98%	98%
Funded	$275	$1,050	$585	1	3	2	100%	100%	100%
Total	**$13,185**	**$10,920**	**$12,860**	**52**	**41**	**45**	**84%**	**78%**	**85%**

* Underwriting

Exhibit 18.1 Mortgage Pipeline Status by Milestone, June through August 2024.* Underwriting

	Pipeline %		
Mortgage Purpose	Jun-24	Jul-24	Aug-24
Purchase	60%	50%	55%
Rate/Term Refinance	8%	3%	8%
Cash-out Refinance	32%	47%	37%

Exhibit 18.2 Pipeline by Mortgage Purpose, June through August 2024

	Jun-24			Jul-24			Aug-24		
Loan Program	Volume (x 1,000)	Units	WAVG Note Rate	Volume (x 1,000)	Units	WAVG Note Rate	Volume (x 1,000)	Units	WAVG Note Rate
10yr	$155	1	6.125%	$0	0		$175	1	6.125%
15yr	$875	3	6.950%	$300	1	6.250%	$0	0	
20yr	$1,200	4	6.640%	$1,200	4	6.650%	$2 100	8	6.050%
30yr	$10,955	44	7.050%	$9,420	36	7.040%	$10,585	36	6.625%
Total	**$13,185**	**52**	**6.995%**	**$10,920**	**41**	**6.975%**	**$12,860**	**45**	**6.524%**

Exhibit 18.3 Pipeline by Loan Program, June through August 2024

10 years to 30 years. The TBA securities used to hedge this pipeline will typically have a coupon that is 75 to 100 basis points lower than the weighted average note rate of the loans within the pipeline. This is due to the way MBS are created by the agencies, i.e., the minimum note rate must be 25 basis points above the MBS stated coupon and the maximum is 112.5 basis points.

The TBA Market

The TBA market is fascinating since it represents a little over 90% of trading in all Agency MBS, emphasizing the degree to which originators as well as investors and traders use these securities for hedging or speculative purposes. The securities themselves only exist for a relatively short period of time, usually three-month windows, before they become "specified." As stated by Vickery and Wright, the liquidity of the TBA market improves market functioning and helps mortgage lenders manage risk since it allows them to "lock in" sale prices for new loans as, or even before, those mortgages are originated.[5]

TBA securities are forward contracts where two parties agree upon a price of certain volume of agency MBS to be transacted upon in the future. The

[5] James Vickery and Joshua Wright, "TBA trading and liquidity in the Agency MBS market." *FRBNY Economic Policy Review,* May 2023, 1–18.

specific attributes for consideration by the originator are maturity, coupon, price, par amount, and settlement date. When used for hedging, the originator or hedge manager does not intend to actually deliver anything to the agencies, but rather, the TBA trade is rolled out or paired off prior to the delivery deadline. If the hedge manager is short the TBA, then pairing out of the trade requires a purchase of a like TBA contract prior to the MBS delivery deadline. These positions will net to zero on the dealers' books; however, there will likely be a money difference that will have to be settled with one party owing the other depending on the direction of mortgage rates over the course of the TBA holding period.

Hedging the Pipeline with TBAs

In addition to the estimated pull-through ratios, what must also be considered are the locked note rates along with the terms of the notes. These attributes will influence pull-through ratios, but they mostly drive the type and coupon for the TBA to be used for hedging. Berliner and Fabozzi emphasize the necessity of dynamically adjusting hedge ratios as the mortgage pipeline evolves. Their work highlights the importance of incorporating pull-through rates, loan lock characteristics, and market conditions to optimize hedging strategies and reduce exposure to interest rate volatility.[6]

Coming back to our example, if we assume the lock commitments represented in Exhibit 18.3 are to be sold to Fannie Mae or Freddie Mac, then the TBAs chosen to hedge the pipeline will be based off either the UMBS (Uniform Mortgage-Backed Security) 15-year or 30-year contract. Exhibit 18.4 represents how TBA prices move relative to mortgage rates, with mortgage rates representing the inverse movement of mortgage price. As mentioned previously, the hedge provided by TBAs can be very efficient given the reduction of basis risk and the homogeneity of the underlying assets, but for larger relative rate movements, care must be taken to adjust hedge ratios for the impact of fallout risk.

Exhibits 18.5, 18.6, and 18.7 show the TBA positions that are used to hedge the mortgage pipeline for the three months, respectively. The columns in these exhibits are defined as follows:

- **Coupon**—the stated coupon of the TBAs available to hedge current mortgage pipeline volume.

[6] Berliner and Fabozzi, "Mortgage originator pipeline management.".

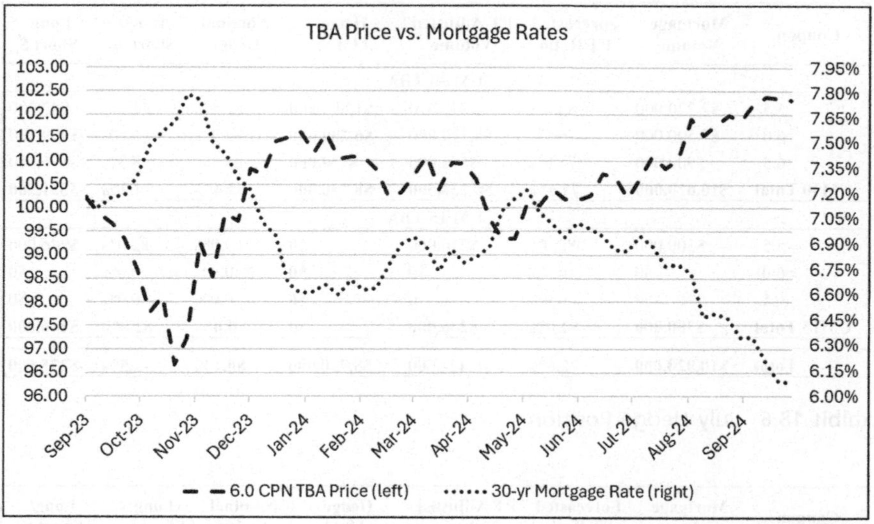

Exhibit 18.4 6.0% Coupon TBA vs. Freddie Mac Weekly 30-year Mortgage Rate Index. *Source* Bloomberg. Calculations made by the author

Coupon	Mortgage Volume	Forecasted PT Ratio	PT Adjusted Volume	Hedge (TBA)	Nominal Hedge	Long/ Short %	Long/ Short $
			UM 30 TBA				
5.5	$2,800,000	78,.%	$2,184,000	**$2,250,000**	80.4%	-2.4%	-$66 000
6.0	$8,255,000	85.7%	$7,072,884	**$7,300,000**	88.4%	-2.8%	-$227 116
6.5	$1,100,000	85.0%	$935,000	**$1,250,000**	113.6%	-28.6%	-$315 000
UM30 Total	**$12,155,000**	**83.8%**	**$10,191,884**	**$10,800,000**	**88.9%**	**-5.0%**	**-$608 116**
			UM 15 TBA				
5.5	$300,000	80.0%	$240,000	**$0**	0.0%	80.0%	$240 000
6.0	$250,000	89.0%	$222,500	**$0**	0.0%	89.0%	$222 500
6.5	$480,000	90.0%	$432,000	**$0**	0.0%	90.0%	$432 000
UM15 Total	**$1,030,000**	**86.8%**	**$894,500**	**$0**	**0.0%**	**86.8%**	**$894 500**
Total	**$13,185,000**	**84.1%**	**$11,086,384**	**$10,800,000**	**81.9%**	**2.2%**	**$286 384**

Exhibit 18.5 June Hedge Position

- **Mortgage Volume**—the amount of mortgages in the pipeline that would be slotted according to the respective TBA coupon. A locked mortgage with a note rate of 6.75%, for example, would most likely be slotted into a TBA with a coupon of 6.0%. This also represents the "long position" of the originator.
- **Forecasted Pull-Through (PT) Ratio**—this represents the weighted average pull-through rate according to where each of the slotted loans is in terms of pipeline milestone.

Coupon	Mortgage Volume	Forecasted PT Ratio	PT Adjusted Volume	Hedge (TBA)	Nominal Hedge	Long/ Short %	Long/ Short $
			UM 30 TBA				
5.5	$2,220,000	83.0%	$1,842,600	**$1,800,000**	81.1%	1.9%	$42,600
6.0	$7,500,000	76.1%	$5,710,900	**$6,200,000**	82.7%	-6.5%	-$489,100
6.5	$900,000	75.0%	$675,000	**$750,000**	83.3%	-8.3%	-$75,000
UM30 Total	**$10,620,000**	**77.5%**	**$8,228,500**	**$8,750,000**	**82.4%**	**-4.9%**	**-$521,500**
			UM 15 TBA				
5.5	$300,000	82.0%	$246,000	**$0**	0.0%	82.0%	$246,000
6.0	$0	0.0%	$0	**$0**	0.0%	0.0%	$0
6.5	$0	0.0%	$0	**$0**	0.0%	0.0%	$0
UM15 Total	**$300,000**	**82.0%**	**$246,000**	**$0**	**0.0%**	**82.0%**	**$246,000**
Total	**$10,920,000**	**77.6%**	**$8,474,500**	**$8,750,000**	**80.1%**	**-2.5%**	**-$275,500**

Exhibit 18.6 July Hedge Position

Coupon	Mortgage Volume	Forecasted PT Ratio	PT Adjusted Volume	Hedge (TBA)	Nominal Hedge	Long/ Short %	Long/ Short $
			UM 30 TBA				
5.5	$4,200,000	89.0%	$3,738,000	**$2,200,000**	52.4%	36.6%	$1,538,000
6.0	$7,000,000	84.4%	$5,909,250	**$7,250,000**	103.6%	-19.2%	-$1,340,750
6.5	$1,410,000	80.0%	$1,128,000	**$1,200,000**	85.1%	-5.1%	-$72,000
UM30 Total	**$12,610,000**	**85.5%**	**$10,775,250**	**$10,650,000**	**84.5%**	**1.0%**	**$125,250**
			UM 15 TBA				
5.5	$250,000	80.0%	$200,000	**$0**	0.0%	80.0%	$200,000
6.0	$0	0.0%	$0	**$0**	0.0%	0.0%	$0
6.5	$0	0.0%	$0	**$0**	0.0%	0.0%	$0
UM15 Total	**$250,000**	**80.0%**	**$200,000**	**$0**	**0.0%**	**80.0%**	**$200,000**
Total	**$12,860,000**	**85.3%**	**$10,975,250**	**$10,650,000**	**82.8%**	**2.5%**	**$325,250**

Exhibit 18.7 August Hedge Position

- **PT Adjusted Volume**—this represents the sum of each loan within the pipeline multiplied by its expected pull-through rate.
- **Hedge (TBA)**—this is the amount of TBA contracts for the respective coupon amount that have been sold short to hedge the PT adjusted long position.
- **Nominal Hedge Position**—the dollar amount of the short TBA position divided by the amount of locked mortgages (long position).
- **Long/Short %**—the net difference between the forecasted pull-through ratio and the nominal hedge position. For a perfect hedge, this difference would be zero.
- **Long/Short $**—the net dollar difference between the PT adjusted volume and the hedge position (TBA).

As the pipeline and the respective hedge progress from June through August, as shown in Exhibits 18.5, 18.6, and 18.7, it is important to think through how the pipeline is impacted by constant change. On a daily basis, loans may be locked, progress from one milestone to the next, become funded, or fall out of the pipeline. The constant change occurring within the pipeline requires persistent monitoring and prudent risk management. Furthermore, this constant change occurs along with the constant change of macro market factors such as interest rates, housing supply and demand, and the job market.

The net long/short position, shown in Exhibits 18.5, 18.6, and 18.7, will be impacted by any one or several of these factors at any given time. For the example shown, we see the net long/short positions progress from 2.2%, –2.5%, and 2.5% for June, July, and August, respectively. The net short position of –2.5% observed in July was partly impacted by the lower pull-through ratio of 77.6%. One of the factors that may have contributed to the lower pull-through ratio is the general decline in market rates observed over the three-month period, peaking at the beginning of June and bottoming at the end of August (see Exhibit 18.4). As rates moved lower, locked borrowers may have chosen to cancel their lock with their would-be lender to obtain a lower rate with a different lender.

Of note in the TBA positions identified by Exhibits 18.5, 18.6, and 18.7 is the absence of UM 15 TBAs purchased to hedge against the shorter 10- or 15-year loans in the pipeline. Most important is that the net long or short position does not exceed the rebalance threshold set by the originator. For example, if the originator maintained a daily long/short percentage threshold of 5%, then all of the hedged pipeline snapshots shown would be in compliance. Therefore, to reduce the amount of trading and therefore trading costs, it may be advantageous to leave smaller components of the pipeline unhedged while ensuring the aggregate pipeline hedge complies with rebalancing limits.

Rather than a monthly update, in practice, these tables would be updated intraday to capture the changes in both the mortgage pipeline and the hedge position. Prudent risk management calls for identified rebalancing limits, which would signal a point at which the secondary market desk would buy or sell TBA to bring the overall long/short position within guidelines. A rebalancing threshold that is too small would result in excessive trading and associated trading costs. A threshold that is too large could lead to the realization of downside risk and an adverse impact to profitability. A rebalancing threshold of 5% would not be uncommon for a typical secondary market desk.

Summary

This case shows how banks and credit unions manage the pipeline of the mortgages they originate on an ongoing basis by transacting in TBA derivatives written on mortgage-backed securities. Thanks to these instruments, mortgage originators can protect against adverse market movements that may arise in the time lapse between the moment the mortgage loans are signed and executed, that is, between the lock and the funding. Risk can be offset by selling TBA contracts with maturities and coupons directionally consistent with the originated note rates.

The case illustrates how originators determine their hedge ratio and tune their implementation strategy depending on the changing conditions, notably the estimated pull-through rate of the mortgages in the pipe in the various stages of the validation process.

This case study serves as a practical guide for investors, in particular mortgage originators, seeking to navigate the complexities of integrating TBA derivatives into their mortgage pipeline management, providing practical insights.

19

Application of FX Options in Portfolio Management

Suprita Vohra

A critical risk associated with foreign investing and the pricing of international assets is foreign exchange (FX) risk. Portfolio managers operate in a multi-currency world where the portfolio often has currency exposure from international investments. Managers' behavior differs in how they measure and hedge currency exposures. Although the bulk of long-term, "real money" investors passively hedge their FX risk exposures, some actively seek to improve efficiency via dynamic hedging. Yet, others deal with FX as an asset class aiming to derive alpha returns by active allocation to FX trading. From a product perspective, most portfolio managers employ FX spot- and forward contracts as their primary hedging tools. Progressively, FX options provide portfolio managers with flexible risk/return profiles that are more likely to attain specific investment and behavioral objectives.

Here, we explore the use of FX options as a strategic tool for managing currency risks in portfolio management. As portfolios increasingly encompass international assets across multiple currencies, managing FX exposure becomes essential to protecting returns and achieving investment objectives. FX options offer flexibility and precision, allowing portfolio managers to address various risks associated with currency volatility while tailoring their hedging strategies to specific investment needs.

S. Vohra (✉)
Financial Professional Specializing in Foreign Exchange and Interest Rate Derivatives, Barclays, Singapore
e-mail: suprita.vohra@gmail.com

F. J. Fabozzi and M. de Jong (eds.), *Derivatives Applications in Asset Management*,
https://doi.org/10.1007/978-3-031-86354-7_19

The case begins by covering a few FX option concepts, in particular delta, volatility, and moneyness, which underpin FX options' pricing and risk assessment. (Further information about the mechanics of FX options is provided in Chapter 4). It then illustrates these principles through case studies, showing how FX options can enhance portfolio performance by mitigating FX risk in different market conditions. Examples such as hedging the internal rate of return in USD for foreign currency-denominated assets highlight how options like at-the-money (ATM) options, average rate options, and contingent options provide portfolio managers with versatile tools to manage and capitalize on currency exposures.

Additionally, we discuss advanced strategies like dynamic hedge ratio management and contingent FX options for cross-border investments and mergers, emphasizing the adaptability of FX options in meeting complex portfolio requirements. Together, these insights offer a comprehensive view of FX options as integral instruments for effective risk management in a globally diversified investment environment.

FX Option Basics

We first describe an option's delta, which is the starting point of any option pricing. The delta of an at-the-money FX forward option is approximately 50%. In interbank dealing, strike prices are often set to an exchange rate such that delta equals 25%. A 25-delta (denoted by 25d) call corresponds to a call option with a Black–Scholes delta of 0.25, and a 25-delta put corresponds to a put option with a Black–Scholes delta of -0.25. A property of delta, which makes it a convenient metric for moneyness, is the following: for a 25-delta call and a 25-delta put with the same maturity and the same implied volatility, the strike prices of the two options are an equal percentage distance from the current forward exchange rate.

Out-of-the-money (OTM) call options often have different implied volatilities from analogue OTM puts, suggesting that the market considers directional bias in exchange rates. The market refers to these phenomena as the "volatility smile" due to the characteristic shape of the implied volatilities plot of options with a given maturity against delta.

It is well known that FX markets exhibit several stylized characteristics, such as a forward premium bias, leptokurtosis, heteroscedasticity, autocorrelation, and mean-reversion. These characteristics play a role in the application of FX options in a portfolio context. For example, almost all major currencies

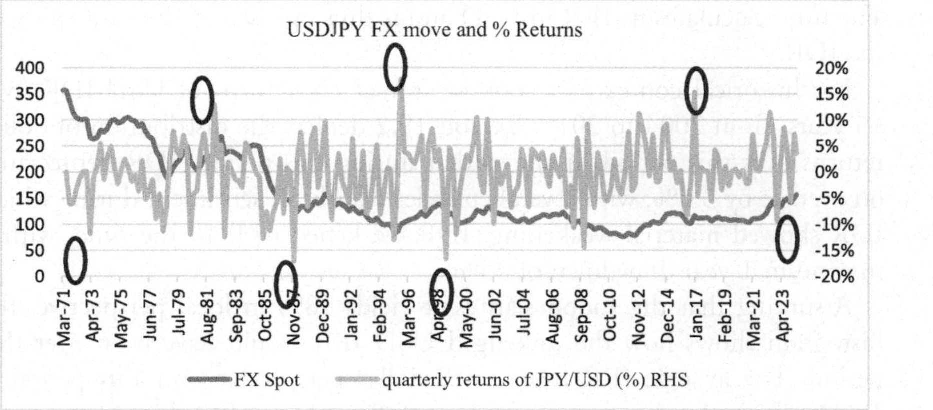

Exhibit 19.1 Jump behavior of FX: USD/JPY

are prone to jump risk (Exhibit 19.1). These are particularly evident during stress in financial markets, which is difficult to predict and model.

Such sharp FX moves can have a material impact on portfolio returns. Conventional wisdom would dictate hedging all the risks that are not core to the portfolio-stated strategy. If the investment mandate does not include generating returns from currency risks, then all such currency risks should be hedged away. However, in practice, that is rarely the case for various reasons. Besides, the decision-makers often exhibit heterogeneous behavior such as shortfall aversion, money illusion, and regret risk, among others, which are asymmetrical in nature. Hence, a hedging strategy needs to provide protection against risk stemming from those asymmetries that are detrimental to the objectives of the portfolio performance. Options have an asymmetric payoff and, hence, often suit such objectives.

Applications

In this section, we illustrate applications of FX options in a portfolio context.

Yield Protection Using FX Options

For a USD-denominated fund investing in a non-US asset, FX risks, if left unhedged, impact the yield, as quantified by the fund's Internal Rate of Return (IRR). In this case study, we have looked at the example of an investment made in an Indonesian asset denominated in IDR (Indonesian rupiah).

The fund calculates its IRR in USD and is thus exposed to the weakening of the IDR.

For historical context, we look at annual FX returns of USD-IDR over 15 years, from 2004 to 2019. Exhibit 19.2 depicts the distribution of dollar returns over this period. It shows that during this period, IDR depreciated on average by 3.6%, with several episodes of risk-off sentiment during which IDR showed material weakening. IDR weakened 67% of the time, with a maximum 1-year drawdown of 35%.

Assuming that the Indonesian asset yields 18% in local perspective, the histogram shows how the unhedged USD IRR would have been over this period. The average IRR from a US dollar perspective over this period is 14.8%, driven by significant periods of IDR weakness. In a third of the years, the USD IRR goes below 10% and even turns negative in 8% of the cases.

Assuming the entry USD-IDR rate is 14,100 Rupiahs to the dollar, Exhibit 19.3 depicts the impact on the yield in dollar perspective (USD IRR) at various FX spots. It only takes an IDR weakening of 2,550 Rupiahs for it to become negative. The FX impact is significant.

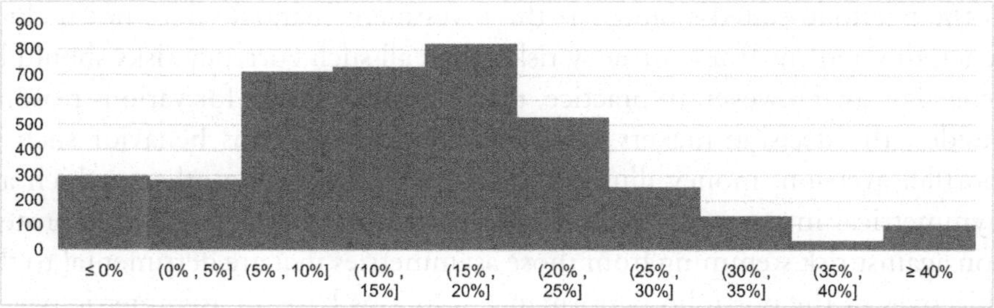

Exhibit 19.2 Historical simulation of USD IRR, 2004–2019

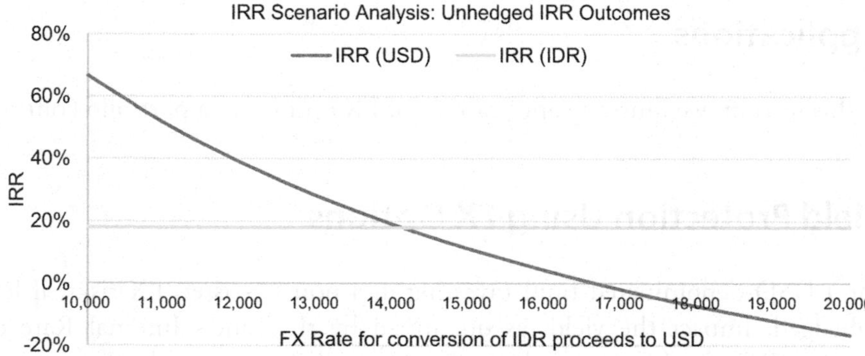

Exhibit 19.3 Unhedged IRR in dollar perspective across various FX Scenarios

For a shortfall-averse risk manager, this is a critical issue. The manager would want to protect, at a minimum, against the key reference point, below which the portfolio returns would be sub-optimal. This can be done via FX forwards, or FX options. In Exhibits 19.4, 19.5 and 19.6, we look at the effectiveness of both in the context of portfolio shortfall, all else equal. Exhibit 19.4 shows the impact of hedging the 1-year IRR through a 1-year FX forward. Tenor mismatches are assumed absent for this analysis to bring out the hedge instrument-specific features.

Hedging via an FX forward will lock in the effective USD IRR, so that no FX movement will impact the locked-in $IRR. However, a sunk cost is associated with this forward hedging, which is a result of the market implied interest rate differential. This cost immediately and adversely impacts the IRR, moving it from 18% in IDR terms to 12.9% in USD terms. If IDR were to stay stable or appreciate against USD, a forward hedge would not allow to benefit from that.

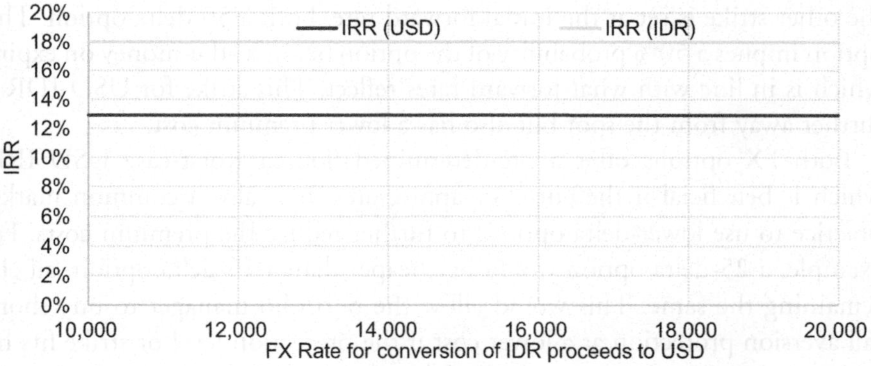

Exhibit 19.4 Hedged USD IRR using FX Forward

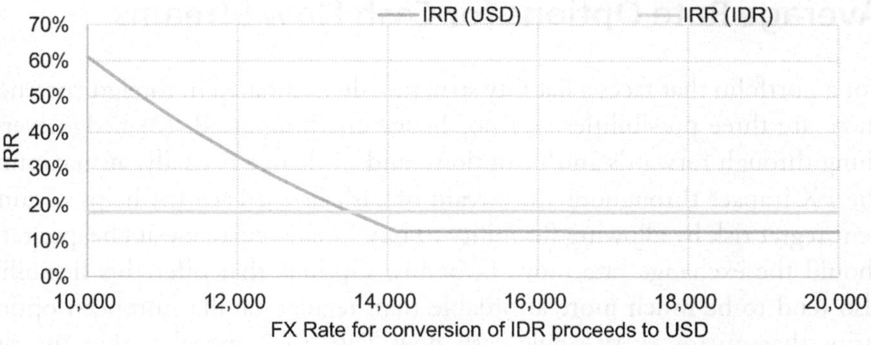

Exhibit 19.5 Hedged USD IRR using FX Option: Strike At-The-Money-Spot (ATMS)

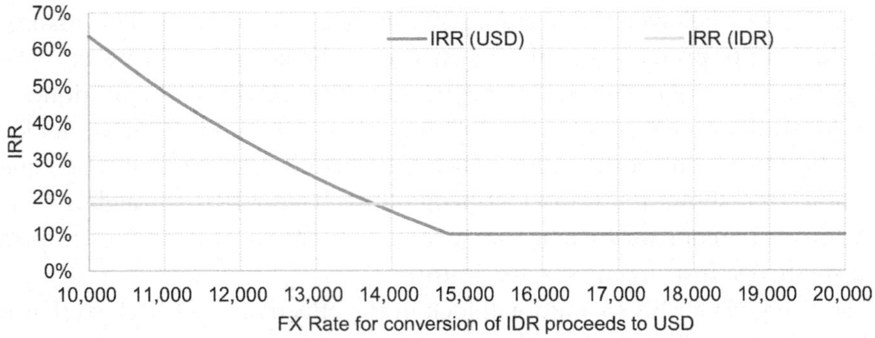

Exhibit 19.6 Hedged USD IRR using FX Option: Strike At-The-Money-Forward (ATMF)

Using FX options results in a non-linear IRR profile. Exhibits 19.5 and 19.6 show the impact on USD IRR when FX risk is hedged using a 1-year USD call IDR implemented with two different strikes. One strike is chosen to be at-the-money-spot or initial spot with a higher premium cost, while the other strike is set at the initial forward rate, both a 50-delta option. This option implies a 50% probability of the option being in-the-money on expiry, which is in line with what forward rates reflect. This strike for USD-IDR is further away from the spot but also has a lower premium cost.

Both FX options offer a pre-determined floored worst-case USD IRR, which is beneficial if the currency appreciates. It is also a common market practice to use lower-delta options to further reduce the premium costs. For example, a 25-delta option would be cheaper than a 50-delta option, all else remaining the same. This would allow the portfolio manager to buy shortfall aversion protection at a lower cost if the protection level or strike fits his hedging objectives.

Average Rate Options for Cash Flow Streams

For a portfolio that faces a liability structure denominated in foreign currency, there are three possibilities: (1) not hedge anything at all, (2) hedge everything through forwards and/or options, and (3) hedge partially, at maximum the FX impact throughout the stream of cash flows. Path (3) helps circumvent regret risk by allowing flexibility to buy foreign currency at cheaper rates should the exchange rate move favorably. Options that offer this flexibility also tend to be much more affordable than regular vanilla European option strips that mirror every single cash flow. Path (3)'s appeal is that the risk manager is often not interested in buying foreign currency at a specified level for each cash flow. The manager is more concerned about the overall costs of managing the liability payments and wishes to avoid costs exceeding a certain level.

One type of option that helps achieving path (3) is the average/Asian option, which payoffs are determined by certain averages of the underlying asset prices during a specified time period before the expiration date; they are also called average price or average rate options. A company can use Asian options to reduce its risk in buying foreign currency by buying a call whose payoff depends on the difference between the exercise price and the average exchange rate. If the average exchange rate increases, the company can get some compensation thanks to the option for the loss incurred in holding foreign currency.

An illustrative application of an Average Rate FX Option is as follows. An Average Rate Put protects against a sustained FX weakness over a period of time. Unlike vanilla puts, where the payoff depends on the final spot rate at maturity, here, the payoff is directly linked to the average spot rate. This is suitable when the need for protection is not for a specified date/tenor but lasts over a period of time. In periods when the expectations are a sustained weakness of emerging markets currencies such as IDR, an average rate option makes sense and is cost-effective by being materially cheaper than a vanilla option. Exhibit 19.7 gives indicative pricing. An average rate option may not pay off if the average spot rate over the tenor is below the strike. Hence, if IDR weakens only near the end of the tenor period for example, a vanilla option will capture that in the payoff, but an average rate option would not.

Similar to the previous example, an average rate FX option strike can be chosen to suit specific objectives. In the below example, a strike is selected for the IDR/USD rate at 20,000, but it can just as easily be a 25-delta strike or any other level, depending on the risk manager's view and cost budget.

1Y Option	Bought IDR Average Put Strikes (Absolute)	Final Fixing Rate determination	Cost (USD % upfront)
Average Rate IDR put	20,000	Average of weekly fixings starting from T+1w to T+1y	0.90%
Vanilla IDR Put	20,000	Final Fixing Rate Observed at T+1y	2.15%

Exhibit 19.7 Indicative Pricing of an Average Rate FX Option

Using Options as Insurance Strategies

Portfolio decisions are made using valuation models with several assumptions, under which those related to FX. For a multi-year investment, the model needs to estimate the returns under several FX outcomes. Usually, the returns are stress tested to be above hurdles for a reasonable weakening of the local currency, say 3–5% per annum. Hence, the underlying asset performance, and thus the IRR, is built to be resilient to ordinary fluctuations of the currency. If the currency weakens severely, then there are a few possible adverse outcomes. The underlying asset performance itself may weaken below its target local currency IRR. The portfolio may then have to support the asset through additional cash injections. This is particularly relevant for private equity funds where the underlying asset is an operating company. If the returns and valuations fall considerably, there is a substantial cost for the portfolio in managing that asset's risks. In that case, a hedge that possibly provides a pre-defined fixed payoff in USD is often helpful in managing the investment.

Exhibit 19.8 provides an example. A range of low-delta options are used for such type of insurance strategies with multiple cash injections. Chinese currency (CNH) 10-delta options are commonly seen in this context, and are relatively actively traded in the market.

This is a proxy hedge, that is, it assumes that a material weakening of the currency is associated with a material weakening of the underlying asset. There are plenty of real-life examples where this is often the case, but also plenty of exceptions. Hence, applying this kind of strategy is best suited after careful analysis of the underlying asset, the macroeconomics, and the fundamental drivers of the local currency.

Context	If net margins are at risk with CNH weakness, beyond say 10%
Solution	Buy an option that pays out a pre-determined gain if CNH weakens more than 10% in 1 year
Cost-Payout	10% (e.g., for a possible payout of $10 million, cost of this insurance option today is $1 million)
Reference:	Spot FX rate: 6.96 CNH/USD, 10% weakening implies 7.656 CNH/USD after 1 year

Exhibit 19.8 Using FX Option as Insurance: Illustrative example

Context	A USD Portfolio needs FX tail protection beyond 10% CNH weakness
Solution	Buy a CNH put USD call for 6 months with Strike 10% above spot
Contingent Feature	If CNH materially appreciates instead, no premium is payable, option lapses
Contingent Premium	0.75%, which is payable only if CNH is above 6.80 at maturity
Reference:	Spot FX Rate: 7.09 CNH/USD, 10% weakening implies 7.80 CNH/USD after 6 months

Exhibit 19.9 Using FX Option as Contingent Insurance: Illustrative example

Paying for Insurance When Needed

Risk managers must balance the cost of paying for every event risk against the cost of doing so. As a result, they would behaviorally avoid options that are expensive or have a high upfront cost. A contingent premium allows the premium to be payable only if a pre-defined event occurs. Exhibit 19.9 offers an illustrative example of how such a contingent insurance FX option would work.

The economic rationale is that a material CNH strength move would not require the hedge; hence, a refund of the premium reduces the hedge's regret risk.

The risk manager can also use compound options, which are options written on other standard options. As a result, a compound option has two expiration dates and two strike prices. Compound options are often used to hedge complex investments contingents on other conditions. The buyer of a compound option normally pays an initial upfront premium for an option they may need later. The buyer will only have to pay an additional premium if this option is needed. If the buyer finds this option unnecessary, the buyer can simply give up the right.

Monetize Indifference Utility Between Currencies

Internationally invested portfolios are liable to have multiple currency exposures. These exposures can arise from cross-border investments, cash holdings in multiple currencies, or financing at the portfolio level in multiple currencies.

There appears to be considerable heterogeneity in hedging behavior when managing multiple currency exposures. Popular frameworks are (1) a full hedge, leaving no portfolio holding unhedged, (2) a hedging program that includes basket hedging or dynamic hedging through optimization tools, or (3) no hedge, in the view, often rightly so, that several currency exposures in different directions and quantities lead to a well-diversified portfolio in terms of currency risks. In the latter approach, any one currency is deemed unlikely to adversely impact the overall portfolio. Depending on the risk manager and portfolio composition, each of the above strategies has its merits and demerits. A detailed discussion of that is outside the scope of this case study. However, highlighting some of the monetizing opportunities that arise from such hedging frameworks is worthwhile.

For example, a portfolio may contain cash holdings in two or three currencies for various reasons (e.g., operational ease, legacy reasons, cross-border controls). The risk manager may need to keep a certain minimum portion in each currency (say 25% in each of two currencies, euro (EUR) and Swiss franc (CHF) for example). Beyond that, the manager may be indifferent to holding the cash in ratios of 50% each or 25%/75% or 75%/25%, etc. This is an example of inherent portfolio optionality. An indifference option can monetize this optionality to generate additional yields on the cash. In return, the cash holdings either stay the same or change to reflect a higher weight in the weaker currency. This is done via an FX option on EUR/CHF, with illustrative pricing, shown in Exhibit 19.10.

Exhibit 19.10 illustrates how selling an option can serve investor objectives with inherent optionality. In this example, the intrinsic optionality is the investor's neutral preference between holding cash in EUR vs CHF within a range of 25% and 75%. If the starting point of the cash holding is 50% CHF and 50% EUR, then including this option allows the investor to enhance overall cash yield by monetizing this neutral preference by selling the above EURCHF FX option. The EUR notional for this FX option equals 25% of the overall cash holding.

Upon expiry, if on one hand the option gets exercised, the investor will have cash in 75% CHF and 25% EUR. On the other hand, if the option

Context	Client has cash balances in EUR, CHF
Solution	Sell a EUR call /CHF put for 1Y with Strike = Spot
Payoff	If EUR appreciates, client gets the EUR converted into CHF at the strike
Premium	1.75% p.a which adds to the low/negative yield of the cash balance
Consideration	The excess yield comes at a price of giving up the appreciating currency. However, this is mitigated if the treasurer is indifferent between the two currencies (i.e., is not getting the benefit of holding an appreciating currency). Furthermore, the strike can be chosen such that the yield benefit is higher than the forecasted appreciation of the sold currency. In this example, if EUR appreciates less than 1.75% in the year, this trade overall improves the return for the cash.

Exhibit 19.10 Indifference FX Option: EUR/CHF

lapses, then the previous cash holding stays the same, i.e., 50% CHF and 50% EUR. In return, the investor earns the option premium of 1.75% p.a. on the EUR notional, adding to the overall yield. The risk, of course, is if EUR appreciates materially. In that instance, the investor gets converted into holding a greater portion of cash in CHF, which is the weaker currency compared to EUR. The investor may be comfortable with this risk given the neutral preference mentioned above; however, often a sustained structural weakness of a currency can lead to a change in such a preference. Hence, using this strategy of enhancing yield using sold FX options should be carefully assessed in terms of suitability to long-term portfolio objectives.

Using FX Options to Hedge Contingent Risks

Asset managers can make investments by buying a stake in a company. For cross-border mergers and acquisitions (M&A) transactions, a US asset manager may invest from the portfolio's USD fund into an M&A in another currency (e.g., JPY, EUR). In such transactions, there is a timeline from the signing of the M&A agreement till the closing of the deal when the FX conversion is needed to settle the investment purchase. However, the FX rate is often locked in at the time of signing. The sign-to-close period can often be as long as 6–12 months, during which the purchaser is vulnerable to adverse FX moves.

Additionally, the probability of successfully completing the M&A deal is rarely 100%, as an M&A agreement is subject to several completion conditions, which, if not met, would result in an unsuccessful deal. These closing conditions can range from regulatory approvals to material adverse change clauses, breach of warranties, other termination rights, or an interloper coming in with a counterbid.

Traditional solutions such as FX forwards are ill-equipped to be effective risk hedges in such situations. Hence, a deal-contingent FX hedge is the preferred instrument to manage these "M&A closing"-linked FX risks. As the name suggests, the key feature of this hedge is that it exists if the exposure materializes (M&A successfully closes) and falls away if the exposure does not materialize (M&A is unsuccessful).

A deal-contingent FX solution combines FX forward plus a cancellation option. All other features are known on day 1: the tenor, notional, hedge rate, etc. This provides the acquirer with certainty about the USD value of the investment at the closing date.

Context	US Corporate making an acquisition in Australia, deal is being funded by USD
Solution	Sell USD buy AUD aligned with M&A dates, contingent on deal closing
Payoff	US Acquiror has a known upfront FX rate for conversion of USD into AUD
Price	Deal Contingent Pricing is the FX Forward rate adjusted for the completion risk premium

Exhibit 19.11 Deal-Contingent FX Hedge for Event Risks: M&A as an Example

Contingent hedges have historically been used to manage FX and interest rate risks in M&A transactions. In recent years, they have also expanded to hedge a range of other underlying deals, including infrastructure and project finance deals, IPOs, and take-privates. Exhibit 19.11 offers an example application of such a solution in the M&A context.

The above exhibit shows a real-world application of how a deal-contingent works. Consider an M&A situation where a US corporate is acquiring an Australian asset. Such M&A deals are contracted using a "Sale and Purchase Agreement" or SPA. The SPA is usually inked in terms of the currency of the asset being bought. There are sometimes exceptions, but the predominant practice is for the acquirer to pay the seller in a currency that is native to the seller. In this illustration, that currency is Australian dollar (AUD). Hence, the purchase price in the SPA would likely be contracted in AUD at the time of signing.

For the US acquirer, this results in an FX exposure, especially if USD funds are used for this acquisition. This FX rate is typically referenced as the rate prevailing at the time of signing. As explained above, there is usually a time lag between signing (when the FX rate is determined) and closing (when the purchase consideration is actually settled). If AUD appreciates between signing and closing, the US acquirer would have to arrange for more USD funding on the closing date for the same AUD consideration. This can be a material FX risk for large M&A transactions, which often run into billions of dollars. Thus, there is a keen desire to manage and mitigate this risk. A deal-contingent FX hedge would allow the US acquirer to lock in a pre-determined FX rate of USD per AUD at the time of signing. This FX rate is then used to settle funds at the time of closing, giving the acquirer certainty of USD funds needed at the time of settlement.

This hedge is different from a simple FX forward because an FX forward is a contractual obligation without condition, while a deal-contingent FX forward is a contractual obligation with conditionality on the M&A deal closing. For any pre-specified reasons (such as regulatory approvals, shareholder approvals, counter bidder offer, etc.), if the underlying M&A deal does not close by its end date, then the deal-contingent FX hedge also ceases to exist and is not longer a contractual obligation for the acquirer to settle. This is very helpful as it matches the FX hedge to the FX exposure.

Since the FX exposure is contingent and conditional, it makes sense for the FX hedge to be also contingent and conditional. This is a popular tool in several cross-border M&A transactions. A key question is how banks price and risk manage such a conditionality, which can rely on several factors that are not directly hedgeable in the market. M&A transactions that are contingent on shareholder approvals may succeed or fail depending on how shareholders assess the price, the new ownership, the future proposed strategy, etc. These factors make it hard to quantify the risk, and hence, the probability of deal closing. This is an important risk consideration that is undertaken by experts within the banks that are well-versed across both M&A transactions and incorporate those risks into FX pricing. An extensive assessment includes a historical track record of approvals needed for the M&A transaction, specifics of the M&A deal, termination rights, and so on. A detailed description of this pricing is out of the scope for this paper but worth noting that this is a growing space of application of FX hedging.

Using FX Options to Run a Flexible Hedge Ratio Program

Asset managers and corporate treasurers run a hedge policy driven by a few key parameters: hedge ratio, hedge tenor, nature of underlying exposure, and use of various hedging products. The hedge ratio parameter is key and is often defined as a band (e.g., 70–90%, 50–75%). These bands act as guardrails for the risk hedger to achieve a minimum hedge ratio while using discretion within the band. This discretion is helpful when opportunistically targeting market views, trends, or target levels. Often, these hedge ratio bands vary by tenor. As the certainty of exposure is highest in near term, the shorter tenor hedge ratios tend to be higher than those of longer tenors. Covered options are a good way to monetize the latent optionality inherent within these hedge bands.

An illustrative example is shown in Exhibit 19.12. We take the case of a US asset manager who needs to hedge their INR exposure in a portfolio. The exposure is multi-year, due to long-term investments yielding dividends and interest income in the local currency. An illustrative target hedge ratio ladder would look like Exhibit 19.13, with a hedge ratio band of minimum and maximum thresholds, which move lower as we go further out in tenor. The asset manager can use forwards to hedge the minimum threshold. Beyond this, the asset manager has flexibility. The asset manager can choose not to hedge any further, especially if the view is that INR may strengthen and wishes that the exposure benefits from that.

Alternatively, if the portfolio manager does not have a strong view, selling covered options to take advantage of the hedge ratio band flexibility can be selected. The covered options could be selling USD put INR calls, with tenor and strikes customized to suit specific targets and objectives. The strike of the options is often lower than current market levels, such that if they get exercised, the portfolio benefits from an average lower FX rate of hedging while getting close to the upper hedge ratio band. The portfolio also earns a premium by selling such options. The portfolio manager is at the maximum hedge ratio threshold if all the options are exercised. Exhibit 19.13 illustrates the evolution of this strategy across various scenarios.

In this illustration, FX options are used to opportunistically increase hedge ratios if the FX rates move lower while also generating premium earnings, which can be attractive offsets to hedging costs elsewhere. The target hedge ratios are defined as a minimum–maximum band in a reducing trajectory to reflect the higher certainty of exposures in the near term. This reflects prevalent practice where for FX exposures in the 3–6 months tenor, target hedge ratios are high in the 75–100% range. In the 1Y tenor, it can often be lower, such as the 50–75% range in the above example, and going further

Context	US asset manager hedging INR exposure out to five years. Target hedge ratios as given in Exhibit 13.
Solution	Hedger sells INR buys USD forwards to satisfy the minimum hedge ratio bank level and sells covered options (USD puts) with strike at target levels.
Payoff	The hedge ratios will move higher if markets move through the asset manager's target levels and the options are exercised.
Price	Receive premium from selling covered options.

Exhibit 19.12 Dynamic Hedge Ratio management using FX options

Hedge Ratio / Tenor	3m	6m	1y	2y	5y
Min Target	75%	75%	50%	25%	25%
Max Target	100%	90%	75%	50%	40%
Forwards used to achieve min	75%	75%	50%	25%	25%
Covered options for incremental	25%	15%	25%	25%	15%
Hedge Ratio if options not exercised	75%	75%	50%	25%	25%
Hedge Ratio if options exercised	100%	90%	75%	50%	40%

Exhibit 19.13 Target Hedge Ratio for INR-USD exposures: An example

lower in the 2Y and 5Y tenors. This kind of ladder can take on multiple variations, differing by currency as well as nature of exposures. Since the minimum target hedge ratio is efficiently achievable using FX forwards, the above example uses INR/USD FX forwards to obtain that. The risk manager can then opportunistically sell covered options in the form of USD put INR calls across tenors and strikes to manage the hedge ratio to stay within the upper maximum band. There is a wide range of strikes possible for such options. The choice of appropriate strike depends on the risk manager's view on INR/USD, their ability to use FX options within their mandate of eligible products, and the target average hedge rate that they wish to achieve for their hedging.

Summary

This case delves into the strategic use of FX options in managing currency risks within portfolio management, especially in multi-currency investment contexts. It begins by emphasizing the importance of FX options in mitigating the impact of FX fluctuations on international investments, detailing key option concepts like delta, volatility, and moneyness. These elements form the basis for constructing volatility profiles, which allow portfolio managers to tailor their risk exposures based on market movements and hedge against adverse currency shifts. Through these tools, managers can effectively price and manage FX options, accounting for market nuances like the volatility smile.

Several case studies are provided to illustrate the practical application of FX options. One case explores hedging techniques for a US dollar portfolio investing in foreign assets, in particular one denominated in Indonesian Rupiah. It compares different hedging tools, including FX forwards, at-the-money FX options, and average rate (Asian) options. It highlights how each approach impacts the internal rate of return depending on currency movements. Overall, the cases underscore the need for portfolio managers to balance risk mitigation with cost-effectiveness, such as using average rate options when sustained currency weakness is anticipated, as they are generally more cost-efficient than standard options.

The case studies also discuss some advanced strategies like using contingent FX options for M&A purposes and other cross-border transactions, which only activate if the currency exposure materializes, offering cost-efficient protection. Additionally, the cases introduce a dynamic hedge ratio management, where managers can adjust hedge ratios based on target levels and market views by selling covered options within preset threshold bands. This flexibility enables portfolio managers to monetize currency exposures effectively, adapt to market conditions, and maintain optimal hedge ratios, making FX options an integral part of a sophisticated risk management strategy in global portfolios.

20

FX Forward Contracts for Portfolio Management Applications

Redouane Elkamhi, Jacky S. H. Lee, and Marco Salerno

This case demonstrates the use of foreign exchange (FX) forward contracts for managing the currency risks that institutional portfolios face. These derivative instruments offer tools for mitigating the impact of fluctuating currency rates on international investments, allowing portfolio managers to hedge against potentially adverse currency movements that could affect investment returns. For example, a portfolio holding European stocks but based in the United States could suffer currency losses if the euro depreciates against the dollar. Through FX forwards, a portfolio manager can lock in today's exchange rate for a future transaction, ensuring that the portfolio value remains stable despite changes in the exchange rate.

R. Elkamhi
Rotman School of Management, University of Toronto, Toronto, ON, Canada

J. S. H. Lee (✉)
Total Portfolio Group at Healthcare of Ontario Pension Plan (HOOPP), Toronto, ON, Canada
e-mail: jlee5@hoopp.com

M. Salerno
Abu Dhabi Investment Authority, Abu Dhabi, UAE

F. J. Fabozzi and M. de Jong (eds.), *Derivatives Applications in Asset Management*,
https://doi.org/10.1007/978-3-031-86354-7_20

Use of FX Forward Contracts

A portfolio manager can use FX forward contracts in various ways. Let's start with a description of FX forward contracts.

When managing a portfolio's FX exposure, the primary objective is reducing the potential risk of currency fluctuations. This goal is particularly crucial for portfolios containing international investments because changes in currency values can significantly impact overall returns. One effective strategy for mitigating currency-related risks in a portfolio with substantial foreign currency exposure is to utilize FX forwards.

For instance, consider a scenario where a pension fund manager must oversee a portfolio's FX exposure to align it with a specific investment objective. In an environment where the home currency is expected to experience significant fluctuations against foreign currencies, effectively managing this exposure becomes paramount.

A Simple Example of Currency Risk Management with FX Forwards

Let's look at a simple illustration before we move on to a more detailed case. Suppose a US-based portfolio manager is overseeing a portfolio with substantial investments in European assets, creating exposure to the euro (EUR) against the US dollar (USD). Further, assume that on a specific date, the portfolio's value in USD equivalent is \$10 million. The portfolio's current FX exposure is significant due to its holdings in euro-denominated assets.

Now, assume that the manager is seeking to hedge against fluctuations in the exchange rate between the euro and the US dollar. To achieve this, the portfolio manager decides to hedge 50% of the portfolio's euro exposure using FX forwards and assume the following:

- *Current portfolio exposure (priced in USD) in the currency EUR*: Denote the current portfolio exposure to assets denominated in EUR as P_{EUR}. When priced in US dollars, the portfolio value P_{EUR} is \$10 million (USD equivalent).
- *Percentage of exposure to hedge*: Denoted as H, in this case, 50%.
- *Amount to hedge*: This is the amount of exposure in euros the manager wants to hedge, which would be $P_{EUR} \times H = \$10 \text{ million} \times 50\% = \$5$ million (USD).

- *Agreed rate in FX forward contract (EUR/USD)*: Assume that the agreed rate for the FX forward, denoted as, is 1.20 EUR/USD. That is, 1 EUR can be exchanged for 1.20 USD.
- *Equivalent amount in euros to be hedged*: This is the amount in euros corresponding to the USD amount being hedged. This would be 5 *million USD*/1.20 = 4.17 million (EUR).
- *Maturity of the contract:* For simplicity, assume a 6-month maturity.
- *Contract execution.* The manager enters into an FX forward contract to sell 4.17 million in euros for 5 million in US dollars (effectively at the rate of 1.20 EUR/USD), to be executed in 6 months. This contract guarantees that regardless of future EUR/USD exchange rate fluctuations, the manager will exchange 4.17 million in euros for US dollars at the agreed rate, thereby mitigating the risk of euros depreciation against the US dollar for the hedged portion of the portfolio.

Controlling FX exposure through FX forwards allows portfolio managers to manage the impact of currency fluctuations on their investments strategically. By locking in exchange rates for future dates, managers can more accurately forecast and mitigate potential risks associated with currency movements, ensuring that the portfolio's performance aligns more closely with its intended investment objectives.

Controlling the FX Exposure of a Portfolio: A Real-Life Illustration

In this example, we explore the management of FX exposure in an international equity portfolio. The portfolio's net asset value (NAV) at time 0 is $1 million US dollars and is exposed to international equities across various regions. The portfolio in our illustration includes the following:

- The Standard & Poor's 500 (S&P 500) is a capitalization-weighted stock market index that measures the performance of 500 of the largest publicly traded companies in the United States.
- The Euro STOXX 50 is a stock market index representing 50 large European companies (based on market capitalization) that operate in the Eurozone.

- The Financial Times-Stock Exchange 100 Share Index (FTSE 100) is a U.K. stock market index that represents the 100 largest publicly traded companies on the London Stock Exchange, ranked by market capitalization.
- The S&P/TSX Composite is a capitalization-weighted index designed to measure the market activity of stocks listed on the Toronto Stock Exchange (TSX).
- The Tokyo Stock Price Index (TOPIX) is a capitalization-weighted index of all companies listed on the First Section of the Tokyo Stock Exchange.
- The S&P/ASX 200 measures the performance of the 200 largest index-eligible stocks listed on the Australian Securities Exchange (ASX) by market capitalization.

The composition of the portfolio is as follows:

	S&P 500	EURO STOXX 50	FTSE 100	S&P/TSX Composite	TOPIX	S&P/ASX 200
Portfolio weights	50%	10%	10%	10%	10%	10%

At the initial assessment (Time 0), the US dollar amount allocated to each segment of the portfolio is based on the weights above. For example, the S&P 500, with a 50% weight, allocates $500,000 in USD. Similarly, each of the other indices allocates $100,000 in USD, making up the remaining 50% of the portfolio. These exposures are acquired through purchases of exchange-traded funds (ETFs). These ETFs are traded in their local currencies: S&P 500 in US dollars, EURO STOXX 50 in euros, FTSE 100 in British pound sterling (GBP), S&P/TSX Composite in Canadian dollar (CAD), TOPIX in Japanese yen (JPY), and S&P/ASX 200 in Australian dollars (AUD).

Changes occur in the ETF prices and the FX spot rates between time 0 and time 1 (i.e., 1 month). These changes affect the value of the portfolio's international components. The ETF prices at both times, alongside the FX spot rates, are critical for assessing the portfolio's performance and its exposure to currency risk.

Portfolio Performance When Currencies are Unhedged

Let's first look at the portfolio's performance when currencies are unhedged. Consider the following ETF prices and FX spot rates shown in Exhibit 20.1.

	ETF Prices		FX Spot Rates		
	Time 0	Time 1	FX Spot (1 USD to)	Time 0	Time 1
S&P 500	$458.08	$450.63	EUR	0.9093	0.9223
EURO STOXX 50	44.81 €	43.15 €	GBP	0.7791	0.7891
FTSE 100	£742.93	£724.73	CAD	1.319	1.3508
S&P/TSX Composite	CAD $32.57	CAD $32.12	JPY	142.29	145.54
TOPIX	¥2,376	¥2,384	AUD	1.4888	1.5423
S&P/ASX 200	AUD $29.39	AUD $29.16			

Exhibit 20.1 ETF prices and FX spot rates

The amount in local currency and the number of shares of each ETF are calculated based on the time 0 prices and FX spot rates. In this example, we allow for fractional shares. The number of shares is determined by dividing the dollar amount in local currency by the ETF price at time 0. Exhibit 20.2 shows a detailed breakdown of these values.

Suppose the manager does not hedge the FX exposure of the portfolio. In that case, the profit and loss (P&L) will be influenced by the changes in the local values of the equity indices and the movements due to changes in FX rates. To understand the impact of these components, we can examine the portfolio's value at time 1. Exhibit 20.3 shows the portfolio breakdown at time 1. Here is how the values in the Exhibit 20.3 are determined:

Column 2: *Local Amount*: This column shows the value of each investment at time 1 in its local currency. It reflects the change in the equity index value only. For example, the value of an investment in the S&P 500 is $491,868.23, the value of an investment in the FTSE 100 is £76,001.39, etc.

Column 3: *USD Amount* (*time 1 FX spot*): This column presents the value of each investment converted to US dollars at the FX spot rate at time 1. It includes both the change in equity value and the impact of FX rate changes. For example, the value of the investment in the FTSE 100 is $96,314.02, which is equal to the value of the investment in GBP at time 1 (£76,001.39, shown in column 2) divided by the FX sport rate at time 1 (0.7891 GBP for 1 US dollar).

Index	USD Amount	Local Amount	Shares
S&P 500	$500,000	$500,000.00	1,091.51
EURO STOXX 50	$100,000	90,930.00 €	2,029.23
FTSE 100	$100,000	£77,910.00	104.87
S&P/TSX Composite	$100,000	CAD $131,900.00	4,049.74
TOPIX	$100,000	¥14,229,000	5,988.64
S&P/ASX 200	$100,000	AUD $148,880.00	5,065.67
Portfolio	**$1,000,000**		

Exhibit 20.2 Portfolio composition at Time 0

Column 4: *USD Amount* (*time 0 FX spot*): The value of each investment is converted to US dollars using the FX spot rate at time 0 in this column. This isolates the effect of the equity index value change, excluding FX rate fluctuations. For example, the value of the investment in the FTSE 100 is $97,550.24, which is equal to the value of the investment in GBP at time 1 (£76,001.39, shown in column 2) divided by the FX sport rate at time 0 (0.7791 GBP for 1 US dollar).
Column 5: *USD Amount* (*FX change only*): This column shows the value of the initial investment converted to USD using the time 1 FX rate. It highlights the impact on the portfolio if only the FX rates had changed, while keeping the equity values constant. For example, the value of the investment in the FTSE 100 is $98,732.73, which is equal to the value of the investment in GBP at time 0 (£77,910.00) divided by the FX sport rate at time 1 (0.7891 GBP for 1 US dollar).

Exhibit 20.4 provides a comprehensive performance analysis, factoring in both local equity movements and FX rate fluctuations. This analysis is crucial for understanding how different components contribute to the overall P&L of the portfolio. The exhibit presents the following measures:

Column 2: *P&L* (*FX & Local*): This P&L, measured in US dollars, represents the total unhedged profit and loss. It reflects the combined effects of changes in the local ETF prices and FX movements. This component indicates a total loss of −$26,711.02, translating into a −2.67% decline of the portfolio's NAV in US dollars.
Column 3: *P&L* (*Local*): This P&L, measured in US dollars, isolates the profit and loss arising solely from local ETF price movements, assuming that the FX rate is unchanged. This part of the analysis reveals that a large component of the losses, amounting to −$16,113.58 or −1.61%, are attributed to local market movements rather than FX fluctuations.

(1) Investment	(2) Local Amount	(3) USD Amount (time 1 FX spot)	(4) USD Amount (time 0 FX spot)	(5) USD Amount (FX change only)
S&P 500	$491,868.23	$491,868.23	$491,868.23	$500,000.00
EURO STOXX 50	87,561.47 €	$94,938.17	$96,295.47	$98,590.48
FTSE 100	£76,001.39	$96,314.02	$97,550.24	$98,732.73
S&P/TSX Composite	CAD $130,077.62	$96,296.73	$98,618.36	$97,645.84
TOPIX	¥14,276,909	$98,096.12	$100,336.70	$97,766.94
S&P/ASX 200	AUD $147,714.90	$95,775.72	$99,217.42	$96,531.15
Portfolio		**$973,288.98**	**$983,886.42**	**$989,267.15**

Exhibit 20.3 Portfolio Breakdown at Time 1

(1) Investment	(2) P&L (FX & Local)	(3) P&L (Local)	(4) P&L (FX)	(5) Interaction term
S&P 500	-$8,131.77	-$8,131.77	$0.00	$0.00
EURO STOXX 50	-$5,061.83	-$3,704.53	-$1,409.52	$52.22
FTSE 100	-$3,685.98	-$2,449.76	-$1,267.27	$31.04
S&P/TSX Composite	-$3,703.27	-$1,381.64	-$2,354.16	$32.53
TOPIX	-$1,903.88	$336.70	-$2,233.06	-$7.52
S&P/ASX 200	-$4,224.28	-$782.58	-$3,468.85	$27.15
Portfolio	**-$26,711.02**	**-$16,113.58**	**-$10,732.85**	**$135.41**
Portfolio in %	**-2.67%**	**-1.61%**	**-1.07%**	**0.01%**

Exhibit 20.4 P&L Breakdown (all figures in USD)

Column 4: *P&L* (*FX*): This P&L, measured in US dollars, specifically represents the loss attributable to changes in FX rates only, which for this portfolio amounts to −$10,732.85, contributing to a −1.07% decline.
Column 5: *Interaction Term*[1]: This term captures the interaction effect between local equity movements and FX rate changes. The overall interaction effect is relatively small ($135.41 or 0.01%), indicating that the combined impact of equity and FX changes does not significantly deviate from their individual effects. The interaction term is computed as the P&L (FX & Local) minus P&L (Local) minus P&L (FX).

The P&L for S&P 500 is entirely due to local market movements, as indicated by the value of zero for FX P&L. For EURO STOXX 50, FTSE 100, S&P/TSX Composite, and S&P/ASX 200, losses are a combination of local market and FX rate changes, with the FX P&L contributing significantly to the total loss. The TOPIX is different because it shows a positive Local P&L in US dollars, but this gain is more than offset by FX losses.

The row "Portfolio in %" shows the percentage change concerning the portfolio value at time 0 (i.e., $1,000,000). The P&L if the portfolio was not hedged (FX and Local P&L) shows that the return would have been −2.67%. Without FX risk (i.e., FX rates held constant), the P&L would have been −1.61%.

[1] This term is referred to as the "cross-product" in Gary P. Brinson and Nimrod Fachler, "Measuring Non-US Equity Portfolio Performance," *Financial Analysts Journal*, 42(4), 1985, pp. 73–76. However, we prefer to use "Interaction term," as it is more commonly used today.

Portfolio Performance When Currencies are Hedged

In our illustration, the portfolio manager can use FX forwards to effectively manage the FX risk inherent in the international equity portfolio. At time 0, the manager can use FX forward contracts with a 1-month maturity, aligning with the timeframe of the analysis (maturing at time 1). These contracts allow for locking in exchange rates at a future date, providing a hedge against potential adverse movements in currency values.

Suppose that the portfolio manager observes the following forward rates with a 1-month maturity in Exhibit 20.5.[2]

The hedging strategy involves entering into forward contracts for each currency in the portfolio, corresponding to the portfolio's exposure to that currency. The objective is to mitigate the risk of currency depreciation against the US dollar. The forward rate essentially "locks in" the exchange rate for the amount of foreign currency exposure at time 0, which will be converted back to US dollars at time 1.

Exhibit 20.6 illustrates the results of hedging the FX exposure of an international equity portfolio using FX forwards. The hedging is executed for all components of the portfolio except the S&P 500, which is denominated in US dollars and, therefore, does not require FX hedging. Below we break down the exhibit to understand the results:

> Column 2: *Foreign Currency sold forward at Time 0, due in 1 month.* This column displays the leg of the FX forward that pertains to the foreign (local) currency. The unhedged portfolio has a "long exposure" to various local currencies. For an investor using the US dollar as their base currency, having a "long" exposure in currency X implies that the investor realizes gains when currency X strengthens against the US dollar. Conversely, the investor experiences losses

FX Forward (1 USD to)	Time 0
EUR	0.9079
GBP	0.7790
CAD	1.3184
JPY	141.5451
AUD	1.4870

Exhibit 20.5 FX Forward Rates (1-month)

[2] FX Forward rates for this example are sourced from Bloomberg and they are determined using the arbitrage-free price relationship between interest rates of the two currencies and the current spot rate. For example, for the forward rates on EUR/USD, the Bloomberg ticker "EUR1M BGN Curncy" was used.

when currency X depreciates against the US dollar. To hedge these exposures to local currencies, the portfolio manager entered into a forward contract that is short the local currency and is long US dollar.[3] In other words, the portfolio manager sold the local currencies in the FX forward contracts to lock in the FX rates. For example, the FX forward contract to hedge the currency exposure of EURO STOXX 50 requires the portfolio manager to sell 90,930.00 € of Euros for $100,154.20 US dollar, due in 1 month.

Column 3: *USD brought forward at Time 0, due in 1 month.* This column displays the leg of the FX forward that pertains to the US currency. Essentially, this amount is the predetermined value for the foreign currency converted back to US dollars using the forward FX rate, effectively "locking in" this rate through the forward contract. For example, for the EUR currency hedge position, the 90,930.00 € euros divided by the forward FX rate of 0.9079 yields the forward US dollar amount of $100,154.20.

Column 4: *Cost of Foreign Currency at Time 1, in the spot market*: This column represents, at Time 1, the value of the foreign currency that is sold with the FX forward in the spot FX market. At maturity, given the properties of forward contracts, the FX forward rate is equal to the FX spot rate.

Column 5: *FX Forward P&L*: The profit or loss for the FX forward, calculated as the difference between the values of the foreign currency sold forward at Time 0, due in 1 month, and spot FX rate observed at Time 1. A positive value indicates a gain from hedging. The FX forward on euro shows a gain of $1,563.72 from hedging. Theoretically, the P&L comes from the fact that the counterparty of the FX forward contract pays the portfolio manager the agreed-upon USD amount for the foreign currency. Simultaneously, the portfolio manager purchases the required amount of foreign currency with US dollars in the spot FX market and delivers the foreign currency to the counterparty. The difference in the US dollar amounts is the P&L. For example, the counterparty pays the portfolio manager $100,154.20 USD for 90,930.00 EUR. The portfolio manager buys 90,930.00 EUR using only $98,590.48 USD. Since the portfolio manager uses fewer funds to buy the EUR than received from the counterparty, the profit of this transaction is $1,563.72 in USD.

Column 6: *Slippage*: This is the sum of the FX Forward P&L shown in Exhibit 20.6 and the P&L (FX) shown in Exhibit 20.4. This represents the P&L due to the forward rate shown in Exhibit 20.5 being different from the spot rate

[3] A FX forward contract has two legs: the short leg indicates the currency with a short position (i.e., negative exposure) and the long leg indicates the currency with a long position (i.e., positive exposure). For example, consider a portfolio manager that enters into an FX forward contract that is long US dollar and short Euro. Such FX forward will generate profits for the portfolio manager when the US dollar appreciates (i.e., when the Euro depreciates). On the other hand, this FX forward will generate losses for the portfolio manager when the US dollar depreciates (i.e., when the Euro appreciates).

(1) Currency	(2) Foreign Currency sold forward at Time 0, due in 1 month	(3) USD brought forward at Time 0, due in 1 month	(4) Cost of Foreign Currency at Time 1, in the spot market	(5) FX Forward P&L	(6) Slippage
EUR	€-90,930.00	$100,154.20	-$98,590.48	$1,563.72	$154.20
GBP	-£77,910	$100,012.84	-$98,732.73	$1,280.10	$12.84
CAD	-CAD $131,900	$100,045.51	-$97,645.84	$2,399.67	$45.51
JPY	-¥14,229,000	$100,526.26	-$97,766.94	$2,759.33	$526.26
AUD	-AUD $148,880	$100,121.05	-$96,531.15	$3,589.89	$121.05
Total		**$500,859.86**	**-$489,267.15**	**$11,592.72**	**$859.86**
Total in %				**1.16%**	**0.09%**

Exhibit 20.6 FX Hedges (all figures in USD)

at Time 0 shown in Exhibit 20.1. For the FX Forward on EUR, slippage is $154.20.

Overall, Exhibit 20.6 shows that the portfolio P&L from its FX forwards is $11,592.72. Slippage shows that the P&L from the FX forwards more than offsets the loss shown by the FX P&L of the portfolio (see Exhibit 20.4, column P&L (FX)) by $859.86.

Basis Risk. Basis risk in the context of FX forwards refers to the risk that arises from the mismatch between the hedging instrument (i.e., the FX forward) and the underlying exposure it is supposed to hedge (i.e., the FX exposure of the investment). In other words, it is the risk that the hedge will not perfectly offset the risk of the underlying exposure. Basis risk occurs when there is a difference in the terms of the FX forward contract and the underlying exposure. This can happen in several ways:

- *Maturity Mismatch*. The forward contract might have a different maturity date compared to the timing of the underlying exposure.
- *Amount Mismatch*. The notional amount of the forward contract might not match exactly with the amount of the exposure.
- *Rate Mismatch*. Rate mismatch occurs when the change in the forward exchange rate is different from the change in the FX spot rate, as in our example.

To conclude our illustration, we compare the Local P&L (i.e., the P&L assuming FX rates did not move) with the Actual P&L of the FX-hedged portfolio (i.e., the actual portfolio performance plus the impact of hedging via FX forwards). Ideally, if the hedge was perfect, the Actual P&L with the hedge should match the Local P&L. However, there is typically some deviation in

Investment	[A] Asset P&L (Local)	Asset P&L (FX)	Hedge P&L (FX)	Net P&L (FX)	Interaction term	[B] Total	Total Slippage ([B] - [A])
S&P 500	-$8,131.77	0	0	0	0	-$8,131.77	
EURO STOXX 50	-$3,704.53	-$1,409.52	$1,563.72	$154.20	$52.22	-$3,498.11	$206.42
FTSE 100	-$2,449.76	-$1,267.27	$1,280.10	$12.84	$31.04	-$2,405.88	$43.88
S&P/TSX Composite	-$1,381.64	-$2,354.16	$2,399.67	$45.51	$32.53	-$1,303.60	$78.04
TOPIX	$336.70	-$2,233.06	$2,759.33	$526.26	-$7.52	$855.44	$518.74
S&P/ASX 200	-$782.58	-$3,468.85	$3,589.89	$121.05	$27.15	-$634.38	$148.20
Portfolio	**-$16,113.58**	**-$10,732.85**	**$11,592.72**	**$859.86**	**$135.41**	**-$15,118.30**	**$995.28**
Portfolio Return in % of Fund NAV	**-1.61%**	**-1.07%**	**1.16%**	**0.09%**	**0.01%**	**-1.51%**	**0.10%**

Exhibit 20.7 Currency Hedging Effectiveness (all figures in USD)

practice (i.e., slippage) due to the basis in the FX forward contracts and the interaction term.

The analysis shown in Exhibit 20.7 reveals the effectiveness of the FX hedging strategy. The Net FX P&L, which is simply the sum of Asset FX P&L and FX Forwards P&L, clearly shows how the hedging, through FX forwards, has in most cases more than compensated for the fluctuations of FX movements on the portfolio.

The total slippage is the difference between the local P&L and the actual P&L of the FX-hedged portfolio. This slippage arises because the FX forwards are not a perfect hedge due to the presence of the FX basis and the interaction term.

The final row of Exhibit 20.7, depicting the portfolio's return as a percentage of the fund's Net Asset Value, shows that the hedged portfolio's return of −1.51% is closely aligned with the Local P&L return of −1.61%. This starkly contrasts the portfolio's performance if there were no FX hedges, which would have shown a return of −2.67%, as discussed above. This indicates that the hedging strategy effectively reduced the impact of adverse FX movements on the portfolio's overall performance.

Summary

In this case, we demonstrate how institutional investors manage currency risk in global portfolios using FX forward contracts. These derivatives play an essential role in stabilizing returns by reducing the impact of exchange rate fluctuations on international investments. Currency risk management is crucial because shifts in currency values can significantly affect portfolio performance.

The real-world case underscores the practical application of FX forwards, showcasing their ability to "lock in" exchange rates and provide robust protection against adverse currency movements. By employing tailored currency hedging strategies, portfolio managers mitigate risks and position their portfolios to leverage favorable market conditions, potentially enhancing overall returns.

Part III

Leverage and Exposure Management

21

Exploring the Mechanics and Applications of Equity Swaps in Investment Portfolio

Christopher Small and Andrew Weisman

Equity swaps are versatile financial instruments that allow investors to exchange the returns of an equity index, a basket of stocks, or individual equities for a different set of cash flows, such as a fixed or floating interest rate. These instruments provide a cost-effective way to achieve desired equity exposure, rebalance portfolios, or manage risk without directly trading the underlying securities. Using equity swaps, portfolio managers can maintain operational efficiency while adapting to market conditions and strategic objectives.

This case focuses on the practical application of equity swaps in portfolio management. It highlights how these instruments can address transaction costs, liquidity constraints, and exposure adjustments. Through a detailed scenario, it explores equity swaps' mechanics, benefits, and limitations, providing actionable insights for portfolio managers. The discussion sets the stage for understanding how these instruments enhance returns, manage risk, and streamline portfolio operations.

C. Small
Director of Trading at Windham Capital Management, LLC, Boston, USA

A. Weisman (✉)
Market Revealed Preference, Boston, MA, USA
e-mail: abweisman1@gmail.com

F. J. Fabozzi and M. de Jong (eds.), *Derivatives Applications in Asset Management*,
https://doi.org/10.1007/978-3-031-86354-7_21

Applications of Equity Swaps

An equity swap is a financial derivative contract between two parties to exchange two sets of cash flows over a defined period. One cash flow is based on the performance of specific assets, like an equity index, a customized basket of equities, or even a single stock. The second cash flow is typically a fixed financing payment.

Equity swaps can be customized to suit the specific needs and investment objectives of the involved counterparties, including the choice of the equity index or specific equities, the type and tenor of the interest rate, and the period over which the swap is in effect. Swaps are widely used by corporations, institutional investors, and hedge funds. Given their flexibility, equity swaps can be used for several purposes.

Speculation

Portfolio managers seeking to speculate can use equity swaps to bet on a stock's future performance or a basket of stocks without owning the underlying assets. If portfolio managers anticipate a rise in stock values, they can enter a long swap position to receive the equity performance while paying a fixed financing cost. Conversely, if they expect stock values to decline, they can enter a short swap position to pay the equity performance and receive a fixed financing rate of return.

Hedging

Portfolio managers can use equity swaps to hedge against potential losses in their positions. If a portfolio manager holds a position in a particular stock and is concerned about a short-term decline in market value, they can enter a short equity swap position. The investor would be responsible for paying the equity performance. In return, they would receive the fixed financing payments. If the asset price falls, the short swap position will receive both the financing payments and the absolute value of the stock's decline. Given that they are hedging a preexisting investment, using the swap would be the economic equivalent of temporarily selling out of their existing stock investment. When the swap term is complete, it would be the economic equivalent of repurchasing the stock investment. In this example, the swap is used to temporarily sell out of the equity investment without doing so.

Asset Allocation

Portfolio managers can use equity swaps to adjust their asset allocation without buying or selling the underlying securities. This can be particularly useful for large institutional investors looking to rebalance their portfolios efficiently or temporarily change their exposure to specific asset classes.

Leverage

Equity swaps can achieve leverage in an investment portfolio. Swap investors often do not need to provide 100% of the capital for their swap investment value. For example, they might only be asked to provide $2.5 million for a $10 million position. This means that investors can gain more exposure to the equity markets than their capital investment would typically allow. This can amplify gains and losses, making it a strategy with higher risk but potentially higher return.

Accessing Restricted Markets

Equity swaps can expose portfolios to markets or securities that are otherwise difficult to access due to regulatory restrictions, high entry costs, or other barriers. By entering into a swap with a counterparty that has access to these markets, investors can gain exposure to the returns of the desired assets without directly acquiring them.

Tax Efficiency

Equity swaps can offer tax advantages in some jurisdictions. For example, using equity swaps can sometimes defer or reduce capital gains taxes compared to directly buying and selling the underlying equity. This is a more complex use of swaps that is beyond the scope of this discussion.

Income Generation

Portfolio managers can use equity swaps to generate income by receiving regular interest payments. Suppose a portfolio manager has invested in a basket of equities. In that case, they can enter into a short swap agreement as the interest rate owner, where the reference asset is the equity basket that they currently own. They now receive steady interest payments and avoid the volatility of their equity portfolio. This example has the same effect as the hedging transaction but is done with an income objective.

Operational Risk Management and Efficiency

Portfolio managers can buy or sell a swap to improve operational efficiency. Equity swaps are frequently based on broad equity baskets or indices. Portfolio managers can transact in a single instrument (the swap) with a single price that is tied to the market value of a more complex and comprehensive basket of securities rather than buying or selling and managing potentially hundreds of individual securities.

Investing in an index directly could mean significant operational responsibilities regarding accounting systems, risk systems, ongoing corporate action monitoring, index monitoring, and general maintenance. By entering into a swap, portfolio managers can rely on the trade execution infrastructure of a large, well-resourced trading counterparty such as major money center or investment banks. If properly overseen by the portfolio manager, this can reduce transaction costs and limit the scope of mishandling a trade during execution, booking, or maintenance. Maintenance of large stock positions, mainly when shorting a large basket of stocks, can be demanding and time-consuming in that they require ongoing accounting adjustments associated with such things as stock splits and equity dividend payments.

Return Enhancement

One use of swaps to control operational risk while enhancing returns is related to securities lending. Securities lending occurs when a stockowner (or other securities) temporarily lends it to a borrower. Financial institutions, such as hedge funds or investment banks, typically borrow stocks to sell them short, cover a failed trade, or hedge an extended position. In return for lending out their securities, the stockowner receives a securities lending fee, which can enhance their overall returns for their investment portfolio.

Securities lending, however, introduces additional risks, including counterparty risk and additional operational risk, to name a few. Counterparty risk is introduced due to the possibility of a borrower defaulting on their obligation to return the borrowed securities. Operational risk occurs due to potential failures in processes, systems, or controls within the securities lending program, such as errors in record-keeping, mismanagement of collateral, or failures in managing corporate actions on the lent securities. By using a swap to own the stock rather than buying it directly, one can transfer the operational risks associated with securities lending to the swap counterparty in exchange for sharing in some of the securities lending revenues. This allows for some return enhancement from securities lending while eliminating operational risk.

Mechanics of Equity Swaps

The structure of an equity swap involves two legs: an equity leg and an interest rate or financing leg. It is possible but less common that both legs involve equities. For a typical example of an equity swap, see Exhibit 21.1.

The equity leg is tied to the return of a specific equity or basket of equities. The returns include capital gains or losses due to price appreciation or depreciation and dividends from the underlying equity or equity basket. The investor in this leg of the swap benefits from the performance of the selected equities, receiving the returns as if they owned the underlying assets directly.

The interest rate or financing leg is typically linked to a fixed or floating interest rate. The cash flows on this leg are determined by applying the agreed-upon interest rate to a notional principal amount, i.e., the dollar value

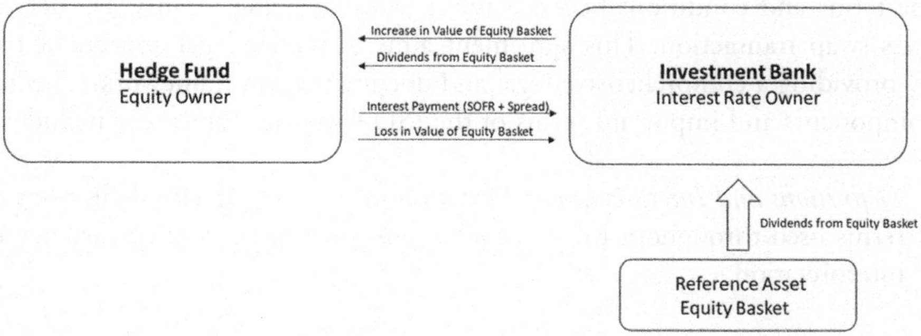

Exhibit 21.1 Hedge Fund Goes Long an Equity Basket Using a Swap

of the selected equity or equity basket at the contract's start. The interest rate is typically tied to a benchmark rate such as the Secured Overnight Funding Rate (SOFR) or the Federal Funds rate. Still, in rarer cases, it could be tied to a longer-maturity fixed-income asset. The investor in this leg of the swap typically receives a cash flow based on the principal value of the equity asset and the applicable interest rate. Note that a longer fixed-income reference asset duration could produce a capital loss for the owner of this leg if interest rates were to move higher. Similarly, if interest rates are negative, the owner of the interest rate leg will have a negative cash flow.

At the heart of an equity swap is exchanging these two cash flows without needing either party to hold the underlying assets. Swap investors can gain exposure to or hedge against equity market performance, manage interest rate risk, or achieve specific financial objectives without the complexities and costs associated with direct investment or additional financing arrangements.

Nomenclature and Mechanics

The acronym "ISDA" stands for the International Swaps and Derivatives Association (ISDA), which is a trade organization that was founded in 1985 to represent participants in the derivatives market, including banks, investment managers, government and supranational entities, insurance companies, and corporations. The organization, known as ISDA, is most famous for its role in creating standardized contracts for derivatives transactions, such as the ISDA Master Agreement, typically referred to as "the ISDA," which is used globally to govern over-the-counter (OTC) derivatives transactions, such as equity swaps.

The two primary documents governing a swap transaction are the ISDA Master Agreement and the Schedule and Credit Support Annex (CSA).

The ISDA Master Agreement is a standardized document that outlines the terms and conditions between two parties engaging in an OTC derivatives swap transaction. This agreement aims to reduce legal and credit risk by providing a comprehensive legal and documentation framework. The key components and important terms of the ISDA Master Agreement include:

- *Definitions and Interpretations:* This section provides precise definitions of terms used throughout the agreement, ensuring clarity and consistency in interpretation.

- *Representations and Warranties*: Both parties make certain representations and warranties regarding their legal capacity, authority, and compliance with laws and regulations to enter into transactions.
- *Covenants:* These are the parties' ongoing obligations during the life of the agreement, such as the obligation to provide timely notice of certain events.
- *Events of Default and Termination Events*: This crucial section lists conditions under which one party may terminate the agreement due to the other party's failure to perform its obligations or other specified events, such as bankruptcy or failure to pay.
- *Closeout and Netting*: This portion of the agreement provides mechanisms for calculating and netting off obligations in the event of a termination. This process reduces credit risk by allowing the non-defaulting party to offset positive and negative exposures to the defaulting party.
- *Transfer and Assignment*: Terms under which parties may or may not assign their rights and obligations under the agreement to third parties.
- *Governing Law and Jurisdiction:* Specifies the law governing the agreement and the jurisdiction for resolving disputes.
- *Taxation*: Outlines the parties' responsibilities concerning the withholding and payment of taxes.

In addition to the Master Agreement, parties typically complete a schedule known as the Schedule and Credit Support Annex (CSA) that specifies additional terms, elections, and amendments to the Master Agreement to tailor it to their specific transaction. The CSA defines items such as eligible collateral, collateral valuation, and daily margin guidelines.

Important Features of an ISDA

The ISDA Master Agreement governs the exchange of cash flows between parties, typically covering issues related to the performance of an equity investment (like a stock or a basket of stocks) versus a fixed or floating interest rate. Important considerations specific to equity swaps might include:

- *Equity Definitions*: The agreement might include specific definitions related to equity swaps, such as how dividends and stock splits are treated.
- *Valuation and Payment Dates:* The agreement will specify how and when the equity and interest components of the swap are valued and when payments are due.

- *Termination and Early Termination*: The conditions under which the equity swap can be terminated early and how the termination amount is calculated.

The ISDA Master Agreement and its associated documents provide a robust framework that helps manage the potentially complex risks associated with equity swaps. Now let's consider a real-world example.

Swap Example

A portfolio manager (PM) wishes to capture exposure to the MSCI Daily Total Return Gross Small Cap World USD. Investment index provider MSCI creates this index. MSCI maintains numerous indices by identifying ordinary and preferred shares, share equivalents, and real estate investment trusts that are investable, accessible to global investors, and sufficiently liquid, and then creates identifiable indexes that investors can analyze, track, and invest in. Their indexes can be broadly based or categorized into geographies, sizes, sectors, industries, themes, or combinations thereof. In this example, the portfolio manager wishes to capture the total return of global small-cap equities. About 4,150 securities in this index cover the 85–99th percentiles of free-float market capitalization in 23 developed international markets. The index is denominated in US dollars. The index is theoretical and not directly investable. A portfolio manager can attempt to capture the index performance by purchasing and managing the 4,150 index constituents directly or by buying a mutual fund, ETF, or derivative instrument that aims to track the index.

In the example presented below, a portfolio manager enters a swap transaction with a broker-dealer (BD) whereby the BD agrees to pay the performance of the index (the equity, i.e., floating leg), and the portfolio manager agrees to pay a financing cost (the interest rate, i.e., fixed leg). Simply put, the portfolio manager gets long an equity index, in this case, the MSCI World Small Cap Total Return Index, and does so through a swap.

The swap agreement entered is governed by two key documents: an ISDA and an associated CSA. The details of these contracts are negotiated before initiating the investment and include the specification of an equity index, a financing benchmark, a financing spread,[1] index pricing, execution fees, initial and variation margin, and the duration of the agreement.

[1] Typically, when an interest rate is specified, the holder of the equity leg pays that interest rate plus some additional amount known as the spread, for example SOFR plus 50 basis points.

The case presented in Exhibit 21.2 is a sample real-world swap investment that was initiated on August 31, 2022, and closed on September 30, 2022. The initial (opening) terms and pricing are shown in the section titled "TRADE OPEN." The closing details of the swap investment are presented under "TRADE CLOSE." In both cases, there is a trade date (when the transaction occurred), a settlement date (when all relevant transfers of assets are completed), and all transaction costs and pricing information.

In the section titled "TRADE LIFECYCLE," details are provided concerning the various cash flows required to initiate, maintain, and close the swap. Cash flows related to retaining the swap will depend on its ongoing performance. In straightforward terms, if the swap is profitable, the BD will send money to the investor; if it is unprofitable, the portfolio manager will send more money (post more collateral) to the BD.

Finally, the calculation of the investment's net returns is presented toward the end of the TRADE LIFECYCLE section. In this example, the portfolio manager lost approximately \$2.35 million. Let's hope this was a hedging transaction!

Portfolio Case Study

In this case study, we consider a situation where a manager intends to add risk factor exposure, small-cap stocks (SC), to an existing S&P 500 stock portfolio (SP). The portfolio manager has decided to use an equity swap that efficiently provides the economic equivalent of allocating a small-cap index for operational simplicity. The manager has been asked to structure a portfolio that will provide returns that do not divert too radically from the original investment mandate. The portfolio manager must build a new combined portfolio with a 2% tracking error versus the SP benchmark. Tracking error (TE) is defined as the standard deviation of the return difference between the portfolio ($R_{portfolio}$) and the benchmark (R_{SP}):

$$TE = \sqrt{Var\left(R_{portfolio} - R_{SP}\right)} \tag{21.1}$$

For a given covariance structure between the S&P 500 index and the small-cap index, the portfolio allocation that satisfies the condition is uniquely determined. In particular, using the following assumed realistic values:

- standard deviation of SP returns $\sigma_{SP} = 16\%$,
- standard deviation of SC returns $\sigma_{SC} = 18\%$,

TRADE OPEN:

Dates	Trade Date (TD1)	08/31/22
	Settle Date (SD1)	09/02/22
Floating Leg Payer	Index	MSCI Daily Total Return Gross Small Cap World USD
	Notional Amount	23,607,707
	Initial Price	620.994
Fixed Leg Payer	Index	US Federal Funds Effective Rate
	Spread to Index	0.42%
	Convention	ACT/360
Other Details	Opening Execution Fee	0.00%
	Closing Execution Fee	0.02%
	Initial Margin Amt BD	0%
	Initial Margin Amt PM	25%
	Transfer Minimum Amt	250,000
	Transfer Rounding Amt	10,000

TRADE CLOSE:

Dates	Trade Date (TD2)	09/30/22
	Settle Date (SD2)	10/04/22
	Closing Price	557.572

TRADE LIFECYCLE

- Trade opened 08/31/22.
- PM wires 5,901,927 to the BD on T+1 to cover the initial margin requirements, this is 25% of starting exposure value.
- Both parties monitor the swap value on a daily basis and adjust posted collateral if needed
  - If the value of swap and posted collateral drifts below the required initial margin amount by greater than 250,000, then the BD can request additional funds to "true up" the margin balances, rounded to the nearest 10,000.
  - If the value of swap and posted collateral drifts above the required initial margin amount by greater than 250,000, then the PM can withdraw the accumulated gains, rounded to the nearest 10,000.
- Trade closed 09/30/22.
- Floating equity index performance leg calculation
  - Notional Amount * [(Closing Price +/- Fees)/(Starting Price +/- Fees)- 1)]
  - 23,607,707.90 * [(557.572-557.572*0.02%)/(620.994-620.994*0.00)-1)]
  - (2,415,289.99)
- Fixed financing leg calculation
  - Notional Amount * [(Calendar-day average rate from SD1 with lookback two business days to SD2 with lookback two business days) + (Spread) / (360 days) * (number of days from SD1 to SD2)]
  - 23,607,707 * [(2.5175% + 0.42%) / 360 * 32)]
  - 61,642.35
- Net transaction
  - PM pays BD for 2,353,647.64 trade loss.
  - BD pays back PM the initial margin amount of 5,901,927 plus/minus any amounts. Transferred during swap lifetime because the contract is closed.

Exhibit 21.2 Sample Real-World Swap Investment: Initiated on August 31, 2022, closed on September 30, 2022

- correlation coefficient of SC to SP $\rho = 0.85$,

the resulting weights w_{SC} to SC and $w_{SP} = (1 - w_{SC})$ to SP, that solve for a targeted tracking error of 2%, are $w_{SC} = 0.21$ and $w_{SP} = 0.79$. The interested reader can verify, manually or in Excel. Since

$$
\begin{aligned}
R_{portfolio} &= w_{SC}R_{SC} + (1 - w_{SC})R_{SP}, \textit{ and thus} \\
R_{portfolio} - R_{SP} &= w_{SC}(R_{SC} - R_{SP}),
\end{aligned} \tag{21.2}
$$

the variance of the return difference is

$$
\begin{aligned}
Var\left(R_{portfolio} - R_{SP}\right) &= w_{SC}^2\sigma_{SC-SP}^2 where \sigma_{SC-SP}^2 \\
&= \sigma_{SC}^2 + \sigma_{SP}^2 - 2\rho\sigma_{SC}\sigma_{SP}
\end{aligned} \tag{21.3}
$$

Taking the square root of both sides in Eq. (21.3), we derive the decision variable as follows.

$$
w_{SC} = TE/\sqrt{\sigma_{SC}^2 + \sigma_{SP}^2 - 2\rho\sigma_{SC}\sigma_{SP}} \tag{21.4}
$$

It is worth noting a few things. First, by specifying the desired weights as w_{SC} and $(1 - w_{SC})$, the math is greatly simplified while abnegating the need for a constraint requiring the weights to sum to 1. However, if one were to impose additional constraints such as a maximum allocation constraint, or simultaneously attempt to solve for more than one additional risk factor allocation, or allowing for leverage, then an analytical solution may not be possible, and the use of an optimizer will be required. Finally, a targeted tracking error of 2% does not imply that out-of-sample deviations of the new portfolio from the benchmark will not exceed 2%; it implies that the expected standard deviation of the tracking error is 2%.

Summary

This case explains how equity swaps can be a strategic tool for portfolio managers to achieve specific investment objectives while managing operational constraints and risk. It focuses on a portfolio manager overseeing a portfolio that tracks the S&P 500 Total Return Index and aims to introduce a small-cap factor tilt—a well-documented risk factor. Using an equity swap, the portfolio manager efficiently adjusts the portfolio allocation to incorporate the desired exposure without directly trading the underlying securities.

This approach minimizes transaction costs and operational complexity while closely aligning with the benchmark.

The case demonstrates the mechanics of the equity swap, including its cash flow structure, and evaluates the strategy's performance outcomes. By carefully aligning the swap exposure with strategic goals, the portfolio achieves the desired factor tilt while controlling tracking error relative to the benchmark. The performance analysis underscores the cost-effectiveness and operational efficiency of equity swaps. It offers valuable insights for portfolio managers seeking to implement tactical adjustments or enhance diversification in their investment strategies. This case highlights the versatility of equity swaps as a tool for modern portfolio management.

22

Cash Equitization in Global Equity and Multi-Asset Portfolios

Eddie Cheng and Wai Lee

Cash equitization is an essential tool in portfolio management, offering a solution to the performance challenges posed by cash drags, i.e., the reduction in returns caused by holding uninvested cash.[1] For investment vehicles like mutual funds, a cash drag can significantly impact the portfolio's ability to achieve its target returns relative to benchmarks and peers. This issue becomes especially critical during periods of low or negative interest rates, when the opportunity cost of holding cash is particularly pronounced. To address this, portfolio managers increasingly rely on cash equitization strategies, primarily using liquid derivatives such as futures, to maintain market exposure and align with the investment objectives.

This case examines the application of cash equitization in managing the daily cash flows within a portfolio, focusing on the Allspring Global Equity Enhanced Income Fund (GEEI). Through a combination of theoretical insights and practical examples, it explores how derivatives like S&P E-mini futures can be used to replicate the target portfolio exposures effectively.

[1] It has become the industry convention that the word "equitize" applies to all asset classes, including equities. Therefore, the same cash management strategy in a fixed-income fund is also referred to as cash equitization regardless of whether equities are in the holdings.

E. Cheng (✉) · W. Lee
Allspring Global Investments, London, UK
e-mail: eddie.cheng712@gmail.com

F. J. Fabozzi and M. de Jong (eds.), *Derivatives Applications in Asset Management*, https://doi.org/10.1007/978-3-031-86354-7_22

The discussion highlights the benefits of this approach, including cost-efficiency, operational simplicity, and the ability to mitigate risks associated with cash flow volatility. Additionally, it addresses the broader implications of cash equitization in global multi-asset portfolios, emphasizing its role as a bridge between short-term liquidity management and long-term investment strategies.

Understanding the Cash Drag and Cash Equitization

Portfolio managers often contend with the operational challenge of managing daily cash flows from investor activities such as subscriptions, redemptions, and income distributions. These cash flows require portfolio managers to deploy or withdraw capital efficiently. While maintaining some cash holdings is necessary for liquidity and operational flexibility, excess cash positions can lead to a phenomenon known as "cash drag." This occurs when cash held within the portfolio earns lower returns than the invested assets, reducing the portfolio's overall performance relative to its benchmarks or peers.

The impact of a cash drag can be significant, particularly in periods of low or negative interest rates. For example, in a portfolio where securities yield 10% while cash yields 5%, a 5% cash holding results in a return drag of 0.25% annually. This seemingly small figure can erode the portfolio's competitive performance, especially with respect to the management fees charged to investors. Consequently, addressing the cash drag is a critical task for portfolio managers striving to maximize returns while managing liquidity needs.

Cash equitization offers an effective strategy to mitigate the cash drag by using derivatives to replicate in part the portfolio's intended market exposures. Instruments such as futures, forwards, swaps, and exchange-traded funds are commonly employed in this process. Exchange-listed futures contracts are particularly advantageous due to their liquidity, standardized structures, and their cost-efficiency. For instance, futures based on equity indices or government bonds provide a straightforward means to align cash holdings with the broader portfolio objectives, thereby minimizing opportunity costs without requiring direct trading of the underlying securities.

Cash equitization typically involves selecting appropriate derivatives to approximate the risk and return characteristics of the portfolio's underlying assets. Managers consider factors such as liquidity, operational simplicity, and the alignment of the derivatives' exposures with the portfolio's benchmark. The objective is not to replace the long-term investment strategy but to serve as a temporary means to bridge the gap between daily cash management and the deployment of assets into their intended investments.

Illustration

For simplicity, we illustrate cash equitization by trading exchange-listed futures contracts only to achieve the returns and risk characteristics of a portfolio.

Here, we will describe the cash equitization process of the Allspring Global Equity Enhanced Income Fund, GEEI, which is a sub-fund of the Allspring (Lux) Worldwide Fund. In addition, we will highlight other considerations regarding cash equitization in funds with multiple asset classes and currencies. First launched in July 2020, GEEI is managed by the Systematic Core Equity team at Allspring Global Investments.[2] The fund, benchmarked to the MSCI All Country World Index (ACWI), seeks to deliver a high level of current income (distribution yield) along with a long-term capital appreciation by investing in a well-diversified portfolio of global stocks and an actively managed options overlay designed to generate additional income by selling out-of-the-money index call options. Based on the prevailing market conditions, the fund is currently managed to target a yield of 6% per annum.[3]

On January 30, 2024, at 15:28:00 CST (21:28:00 GMT, 22:28:00 CET),[4] as part of the daily portfolio management routine, the Allspring Accounting team and the GEEI portfolio management team received an electronic notification of cash flows with a time 22:15:23 CET (15:15:23 PST, 21:15:23 GMT) stamped by the fund's custodian passing along the following information:

- Trade Date: 30 January, 2024
- Value Date: 2 February, 2024

---

[2] Allspring Global Investments™ ("Allspring") is the trade name for the asset management firms of Allspring Global Investments Holdings, LLC, a holding company indirectly owned by certain private funds of GTCR LLC and Reverence Capital Partners, L.P. These firms include, but are not limited to, Allspring Global Investments (UK) Limited ("Allspring UK") an investment management company, authorized and regulated by the UK Financial Conduct Authority (FCA), and Allspring Global Investments Luxembourg S.A ("Allspring Luxembourg"), authorized and regulated by the CSSF.

[3] A target is indicative only, is not guaranteed, and does not consider fees or charges that will reduce returns. The targeted yield is based on prevailing market conditions and subject to change. There is no guarantee that the targeted yield, or any other level of income or returns, will be generated.

[4] Unless otherwise stated, when other time zones were used in actual communication to preserve as many facts of the execution as possible, we use CST time zone for ease of trading time reference in this case illustration.

- Cash Inflow: $ 8,606,937.73
- Cash Outflow: $ 12,319.27

Cash Equitization for Global Equity Exposures

Since its launch on May 31, 1990, the MSCI ACWI has become one of the most widely followed global equity index benchmarks. It currently captures about 85% of the global investable public equity universe, with more than 2,600 large and mid-cap stocks across 23 developed and 24 emerging markets, respectively. The United States, the largest country, and Information Technology, the largest sector, account for about 65 and 25% of the index, respectively.

MSCI ACWI Net Total Return (NTR) Index futures contracts are listed and traded on the Intercontinental Exchange® (ICE), the leading exchange for MSCI Index Futures, offering exposure to the MSCI ACWI. At the time of writing, open interest and trade volume of the current MSCI ACWI NTR Index futures contracts named L3Z24 Dec' 24 are below 50,000 and 200, respectively. It is possible to combine other MSCI index futures for a cash equitization, but their liquidities are not as ample as their US counterpart, i.e., the S&P E-mini contracts, when adjusted for contract values.

In addition, several developed markets' stock indices have liquid futures contracts that can be used together with the US stock index futures in a cash equitization of a global equity fund. The trading, including these instruments' rolling, middle- and back-office operations, is straightforward. However, unless there is a time during the day that all these futures contracts are actively traded, market moves during off trade hours among these markets can cause implementation slippage if trade execution is non-synchronized and far apart.

Given the daily horizon of the fund at hand, the reasonable size of daily net flows, the high correlations among stock markets, and the fact that the United States accounts for approximately 65% of the ACWI, the S&P 500 has proven to be an effective proxy for other stock market indices in the cash equitization process, even accounting for some degree of currency effects. Some textbooks suggest that the market betas of the assets should be estimated in an attempt to account for different market volatilities when determining the number of contracts to trade. In our experience working with a daily horizon, such adjustments are immaterial to the effectiveness of cash equitization when other factors dominate.

Another point worth considering is that cash equitization is a useful process for the portfolio management team to bridge the gap between maintaining market exposures and excessive trading over short time horizons (e.g., a couple of days). The portfolio management team will then actively deploy that cash into the appropriate investment as soon as possible to achieve the investment objective. This also mitigates the short-term risk of using US stock index futures to fulfill wider exposures.

Liquid Derivatives to Be Considered for Fixed-Income Cash Equitization

The GEEI team uses the S&P E-mini futures contracts for cash equitization. The CME Globex trading sessions for the S&P E-mini futures contracts are Sunday 17:00 CST to Friday 16:00 CST with a daily maintenance period from 16:00 CST to 17:00 CST. That gives the GEEI team about 30 minutes to execute the cash equitization trade before the E-mini futures trading session day closes.

The S&P 500 E-mini futures contract with settlement in March 2024, named the ESH4, offers exposure to the S&P 500 Index in an accessible package. In the ESH4, the "ES" stands for the E-mini S&P 500 futures, the "H" is a code for the expiration month of the contract ("H" being the letter code for March), and "4" indicates the year 2024. As the cash inflow was more than the cash outflow, resulting in a positive net cash flow for the day, cash equitization would require taking a long position in the futures contracts. The following sections describe how the decisions regarding the cash equitization trade were made.

Which S&P E-Mini Contracts

At the time of the trade, a multiple of S&P E-mini futures contracts were available. Exhibit 22.1 shows the trade recap details of four such contracts around 15:37:00 CST, soon after the GEEI team received the flows email notification.[5]

From a liquidity standpoint, the nearby contract ESH4 Mar' 24 was the clear choice of execution with the highest total number of outstanding

[5] Not all contracts were traded at the same second, so we select quotes of the contracts around the same time 15:37:00 CST for illustration.

Jan 30, 2024 ~15:37:00 CST	ESH4 Mar' 24	ESM4 Jun' 24	ESU4 Sep' 24	ESZ4 Dec' 24
First Trade	12/17/2021	3/18/2022	6/20/2022	6/7/2021
Last Trade	3/15/2024	6/21/2024	9/20/2024	12/20/2024
Valuation Date	3/15/2024	6/21/2024	9/20/2024	12/20/2024
Trade Recap Time	15:36:45 CST	15:37:08 CST	15:37:08 CST	15:37:51 CST
Open Interest	2270115	28144	2777	2732
Volume	1065313	5149	120	19
Bid / Ask	4938.75 / 4939.00	4994.50 / 4995.25	5042.00 / 5044.00	5080.00 / 5093.00
Bid-Ask Spread	0.25	0.75	2.00	13.00

Exhibit 22.1 Trade Recap Details of S&P E-mini Futures Contracts

contracts known as open interests, and trading volume, leading to a much tighter bid-ask spread than the other contracts. In most cases, regardless of asset classes and instruments, the nearby contract is usually the contract of choice, except when rolling is considered. We will briefly discuss futures contracts rolling in a subsequent section.

Contract Value of ESH4 Mar' 24

Next, the value of each contract of ESH4 Mar'24 can be computed based on the set of contract parameters pre-defined by the exchange. For all the S&P E-mini futures contracts, the contract value is equal to 50 times the price of the underlying S&P 500 index. Take the closing price of the S&P 500 index on January 30, 2024, at 4924.97, for example,

Contract Value of ESH4 Mar' 24 = $50 4924.97 = $246,248.50.

Likewise, the value of a 1-point move in the contract price is $ 50. For a tick size of 0.25, therefore, each tick value is $12.50 ($50 0.25).

The Number of Contracts to Trade

Once the instrument of choice is determined, the GEEI team computes the number of ESH4 Mar' 24 contracts to trade, considering the current cash holdings, futures collateral, inflow and outflow, and the current number of futures contracts in the portfolio, among other considerations. For ease of illustration, we define the following variables with brief explanations.

C = Current cash holdings
FC = Futures collateral
NCF = Net cash flow of the day = Cash Inflow – Cash Outflow
CV = Contract value
NH = Number of contracts to hold
N = Current number of contracts

NT = Number of contracts to trade = $NH - N$

Trading futures contracts requires collateral for the initial margin call and the maintenance margin. All current cash holdings, whether they be residual from previous trades or intentionally for other purposes, should be considered in combination with the daily cash flows. Depending on the volatility and the price level of the underlying assets, among other factors, margin requirements per contract are subject to change at any time. Currently, the maintenance margin for S&P E-mini contracts is $11,800 per contract, which is about 5% of the contract value.

With current cash holdings C of $832,520, total futures collateral (*FC*) of $20,192,377, net cash flow (*NCF*) of the day $ 8,594,619 as the difference between inflow of $8,606,938 and outflow of $ 12,319, and 82 (*N*) contracts of ESH4, the number of ESH4 contracts to trade is determined by $NT = NH - N = (C + FC + NCF)/CV =$ (\$832,520 + \$20,192,377 + (\$8,606,938 − \$12,319))/(\$246,248.50) − 82 = 38 rounding down to 38 contracts to trade. After reviewing and verifying the accuracy of the output, the team confirmed the trade and generated the trade file for the applicable order management system (OMS). The team then verified the file for accuracy, uploaded it, received necessary approvals, and sent the trade file to the trading desk for execution.

With market movements and daily cash flows in and out of the fund, the number of contracts to hold and trade daily is determined using the same process as part of the daily portfolio management routine. Prompt execution in a cost-effective manner can assure well-managed market exposures, given the deep liquidity and low execution costs of the futures markets trade every day, which is determined using the same process as part of the daily portfolio management routine. Given the deep liquidity and low execution costs of future markets, prompt execution can be cost-effective and can ensure well-managed market exposure.

Other Considerations

Several other considerations in implementing cash equitization are briefly discussed below.

Rolling Futures Contracts

As the ESH4 Mar' 24 contracts held by the GEEI fund will be last traded on March 15, 2024, the team must roll the contracts before the last trading day to avoid settlement of the existing contracts. To help the team implement a futures contracts roll, the team utilizes the Roller tool developed in-house, which identifies what futures contracts are currently in the portfolio and the next futures contracts to be rolled into, which are in the case at hand the ESM4 Jun' 24 contracts.

The first trade dates, the last trade dates, and the open interests of the current and the next contracts are updated daily and in real-time. As it approaches the last trade date of the current contracts, the open interest and trade volume of the next contract typically pick up. The Roller tool will alert the team when the next contracts' open interest reaches 67% of the current contracts' open interest, a level that reflects sufficient liquidity of both contracts so that the team can review and decide the timing of the roll execution. At the time of writing, it was still too early to see material pickup in the open interest and the ESM4 Jun' 24 trading volume. For the sake of illustration, therefore, we refer to the roll from holding the previously expired ESZ3 Dec' 23 contracts into the current ESH4 Mar' 24 contracts.

Exhibit 22.2 tabulates the open interest of the two contracts two weeks before the last trade date, December 15, 2023, of the ESZ3 Dec' 23. Exhibit 22.3 plots the history of open interests of the two contracts and the next contract ESM4′ 24.

About a week before the last trade date December 15, 2023, of the ESZ3 Dec' 23 contracts, we started to notice material changes in the open interest of the contracts. On December 11, 2023, the open interest of the ESH4 Mar' 24 contracts began to exceed that of the ESZ3 Dec' 23 contracts. Based on the assessment of trading volume, among other considerations, the ESZ3 Dec' 23 contracts were rolled into the ESH4 Mar' 24 contracts during December 12, 2023 trading sessions. Once trades were settled, the GEEI

	ESZ3 Dec' 23	ESH4 Mar' 24
01/12/2023	2230022	72196
04/12/2023	2185454	91539
05/12/2023	2180591	125227
06/12/2023	2158907	174372
07/12/2023	2098544	290299
08/12/2023	1686069	750582
11/12/2023	1119150	1511607
12/12/2023	765586	1895463
13/12/2023	616726	2037855
14/12/2023	520112	2142203
15/12/2023	500520	2123223

Exhibit 22.2 Open Interest of ESZ3 Dec' 23 and ESH4 Mar' 24

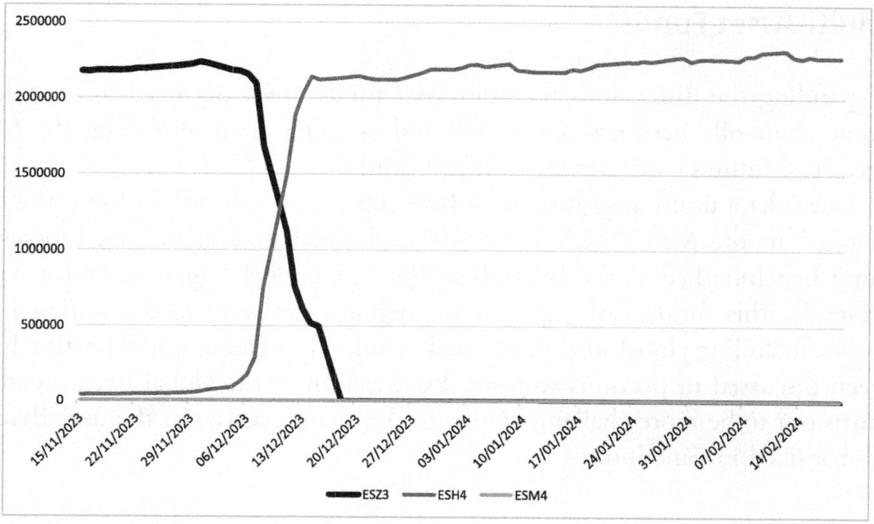

Exhibit 22.3 Open Interest of ESZ3 Dec' 23, ESH4 Mar' 24, and ESM4 Jun' 24

team started to monitor the open interest of the next ESM4 Jun' 23 contracts in determining the next roll date.

Fine Tuning Positions

In our illustration, the number of contracts of ESH4 Mar' 24 to trade was rounded to the whole number 38. Given a certain fund size, the rounding is relatively insignificant on the effectiveness of cash equitization. For funds with smaller sizes, however, more fine-tuning of positions will be helpful for the accuracy of cash equitization in proxying the returns and risk characteristics of the underlying securities in the portfolio. For instance, the contract values of the Micro E-mini futures contracts are 5 times, in contrast to the 50 times, the price of the underlying S&P 500 index. In other words, Micro E-mini's contract values are only 10% of that of the E-mini contracts. A 10-point move in the S&P 500 index changes the value of the Micro E-mini by $ 50, instead of $ 500 in the case of the E-mini, making it a better instrument for cash equitization for funds with smaller sizes. Other than smaller contract values, the same cash equitization process can be applied to the current Micro E-mini contracts, including the contract roll.

Multi-Asset Funds

Expanding the discussions to multi-asset funds, investors need to consider some trade-offs between complexity and accuracy in determining the full basket of futures contracts for cash equitization.

Consider a multi-asset fund with 60% allocated to the GEEI fund benchmarked to the MSCI ACWI and 40% allocated to a global fixed-income fund benchmarked to the Bloomberg Barclays Global Aggregate Index. For example, this fund's cash equitization requires exposure to the underlying assets, including global stocks and fixed income. The global stocks portion has been discussed in previous sections. Equitization of the global fixed income turns out to be more challenging due to the characteristics of the underlying global fixed-income index.

Cash Equitization for Global Fixed-Income Exposures

The Bloomberg Barclays Global Aggregate Index in both hedged and unhedged versions is a widely followed index made up of twenty-eight local currency markets that currently includes treasury, government-related, corporate, and securitized fixed-rate bonds from both developed and emerging markets issuers. The Index exposes investors to duration, credit, currency, liquidity factor risks, and issuer-specific risks. Due to the multi-dimensional risk nature of the index, there is no single exchange-traded futures contract available for this index. However, if desirable, investors can use a combination of government bond futures to capture duration, credit futures for credit spread risks, currency futures or forwards for currency exposures, among others, to create a reasonably close proxy to the index.

What and how many of these instruments are to be used is subject to different trade-offs between the operational complexity and the desire for a close approximation, as discussed in Dynkin, Gould, and Konstantinovsky.[6] We will continue focusing on cash equitization that is meant for a reasonably short horizon.

---

[6] Dynkin, Lev, Anthony Gould, and Vadim Konstantinovsky, "Replicating Bond Indices With Liquid Derivatives," *Journal of Fixed Income*, *14*(4), 2006, 7–19.

Liquid Derivatives to Be Considered for Fixed-Income Cash Equitization

As highlighted earlier, when investors engage in cash equitization activities, whether due to the desire to shift the asset allocation quickly or managing exposures to smooth the impacts of inflows or outflows, the process's speed, cost, simplicity, and effectiveness are among the most important considerations. It is, therefore, advantageous to use derivatives, mainly exchanged traded futures, as the building blocks for equitization given their liquid, transparent, exchange-traded, unfunded, and low transaction cost features. Exhibit 22.4 shows a set of liquid futures representing three main risk factors underlying the Bloomberg Barclays Global Aggregate Index: duration, currency, and credit.

- **Duration**: This is one of the most important risk factors for the Bloomberg Barclays Global Aggregate Index. Historically, the 10-year US Treasury note futures have been an effective instrument to proxy the global duration risk and are one of the most liquid and traded futures. However, as Central Banks around the world could diverge in their policymaking in various stages of their respective economic cycles, some investors may wish to cover a broader range of duration risks in their replicating baskets. Exhibit 22.4 shows a selection of liquid global bond futures representing material risk exposures in the Bloomberg Barclays Global Aggregate Index.
- **Currency**: When the target exposure is the *unhedged version* of the Bloomberg Barclays Global Aggregate Index, currency risks must be considered. In general, it is more challenging to select the currency proxy as there is no dominant "global currency beta," unlike in the cases of duration or equity beta. Exhibit 22.4 provides some liquid currency futures to which the Index has material exposures as part of the replicating instruments.
- **Credit Spread**: To proxy the credit spread risks in the Bloomberg Barclays Global Aggregate Index, investors can use a basket of over-the-counter (OTC) credit default swaps (CDS) or the credit default swap index (CDX) for the US and emerging markets exposures, and the iTraxx for the Europe, Japan, non-Japan Asia, and Australia exposures. Recently, we have started to see the emergence of credit futures, which helps reduce operational complexity. Exhibit 22.4 shows one such example, namely the DBH1, which is the futures contracts for the Bloomberg US Corporate Investment Grade Duration Hedged Index. Including credit futures improves the tracking effectiveness of the replicating basket and maintains the operation requirement's simplicity and consistency.

Main Risk Factor	Futures	Generic Bloomberg Ticker	Exchange	Open Interest	Trading Volume
Duration	10 Year US Treasury Note	TY1 Comdty	Chicago Board of Trade	4,589,527	1,819,795
	10 Year Canada Bond	CN1 Comdty	Montreal Exchange	613,294	117,220
	10 Year Euro Bund	RX1 Comdty	Eurex	1,288,430	1,351,872
	10 Year Japanese Bond	JB1 Comdty	Osaka Exchange	176,015	9,189
	10 Year Australian Bond	XM1 Comdty	ASX Trade24	1,058,731	84,389
	Long Gilt	G 1 Comdty	ICE Futures Europe Financials	858,619	401,311
Currency	Euro Foreign Exchange	EC1 Curncy	Chicago Mercantile Exchange	639,808	162,497
	British Pound Currency	BP1 Curncy	Chicago Mercantile Exchange	219,589	124,923
	Japanese Yen Currency	JY1 Curncy	Chicago Mercantile Exchange	223,008	98,338
	Standard USD/CNH	CHY1 Curncy	Chicago Mercantile Exchange	648	332
	Canadian Dollar Currency	CD1 Curncy	Chicago Mercantile Exchange	322,322	52,601
	Australian Dollar Currency	AD1 Curncy	Chicago Mercantile Exchange	182,067	75,493
Credit	Bloomberg US Corporate Investment Grade Duration Hedged	DHB1 Index	Chicago Board of Trade	404	124

Exhibit 22.4 Selected set of liquid futures contracts as underlying risk factors of the Bloomberg Barclays Global Aggregate Index. *Source* Data obtained from Bloomberg as of 30/10/2024

Approaches to Replicate the Fixed-Income Exposures for Cash Equitization

Again, the primary purpose of cash equitization is to allow the portfolio management team to find a balance between swiftly establishing market exposures and avoiding unnecessary trading over a short period, as the desired exposures, such as cash-based instruments, will be deployed shortly.

Example of Min. Tracking Error Replicating Baskets		Bloomberg Barclays Global Aggregate Hedged Index			Bloomberg Barclays Global Aggregate Unhedged Index		
		A	B	C	D	E	F
Main Risk Factor	Futures	Bond (UST only) Futures	Bond Futures	Bond + Credit Futures	Bond (UST only) + Currency Futures	Bond + Currency Futures	Bond + Currency + Credit Futures
Duration	10 Year US Treasury Note	76%	48%	48%	67%	35%	46%
	10 Year Canada Bond	-	12%	10%	-	21%	19%
	10 Year Euro Bund	-	11%	12%	-	1%	0%
	10 Year Japanese Bond	-	8%	9%	-	9%	15%
	10 Year Australian Bond	-	0%	0%	-	1%	0%
	Long Gilt	-	2%	0%	-	0%	0%
Currency	Euro Foreign Exchange	-	-	-	16%	11%	17%
	British Pound Currency	-	-	-	11%	10%	0%
	Japanese Yen Currency	-	-	-	11%	14%	15%
	Standard USD/CNH	-	-	-	9%	15%	9%
	Canadian Dollar Currency	-	-	-	14%	19%	12%
	Australian Dollar Currency	-	-	-	6%	3%	3%
Credit	Bloomberg US Corporate Investment Grade Duration Hedged	-	-	29%	-	-	31%

Exhibit 22.5 An illustration of replicating baskets based on a minimum-tracking-error approach (October 2022 to September 2024). *Source* Allspring, Bloomberg

	Bloomberg Barclays Global Aggregate Hedged Index	Replicating Basket			Bloomberg Barclays Global Aggregate Unhedged Index	Replicating Basket		
		A Bond (UST only) Futures	B Bond Futures	C Bond + Credit Futures		D Bond (UST only) + Currency Futures	E Bond + Currency Futures	F Bond + Currency + Credit Futures
Monthly Standard Deviation	1.50%	1.45%	1.47%	1.49%	2.41%	2.38%	2.39%	2.40%
Monthly Tracking Error		0.39%	0.30%	0.21%		0.34%	0.27%	0.23%
Number of Instruments		1	6	7		7	12	13

Exhibit 22.6 Risk statistics summary between target indices and their replicating baskets (October 2022 to September 2024). *Source* Allspring, Bloomberg

Keeping this main purpose in mind, practitioners often consider an *exposure-matched approach* and a *minimum-tracking-error approach* for equitization.[7]

- *Exposure-matched approach*: Breaking down the index into its duration, currency, and spread exposures across different regions, investors then select the corresponding liquid derivatives.
- *Minimum-tracking-error approach*: Aiming to minimize the expected tracking error between the index and the replicating basket (as an example shown in Exhibit 22.4), the optimization process with a risk model as input determines the appropriate exposures of each liquid derivative to be included in the replicating basket.

The Bloomberg Barclays Global Aggregate Index is exposed to risk factors, as discussed above, as well as idiosyncratic risks of a large number of underlying securities. The *exposure-matched approach* provides clear transparency and stability of the replicating basket. However, breaking the index down to each risk dimension and mapping them onto their respective liquid derivatives is not a trivial task, especially given the limitation and the availability of some liquid derivatives. In contrast, the optimization-based *minimum-tracking-error approach* can be more efficient. However, constructing its replicating basket could be less transparent and subject to the stability of historical relationships among the risk factors and securities.

Examples of Constructing a Fixed-Income Replicating Basket for Cash Equitization

In this section, using monthly data from October 2022 to September 2024 as the sample period in computing tracking errors, we demonstrate how to apply the *minimum-tracking-error approach* to construct replicating baskets for cash equitization for The Bloomberg Barclays Global Aggregate Hedged Index and The Bloomberg Barclays Global Aggregate Unhedged Index, respectively, with the same set of liquid futures shown in Exhibit 22.4. For each bond index, three replicating baskets with increasing instruments are constructed to capture a broader range of risk factors. The hedged index does not have explicit currency exposures, so currency futures are not included in the replicating universe.

---

[7] Tracking error measures the variability, often proxied by the standard deviation, of the return differences between the index to be replicated and its replicating basket.

Comparing the Effectiveness of Replicating Baskets

To evaluate the effectiveness of the different replicating strategies, we focus on their tracking errors to the targeted indices. As we confine our analysis to futures contracts, given their standardized formats and generally high liquidities in the selected universe, the number of instruments used in each basket could be a good proxy for the degree of operation complexity and transaction costs.

In the case of equitizing The Bloomberg Barclays Global Aggregate Hedged Index, all three replicating baskets (A, B, C) have a volatility similar to the index's volatility. In terms of the tracking errors, even using only one bond futures (10-Year US Treasury Note) in replicating basket A tracks the well-diversified index reasonably well, with a monthly tracking error at 39 bps. This is consistent with the well-documented fact that duration is the dominant risk driver of the Bloomberg Barclays Global Aggregate Hedged Index. As we expand our replicating universe to six different bond futures in the replicating basket B to cover the regional duration differences in the index, we see a moderate reduction in tracking error from 39 to 30 bps. This reflects a reasonable degree of correlation among global government bond markets. On the other hand, including the credit futures to capture the credit spread risks of the index in the replicating basket C helps further reduce the tracking error to 21 bps.

The case of equitizing The Bloomberg Barclays Global Aggregate Unhedged Index shows a similar pattern. All replicating baskets (D, E, F) have a similar volatility to the index's. Including more instruments reduces the tracking errors, similar to the case of the hedged index. However, given the need to include a basket of currencies exposed to the index, the higher operational complexity and transaction costs deserve more consideration in determining the replicating basket.

Summary

This case underscores the pivotal role of cash equitization in portfolio management, particularly in mitigating the impact of a cash drag on performance. Fund managers can effectively replicate underlying portfolio securities' risk and return characteristics by utilizing liquid derivatives such as futures and swaps. This process ensures portfolios maintain their intended market exposures, even during fluctuating cash inflows and outflows.

The application of cash equitization extends beyond single-asset funds to global and multi-asset portfolios, where complexity increases due to diverse benchmarks and risk factors. For fixed-income portfolios, innovative approaches like exposure-matched and minimum-tracking-error replicating baskets provide fund managers with tools to approximate benchmark exposures across dimensions such as duration, credit spreads, and currency risks. These strategies highlight the trade-offs between operational simplicity and tracking precision, allowing managers to align the approach with portfolio objectives and resources.

Cash equitization is a strategic bridge in portfolio management, balancing the need for swift market exposure with cost-efficiency and operational feasibility. By leveraging advancements in liquid derivatives, fund managers can enhance portfolio efficiency and deliver better investor outcomes, particularly in managing short-term liquidity and maintaining alignment with investment objectives.

23

Quantifying Event Risk with Equity Options

Robert Harlow

This case describes strategies for quantifying and trading event risk using equity options, focusing on how anticipated events—such as earnings announcements, elections, and policy meetings—can drive market volatility. Traditional models, such as the Black–Scholes model, often fall short in capturing these volatility shifts, as they typically assume a constant volatility over time. In reality, volatility fluctuates significantly around important events, leading to unique market dynamics that traders can leverage. By analyzing implied volatilities from options with overlapping maturities, it is possible to estimate forward implied volatility, providing insights into market expectations for volatility changes over these event-driven periods.

Through a practical case study involving Amazon stock (AMZN) ahead of an earnings announcement, the document examines two trading strategies designed to capture this event risk: one that involves buying a straddle expiring after the announcement and another that combines this position with a short straddle expiring before the announcement. The illustration emphasizes the critical importance of dynamic position management by evaluating the profitability and challenges of these strategies, particularly in light of volatility forecasts and market reactions. Adjusting option exposures as market expectations shift can significantly influence outcomes, highlighting the nuanced approach needed to trade around key events effectively.

R. Harlow (✉)
Global Multi-Asset Research at T. Rowe Price, Baltimore, USA
e-mail: Robert.Harlow@troweprice.com

F. J. Fabozzi and M. de Jong (eds.), *Derivatives Applications in Asset Management*,
https://doi.org/10.1007/978-3-031-86354-7_23

Defining Event Risk

Event risk is the risk of adverse asset-price movements associated with a discrete event with a known date, but unknown outcome. Often, these events are associated with the unveiling of material information to the investing community. The materiality of the information means that it is often likely to substantially affect asset prices. Examples include earnings announcements, elections, Central Bank policy decisions, macroeconomic data releases, and drug trial results.

In many cases, an asset's price behavior prior to an event is quite different than after the event. Markets process the information revealed by events through the actions of millions of individual participants, all of whom process at different speeds, with different risk preferences, and with different interpretations as to what the revealed news means for asset pricing in future. When an event reveals surprising information, it can take time for markets to reach a new equilibrium.

Option markets provide a valuable way to measure and trade event risk prior to the occurrence of the event itself. The presence of a dense option term structure provides valuable information on an asset's entire distribution both from now to an event and for sub-periods in-between. Even for investors that do not have a view on an event, it can still be helpful to understand what the market-implied view is.

Challenges in Forecasting Event-Driven Volatility

Most financial measures of risk center on volatility. Further, volatility is often assumed to be constant over a period, such as in the Black–Scholes model. However, Black–Scholes, and even some more complex variants that allow for drift in implied volatility, often miss the mark when it comes to measuring event risk in practice. Real asset prices exhibit non-constant volatility in a variety of ways. This includes volatility clustering, or the tendency of high volatility today begetting high volatility tomorrow, and the tendency of volatility to jump, or change abruptly following the arrival of new information.

The fundamental challenge of using full-period implied volatility estimates around discrete events is that they reflect an average expectation from different distributions. Often, this is an average of a lower-risk distribution prior to an event and a higher-risk distribution after and including the event. Even if a volatility estimate of 25% over a full period were accurate, it is often helpful to know that that 25% is, for example, an average of 50% volatility in the last third of the period and substantially lower than 25% volatility in the first two-thirds of the period.

Introduction to Forward Implied Volatility as a Solution

Forward implied volatility allows for isolating the anticipated volatility over specific future periods by leveraging options with overlapping maturities. For instance, if options expire just before and just after an earnings announcement, forward implied volatility can be calculated to reflect expected volatility solely in the days surrounding the event. This level of precision is beneficial when the event is likely to cause notable price swings, enabling traders to focus on event-driven risks and opportunities.

There are three advantages that using forward implied volatility offers rather than traditional implied volatility, especially in the context of event-driven trading. First, it measures volatility expectations specifically around anticipated events rather than averaging over a longer time frame. Second, it provides portfolio managers and traders with a way to measure and manage hedges around an event, allowing for tailored risk-management strategies that often come at lower cost. Finally, traders looking to capitalize on event-driven volatility expectations can use forward implied volatility to structure trades that align with their expectation of event-driven price movements.

To calculate forward variance, we assume that the variance of asset returns for non-overlapping time-periods is independent. This assumption means that the total variance over a period is equal to a time-weighted average of the variance over sub-periods. Suppose that we have both an estimate of the total variance between now and time T, and an estimate of the total variance between now and time t, where $t < T$. Our independence assumption allows us to write formula 23.1:

$$\sigma^2_{0,T} = \frac{t}{T}\sigma^2_{0,t} + \frac{T-t}{T}\sigma^2_{T-t,T} \tag{23.1}$$

The term $\sigma^2_{T-t,T}$ on the right side of the equation is the forward variance and reflects the variance between time t and T. If we solve for that term and take a square root, we arrive at formula 23.2 for the forward volatility.

$$\sigma_{T-t,T} = \sqrt{\frac{T}{T-t}\sigma^2_{0,T} - \frac{t}{T-t}\sigma^2_{0,t}} \tag{23.2}$$

Case Study: Amazon Earnings Announcement

As an example, consider Amazon stock, ticker AMZN, which closed at $127.12 on 2023–09–29. AMZN had an upcoming earnings announcement on 2023–10–26 after the close of trading and had a strip of options expiring on 2023–10–20 *prior* to the earnings announcement and a strip of options expiring on 2023–10–27 *after* the announcement. The implied volatility of near-the-money options on AMZN for 2023–10–20 was 30.3% and the implied volatility of near-the-money options on AMZN for 2023–10–27 was 37.4%. The time to expiry for the 2023–10–20 options was 0.0575 years, and the time to expiry for the 2023–10–27 options was 0.0767 years.

Plugging in values to (23.2) for our AMZN[1] example yields

$$0.5327 = \sqrt{\frac{0.0767}{(0.0767 - 0.0575)} * 0.374^2 - \frac{0.0575}{(0.0767 - 0.0575)} * 0.303^2}$$

This means that between 2023–09–29 and 2023–10-20, market participants expected a volatility of 30% and between 2023–10-20 and 2023–10-27, i.e., the time-period that contains the earnings announcement, market participants expected an annualized volatility of 53%.

As it turns out, the annualized realized volatility over the entire period was 42%, with an annualized realized volatility of 29.7% between 2023–09–29 and 2023–10–20 and an annualized realized volatility of 72% in the period 2023–10–20 through 2023–10–27, including a 6% move after the earnings announcement. This means that even though market participants were pricing in almost double the volatility (and triple the variance) in the portion of the period that included the earnings announcement, it was still underestimated by market participants as of 2023–09–29.

However, as we will see, capturing these differences in practice is not always easy. Suppose that on 2023–09–29 an investor thought that the market was under-appreciating volatility around the upcoming AMZN earnings announcement and options were trading that expire on both 2023–10–20 and 2023–10–27. The investor would consider two potential positions that attempt to implement this belief:

[1] Generally, estimates of implied volatility on an underlying should be calculated using a weighted average of the implied volatilities across all traded strikes, consistent with the methodology used to calculate CBOE's VIX Index. We use near-the-money options as a simplification to illustrate the methodology.

1. *Position 1*: buying a straddle that expires on 2023–10–27, the day after earnings were announced. This is a bet on *total* volatility over the period.
2. *Position 2*: buying a straddle that expires the day after earnings were announced on 2023–10–27 and *selling* a straddle expiring prior to the earnings announcement with an expiration date of 2023–10–20. This is a bet on *forward* volatility *between* 2023–10–20 and 2023–10–27. When the short straddle part of this position expires on 2023–10–20, the only remaining position is a long straddle in the 2023–10–27 expiry, identical to position 1.

A straddle is an option structure that involves buying equal amounts of a call option and put option of the same strike price, often with a strike price that is close to the prevailing market price of the underlying stock. This structure is "long volatility" in two primary ways: its value will *increase* on a mark-to-market basis as volatility expectations, defined by implied volatility, increase,[2] and its final payoff will increase if there is a large move in the underlying stock.[3]

Expanding on the scenario described in the forward volatility example above, the investor will use the option prices in Exhibit 23.1 to evaluate the two positions above. The investor selects options with a strike price of $127 as those are nearest to the closing price on 2023–09-29 of $127.12.

Note that the prices for the first two options are set to their payouts at expiration on and after 2023–10-20. For instance, the put payout formula determined the 127 strike put that expired on 2023–10-20: max(0, 127 – 125.17) = $1.83.[4]

To build position 1, we would purchase one unit of 2023–10-27 127 C and one unit of 2023–10-27 127 P for a total upfront cost of $10.53. To build position 2, we would buy the same options as in position 1 and additionally sell one unit of 2023–10-20 127 C and 2023–10-20 127 P for a total upfront cost of $3.12 ($10.53 – $3.93 – $3.48). Exhibit 23.2 shows each position's resulting profit-and-loss (P&L).

Surprisingly, both positions lost money (–$9.79 for position 1 and –$4.21 for position 2), even though they were "right" on volatility! Full-sample realized volatility for the period was 42% annualized relative to 37% implied on 2023–09–29 when position 1 was purchased, and the realized volatility

---

[2] This is exposure to the Greek factor "vega", or the sensitivity of option prices to changes in implied volatility.

[3] This is exposure to the Greek factor "gamma", or the sensitivity of option price to *squared* changes in the underlying price.

[4] We assume these prices are for cash-settled European options. In this case, we do not make any interest rate assumptions given the short holding period.

Date	AMZN	2023-10-20 127 C	2023-10-20 127 P	2023-10-27 127 C	2023-10-27 127 P
2023-09-29	$127.12	$3.93	$3.48	$5.58	$4.95
2023-10-02	$129.46	$5.15	$2.41	$6.73	$3.85
2023-10-03	$124.72	$2.86	$4.78	$4.42	$6.20
2023-10-04	$127.00	$3.65	$3.23	$5.27	$4.70
2023-10-05	$125.96	$2.96	$3.75	$4.73	$5.35
2023-10-06	$127.96	$3.65	$2.45	$5.35	$4.00
2023-10-09	$128.26	$3.65	$2.14	$5.40	$3.75
2023-10-10	$129.48	$4.17	$1.46	$5.95	$3.10
2023-10-11	$131.83	$5.85	$0.75	$7.48	$2.25
2023-10-12	$132.33	$6.02	$0.57	$7.70	$2.11
2023-10-13	$129.79	$4.10	$1.22	$6.80	$3.75
2023-10-16	$132.55	$6.08	$0.31	$8.32	$2.40
2023-10-17	$131.47	$4.90	$0.34	$7.48	$2.76
2023-10-18	$128.13	$2.38	$1.15	$5.48	$4.12
2023-10-19	$128.40	$2.12	$0.59	$5.65	$4.00
2023-10-20	$125.17	$0.00	$1.83	$3.77	$5.42
2023-10-23	$126.56	$0.00	$1.83	$4.15	$4.62
2023-10-24	$128.56	$0.00	$1.83	$5.35	$3.62
2023-10-25	$121.39	$0.00	$1.83	$2.63	$8.20
2023-10-26	$119.57	$0.00	$1.83	$1.77	$8.97
2023-10-27	$127.74	$0.00	$1.83	$0.74	$0.00

Exhibit 23.1 Option Pricing for 127 Strike Calls and Puts Expiring on 2023–10-20 and 2023–10-27

Date	AMZN	Position 1	Position 2	Cumulative P&L 1	Cumulative P&L 2
2023-09-29	$127.12	$10.53	$3.12	$0.00	$0.00
2023-10-02	$129.46	$10.58	$3.02	$0.05	-$0.10
2023-10-03	$124.72	$10.62	$2.98	$0.09	-$0.14
2023-10-04	$127.00	$9.97	$3.09	-$0.56	-$0.03
2023-10-05	$125.96	$10.08	$3.37	-$0.45	$0.25
2023-10-06	$127.96	$9.35	$3.25	-$1.18	$0.13
2023-10-09	$128.26	$9.15	$3.36	-$1.38	$0.24
2023-10-10	$129.48	$9.05	$3.42	-$1.48	$0.30
2023-10-11	$131.83	$9.73	$3.13	-$0.80	$0.01
2023-10-12	$132.33	$9.81	$3.22	-$0.72	$0.10
2023-10-13	$129.79	$10.55	$5.23	$0.02	$2.11
2023-10-16	$132.55	$10.72	$4.33	$0.19	$1.21
2023-10-17	$131.47	$10.24	$5.00	-$0.29	$1.88
2023-10-18	$128.13	$9.60	$6.07	-$0.93	$2.95
2023-10-19	$128.40	$9.65	$6.94	-$0.88	$3.82
2023-10-20	$125.17	$9.19	$7.36	-$1.34	$4.24
2023-10-23	$126.56	$8.77	$6.94	-$1.76	$3.82
2023-10-24	$128.56	$8.97	$7.14	-$1.56	$4.02
2023-10-25	$121.39	$10.83	$9.00	$0.30	$5.88
2023-10-26	$119.57	$10.74	$8.91	$0.21	$5.79
2023-10-27	$127.74	$0.74	-$1.09	-$9.79	-$4.21

Exhibit 23.2 Value and P&L of Positions 1 and 2

between 2023–10–20 and 2023–10–27 was 72% despite a forward realized volatility estimate of 53% on 2023–09–29.

Analysis of Amazon Case Study

Most great investors perform "post-mortems" of their decisions regardless of whether an outcome is positive or negative. While it is always possible in investing for an individual decision to be good and an outcome to bad and vice versa, decisions are rarely perfect and revisiting them provides an opportunity to learn regardless of outcome. In this section, we seek to understand why the trades above did not work.

First, consider each position's primary exposure to the underlying, or delta. Deltas for each option and positions 1 and 2 are displayed in Exhibit 23.3. Note that option Greeks are additive, so the net delta of any option structure is simply the sum of all the underlying position deltas. For example, on 2023–09–29, position 1 has a net delta of $0.08 = 0.54 + (-0.46)$.

One of the primary challenges with both positions is that even though there was a lot of volatility over the period, the total squared move in the underlying stock was quite small over the full period: the stock closed at \$127.12 on 2023–09–29 and \$127.74 on 2023–10–27. This was due to a

Date	AMZN	2023-10-20 127 C	2023-10-20 127 P	2023-10-27 127 C	2023-10-27 127 P	Position 1	Position 2
2023-09-29	$127.12	0.54	-0.47	0.54	-0.46	0.08	0.01
2023-10-02	$129.46	0.63	-0.37	0.61	-0.39	0.22	-0.04
2023-10-03	$124.72	0.43	-0.58	0.47	-0.54	-0.07	0.08
2023-10-04	$127.00	0.53	-0.48	0.53	-0.47	0.06	0.01
2023-10-05	$125.96	0.48	-0.53	0.50	-0.5	0	0.05
2023-10-06	$127.96	0.58	-0.43	0.56	-0.44	0.12	-0.03
2023-10-09	$128.26	0.59	-0.41	0.57	-0.43	0.14	-0.04
2023-10-10	$129.48	0.67	-0.33	0.62	-0.38	0.24	-0.10
2023-10-11	$131.83	0.78	-0.21	0.69	-0.31	0.38	-0.19
2023-10-12	$132.33	0.83	-0.17	0.71	-0.29	0.42	-0.24
2023-10-13	$129.79	0.70	-0.31	0.61	-0.39	0.22	-0.17
2023-10-16	$132.55	0.85	-0.12	0.70	-0.3	0.4	-0.33
2023-10-17	$131.47	0.85	-0.15	0.67	-0.33	0.34	-0.36
2023-10-18	$128.13	0.61	-0.38	0.56	-0.44	0.12	-0.11
2023-10-19	$128.40	0.67	-0.31	0.57	-0.43	0.14	-0.22
2023-10-20	$125.17	0	0	0.46	-0.54	-0.08	-0.08
2023-10-23	$126.56	0	0	0.5	-0.5	0	0
2023-10-24	$128.56	0	0	0.57	-0.43	0.14	0.14
2023-10-25	$121.39	0	0	0.34	-0.66	-0.32	-0.32
2023-10-26	$119.57	0	0	0.27	-0.74	-0.47	-0.47

Exhibit 23.3 First-order exposure (delta) of each leg and position

mean-reversion effect that manifested over the period. A challenging aspect of managing a book of options is that Greeks change all the time, so most option books are managed dynamically rather than set and forget. As an example of how dynamic management would have helped in this case, both positions had a net delta of –0.47 going into the earnings announcement, meaning that by the time the earnings announcement was going to hit the market, most of the risk of the position was driven by an outright short position of –0.47 shares. A purer bet on volatility would have included maintaining delta neutrality at each time step. Going into the after-market announcement on 2023–10–26, this would have included buying 0.47 shares on 2023–10–26 at $119.57, which would improve the P&L of either position given the large move to the upside, with AMZN closing at $127.74 on 2023–10–27.

Another primary challenge with both positions' hold-to-maturity approach is the path forward that volatility took over the period. Exhibit 23.4 leverages Eq. (23.2) to compute forward volatility at each time step.

Exhibit 23.4 sheds some light on another important market dynamic that explains the results from Exhibit 23.2. Forward volatility was substantially bid up from 53% on 2023–09–29 to over 170% on 2023–10–26, when the close right before earnings were released. Investors went from underpricing earnings volatility to *overpricing* an earnings move substantially. This is also visible

Date	2023-10-20 Volatility	2023-10-27 Volatility	Forward Volatility
2023-09-29	30.34%	37.41%	53.27%
2023-10-02	31.78%	38.53%	52.01%
2023-10-03	34.38%	40.80%	53.27%
2023-10-04	32.34%	39.17%	51.47%
2023-10-05	32.57%	40.57%	53.85%
2023-10-06	30.21%	38.06%	50.20%
2023-10-09	32.06%	40.06%	50.12%
2023-10-10	30.72%	39.72%	49.83%
2023-10-11	31.67%	40.72%	50.01%
2023-10-12	30.76%	41.44%	50.98%
2023-10-13	33.57%	51.18%	64.13%
2023-10-16	38.50%	53.76%	60.78%
2023-10-17	37.95%	55.82%	61.92%
2023-10-18	45.17%	59.73%	63.28%
2023-10-19	45.89%	63.47%	65.59%
2023-10-20	0.00%	65.30%	65.30%
2023-10-23	0.00%	82.83%	82.83%
2023-10-24	0.00%	96.12%	96.12%
2023-10-25	0.00%	134.29%	134.29%
2023-10-26	0.00%	171.67%	171.67%
2023-10-27	0.00%	0.00%	0.00%

Exhibit 23.4 Implied and Forward Implied Volatility

in position 2's cumulative P&L, which steadily grows until being erased on the post-announcement move.

With the benefit of hindsight, the best decision would have been to exit position 2 as market expectations began to predict moves that may have seemed "unrealistic" to the investor.

Summary

The case focuses on leveraging equity options to manage and profit from market event risk. The limitation of traditional models, like the Black–Scholes model, in accounting for non-constant volatility around anticipated events (e.g., earnings announcements, elections, Fed policy meetings), is discussed. To deal with this limitation, forward implied volatility is introduced, a technique that uses options with overlapping maturities to estimate expected volatility changes around these events. Through a case study on Amazon (AMZN), we showed the use of forward implied volatility to predict market reactions to an earnings announcement.

Two trading strategies are examined—one involves buying a straddle that expires after the earnings announcement. At the same time, the other combines buying a post-earnings straddle with shorting a pre-earnings straddle. These positions are used to evaluate performance and assess profitability based on volatility forecasts. Ultimately, both strategies result in losses due to a market mean-reversion effect and the complexities of managing "Greeks" (option sensitivities such as delta). The analysis highlights that forward volatility rose sharply leading up to the event, which impacted profitability due to post-announcement adjustments. This discussion underscores the importance of dynamically managing option positions and adjusting exposure as market expectations evolve, particularly when trading around significant events.

24

Hedging Interest Rate Risk in High-Yield Bonds

Alexander Rudin

Hedging interest rate exposure in bond portfolios presents complex challenges that require careful consideration of objectives and methodologies. This case explores the nuances of hedging in the context of a high-yield bond portfolio, providing insights into the theoretical foundations and practical applications of hedging strategies. The primary focus is determining an optimal hedge ratio that balances risk reduction with performance objectives.

The case begins with a detailed explanation of the key principles of hedging, including the mathematical framework for calculating hedge ratios and the trade-offs in implementing such strategies. It then transitions to the specific challenges of applying these principles to high-yield bonds, where traditional measures like duration can lead to unexpected outcomes due to the unique behavior of credit spreads and interest rates. Using historical data and illustrative examples, the case examines the effectiveness of hedging strategies, including using Treasury futures as hedging instruments.

The analysis culminates in discussing empirical results, highlighting instances where hedging increased portfolio volatility rather than reducing it. The case also guides how to address the discrepancies between analytical and empirical durations, emphasizing the importance of understanding the relationship between interest rates and credit spreads. By examining theoretical and empirical perspectives, this case equips portfolio managers with

A. Rudin (✉)
Global Head of Multi-Asset and Fixed Income Research, State Street Global Advisors, Boston, USA
e-mail: Alexander_Rudin@ssga.com

F. J. Fabozzi and M. de Jong (eds.), *Derivatives Applications in Asset Management*,
https://doi.org/10.1007/978-3-031-86354-7_24

a comprehensive framework for evaluating the effectiveness of interest rate hedging in high-yield portfolios.

Determining the Objective for Hedging

The primary goal of hedging is to immunize the portfolio against specific market exposures, such as interest rate fluctuations. Without hedging, portfolio returns would correlate with these market changes. The mathematical expression of this objective involves calculating the hedge ratio, which minimizes the variance of the hedged returns.

Suppose the portfolio manager's objective is to hedge interest rate exposure for a corporate bond portfolio. To do that, the manager must select an investable "hedge asset" that represents that interest rate exposure. For example, a Treasury bond portfolio of similar duration might be chosen. We will use the following notation:

β^* = hedge ratio, that is the amount of hedge asset that is needed to immunize a portfolio against market exposure per unit of that portfolio.

r_i = returns on the unhedged portfolio.

x_i = returns of the hedge asset.

As noted above, we will hedge the corporate bond portfolio against interest rate movements using a Treasury bond portfolio with a similar duration. The objective is then to find a hedge ratio, β^* that minimizes the variance of the hedged portfolio's returns or $r_i - \beta x_i$. It can be shown that such hedge ratio is

$$\beta^* = \rho_{xr} \frac{\sigma_r}{\sigma_x}, \tag{24.1}$$

where

ρ_{xr} = correlation coefficient between the portfolio returns and the hedge asset (the Treasuries).

σ_r= volatility of the unhedged portfolio returns.

σ_x = volatility of the hedge asset returns.

It is important to note that minimizing variance does not necessarily mean maximizing the risk-adjusted returns. The latter can be assessed by calculating the Sharpe ratio of the hedged strategy, which can be done using the following expression:

$$SR_H = SR_r \frac{1 - \rho_{xr}(SR_x/SR_r)}{\sqrt{1 - \rho_{xr}{}^2}} \tag{24.2}$$

where
SR_r = Sharpe ratio of the unhedged strategy ($SR_r = \frac{\mu_r}{\sigma_r}$).
SR_x = Sharpe ratio for the hedge asset ($SR_x = \frac{\mu_x}{\sigma_x}$).

The effectiveness of the hedge depends on the correlation between the hedge and the strategy (ρ_{xr}), as well as the individual risk-adjusted returns (i.e., Sharpe ratio). The decision to hedge hinges on a trade-off between reduced risk and potential return reductions.

When hedging, the portfolio manager replaces a portfolio that is long the strategy with a portfolio that is long the strategy and short the hedge. If hedging adds to the returns ($SR_x < 0$) or is costless ($SR_x = 0$), then hedging is always warranted ($SR_H > SR_r$). Unfortunately, those situations are rare.

More commonly, the hedge asset has a positive expected return ($SR_x > 0$) and hedging incurs costs. Assuming that all Sharpe ratios are positive and correlation ρ_{xr} is positive as well (which provides the original motivation to hedge), hedging according to the Eq. (24.1) improves risk-adjusted returns of the unhedged strategy ($SR_H > SR_r$) only if

$$\rho_{xr} > \frac{2S}{1+S^2}, \tag{24.3}$$

where $S = \frac{SR_x}{SR_r}$.

Equation (24.3) quantifies the trade-off between returns lost and risk reduction gained. In practice, bond portfolio managers aim to deploy hedging strategies only if they believe the condition given by Eq. (24.3) is satisfied.

Determining the Hedge Ratio

Equation (24.1) provides an empirical method for determining the hedge ratio—using historical data to evaluate standard deviations and correlations between the strategy and the hedge to find the optimal value β*. However, this approach presents an immediate challenge: empirical estimates are often noisy and dependent on the calculation method. For example, the hedger might use exponentially weighted volatility or moving window volatility and consider daily, weekly, or monthly returns over various horizons. Different methods can lead to different outcomes, creating uncertainty about which method—and, in turn, which hedge ratio—to use in a specific situation.

Bond portfolio managers often rely on analytical rather than empirical methods for hedge ratio evaluation to avoid this uncertainty. Analytically computed (and thus well-defined) duration is often used to calculate hedge ratios—we will explain this process later. While such an analytical approach is often well-justified, it can sometimes fail. We will demonstrate an illustrative example of hedging rate exposure in the high-yield bond market, where relying on duration deviates so far from empirical reality that it becomes counterproductive.

Hedging Interest Rate Exposure in High-Yield Bonds

This illustration demonstrates the potential complexities in determining the correct hedge ratio for interest rate exposure in credit portfolios. The measure of a bond and bond portfolio's exposure to interest rates is duration. We will use the Bloomberg US Corporate High Yield Bond Index (Bloomberg ticker LF98TRUU) for our example, denoted HY index, as this index is often used as a benchmark for the high-yield corporate bond space in the US. The duration of that index was 3.15 years as of 12/31/2023 and varied roughly between three and five years in the last two decades. Duration appears to be an ideal choice as an *analytical* hedge ratio if eliminating the effect of rates on high-yield bond holdings is sought. Let's build a hedging strategy under this assumption.

Mechanically, an analytical hedge ratio is simply a ratio of credit portfolio duration to the duration of the Treasury portfolio we chose as a hedge. If—as it often is the case—our Treasury portfolio maintains a duration that is an exact match to the credit portfolio duration, such an analytical hedge ratio becomes equal to one. In that case, the interest rate hedging process entails shorting \$1 in duration-matching Treasuries for every \$1 of our credit exposure. The result of this popular hedging strategy has a special name, "excess returns" of the credit portfolio.

If we hedge interest rate exposure using derivatives, 5-year Treasury bond futures (Bloomberg ticker FV1 COMB) are a solid choice. These futures are liquid, and their duration is comparable to that of the high-yield bond index. A realistic hedging strategy could be implemented: Assume \$100 million was invested in the high-yield bond index at a given time and has been continuously held since, with interest income reinvested into additional index holdings. We could hedge the interest rate exposure of those holdings by utilizing bond futures and using duration calculated by the index provider as a guide for the number of futures contracts to buy.

	The Bloomberg US Corporate High Yield Bond Index	5-Year US Treasury Note Futures	Generic 5y Treasury Duration	High Yield Index Duration	HY Total Returns	(Duration) Hedge Performance	Hedged Returns
1/31/2023	2269.3	109.2	3.6	3.8	3.8%	1.1%	2.7%
2/28/2023	2240.1	106.7	4.2	3.8	-1.3%	-2.5%	1.2%
3/31/2023	2264.0	109.5	3.6	3.7	1.1%	2.4%	-1.4%
4/30/2023	2286.6	109.7	3.5	3.6	1.0%	0.2%	0.8%
5/31/2023	2265.7	108.5	3.8	3.6	-0.9%	-1.2%	0.3%
6/30/2023	2303.6	106.9	4.2	3.5	1.7%	-1.3%	3.0%
7/31/2023	2335.4	106.8	4.2	3.5	1.4%	-0.1%	1.5%
8/31/2023	2341.9	106.4	4.3	3.5	0.3%	-0.3%	0.6%
9/30/2023	2314.2	105.2	4.6	3.5	-1.2%	-1.0%	-0.2%
10/31/2023	2287.2	104.5	4.9	3.6	-1.2%	-0.5%	-0.7%
11/30/2023	2390.8	106.4	4.3	3.4	4.5%	1.3%	3.2%
12/31/2023	2480.0	108.7	3.8	3.2	3.7%	1.7%	2.0%

Exhibit 24.1 Example of hedging interest rates in high-yield bonds. *Data source* Bloomberg. Returns calculations made by the author

Now, let us walk through a calculation in more detail. Exhibit 24.1 shows relevant data for 2023. The first four columns come directly from Bloomberg (or another data provider) and show the value of the high-yield bond index (inclusive of accrued interest), prices of 5-year Treasury bond futures, duration of a generic 5-year Treasury bond, and that of the high-yield bond index.

The fifth column contains calculated month-on-month returns of the high-yield index. They can be calculated from the first column in the exhibit. For example, total return on 12/29/2023 is [(2480.0/2390.8) – 1] or 3.7%.

Calculation of values in the sixth column—Hedge Performance—involves three steps.

First, we need to calculate the analytical hedge ratio as described above—as a ratio of the duration of the HY index and of our chosen hedge, the 5-year Treasury Note Futures. Continuing with the 12/29/2023 example, such analytical hedge ratio is [3.4/4.3] or 0.79. Note that we have utilized duration values from the previous month (Nov 2023) to eliminate look-ahead bias.

Then, we need to calculate the month-on-month returns of the hedged asset itself. For December 2023, such return is [(108.7/106.4) – 1] or 2.16%.

Finally, the performance of our duration hedge is a product of the hedge asset return and the amount of this asset that we hold, which is determined by the hedge ratio. For December 2023, this yields [2.16% 0.79] or 1.7%.

The last column of the table provides Hedged Returns, which are high-yield returns minus the hedge performance. December 2023 yields 3.7% – 1.7% = 2.0%.

Exhibit 24.2 shows the cumulative performance of the unhedged strategy versus the hedged one over the past 20 years, leading to an interesting observation: the hedged strategy, intended to reduce risk, was more volatile than the unhedged one. Simple calculations confirm this: the annualized volatility

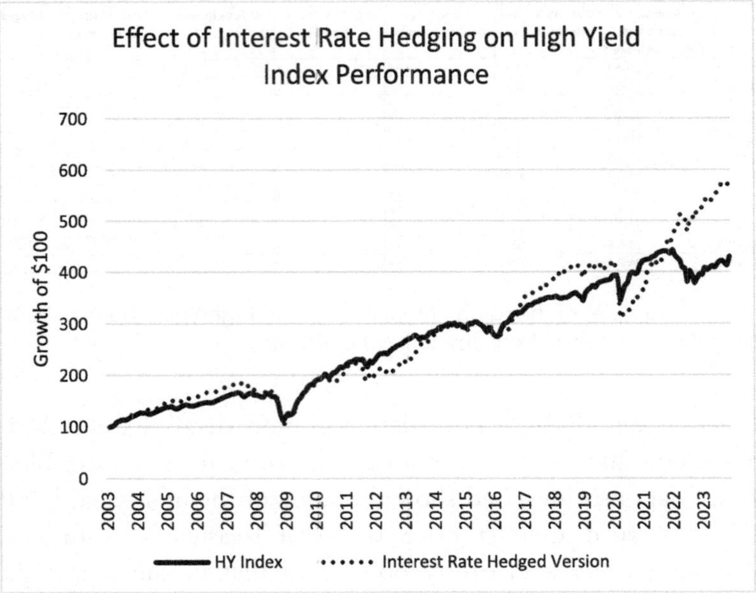

Exhibit 24.2 Effect of interest rate hedging on high-yield index performance

of the index itself was 9%, while the supposedly hedged strategy exhibited an annualized volatility of 13%!

Discussion and Concluding Remarks

How can that be? The answer lies in the choice of the hedge ratio based on duration. A corporate bond's price is the present value of cash flows expected by the bondholder. The discount rate for such present value calculation is the sum of the Treasury rate and the so-called option-adjusted spread (OAS); that is,

$$Y = Treasury\_Rate + OAS \tag{24.4}$$

Duration measures the sensitivity of bond prices to changes in Treasury rates, holding everything else constant. However, a simple test shows that things are not constant when interest rates change. There is a strong negative correlation between interest rate changes and option-adjusted credit spreads. When the market anticipates challenges to future growth, credit spreads tend to widen in anticipation of credit losses and a general increase in risk premia.

Simultaneously, rates tend to drop as investors expect more accommodative monetary policy, which tends to amortize the widening effect.

This push–pull relationship is evident for all corporate bonds, but in the case of high-yield bonds, interest rates and credit spread fluctuations tend to offset each other significantly. As a result, the "empirical duration" of high-yield bonds (defined as the empirically observed ratio of bond price changes to rate changes) tends to be much lower than the analytical duration reported by index providers. For the period considered (2003–2024), while the average analytical duration was over four years, the empirical duration of the high-yield bond index was not only much smaller but went into the negative territory (the empirical duration over this period was an estimated minus 0.41).

The lesson learned here is that choosing a hedge ratio is critical and often requires careful consideration. In our illustration, the most obvious choice, such as analytical duration, may be ineffective, resulting in counterintuitive consequences.

Summary

This case study examines the complexities of hedging interest rate exposure in high-yield bond portfolios, focusing on the trade-offs between risk reduction and performance. Using a blend of theoretical frameworks and empirical analysis, the case highlights the challenges of applying traditional measures like duration to high-yield bonds. Key insights reveal that high-yield bonds often exhibit unique behaviors, such as a strong negative correlation between interest rate changes and credit spreads, which can undermine the effectiveness of duration-based hedging strategies.

The case demonstrates through detailed examples and historical data how using Treasury futures as a hedging instrument can lead to counterintuitive outcomes, including increased portfolio volatility. These findings underscore the importance of distinguishing between analytical and empirical durations and adapting hedging strategies to the specific dynamics of high-yield bonds. This case offers valuable lessons for portfolio managers seeking to optimize their hedging strategies in a high-yield context by providing a practical framework and real-world examples.

25

The Role of Futures in Tactical Asset Allocation: Managing Market Exposure

Scott Hixon

This case demonstrates the role of futures in tactical asset allocation, highlighting their value for portfolio managers seeking flexibility, cost-efficiency, and precision in adjusting market exposures. It begins by explaining how futures contracts function across asset classes like equities and treasuries, detailing their pricing structures and unique benefits.

Top-down asset allocation generally refers to the periodic shifting of portfolio exposures from one group of asset classes to another in hopes of generating returns greater than a stated benchmark. However, the "how" of shifting asset class exposures is often neglected, and details matter. This discussion will focus on using futures contracts to introduce tactical allocation shifts to a balanced portfolio. However, before starting, a key aspect of trading futures contracts is understanding their price conventions.

Futures contracts are popular tactical allocation tools for portfolio managers for several reasons. Futures contracts typically have lower transaction costs than trading the underlying assets directly, including lower commissions and tighter bid-ask spreads. Futures allow portfolio managers to gain significant exposure to an asset class with a relatively small initial investment, known as the margin. Futures markets are highly liquid, enabling managers to enter and exit positions quickly without significantly impacting

S. Hixon (✉)
Senior Portfolio Manager and Head of Research for Invesco's Global Strategies Team, Atlanta, USA
e-mail: Scott.Hixon@invesco.com

F. J. Fabozzi and M. de Jong (eds.), *Derivatives Applications in Asset Management*,
https://doi.org/10.1007/978-3-031-86354-7_25

the market price, which is a crucial feature for implementing tactical asset allocation shifts.

Futures-Based Asset Allocation

In tactical asset allocation, futures contracts are a powerful tool for making swift, cost-effective adjustments to portfolio exposures. The following case studies illustrate practical applications of futures in a balanced portfolio, beginning with a standard 60/40 allocation model. This illustration demonstrates how futures can streamline allocation shifts between asset classes, reducing the need for extensive individual trades and allowing for more precise exposure control. By examining the 60/40 portfolio and beyond, we explore how futures contracts enable dynamic adjustments that align with both strategic and tactical investment goals.

Standard 60/40 Portfolio Illustration

Consider a simple portfolio allocated 60% to global equities (benchmarked to the MSCI World Equity Index) and 40% invested in US Long-Term Treasuries. This portfolio may be created using individual securities to replicate the underlying benchmark exposures and suggests that allocation decisions may need to buy or sell many securities to shift the allocation toward or away from equities or bonds. An alternative to trading individual securities may be to use standard futures contracts to affect the asset allocation shift. The purpose of this case study is to describe how futures may be used to shift the asset allocation of a multi-asset portfolio efficiently.

Futures contracts bring several obvious benefits to the implementation of asset allocation decisions. First, explicit transaction costs (commissions and bid/ask spreads) are generally small. Second, they have standard contract sizes, which makes including them in a portfolio straightforward. For example, the MSCI World Index futures contract is tied to the MSCI World Net Total Return USD Index and trades at a price equal to $10 times the underlying index level. As of December 31, 2023, this means that one contract is equal to $89,347.98 ($10 8,934.795). US long-bond futures prices are based on 20-year, 6% US Treasury bonds with a face value of $100,000. As of December 31, 2023, the long-bond futures contract was priced at $124.9375 (US bond futures are priced in increments of 1/32), meaning that one long-bond futures contract equaled $124,937.50.

The last obvious benefit of futures is that they are generally unfunded investments. Unlike stocks and bonds, where the full value of the purchase amount is usually required upfront, futures contracts can be purchased with a small initial cash outlay. This small outlay is referred to as the initial margin requirement. Following the initial purchase, futures contracts are usually cash-settled daily against the initial margin requirement unless the balance falls below a minimum margin requirement where additional collateral must be posted to maintain the position.

For this case study, we will assume that we have an investment of $200 million. Under a traditional approach, the investor might allocate $120 million (60%) to individual equity securities and $80 million (40%) to purchase long-term bonds. However, we might assume that the investor would like to allocate tactically between stocks and long-term bonds over time and that $10 million is the initial margin requirement. Under this assumption, the portfolio might be allocated $120 million to global equities (benchmarked against the MSCI World Index), $70 million to long-term bonds, and $10 million to cash as the initial margin requirement. The portfolio is underinvested by 5% in long-term bonds relative to the benchmark (40%). Without an active view, the investor may "fix" the allocation shortfall to bonds by buying bond futures contracts equal to $10 million. Recall that as of December 31, 2023, the bond futures contract was priced at $124.9375 and that each contract has a value of $124,937.50. By purchasing 80 ($10 million/$124,937.50) futures contracts, the investor has increased their long-bond allocation by approximately $10 million to reach the benchmark allocation of 40%.

Exhibit 25.1 highlights the difference between the traditional allocation and the futures-based allocation. Because of the standard contract size, the investor cannot "exactly" replace the $10 million cash with long-term bond exposure. Purchasing 81 contracts would over-allocate to bonds and result in leverage at the total portfolio level. Including futures, the portfolio allocation equals 60% equity and 40% bond.

Increasing Equity Allocation Using Futures

Now consider a situation where the investor wishes to express the view that global equities will outperform bonds and would like to shift the allocation mix by 5% from bonds to stocks. This view requires that $10 million be moved from the bond allocation to stocks. Since each MSCI World Index futures contract is equal to $89,347.98 (as of December 31, 2023), the

	Traditional Portfolio	Futures-Based Portfolio	# of Futures Contracts
Cash Equity Allocation	$120,000,000	$120,000,000	
Cash Bond Allocation	$80,000,000	$70,000,000	
Bond Futures Allocation	$0	***$9,995,000***	***+80***
Cash Margin	$0	$10,000,000	
Total (excl. Cash Margin)	$200,000,000	$199,995,000	
Total Equity	$120,000,000	$120,000,000	
Total Bond	$80,000,000	$79,995,000	

Exhibit 25.1 Adding Bond Futures to the Traditional Portfolio

investor should purchase 111 contracts (111$89,347.98 = $9,917,625.78). Again, because of the standard contract size, the full amount of $10 million is impossible without introducing a small amount of leverage to the portfolio. Simultaneously, the 80 contracts of long-bond futures should be sold to reduce the bond allocation by $9,995,000. Exhibit 25.2 illustrates how the portfolio has changed.

	Futures-Based Portfolio	# of Futures Contracts	Adjusted Futures-based Portfolio	# of Futures Contracts
Cash Equity Allocation	$120,000,000		$120,000,000	
Equity Futures Allocation			***$9,917,626***	***+111***
Cash Bond Allocation	$70,000,000		$70,000,000	
Bond Futures Allocation	$9,995,000	+80	***$0***	***0***
Cash Margin	$10,000,000		$10,000,000	
Total (excl. Cash Margin)	$199,995,000		$199,917,626	
Total Equity	$120,000,000		$129,917,626	
Total Bond	$79,995,000		$70,000,000	

Exhibit 25.2 Increasing the Equity Allocation Using Index Futures

Decreasing Equity Allocation Using Futures

After purchasing 111 equity futures contracts and selling 80 bond futures contracts, the portfolio is allocated 64.98% to equities and 35.01% to bonds. Using standard futures contracts makes the implementation of the asset allocation decision much more accessible versus the alternative of increasing the equity allocation through the purchase of many individual stock positions. Finally, the active allocation decision has changed to overweigh bonds versus stocks by 5% versus the original 60/40 portfolio. In this scenario, the investor prefers to allocate $90 million to bonds and $110 million to equities. Exhibit 25.3 shows the difference versus the 60/40 portfolio.

After shorting 111 equity futures contracts and buying 159 bond futures contracts, the portfolio is allocated as 55.06% equity and 44.94% bonds. An additional comment should be highlighted in this example. Under the first scenario (see Exhibit 25.1), a 5% allocation to bond futures resulted in the purchase of 80 contracts, while, under the latest scenario, an additional 5% allocation is only a further 79 contracts rather than an additional 80 contracts. The one contract difference relates to the difference in value between the equity and bond futures contracts. The bond futures contract has a higher value than the equity contracts ($124,937.50 versus $89,347.98). If the portfolio held 160 bond contracts, the total value of the futures exposure plus the underlying cash investment exposure would exceed the $200 million portfolio value. In these cases, the number of contracts should be adjusted to ensure no portfolio leverage.

	Futures-Based Portfolio	# of Futures Contracts	Adjusted Futures-based Portfolio	# of Futures Contracts
Cash Equity Allocation	$120,000,000		$120,000,000	
Equity Futures Allocation			***-$9,917,626***	***-111***
Cash Bond Allocation	$70,000,000		$70,000,000	
Bond Futures Allocation	$9,995,000	+80	***$19,865,063***	***+159***
Cash Margin	$10,000,000		$10,000,000	
Total (excl. Cash Margin)	$199,995,000			
Total Equity	$120,000,000		$110,082,374	
Total Bond	$79,995,000		$89,865,063	

Exhibit 25.3 Decreasing the Equity Allocation Using Index Futures

Tax Considerations and Efficiency in Tactical Allocation

The tax treatment of futures contracts is worth discussing as they relate to tactical allocation decisions within taxable portfolios. Futures contracts benefit from a unique and favorable tax treatment based on the 60/40 rule. This rule means that 60% of the gains or losses associated with a position are treated as long-term capital gains or losses, while 40% are treated as short-term capital gains or losses. This treatment, along with the transaction cost benefits mentioned earlier, suggests that futures contracts are ideal for tactical investment horizons of less than one year since a capital gain on holding physical stocks or bonds for less than a one-year period is considered short-term and taxed at ordinary income tax rates. While holding periods of longer than a year may negate the tax benefits of futures contracts, the transaction cost differences between buying or selling physical securities and futures contracts should be examined before concluding whether trading physical securities are preferable to futures contracts for longer-term tactical views.

Summary

This case emphasizes futures as a strategic asset allocation tool, focusing on scenarios where futures enhance the ability to adjust portfolio exposures. Using detailed examples, it showcases the application of futures to achieve desired equity and bond allocations. It demonstrates how portfolio managers can tactically shift portfolio weights without extensive trades in individual securities. Furthermore, it discusses the tax advantages of futures under the 60/40 rule, making them especially appealing for short-term tactical decisions. This analysis positions futures as indispensable for cost-effective, flexible, and tax-efficient portfolio adjustments.

26

Use of Derivatives in Overlays: Downside Protection and Upside Capture

William Cazalet, Dimitri Curtil, and James Stavena

This case examines the strategic use of derivatives, specifically focusing on their role in overlay strategies designed to enhance portfolio returns while managing risk. Using listed derivatives such as futures and options, portfolio managers can implement tactical asset allocation (TAA) overlays that allow exposure to a broad array of asset classes without disrupting the core portfolio's structure. By doing so, portfolio managers can achieve greater diversification and generate additional returns independently of the benchmark index, a concept often referred to as "portable alpha."

The case delves into the mechanics of implementing TAA overlays, exploring the use of equity index futures, government bond futures, and options in combination with a core equity portfolio. Key considerations such as basis risk, initial margin requirements, and duration mismatches are addressed to provide a comprehensive understanding of these strategies. Furthermore, the case highlights the benefits and challenges of using options for downside protection and upside capture, illustrating their effectiveness during market stress periods such as the COVID-19 pandemic.

W. Cazalet · D. Curtil (✉) · J. Stavena
Newton Investment Management, San Francisco, CA, USA
e-mail: dimitri.curtil@newtonim.com

F. J. Fabozzi and M. de Jong (eds.), *Derivatives Applications in Asset Management*,
https://doi.org/10.1007/978-3-031-86354-7_26

Core Portfolio: Equity Index

The core portfolio in our illustration worth $10 million in total is comprised of a physical equity position of $8.5 million plus a residual position of $1.5 million, equitized by using E-mini S&P 500 futures contracts listed on the Chicago Mercantile Exchange (CME).[1]

For the physical component, the portfolio manager will simply purchase the stocks that comprise the S&P 500 Index, in the appropriate weights, or purchase an ETF (e.g., the iShares Core S&P 500 ETF[2] or the SPDR S&P 500 ETF Trust), with a combined value of $8.5 million. For the residual component, assume that, with the S&P 500 Index at 5,165, the CME's E-mini S&P 500 futures 3-month contract trades at 5,243.50. To achieve an exposure as close as possible to $1.5 million, the portfolio manager will need to purchase:

$$\text{Number of contracts} \times \text{Contract multiplier} \times \text{Futures price} \cong \$1,500,000$$

The contract multiplier for the E-mini S&P 500 is 50. Substituting into the above equation, we get.

$$\text{Number of contracts} \times 50 \times \$5,243.50 \cong \$1,500,000$$

Solving for the number of contracts we get

$$(\sim \$1,500,000)/(50 \times \$5,243.50) = 5.72 \cong 6 \text{ contracts}$$

The core portfolio is summarized in Exhibit 26.1.

Because the portfolio manager is long futures for the residual component of the core portfolio, the only up-front cash outlay related to the residual is

Security/Instrument	*Quantity*	*Price*	*Multiplier*	*(Notional) Value*	*% alloc.*
S&P 500® Index portfolio				$8,500,000	85%
E-mini S&P 500 3-month futures contract (CME)	6	$5,243.50	50	$1,573,050	~15%
Combined			**Total**	**$10,073,050**	

Exhibit 26.1 Core portfolio

[1] The specifications for the E-mini S&P 500 futures contract are available on the CME's website: https://www.cmegroup.com/markets/equities/sp/e-mini-sandp500.contractSpecs.html.

[2] The symbol for the iShares Core S&P 500 ETF is IVV; the symbol for the SPDR S&P 500 ETF Trust is SPY.

the initial margin that must be posted with the exchange as collateral for each contract. The CME's initial margin requirement per E-mini S&P 500 futures contract is $12,980, so the total initial margin required is:

$$6 \text{ contracts} \times \$12,980 = \$77,880$$

This means that, of the initial $10 million cash invested, $1,422,120[3] remains available for the TAA overlay; this will be used principally for managing the collateral associated with the derivative instruments used to implement the overlay.

Why does the portfolio manager not implement the entire core portfolio using futures? The short answer is basis risk. Recall that to maintain exposure to an underlying asset, such as an equity index, futures contracts must be rolled—that is, the portfolio manager must replace the exposure from the currently held futures contract with exposure from one with a further-out maturity before the currently held contract expires. This typically occurs on a quarterly cycle. The practice of rolling futures contracts from one maturity to the next introduces basis risk—the risk that there is a mismatch between the theoretical fair value of the futures contract and its actual quoted price, relative to the price of the underlying asset. While any mismatch for an index as liquid as the S&P 500 Index is likely to be minimal, the portfolio manager will still want to balance the utility of using futures to free up cash to implement a TAA overlay with any potential basis risk that exposure to futures contracts entails; limiting exposure to futures will keep such a risk contained.

Tactical Asset Allocation Overlay

Let's assume the overlay will add TAA exposure using listed derivatives on the S&P 500 Index and long-dated U.S. Treasury bonds. The portfolio manager anticipates that, at present, the S&P 500 carries a positive risk premium relative to both long-dated U.S. Treasury bonds and cash, presuming that large capitalization equities return more than both government bonds and short-term cash investments over the next 12 months. The portfolio manager also anticipates that bonds carry a positive risk premium relative to cash (also known as the term premium), suggesting that government bonds will return more than cash over the next 12 months.

[3] $10 million initial investment—$8.5 million physical stock portfolio—$77,880 initial margin on E-mini S&P 500 Index futures contracts.

Assume further that the portfolio manager regards bonds as a reasonable hedge to equities—that is, equities and bonds tend to be negatively correlated. If equities fall, bonds will likely rise as portfolio managers seek safety and so cushion the negative impact of the fall. On that basis, the portfolio manager implements the TAA overlay with a 20% allocation to equities (S&P 500) and a 10% allocation to bonds (U.S. Long Treasury Index).

Several permutations of derivatives enable us to achieve the desired exposures for the overlay; in this example, we explore two of them.

Simple Overlay: Equity Index and Government Bond Futures

The active TAA component can be overlaid on top of the core portfolio using S&P 500 futures and U.S. Treasury bond futures. The portfolio manager uses the CME's E-mini S&P 500 futures contract. Using the same prices as were used earlier to achieve an exposure as close as possible to \$2 million, and using the same calculation as for the core portfolio futures position, the portfolio manager will need to go long:

$$(\sim \$2,000,000)/(50 \times \$5,243.50) = 7.63 \cong 8 \text{ contracts}$$

For the fixed-income portion of the portfolio manager's tactical asset allocation, CME-listed U.S. Treasury bond futures[4] are used to gain exposure to the Bloomberg U.S. Long Treasury Index; the index measures the performance of U.S. dollar-denominated, fixed-rate, nominal debt issued by the U.S. Treasury with a maturity greater than 10 years.

Because the U.S. Treasury bond futures contract is based on bonds that have a remaining term to maturity of at least 15 years and less than 25 years from the first day of the futures delivery month, there will be a mismatch between its duration and the duration of the index, which captures the performance of any U.S. Treasury bond with a maturity of more than 10 years. The portfolio manager must therefore consider this duration mismatch between the futures contract (instrument) and the index when calculating how many futures contracts to go long.

Assume that the duration of the U.S. Treasury bond future is currently 11.39 years, while the duration of the Bloomberg U.S. Long Treasury Index is currently 15.05 years. With the U.S. Treasury bond futures contract trading

[4] The specifications for the U.S. Treasury bond future are available on the CME's website: https://www.cmegroup.com/markets/interest-rates/us-treasury/30-year-us-treasury-bond.contractSpecs.html.

Security/Instrument	*Quantity*	*Futures Price*	*Multiplier*	*Notional*	*% alloc.*
E-mini S&P 500 3-month futures contract (CME)	8	$5,243.50	50	$2,097,400	~20%
U.S. Treasury bond 3-month futures contract (CME), duration-adjusted	11	$118.4375	1,000	$985,982[6]	~10%
Combined			**Total**	**$3,083,382**	

Exhibit 26.2 TAA portfolio with stock and bond allocations

at $118'14,[5] to achieve an exposure as close as possible to $1 million, the portfolio manager will need to go long:

$$\text{Number of contracts} \times \text{Contract multiplier} \times \text{Futures price} \\ \times (\text{Instrument duration}) / (\text{Index duration}) \cong \$1,000,000$$

Solving for the number of contracts:

$$(\sim \$1,000,000)/(1,000 \times \$118.4375) \times 15.05/11.39 = 11.16 \cong 11 \text{ contracts}$$

The TAA overlay portfolio using only futures for implementation is summarized in Exhibit 26.2.

As with the core portfolio, the CME's initial margin requirement per E-mini S&P 500 Index futures contract is $12,980, so the total initial margin required is:

$$8 \text{ contracts} \times \$12,980 = \$103,840$$

Initial margin must also be posted for the U.S. Treasury bond futures contract; its margin requirement is $4,290 per contract, so the total initial margin required is:

$$11 \text{ contracts} \times \$4,290 = \$47,190$$

Total initial margin requirement is therefore $103,840 + $47,190 = $151,030.

[5] The contract has a minimum price fluctuation of 1/32nd of one point (1% of par); based on a face value of $100,000, this implies a minimum price fluctuation of $31.25. A futures price of 118' 14 therefore translates to $118.4375.

Combined Exposure

Because all the exposures in the combined core portfolio and TAA overlay are fixed exposures (sometimes referred to as delta 1), the return profile from the combined exposure of the core portfolio and the simple overlay will be linear—it will reflect the change in value of the underlying instruments in both portfolios weighted by the exposure to each. Exhibit 26.3 visualizes the combined exposure of the core portfolio and TAA overlay implemented using physical securities and futures, split between stocks and bonds.

Alternative Overlay: Index Futures and Options

The drawback of a delta-one overlay as described above is that it leaves the portfolio manager no opportunity to reduce exposure in a timely manner in case of adverse market movements to avoid significant losses. Instead, the portfolio manager may implement the same overlay but use both listed futures and call options on futures to build the TAA overlay.

In case of unanticipated adverse market movements, the portfolio manager can benefit from the convex payoff profile of a long call option position.

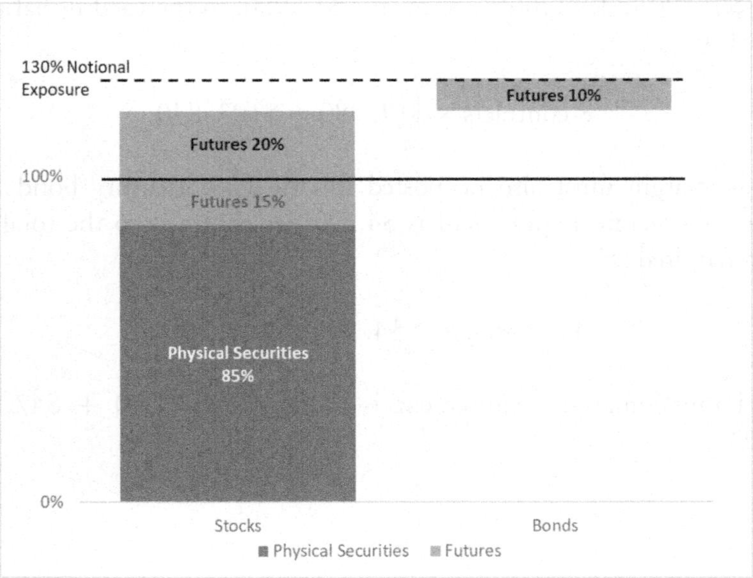

Exhibit 26.3 120% Stock and 10% bond allocation with TAA overlay implemented using futures

Benefiting from Call Option Convexity in a TAA Overlay Strategy

Call options with different strike prices (and, therefore, different deltas) can be deployed to provide both downside protection and upside participation in environments where a portfolio manager is uncertain about the direction of the equity market. The portfolio manager will thereby benefit from the options' convex payoff profile.

Option convexity refers to the non-linear nature of the relationship between the value of an option and its underlying asset. When a portfolio manager purchases a call option, exposure to the underlying will benefit from positive convexity, meaning the portfolio manager's exposure to the underlying equity index increases in a rally, and decreases in a sell-off, as the delta of the call options moves up and down, respectively, with the underlying index level.

One possible version of the TAA overlay (+20% stocks /+10% bonds) that substitutes some options (or convex payoffs) for futures to implement the active weights may look as follows:

Assuming again that 3-month expiry E-mini S&P 500 futures are trading at \$5,243.50 and U.S. Treasury Bond futures are trading at \$118.4375, the portfolio manager will allocate:

- a notional amount of \$2 million (20% of initial capital) to a 3-month 4,450[6] call option on the E-mini S&P 500 futures,[7]
- a notional amount of \$1 million (10% of initial capital) to U.S. Treasury bond futures.

The combination of the core portfolio and the TAA overlay implemented using physical securities, futures, and options on futures is visualized in Exhibit 26.4.

The E-mini S&P 500 options on futures have a contract multiplier of 50 per index point so, to achieve a notional exposure as close as possible to \$2 million, the portfolio manager will need to purchase:

$$\text{Number of call options} \times \text{Contract multiplier} \times \text{Futures price} \\ \times \text{Option delta} \cong \$2,000,000$$

[6] Strike selected: 15% in-the-money (vs. futures price) with 90 delta.

[7] The specifications for the option on the E-mini S&P 500 futures are available on the CME's website: https://www.cmegroup.com/markets/equities/sp/e-mini-sandp500.contractSpecs.options.html#optionProductId=138.

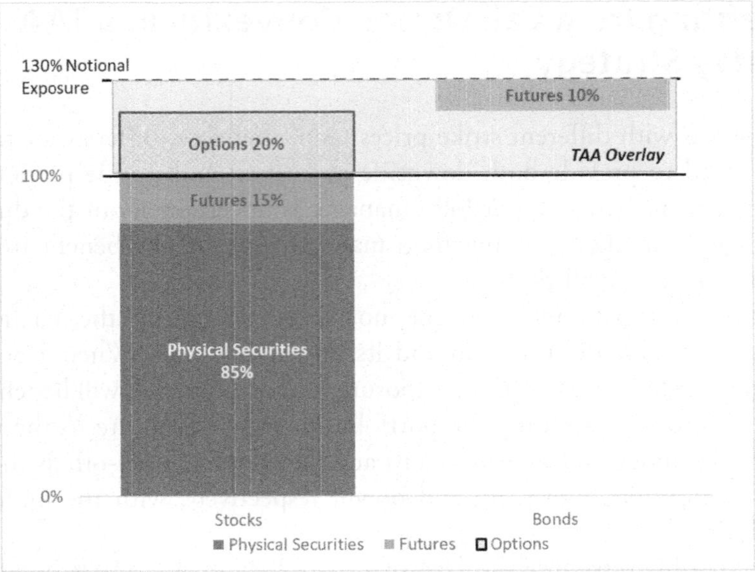

Exhibit 26.4 120% Stock and 10% Bond Allocation with TAA Overlay Implemented Using Options for Stocks and Futures for Bonds

Solving for the number of call options.

$$\$2,000,000/(50 \times \$5,243.50 \times 0.90) = 8.48 \cong 8 \text{ contracts}$$

The offer price for the 3-month 4,450 E-mini S&P 500 Index call option on futures is $803.75. As with the futures contract, the multiplier is 50. The total cost of the call option position will therefore be:

$$8 \text{ contracts} \times 50 \times \$803.75 = \$321,500$$

The U.S. Treasury bond futures contract is the same as in the previous example; with an allocation of $1 million, the portfolio manager will need to go long 11 contracts. The combined futures and options TAA overlay portfolio is shown in Exhibit 26.5.

Properties of Option Convexity in a TAA Overlay Strategy: 2020—COVID-19 Pandemic

The following illustration demonstrates the convex properties of equity index call options in the context of a TAA overlay strategy for delivering downside protection during a market correction and upside participation during a

Security/Instrument	Quantity	Futures Price	Multiplier	Notional	% alloc.
E-mini S&P 500 option on futures – 3-month 4,325 call options, adjusted for delta of 0.90	8	$5,243.50	50	$1,887,660	~20%
U.S. Treasury Bond 3-month futures contract (CME), duration-adjusted	11	$118.4375	1,000	$985,982	~10%
Combined			**Total**	**$2,873,642**	

Exhibit 26.5 Combined Futures and Options TAA Overlay Portfolio

market rally. The illustration covers the period from the start of 2020 to early September, when the market had reached a new high point.

The COVID-19 pandemic that originated in early 2020 had a dramatic impact on economies and markets. In the United States, the S&P 500 Index started the year strongly and had risen by just over 5% by the third week of February. But as the first deaths from the virus in the United States occurred during February and market participants began to grasp the potential severity of the outbreak, and its broader ramifications, the index fell sharply, losing just over a third of its value from its peak in just over four weeks.

In the weeks following the outbreak of the virus, the U.S. Treasury and the Federal Reserve Bank took extraordinary fiscal and monetary measures to stabilize both the economy and the stock market.[8] The S&P 500 Index rallied and, by early June, had climbed back to the level at which it had begun in 2020. The index consolidated in late June before resuming its rally to a new high in early September. The following illustration covers the option positioning for an actual TAA overlay strategy over this period, from January 1 to September 2, 2020.

The strategy in this illustration comprised a core S&P 500 Index portfolio, supplemented by a TAA overlay strategy using S&P 500 futures and options as well as U.S. Treasury bond futures.[9] Because the strategy could not borrow to fund overweight exposures, it used call options where exposure to the S&P 500 Index exceeded 100%.

[8] In the United States, the pandemic was met with massive monetary and fiscal stimulus: on March 3, 2020, the Federal Reserve (Fed) cut its fed funds target rate band from 1.75% to 1.25%, followed by a further cut on March 15, taking the target band to 0.00% - 0.25%; the Fed also announced a $700 billion quantitative easing program on the same day, followed by a program to buy up to $1 trillion of commercial paper to underwrite the continued flow of credit in the U.S. economy. On the fiscal front, the U.S. Senate passed the $2 trillion CARES Act on March 25, 2020, signed into law on March 27. The $484 billion Paycheck Protection Program followed in late April 2020.

[9] While the TAA overlay comprises both (1) call options on equity index futures and (2) bond futures, we only explore the role of the call options on equity index futures in this illustration.

First Quarter of 2020

The portfolio manager's strategy began the year with a net exposure of approximately 111% to the S&P 500; the exposure comprised physical securities (equity index portfolio), futures, and options. The call options embedded in the strategy at the start of the year were deep in-the-money, with deltas of 0.89 and 0.95, for a weighted-average delta of 0.92. The notional amount allocated to call options was 15% or, on a delta-adjusted basis, 13.9%. The in-the-money call options enabled the strategy to participate in market upside, while providing downside protection in the event of a sharp fall in the equity market; the options, along with the futures hedging their delta, effectively created a put option on a strategy that was, overall, overweight equities.

In January, the S&P 500 ended the month flat after rising 3% by mid-month. The portfolio manager had started the year with February 2850 and March 2950 call options but rolled the February calls to March 3000 calls (delta: 0.87) and added February 3350 and March 3370 calls (deltas: 0.26 and 0.29, respectively) early in the month. The rationale for adding out-of-the-money call options was their comparative cheapness (as measured by implied volatility) relative to the March 2950 and February 3350 call options; the weighted-average options delta fell to 0.66, due to the inclusion of the out-of-the-money call options in the portfolio.

In early February, as the S&P 500 Index continued to rise, the portfolio manager rolled the March 2950 call options to April 3050 call options (delta: 0.83) and purchased March 3410 call options (delta: 0.31), for a weighted-average options delta of 0.69. On February 19, 2020, the S&P 500 Index closed at 3,386.15; it then fell almost 1,150 points (34%) over the next four weeks to close at 2,237.40 on March 23. Over the same period, volatility, as measured by the VIX Index, spiked from the mid-teens to over 80. Exhibit 26.6 shows the level of the VIX Index between January 2, 2020, and September 2, 2020.

During this period, the option delta of the TAA overlay fell from a weighted-average 0.76 to, effectively, zero. The March 3000 call option was sold at a delta of 0.54, while the March 3370 and 3410 call options were allowed to expire because they had no value (i.e., their delta was zero). The April 3050 call options also expired worthless.

By the end of March 2020, the TAA strategy had adjusted from an overweight exposure of 115% to a modest underweight exposure to the S&P 500 (comprised of a 77.3% position in the equity index portfolio, a 20.8%

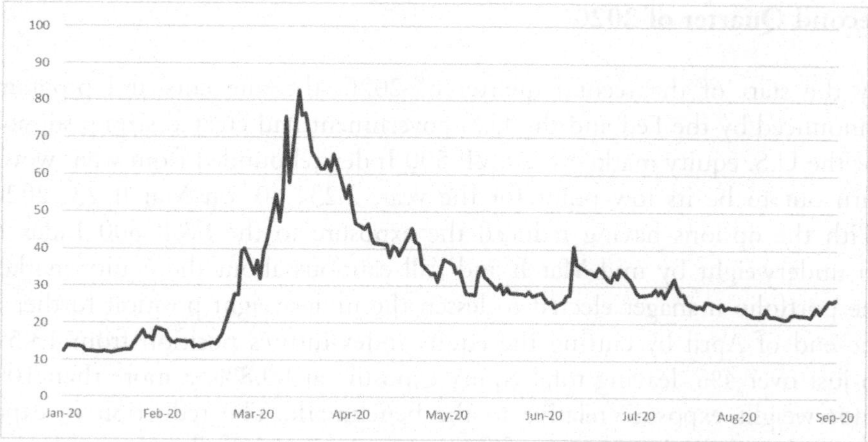

Exhibit 26.6 CBOE VIX Index—01/02/2020–09/02/2020

position in equity index futures and a negligible position (0.1%, on a delta-adjusted basis) in options on equity index futures, for a total equity exposure of 98.2%). The call options had effectively de-risked the portfolio's net equity exposure.

Exhibit 26.7 sets out the exposures of the various components (physical index portfolio, index futures, call options on index futures) of the strategy on the first trading day (1/2/2020) of the first quarter of 2020, followed by exposures on each day that the option exposure was adjusted via a sale or purchase, and the exposures on the last trading day of the quarter (3/31/2020). It also shows the combined option delta and how it changed during the quarter.

		1/2/2020	1/10/2020	1/13/2020	2/4/2020	2/6/2020	2/13/2020	3/6/2020	3/20/2020	3/31/2020
	S&P 500 Index	***3,244.67***	***3,281.81***	***3,271.13***	***3,280.61***	***3,344.92***	***3,365.90***	***2,954.20***	***2,431.94***	***2,614.69***
S&P 500 Index Portfolio		78.7%	79.7%	79.7%	78.9%	78.9%	79.9%	78.2%	78.7%	77.3%
S&P 500 E-mini Futures		18.2%	18.6%	17.4%	18.1%	18.9%	16.2%	23.1%	19.6%	20.8%
S&P 500 E-mini Options on Futures	Feb-20 2850	7.2%								
	Feb-20 3350		0.9%	1.3%	1.3%					
	Mar-20 3000		6.6%	6.8%	6.9%	7.0%	7.2%			
	Mar-20 3370			1.4%	1.5%	2.1%	2.6%	0.0%		
	Apr-20 3050				6.3%	6.5%	6.7%	2.9%	0.1%	0.1%
	Mar-20 2950	6.7%	6.9%	7.0%						
	Mar-20 3410					1.5%	1.9%	0.0%		
Combined option delta		***0.92***	***0.71***	***0.66***	***0.64***	***0.69***	***0.74***	***0.18***	***0.02***	***0.02***
Combined S&P 500 Exposure		**110.8%**	**112.8%**	**113.7%**	**113.0%**	**115.0%**	**114.5%**	**104.3%**	**98.5%**	**98.3%**

Exhibit 26.7 Changes to Equity Component of TAA Strategy during First Quarter of 2020

Second Quarter of 2020

By the start of the second quarter of 2020, the rate cuts and programs announced by the Fed and the U.S. government had created strong support for the U.S. equity market: the S&P 500 Index rebounded from what would turn out to be its low point for the year, 2,237.40, on March 23, 2020. With the options having reduced the exposure to the S&P 500 Index to an underweight by mid-March and still cautious about the equity market, the portfolio manager elected to lessen the underweight position further at the end of April by cutting the equity-index-futures position from 13.5% to just over 4%, leaving total equity exposure at 89.8%, a more than 10% underweight exposure relative to the benchmark. The reduction in exposure included eliminating out-of-the-money April 3050 calls, whose delta had fallen to zero.

However, recognizing the potential positive impact of ongoing monetary and fiscal stimulus on equities and the attendant risk of not participating in an equity market rally, the portfolio manager purchased out-of-the-money May 3150 call options (initial delta: 0.12) in late April, and added June 3100, July 3150, and August 3150 calls (initial deltas: 0.21, 0.18, 0.19, respectively) in early May.

The relatively low delta on the out-of-the-money call options enabled the strategy to re-risk quickly as the equity market continued to recover during May—the weighted aggregate delta of the options rose from 0.12 in late April to 0.60 during the first week of June. With the VIX falling, but still in the high 20s/low 30s, out-of-the-money call options were trading at more attractive levels of implied volatility than either at-the-money or in-the-money call options. The out-of-the-money call options (with no delta hedge) effectively created a comparatively cheap call option on a strategy that was, at this point, underweight equities, enabling it to participate in any equity market recovery.

Between June 8 and June 11, however, the S&P 500 fell 230 points over a few days, and the VIX briefly spiked from 25 to over 40. The weighted aggregate delta of the call options fell from 0.60 to 0.36. Still, as the market resumed its rise toward the end of June, the convex payoff profile of the call options enabled the strategy to participate further in the rally.

Exhibit 26.8 sets out the exposures of the various components (index portfolio, index futures, call options on index futures) of the strategy on each day that the option exposure was adjusted via a sale or purchase and the exposures on the last trading day of the quarter (6/30/2020). It also shows the combined option delta and how it changed during the quarter.

	4/17/2020	4/29/2020	4/30/2020	5/8/2020	5/11/2020	5/12/2020	5/29/2020	6/2/2020	6/30/2020
S&P 500 Index	***2,842.43***	***2,918.46***	***2,930.91***	***2,908.83***	***2,915.46***	***2,939.50***	***3,025.17***	***3,064.78***	***3,050.20***
S&P 500 Index Portfolio	82.0%	84.7%	84.7%	84.9%	85.0%	84.7%	87.1%	87.2%	84.9%
S&P 500 E-mini Futures	16.5%	7.6%	4.2%	3.6%	2.9%	2.1%	1.3%	1.2%	3.7%
Apr-20 3050									
May-20 3150		0.9%	0.8%	0.4%	0.3%	0.2%			
Jun-20 3100				0.7%	0.6%	0.3%	1.3%		
Jul-20 3150					0.6%	0.4%	1.0%	1.2%	1.2%
Aug-20 3150						0.6%	1.2%	1.4%	1.4%
Sep-20 3150								1.4%	1.5%
Combined option delta		**0.12**	**0.08**	**0.08**	**0.09**	**0.08**	**0.36**	**0.40**	**0.41**
Combined S&P 500 Exposure	**98.4%**	**93.1%**	**89.8%**	**89.6%**	**89.4%**	**88.4%**	**92.0%**	**92.5%**	**92.8%**

Exhibit 26.8 Changes During Second Quarter of 2020

Third Quarter of 2020

As the S&P 500 Index continued to recover, the portfolio manager rolled the July 3150 calls into August 3200 calls in early July and shortly afterward sold the August 3150 call position at a delta of 0.60. Retaining the September 3150 calls, the portfolio manager rolled the August 3200 calls into September 3300 calls, at a delta of 0.43. From the start of the third quarter to early September, the index had added almost 500 points, a gain of 16.2%, peaking at 3,543.76 on 9/2/20.

Exhibit 26.9 sets out the exposures of the various components (physical index portfolio, index futures, call options on index futures) on each day that the option exposure was adjusted via a sale or purchase, from the start of the quarter up to and including 9/2/2020. It also shows the combined option delta and how it changed during the period.

Exhibit 26.10 illustrates the portfolio's exposure to the instruments it contains—the stock index portfolio, equity index futures, and call options on equity index futures—as well as the weighted-average delta of the call options, and the performance of the S&P 500 Index. The call options were especially effective in systematically de-risking the strategy by reducing the equity exposure from overweight to underweight during the sharp drawdown the equity market experienced from late February to mid-March.

By calculating the net income from the options—that is, the cost of purchasing the options together with proceeds from selling them and associated financing costs—the portfolio manager can determine their net contribution to overall returns. Exhibit 26.11 shows that the net contribution from using call options was about 1%, with most of the contribution being realized during the market drawdown. The use of options also helped the strategy to re-risk—while they did not contribute further to returns during the market recovery, they maintained the gains realized during the market drawdown.

	7/2/2020	7/17/2020	7/27/2020	7/29/2020	8/3/2020	8/5/2020	8/21/2020	9/2/2020
S&P 500 Index	***3,143.64***	***3,224.21***	***3,219.84***	***3,227.22***	***3,288.26***	***3,317.37***	***3,386.01***	***3,543.76***
S&P 500 Index Portfolio	85.0%	85.1%	85.1%	85.0%	85.1%	83.3%	84.7%	84.8%
S&P 500 E-mini Futures	3.9%	3.9%	4.2%	4.9%	4.8%	6.6%	5.4%	5.4%
Aug-20 3150	1.6%							
Aug-20 3200	1.4%	1.8%	2.0%					
Sep-20 3150	1.7%	4.0%	4.2%	4.4%	4.7%	5.0%	5.9%	6.5%
Sep-20 3300				1.5%	1.8%	1.9%	2.4%	3.1%
Nov-20 3550								
Dec-20 3600								
Combined option delta	**0.46**	**0.58**	**0.61**	**0.58**	**0.63**	**0.68**	**0.81**	**0.94**
Combined S&P 500 Exposure	**93.5%**	**94.9%**	**95.4%**	**95.8%**	**96.3%**	**96.8%**	**98.4%**	**99.9%**

Exhibit 26.9 Changes during third quarter of 2020

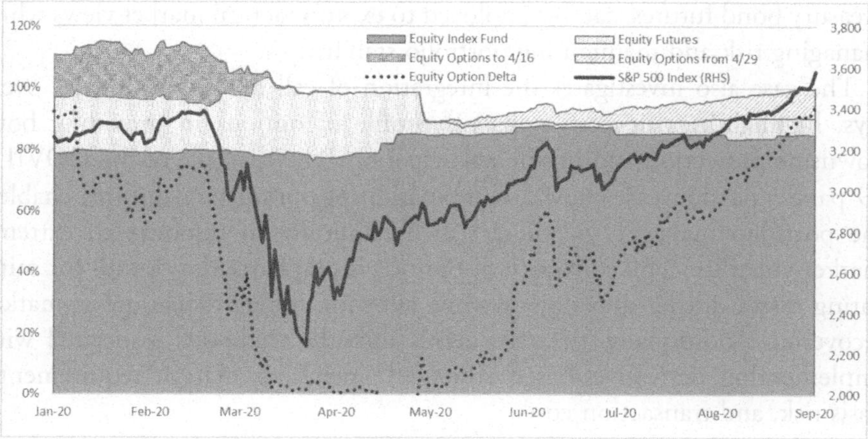

Exhibit 26.10 Equity exposure by security/instrument type, equity option weighted-average delta, and S&P 500 Index performance, 01/02/20–09/02/20

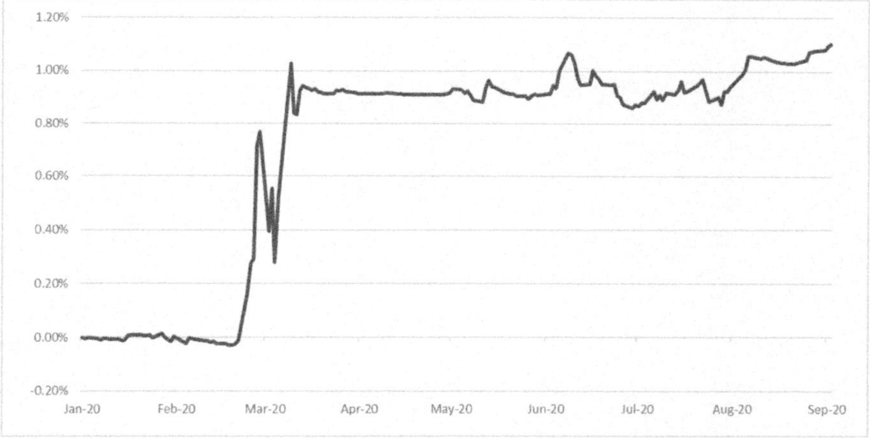

Exhibit 26.11 Net contribution from call options, 1/02/20–9/02/20

Summary

This case illustrates the strategic use of listed derivatives in constructing TAA overlays for invested portfolios, specifically futures and options. The analysis begins by detailing the implementation of a core equity portfolio supplemented with derivatives to achieve efficient exposure to this asset class while preserving liquidity. Through practical illustrations, the case demonstrates how derivatives, such as equity index futures and long-dated U.S.

Treasury bond futures, can be employed to express tactical market views while managing risk and maintaining portfolio stability.

The case also investigates the integration of call options into TAA overlays, highlighting the convex payoff profile of options in providing both downside protection and upside participation. The example of the COVID-19 pandemic showcases how a combination of options and futures enabled the portfolio manager to adjust risk dynamically in response to extreme market volatility. The convexity of options is emphasized as a tool for mitigating losses during drawdowns while allowing for participation in market recoveries. Additionally, the case delves into the trade-offs associated with implementing derivatives-based strategies, including margin requirements, basis risk, and transaction costs.

27

Currency Hedging with a Derivatives Overlay

Kari Vatanen

Currency hedging plays a critical role in institutional portfolios by mitigating the impact of currency fluctuations on portfolio returns. When investments span multiple countries, currency movements can either amplify or erode returns, depending on the direction of exchange rate changes. Institutions face the challenge of determining how much of their foreign currency exposure to hedge and how best to implement a hedging strategy.

A currency hedging policy can help reduce the uncertainty caused by exchange rate volatility. However, the effectiveness of such a policy depends on the portfolio's structure, the specific risks posed by currency movements, and the costs associated with implementing and maintaining a hedge.

Institutional investors must also consider the broader implications of currency hedging, such as its impact on cash flow predictability, regulatory requirements, and the overall risk-return profile of the portfolio. By carefully designing and implementing a hedging strategy, investors can enhance portfolio stability while navigating the complexities of global financial markets.

Currency hedging strategies typically involve using derivatives to offset foreign exchange risk. These strategies can range from simple static hedges to more dynamic, actively managed approaches that adjust to market conditions. The growing use of centralized currency hedging overlays reflects the increasing recognition of the need to manage currency risk comprehensively across a portfolio.

K. Vatanen (✉)
Elo Mutual Pension Insurance Company, Espoo, Finland
e-mail: kari.vatanen@elo.fi

F. J. Fabozzi and M. de Jong (eds.), *Derivatives Applications in Asset Management*,
https://doi.org/10.1007/978-3-031-86354-7_27

Currency Derivatives for Hedging

Currency derivatives are essential for managing foreign exchange (FX) risk in institutional portfolios. These financial instruments allow investors to hedge against unfavorable currency movements, protecting the value of international investments. The most used derivatives for currency hedging include forwards, futures, swaps, and options, each with unique characteristics and use cases. By understanding the advantages and limitations of these derivatives, institutional investors can better align their currency hedging strategies with portfolio objectives and market conditions.

- *Currency forwards* are customized contracts between two parties to exchange a specified amount of one currency for another at a predetermined exchange rate on a future date. These over-the-counter (OTC) instruments offer flexibility regarding contract size and maturity but involve counterparty risk unless collateralized.
- *Currency futures* are standardized contracts traded on exchanges, requiring daily margining to mitigate counterparty risk. Although less flexible than forwards, their liquidity and transparency make them a preferred choice for certain institutional investors.
- *Currency swaps* involve exchanging principal and interest payments in one currency for those in another over a defined period. These instruments are often used to manage longer-term currency exposures or to reduce financing costs in multiple currencies.
- *Currency options* provide the right, but not the obligation, to exchange currencies at a specified rate on or before a set date. These instruments allow investors to hedge downside risk while retaining the potential to benefit from favorable currency movements, although they involve higher upfront costs than forwards or futures.

The choice of a derivative depends on several factors, including the portfolio manager's specific hedging needs, regulatory constraints, and cost considerations. While forwards and swaps are popular for their flexibility, futures, and options, offer benefits like standardized pricing and additional protection against adverse currency movements.

Currency forwards and swaps are OTC instruments, offering greater customization but exposing investors to counterparty risk. In contrast, exchange-traded instruments, such as futures and specific options, provide a standardized framework with lower counterparty risk due to the involvement of clearinghouses. As regulatory changes like central clearing requirements evolve, institutions must carefully weigh the trade-offs between customization, liquidity, and risk when selecting currency derivatives for hedging.[1]

Currency Hedging Overlay

A currency hedging overlay offers a centralized and systematic approach to managing FX risk across an institutional portfolio. This strategy involves using derivatives, such as forwards, futures, or swaps, to neutralize or reduce currency exposures arising from international investments. By centralizing currency management, the overlay separates the handling of FX risk from the broader asset allocation process, improving operational efficiency and risk control.

A currency overlay consolidates FX risk management into a unified framework. This approach ensures consistency across the organization by removing the need for individual portfolio managers to make independent currency decisions. Additionally, a centralized strategy enhances the ability to monitor and manage aggregate FX exposures, providing greater transparency and control. For large institutional portfolios, this centralized oversight reduces duplication of effort and avoids conflicting currency positions that may arise from disparate strategies within the organization. Aligning currency management with the portfolio's overall risk and return objectives creates a more cohesive strategy.

Implementing a currency overlay provides several key benefits. First, it reduces portfolio volatility caused by currency fluctuations, leading to more predictable returns. Second, it streamlines the execution of currency hedging strategies by centralizing operations, which improves efficiency. Third, it enables institutions to negotiate better pricing on derivatives and manage margin and collateral requirements more effectively, lowering costs.

To successfully implement a currency overlay, institutions must define a clear hedging policy that outlines objectives, acceptable instruments, and target hedging ratios. Advanced technology and systems are also critical for monitoring exposures, executing trades, and reporting on the overlay's effectiveness. Whether internal or external, skilled personnel are necessary to navigate the complexities of currency markets and derivatives. An effective overlay strategy also requires strong governance structures to oversee

[1] The impact of regulatory changes and transaction costs on the effectiveness of hedging strategies is extensively discussed in Gueorgui S Konstantinov, Frank J Fabozzi, and Joseph Simonian, *Quantitative Global Bond Portfolio Management*, Singapore: World Scientific Press, 2023. For example, Chapter 4 notes how the increasing shift toward electronic trading and centralized clearing has enhanced transparency but also introduced complexities in hedging emerging market currencies.

operations, ensure regulatory compliance, and adapt to changing market conditions.

A well-defined currency hedging policy is the cornerstone of an effective overlay. It ensures alignment with institutional objectives and provides a framework for consistent decision-making. A currency hedging overlay enhances portfolio stability, improves operational efficiency, and strengthens currency risk management.

Implementing a Currency Hedging Overlay

Institutional investors tend to establish a currency hedging policy in their strategic investment planning process. This process defines the long-term investment objectives of the institution, considering risk tolerance and other potential investment constraints. The result is an investment plan that outlines the long-term strategic allocation, portfolio diversification objectives, and asset classes to be used, including allocation constraints. The strategic allocation also defines the international diversification of the portfolio, which entails currency risk. For this reason, a currency hedging policy is typically part of the investment plan.

The first step in determining the need for currency hedging is identifying and quantifying the currency exposures in the entire portfolio. Exhibit 27.1 shows the currency breakdown for a hypothetical European institutional investor's portfolio. Currency exposures are aggregated across all asset classes, resulting in an overall picture of all currency exposures. The second column shows the total value of the portfolio assets in each currency. The third column shows the current exchange rate used to translate the values of the foreign currency investments into the investor's home currency, the euro. The fourth column shows the currency allocation of the portfolio in euros for each currency, and the fifth column shows the currency exposure as percentages of the portfolio.

The currency hedging policy defines the proportion of exposure to be hedged and the target level for open currency exposure for each currency. Determining the optimal hedging ratio is a foundational step in implementing a currency overlay. This ratio is typically derived by balancing the reduction in portfolio variance against the costs of hedging, which include transaction fees, collateral requirements, and the opportunity costs of foregoing favorable currency movements. For instance, minimizing variance can involve considering factors like the base currency's volatility, foreign asset

Currency	Value of Assets in Local Ccy	Spot FX Rate	Value of Assets in Eur	Allocation to Currency	Hedging Ratio	Exposure to Hedge	Open FX Exposure	Open FX Allocation
EUR	382,067,352	1	382,067,352	43.7%	-	-	-	-
USD	327,150,197	1.0846	301,632,120	34.5%	50%	150,816,060	150,816,060	17.3%
JPY	8,651,998,244	170.62	50,709,168	5.8%	100%	50,709,168	0	0.0%
GBP	37,963,156	0.8514	44,589,096	5.1%	75%	33,441,822	11,147,274	1.3%
CHF	26,534,009	0.979	27,103,176	3.1%	100%	27,103,176	0	0.0%
CAD	42,654,454	1.4784	28,851,768	3.3%	75%	21,638,826	7,212,942	0.8%
AUD	38,494,291	1.6307	23,605,992	2.7%	100%	23,605,992	0	0.0%
SEK	179,753,334	11.4221	15,737,328	1.8%	100%	15,737,328	0	0.0%
Total			874,296,000	100.0%			169,176,276	19.4%

Exhibit 27.1 Example portfolio

correlations, and market liquidity. This step ensures that the overlay effectively reduces risk while maintaining alignment with the portfolio's broader investment objectives.

Exhibit 27.1 illustrates a sample framework for defining a currency hedging policy, highlighting the allocation of open exposures and target hedging ratios across multiple currencies. This framework provides a structured approach to understanding and managing currency risks at a portfolio level. The sixth column in Exhibit 27.1 shows the target hedging ratio for each currency, and the seventh column shows the amount in euros to be hedged for each currency. The last two columns display the target level for open currency exposure in euros and percentages for each currency. Additionally, Exhibit 27.2 details the influence of currency betas and hedging costs on determining optimal hedging ratios. These exhibits serve as practical guides for aligning theoretical principles with operational decisions.

In addition to the target level of open currency exposure, a range is typically defined on either side of it, within which the open currency exposure may fluctuate according to the currency hedging policy. The currency hedging policy also often specifies the acceptable instruments used for currency hedging.

There is no single approach to defining the optimal currency hedging ratio for a portfolio of multiple currencies. The hedging costs of different currencies can vary significantly over time, as can their ability to diversify the risk of the overall investment portfolio. Different investors may have very different objectives regarding their exposure to currency risk, and the regulatory constraints on each institutional investor significantly impact their currency hedging policy.

A simple way to determine the optimal hedging ratio is to minimize the return variance between the open currency exposure and the underlying assets in the portfolio. The currency exposure that minimizes the return variance of the underlying portfolio is equal to the currency beta to the underlying

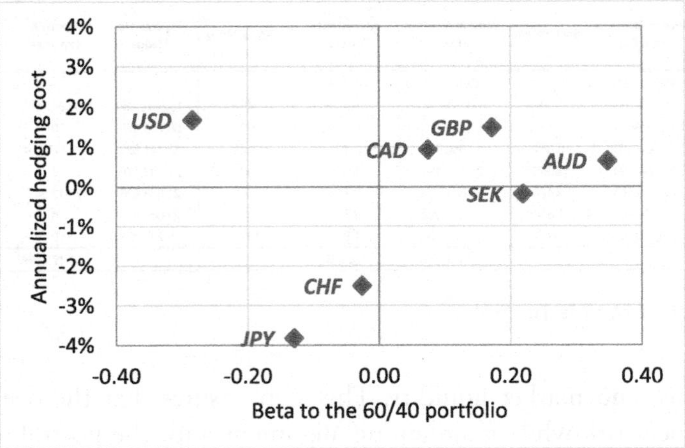

Exhibit 27.2 Currency beta to 60/40 portfolio and the hedging cost (Estimations made by the author. The betas have been estimated from the weekly data points of currency spot rates over a five-year period from 5/2019 to 5/2024. The hedging costs have been calculated from the three-month forward and spot rates of the currency pairs against the euro in May 2024)

portfolio. More specifically, the beta of a single currency is the correlation between the currency and the entire portfolio, scaled by the ratio of their volatilities.

$$\text{Variance minimizing hedging ratio} = \rho_{(\text{FX, Portfolio})} \times \sigma_{(\text{FX})} / \sigma_{(\text{Portfolio})} = \beta_{(\text{FX, Portfolio})}$$

In addition to the risk caused by open currency exposures, the optimal currency hedging ratio for institutional investors is affected by the hedging cost of each currency. Hedging cost is priced into the value of the currency forward and it is the ratio of market interest rates between the two currency areas. The currency forward is priced according to the following formula:

$$\text{Forward rate} = \text{Spot rate} \times \left(1 + \text{foreign interest rate}\right) / \left(1 + \text{domestic interest rate}\right).$$

The currency hedging cost for the tenure of the forward is calculated with the formula:

$$\text{Hedging Cost} = (\text{Forward price} - \text{Spot price}) / \text{Spot price}.$$

Exhibit 27.2 shows the currency betas for a hypothetical European 60/40 portfolio and the hedging costs for a euro-based investor. Currency beta represents the variance-minimizing open currency exposure as previously described. The annualized hedging costs are calculated directly from the forward prices and tend to fluctuate according to the market interest rates. In practice, the optimal hedging ratio is determined by considering the costs and the ability to reduce the portfolio's risk through currency hedging. Additionally, the potential regulatory capital charge from open currency positions may influence the optimal currency hedging ratio choice for institutional investors.

For example, having open exposure in USD reduces the risk of a European 60/40 portfolio and the hedging cost is positive. Therefore, it is rational for a euro-denominated investor to maintain some level of USD exposure, considering regulatory capital charges. Conversely, the hedging cost for JPY is notably negative, resulting in a positive gain from hedging. Exposures in SEK and AUD increase portfolio risk, but their hedging costs are manageable, making full hedging feasible.

Factors Affecting Currency Hedging Decisions

Several factors influence the design and implementation of a currency hedging strategy, shaping how institutions manage FX risk within their portfolios. These factors include regulatory constraints, hedging costs, portfolio objectives, and market conditions, each of which plays a significant role in determining the approach to currency risk management.

Regulatory constraints are a critical consideration for institutions operating in highly regulated environments. For example, capital adequacy requirements may impose additional costs or limitations on hedging activities. Regulatory frameworks often dictate the instruments that can be used, the level of leverage permitted, and reporting requirements for hedging activities. Institutions must ensure that their hedging strategies comply with these rules while still achieving their desired risk management outcomes.

Hedging costs are another significant factor in the decision-making process. These costs include transaction fees, margin requirements, and opportunity costs associated with hedging. For example, interest rate differentials between currencies can impact the forward points in currency forwards or swaps, increasing the overall cost of the hedge. High costs can erode the benefits of reduced volatility, leading some institutions to adopt partial hedges or selective strategies that target the most significant exposures.

Portfolio objectives and risk tolerance also heavily influence hedging decisions. Institutions with a lower risk tolerance may prioritize stability and predictability, favoring higher hedging levels. Conversely, investors with a longer investment horizon and higher risk tolerance may accept greater exposure to currency risk in pursuit of potential returns. The specific investment goals of the portfolio, whether focused on capital preservation or growth, further shape the extent and nature of currency hedging.

Market conditions, such as currency volatility, liquidity, and interest rate environments, are dynamic factors that affect the cost and feasibility of hedging. During periods of high volatility, hedging may become more expensive, prompting some institutions to reconsider the scope or timing of their hedging activities. Similarly, liquidity constraints in particular currency markets may limit the ability to execute or maintain a desired hedging position.

Finally, the availability of internal resources and expertise is practical in determining whether to manage currency hedging in-house or outsource it to external specialists. Institutions with significant scale and internal expertise may find it cost-effective to manage hedging internally. In contrast, others may prefer to engage external overlay managers to handle the complexity and operational requirements.

By considering these factors, institutions can design hedging strategies that align with their operational capabilities, investment goals, and market conditions. Effective currency hedging decisions require balancing risk and managing the costs and operational challenges associated with hedging activities.

Internal vs. External Management of Currency Overlays

Institutions must decide whether to manage a currency hedging overlay internally or outsource it to external specialists. This decision depends on various factors, including the institution's resources, expertise, and the complexity of the hedging strategy. Each approach has distinct advantages and challenges, and the choice often reflects the organization's specific operational and strategic goals.

Internal management of currency overlays provides institutions with greater control over the hedging process. This approach lets portfolio managers directly align currency hedging decisions with the investment strategy and risk tolerance. By keeping the process in-house, institutions can customize their hedging strategies to suit unique portfolio needs and respond quickly to changes in market conditions. However, internal management requires substantial resources, including skilled personnel, advanced technology systems, and robust risk management frameworks. The lack of these resources can lead to inefficiencies or increased operational risk.

On the other hand, outsourcing the currency overlay to external managers offers access to specialized expertise and operational efficiency. External overlay managers are typically well-versed in currency markets and derivatives, enabling them to execute hedging strategies effectively and cost-efficiently. These specialists often provide sophisticated tools for monitoring and reporting FX exposures, which can enhance transparency and decision-making. Additionally, external managers can leverage economies of scale to reduce transaction costs and negotiate better terms for derivatives. However, outsourcing involves additional fees and may result in less direct control over the hedging process, which can be a drawback for institutions with specific or complex requirements.

The decision between internal and external management also hinges on the institution's scale and level of activity in currency markets. Large institutions with diversified international portfolios may have the resources and expertise to manage hedging internally, whereas smaller organizations may find outsourcing more practical and cost-effective. Moreover, regulatory requirements, such as those mandating independent oversight or third-party validation, can influence the decision.

For some institutions, a hybrid approach may be optimal. In this model, certain aspects of the hedging process, such as policy design and oversight, are managed internally, while the execution of hedging transactions is outsourced to external specialists. This approach combines the benefits of internal control with the expertise and efficiency of external management.

Ultimately, the choice between internal and external management depends on the institution's strategic priorities, operational capabilities, and the specific demands of its currency exposure. Both approaches can effectively reduce FX risk, provided they are implemented with a clear policy framework and ongoing evaluation to ensure alignment with broader investment objectives.

Summary

Currency hedging is a critical tool for managing FX risk in institutional portfolios, and its implementation requires careful consideration of various factors. A centralized currency hedging overlay streamlines currency risk management, separating it from broader asset allocation decisions. The choice of hedging ratio, informed by portfolio objectives and risk tolerance, balances risk reduction with the costs of hedging, such as transaction fees and interest rate differentials. Different derivatives, including forwards, swaps, futures, and options, provide the instruments for executing hedging strategies, each with unique advantages depending on the portfolio's requirements and market conditions.

The decision to manage a currency hedging overlay internally or outsource it to external managers hinges on institutional resources, expertise, and operational scale. Internal management offers direct control and alignment with investment objectives but demands significant infrastructure and skilled personnel. External managers bring specialized knowledge and cost efficiencies, leveraging economies of scale and advanced tools for monitoring and execution. Some institutions may adopt a hybrid approach, combining internal oversight with outsourced execution to balance control and efficiency. Ultimately, effective currency hedging depends on aligning strategy with institutional capabilities and market dynamics while maintaining flexibility to adapt to evolving conditions.

Part IV

Income Enhancement Strategies

28

Managing Path Dependency and Balancing Yield in Option Income Strategies

John Burrello

Path dependency is a defining characteristic of option income strategies, in particular of covered call and cash-secured put strategies, influencing how returns are generated and managed over time. Unlike traditional investments, options rely on point-to-point dynamics, where both the sequence and timing of price movements determine the outcome. This dependence can lead to inconsistent results, as we observe in strategies like the CBOE S&P 500 BuyWrite Monthly Index (BXM), which follows a single-path framework tied to fixed option expirations; the BXM occasionally declines during rising markets and underperforms the S&P 500 Index during declining markets. Both of these scenarios are contrary to covered call strategy expectations.

Simultaneously, balancing yield and total return poses a key challenge for portfolio managers pursuing such strategies. While high distribution yields may seem attractive, they often come at the expense of long-term capital growth, leading to capital erosion if not carefully managed. This case examines the dual challenges of path dependency and yield management, emphasizing the importance of laddering strategies and setting realistic yield targets to ensure portfolio sustainability. By exploring numerical examples, historical data, and practical solutions, the case provides a comprehensive framework for addressing these issues.

J. Burrello (✉)
Invesco Global Strategies, Atlanta, GA, USA
e-mail: John.Burrello@invesco.com

F. J. Fabozzi and M. de Jong (eds.), *Derivatives Applications in Asset Management*,
https://doi.org/10.1007/978-3-031-86354-7_28

Path Dependency in Option Income Strategies

Path dependency is a critical feature of option income strategies, where expiration dates inherently negate the ability to buy and hold, and outcomes depend on the sequence of underlying asset price movements between initiating and closing option trades. For example, BXM systematically writes monthly at-the-money (ATM) S&P 500 index call options at fixed expirations on the third Friday of each month. While this strategy generates income from premiums, its performance is highly sensitive to the timing and trajectory of market movements between third Fridays. During periods of rapid market rallies, the capped upside of ATM options prevents full participation in growth, while in declining markets, the collected premiums may not sufficiently offset portfolio losses.

Challenges of Single-Path Strategies

Left unchecked, this type of path dependency can lead to inconsistent results. On the surface, one might assume a covered call strategy should increase in value but underperform the underlying asset in up markets, and decline but outperform the underlying asset in down markets.

However, single-path strategies, such as BXM, are inherently inflexible and heavily dependent on market conditions between specific expiration dates. By design, these strategies tie all trades to a fixed schedule, initiating and closing options on predetermined dates. This rigidity makes them particularly vulnerable to adverse market movements, as performance is disproportionately affected by the timing of price changes. Historical data highlight the limitations of the BXM: since 1990, the strategy has consistently declined in at least one up market and underperformed the S&P 500 in at least one down market annually.

Exhibit 28.1 provides a detailed comparison of single-path and daily laddered covered call strategies, showcasing the practical advantages of diversification. The exhibit's scatter plot reveals that single-path strategies exhibit significant variability in returns, with non-intuitive underperformance during both market rallies and declines. Conversely, the laddered strategy smooths returns by diversifying expiration dates and strike levels, reducing reliance on any single market outcome. This visual evidence underscores the weaknesses of single-path strategies and highlights the necessity of employing alternative approaches to manage path dependency.

The inherent challenges of single-path strategies emphasize the need for techniques that mitigate these risks. Without diversification, such strategies

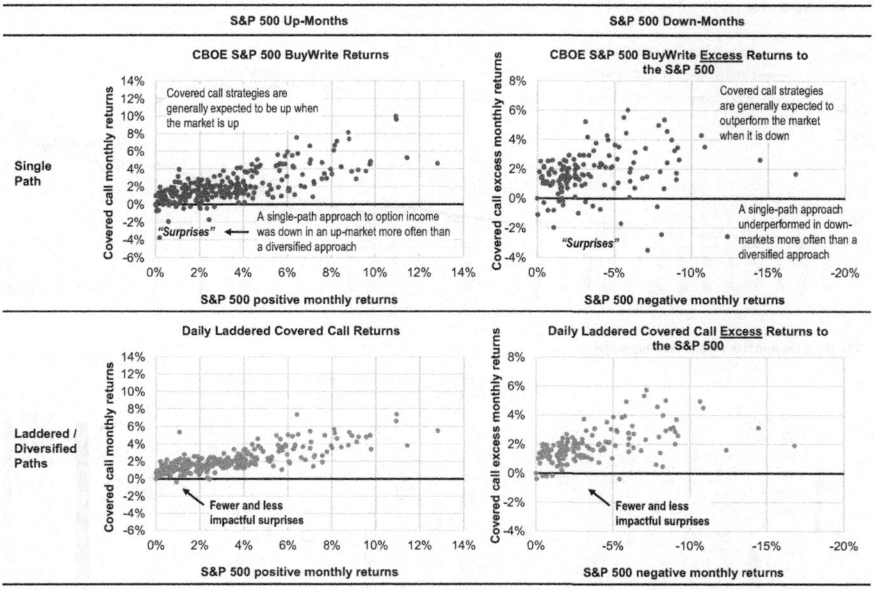

Exhibit 28.1 Single-path and daily laddered covered call strategy returns in up and down markets

remain highly vulnerable to timing-related issues, leading to inconsistent and often suboptimal outcomes. As detailed in the next section, laddering offers a robust solution to these challenges by introducing diversification into option income strategies.

Mitigating Path Dependency Through Laddering

Laddering is a practical and effective solution to mitigate the risks of path dependency in option income strategies. Unlike single-path strategies that rely on fixed expirations and trade dates, laddering involves staggering option expirations and strike levels across different time frames. This approach reduces reliance on specific market outcomes, creating a smoother income stream and a more resilient portfolio structure.

Exhibit 28.2 highlights the significant benefits of laddering by combining one-month period for each trading day of the month. The results demonstrate that laddered strategies reduce return variability compared to single-path strategies, which depend heavily on specific market conditions at expiration. By diversifying expirations and strikes, laddering ensures a steady flow of income while minimizing the impact of adverse market events. The laddering approach may also improve liquidity, enabling portfolio managers

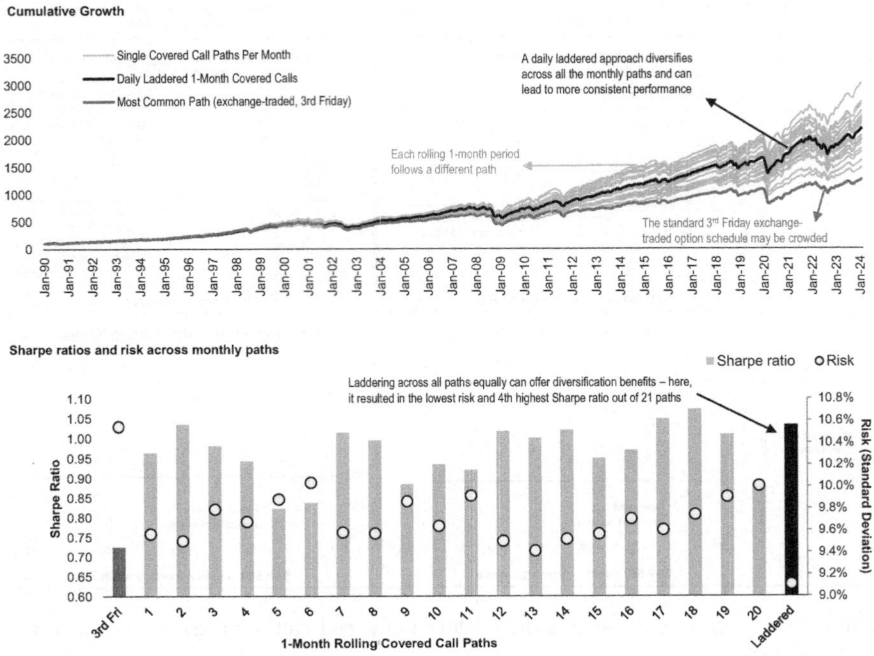

Exhibit 28.2 Summary performance statistics

to incrementally adjust their portfolios more effectively in response to market changes. This makes laddering an indispensable tool for managing path dependency and achieving consistent portfolio performance.

By diversifying option expirations, laddering distributes the timing of premium collection and capital deployment. This approach is similar to techniques used in bond laddering, where maturities are spread out to minimize reinvestment risk, or dollar-cost averaging, which smooths the cost basis of investments over time. Laddering diversifies unpredictable market movements, ensuring that no single expiration or strike significantly impacts overall performance.

Balancing Yield and Growth

Balancing yield and total return is essential for the long-term success of option income strategies. Total return, which includes both income generation and capital appreciation, offers a more comprehensive measure of portfolio performance than yield alone. While high distribution yields may appeal to income-focused portfolio managers, they can jeopardize a portfolio's sustainability if those yields consistently exceed its growth rate.

Historical performance data reinforces the critical need for realistic yield targets. The S&P 500 has delivered an average annualized return of approximately 11% over the long term, while the BXM, constrained by its capped upside potential, has achieved returns closer to 8.6%. Portfolios targeting yields significantly above their long-term expected returns risk depleting their capital over time as distributions outpace the portfolio's growth.

Exhibit 28.3 provides critical visual evidence of how yield targets impact portfolio longevity. The simulation compares two covered call strategies: one targeting an 11% yield and another targeting an 8% yield. Over time, the 11% strategy consistently depletes capital as distributions exceed the portfolio's growth rate. In contrast, the 8% strategy aligns closely with market returns, allowing for sustainable distributions while growing capital. These results underscore the importance of aligning yield targets with achievable growth rates to ensure the portfolio's long-term viability. Excessive yield targets jeopardize the portfolio's ability to generate future returns.

Maintaining realistic yield targets is critical to avoiding these pitfalls. Achieving a sustainable balance between yield and growth requires careful portfolio management, particularly in selecting option strike prices and managing option notional size. For instance, selling out-of-the-money (OTM) call options allows portfolio managers to capture more market growth potential while generating premium income. Conversely, ATM options increase premium income but cap upside potential, which may be detrimental in a bull market.

Portfolio managers should aim for yields that reflect their portfolio's growth potential, ensuring income objectives do not undermine long-term capital preservation. By focusing on total return, portfolios can achieve a sustainable balance between income and growth, providing steady income

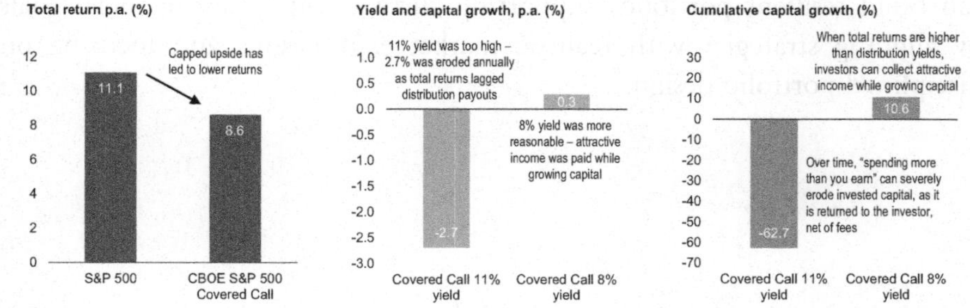

Exhibit 28.3 Simulated covered call strategies with 11% and 8% yield targets, and their impact on capital growth

streams while maintaining the integrity of the capital base. The guiding principle is simple yet vital: "Don't spend more than you earn."

Summary

Option income strategies are powerful tools for generating consistent income, but their success depends on effectively managing path dependency and balancing yield with total returns. The inherent path dependency in options can lead to unpredictable outcomes, especially in single-path strategies like the CBOE S&P 500 BuyWrite Monthly Index (BXM). Diversification techniques, such as laddering, provide a robust solution by spreading option expirations and strike levels, reducing risk, and creating smoother income streams.

Setting realistic yield targets that align with historical market returns is equally critical. Excessive distribution yields, while appealing in the short term, lead to capital erosion and undermine the portfolio's long-term sustainability. Numerical examples and simulations, such as those comparing 8% and 11% yield targets, clearly demonstrate the risks associated with prioritizing yield over total return. By adopting disciplined portfolio management practices, including sustainable distribution policies and diversification through laddering, investors can achieve a balance that meets immediate income needs while preserving capital for future growth.

The ultimate goal of any option income strategy is to achieve a balance between generating immediate income and preserving the portfolio's long-term growth potential. Prioritizing total return over excessive yield targets ensures that investors can maintain sustainable distribution policies while avoiding the risks of capital erosion. Techniques such as laddering, which diversifies expiration dates and strike levels, provide a practical solution to manage path dependency and enhance portfolio stability. Portfolio managers can build resilient portfolios supporting current and future financial goals by aligning strategies with realistic market expectations and focusing on disciplined portfolio design.

29

Harvesting Volatility Risk Premium with Equity Index Options

Kari Vatanen

The Volatility Risk Premium (VRP) has emerged as a cornerstone concept in modern derivatives-based asset management, offering investors a potential source of consistent returns through systematic options strategies. At its core, the VRP reflects the tendency of ex-ante implied volatility—embedded in option prices—to exceed the ex-post realized volatility of the underlying asset. This difference arises because market participants demand compensation for bearing the uncertainty and risk associated with volatile markets. By systematically harvesting this premium, asset managers can generate returns uncorrelated with traditional equity and fixed-income strategies, making VRP-focused approaches highly appealing for portfolio diversification.

This case study describes a specific strategy to capitalize on the VRP: the one-month at-the-money (ATM) straddle on the S&P 500 index, dynamically hedged with futures to manage directional risk. The strategy involves selling both call and put options and using daily delta hedging to minimize exposure to the underlying asset's price movements. The primary goal is to capture the VRP embedded in option premiums while mitigating potential losses from adverse market moves.

The case highlights both the opportunities and challenges associated with harvesting the VRP. On the one hand, the strategy's potential for stable risk-adjusted returns has made it a cornerstone in the toolkit of sophisticated asset managers. On the other hand, the approach requires careful management of

K. Vatanen (✉)
Elo Mutual Pension Insurance Company, Espoo, Finland
e-mail: kari.vatanen@elo.fi

F. J. Fabozzi and M. de Jong (eds.), *Derivatives Applications in Asset Management*,
https://doi.org/10.1007/978-3-031-86354-7_29

risks, including sharp spikes in market volatility, significant drawdowns, and liquidity considerations.

The analysis presented here comprehensively examines the strategy's mechanics, performance, and practical implications. By detailing a real-world application of VRP harvesting, this case study offers valuable insights for asset managers seeking to incorporate equity index options into their portfolios.

The Economic and Structural Foundations of the VRP

At its core, the VRP emerges from the risk transfer process between market participants. Institutional investors, such as pension funds and insurers, often seek protection against downside risks, especially during periods of heightened uncertainty. This demand for insurance creates a consistent bid for options, thus embedding a risk premium into their prices. Sellers of options—typically hedge funds, proprietary trading desks, and other liquidity providers—are compensated for bearing this risk. This asymmetry between risk-seeking sellers and risk-averse buyers is the primary driver of the VRP.

Additionally, market inefficiencies play a role. Option pricing models, while sophisticated, often overestimate future realized volatility due to the inclusion of risk premiums and conservative assumptions about tail risk. These biases tend to accentuate the persistence of the VRP.

Its persistence is also supported by several structural factors inherent in financial markets. Hedging demand from institutional investors that use options to protect against adverse market outcomes creates consistent upward pressure on implied volatility. Regulatory constraints often impose these investors to maintain hedged positions, fueling the systematic demand for options. Behavioral tendencies, such as loss aversion and the overestimation of rare events, accentuate the consistent overpricing of volatility in options markets. Furthermore, the liquidity premium demanded by option sellers, who must hold capital to back their positions, adds another layer to the pricing dynamics.

The VRP has been observed consistently across multiple asset classes, including equities, fixed income, and commodities. Research shows that, over long horizons, strategies designed to exploit the VRP—such as selling straddles or variance swaps—tend to generate positive risk-adjusted returns. However, seizing this premium is not without risks, as market dislocations and volatility spikes can lead to significant drawdowns for VRP-based strategies.

Harvesting the VRP

There are several ways to harvest the volatility risk premium via options. A straightforward way is to sell naked out-of-the-money (OTM) options, collect the premium, and expect them to expire worthless. The strategy works well up to the point that the option strike is met due to a sudden market move, which can result in significant losses. It is more sensible to hedge the options sold either with a dynamic delta protection, or to buy more distant OTM options as a way to guard against significant market movements.

Short Straddle and Strangle Strategies

A typical way to harvest the volatility risk premium is by selling either straddles or strangles, and hedge the delta of the option strategy. A short straddle involves selling an at-the-money (ATM) call and put with the same strike price, while a short strangle involves selling an OTM call and put with different strike prices. Exhibit 29.1 shows the payoff functions of the short straddle- and short strangle strategies. The delta risk of the strategy is typically hedged at least on a daily basis. The delta risk of an option strategy refers to the sensitivity of the value to small changes in the price of the underlying asset and fluctuates as the price of the underlying asset changes.

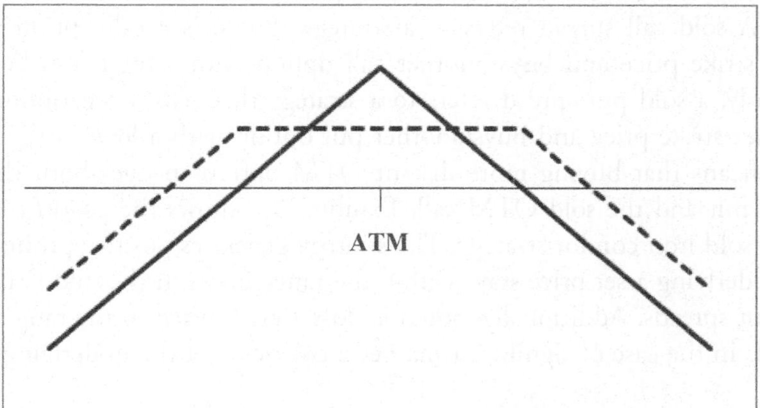

Exhibit 29.1 Payout function of short straddle and short strangle (The horizontal axis represents the options' strike price relative to the underlying asset (ATM) price. The vertical axis represents the value of the option strategy at expiration. The value of the option strategy is positive above the horizontal axis and negative below the horizontal axis)

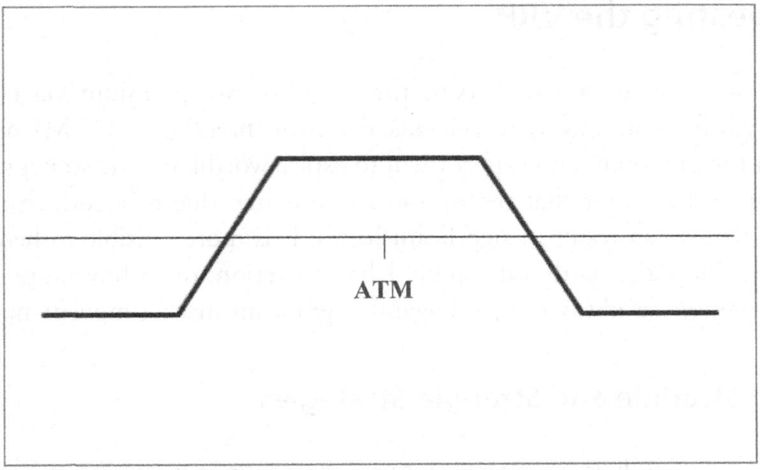

Exhibit 29.2 Payout function of a short iron condor (The horizontal axis represents the options' strike price relative to the underlying asset (ATM) price. The vertical axis represents the value of the option strategy at expiration. The value of the option strategy is positive above the horizontal axis and negative below the horizontal axis)

Iron Condors as a Safer Alternative

An alternative safer way to collect the volatility risk premium is to sell iron condors, either with or without delta hedging. An iron condor involves selling both an OTM call spread and an OTM put spread on the same underlying asset. A sold call spread refers to a strategy that sells a call option with a lower strike price and buys another call option with a higher strike price. Similarly, a sold put spread refers to a strategy that sells a put option with a higher strike price and buys another put option with a lower strike price. This means that buying more distant OTM options hedges both the sold OTM put and the sold OTM call. Exhibit 29.2 shows the payoff function of the sold iron condor strategy. The strategy generates positive profits when the underlying asset price stays within the range between the sold OTM call and put spreads. Additionally, potential losses are limited to the range of the spreads in the case of significant market movements of the underlying asset.

Case Study: One-Month ATM Straddle on the S&P 500

We present an example of harvesting the volatility risk premium by selling one-month ATM straddles on the S&P 500 index while delta hedging the position on a daily basis. Let's assume that we sell 25 contracts of exchange-listed January 2023 ATM call and put options just after the opening on

January 3, 2023. The options will expire at the opening on January 20. The strike price of the options is the closest available strike of listed options to the opening market price of the S&P Index, which is 3,850 on January 3, 2023.

Exhibit 29.3 shows the relevant data on a daily basis, including the implied volatility, the option prices and deltas, the value of 25 contracts of sold straddles, and the number of futures needed to hedge the straddles. The implied volatility used to price options is proxied by the daily values of the VIX index.[1] Call and put option prices are calculated daily, and the straddle price combines the call and the put. Similarly, option deltas are calculated daily for both call and put options, and the sum of the option deltas describes the total delta of the straddle strategy.

The sold straddle strategy is assumed to contain 25 contracts of sold calls and 25 contracts of sold puts. For listed S&P 500 index options, the contract size is 100 times the underlying option price, so one unit of the straddle has the value of 100 × straddle price. Thus, the value of 25 contracts of the sold straddle is −25 × 100 × straddle price. The dollar value of the sold straddle strategy changes daily according to the call and put prices, which is indicated in the column "Value of 25 Sold Straddles" of Exhibit 29.3. Daily profit/loss from the initial date is shown in the column "Change in Value."

In this case, the nominal value of the sold straddle strategy is 25 × 100 × 3,850 (option strike), which is 9,625,000 USD. The nominal value captures the total value of the underlying asset that the option represents. The sold straddle strategy generates a profit of 235,046 USD (bottom of column "Change in Value") in this short period without delta hedging.

Delta hedging requires a regular calculation of the open delta position of the sold straddle strategy. First, a daily delta must be calculated for both the sold call option and the put option. Second, the delta of the straddle is the

Date	S&P 500 Open Price	Implied Volatility	Call Price	Put Price	Straddle Price	Value of 25 Sold Straddles (in USD)	Change in value (USD)	Call Delta	Put Delta	Total Delta to Hedge (USD)	Number of futures to Hedge	P/L of Delta Hedging (USD)
1/3/2023	3,853.30	23.09	80.40	72.62	153.02	-382,546		53 %	-47 %	-502,433	3	
1/4/2023	3,840.40	22.93	70.88	76.25	147.13	-367,825	14,721	50 %	-50 %	39,589	0	-1,975
1/5/2023	3,839.70	22.2	65.81	72.15	137.96	-344,895	37,651	49 %	-51 %	108,627	-1	-1,975
1/6/2023	3,823.40	22.69	57.09	79.99	137.08	-342,699	39,847	45 %	-54 %	853,408	-4	-1,146
1/9/2023	3,910.80	21.75	95.66	32.00	127.66	-319,138	63,408	67 %	-32 %	-3,420,243	17	-18,469
1/10/2023	3,888.60	22.22	79.69	38.48	118.17	-295,426	87,120	62 %	-38 %	-2,352,413	12	-37,567
1/11/2023	3,932.30	20.8	103.83	19.19	123.02	-307,550	74,996	75 %	-25 %	-4,964,665	25	-11,507
1/12/2023	3,977.60	21.56	139.31	9.65	148.96	-372,405	10,141	85 %	-15 %	-7,041,331	35	44,782
1/13/2023	3,960.60	19	119.52	7.12	126.64	-316,610	65,936	87 %	-13 %	-7,245,535	37	14,555
1/17/2023	3,999.30	19.89	150.50	0.43	150.93	-377,322	5,224	98 %	-2 %	-9,665,261	48	84,142
1/18/2023	4,002.20	19.28	152.77	0.05	152.82	-382,049	497	100 %	0 %	-9,941,687	50	90,445
1/19/2023	3,911.80	20.43	63.29	1.23	64.52	-161,293	221,253	93 %	-7 %	-8,474,678	43	-136,240
1/20/2023	3,909.00	20.28	59.00	0.00	59.00	-147,500	235,046	100 %	0 %	-9,772,500	50	-142,836

Exhibit 29.3 Daily evolution of the sold straddle with a delta hedge

[1] The VIX, short for Chicago Board Option Exchange (CBOE) Volatility Index, measures the implied price volatility of the S&P 500 index.

sum of the call and put deltas. The total open delta position for 25 contracts of sold straddles is $-25 \times$ contract size (100) $\times$ straddle delta $\times$ underlying S&P 500 price. Exhibit 29.3 shows daily values of the call and put deltas and the total open delta position for 25 contracts of sold straddles.

The total open delta position is the amount of directional risk that should be hedged daily with futures if you intend to maintain the strategy fully delta hedged. Let's assume that we are using S&P 500 e-mini futures with a contract size of 50 for hedging. Then the underlying value of one S&P 500 e-mini future contract is $50 \times$ index value. To calculate the number of contracts needed to hedge the total delta position, we use the equation:

$$Number of future contracts = Total delta\ position\ to\ hedge / (\text{contract size (50)} \times index value).$$

The last two columns of Exhibit 29.3 present the daily number of S&P 500 e-mini futures contracts needed to hedge the total delta position of the sold straddle strategy and the cumulated profit/loss from the futures used for delta hedging. Delta hedging costs 142,836 USD (bottom right column) in this case, but it significantly reduces the daily volatility and potential losses of the total strategy, as can be seen next in Exhibit 29.4.

Exhibit 29.4 shows the total profit/loss of the sold straddle strategy with delta hedging. Sold straddles generate a positive profit for the whole investment period, but there is some volatility during the period due to changes in option market prices. The delta hedge generates some loss for the entire

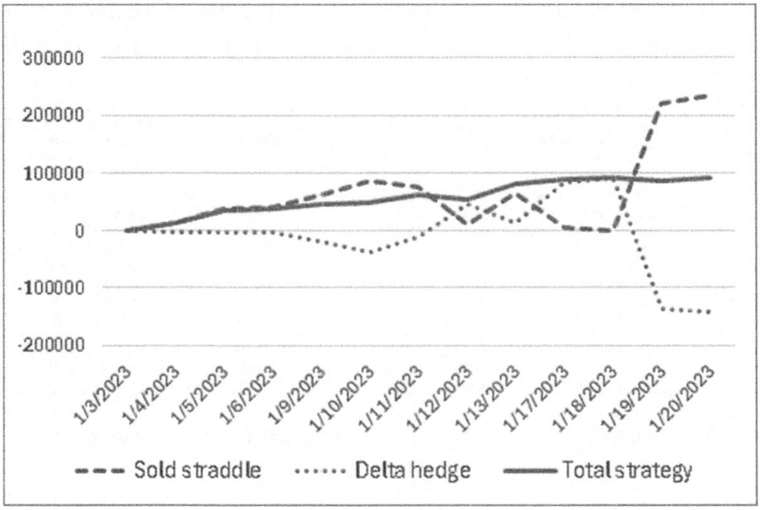

Exhibit 29.4 Profit/loss of the sold straddle with a delta hedge

investment period, but hedging reduces losses on the sold straddles and decreases the volatility of the overall strategy. The sold straddle strategy with delta hedging produces a positive profit of USD 92,210 with relatively low daily volatility.

Enhancements to Risk Management

The above example shows how the VRP can be harvested by selling options and hedging the changes in option market prices with futures. Because the implied volatility of options is usually higher than the realized volatility of the underlying asset, option selling can generate positive returns over time. While selling volatility generates relatively steady returns over the longer term, rapid market movements and sudden increases in volatility can result in substantial losses. Therefore, effective delta hedging is of great importance for the risk management of the strategy.

Delta hedging can be enhanced by increasing the frequency of hedging from daily to intraday, allowing it to react more quickly to sudden market changes. A more dynamic hedging strategy can also better account for intraday changes in the implied volatility and gamma exposure of options, leading to more efficient risk management.

Another way to enhance the risk management of option selling strategies is to diversify the strikes and the timing of selling the options. Instead of once a month, a smaller fraction of at-the-money straddles can be sold on a daily basis, resulting in a strip of options sold at different strike levels. In this case, the payoff function of several sold call and put options with different strikes and delta hedging starts to approach the payoff function of a variance swap. A variance swap is another efficient way to harvest the volatility risk premium, but we leave it outside the scope of this case study.

Summary

This case study describes and illustrates strategies for capturing the VRP using equity index options. The VRP arises from the consistent difference between the implied volatility embedded in option prices, and realized volatility of the underlying asset. This gap, resulting essentially from market participants' risk aversion and demand for protection, creates a systematic opportunity for other participants to generate returns by selling options while actively managing risk.

The study highlights how to use short straddles and strangles, which involve selling options to collect premiums while managing directional risk through dynamic hedging with futures. These strategies capitalize on the premium embedded in implied volatility but require disciplined risk management to avoid significant losses during market turbulence. Safer alternatives, such as iron condors, incorporate defined risk-reward structures by pairing sold options with further out-of-the-money hedging positions, providing enhanced risk control.

A central component of the case is the detailed analysis of a one-month ATM straddle strategy on the S&P 500. This example demonstrates the mechanics of option selling and dynamic delta hedging, illustrating how to systematically harvest the VRP. The study outlines the daily adjustments required to maintain a neutral position, offering insights into the operational and risk considerations for implementing such strategies.

The case also examines refinements to these approaches, such as increasing hedging frequency and diversifying strike prices and expiration timings, which can enhance returns and reduce volatility exposure. While these enhancements improve performance, they underscore the importance of careful management in mitigating the risks associated with sudden market shocks or volatility spikes.

30

Augmenting Covered Call Returns with Stock Index Options

Anil Sood

Portfolio managers widely use covered call strategies to generate additional income on equity holdings, particularly for stocks with a high-growth potential and significant implied volatility. In this case, we explore an innovative approach to enhancing returns from a covered call strategy by integrating stock index options. Using Nvidia—a growth stock with exceptional performance—as the primary focus, the case examines how a portfolio manager can maximize risk-adjusted returns while mitigating the unique risks associated with high-growth equities.

The analysis introduces the fundamental mechanics of covered calls and explains how implied volatility influences option pricing. It contrasts single-stock options with index options, highlighting the differences in implied volatility skews and how these dynamics impact pricing and strategy selection. With Nvidia as a case study, the discussion delves into the practical challenges of executing covered calls on high-growth stocks. It proposes a hedging technique involving index call options to offset the risks inherent to the short call position.

The case covers Nvidia's implied volatility dynamics and their implications for covered call strategies. It also examines how single-stock and stock index options differ, focusing on volatility skews and pricing. A central theme is integrating S&P 500 index call options as a hedging tool to manage the

A. Sood (✉)
Ernst & Young U.S. LLP, New York, NY, USA
e-mail: sood_anil@outlook.com

F. J. Fabozzi and M. de Jong (eds.), *Derivatives Applications in Asset Management*,
https://doi.org/10.1007/978-3-031-86354-7_30

downside risk of the short call position in a covered call position. Additionally, the case includes a real-life example demonstrating position sizing, cash flow neutrality, and delta alignment to achieve optimal results.

By the end of this case, readers will gain insight into advanced techniques for managing covered call strategies on high-growth stocks, and into the role of index options in improving risk-weighted returns. The discussion underscores the importance of evaluating features such as price correlation, beta, and option premiums to design robust and adaptive strategies.

Covered Call Strategy

Since Nvidia's stock has rallied significantly and consistently from the second quarter of 2023 to the first quarter of 2024, the portfolio manager, while generally optimistic, wants to mitigate downside risk by generating additional income from owning Nvidia shares. There are two primary methods to achieve this:

- *Securities Lending*: The first is temporarily lending the security to another party (the borrower) in exchange for a fee. This arrangement allows the portfolio manager to earn income while retaining stock ownership.
- *Covered Call*: The second strategy is to sell out-of-the-money call options. By doing this, the portfolio manager gives someone else the right to buy the Nvidia stock at a predetermined price (the strike price) before a specified date (the expiration date). In return, the portfolio manager receives a premium. As long as the stock price remains below the strike price, the option expires worthless and the portfolio manager keeps the premium, contributing to the total return.

Both strategies sound reasonable; the portfolio manager finds selling out-of-the-money call options more lucrative due to the high implied volatility in Nvidia stock. Selling call options on an asset while simultaneously holding a long position in the asset is called covered call. The underlying stock is the "cover," as it ensures that the seller can deliver the shares if the buyer chooses to exercise the call option.

Implied volatility reflects the expected magnitude of market movements in future. A high implied volatility in options suggests that traders anticipate considerable movement in the underlying stock prices, either upwards or downwards. This can indicate a forthcoming event that may lead to a significant rally or a sharp sell-off.

Index Options Versus Single Stock Options

Index options generally exhibit a much lower implied volatility compared to individual stocks. Moreover, the implied volatility on the out-of-money (OTM) put side is typically higher than that on the OTM call side, attributed to the high demand for OTM puts by asset managers worldwide seeking portfolio hedging. Conversely, there is minimal interest in profiting from a sudden market upswing, that is, the call side. The stylized fact that a market index falls more rapidly than it rises dampens the demand for index call options, further reducing their implied volatility skew and making OTM calls much cheaper than puts.

Having discussed implied volatility in the context of index options, let's consider stock options. Generally, the implied volatility level is influenced by historical realized volatility; however, unlike index options, the higher demand for OTM puts over OTM calls does not always hold. For stocks with diversified businesses, such as Microsoft, the implied volatilities (IVs) for OTM calls and OTM puts are relatively equal. Conversely, a stock like Nvidia showing unidirectional price trends tend to exhibit higher OTM call option premiums than OTM puts for the equivalent moneyness, resulting in a positive implied volatility skew. This discrepancy is not solely due to a higher demand for call options—as there is no inherent need to buy calls like there is for OTM puts, which are used for hedging cash positions. Rather, the increased implied volatility on the OTM call side is primarily because option sellers are wary of the shorting of high-growth stocks that have been consistently rising.

Market participants' combined expectations and actions are the main factors behind the volatility skew. When investors anticipate a substantial price swing in a particular direction, they may be inclined to pay higher prices for options that benefit from such a movement. This heightened demand can increase those options' implied volatility (IV), resulting in a skew.

Hedging the Short Call in the Covered Call Strategy

The anticipated return-over-risk of the covered call strategy adopted by the portfolio manager, who is bullish on Nvidia stock, can be amplified by hedging the downside risk of the short position on the call option. One way of hedging the short call on Nvidia is to go long on an instrument that is correlated with Nvidia yet has a much lower implied volatility, thereby

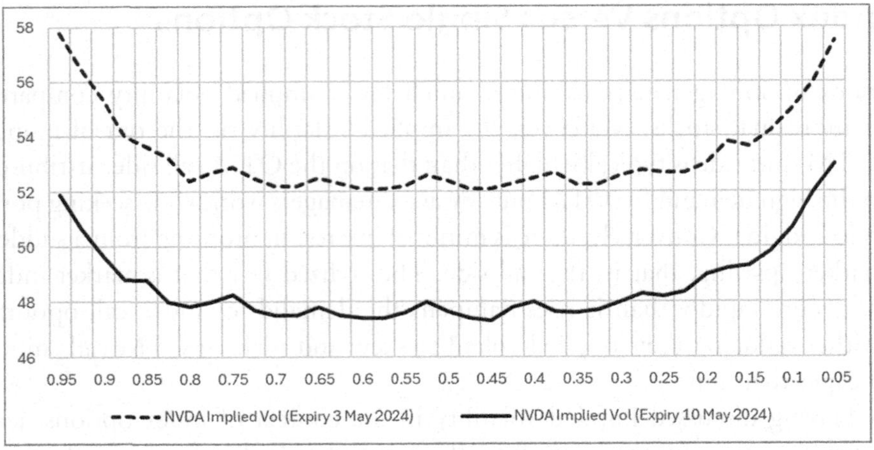

Exhibit 30.1 Nvidia Implied Volatility Smile/Skew for the expirations of May 3, 2024, and May 10, 2024, at the close of business on April 30, 2024 (The horizontal axis represents the options' strike price as a percentage of the underlying stock price (moneyness). The vertical axis represents the options' implied volatility)

keeping the hedging costs low. Based on what we observe in the implied volatility dynamics of index options, the S&P 500 call options are a perfect candidate for hedging the short Nvidia call.

As shown in Exhibit 30.1, as of the close of business on April 30, 2024, the volatility structure of Nvidia is a nice smile. Before that date, it had been a skew, with out-of-the-money (OTM) calls being much more expensive than OTM puts for the same moneyness. The skew has become a smile as the Nvidia price stabilized after an uninterrupted several-month rally. In April 2024, we observe a slight skew as the implied volatility (IV) for a 10% delta is higher than for a 90% delta. On the flipside, the volatility skew in the S&P 500 options, as shown in Exhibit 30.2, is the opposite, with OTM puts being more expensive than OTM calls.

In summary, the aggregate returns from this modified strategy would consist of returns from the cash position, the short call in the underlying stock plus the long call on the index.

A Real-Life Example

To determine position sizing, the portfolio manager should set two constraints. One is to make the aggregate option position cash flow neutral in case the underlying stock and the index surpass their respective strikes. Since the S&P 500 index value is approximately 6 times the Nvidia price,

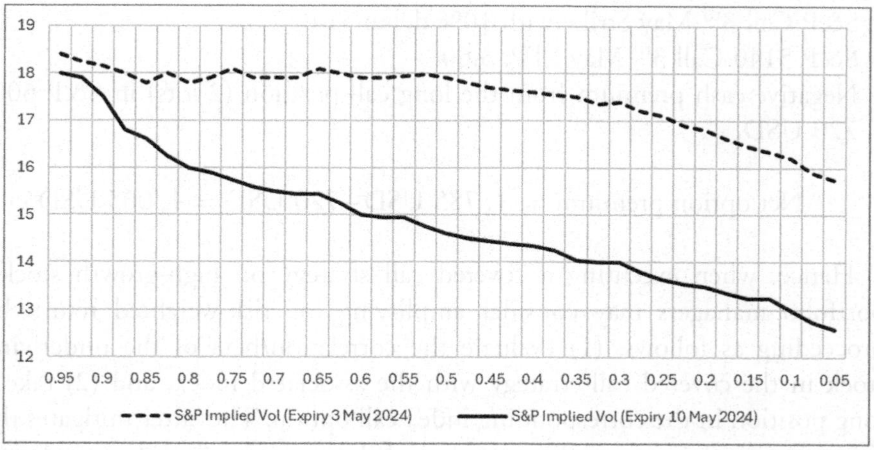

Exhibit 30.2 S&P 500 Implied Volatility Skew for the expirations of May 3, 2024, and May 10, 2024, at the close of business on April 30, 2024 (The horizontal axis represents the options' strike price as a percentage of the underlying stock price (moneyness). The vertical axis represents the options' implied volatility)

and Nvidia's 5-year monthly beta is an estimated 1.74, the portfolio manager should go long two contracts in the S&P 500 call option for every seven short contracts of Nvidia.

- Beta (Nvidia) = 1.74
- Number of Nvidia Contracts = 7
- Index Value Multiplier = 6
- Ratio = Beta (Nvidia) * Number of Nvidia Contracts / Index Value Multiplier = 2.03 = ~2.

Second, the portfolio manager should keep the delta of both the long and short positions similar to ensure that both the stock and the associated index have the same probability of breaching the respective strike prices.

Consider the following market data as of the close of business on April 30, 2024, and the associated position data:

- Nvidia Last Traded Price (LTP): 864.02 USD
- Cash position: 700 shares equivalent to 604,814 USD
- Nvidia Call 3rd May Strike with 10% delta: 935
- Nvidia 935 Call 3rd May LTP: 2.55
- Positive cash premium from the short call position (7 lots) in Nvidia: 7 * 255 USD = 1,785 USD
- S&P 500 LTP: 5035.69

- S&P Call 3rd May Strike with 10% delta: 5140
- S&P 5140 Call 3rd May LTP: 3.60
- Negative cash premium from the long call position (2 lots) in S&P 500: 720 USD.

$$\text{Net option premium} = 1,785\ \text{USD} - 720\ \text{USD} = 1,065\ \text{USD}$$

Hence, when executing a covered call strategy on high-growth stocks, portfolio managers may consider amplifying the risk-weighted return by proceeding as follows: (1) evaluate the correlation/beta of the underlying stock in the covered call strategy with the associated index, and (2) take a long position in the corresponding index call option. The latter mitigates the risk stemming from the call component of the covered call, if the correlation is reasonably positive.

Summary

This case examines an innovative approach to enhancing the performance of covered call strategies by incorporating stock index options. It uses Nvidia—a high-growth stock known for its strong performance and high implied volatility—as the primary example. The discussion highlights the fundamental mechanics of covered calls, emphasizing the role of implied volatility in option pricing, and explores the risks and opportunities of executing such strategies on high-growth equities.

The case explains how volatility skews and pricing differences shape the strategy design by contrasting single-stock options with index options. It further introduces the integration of S&P 500 index call options as a hedging mechanism to mitigate the downside risk of short calls while maintaining cash flow neutrality and delta alignment. The analysis demonstrates optimal position sizing and strategy execution, ensuring risk-adjusted returns.

This case provides practical insights into managing covered call strategies on high-growth stocks while leveraging stock index options to improve portfolio outcomes. It also underscores the importance of evaluating correlation, beta, and option premiums to build robust, adaptive strategies that balance income generation with risk management.

31

Targeting Options-Based Income with Puts and Calls

John Burrello and Han Liang

Options-based income strategies offer investors a flexible and differentiated source of returns for achieving income objectives. Covered calls and cash-secured puts are two foundational strategies that allow for consistent premium generation while participating in market movements. By leveraging these tools, investors can create portfolios that balance income generation with risk management.

This case illustrates the mechanics of covered calls and cash-secured puts, focusing on how they can be used to target specific income levels. The analysis delves into three approaches to income targeting: adjusting strike prices, modifying portfolio weights, and combining covered calls with cash-secured puts. Each method is evaluated based on key performance metrics such as total premium income, risk-adjusted returns, and downside risk.

Additionally, the case examines the impact of volatility skew on option pricing and income generation, providing insights into how investors can optimize their strategies in varying market conditions. Practical recommendations help portfolio managers align their options strategies with financial goals, balancing short-term income needs with long-term portfolio stability.

J. Burrello (✉) · H. Liang
Invesco Global Strategies, Atlanta, GA, USA
e-mail: John.Burrello@invesco.com

F. J. Fabozzi and M. de Jong (eds.), *Derivatives Applications in Asset Management*,
https://doi.org/10.1007/978-3-031-86354-7_31

Covered Calls and Cash-Secured Puts

The two most common option income strategies are covered calls and cash-secured puts. Newcomers to option income investing may not realize that these two strategies have the same payoff profile when implemented with the same strike price and expiration date. They are often implemented with at-the-money strikes with one month to expiration, and investors should expect very little difference between covered calls and cash-secured puts when they share these characteristics.

If covered calls and cash-secured puts are so similar, which is the most effective option structure for an income strategy? When consistent yield and market participation are key objectives, it can be beneficial to use both. There are three primary reasons:

1. The flexibility to adjust call and put strikes, above and below the market, allows for more balanced and consistent yields and market participation profiles.
2. A combination of fully covered out-of-the-money calls and puts tends to have higher income potential than out-of-the-money covered calls alone.
3. A combination tends to offer more downside cushion potential than covered calls alone.

A common pitfall of option income strategies is in considering the relationship between market volatility and yields. When market volatility is high, yields are high, but they drop significantly when markets normalize. These fluctuations in yields are most pronounced when a strategy repeatedly sells options with the same strike prices, regardless of market conditions.

Offering a more consistent stream of income can be valuable to investors for planning purposes. Also, when option income funds are part of broader income-oriented portfolios, reliable yield expectations can make it easier to use in a broad portfolio context. How can investors achieve smoother income across different market volatility environments? Rather than always targeting the same strike price, which results in highly variable income, they can systematically adjust strikes to meet income objectives more consistently.

Does the market participation profile change with adjustments in strike prices? Yes, this is where the risk and return profiles of covered calls and cash-secured puts start to diverge. Income, upside, and downside participation levels can all be customized through flexible option strike selection. For example, shifting covered call strikes up and above the current market price (out-of-the-money, or "OTM"[1]) can allow for more upside potential than at-the-money (ATM) covered calls but less income and downside cushion. In other words, the further call strikes are moved away from the current market level, the more equity-like the covered call strategy becomes. Conversely, shifting cash-secured put strikes below the current market price can offer more downside cushion than their ATM counterparts, but less income and upside. The further the put strikes are moved, the more cash-like the cash-secured put strategy becomes. As call strikes are shifted upward, growth potential is increased; as put strikes are shifted downward, defensive characteristics are increased—they are initially offsetting.[2]

This means an investor can maintain more consistency and balance with market participation *and* yield when using both calls and puts—it does not require choosing stability in one or the other. If only adjusting call *or* put strikes to help stabilize yields, portfolios can end up with wider ranges of market participation than intended. In other words, adjusting only one side of the market can create lopsided performance profiles.

Practical Applications for Portfolio Managers

The implications of the above concepts can be seen by comparing three illustrative option income strategies on the S&P 500, each targeting a yield that is 5% higher than the S&P 500 dividend yield. These strategies assume a laddering approach for option income holdings across 20 expiration chains over a four-week lifecycle, aiming to minimize the effect of path dependency. Many option income strategies are designed to be defensive in nature. Therefore, the weights of the option holdings across the three strategies have been calibrated to have ex ante underlying market exposure of 0.75, assuming ATM strikes as a starting point before strikes or weights are forced to adjust to meet the yield target. The three strategies are as follows:

---

[1] At-the-money (ATM), out-of-the-money (OTM), and in-the-money (ITM) calls are struck at, above, and below the current market level, respectively. Puts are the opposite. ATM and OTM options tend to be more liquid and commonly used in option income strategies than ITM options.

[2] When selecting call and put strikes with the same deltas, the initial exposure nets to zero. Frequent laddering helps to consistently reset net exposures to zero, allowing for relatively stable market beta without delta hedging.

Strategy 1: Adjust Call Strikes to Target Yield

Sell 50% notional 1-month SPX calls against a fully invested passive S&P 500 equity portfolio. Adjust the strike prices of the calls dynamically to reach the target yield of SPX + 5%.

Strategy 2: Adjust Call Weights to Target Yield

Sell 1-month ATM SPX calls against a fully invested passive S&P 500 equity portfolio. Dynamically adjust the notional weights of ATM calls to achieve the target yield of SPX + 500 basis points.

Strategy 3: Adjust Call and Put Strikes to Target Yield

Sell 25% notional 1-month OTM SPX calls on 75% S&P 500 index holdings, along with 25% of 1-month OTM SPX puts on 25% cash holdings. Dynamically adjust the strike prices of both puts and calls to have symmetrical delta values (e.g., 0.3 delta for calls and -0.3 delta for puts) to meet the target yield of SPX + 500 basis points. This method is equivalent to a combination of 50% equity holdings, 25% covered calls and 25% cash-secured puts, using variable strikes but maintaining symmetrical deltas.

Performance Analysis of Strategies

When simulating these three strategies, prioritizing the yield target leads to variations in market participation stability. A primary objective of many option income strategies is beta reduction relative to underlying markets. Therefore, stability of beta reduction is crucial when incorporating these strategies into broader portfolios, as a variable beta profile can create unstable portfolio risks and present significant asset allocation challenges. For this comparison, a 3-year rolling beta to the S&P 500 index was used as a proxy for market participation over a 35-year period. The results, shown in Exhibit 31.1, indicate that the strategy using both puts and calls with variable strikes and symmetrical deltas tends to have a more concentrated beta distribution and more stable risk reduction. Market participation is lower than the "calls only" approaches and is maintained closer to the initial beta calibration at 0.75.[3] Meanwhile, the two strategies that employ only call options exhibit higher overall market risk and a more volatile market exposure, with the distribution of the rolling beta displaying a broadly spread, two-humped shape.

From a performance perspective, the strategy that employs both OTM calls and puts shows significantly lower beta, volatility, and drawdowns. This strategy's beta profile is more stable, yet it offers better upside/downside capture asymmetry, as measured by the "Participation Ratio" (upside capture/downside capture) as shown in Exhibit 31.2. It also exhibits a higher Sharpe ratio than the S&P 500 and the two strategies that only use calls.

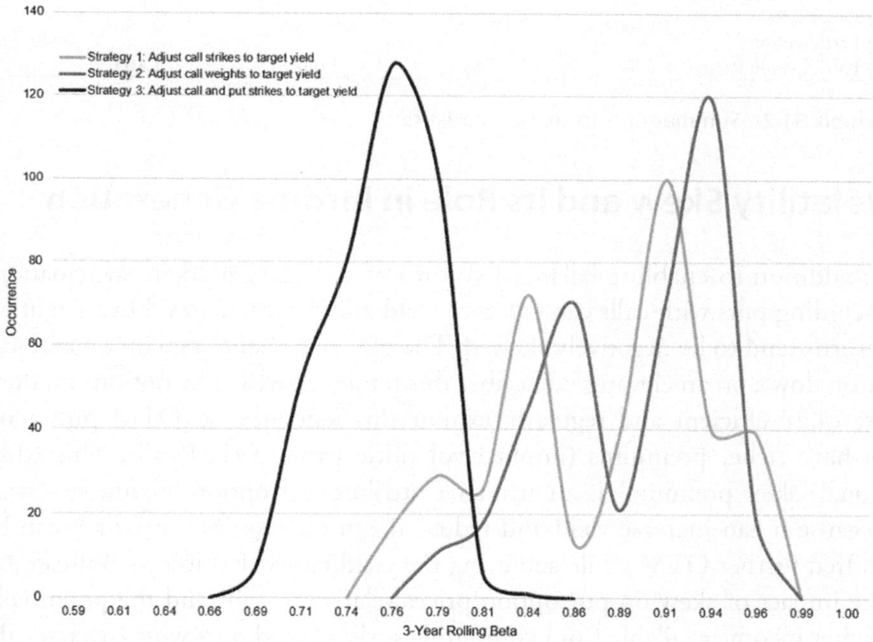

Exhibit 31.1 Distribution of beta

[3] Initial beta calibration can be set at any level according to investor preferences and utility functions. Our objective is to illustrate the variability of the beta profile across different option income design choices. We use 0.75 here to represent a beta profile similar to commonly used defensive equity exposures like out-of-the-money covered call strategies and low volatility factor equity portfolios.

	100% S&P 500 Index Total Return	**Strategy 1** 100% S&P 500 Index + 50% Short Calls with Variable Strikes	**Strategy 2** 100% S&P 500 Index + ATM Short Calls with Variable Weights	**Strategy 3** 75% S&P 500 Index + 25% Puts and Calls with Variable Strikes
Correlation to S&P 500	1.000	0.993	0.997	0.995
Beta to S&P 500	1.000	0.897	0.914	0.765
Max 3Y Beta	1.000	0.962	0.954	0.829
Min 3Y Beta	1.000	0.752	0.790	0.680
Vol 3Y Beta	0.00%	19.98%	15.68%	9.40%
Annual Return	10.70%	10.53%	10.35%	9.98%
Annual Volatility	14.87%	13.43%	13.62%	11.43%
Sharpe Ratio	0.517	0.560	0.539	0.612
Max Drawdown	-50.95%	-47.39%	-48.31%	-39.96%
Upside Participation	100.00%	91.25%	91.74%	80.27%
Downside Participation	100.00%	87.08%	88.85%	72.80%
Participation Ratio	1.000	1.048	1.032	1.103

Exhibit 31.2 Summary performance statistics

Volatility Skew and Its Role in Income Generation

In addition to enabling balanced control of yield and market participation, including puts with calls can enhance yield and defensiveness. Equity market returns tend to be negatively skewed. The old adage "stocks go up on an escalator, down on an elevator" describes this tendency well. The options markets are quite efficient and regularly exhibit this tendency, so OTM puts tend to have richer premiums (implied volatilities) than OTM calls. This additional "skew premium" is an attractive attribute for option income investors because it can increase yield and reduce downside risk, as put strikes can be shifted further OTM while achieving the yield target. Exhibit 31.3 illustrates the impact of skew on put option prices relative to calls and the potentially higher income available from combining cash-secured puts with covered calls relative to a portfolio constrained to covered calls alone.

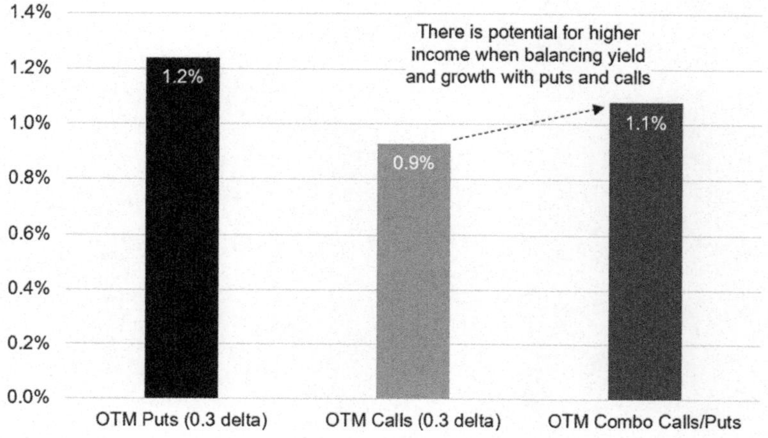

Exhibit 31.3 Average monthly S&P 500 option premiums for out-of-the-money calls and puts with the same market sensitivities (0.3 delta), January 1990 to March 2024

Summary

This case examines options-based income strategies, focusing on the practical application of covered calls and cash-secured puts to generate consistent income while managing risk. The case explores three approaches to targeting specific income levels through detailed examples and analysis: adjusting strike prices, modifying portfolio weights, and combining covered calls with cash-secured puts. Each strategy is evaluated based on performance metrics such as total premium income, risk-adjusted returns, and downside risk.

The case also highlights the role of volatility skew in influencing option pricing and income potential. By leveraging insights into skew dynamics, investors can optimize their strategies for varying market conditions. Practical recommendations demonstrate how to align options strategies with financial goals and balance short-term income needs with long-term portfolio stability.

This comprehensive approach equips investors and portfolio managers with the tools and techniques needed to design effective options-based income strategies, ensuring robust performance across diverse market environments.

32

Efficiently Replicating Corporate Bond Returns with CDS Indices

Johan Duyvesteyn, Patrick Houweling, and Lodewijk van der Linden

This case study explores using credit default swap (CDS) indices as an efficient and cost-effective alternative to traditional corporate bond portfolios. It examines how CDS indices like the CDX and the iTraxx allow portfolio managers to replicate corporate bond market exposure with enhanced liquidity, lower transaction costs, and operational flexibility. The study demonstrates how combining CDS indices with government bonds provides a viable strategy for replicating the risk-return profile of corporate bond indices while mitigating some of the challenges associated with physical bond investments, such as illiquidity and high transaction costs.

Key insights include comparing traditional corporate bond- and derivatives-replicated portfolios, revealing that the latter offers similar returns with reduced volatility and lower default rates. The case highlights the advantages of using CDS indices when diversifying exposures, implementing dynamic beta allocations, and when going through periods of market distress. Despite these benefits, the case does indicate there to be an additional tracking error associated with using CDS indices, and discusses the implications of that for asset managers who benchmark against physical bond indices. Ultimately, this study provides an in-depth examination of the strategic value of CDS indices in modern portfolio management.

J. Duyvesteyn (✉) · P. Houweling · L. van der Linden
Quant Fixed Income, Robeco, Rotterdam, The Netherlands
e-mail: J.Duyvesteyn@Robeco.nl

F. J. Fabozzi and M. de Jong (eds.), *Derivatives Applications in Asset Management*,
https://doi.org/10.1007/978-3-031-86354-7_32

The Mechanics of CDS Index Replication

Traditionally, portfolio managers gain exposure to the corporate bond market by investing in physical bonds. By constructing a well-diversified portfolio issued by companies from various sectors and regions and with different maturities and credit ratings, investors can expect to earn market-like returns. However, they should be conscious of the challenges of constructing and maintaining such a traditional portfolio regarding individual corporate bonds' liquidity and transaction costs. This is especially true in the high-yield segment of the corporate bond market, particularly in times of market distress, when selling physical bonds can be prohibitively costly. An alternative, more cost-efficient way to gain exposure to the corporate bond market is by investing in derivatives instead of physical bonds. In this case study, we describe the pros and cons of the derivatives-based method.

A corporate bond's yield can be decomposed into a government bond yield and a credit spread that compensates for the credit risk of the specific company. An investor can efficiently replicate exposure to the interest rate risk part by buying government bonds. The credit risk part may be replicated using credit default swaps (CDS). A CDS is a derivative contract that exposes its holder to the credit risk of the underlying company. The position of 'protection sellers' in a CDS is very similar to the holders of a corporate bond: they receive a regular payment (the premium on the CDS contract, respectively, the coupon on the physical bond) if the company survives, but suffer a loss when the company defaults and the market price of the bond drops to the recovery value.

Comparable to single-name corporate bond default swaps, information services provider IHS Markit has created CDS indices, designed as equally weighted baskets of individual CDS contracts. For companies in North America, these CDS indices are called CDX, and for European companies, iTraxx. Separate indices exist for investment-grade (IG) and high-yield (HY), creating thus four CDS indices that cover the four main corporate bond market segments. The selection of the index constituents is rules-based, most importantly applying liquidity criteria and limiting sector weight deviations versus the physical market index counterparts. Also, companies for which a credit event has occurred will be excluded, as are distressed companies with a too wide spread.[1] The constituents are updated twice per year (in March and September) when new CDS indices are released with a reset maturity

[1] More details on the construction of the CDS indices can be found on the Markit website: https://www.markit.com/Documentation/Product/ITraxx and https://www.markit.com/Documentation/Product/CDX.

	North America			Europe		
	Name	Constituents	Coupon	Name	Constituents	Coupon
Investment grade	CDX IG	125	100 bps	iTraxx Europe	125	100 bps
High Yield	CDX HY	100	500 bps	iTraxx Crossover	75	500 bps

Exhibit 32.1 Overview of CDS index contracts

of 5.25 years. Exhibit 32.1 provides an overview of the four leading CDS indices, displaying the number of index members and their standardized coupon.

While a corporate bond index consists of thousands of relatively illiquid individual bonds, and corporate bond index futures are still an infrequently traded illiquid phenomenon, a CDS index can be traded in a single transaction and at large volumes. This makes it very time- and cost-efficient to get exposure to a diversified basket of companies. CDS indices are in that sense comparable to equity index futures.

Exhibit 32.2 compares the average trading volume in the high-yield bond market with that of the high-yield CDS indices between 2014 and 2024. The average weekly trading volume in the high-yield bond market has been USD 34 billion, compared to almost USD 41 billion for the two high-yield CDS indices. As the high-yield bond market consists of thousands of individual bonds, the average volume per instrument thus makes a huge difference. Also, the average trading cost is 5–10 times higher for bonds. In the past, CDS indices were traded bilaterally, meaning that in addition to the credit risk of the CDS index' constituents, the investor also incurred exposure to the credit risk of the counterparty. Currently, central clearing is the most common way of trading CDS indices, offloading the counterparty risk to the clearinghouse.

	High Yield Bonds	High Yield CDS indices
Total weekly trading volume	USD 34.0 billion	USD 40.6 billion
Weekly volume per instrument	USD 17.0 million	USD 20.3 billion
Transaction costs	40-60 bps	5-10 bps

Exhibit 32.2 Trading volumes and costs of high-yield bonds and CDS indices (*Source* Bloomberg, Robeco. Sample period: April 2014 - April 2024. The DTCC and TRACE register the average weekly trading volume of CDS indices and all US high-yield corporate bonds. Weekly volume per instrument is divided by the respective number of instruments)

Benefits and Trade-Offs of CDS Index Strategies

Next, we illustrate how corporate bond market exposure can be replicated with a combination of CDS indices and government bonds. Exhibit 32.3 compares a traditional high-yield corporate bond portfolio to a derivatives-replicated portfolio using CDS indices. The traditional portfolio worth USD 200 million is invested evenly between US and European corporate bonds. The derivatives-replicated portfolio gets its credit risk exposure to the US and Europe via the CDX HY and iTraxx Crossover contracts; the government bond exposure is obtained by investing in US Treasuries and high-rated European government bonds. CDS indices provide leverage, in particular, USD 10 million invested in the CDS indices gives around USD 200 million in exposure. The exact leverage (market value) depends on the credit spread's prevailing market level versus the CDS index coupon: the CDS index contract has a positive market value when the market spread is below its coupon and a negative market value vice versa. Even though the money invested in the CDS indices cannot be invested in government bonds, the portfolio duration can be aligned with the bond benchmark by buying government bonds with a higher duration or adding long positions in government bond futures.

Exhibit 32.4 compares the high-yield CDS indices' rating, sector- and country distributions to the physical high-yield corporate bond market, as represented by the Bloomberg Global High-Yield Corporate Bond Index. We create the global CDS index portfolio by applying a 50% weight to iTraxx Crossover and CDX HY. The distributions show similarities and differences. The rating profile is roughly in line. As to the sector distribution, the zero weight in the banking sector stands out, which is caused by banks not being included in the construction of the CDS indices. In the country distribution, we see that the CDS indices have a smaller exposure to the United States and larger exposures to European markets due to the 50–50 weighting scheme that we have applied to CDX HY and iTraxx Crossover in this illustration.

	Traditional Portfolio		Derivatives-Replicated Portfolio	
	Market Value	Credit risk exposure	Market Value	Credit risk exposure
US HY corporate bonds	100	100		
European HY corporate bonds	100	100		
US Treasuries			95	
CDX HY			5	100
European government bonds			95	
iTraxx Crossover			5	100
Total	200	200	200	200

Note: Numbers in million USD

Exhibit 32.3 Overview replication corporate bond market (*Note* Numbers in million USD)

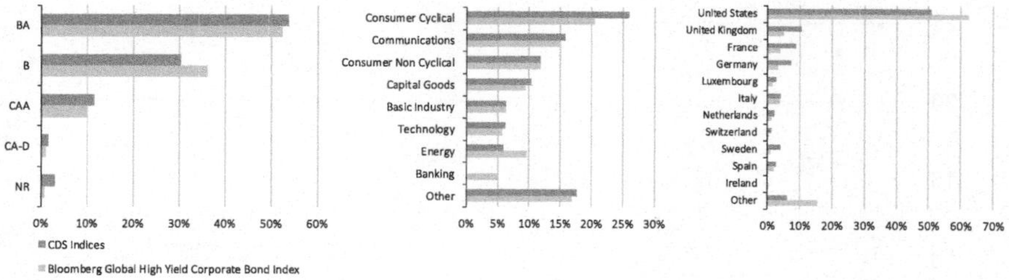

Exhibit 32.4 Distribution Derivatives-Replicated Portfolio and Traditional Portfolio (*Source* Bloomberg, Robeco. December 2023)

With a larger weight in the CDX HY contract, the exposure to the US in the derivatives-replicated portfolio could be matched with the bond index. Note that the CDS indices do not cover emerging markets (in the "Other" category).

Comparative Analysis: Corporate Bonds vs. CDS Indices

Finally, we compare the historical performances of the derivatives-replicated and traditional portfolios. Exhibit 32.5 shows these portfolios' historical annualized return, volatility, and yield for investment-grade and high-yield from 2004 to 2024.

Over the observation period, the total return of the derivatives-replicated portfolio has been somewhat higher than the return of the traditional portfolio, while the volatility has been substantially lower, both for investment grade and for high yield. The volatility difference is mainly due to the larger credit spread widening in the traditional bond market in severe crisis periods like the 2007–2008 Global Financial Crisis and the COVID turmoil in 2020 when physical corporate bonds started carrying an illiquidity premium that

		Total return	Volatility	Yield	Correlation	Tracking error
IG	Derivatives	4.12%	4.24%	2.9%	79%	3.29%
	Traditional	4.08%	5.35%	3.6%		
HY	Derivatives	8.68%	7.69%	6.6%	77%	5.92%
	Traditional	7.53%	9.16%	7.4%		

Exhibit 32.5 Historical return, volatility, yield, and correlation (*Source* Bloomberg, JP Morgan DataQuery, Robeco. July 2004 - April 2024. Bond returns are based on Bloomberg corporate bond indices for the US and Pan Europe. The derivatives-based portfolio is constructed by assigning 50% weights to the US and Europe, for both the government bonds and the CDS indices)

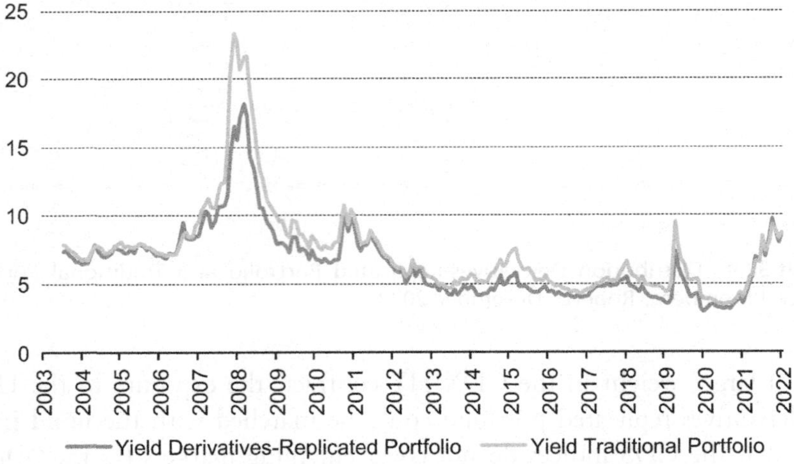

Exhibit 32.6 Yield of Derivatives-Replicated Portfolio and Traditional Portfolio (*Source* Bloomberg, JP Morgan DataQuery, Robeco. June 2004-April 2024)

is not apparent in the credit spreads of the more liquid CDS indices. See Exhibit 32.6 for an illustration of the historical yield development for the high-yield market.

As shown in Exhibit 32.5, the average yields are also influenced by this pattern, showing higher levels for the traditional portfolios. The monthly return correlation between the derivatives-replicated and traditional portfolios was close to 80%, suggesting that CDS and bond indices largely co-move. However, their returns and yields occasionally deviate, especially during the aforementioned crisis periods and their subsequent recoveries. These crisis periods are also the main driver of a considerable tracking error of the derivatives-replicated portfolio versus physical bonds, attaining about 3% for investment-grade and 6% for high-yield. This introduces a *relative* risk for portfolio managers who benchmark their investments against a physical bond index.

Risk Considerations in Using CDS Indices

A characteristic of the high-yield market is the occurrence of default events and here we again find a remarkable difference between physical corporate bond indices and CDS indices. The historical annual default rate of the high-yield CDS indices has been 1.3%, while the rate for the physical high-yield index has been twice as high at 2.6%. Exhibit 32.7 shows that this is mainly due to the much higher default rate for the bond index in crisis periods like

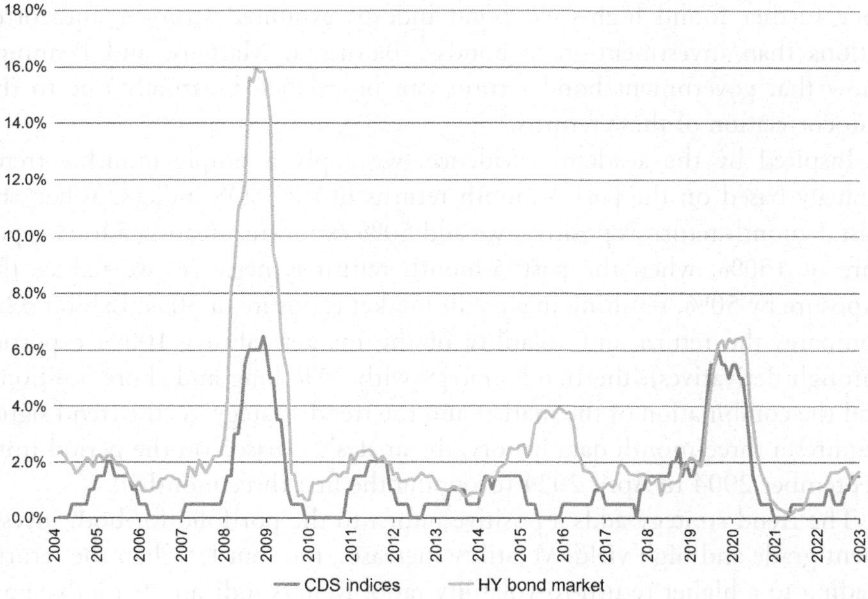

Exhibit 32.7 12-month rolling default rates of CDS indices and high-yield bonds (*Source* Bloomberg, Robeco. June 2004-December 2023)

2008 and 2015, while during the COVID period the default rates were more similar. Another reason for the lower default rate is the removal of distressed names in the semi-annual index rebalance of the CDS indices.

Dynamic Beta Allocation

As shown in Exhibit 32.2, CDS indices can be traded in large quantities and with much lower transaction costs than corporate bonds. The derivatives, therefore, offer portfolio managers the flexibility to steer their credit beta allocation dynamically over time. We give an example of such a strategy.

Stevens, Clinebell, and Kahl found an autoregressive pattern for corporate bond excess returns over different holding periods.[2] Hong, Lin, and Wu confirmed significant autocorrelations in investment-grade and high-yield indexes for both total returns and total returns over the risk-free rate;

[2] Jerry L. Stevens, John M. Clinebell, and Douglas R. Kahl, "Time Series Estimation of the Bond Default Risk Premium," *Quarterly Review of Economics and Finance*, 36(4), 1996, 475–484.

they further found high-yield bond indexes exhibited stronger autocorrelations than investment-grade bonds.[3] Baltussen, Martens, and Penninga show that government bond returns can be predicted partially due to the autocorrelation of these returns.[4]

Inspired by the academic evidence, we apply a simple monthly trend strategy based on the past 3-month returns of the CDS indices. When the past 3-month return is positive, we add 50% exposure, creating a total exposure of 150%; when the past 3-month return is negative, we reduce the exposure by 50%, resulting in a credit market exposure of 50%. Exhibit 32.8 compares the return and volatility of the market (always 100% exposure through derivatives), the trend strategy with 50% long and short positions, and the combination of the market and the trend strategy. As the trend signal requires a three-month data history, the analysis is based on the period from September 2004 to April 2024 (dropping the first three months).

The trend strategy adds a positive return to the portfolio for both investment grade and high yield. Volatility increases, too, but less than the return, leading to a higher return-to-volatility ratio. Results indicate that a dynamic beta allocation based on a simple trend strategy improves the gross return with limited additional risk. CDS indices enable the opportunity to steer the credit beta allocation dynamically over time, aiming to reduce losses when the market declines (lower beta) and to benefit more from strong market environments (higher beta).

		Return	Volatility	Ratio
IG	Market	4.00%	4.25%	0.94
	Trend strategy	0.83%	2.59%	0.32
	Combination	4.83%	4.78%	1.01
HY	Market	8.47%	7.72%	1.10
	Trend strategy	2.29%	3.80%	0.60
	Combination	10.76%	7.93%	1.36

Exhibit 32.8 Added value dynamic beta allocation (*Source* Bloomberg, JP Morgan DataQuery, Robeco. September 2004–April 2024. "Market" is based on the derivatives-based portfolio first introduced in Exhibit 32.5. "Trend strategy" is based on 50% long and short positions in both the US and Europe based on the sign of the past 3-month return. "Combination" is the sum of the market and trend strategy. Ratio is defined as the return divided by the volatility)

[3] Yongmiao Hong, Hai Lin, and Chunchi Wu, "Are Corporate Bond Market Returns Predictable? *Journal of Banking & Finance*, 36(8), 2011, 2216–2232.

[4] Guido Baltussen, Martin Martens, and Olaf Penninga, "Predicting Bond Returns: 70 Years of International Evidence," *Financial Analysts Journal*, 77(3), 2021, 133–155.

Summary

This case study examines the use of credit default swap (CDS) indices as an efficient and effective alternative to physical corporate bond portfolios. By analyzing empirical results over the past two decades, the study highlights the advantages of CDS indices in terms of performance, risk management, and operational efficiency. Although CDS indices and derivatives are sometimes perceived as risky, the findings suggest the opposite: CDS indices deliver similar returns to physical corporate bonds while exhibiting lower volatility, a lower default rate, better liquidity, and lower transaction costs.

CDS indices also offer portfolio managers the flexibility to implement dynamic beta allocations in a time- and cost-efficient manner, enabling a higher return from active management. While CDS indices exhibit large relative risk (tracking error) for portfolio managers who benchmark against physical bond indices, patient managers focusing on long-term results may benefit from comparable returns with reduced volatility and fewer defaults. The case underscores the strategic value of CDS indices in replicating corporate bond exposure, allowing managers to overcome challenges such as illiquidity and high costs associated with physical bond portfolios. This analysis provides a comprehensive perspective on how CDS indices can enhance portfolio construction while addressing concerns about their perceived risks.

33

Using Credit Default Swaps to Enhance the Return-to-Risk Profile of Buy-and-Hold Bond Portfolios

Marielle de Jong

This case study examines how credit default swaps (CDS) can enhance the return-to-risk profile of buy-and-hold bond portfolios. Although buy-and-hold strategies are typically associated with passive investment, CDS overlays introduce a level of active management, protecting against issuer defaults while preserving the portfolio's yield objectives. The analysis is grounded in a hypothetical portfolio of 30 bonds and incorporates quantitative methods to evaluate performance with and without CDS overlays.

The study adopts the framework developed by Barclays' Quantitative Portfolio Strategy (QPS) Group, which emphasizes yield-to-maturity for return estimates and tail-risk measures such as Value at Risk (VaR) and Conditional Value at Risk (CVaR) for risk assessment. These measures are derived using Monte Carlo simulation techniques, supported by stylized default probability tables. The use of CDS is further contextualized through its application to the Credit Suisse bond position.

This case demonstrates the tradeoffs involved in balancing risk mitigation and return optimization in fixed-income portfolios through a combination of simulation results and cash flow projections. The study concludes with broader reflections on the implications of CDS use in asset management, referencing key market developments such as the collapse of Credit Suisse in 2023, which underscored the critical role of derivatives in modern financial strategies.

M. de Jong (✉)
Grenoble Ecole de Management, Paris, France
e-mail: marielle.de-jong@grenoble-em.com

F. J. Fabozzi and M. de Jong (eds.), *Derivatives Applications in Asset Management*,
https://doi.org/10.1007/978-3-031-86354-7_33

Portfolio Description

The portfolio analyzed in this case consists of 30 corporate bonds with staggered maturities between 2020 and 2024, designed to serve as an annuity fund by generating regular cash flows over the investment horizon. The bonds, shown in Exhibit 33.1, are primarily out-of-the-money convertibles chosen for their low delta, which makes conversion into equity unlikely. These bonds trade at a discount, and the portfolio seeks to capitalize on this premium by holding them to maturity. Notably, all bonds are equally weighted except for the Credit Suisse bond, which carries a larger weight for illustrative purposes.

The structure of the portfolio ensures that the maturities are evenly distributed, allowing for stable cash flows throughout the holding period. These cash flows are depicted in Exhibit 33.2, which highlights biannual redemptions and annual fund payouts. The first four years' payments fully reimburse the nominal investment, while the residual sum paid in the final year reflects the portfolio's yield-to-maturity. For this portfolio, the maximum upside yield in a zero-default scenario is 3.39%, contingent upon the reinvestment of all intermediate cash flows at the same yield rate over the entire period.

The portfolio assumes a degree of exposure to credit events in managing risk, as the principal risk arises from potential defaults. To estimate default probabilities, this analysis employs a stylized version of default probability tables based on credit ratings, as shown in Exhibit 33.3. These probabilities are incorporated into Monte Carlo simulations to project cash flow outcomes under varying default scenarios. The methodology accounts for recovery rates, assumed to be 30% overall in this case, which aligns with industry conventions for corporate bond defaults.

The portfolio's design and structure demonstrate the fundamental principles of buy-and-hold investing, including the importance of maintaining a steady cash flow and adhering to liability-driven objectives. Depending on the client's goals, hedging requirements may vary. For instance, portfolios integrated into liability-driven investment strategies necessitate high hedge ratios to ensure payouts align with obligations. By contrast, open mandates offer portfolio managers greater flexibility to adjust hedge ratios, as illustrated through the partial CDS overlay applied to the Credit Suisse bond. This overlay, analyzed in later sections, exemplifies how CDS can serve as a tactical tool for optimizing the return-to-risk profile of fixed-income portfolios.

Issuer name	Weight	Rating	Coupon	Maturity	Yield
Huazhu	3.1	BBB	0.375	02/11/2020	3.2
Vodafone	3.1	BBB	0	26/11/2020	1.6
Lenovo	3.1	BBB-	3.375	24/01/2021	3.4
Technip	3.1	BBB	0.875	25/01/2021	2.2
Teva Pharma	3.1	BB	0.25	01/02/2021	4.2
Relo	3.1	BBB	0	22/03/2021	4.5
Verint Systems	3.1	BB	1.5	01/06/2021	2.2
Siem Ind	3.1	BB	2.25	02/06/2021	13.8
Bekaert	3.1	BB+	0	09/06/2021	4.2
Valeo	3.1	BBB-	0	16/06/2021	2.4
Orange	3.1	BBB+	0.375	27/06/2021	1.6
Twitter	3.1	BB	1	15/09/2021	2.5
Iindra	3.1	BB-	1.25	07/10/2021	3.3
Almmitall	3.1	BB-	0.25	14/12/2021	2.7
Telecom Italia	3.1	BB+	1.125	26/03/2022	2.2
Fireeye	3.1	BB-	1.625	01/06/2022	4.5
Luye Pharma	3.1	BB-	1.5	09/07/2022	6.8
Int Cons Airline	3.1	BBB-	0.625	17/11/2022	6.9
Brenntag	3.1	BBB-	1.875	02/12/2022	2.3
Bosideng	3.1	BB+	1	17/12/2022	14.9
Nutanix	3.1	BB-	0	15/01/2023	4.9
Supernus Pharma	3.1	BB-	0.625	01/04/2023	5.0
New Relic	3.1	BB+	0.5	01/05/2023	1.6
Intercept Pharma	3.1	BB-	3.25	01/07/2023	8.7
Macquarie Infra	3.1	BB	2	01/10/2023	6.4
Ares Captial	3.1	BBB-	4.625	01/03/2024	5.2
Dish Network	3.1	B	2.375	15/03/2024	5.1
Herbalife	3.1	BB-	2.625	15/03/2024	3.0
Jazz	3.1	BB	1.5	15/08/2024	3.7
Credit Suisse	10.0	BBB	1.25	17/07/2024	1.1

Exhibit 33.1 Buy-and-hold bond portfolio as of June 18, 2020 (*Data source* Bloomberg. All coupons are semi-annual, except those of Credit Suisse that are annual. Figures are in percentages. Bond selection was made by the author)

Risk and Return Metrics

The evaluation of risk and return for a buy-and-hold portfolio requires metrics that reflect its unique characteristics, particularly the asymmetric risks associated with credit events. This case employs the framework developed by Barclays' Quantitative Portfolio Strategy (QPS) Group, which emphasizes yield-to-maturity for returns and tail-risk measures such as Value at Risk (VaR) and Conditional Value at Risk (CVaR) for assessing risk.

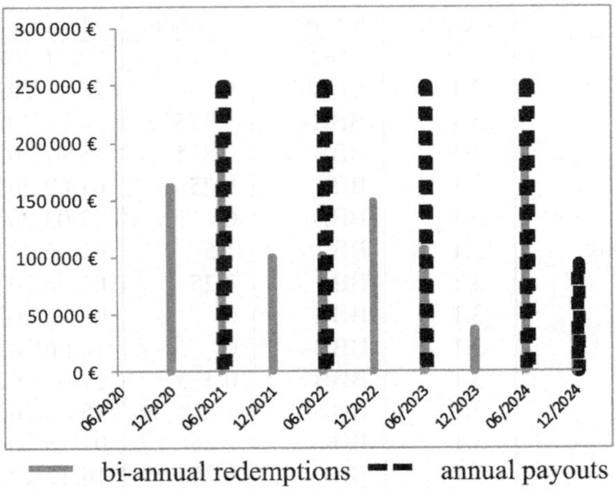

Exhibit 33.2 Portfolio redemption schedule (Schedule established by the author)

Rating	1 year	2 years	3 years	4 years	5 years
AAA	0%	0%	0%	0%	0%
AA	0%	0%	0%	0.25%	0.50%
A	0%	0.25%	0.50%	0.75%	1%
BBB	0.25%	0.50%	0.75%	1%	2%
BB	1%	3%	5%	7%	9%
B	4%	8%	13%	18%	22%

Exhibit 33.3 Stylized version of the default probability table (Stylized table produced by the author)

Return Metric: Yield-to-Maturity

Yield-to-maturity, denoted YTM, is a standard measure of return for fixed-income portfolios, calculated under the assumption that all intermediate cash flows are reinvested at the same yield rate throughout the investment period. As shown in Exhibit 33.2, the portfolio's maximum upside yield is 3.39%, achievable in a scenario where no defaults occur. While this metric provides a useful benchmark, it is based on assumptions about reinvestment that may not hold under real-world conditions, as highlighted later in the analysis.

Panel A: No CDS hedge

# defaults	# occurrences	yield
0	3606	3.39%
1	3894	2.52%
2	1855	1.61%
3	540	0.68%
4	90	-0.34%
5	13	-1.52%
6	2	-2.19%
Average		**2.54%**
	loss	
CVaR	€7,824	-0.78%

Panel B: Partial CDS hedge

# defaults	# occurrences	yield
0	3645	3.40%
1	3898	2.52%
2	1829	1.61%
3	528	0.66%
4	86	-0.35%
5	12	-1.51%
6	2	-2.39%
Average		**2.54%**
	loss	
CVaR	€396	-0.04%

Exhibit 33.4 Monte Carlo simulation results

Risk Metrics: VaR and CVaR

Evaluating risk and return for the portfolio requires metrics tailored to the asymmetrical risks inherent in credit events. This analysis employs the framework developed by Barclays' QPS Group, emphasizing yield-to-maturity as the return metric and tail-risk measures, including VaR and CVaR, for risk assessment.

VaR and CVaR capture the asymmetric downside risks posed by defaults. VaR estimates the maximum potential loss at a specific confidence level (e.g., 99%), while CVaR measures the average loss beyond this threshold. For this portfolio, simulations indicate a 99% VaR of €2,062 and a CVaR of €7,824, as detailed in Panel A of Exhibit 33.4. These figures highlight the potential severity of losses in extreme scenarios.

Monte Carlo Simulation

Monte Carlo simulations were employed to estimate risk metrics by modeling thousands of default scenarios for the bonds in the portfolio. Following the methodology outlined by Raunig and Scheicher,[1] the simulation uses each bond's default probability, derived from its credit rating as shown in Exhibit 33.3, and assumes a recovery rate of 30%. This approach enables a comprehensive assessment of potential outcomes, incorporating the asymmetrical risks posed by credit events.

The use of Monte Carlo methods allows for the probability-weighted estimation of both VaR and CVaR, providing insights into extreme downside scenarios. By simulating a wide range of potential default patterns, the portfolio's risk profile is thoroughly examined, offering a robust foundation for evaluating the impact of the CDS overlay in subsequent sections.

[1] Burkhard Raunig, and Martin Scheicher, M. "A Value at Risk Analysis of Credit Default Swaps." Bundesbank *Series* 2 *Discussion Paper No. 2008, 12.*

Importance of Tail-Risk Measures

The significance of tail-risk measures such as CVaR lies in their ability to quantify extreme losses beyond the VaR threshold. Exhibit 33.4 demonstrates the compounding effect of multiple defaults, underscoring the importance of understanding risks in buy-and-hold portfolios where credit events disproportionately impact outcomes.

This analysis of risk and return metrics provides a foundation for evaluating the impact of the CDS overlay in subsequent sections, where the results of these simulations are extended to incorporate derivatives-based risk mitigation.

Credit Default Swaps Overlay

Integrating a CDS overlay into a buy-and-hold portfolio introduces an active risk management dimension, allowing investors to target specific credit risks while preserving overall return objectives. This section examines the structure of the CDS overlay and its impact on the portfolio.

CDS Instrumentation and Structure

In this case, the CDS overlay targets the Credit Suisse bond position, protecting against default risk. As detailed in Exhibit 33.5, several CDS options were available for this bond as of June 18, 2020, offering variations in seniority, coupon rates, and restructuring clauses. For this analysis, a senior CDS with a 5% running coupon and a four-year tenor was selected. The backloaded payment structure, which is typical for a CDS, results in a buy-and-hold investment in a near-zero net present value at inception, minimizing the initial cost while maintaining effective protection.

Tier	Coupon	Clause	Upfront
SNRFOR[1]	1%	CR14[3]	-2.4%
SNRFOR	1%	MM14[4]	-2.4%
SNRFOR	5%	CR14	-18.6%
SNRFOR	5%	MM14	-18.6%
SUBLT2[2]	1%	MM14	-1.1%
SUBLT2	5%	MM14	-17.2%

Exhibit 33.5 CDS instruments written on Credit Suisse on June 18, 2020 (*Data source* IHS Markit. 1. Senior unsecured/foreign debt for sovereigns; 2. Subordinated/lower tier-2/debt for banks; 3. Old/full restructuring; 4. Modified restructuring)

Simulation Results with CDS Overlay

As outlined in the Risk and Return Metrics section, Monte Carlo simulations were used to evaluate the impact of the CDS overlay. These simulations showed that the default modeling framework was extended to incorporate the CDS, reducing the Conditional Value at Risk (CVaR) at the 99% confidence level from €7,824 to €396, as shown in Panel B of Exhibit 33.4. Importantly, the yield-to-maturity remained unaffected at 2.54%, demonstrating the overlay's ability to mitigate risk without compromising returns.

Cost and Value of the CDS

The CDS overlay involves an upfront inflow due to its negative initial price, offset by periodic coupon payments over its four-year tenor. While the nominal cost of the CDS is €2,634 on a €1 million investment, its contribution to risk mitigation is evident in the significantly reduced CVaR, making it particularly valuable for liability-driven portfolios where downside protection is a priority.

Historical Context: Credit Suisse Collapse

The collapse of Credit Suisse in 2023 underscores the practical importance of CDS instruments in managing systemic risks. As noted by Nolan,[2] UBS acquired most of Credit Suisse's bonds, but certain subordinated bonds defaulted, creating significant disruptions in the Swiss CDS market. This event illustrates the critical role of CDS in protecting portfolio stability during periods of market stress.

Strategic Implications

This case demonstrates how CDS overlays can enhance the risk management of buy-and-hold portfolios by selectively addressing credit risks. While the targeted protection reduces tail risks without materially affecting expected returns, the overlay also introduces complexities in cash flow management and valuation that must be carefully considered within the broader portfolio strategy.

[2] Gavin Nolan, "A Swiss CDS Story. "*S&P Global Market Intelligence, March 23, 3023.* Retrieved from https://www.spglobal.com/marketintelligence/en/mi/research-analysis/a-swiss-cds-story.html.

Analysis of Results

The incorporation of a CDS overlay significantly alters the return-to-risk profile of the portfolio, as evidenced by the Monte Carlo simulation results. This section evaluates these changes, focusing on their practical implications for portfolio performance and risk management.

Performance without CDS Overlay

As detailed in Panel A of Exhibit 33.4, the portfolio without a CDS overlay faces substantial downside risk. While the maximum upside yield of 3.39% is achievable in a zero-default scenario, the expected return, or probability-weighted yield, is reduced to 2.54% due to the likelihood of defaults. The portfolio's risk metrics highlight this vulnerability, with a 99% VaR of €2,062 and a CVaR of €7,824, reflecting potential severe losses in extreme cases. These risks stem primarily from the inclusion of lower-rated bonds, as outlined in Exhibit 33.3.

Performance with CDS Overlay

The introduction of the CDS overlay mitigates extreme downside risks, particularly for the Credit Suisse bond, as shown in Panel B of Exhibit 33.4. The CVaR at the 99% confidence level improves significantly, dropping from €7,824 to €396, demonstrating the CDS's effectiveness in limiting losses during credit events. Importantly, the expected return remains steady at 2.54%, as the backloaded structure of the CDS offsets its nominal cost.

Interpretation of Results

The CDS overlay provides substantial value for liability-driven portfolios, where downside protection is critical. By reducing extreme losses without impacting the portfolio's yield-to-maturity, the overlay aligns well with risk-averse investment mandates. For portfolios with more flexible objectives, however, the cost–benefit tradeoff of the CDS must be carefully considered, particularly given its nominal cost of €2,634.

Strategic Insights for Portfolio Management

The results highlight the importance of tailoring CDS overlays to the specific objectives of the portfolio. By targeting issuer-specific risks, such as those associated with Credit Suisse, the overlay enhances the portfolio's resilience to adverse credit events. However, portfolio managers must also account for the implications of the CDS on cash flow management and overall valuation when integrating derivatives into a broader strategy.

Relevance to Market Events

The Credit Suisse collapse in 2023 provides a compelling illustration of the practical importance of CDS instruments. As detailed in the Credit Default Swaps Overlay section, this event underscores the systemic risks that CDS can help mitigate, particularly during periods of heightened market volatility.

Summary

This case study demonstrates how CDS can be used as an effective tool for managing and enhancing the return-to-risk profile of buy-and-hold bond portfolios. By focusing on a hypothetical portfolio of 30 bonds, the analysis highlights both the opportunities and challenges associated with integrating CDS into fixed-income strategies.

Including a CDS overlay targeting the Credit Suisse bond significantly reduced the portfolio's downside risk, as evidenced by the lower CVaR. At the same time, the yield-to-maturity remained unaffected, underscoring the overlay's ability to protect without compromising returns. These findings align with the framework developed by Barclays' QPS Group, emphasizing the importance of tail-risk measures in evaluating fixed-income portfolios.

The analysis also reveals the limitations of standard metrics such as yield-to-maturity, which rely on strong assumptions about reinvestment and cash flow management. As noted in the Monte Carlo simulation methodology, these assumptions may not always hold in practice. Furthermore, the stylized default probabilities used in the simulation provide a useful framework but may oversimplify the complex dynamics of credit risk.

The collapse of Credit Suisse in 2023, mainly due to its implication in the Archegos fund (see Chapter 2), underscores the practical relevance of CDS in modern financial strategies. This event highlighted systemic vulnerabilities and the critical role of derivatives in mitigating market disruptions. By offering targeted protection against issuer-specific risks, CDS overlays provide a valuable tool for ensuring portfolio stability during periods of heightened volatility.

The use of CDS in buy-and-hold portfolios depends on the specific objectives and constraints of the investment strategy. CDS overlays can offer significant value for liability-driven mandates where downside protection is paramount. For more flexible mandates, the cost–benefit analysis of CDS use requires careful evaluation, considering nominal and present-value metrics. This case study serves as a practical guide for investors seeking to navigate the complexities of integrating CDS into fixed-income strategies, providing theoretical and applied insights.

Index

F. J. Fabozzi and M. de Jong (eds.), *Derivatives Applications in Asset Management*, https://doi.org/10.1007/978-3-031-86354-7

T

U

V

Y

The manufacturer's authorised representative in the EU is Springer Nature Customer Service Centre GmbH, Europaplatz 3, 69115 Heidelberg, Germany. If you have any concerns regarding our products, please contact ProductSafety@springernature.com

Printed and bound by CPI Group (UK) Ltd, Croydon, CR0 4YY
30/09/2026
02225565-0020